BIRTH OF THE LEVIATHAN

BIRTH OF THE LEVIATHAN

BUILDING STATES AND REGIMES IN MEDIEVAL AND EARLY MODERN EUROPE

THOMAS ERTMAN

Harvard University

CAMBRIDGE
UNIVERSITY PRESS

PUBLISHED BY THE PRESS SYNDICATE OF THE UNIVERSITY OF CAMBRIDGE
The Pitt Building, Trumpington Street, Cambridge CB2 1RP, United Kingdom

CAMBRIDGE UNIVERSITY PRESS
The Edinburgh Building, Cambridge CB2 2RU, United Kingdom
40 West 20th Street, New York, NY 10011–4211, USA
10 Stamford Road, Oakleigh, Melbourne 3166, Australia

© Thomas Ertman 1997

First published 1997

Printed in the United States of America

Typeset in Baskerville

Library of Congress Cataloging-in-Publication Data
Ertman, Thomas.
Birth of the leviathan : building states and regimes in medieval
and early modern Europe / Thomas Ertman.
p. cm.
Includes bibliographical references and index.
ISBN 0–521–48222–4. – ISBN 0–521–48427–8 (pbk.)
1. Europe – Politics and government. 2. Europe – Constitutional
history. 3. Local government – Europe – History. 4. Comparative
government. I. Title.
JN5.E77   1997
320.94 – dc20   96–19582
CIP

*A catalog record for this book is available from
the British Library*

ISBN 0–521–48222–4 hardback
ISBN 0–521–48427–8 paperback

FOR SUSAN

CONTENTS

7.   CONCLUSION   317

TABLES

ACKNOWLEDGMENTS

This book began life as a doctoral dissertation written in the Sociology Department at Harvard University under the title "War and Statebuilding in Early Modern Europe." The dissertation's principal aim was to analyze the impact of sustained warfare on the methods of administration, finance, and military organization employed in England, France, Spain, and Prussia from about the 14th century to 1789. After I took up a position in the Harvard Government Department in 1990, persistent questioning by my colleagues there led me to rethink that project and direct my attention to a set of issues with much broader resonance for political science: namely, why had some states developed in a constitutionalist direction during the formative centuries of European statebuilding, while others had become absolutist? And why had military pressures driven some states to construct effective, proto-modern bureaucracies, while others remained wedded to administrative methods that seemed highly dysfunctional? In order to address this subject in a satisfactory way, I was forced to expand substantially the scope of my research in terms of both the cases examined and the period covered. In consequence, little now remains of the original dissertation. I hope the results justify these efforts.

Over the last five years, I have incurred many debts. The Clark and Milton Funds of Harvard University provided support which allowed me to make several crucial, short research trips to Europe. The Center for European Studies most generously provided additional travel funds during a semester of leave, over the course of which I was able to write a good portion of this book. The Institute of Historical Research in London placed its vast resources at my disposal and provided an intellectual home away from home.

Many scholars and colleagues have sought to improve this study through their comments and criticisms. I am deeply grateful to my *Doktormutter*, Professor Theda Skocpol. Her course on revolutions, which I took in 1977, first fired my interest in problems of history and politics, and her own works have been a constant source of inspiration ever since. Orlando Patterson and John A. Hall both encouraged me to think in the widest possible terms, unconstrained by disciplinary boundaries. Alberto Alesina, Henry Brady, David Collier, Jonah Levy, Bob Powell, Robert Putnam, and John Zysman valiantly read much or all of the manuscript at a crucial moment and forced me to clarify my thinking on many points. Peter Dickson, David Laitin, Paul Langford, Paul Lucas, Gerhard A. Ritter, Lawrence Stone, Charles Tilly, and the participants in seminars at Harvard, M.I.T., Princeton, Berkeley, Oxford, and the University of Munich provided insightful feedback on various versions of the argument. Edwina Barvosa helped with the preparation of the final text and Mala Htun provided invaluable editorial assistance.

Sam Cohn, Matthew Evangelista, Ann Goldgar, Roger Gould, Gary Herrigel, Percy Lehning, Lella Pileri, Carlo Ruzza, Barbara Schinko, Annette Schlagenhauff, Rosemary Taylor, Genevieve Warwick, and Christoph Wielepp offered unstinting moral support and intellectual stimulation while this book was taking shape. John Brewer, Eckhart Hellmuth, Jo Innes, and above all Peter Hall, friends and mentors all, deserve special mention. Without the faith which they showed in this project from the very beginning it never would have gotten off the ground. Andy Markovits has been there through thick and thin, and the same is true in even greater measure of my family – and most especially my mother, whose belief in me has been a constant source of strength.

My greatest debt, however, is to my wife, Susan Pedersen. Despite a burden of academic obligations far heavier than my own, she read the entire manuscript several times, helped out with tasks large and small, and constantly revived my sagging spirits. By casting an historian's skeptical eye over many of my assertions, she more than anyone else forced clarity upon my muddled ideas. She has had a hand in nearly everything that is of value in this work. Its shortcomings are entirely my own. I dedicate this book to her in love and gratitude.

BIRTH OF THE LEVIATHAN

——— ༼༽ ———

INTRODUCTION

We live in a great age of statebuilding. With the disintegration of the last colonial empires, the second half of this century has witnessed the birth of dozens of new nations in Asia, Africa, and eastern Europe. The high incidence among these young states of dictatorship, corruption, and separatist threats to central authority has lent added relevance to one of the central questions of political science: how is it possible, under conditions of rapid social and economic change, to construct stable and legitimate governments and honest and effective systems of public administration and finance, all while maintaining an often fragile national unity?

The European statebuilding experience, the only case of sustained political development comparable in scale and scope to the one unleashed by the recent wave of state formation, can cast new light on this question. Between the fall of the Roman Empire and the French Revolution, Europe witnessed the creation of scores of new polities where once a single empire had held sway. Across the length and breadth of the continent, successive generations of leaders were confronted with the arduous task of constructing stable governance structures and state apparatuses capable of unifying often diverse territories in the face of both internal and external threats and of continuous market expansion, urbanization, and social and religious upheaval. Yet despite the similarity of the challenges involved, and the relatively homogeneous cultural setting in which Europe's rulers sought to meet them, the durable state structures which emerged by the end of the early modern period were anything but uniform in character. The political system of Louis XIV's France or Frederick the Great's Prussia could not have been more different from that of Pitt's Britain, not to mention the Poland of the *liberum veto*. The institutions through which government policy was implemented and enforced also varied substantially across these countries. Such contrasts in the area of political regime and of administrative infrastructure in turn corresponded to divergent levels of domestic stability and international power and influence.

Over the past several decades, social scientists have redoubled their efforts to explain the process of European statebuilding. They have done so in order not only to understand more fully the continent's fate during the most recent period of its history, but also to generate insights relevant to today's statebuilders. The beginnings of this recent literature, which encompasses contributions from historical sociologists, economists, and historians as well as political scientists, can be traced back to the mid-1960s, when the Social Science Research Council initiated a large-scale project on the comparative development of states and nations which resulted in several studies with a substantial European focus, most notably the volume edited by Charles Tilly entitled *The Formation of National States in Western Europe*.[1] At the same time, Stein Rokkan was drawing up his "conceptual map of Europe," which sought to provide a framework for analyzing long-term political change across the continent from the medieval period into the 20th century.[2] Perry Anderson's seminal *Lineages of the Absolutist State* appeared in 1974.[3]

In 1985, Theda Skocpol lent this field of research a new dynamism with her call to "bring the state back in[to]" the social sciences and take historical cases and data seriously.[4] More recently Charles Tilly, John A. Hall, Michael Mann, Aristide Zolberg, Margaret Levi, Brian Downing, Robert Putnam, and Hendryk Spruyt, among others, have all contributed

[1]   Charles Tilly (ed.), *The Formation of National States in Western Europe* (Princeton: Princeton University Press, 1975). Two other volumes from this project with direct bearing on the subject of this book are: Leonard Binder et al. (eds.), *Crises and Sequences in Political Development* (Princeton: Princeton University Press, 1971); and Raymond Grew (ed.), *Crises of Political Development in Europe and the United States* (Princeton: Princeton University Press, 1978).

[2]   Stein Rokkan, "Cities, States and Nations: A Dimensional Model for the Study of Contrasts in Development," in: S. N. Eisenstadt and Stein Rokkan (eds.), *Building States and Nations*, 2 vols. (Beverly Hills: Sage, 1973), vol. I, pp. 73–97; idem, "Dimensions of State Formation and Nation-Building: A Possible Paradigm for Research on Variations within Europe," in: Tilly, *Formation*, pp. 562–600; idem, "Territories, Nations, Parties: Toward a Geoeconomic-Geopolitical Model for the Explanation of Variations within Western Europe," in: Richard Merritt and Bruce Russett (eds.), *From National Development to Global Community* (London: George Allen & Unwin, 1981), pp. 70–95.

[3]   Perry Anderson, *Lineages of the Absolutist State* (London: New Left Books, 1974). Other works on European statebuilding published around this time include: Richard Bean, "War and the Birth of the Nation State," *Journal of Economic History*, vol. 23, no. 1 (March 1973), pp. 202–221; Gianfranco Poggi, *The Development of the Modern State* (Stanford: Stanford University Press, 1978); Ronald Batchfelder and Herman Freudenberger, "On the Rational Origins of the Modern Centralized State," *Explorations in Economic History*, vol. 20 (1983), pp. 1–13; Anthony Giddens, *The Nation-State and Violence* (Berkeley: University of California Press, 1985).

[4]   Theda Skocpol, "Bringing the State Back In: Strategies of Analysis in Current Research," in: Peter Evans, Dietrich Rueschemeyer, and Theda Skocpol (eds.), *Bringing the State Back In* (Cambridge: Cambridge University Press, 1985), pp. 3–37.

important new books and articles with an historical focus on European political development.[5] Studies by Stephen Krasner, David and Ruth Collier, and Douglass North on the character and dynamics of long-term political and economic change have added a further theoretical dimension to this literature.[6] The work of all of these authors has drawn on the classic texts of Tocqueville, Weber, Norbert Elias, and especially those of Otto Hintze, a selection of whose essays were published in English for the first time in 1975.[7]

This extensive new literature has greatly advanced our knowledge of European political development and of statebuilding more generally. A broad consensus now exists among those active in this field on a number of points concerning the European case. In the first instance, further support has been provided for Weber's contention that what set the early modern West apart from other great civilizations was the combination of a distinctive kind of polity – the exceptionally penetrative sovereign, territorial state[8] – and a dynamic market economy which

[5] Charles Tilly, "War Making and State Making as Organized Crime," in: Evans et al., *Bringing the State Back In*, pp. 169–191; Charles Tilly, *Coercion, Capital and European States A.D. 990–1990* (Oxford: Basil Blackwell, 1990); John A. Hall, *Powers and Liberties* (Harmondsworth: Penguin, 1986); Michael Mann, *The Sources of Social Power. Volume I: A History of Power from the Beginning to A.D. 1760* (Cambridge: Cambridge University Press, 1986); see also his earlier article: "State and Society 1130–1815: An Analysis of English State Finances," *Political Power and Social Theory*, vol. 1 (1980), pp. 165–208; Aristide Zolberg, "Strategic Interaction and the Formation of Modern States: France and England," in: Ali Kazancigil (ed.), *The State in Global Perspective* (London: Gower, 1986), pp. 72–106; Margaret Levi, *Of Rule and Revenue* (Berkeley: University of California Press, 1988); Brian Downing, "Constitutionalism, Warfare, and Political Change in Early Modern Europe," *Theory and Society*, vol. 17, no. 1 (January 1988), pp. 7–56; idem, *The Military Revolution and Political Change: Origins of Democracy and Autocracy in Early Modern Europe* (Princeton: Princeton University Press, 1992); Robert Putnam, *Making Democracy Work: Civic Traditions in Modern Italy* (Princeton: Princeton University Press, 1993); Hendrik Spruyt, *The Sovereign State and Its Competitors* (Princeton: Princeton University Press, 1994).

[6] Stephen Krasner, "Approaches to the State: Alternative Conceptions and Historical Dynamics," *Comparative Politics*, vol. 16, no. 2 (January 1984), pp. 223–246; idem, "Sovereignty: An Institutional Perspective," *Comparative Political Studies*, vol. 21, no. 1 (April 1988), pp. 66–94; Ruth Berins Collier and David Collier, *Shaping the Political Arena* (Princeton: Princeton University Press, 1991), pp. 27–39; Douglass North and Robert Paul Thomas, *The Rise of the Western World* (Cambridge: Cambridge University Press, 1973); Douglass North, *Structure and Change in Economic History* (New York: W. W. Norton, 1981); idem, *Institutions, Institutional Change and Economic Performance* (Cambridge: Cambridge University Press, 1990).

[7] Otto Hintze, *The Historical Essays of Otto Hintze*, Felix Gilbert (ed.) (New York: Oxford University Press, 1975).

[8] Following Spruyt, *Sovereign State*, I have chosen to use the terms "sovereign, territorial state" or just "territorial state" to designate the qualitatively new kind of polity which came to full maturity in early modern Europe. Alternative terms used by other authors include "organic state" (John Hall, Michael Mann), "national state" (Charles Tilly, Patricia Crone), "nation-state" (Douglass North, E. L. Jones), and "modern state" (much of the German historical literature). However, these other terms carry with

permitted a breakthrough to self-sustaining growth and hence escape from periodic Malthusian crises. Wide agreement can also be found on the factors which led to this unique Western outcome: a favorable geographic and ecological setting, a multiplicity of competing political units, and the unifying and restraining force of Christianity.[9] Various models have been proposed which detail how these factors interacted to produce a set of features shared by all medieval and early modern polities.[10] Furthermore, it is now generally accepted that the territorial state triumphed over other possible political forms (empire, city-state, lordship) because of the superior fighting ability which it derived from access to both urban capital and coercive authority over peasant taxpayers and army recruits.[11]

Finally, a number of authors have taken up the task which is of greatest relevance to political science, namely, developing a general theory of statebuilding in medieval and early modern Europe capable of explaining variations in political regime and administrative and financial infrastructure within the dominant form of the territorial state, which accounted for nearly all of the continent's polities at the end of the early modern period.[12] These authors have argued convincingly that war, sometimes in combination with other factors, was the principal force behind attempts by rulers both to alter political systems and to expand and rationalize state apparatuses in the interest of military competitiveness.

Yet the theories proposed to explain variations in outcome have remained unsatisfactory for a number of reasons. First, this literature has paid too little attention to the role played by different kinds of representative institutions in the failure or triumph of royal plans to introduce

them misleading overtones linked to their use in another literature to refer to the very different 19th- and early 20th-century European state. On the usage of "modern state" to refer to a quantitatively new kind of polity which came to full maturity across the continent around 1500, see: Werner Näf, "Frühformen des 'modernen Staates' im Spätmittelalter," in: Hans Hofmann (ed.), *Die Entstehung des Modernen Staates* (Köln: Kiepenheuer & Witsch, 1967), pp. 101–114.

[9] See: Hall, *Powers and Liberties*; Mann, *Sources*, vol. I; E. L. Jones. *The European Miracle*, 2nd ed. (Cambridge: Cambridge University Press, 1987); and Patricia Crone, *Pre-Industrial Societies* (Oxford: Basil Blackwell, 1989).

[10] Norbert Elias, *Ueber den Prozess der Zivilisation*, 2 vols. (Frankfurt am Main: Suhrkamp, 1976) [originally published in 1939]; Poggi, *Development of the Modern State*; idem, *The State: Its Nature, Development and Prospects* (Stanford: Stanford University Press, 1990); Mann, *Sources*, vol. I.

[11] Tilly, *Formation*; idem, *Coercion, Capital*; Rokkan, "Cities, States"; idem, "Dimensions of State Formation"; idem, "Territories, Nations, Parties"; Spruyt, *Sovereign State*.

[12] In addition to the works of Tilly, Mann, Downing, Anderson, and Zolberg cited above, see also the classic essays of Otto Hintze found in Gilbert (ed.), *Historical Essays of Otto Hintze*, and the more extensive collection found in: Otto Hintze, *Staat und Verfassung*, ed. Gerhard Oestreich (Göttingen: Vandenhoeck & Ruprecht, 1970).

absolutism and in the subsequent development of state infrastructures. Second, these theories have proved too willing to link one kind of political regime with only one kind of state apparatus – absolutism with "bureaucracy" and constitutionalism/parliamentarism with the absence thereof – when in fact, as will be shown below, constitutionalism could just as well be associated with bureaucracy and absolutism with nonbureaucratic forms of administration. Finally, such theories have underplayed the prevalence of dysfunctional, "patrimonial" institutional arrangements like the sale and traffic in offices within the apparatuses of many early states, and have thus underestimated the substantial difficulties involved in constructing proto-modern bureaucracies in response to geomilitary pressures. One of the principal reasons for these shortcomings has been that case selection has often proved to be too narrow to encompass the full range of early modern outcomes in both the political and the administrative sphere.

This book proposes a new general theory of statebuilding in medieval and early modern Europe which seeks to avoid such shortcomings by considering the widest possible range of cases, from England in the west to Hungary and Poland in the east, and from Sweden and Denmark in the north to the states of Iberia and Italy in the south.[13] It

---

[13]   Before proceeding further, I should say a bit more about the logic underlying case selection in this book. In an effort to hold constant as many independent variables as possible, I have limited the scope of this analysis to "western Christendom," or the area of the European continent which was Catholic during the middle ages and Catholic or Protestant thereafter. As the work of authors like John Hall, Patricia Crone, and E. L. Jones mentioned above has shown, this area – which would include all of present-day western and central Europe as far east as Poland, Hungary, and Slovakia, but exclude Russia, Ukraine, the Balkans, and Turkey – exhibited a high degree of cultural, social, and, to a lesser extent, economic homogeneity prior to 1500, a homogeneity which persisted even after the Reformation destroyed the unity of the western Church. For this reason, unless otherwise specified, "Europe" throughout the remainder of the text will mean "western Christendom" in the sense just defined.

Following this same principle of maximizing underlying commonalities, I will also seek to account for political and institutional variations among polities of a roughly similar kind, namely territorial states. This means excluding the three city-republics of Italy (Venice, Genoa, and Lucca) and the city-states of Germany from the analysis because their internal organization, and hence their developmental trajectory, was entirely different from that of all other European states. The same is also true of the more than 200 "midget states" and 1,500 autonomous territories of the imperial knights found within the 18th-century Holy Roman Empire which possessed the character of overblown private estates; and of the Swiss Confederation and the Dutch Republic, both of which were confederal entities in which sovereignty rested with the constituent territories (cantons or provinces) rather than with the center.

Having eliminated these nonterritorial states, only about thirty-odd cases remain, depending on how many of the smaller German polities are included. Thus, the following states are considered in this analysis, even if sometimes only in a minimal way: England/Britain, France, Portugal, Spain, Savoy, Tuscany, Naples, Denmark-Norway, Sweden-Finland, Poland, Hungary, Brandenburg-Prussia, Austria, Saxony, Bavaria,

argues that three factors – the organization of local government during the first few centuries after state formation; the timing of the onset
of sustained geopolitical competition; and the independent influence
of strong representative assemblies on administrative and financial
institutions – can account for most of the variation in political regimes
and state infrastructures found across the continent on the eve of the
French Revolution. In the remainder of this introductory chapter, I will
present this argument in greater detail by first re-specifying the full
range of 18th-century outcomes to take into account a wider case selection. I will then evaluate the ability of current theories to explain these
outcomes before presenting my own alternative argument in three steps.

EARLY MODERN STATES: FOUR TYPES

For almost a century, it has been conventional to think of the development of the European state in terms of two models. One, usually associated with France or Germany, is characterized by absolutist rule and
a large state bureaucracy and defense establishment. The other, most
often linked to Britain, features constitutional or parliamentary government and administration through local justices of the peace without
much in the way of a central bureaucracy or standing armed forces.
Bureaucratic absolutism is thus counterposed to a parliamentary night-
watchman state.

One of the most important points of the present book is to expose
this as a false dichotomy. I do so by breaking down the state into two
component dimensions, one related to government or regime type and
the other to the character of the state apparatus. Two different kinds
of political regimes can be found among the territorial states of 18th-
century Europe, the absolutist and the constitutional. In an absolutist
regime, the ruler unites both executive and legislative powers in his or
her own person; whereas in a constitutional regime[14] the legislative
prerogative is shared by the ruler and a representative assembly. This

---

Württemberg, Hannover, Hessen-Kassel, Mecklenburg-Schwerin, Baden, the Palatinate,
Cologne, Trier, Mainz, Würzburg, Münster, Bamberg, Eichstätt, Augsburg, and Salzburg.
  For methodological guidelines, I have drawn principally upon: Theda Skocpol and
Margaret Somers, "The Uses of Comparative History in Macrosocial Inquiry," in:
Theda Skocpol, *Social Revolutions in the Modern World* (Cambridge: Cambridge Univer-
sity Press, 1994), pp. 72–95; and David Collier, "The Comparative Method," in: Ada
Finifter (ed.), *Political Science: The State of the Discipline II* (Washington: American Political
Science Association, 1993), pp. 105–119.

[14] This is the term used by Michael Mann and it seems preferable to Hintze's "parlia-
mentarism," since the latter is most commonly employed to refer to a 19th- and 20th-
century form of government which differed substantially from that found in most
non-absolutist states of the early modern period. Fortescue's contemporary category
"limited monarchy" (see next footnote) is more accurate, but also more cumbersome.

contrast was recognized at a very early date by contemporary commentators. Thus in 1476, the English statesman and political theorist Sir John Fortescue distinguished in his tract *The Governance of England: Otherwise Called the Difference between an Absolute and a Limited Monarchy* between states (like France) in which the king "mey rule his people bi suche lawes as he makyth hym self" and those (like England) in which the king "may not rule his people bi other lawes than such as thai assenten unto." For Jean Bodin, writing a century later, a sovereign's exclusive possession of the power of legislation was the defining feature of absolutism.[15] Using this criterion, 18th-century France, Spain, Portugal, Savoy, Tuscany, Naples, Denmark, and the German principalities – all of whose rulers enjoyed such a legislative prerogative – must be classified as absolutist; whereas Britain, Hungary, Poland, and Sweden,[16] where no new laws could be made without the approval of a national representative assembly, can all be considered constitutional.

It is more difficult to classify states according to the character of their infrastructures, the second dimension of variation, because of what at first glance seems like the bewildering multiplicity of organizational forms found in this area. Following Max Weber, I will differentiate between patrimonial and bureaucratic infrastructures.

As is well known, Weber was especially interested in the dynamic of development within state apparatuses. In *Economy and Society* and other writings, he identifies a particular pattern of conflict and change within the patrimonial states associated with many of the world's great civilizations, including the medieval and early modern West. For Weber, a constant struggle between patrimonial rulers and various elite groups (nobles, clerics, educated laymen, financiers) over the control of the

---

[15] Sir John Fortescue, *The Governance of England: Otherwise Called the Difference between an Absolute and a Limited Monarchy*, edited by Charles Plummer (Oxford: Clarendon, 1885), p. 109; Jean Bodin, *Les Six Livres de la République* (Aalen: Scientia Verlag, 1977), p. 221.

[16] Sweden poses some difficulties of classification along this dimension. Throughout most of the 18th century, from 1719 to 1772, the country was ruled by a constitutional form of government in which the four-chamber Riksdag, Sweden's national representative assembly, was as powerful as, if not even more powerful than, the contemporaneous British Parliament. After 1772, however, King Gustav III succeeded in greatly reducing those powers, and the period between 1772 and 1809 is sometimes referred to as one of "absolutism" in Sweden. Yet it should be emphasized that until at least 1789 Riksdag approval was still necessary – in fact as well as in theory – for new laws and new taxes, and hence it does not seem reasonable to classify the country as "absolutist" even for these decades. In the discussion in Chapter 6 below, I will, however, seek to explain both why a constitutional regime emerged in Sweden and why that regime proved less durable than that of the British. For a concise discussion of Swedish constitutional practices and changes during this period, see: Michael Metcalf (ed.), *The Riksdag: A History of the Swedish Parliament* (New York: St. Martin's, 1987), pp. 112–164.

"means of administration" lies at the heart of the statebuilding process in these polities.

That statebuilding process begins when the small staff of a ruler's household is no longer capable of carrying out all of the tasks of governing. A more extensive administrative apparatus must be constructed which can no longer be supervised directly by the ruler or manned solely by his personal dependents.[17] Establishing such an organization requires the cooperation of those groups in society which possess the resources necessary for infrastructural expansion, namely administrative, financial, and military expertise, ready cash, and the personal authority associated with high social standing. These groups in turn seek to negotiate or extract terms of service which will protect and/or extend their privileges, status, and income in the face of the potentially unlimited and arbitrary authority of the patrimonial monarch or prince. The best way to do this is to gain security of tenure and some control over the choice of a successor in one's office, so as to permit that office to be passed on to a family member or client.

In some cases, an elite group in fact succeeds in transforming the administrative positions it occupies into the group's private patrimony rather than that of the ruler. What results is a kind of state apparatus which Weber clumsily refers to as "stereotyped" (or, as Bendix translates it, "typified") patrimonial administration (*stereotypisierte Patrimonialverwaltung*). The "appropriation" at the heart of this apparatus can take a variety of forms, depending on the elite group involved: "proprietary officeholding," where government officials gain legally recognized property rights over their administrative positions; tax farming and other kinds of "enterprising," in which private businessmen take over various state functions and run them for their own profit; and "local patrimonialism," where elites (usually landed nobles, but sometimes also urban oligarchs), acting through local government offices which they collectively monopolize, extend the authority which they already exercise over their own dependents to all inhabitants of a given region.

In certain other circumstances, which Weber unfortunately never specifies but upon which I hope to cast some light in this book, rulers successfully resist the appropriating designs of their elite staffs and retain the right to remove officials at will. If such rulers then use the powers they have retained to create a formal hierarchy of positions and

---

[17] Max Weber, *Economy and Society* (Berkeley: University of California Press, 1978), pp. 1010–1064, 1085–1090; idem, "Politics as a Vocation," in: H. H. Gerth and C. Wright Mills (eds.), *From Max Weber* (New York: Oxford University Press, 1946), pp. 77–128, here at pp. 80–82. See also Reinhard Bendix, *Max Weber: An Intellectual Portrait* (Berkeley: University of California Press, 1977), pp. 341–356. The discussion which follows is based on these sources.

fill those positions with candidates possessing special educational qualifications, then the groundwork will have been laid for the eventual
emergence of a modern, rational-legal bureaucracy. However, such a
bureaucracy can only become a full-fledged reality when the possibility
of arbitrary intervention on the part of the ruler has been eliminated
by the introduction of a set of standard operating procedures subject
to the strictures of a formalized, impersonal administrative law.

State infrastructures approximating the Weberian ideal-type of the
modern bureaucracy first made their appearance in Europe prior to
the French Revolution, though they were only perfected in the course
of the 19th century. It is often claimed that the continent's absolutist
political regimes pioneered the construction of such proto-modern
bureaucracies, but the specialized historical literature has demonstrated
that this is only partially true. In the absolutist polities of the German
territorial states and post-1660 Denmark, hierarchically organized infrastructures manned by highly educated officials without any proprietary claims to their positions were indeed in place by the 18th century,
and tax farming was all but unknown in these countries.[18]

However, proto-modern bureaucracies were to be found not only in
absolutist Germany and Denmark, but in constitutional Sweden and
Britain as well, though the latter also possessed remnants of proprietary
officeholding in certain government departments such as the Exchequer and the royal household.[19] Furthermore, and in sharp contrast to
the situation which obtained in their central and northern European
counterparts, the infrastructures of Latin Europe's[20] absolutist states
(France, Spain, Portugal, Savoy, Tuscany, Naples) were clearly patrimonial
in character. Not only did proprietary officeholding – often in its most
pronounced form (full heritability of office) – dominate across this
entire region, but tax farmers and other private businessmen fully controlled these countries' financial affairs.[21]

---

[18] Michael Stolleis, "Grundzüge der Beamtenethik," in: idem, *Staat und Staatsräson in der
Frühen Neuzeit* (Frankfurt: Suhrkamp, 1990), pp. 197–231; Birgit Bjerre Jensen,
Udnaevnelsesretten i Enevaeldens Magtpolitiske System 1660–1730 (Copenhagen: Riksarkivet/
G. E. C. Gads Forlag, 1987), pp. 328–330 and passim. Further references can be found
in Chapters 5 and 6 below.

[19] John Brewer, *The Sinews of Power* (London: Unwin Hyman, 1989), pp. 69–70 and
passim. For a more extended discussion of the significance of John Brewer's findings
for attempts to understand political development in early modern Europe, see my:
"*The Sinews of Power* and European State-building Theory," in: Lawrence Stone (ed.),
An Imperial State at War (London: Routledge, 1993), pp. 33–51.

[20] I employ "Latin Europe" throughout this book as a collective term encompassing
France, the southern Netherlands, and the Iberian and Italian peninsulas.

[21] In general, see the two recent comparative collections: Klaus Malettke, *Aemterkäuflichkeit:
Aspekte Sozialer Mobilität im Europäischen Vergleich (17. und 18. Jahrhundert)* (Berlin:
Colloquium Verlag, 1980); and Ilja Mieck (ed.), *Aemterhandel im Spätmittelalter und im*

Table 1. *Outcomes to Be Explained: States of 18th-Century Western*
Christendom Classified by Political Regime and Infrastructural Type

		Political regime	
		Absolutist	*Constitutional*
Character of state infrastructure	*Patrimonial*	France, Spain, Portugal, Tuscany, Naples, Savoy, Papal States (Latin Europe)	Poland, Hungary
	Bureaucratic	German Territorial States, Denmark	Britain, Sweden

Finally, the great non-absolutist kingdoms of east-central Europe –
Hungary and Poland – exhibited yet another variation. Unlike constitutionalist Britain and Sweden, they did not construct proto-modern
bureaucracies, but rather by the end of the early modern period had
come to possess infrastructures organized along local patrimonialist
lines. In practical terms this meant that organs of local government
staffed exclusively by nonprofessional members of the local nobility
carried out nearly all government functions, including the administration of justice, tax assessment and collection, and military recruiting.[22]

The polities of early modern Europe considered in this book can
thus be grouped into four distinct types according to different combina-
tions of political regime and state infrastructure (see Table 1).

COMPETING EXPLANATIONS

Five authors – the historian Otto Hintze, the historical sociologists
Charles Tilly, Michael Mann, and Perry Anderson, and the political
scientist Brian Downing – have developed broad-ranging theories concerning statebuilding in medieval and early modern Europe which offer
competing explanations for variations in political regime and in the

---

16. Jahrhundert (Berlin: Colloquium Verlag, 1984); as well as the older study by K. W.
Swart, *Sale of Offices in the 17th Century* (Utrecht: HES Publishers, 1980). See also the
pathbreaking work on the French case: Daniel Dessert, *Argent, Pouvoir et Société au
Grand Siècle* (Paris: Fayard, 1984).

22 Heinrich Marczali, *Ungarische Verfassungsgeschichte* (Tübingen: J. C. B. Mohr, 1910),
pp. 93–103, 112–113; Stanislaus Kutrzeba, *Grundriss der Polnischen Verfassungsgeschichte*
(Berlin: Puttkammer & Mühlbrecht, 1912), pp. 60, 113, 121, 131, 134–136, 139–140,
174, 183–190. For further references, see Chapter 6 below.

character of administrative and financial infrastructures. I now turn to a more detailed analysis of these competing explanations, evaluating them both relative to one another and in light of their ability to account for the outcomes specified in Table 1.

At the beginning of his article "Military Organization and the Organization of the State" (1906), Otto Hintze contends that: "It is one-sided, exaggerated and therefore false to consider class conflict the only driving force in history. Conflict between nations has been far more important; and throughout the ages pressure from without has been a determining influence on internal structure."[23] In another piece from the same period entitled "Power Politics and Government Organization," he applies this perspective directly to the study of European political development:

> The different systems of government and administration found among the large European states can be traced back in the main to two types, one of which can be called the English and the other the continental. . . . [The principal difference between them] consists in the fact that on the continent military absolutism with a bureaucratic administration emerges, while in England . . . the older line of development continues . . . and leads to what we usually term parliamentarism and self-government. What then is the cause of this pronounced institutional differentiation? . . . The reason lies above all in the fact that on the continent compelling political imperatives held sway which led to the development of militarism, absolutism and bureaucracy, whereas such pressures were not present in England. . . . It was above all geographic position that had its effects.[24]

This passage represents a classic statement of a widely held, dualistic view of European statebuilding. Thus Hintze views this process as having two divergent outcomes – absolutist government and a bureaucratically organized state infrastructure on the continent, and parliamentary government and nonbureaucratic administration through local notables like justices of the peace ("self-government") in England – and he links these to the degree of sustained military pressure from land forces experienced by particular countries. This pressure is in turn a function of a country's geographic position (more or less exposed) within an historically specific state system in which geopolitical competition normally took the form of war and preparations for war. Put another way, Hintze's argument can be reduced to the following proposition: the greater the degree of geographic exposure to which a given medieval

---

[23] Otto Hintze, "Military Organization and the Organization of the State," in: idem, *Historical Essays*, pp. 178–215, here at p. 183.

[24] Otto Hintze, "Machtpolitik und Regierungsverfassung," in: idem, *Staat und Verfassung*, pp. 424–456, here at pp. 427–428.

or early modern state was subjected, the greater the threat of land warfare; and the greater the threat of land warfare, the greater the likelihood that the ruler of the state in question would successfully undermine representative institutions and local self-government and create an absolutist state backed by a standing army and a professional bureaucracy in order to meet that land threat.

Elegant and parsimonious as it is, Hintze's theory contains two serious deficiencies. First, the relationship he posits between geographic exposure and absolutism on the one hand and geographic isolation and constitutionalism on the other is contradicted by a number of important cases. Thus Hungary and Poland were geographically exposed and subject to extensive military pressure over many centuries from, respectively, the Turks and the Russians, and yet both retained political regimes that were decidedly constitutional. Conversely, Spain was protected from the rest of the continent by the formidable barrier of the Pyrenees and still developed in an absolutist direction.

Second, despite its continuing appeal to many writers on European political development, Hintze's assertion that only absolutist states built bureaucracies and only constitutionalist polities employed nonbureaucratic forms of administration is simply not borne out by the facts. Thus the research of Geoffrey Holmes and John Brewer has shown that while 18th-century Britain did indeed make use – as Hintze claimed – of a highly developed system of participatory local government centered on the county, the hundred, and the borough, it *also* possessed a bureaucratically organized fiscal and administrative infrastructure which was larger in both absolute and per capita terms than that of Frederick the Great's Prussia.[25] Moreover, Brewer has characterized the British Excise

---

[25] Thus Holmes estimates that the English government employed some 12,000 full-time civil servants in the 1720s and 16,000 in the 1760s. Both figures exclude Scottish officials. As such, they are almost certainly underestimates of the total size of the British state apparatus (excluding Ireland). See Geoffrey Holmes, *Augustan England* (London: George Allen & Unwin, 1982), p. 255. See also Brewer, *Sinews*, pp. 36, 65–67.

According to the calculations of Hubert Johnson, the entire Prussian bureaucracy, including local officials like the *Landräte*, numbered no more than 3,100 during the reign of Frederick the Great (1740–1786). See: Hubert Johnson, *Frederick the Great and His Officials* (New Haven: Yale University Press, 1975), pp. 283–288. Since the population of Prussia at the time of Frederick's death was approximately 5.8 million, this implies a per capita total of one official for every 1,871 inhabitants. Using the almost certainly low figure of 16,000 officials and a population total for England, Wales, and Scotland of 8.8 million for the same period yields a comparable British result of one official for every 550 inhabitants. For population figures, see: Walther Hubatsch, *Friedrich der Grosse und die Preussische Verwaltung*, 2nd ed. (Köln: Grote, 1982), p. 233; E. A. Wrigley and R. S. Schofield, *The Population History of England, 1541–1871* (Cambridge: Harvard University Press, 1981), p. 529; Phyllis Deane and W. A. Cole, *British Economic Growth 1688–1959*, 2nd ed. (Cambridge: Cambridge University Press, 1967), p. 6. It should be emphasized here that because complete records of government personnel no longer exist, all of these numbers represent orders of magnitude.

as having "more closely approximated . . . Max Weber's ideal of bureaucracy than any other government agency in eighteenth-century Europe."[26]

If Britain is an example of a constitutionalist polity which succeeded in constructing a bureaucratic infrastructure, then France, Spain, Portugal, and the Italian territorial states represent the opposite case: states with absolutist regimes which, despite constant exposure to military pressure, failed in their attempts to build proto-modern bureaucracies and were left instead with much less effective patrimonial infrastructures dominated by proprietary officeholding, "inside" finance, and tax farming.

More recently, Charles Tilly, Michael Mann, and Brian Downing have proposed theories which attempt to develop a more complex understanding of the way in which the pressures of war called forth the construction of different kinds of state institutions. In his well-known essay "War Making and State Making as Organized Crime," Tilly writes: "Variations in the difficulty of collecting taxes, in the expense of the particular kind of armed force adopted, in the amount of war making required to hold off competitors, and so on resulted in the principal variations in the forms of European states."[27] Tilly later goes on to elaborate on what he means by "variations in the difficulty of collecting taxes":

In the case of extraction, the smaller the pool of resources and the less commercialized the economy, other things being equal, the more difficult was the work of extracting resources to sustain war and other government activities; hence, the more extensive was the fiscal apparatus. . . . On the whole, taxes on land were expensive to collect as compared with taxes on trade, especially large flows of trade past easily controlled checkpoints.[28]

He then uses the divergent cases of Brandenburg-Prussia and England to spell out the practical implications of this new argument for the size and character of state apparatuses:

Brandenburg-Prussia was the classic case of high cost for available resources. The Prussian effort to build an army matching those of its larger Continental neighbors created an immense structure. . . . England illustrated the corollary of that proposition [concerning the ease of resource extraction], with a relatively large and commercialized pool of resources drawn on by a relatively small fiscal apparatus.[29]

Thus while Tilly accepts Hintze's stress on the importance of war and preparations for war as a catalyst for "state making," he calls into question

---

[26] Brewer, *Sinews*, p. 68.   [27] Tilly, "War Making," p. 172.

[28] Ibid., p. 182. This point is echoed in *Coercion, Capital* (p. 60): "In the absence of ready capital . . . rulers built massive apparatuses to squeeze resources from a reluctant citizenry."

[29] Tilly, "War Making," p. 182.

the tight link between the degree of military pressure experienced by
a given country and the size and bureaucratic character of the state
apparatus built in response to that pressure. Drawing on the work of
Gabriel Ardant, Tilly argues instead that the ready availability of easily
taxable resources could act as an intervening variable. In effect, a polity
could avoid bureaucratization and perhaps also absolutism in the wake
of sustained military pressure if, as a result of a high level of economic
development, it had access to abundant commercial revenues.

The broader significance of Tilly's argument is twofold. First, it provides a more sophisticated explanation than that of Hintze by bringing
together both geopolitical and, in a broad sense, economic factors
(available revenue sources, in turn determined by the relative weight of
agriculture and commerce within a given economy) to account for the
distribution of large bureaucratic state apparatuses across the continent
at the end of the early modern period. Second, it hints at a link between
regime type (absolutist/non-absolutist) and the relative abundance of
different revenue sources (commercial or land taxes) that Michael Mann
and Brian Downing bring out more explicitly.

Both the first volume of Mann's *The Sources of Social Power* and Downing's *The Military Revolution and Political Change* advance further the line
of argument put forward by Hintze as later modified and amended by
Tilly. Mann incorporates Tilly's claim that the kind of revenue upon
which a state depended to meet geopolitical exigencies also helped
determine the size and character of its infrastructure. He then goes on
to link these different extractive strategies to particular kinds of political regimes, arguing that absolutist states employed centralized bureaucracies to "mobilize" in a coercive manner monetary and manpower
resources held by a recalcitrant rural population, while more economically developed, constitutional states like England could tax commerce
and the wealth of landed elites without the need for such a bureaucracy.[30] In another publication, Mann makes this point about England
in an even more direct manner: "At the other extreme, a rich trading
country like England could maintain great power status without reaching
a high level of tax extraction and therefore, without a standing army."[31]

While Mann's discussion of variation within European statebuilding
is confined to just a few sections of his massive *The Sources of Social Power*,
Brian Downing has expounded similar ideas at much greater length in
his monograph *The Military Revolution and Political Change*. This book,
which draws on the writings of both Tilly and Mann, presents in its most

[30]   Mann, *Sources*, vol. I, pp. 456, 476, 479.
[31]   Mann, "State and Society," p. 196. Mann explicitly acknowledges his theoretical debt
to Tilly in *Sources*, vol. I, p. 433.

developed form a "fiscal-military" alternative to Hintze's purely geopolitical theory of European statebuilding. Downing summarizes his conclusions as follows:

To put the argument in its barest form, medieval European states had numerous institutions, procedures, and arrangements that, when combined with light amounts of domestic mobilization of human and economic resources for war, provided the basis for democracy in ensuing centuries. Conversely, constitutional countries confronted by a dangerous international situation mandating extensive domestic resource mobilization suffered the destruction of constitutionalism and the rise of military-bureaucratic absolutism.[32]

Though the position outlined above is very close to that of Mann, Downing takes the latter's work one step further by claiming that two other revenue sources in addition to abundant commercial wealth – income extracted from conquered territories and foreign subsidies – could also prevent the "extensive domestic resource mobilization" and ensuing "military bureaucratic absolutism" which was, so both authors believe, the necessary fate of those states dependent entirely on revenue from land taxes.

Though the theories of Tilly, Mann, and Downing are in some respects more sophisticated and richer in detail than that of Hintze, they suffer from some of the same deficiencies as the German historian's work. Thus in their writings as well the cases of Hungary and Poland remain unexplained. Almost entirely lacking in commercial resources, both states should have become absolutist and bureaucratic, but in fact they remained constitutional and nonbureaucratic. The logic of these theories would also lead one to predict that Spain and Portugal, which derived substantial incomes during the crucial "centuries of absolutism" from their American and Asian colonies, would have been able to preserve non-absolutist forms of government, but of course they did not.

Furthermore, like Hintze, the authors under consideration all tend to link one kind of early modern political regime with one kind of infrastructure – absolutism with bureaucracy and constitutionalism with the relative absence thereof – though the argument employed is somewhat different. According to Tilly, Mann, and Downing, absolutist states were those which, under geopolitical pressure, had to rely on land tax receipts to finance their standing armies and, because taxes on land were supposedly difficult to extract from recalcitrant rural populations, such states were forced to construct "bulky bureaucracies" in order to carry out this task. Non-absolutist states, which derived their income

---

[32] Downing, *Military Revolution*, p. 9.

largely from taxes on commerce or their equivalents like foreign subsidies or payments extorted from occupied territories which were alleg-
edly easy to collect, could dispense with such bureaucracies. Thus while
the underlying logic is somewhat different, these theorists' predictions
concerning variations in state infrastructure are in the end nearly identical with those of Hintze, and equally problematic.

The reason for this, as John Brewer's work has shown, is that the
assumption that taxes on commerce were easy to collect and taxes on
land difficult is erroneous. Far from requiring a minimum apparatus,
the collection of commercial revenues in fact demanded a large number
of well-trained personnel with advanced computational skills and a
detailed knowledge both of numerous commodities and of an array of
complex regulations. On the other hand, land taxes were not difficult
to administer, because central governments could dispense with the
time-consuming business of wealth or income assessments and instead
simply demand fixed amounts from each local area. It then fell to government officials or local notables to apportion this tax burden among
the populace in any way which the latter seemed willing to tolerate, and
to appoint the nonprofessional village collectors who were obliged to
extract the sums involved from their neighbors. While states which
derived substantial income from land taxes like France and Castile might
well have possessed very large fiscal apparatuses, this had more to do
with the proliferation of venal offices than with any difficulties involved
in collecting such taxes, as the relatively small number of British and
Prussian officials involved in land tax administration indicates.[33]

Perry Anderson, in his two works *Passages from Antiquity to Feudalism*[34]
and *Lineages of the Absolutist State* has provided yet another general theory
of European statebuilding, one which attempts to combine an aware-
ness of the significance of geopolitical competition shared by all of the
authors mentioned above with a new emphasis on socioeconomic for-
mations and on the legacies of the past in bringing about divergent
political regimes and infrastructures. In *Lineages*, Anderson identifies
three kinds of outcomes to the process of early modern statebuilding:
a milder form of absolutism found in western and southern Europe
(France, Spain) characterized in the administrative sphere by the sale
of offices; a small number of cases (England, the Dutch Republic) in

---

[33] Thus, during the second half of the 18th century, the British were employing between
6,000 and 8,000 staff in departments concerned with commercial taxes, while the
central office coordinating the activities of the amateur land tax commissioners in the
counties numbered just 14 persons. Also, the contemporaneous Prussia of Frederick
the Great employed no more than 500–600 officials at all levels of government to
collect its very substantial land taxes. Brewer, *Sinews*, p. 66; Johnson, *Frederick the Great*,
pp. 283–288; W. R. Ward, "The Office for Taxes, 1665–1798," *Bulletin of the Institute
of Historical Research*, vol. 25, no. 72 (November 1952), pp. 204–212, here at p. 208.
[34] Perry Anderson, *Passages from Antiquity to Feudalism* (London: New Left Books, 1974).

which absolutism was swept away by a precocious "bourgeois revolution"; and finally a harsher, more militarized eastern version of absolutism without the sale of offices found in Brandenburg-Prussia, Austria, and (outside of our universe of cases) Russia.

Anderson traces these divergent outcomes to what he calls the "uneven development of Europe"[35] rooted in the fact that some parts of the continent (latter-day England, France, Iberia, Italy, and southern Germany) had been part of the western Roman Empire prior to the middle ages, whereas others (the remainder of Germany, Scandinavia, eastern Europe) were in effect areas of new settlement. In the former, feudalism emerged independently out of a fusion between Roman and Germanic institutions, leaving a landscape characterized in the 13th century by parcelized sovereignty, autonomous towns, and serf-based agriculture. In the "colonial" east, however, royal authority was stronger, towns weaker, and peasants generally free.

The great crisis of the 14th century, triggered by the disappearance of uncultivated lands and resultant overpopulation in the west, deepened the differences between the two regions. In the western part of the continent, this crisis further weakened serf-based agriculture and noble landlords while strengthening both the towns and royal authority, leading eventually to the creation of royal absolutism as a means of maintaining the basic conditions of reproduction for the feudal aristocracy. Absolutism accomplished this task in two ways. First, it increased the land and people available for noble exploitation through an aggressive program of foreign conquest; and second, it employed the armed forces and bureaucracy created under pressure from military competitors to protect elite property rights.[36] Furthermore, a rising bourgeoisie was "bought off" and "feudalized" through the sale of offices within the growing state apparatus. In England and Holland, however, where commercial development was particularly strong, this bourgeoisie could not be tamed and eventually overthrew absolutism through revolution (the English Civil War and the Revolt of the Netherlands, respectively).[37]

In eastern Europe, by contrast, it was the weakening of the towns and of the independent peasantry as a result of the 14th-century crisis imported from the west which first permitted the local nobility to introduce serfdom at precisely the moment when it was beginning to disappear in western Europe.[38] During the next major exogenous economic crisis, that of the 17th century, military pressure generated primarily by a newly expansionist Sweden forced rulers in Brandenburg-Prussia,

---

[35] Anderson, *Passages*, p. 213.
[36] Anderson, *Passages*, pp. 154–155, 197–209; idem, *Lineages*, pp. 18–31, 51–54.
[37] Anderson, *Lineages*, pp. 11, 33–35, 94–95, 142.
[38] Anderson, *Passages*, pp. 213–214, 246–254, 263–264.

Austria, and Russia to establish bureaucratic-absolutist regimes to counter this external threat. The highly militarized and centralized form
assumed by these states was conditioned by the need to prop up – in
the interest of the nobility – a depressed, serf-based, agricultural system
facing the danger of widespread peasant flight. At the same time, the
absence of a significant commercial class made it possible to avoid
the sale of offices and construct more modern bureaucracies in this
region.[39]

Thus, as will be apparent from this summary, war also plays a central
role in Anderson's model of European political development despite its
nominally neo-Marxist framework, a result he justifies by arguing that
feudalism "was a mode of production founded on extra-economic coercion: conquest, not commerce, was its primary form of expansion."[40]
Yet the very ubiquity of military competition within feudalism means
that war cannot in itself account for the divergent features of the western and eastern absolutist state; rather, this role falls to variations in
socioeconomic structure (absence/presence of serfdom, relative strength
of bourgeoisie/towns), themselves largely rooted in differences in prior
historical experience (presence/absence of a direct Roman inheritance).

Despite its sweep and eloquence, Perry Anderson's analytic history
of the West from the fall of Rome to the French Revolution is also beset
by a number of difficulties. Like all of the other authors discussed,
Anderson is unable to do justice to the Hungarian and Polish cases.
Thus the same two factors which he employs to explain political outcomes in Brandenburg-Prussia and Austria – an underdeveloped
economy characterized by serf-based agriculture and weak towns, and
an acute security threat from more militarily advanced states – were
equally present in both Hungary and Poland. Yet the kind of government and infrastructure which the latter two countries came to possess
– a particularly pronounced variant of constitutionalism and a nonbureaucratic infrastructure built around local patrimonialism – were as
far removed as possible from the militarized, bureaucratic absolutism of
their Germanic neighbors.

Furthermore, Anderson presents no convincing general explanation
as to why the commercial classes in England and the Dutch Republic
proved so much stronger than those in France and Spain, thereby permitting the first two states to throw off absolutism. Also, like the other
authors mentioned earlier, he overlooks the existence of a large, nonproprietary bureaucracy in 18th-century Britain. Finally, his explanation
for differences in infrastructure between western and eastern absolutism
– the relative strength of the "demand" side for offices as determined
by the presence or absence of a strong commercial bourgeoisie – is

---

[39] Anderson, *Lineages*, pp. 195–200, 202–208, 212, 217.   [40] Ibid., p. 197.

ultimately unsatisfactory, because this would imply that the more economically advanced "western" areas of Germany would have developed apparatuses closer to those of France and Spain than those of "eastern" Prussia and Austria. This, however, was not the case.

EXPLAINING VARIATIONS IN EARLY MODERN STATES: THE ARGUMENT

The works discussed above, when taken together, have greatly advanced our understanding of the process of political development among the territorial states of medieval and early modern Europe. They have confirmed the overriding importance of both autonomous economic networks and geopolitical competition to the expansion and internal specialization of the individual European states. Yet the arguments presented in these works have in the end proved unable to explain the full range of outcomes of the process of European statebuilding. Hence a new theory of that process is necessary, one that can account in a more satisfactory way for the distribution of political regimes and state infrastructures found across the continent on the eve of the French and Industrial Revolutions. In sketching the outlines of just such a theory below, I first address the problem of political regimes, then infrastructures, and finally examine the independent influence of representative assemblies on infrastructural development.

Political Regimes

Explaining variations in political regime at the end of the early modern period means accounting for the strength or weakness of particular representative institutions, since it was the powers still held by such institutions which determined whether a given government was headed by a ruler who was relatively constrained (constitutionalism) or unconstrained (absolutism) in his behavior. In effect, this requires explaining why a given national representative assembly was strong enough to resist the endemic attempts by monarchs to monopolize legislative and other powers. The only recent author to address this question directly, H. G. Koenigsberger, declared with some exasperation at the end of his article "Dominium Regale or Dominium Politicum et Regale?": "The blunt truth is that no one has yet come up with an answer to [this] problem, that is, with anything approaching a satisfactory overall theory. I am not able to do this, either."[41] What is more, Koenigsberger remained skeptical

---

[41] Helmuth G. Koenigsberger, "Dominium regale or dominium politicum et regale? Monarchies and Parliaments in Early Modern Europe," in: Karl Bosl (ed.), *Der Moderne Parlamentarismus und seine Grundlagen in der Ständischen Repräsentation* (Berlin: Ducker & Humblot, 1977), pp. 43–68, here at p. 48.

about whether it would *ever* be possible to develop a general theory to explain variations in the strength of representative institutions.

But before succumbing to despair, we should take note of the fact that, as Koenigsberger himself mentions, one person at least offers the beginnings of such a theory, and that person was none other than Otto Hintze. During the 1920s and early 1930s, following his retirement from the University of Berlin, Hintze turned his attention increasingly to the representative assemblies of medieval and early modern Europe, a subject which he had neglected prior to World War I. His new interest may have been prompted by the difficulties that the Hungarian and Polish cases posed for his earlier, geopolitical theory[42] or perhaps it was inspired by the advent of the parliamentary Weimar Republic. For our purposes, the most important result of this new line of research was the short essay "Typologie der ständischen Verfassungen des Abendlandes" ("A Typology of the Representative Regimes of the West"), first published in 1930.[43]

In this essay, Hintze argues that the parliaments or "Estates" of the medieval and early modern West can be divided into two basic (ideal-) types, the "two-chamber" and the "tricurial," according to the system of representation they employed.[44] Into the former category he places the

---

[42] This supposition is supported by the presence among Hintze's papers of a long, unpublished study on Polish constitutional development written during the 1920s. Part of this study has now appeared under the title, "Verfassungsgeschichte Polens vom 16. bis 18. Jahrhundert," in: Hintze, *Staat und Verfassung*, pp. 511–562.

[43] Otto Hintze, "Typologie der ständischen Verfassungen des Abendlandes," in: idem, *Staat und Verfassung*, pp. 120–139. Other essays by Hintze from the 1920s and early 1930s which touch on this topic are: "Die Wurzeln der Kreisverfassung in den Ländern des nordöstlichen Deutschland" (1923), in: ibid., pp. 186–215; "Staatenbildung und Kommunalverwaltung" (1924), in: ibid., pp. 216–241; and "Weltgeschichtliche Bedingungen der Repräsentativverfassung" (1931), in: ibid., pp. 140–185. Only the last of these is contained in the Gilbert volume (pp. 302–353), translated as: "The Preconditions of Representative Government in the Context of World History." For a more extended discussion of Hintze's typology of representative institutions and of critical responses to it, see my essay: "Explaining Variation in Early Modern State Structure: The Cases of England and the German Territorial States," in: John Brewer and Eckhart Hellmuth (eds.), *Rethinking Leviathan: The British and German States of the Eighteenth Century* (Oxford: Oxford University Press, forthcoming).

[44] It is important to stress here that Hintze saw this distinction between "two chamber" and "tricurial" assemblies as *ideal-typical*; i.e., he did not mean to claim that all of the real world assemblies which he assigned to the first category actually possessed two chambers. In fact, as Hintze explicitly states, the division into two chambers was a later development that never came to pass in either Scotland or in medieval Sweden and Denmark. Likewise, it is well known that many "tri-curial" German assemblies came to possess only two chambers due to the disappearance of one or other of the three traditional estates. Yet, Hintze would argue, this variation in the number of chambers in no way affected the *internal organization* of the chambers, which is the real difference he is seeking to highlight through his typology. Given this fact, Hintze's choice of terminology is rather unfortunate.

representative assemblies of, among other states, England, Poland, Hungary, and the Scandinavian countries; and into the latter those of the German territorial states, France, Aragon, Catalonia, Valencia, Naples, and Sicily.[45] What distinguishes these two types of assemblies from one another is not so much the number of chambers they possess as the *internal structure* of those chambers. "Two-chamber" or territorially based bodies like the English Parliament were characterized by an upper house in which members of the higher nobility and clergy sat together, and a lower house made up of chosen representatives of rurally based organs of local government (the counties or their equivalent) and of the self-governing towns. On the other hand, assemblies in the "tricurial" or estate-based system found throughout the German territories and Latin Europe were divided into three or more chambers, each of which contained representatives (or indeed all members appearing personally) of one, and only one, legally privileged status group or estate such as the nobility, the clergy, and the burghers of the self-governing towns.

Hintze's basic contention in his essay is that the territorially based assemblies or parliaments were structurally stronger, and hence better able to resist the blandishments of ambitious rulers, than were status–group-based assemblies or Estates. He does not spell out why this might be so, but at least two reasons come to mind. First, because Estate-based assemblies were by definition strictly divided along status-group lines, the overriding concern of each of the individual chambers which composed such assemblies was to protect and, if possible, extend group-specific privileges. This made it very difficult for the chambers to co-operate among themselves in defense of the rights of the assembly as a whole vis-à-vis its royal master. Conversely, this situation encouraged rulers to negotiate directly with the individual chambers and strike bilateral deals with them. In fact, as we shall see, the chambers were often more than willing to give up rights of co-legislation or even co-taxation as long as the social and economic privileges of their respective status groups were guaranteed.

By contrast, the bicameral or territorially based assemblies were not divided along status-group lines. On the contrary, members of the different orders were mixed together in both chambers: higher aristocrats, clergy, and (in Poland and Hungary) officeholders in the upper house; and greater and lesser nobles, townsmen, and non-noble landowners (England) in the lower house. Furthermore, members of the upper house were frequently bound to their lower-house colleagues through ties of family, patronage, and locality. As a result, it proved far more difficult than in the case of the Estate-based assemblies for

---

[45] Hintze, "Typologie," pp. 124–125.

monarchs to play one chamber off against the other and thereby weaken
the representative body's ability to resist its ruler's ambitions. Put another way, the structure of the territorially based parliaments encouraged cooperation at the level of the entire assembly, whereas in the
status-based Estates such cooperation took place at the level of the
individual chamber, with detrimental consequences for the future of
the assembly as a whole (though not necessarily for its constituent
status groups).

A second reason for the greater resilience of the territorially based
assemblies was that they were inextricably linked to and rooted in
organs of local government. The lower chambers were, after all, made up
of representatives directly selected by county or borough assemblies or
councils, and such representatives were almost always themselves active
participants in local administration. Also, nearly all of the higher nobles
represented in the first chamber were, of course, also active in politics
in the areas in which their estates were located. Territorially based assemblies thus came to be seen both as an extension of and as an agency for
protecting the interests of organs of local government. Such organs
themselves already possessed a distinctly participatory complexion, characterized as they were by the interaction between central government
officials sent to the localities and members of the local (elite) population
who took part in judicial processes, tax assessments, and other government business.

At the same time, local government provided the members of territorially based assemblies with just those resources necessary to mount
an effective defense of such assemblies against overweening royal am-
bition: a ready-made forum in which all of the local political elite could
meet and discuss a common course of action; financial resources such
as local taxes; and even armed forces in the form of the local militia.
Such resources were in fact regularly mobilized to counter real or supposed threats of absolutism on the part of rulers. Prominent examples
include the English and Scottish parliamentary revolts against the Stuarts,
the repeated elite-led uprisings in Hungary against the Habsburgs, and,
more insidiously, the frequent armed noble confederations or *rokoszy*
directed against the Polish kings. The same advantages were not enjoyed by the status-based assemblies, for the simple reason that, aside
from the link between the representatives of the towns and the municipal councils which sometimes selected them, most of their members
possessed no organic connection to any unit of local government other
than the individual landed estates of nobles and ecclesiastics.

How can we explain the existence of these two contrasting types of
assemblies? Here again Hintze provides little assistance. I argue that the
answer lies for the most part in the *divergent experiences* of Latin Europe

and Germany on the one hand and Britain, Scandinavia, Poland, and Hungary on the other during the so-called dark ages between the collapse of the western Roman Empire and the turn of the millennium.[46] In Latin Europe and Germany, leaders of invading Germanic tribes built large-scale states upon the Roman foundations of the *civitas* (city-region), written law codes, an imperial conception of rulership, a highly regulated, noncompetitive market economy, and a caesaro-papist church. Over the coming centuries, as social and economic conditions moved farther and farther away from those that had obtained during antiquity, these foundations became ever weaker as they proved less and less able to provide the basis for political order in an increasingly "medieval" world. The resulting decline in central state authority across Latin Europe and Germany permitted a powerful landed elite of mixed Roman and Germanic origin to appropriate ever more public power and use it to construct autonomous lordly domains centered upon their rural estates.

The failure in Latin Europe and Germany of the Carolingian, Lombard, Visigothic, and Umayyad statebuilding experiments bequeathed a distinctive legacy to the rulers who set about creating a new generation of durable states across these regions between the turn of the millennium and the end of the middle ages: the Capetians of France (1000s/1100s), the Normans of southern Italy (1000s/1100s), the royal houses of *reconquista* Castile, Aragon, Catalonia, Valencia, and Portugal (1000s/1200s) and the hundreds of German noble families who, beginning in the 13th century, sought to construct their own states upon the ruins of the last of the dark age polities, the Ottonian-Salian Holy Roman Empire.[47] In the first instance, the collapse of the large-scale dark age polities encumbered this new generation of state-formers with an extremely fragmented regional and local political landscape, much of

---

[46] The importance of antecedent historical experiences is also stressed in Perry Anderson's model of European statebuilding, for it was the areas in the west of the continent formerly under Roman rule which first developed specifically feudal forms of dependent labor organization, while the non-Roman areas to the east only imported such forms centuries later. However, this divergence in the socioeconomic sphere, while significant in other respects, cannot explain differences in political regime and state infrastructure found in 18th-century Europe.

[47] It was the periodic weakness of a German imperial power built upon outmoded foundations that provided the opportunity for alternative state forms to arise in medieval central Europe. While local lords constructing new princely states were the primary beneficiaries of German imperial weakness, alternative outcomes were possible in those few areas where other social groups were stronger: city-dwellers in northern Italy and parts of Germany, and both city-dwellers and peasants in the northern Netherlands and Switzerland. These groups took advantage of the power vacuum which arose during the decline of Europe's last dark-age polity and formed city-republics and the republican confederation of Switzerland. This explains the fact that all the alternative state forms found within 18th-century western Christendom were located within the medieval boundaries of the Holy Roman Empire.

which lay under the direct control of noble lords large and small and hence beyond the direct influence of the new central authorities.

The response of these new state-formers was to use royal officials as agents with which to rebuild state authority from the center outward against the opposition of long-established, well-entrenched local elites whose power antedated, often by centuries, that of the new ruling houses (*administrative* pattern of local government). This organizational response to the extreme decentralization of power bequeathed by the dark ages was complemented by an intellectual one as sympathetic churchmen responded to the disorder around them by developing, during the course of the 1000s and 1100s, two new models of sociopolitical order – the theories of feudal hierarchy and of the tripartite society of orders – which would be deployed over the coming centuries as potent ideological weapons by statebuilding rulers in Latin Europe and Germany to reestablish central authority in the face of lordly opposition.[48]

By contrast, very different "starting conditions" confronted leaders who sought to build new states in the previously un- or only lightly inhabited areas along the periphery of western Christendom where their peoples had come to settle in the centuries following the demise of the western Roman Empire. Unencumbered by the legacies of dark age, neo-Roman statebuilding in general and opposition from old entrenched elites in particular – rulers in England, Scotland, Norway, Sweden, Denmark, Poland, and Hungary worked together with churchmen, native aristocrats, and other fighting men to form a series of durable new polities in the century and a quarter between 954 (English unification) and 1076 (elevation of a Polish duke to royal status by the pope). These kingdoms were all subdivided into a series of smaller, regular territorial units (the county in England, Scotland, and Hungary; *ziemia* in Poland; *häred/herred* and *landskab* in Scandinavia) where the local free male population itself carried out many tasks of governance (dispensing justice, maintaining order, and organizing local defense and revenue collection) with the help of royal officials sent out from the center (*participatory* pattern of local government).

This divergence in the pattern of *local government* found during the first period of life of those European polities which survived into the 18th century was of immense significance for the future course of European political development. It was this factor which helped determine

---

[48] Georges Duby, *Les Trois Ordres ou l'Imaginaire du Féodalisme* (Paris: Gallimard, 1978), pp. 77–81 et passim; idem, *Le Moyen Âge 987–1460* (Paris: Hachette, 1987), pp. 225–229; Jean-Pierre Poly and Eric Bournazel, *La Mutation Féodale: X^e–XIIe Siècles* (Paris: Presses Universitaires de France, 1980), pp. 298–305; Jean Dunbabin, *France in the Making 843–1180* (Oxford: Oxford University Press, 1985), pp. 256–259.

the type of representative assembly and ultimately the kind of political regime (absolutist or constitutional) that would emerge centuries later within a given state. Thus when the kings of England, Scotland, Sweden, Hungary, and Poland called national representative bodies into existence during the 1200s, 1300s, and 1400s in order to obtain approval for taxes to meet external military threats, they sought to gain the support of the unitary organs of local government found across their realms by asking the counties (or their equivalents) and the self-governing towns to send delegates to deliberate side by side with the leading churchmen and aristocrats of the realm. While in Scotland and medieval Sweden these county and borough representatives always remained together in a single chamber with the bishops and peers, in England, Hungary, and Poland the two groups soon came to form their own separate chambers, thus creating the kind of bicameral assembly most famously embodied in the English/British Parliament.

In Latin Europe and the German states, however, the character of local government was very different. Instead of the orderly pattern of unitary counties and autonomous boroughs within which local freemen took part in judicial inquiries, discussed matters of collective concern in periodic assemblies, and served in the militia, one finds in these regions overlapping and ill-defined catchment areas in which the business of governance was carried out almost exclusively by officials answerable to the center and their assistants with little or no active role for the local population above the village level. As a consequence, the states of Latin Europe and Germany lacked the unitary, participatory organs of rural local government found in the other areas of the continent. Thus, such organs could not serve as the basis for representation, as was the case with the territorially based assemblies. Rather, the tripartite model of society provided the basis for an Estate- (i.e., status-) based form of assembly with only tenuous connections to local government, with all of the consequences for the future of such bodies that this implied.

State Infrastructures

Though differences in the organization of local government resulting from variations in the pattern of state formation go a long way towards explaining why the rulers of Latin Europe and Germany eventually became absolute while their counterparts in Britain, Sweden, Hungary, and Poland were forced to share power with representative assemblies, they cannot account for the fact that France, Spain, the Italian states, and the two eastern European kingdoms had all by the eve of the French Revolution come to possess patrimonial infrastructures of various kinds, whereas the German states and Britain had successfully constructed proto-modern bureaucracies. How can we explain this second pattern of outcomes?

I suggest that we look for inspiration to the neighboring discipline of economic history. Alexander Gerschenkron achieved a major breakthrough in that field when he argued that a static understanding of the industrialization process of the kind dominant during the 1950s and 1960s could not in itself account for the significant differences found across the mature industrial economies of the 20th century. Instead, he pointed out that while all states undergoing industrialization did indeed share many common experiences, variations in outcome could only be explained by the timing ("early" or "late") of the onset of that process in a given state relative to all other states.[49] Thus many of the structural features that today distinguish Britain's economy from that of Germany can be traced back to the fact that the former was the first industrializer, and hence faced no comparable competition in many markets, whereas the latter was forced to build up its economy in a world already profoundly altered by Britain's earlier industrialization. I argue that a similar logic also obtained during the process of European statebuilding and that differences in the timing of the onset of sustaining geopolitical competition go a long way towards explaining the character of state infrastructures found across the continent at the end of the 18th century.

To see why this might be so, we first should remember that the work of Hintze, Tilly, Mann, Downing, and Anderson has already conclusively established that war and preparations for war tended to stimulate the creation of ever more sophisticated state institutions across the continent. Yet what this "consensus" overlooks is that while geopolitical competition may have had a crucial impact on the statebuilding process, the onset of such competition was "nonsimultaneous" – that is, it did not affect all states at the same time. This "nonsimultaneity" proved to be of particular significance for three reasons. First, timing mattered because the range of "technical resources" available to statebuilders did not remain invariant across this period. As all the authors mentioned above emphasize, medieval and early modern rulers responded to sustained (as opposed to merely episodic) geopolitical pressures by seeking

---

[49] The classic statement of this view is Alexander Gerschenkron, "Economic Backwardness in Historical Perspective," in: idem, *Economic Backwardness in Historical Perspective* (Cambridge, Mass.: Harvard University Press, 1962), pp. 5–30, here at pp. 7–11. For an extended discussion and criticism of Gerschenkron's argument in light of more recent research on European industrialization, see: Clive Trebilcock, *The Industrialization of the Continental Powers 1780–1914* (London: Longman, 1981), pp. 8–20, 421–426 and passim.

to construct larger and more specialized administrative and fiscal apparatuses in order to increase their military capacities. Yet the building
blocks with which they attempted to do this – whether in the form of
organizational models, legal concepts, or financial techniques – changed
greatly between the 12th and 18th centuries thanks to the forward
march of "technological progress" in this area.

As a result, states that expanded and differentiated their infrastructures before about 1450 (early statebuilders) often did so using methods and institutional arrangements that became increasingly outmoded
and even dysfunctional as the centuries passed, but that proved very
difficult to replace due to the power of vested interests with a material
and ideological stake in already established institutions.[50] At the same
time, states that were not affected by geopolitical competition – and
hence did not initiate a similar set of structural changes until after
about 1450 (late statebuilders) – possessed the advantage of being able
to adopt the latest techniques of administration and finance.

Second, and even more importantly, the supply of expert personnel
– administrators and those with financial and military expertise –
expanded greatly in the period after 1450 as a result of the proliferation of medieval universities, the growth of commercial and financial
markets, and changes in military technology. Prior to 1450, such personnel could exploit their very strong labor market position, owing to
the scarcity of their skills, to promote institutional arrangements like
proprietary officeholding and tax farming which were much more
beneficial to them than to their royal employers. With the tremendous
increase in the supply of such personnel in the early modern period,
the bargaining position of rulers who built up their state apparatuses
later improved substantially, thereby permitting them to resist more
effectively pressures toward appropriation. Finally, late statebuilders were
also able to learn from the experiences and mistakes of the "pioneers,"
an advantage that the latter, of course, did not share.

The nonsimultaneous onset of endemic conflict affected the various
parts of the continent in different ways. It was in the west and south of
Europe that sustained geopolitical competition first arose among the
polities of Latin Europe and the newly formed kingdoms of England
and Scotland during the course of the 1100s and 1200s, leading rulers
there to begin to construct complex, specialized state infrastructures. In
the relatively primitive conditions of that period, before the full flowering
of the revived Roman law and the medieval universities, the only two

[50] Douglass North has explored the reasons beyond the persistence of inefficient, dys-
      functional institutions over many centuries in his book *Institutions, Institutional Change
      and Economic Performance*.

models of large-scale organization available to statebuilding rulers were
the feudal and the ecclesiastical. The conceptions of office found at the
heart of both organizational models granted quasi-proprietary rights to
officeholders from the start, rights that the latter were able to strengthen
considerably by exploiting to the full their monopoly of scarce administrative skills.

In a similar way, cash-poor rulers often found themselves at the mercy
of the small number of financiers and merchants who possessed liquid
assets to lend during this period. Thus while the monarchies of western
and southern Europe had all, by the late 15th century, succeeded in
constructing impressive fiscal and administrative systems well ahead of
their neighbors to the east and north, the price that they paid for this
precocity was a substantial loss of effective control to proprietary
officeholders, tax farmers, and officeholder-financiers who viewed the
state not only as an instrument of princely power but also as a source
of income and social standing.

By contrast, similar geopolitical pressures did not impinge upon the
late-forming states of Germany and the Northern Netherlands or the
older kingdoms of Denmark, Sweden, Hungary, and Poland until centuries later, during the late 1400s and 1500s. As a result, when rulers
in these areas first attempted to expand and render more sophisticated
their infrastructures, they found themselves in a quite different world,
one filled with universities engaged in training large numbers of students in both canon and Roman law, and one with a much more developed commercial economy offering myriad opportunities for borrowing.
In addition, they also benefited from the practical examples, both good
and bad, furnished by their neighbors to the west and south. These
polities were hence in a better position to resist the kinds of large-scale
appropriation by officeholders and financiers which plagued statebuilding pioneers like France, the Iberian and Italian states, and England, and to attempt to construct instead proto-modern bureaucracies
based upon the separation of office from the person of the officeholder.

The Independent Effect of Parliaments

If differences in the organization of local government and in the timing
of the onset of sustained geopolitical competition had been the only
two factors influencing the distribution of political regimes and state
infrastructural types found across early modern Europe, then one would
expect to see the pattern of outcomes shown in Table 2.

A comparison of this table with Table 1, which summarizes the outcomes as specified in the historical literature, raises a number of important points. First, the organization of local government during the initial

Table 2. *Outcomes That Would Have Occurred If the Character of Local Government and Timing Had Been the Only Factors at Work*

		Type of local government during the first period of statebuilding	
		Administrative Patrimonial	*Participatory* Patrimonial
Onset of sustained geopolitical competition	*Pre-1450*	absolutism (Latin Europe)	constitutionalism (Britain)
	Post-1450	Bureaucratic absolutism (German States)	Bureaucratic constitutionalism (Poland, Hungary, Sweden, Denmark)

phase of statebuilding, itself a result of the antecedent experience of state formation, does a good job of predicting the actual distribution of absolutist and constitutional regimes found in the 18th century.[51]

Second, timing alone is sufficient to account for the kinds of state apparatuses found among the absolutist states: patrimonial infrastructures built around proprietary officeholding and tax farming in the case of France, Spain, Portugal, and the Italian principalities; and nonproprietary, proto-modern bureaucracies among the German states and Denmark. However, the predicted results for England and for Hungary and Poland in the sphere of infrastructures are the opposite of those which actually occurred. Since sustained geomilitary pressure came early to England, it should have been left on the eve of the French Revolution with a patrimonial state apparatus, when in fact it possessed, as John Brewer has shown, an extensive proto-modern bureaucracy. Conversely, Hungary and Poland should, as late statebuilders, have constructed such bureaucracies, but in fact never did so. Rather, almost all state functions in these countries had, by the end of the early modern period, been appropriated by noble-controlled organs of local government, thus leaving them with their own novel form of patrimonialism.

How can these unexpected results be explained? The answer lies in the fact that the presence of a powerful national representative institution acted as an independent influence on the pattern of infrastructural development found among constitutional states, deflecting them from

---

[51] The exception here is Denmark, which enjoyed a participatory pattern of government during the centuries following its formation, yet became an absolutist state after 1660. I will provide a brief explanation for this Danish "exceptionalism" at the end of this introduction, and then again in Chapter 6.

the path they otherwise would have followed had the effects of timing
been able to work themselves out unimpeded. Since such assemblies
were by definition weak or nonexistent in the absolutist states, they
could not play there the role of a third independent variable, which
explains why in these cases timing alone does in fact predict infrastructural outcomes quite accurately. To render more concrete what this
means, let us look briefly at the cases of England and of Hungary and
Poland, before contrasting them with those of the absolutist states of
Latin Europe and Germany.[52]

As mentioned earlier, sustained geopolitical competition came to
affect England very early, during the course of the 1100s. As a result, that
country was among the first to begin to construct a sophisticated state
apparatus in order to meet a foreign military threat, in this case one
from France. Just as the timing argument outlined above would predict,
that apparatus exhibited strong patrimonial tendencies right from the
start. However, with the appearance in the late 1200s of Parliament as
the representative of the participatory county and borough communities, patrimonial practices like proprietary officeholding and tax farming came under intense criticism. The resulting struggle between royal
officials and England's national representative assembly over the character of the growing administrative and financial infrastructure continued intermittently for over three and a half centuries.

The importance of Parliament in countering tendencies towards the
appropriation of office became clear during the late 1400s and 1500s
when the decline of that body in the wake of England's military dis-
engagement from the continent, combined with the replacement of
clerics by laymen in many government positions, led to the consolidation
and spread of proprietary officeholding. The grip of this and other
patrimonial practices on the English state was only permanently overcome when a return to regular, nearly annual meetings of Parliament
after 1660 created conditions which allowed reformers within the central government to construct a new, nonproprietary fiscal-military bureaucracy built around the Treasury, the revenue boards, the Navy Board,
the Admiralty, and the offices of the secretaries of state and secretary-
at-war. Thus by the late 17th century, Parliament was at last able largely
to replace the patrimonial infrastructure which early statebuilding had
initially bequeathed to England with a new administrative apparatus
organized along (proto-) modern bureaucratic lines. In effect, the efforts
of that body in the end permitted Britain to move off a path of development which would have culminated in patrimonial constitutionalism
and instead to enter onto another leading to *bureaucratic constitutionalism.*

---

[52] For supporting evidence for the following arguments, see the detailed discussion of
the countries in question in the chapters which follow.

If the British Parliament acted to prevent the final triumph of patrimonialism in favor of bureaucracy, strong national representative bodies did just the opposite in Hungary and Poland. In contrast to England, these countries did not come under sustained geopolitical pressure until the late 1400s and 1500s, when the Turks began to menace Hungary and the rise of Muscovy/Russia and Sweden permanently threatened Poland. Because of the late onset of such pressures, Hungarian and Polish rulers found themselves – like their counterparts in Germany – in a position to benefit from the administrative, financial, and military progress made since the 12th century and to build state infrastructures in response to foreign military threats that would be less prone to appropriation.

This is indeed exactly what the king Mátyás Hunyadi (reigned 1458 –1490) did in Hungary. During the 1470s and 1480s, he built up a professional army of 28,000 men supported by a nonproprietary bureaucracy staffed by university-educated Humanists. Yet after Mátyás's death in 1490, the Hungarian Diet, acting for the noble-controlled county communities, promptly dismantled this new instrument of royal power and turned over most state functions to local government organs which had now become little more than extended arms of noble power. Similar developments occurred numerous times in Poland from the reign of Sigismund Augustus (1548–1572) through that of Jan Sobieski (1674–1696), with the Sejm (parliament) repeatedly blocking attempts to construct a modern state apparatus that might strengthen royal authority and more effectively defend the country against Russians, Swedes, Turks, and Prussians in favor of retaining most power at the local level, where it could easily be appropriated by the magnates. Thus in both Hungary and Poland, strong national assemblies acted to prevent the bureaucratization that occurred in other late statebuilders such as the German states in order to protect a kind of patrimonialism centered not around proprietary officials and tax farmers, as in Latin Europe, but around continued control by a locally based elite, in this case the landowning nobility. The most tangible consequence of this triumph of *patrimonial constitutionalism* was a decline of military effectiveness in both countries, which led to a partial loss of independence in Hungary and the complete destruction of the state at the hands of its neighbors in Poland.

The reason behind the opposite effect of intervention by representative assemblies in England on the one hand (bureaucratization) and Hungary and Poland on the other (patrimonialization) lies in the fact that because of the early onset of geopolitical competition in the former, a substantial state apparatus with patrimonialist tendencies was already in place *before* the English Parliament ever appeared on the scene in the late 1200s. Since it was already too late to eliminate this apparatus altogether, the goal of representatives in Westminster became to reform it, a task which required many centuries to accomplish. In Hungary and Poland, by contrast, the onset of sustained geopolitical pressures occurred *after* national representative assemblies were already in place, and those assemblies were hence in a position to block altogether the construction of a bureaucratic infrastructure in response to such pressures.

If powerful representative institutions in England, Hungary, and Poland were capable – each in their own way – of altering the path of infrastructual development dictated by the attempt of rulers to respond to the functional exigencies of geopolitical competition alone, the same was not true of the weaker assemblies of Latin Europe and the German states. Like their English counterpart, the Estates of France, the Iberian peninsula, and Italy also railed against the prevalence of patrimonial practices that were the usual concomitant of early statebuilding. Yet with the exception of the Sicilian *parlamento*, by the late 1600s all such assemblies had been swept away following a period of sustained weakness that had lasted several centuries. As a result, proprietary office-holding and other forms of patrimonial organization only grew stronger, leaving this region the homeland of *patrimonial absolutism* until the French Revolution and beyond.

While many more German Estates survived in some form into the 18th century, this was so only because they had chosen to confine their activities entirely to the administration of certain direct taxes, leaving their rulers free to take advantage of their positions as late statebuilders to construct proto-modern bureaucracies active in all other spheres of government. It was this crucial difference in the character of their infrastructures which distinguished the *bureaucratic absolutist* states of early modern Germany from their patrimonial absolutist cousins in Latin Europe.

It should be stressed here that the four concepts introduced above – bureaucratic constitutionalism, patrimonial constitutionalism, patrimonial absolutism, and bureaucratic absolutism – represent *analytic categories* constructed around only two aspects of 18th-century territorial states: political regime and infrastructural type. Hence I make no claim that they capture all salient features of those states even within the political realm, let alone in any other sphere of life. Furthermore, the "fit" between the categories and the empirical cases also varies even as far as political regime and infrastructure are concerned. Thus ancien régime France and Frederician Prussia were more fully realized examples of, respectively, patrimonial and bureaucratic absolutism than were contemporaneous Spain and Saxony.

Mention should also be made of two cases which are explained less well by the three independent variables I have introduced: those of Denmark and Sweden. Both Scandinavian states arose in areas untouched by large-scale, dark-ages state formation, and both subsequently developed patterns of local government which were clearly participatory in nature. Also, neither polity was subjected to sustained geopolitical pressure until quite late, during the 1500s. Hence, based on the arguments presented above, one would expect that both countries would have developed in the direction of patrimonial constitutionalism, and indeed they did so for many centuries. By the 1700s, however, Sweden had emerged as a bureaucratic, rather than a patrimonial, constitutional monarchy, and Denmark had made an even more sudden and startling shift towards bureaucratic absolutism.

While the reasons for these deviations will be explored in greater detail in Chapter 6, suffice it to say here that in both cases powerful contingent events conspired to confound expected paths of development. In Sweden, these took the form of the election of the noble Gustav Vasa to the throne in 1523 under circumstances which allowed him to replace the country's old territorially based assembly with a new, four-chamber body (the Riksdag) containing both territorial and status-based elements.[53] While the Riksdag eventually proved strong enough to maintain its powers of co-legislation and co-taxation through most of the early modern period, it could not prevent the construction by successive Vasas of a nonproprietary bureaucracy closely modeled on those of the German states. This development occurred during the course of the late 1500s and 1600s in the wake of Sweden's new involvement in European power politics.

In Denmark, by contrast, it was the progressive destruction of a participatory form of local government beginning in the middle ages through the immigration of German knights granted lands at feudal tenure which stunted the growth of a powerful, territorially based assembly in that country. Such an alteration in the character of local government laid the groundwork for the royal "coup" of 1660 and the subsequent introduction of a bureaucratic absolutism also inspired by German models.[54]

Thus when due account is taken of the ability of strong representative assemblies to influence infrastructural development directly, the

---

[53] Thus the new Riksdag contained chambers of the nobility, clergy, and the towns just like the Estates of the German states and Latin Europe, but also a fourth chamber of peasants whose representatives were elected by the participatory organs of local government which remained in existence throughout this period. See the detailed discussion on the origins and internal organization of the post-1527 Riksdag in Metcalf, *Riksdag*, pp. 58–60, 66–68, 86–108.

[54] Kersten Krüger, "Absolutismus in Dänemark – ein Modell für Begriffsbildung und Typologie," in: Ernst Hinrichs (ed.), *Absolutismus* (Frankfurt: Suhrkamp, 1986), pp. 65–94; Lucien Musset, *Les Peuples Scandinaves au Moyen Âge* (Paris: Presses Universitaires de France, 1951), pp. 106, 114–115, 118, 266–267, 278–279.

Table 3. *Actual Outcomes Explained When Account Is Taken of the Influence of Parliaments on Infrastructural Development*

		Type of local government during the first period of statebuilding	
		Administrative	*Participatory*
Onset of sustained geopolitical competition	*Pre-1450*	Patrimonial absolutism (Latin Europe)	Bureaucratic constitutionalism (Britain)
	Post-1450	Bureaucratic absolutism (German States)	Patrimonial constitutionalism (Poland, Hungary)

predicted pattern of 18th-century outcomes summarized in Table 3 closely approximates the actual pattern detailed in Table 1.

The argument presented above will be substantiated and developed in much greater detail in the chapters which follow. Chapters 2 and 3 will analyze the emergence and consolidation of patrimonial absolutism in Latin Europe and its inability to reform itself despite endemic financial crises and military defeats. In Chapter 4, I turn to Britain and show how the patrimonial legacy bequeathed by the early onset of geopolitical competition *was* eventually overcome with the help of a strong, territorially based representative assembly. In Chapter 5, I examine the complex subject of political development in central Europe and discuss the emergence of bureaucratic absolutism among the German states, with particular emphasis on the case of Brandenburg-Prussia. Chapter 6 then addresses the cases of Hungary and Poland, where elites organized both in national parliaments and in the regions appropriated much of the power of central government, an outcome with tragic consequences for Poland. Chapter 6 will also explore why Denmark and Sweden eventually deviated from the path of patrimonial constitutionalism which they initially seemed destined to follow. Finally, in Chapter 7, I will discuss some of the broader theoretical implications of the European statebuilding experience.

———— ☙ ————

Chapter 2

THE ORIGINS OF PATRIMONIAL
ABSOLUTISM IN LATIN EUROPE

On the eve of the French Revolution, after over thirteen centuries of post-Roman statebuilding, two common features distinguished the polities of Latin Europe – an area comprising the southern Netherlands, France, and the Iberian and Italian peninsulas – from the other states of western Christendom. First, with the exception of Sicily and the three remaining Italian republics (Venice, Genoa, Lucca), all had long since dispensed with their national representative assemblies. In a word, this was the early modern West's most thoroughly absolutist area. At the same time, however, its rulers, while *de jure* enjoying quite extensive prerogative powers, had lost direct control over much of the administrative, judicial, and financial infrastructure of their realms to proprietary officeholders, officeholder-financiers, and tax farmers. Over the course of many centuries these groups had succeeded in appropriating substantial portions of their respective states' public powers for their own private ends. Thus Latin Europe was the homeland of an early modern state form that I have termed "patrimonial absolutism," an ideal type most closely approximated by ancien régime France.

How is it possible to account for this common outcome to the long process of medieval and early modern political development among a group of countries which, after all, differed greatly in size, wealth, geographic position, and significance within the world of European power politics? This chapter will argue that such an outcome can be explained by two factors: an administrative, nonparticipatory pattern of local government among the new generation of states (Capetian/Valois France, *reconquista* Castile, Aragon and Portugal, Hohenstaufen/Angevin Naples, and Sicily) formed in Latin Europe around the year 1000, which was itself the lasting legacy of failed, dark age attempts at statebuilding within this region; and early geopolitical competition, or the precocious onset of sustained rivalries involving large-scale warfare between these states and the polities surrounding them.

As argued in the first chapter, one of the most far-reaching variations in the process of European political development concerns the difference between those areas comprising the continent's geographic core

(Latin Europe and Germany), where substantial states came into being
and even thrived during the so-called dark ages,[1] and the western,
northern, and eastern peripheries (British isles, Scandinavia, east central Europe) where such polities did not coalesce until the 11th century.
While none of the dark age states of Latin Europe – the most notable
of which were the Visigothic kingdom and the Umayyad caliphate in
Iberia, the Lombard kingdom in Italy, and the Merovingian and
Carolingian realms in Gaul – survived unaltered into the central middle ages, I argue that their prior existence left an indelible mark, in the
form of a predisposition towards absolutism, on the polities which came
to replace them. This was so because failed, dark age states burdened
those successors with a fragmented political landscape which favored
the creation first of a top-down, nonparticipatory pattern of local government and then of structurally weak, corporately organized representative assemblies which proved unable to stand up to attempts of
ambitious rulers to maximize their own power.

While the legacy of previous, unsuccessful attempts at statebuilding
may have pushed the postmillennial kingdoms of Latin Europe in the
direction of absolutism, it was their early exposure to sustained geopolitical pressure which helped determine the precise form which that
absolutism would take. Europe's sudden transformation into a multistate
world after the year 1000 brought with it intense geopolitical competition among its constituent countries. However, the onset of such competition, and the large-scale warfare that regularly accompanied it during
this period, was "nonsimultaneous": it did not occur at the same time
in all parts of the continent. Such competition came first to Latin
Europe and England, western Christendom's most culturally and economically developed areas, and in so doing set off intense statebuilding
efforts there as rulers sought to cope with the demands of war and
preparations for war.

While these efforts turned the states of Latin Europe (along with
their neighbor England) into statebuilding pioneers, it also increased
the dependence of still-fragile polities on the small group of elites in
possession of the administrative, judicial, military, and financial know-
how and resources vital to state expansion. These elites were in turn
able to exploit their strong position, a position only strengthened by
periods of extended warfare, to lay the groundwork for the future

---

[1] Though this expression has rightly gone out of fashion because of the quite mislead-
    ing impression which it conveys about the post-Roman world, I have chosen to use it
    because it is the only available term which covers the whole period from the 5th
    through the 11th centuries. The current practice among historians is to employ "late
    antiquity" for the period 200–700 and "early" or "high middle ages" for the subse-
    quent centuries.

appropriation of vital state functions. Their task was made easier by the still quite limited range of administrative models and market-based financial services available in the 1300s and 1400s.

In this chapter, I first discuss the origins, nature, and decline of the large-scale dark age kingdoms which arose across Latin Europe in the wake of the dissolution of Roman power. I pay special attention to the greatest of these polities, the Carolingian Empire of the Franks. I then examine how the decline of Carolingian power unleashed forces of economic and ecclesiastical renewal which laid the basis for a new wave of state formation around the turn of the millennium, a development which soon turned Europe into a competitive, multistate world. Finally, I show how the early onset of geopolitical competition, when combined with a top-down, administrative pattern of local government that was the legacy of failed dark age state formation, helped place the polities of Latin Europe on the path toward patrimonial absolutism well before the close of the middle ages.

THE LATE ROMAN EMPIRE AND EARLY STATE FORMATION IN VISIGOTH SPAIN, LOMBARD ITALY, AND MEROVINGIAN AND CAROLINGIAN GAUL

Despite popular images of the "fall of the Roman Empire" as a violent, cataclysmic event leading to the demise of classical civilization, modern historiography has stressed the high degree of continuity between the western Empire and the barbarian kingdoms which came to replace it during the course of the 5th and 6th centuries. The late Empire was a highly institutionalized polity headed by an emperor who, in addition to possessing sole powers of legislation, taxation, and military command, exercised tight control over both the (Christian) state church and a nondynamic economy little affected by competitive markets. The foundation upon which this imposing edifice was constructed was the *civitas*, a unit of local government consisting of a city and its often sizable rural hinterland which was at once a political, social, and economic community.

A considerable portion of the surviving Roman sociopolitical infrastructure was taken over by the new Germanic rulers; indeed, it was only this inheritance which allowed them to construct such large and durable successor states so rapidly. However, the exhaustion of the western Empire's financial and manpower resources, the decline of city life, and the devastation wrought by civil wars and invasions had damaged much of that infrastructure. This fact forced barbarian kings to introduce new institutions and methods of governance to raise the capacities of their states within a world slowly moving away from the

social and economic conditions that had obtained during antiquity. Yet
these new institutions and methods, while effective in the medium term,
tended ultimately to weaken the central authority of the Germanic
kingdoms. This development in turn increased the difficulty of containing the power of a wealthy landed aristocracy of mixed Roman and
barbarian origin and channeling their ambitions, as the Empire had
always done, into forms of competition not threatening to the state
itself.

Roman Collapse and the Early Dark Age Kingdoms

While the relative weight of social, economic, and military causes in
bringing about the decline of the western Roman Empire remains in
dispute, one manifestation of that decline is clear enough: the complete disappearance between 406 and 476 of the imperial standing
army in the West as authorities there proved unable to find the men,
money, and supplies necessary to keep this cornerstone of the Roman
state alive.[2] The process leading to this catastrophic outcome was complex and cannot be recounted in detail here. The basic pattern was that
the western authorities were forced to abandon direct control over one
province after another as they found themselves incapable of replacing
garrison and field troops decimated in engagements with barbarians or
in fratricidal conflicts over the imperial succession. Instead, in an ultimately fatal move, the government came to rely almost exclusively on
foederati (allies, federates) to defend the western provinces.

These "allies" were Germanic peoples organized and commanded by
their own leaders who had been settled within the Empire and offered
grants of land and/or taxes with which to support themselves and their
families in return for promises to defend the regions in which they now
lived.[3] Turning to these proven fighters for help must have seemed like
an irresistible proposition to the hard-pressed government of the western

---

[2]   Roger Collins, *Early Medieval Europe 300–1000* (New York: St. Martin's Press, 1991),
      pp. 75–93, especially pp. 89–90; A. H. M. Jones, *The Late Roman Empire 284–602*
      (Baltimore: Johns Hopkins University Press, 1986), pp. 201–202, 1067.
[3]   The technical details surrounding the settlement of federates within the Empire re-
      main a matter of great dispute. Walter Goffart, in his *Barbarians and Romans A.D. 418–
      584: The Techniques of Accommodation* (Princeton: Princeton University Press, 1980),
      argues that the federates were supported in the first instance by grants not of land but
      of Roman tax revenues, and only became landowners much later. Collins, *Early Medi-
      eval Europe*, p. 53, supports Goffart, but Klavs Randsborg, *The First Millennium A.D. in
      Europe and the Mediterranean* (Cambridge: Cambridge University Press, 1991), p. 166,
      and Peter Heather, *Goths and Romans 332–489* (Oxford: Clarendon, 1991), p. 222,
      remain more skeptical. What does not seem in dispute is that by the late 500s the
      federates had become landowners *and* that the Roman system of direct taxation had
      largely disappeared.

Empire, for it brought peoples over to the Roman side who might otherwise have become dangerous enemies, while at the same time providing for the defense of whole regions without the administrative and fiscal burdens imposed by an expensive standing army. Yet the dangers inherent in this novel defense strategy soon became apparent: the resources found in the provinces where federates settled were effectively lost to the authorities in Italy, and this made it all the more difficult to maintain the standing army in those regions still under direct Roman rule, thereby encouraging further use of federates. And once federate leaders had taken control of the provinces they now were to defend, there was nothing to prevent them from extending their authority over Romans living in the area as well, thus transforming themselves from kings of their own people into rulers of territorially defined kingdoms which now arose within the old boundaries of the Empire.

In this way the western government, now based in Ravenna, had by the 460s lost direct control over nearly all of the West outside Italy to federates or rebellious Roman generals supported by federates. The western Empire had in effect been handed over to the barbarians in order to save it from them. Or, as Walter Goffart has put it, "what we call the fall of the western Roman Empire was an imaginative experiment [in defense] that got a little out of hand."[4] The final blow came in 476, when the Germanic general Odovacer overthrew the last western emperor and, with the support of his federate troops, declared himself king of Italy.

The next century witnessed a series of drawn-out conflicts among the newly established Germanic kingdoms and, during the mid-500s, between the Ostrogothic rulers of Italy and the forces of the eastern emperor Justinian, who succeeded in recapturing the old imperial heartland only to lose most of it after 568 to the invading Lombards. By the late 6th century, however, a degree of stability had returned to a West now dominated by three large-scale polities, all of which would prove to be quite durable: the Visigothic kingdom in Spain, which lasted 227 years, from 484 to 711; the Lombard kingdom in Italy, which shared control of the peninsula with a series of isolated Byzantine strongholds and lasted 206 years, from 568 to 774; and the Merovingian kingdom of the Franks in Gaul, which lasted 240 years, from 511 to 751.

The Carolingian Empire

By the mid-600s the effective power of the Merovingian dynasty within the Frankish kingdom was being challenged by the Carolingians, an

---

[4]   Goffart, *Barbarians and Romans*, p. 35.

aristocratic family from the subkingdom of Austrasia, the least developed and most "Germanic" part of Gaul that was centered on the southern Netherlands and the west bank of the Rhine. By that date this rising family, thanks to its substantial wealth and clever marriage alliances, had gained control of the highest office in Austrasia, that of mayor of the royal palace (*maior domus*) and had used this position to consolidate its preeminence in the region. The Carolingians then established themselves as the dominant political force in all of Gaul through the great military victories won first by Pippin II over his rival the *maior domus* of Neustria (battle of Tertry – 687), and then by his son Charles Martel over the hitherto autonomous Alamans, Thuringians, Bavarians, Burgundians, Provençals, and – most spectacularly of all – the invading Umayyad Arabs (battle of Poitiers – 732). The family also followed up these "domestic" successes with an aggressive campaign of foreign expansion leading to the conquest and incorporation into the realm of the Lombard kingdom of Italy in the 770s, of northeastern Spain by 806, and, most significantly, of all of Germany to the river Elbe by 814.[5]

The tremendous personal and (thanks to the Merovingian precedent) family charisma generated by a nearly unbroken string of military successes lasting more than a century was a necessary but not sufficient condition for the removal of the older dynasty from the Frankish throne. Hence in 750 Pippin the Short, Charles Martel's son, turned to Pope Zacharias to help determine whether it would be legitimate to depose the reigning Merovingian Chilperic III. Zacharias, mindful of the importance of Frankish support against his enemies the Lombards, replied that "it would be better to call king the man who had power than the man who was still there without royal power," and in the following year Pippin, with the approval of the Franks, was finally anointed *rex Francorum* by his bishops.[6] This mutually beneficial relationship between Papacy and Frankish power reached its height in 800, when Pope Leo III offered the restored imperial crown to Pippin's son Charlemagne after the latter had rescued Leo from a revolt led by his Roman aristocratic rivals.[7]

---

[5]   On the rise of the Carolingians and their subsequent conquests, see: Rosamond McKitterick, *The Frankish Kingdoms under the Carolingians, 751–987* (London: Longman, 1983), pp. 16–76; Karl Ferdinand Werner, *Histoire de France. Tome I: Les Origines* (Paris: Fayard, 1984), pp. 335–339, 342–349, 363–388; Collins, *Early Medieval Europe*, pp. 157–161, 245–271.

[6]   Quoted in: Janet Nelson, "Kingship and Empire," in: J. H. Burns (ed.), *The Cambridge History of Medieval Political Thought c. 350–c. 1450* (Cambridge: Cambridge University Press, 1988), pp. 211–251, here at pp. 213–214.

[7]   On the complex circumstances surrounding Charlemagne's coronation and its broader significance, see: Judith Herrin, *The Formation of Christendom* (Oxford: Basil Blackwell, 1987), pp. 451–462 and passim; also Collins, *Early Medieval Europe*, pp. 268–274.

The extraordinary string of Carolingian successes which culminated in the coronation of 800 confronted the family with an immense task: maintaining control over a vast, mainly inland, realm in an age of extremely poor communications and in the face of the centrifugal forces of both independent aristocratic power and regional and ethnic diversity. To accomplish this, they could of course draw on the political institutions and practices inherited from their Roman and Merovingian predecessors, suitably modified in keeping both with the much greater size of their kingdom and the changing economic circumstances of the 8th and 9th centuries. The Roman features of Merovingian kingship – the ruler's strong prerogatives in the areas of defense, justice, and lawmaking – were retained and strengthened by the imperial elevation. Charlemagne now came to see himself explicitly as "a new Constantine," adopting as his motto *"renovatio Romani imperii"* and reintroducing elements of Roman iconography and ceremonial, thereby revitalizing a relationship between the late Empire and its barbarian progeny that had slowly faded over the preceding three centuries. On a more practical level, his lawmaking activity increased markedly after 800 in response to what he saw as his imperial vocation as legislator.[8]

At the same time, it is clear that the role played by successive popes in the events of 751 and 800 marked a shift towards a conception of rulership more explicitly Christian than that of either the late Empire or its Visigoth, Lombard, or Merovingian successor states. Indeed, the Carolingians seemed to be prepared to acknowledge for the first time the papal claims to independent moral authority set down in 494 in Gelasius's doctrine of the two swords, and they saw in the protection and propagation of the faith their highest duties as emperors.[9] This piety, which lent the revived empire a militantly Christian tinge, did not prevent the Carolingians either from incorporating the papal territories into their realm or from making full use of the extensive powers traditionally enjoyed by emperors in matters of both ecclesiastical organization and theology. Indeed, they were the true architects of the so-called imperial Church system (*Reichskirchensystem*), later perfected by the Ottonians and Salians in Germany, which saw ecclesiastical institutions more fully integrated into the state than they had been even during the heyday of Constantine and his successors.[10]

---

[8] Werner, *Histoire*, pp. 385–386; Collins, *Early Medieval Europe*, pp. 274–275.

[9] Nelson, "Kingship and Empire," pp. 214–216, 226–227, 230–234; I. S. Robinson, "Church and Papacy," in: Burns, *Cambridge History*, pp. 252–305, here at pp. 291–296; McKitterick, *Frankish Kingdoms*, pp. 35–36; Collins, *Early Medieval Europe*, pp. 258–259.

[10] On the imperial Church system and its origins under the Carolingians, see: Leo Santifaller, *Zur Geschichte der Ottonisch-Salischen Reichskirchensystems* (Wien: Hermann Böhlaus Nachfolger, 1964), especially pp. 20–26. On the role of the Church within

While the Carolingians retained the basic outlines of the administrative system they had inherited from their predecessors, they also altered this system in significant ways. Conflicts during the Merovingian period over the respective powers of the bishop and the count, respectively the highest religious and civilian authority within the *civitas*, had served to undermine the efficacy of local government. Through a series of actions later known as the *divisiones inter episcopatum et comitatum* (divisions between the diocese and the county), Charles Martel took away much land held by episcopal churches in their rural hinterlands, along with various regalian rights which bishops had accumulated, and transferred them to the count, who now became the more important representative of the royal will at the local level. At the same time, however, the privilege of immunity (freedom from the count's judicial authority) enjoyed by the remaining episcopal lands was reconfirmed and even strengthened, and the bishop assigned a new role as a direct agent of royal oversight monitoring the activities of the count.[11]

The cumulative effect of these and subsequent reforms was to shift decisively the locus of power at the local level from the city to the countryside, where both the comital estates and royal monasteries upon which the count relied for material and political support were to be found. Thus the basic building-blocks of the new empire were no longer the cities with their dependent country districts, as had been the case during the Roman and Merovingian periods, but rather the country districts themselves, which might contain within their borders (in addition to some remaining territory held by ecclesiastical immunists) both dependent and autonomous towns. This epochal change was reflected at the linguistic level by a transformation in the usage of the ancient terms *civitas* and *pagus*, with the former coming to mean only "city" and the latter shedding its overtones of "rural hinterland" and becoming instead synonymous with "county" (*comitatus*), the new name for the standard unit of local government throughout the Empire.[12] The administrative

the Carolingian administrative system, see: Karl Ferdinand Werner, "Missus – Marchio – Comes," in: idem, *Vom Frankenreich zur Entfaltung Deutschlands und Frankreichs* (Sigmaringen: Jan Thorbecke, 1984), pp. 109–156, here at pp. 114–122.

[11] Martin Heinzelmann, "Bischof und Herrschaft vom spätantiken Gallien bis zu den karolingischen Hausmeiern. Die institutionellen Grundlagen," in: Friedrich Prinz (ed.), *Kirche und Herrschaft* (Stuttgart: Anton Hiersemann, 1988), pp. 24–82, here at pp. 81–82; Reinhold Kaiser, "Königtum und Bischofsherrschaft im frühneuzeitlichen Neustrien," in: ibid., pp. 83–108, here at pp. 98–99, 104–105; Edward James, *The Origins of France* (London: Macmillan, 1982), p. 202; Werner, "Missus – Marchio – Comes," pp. 118–119.

[12] James, *Origins*, pp. 63, 162; McKitterick, *Frankish Kingdoms*, p. 87; François Louis Ganshof, "Charlemagne et les Institutions de la Monarchie Franque," in: Helmut Beumann (ed.), *Karl der Grosse: Lebenswerk und Nachleben. Band I: Persönlichkeit und Geschichte* (Düsseldorf: Verlag L. Schwann, 1965), pp. 349–393, here at pp. 371–372.

reorganization carried out by the Carolingians thus realigned the structure of the Frankish state with the realities of an early medieval world in which cities were no longer the centers of social and economic life they had been throughout antiquity.

At the heart of this new rural political community centered on the *pagus* stood the *mallus*, the county court, which was presided over by the count, convoked two to three times a year, and attended by all the free men of the district. These general sessions of the *mallus* were supplemented by smaller local sessions which the count held in the course of his regular trips through the county. A further opportunity for the district's political community to gather was provided by the local assemblies or *placita* which the count called together several times a year in order to announce new items of legislation, communicate important news, or discuss problems affecting the county. To assist the count in coping with his extensive workload, Charlemagne provided him with an assistant, the viscount, who carried out the count's duties while the latter was away on campaign or visiting the royal court, as well as a permanent corps of assessors (*scabini*) learned in the law who helped him decide the civil and criminal cases brought before the *mallus*. In addition to his function as chief judge and political leader of the district, the count was also responsible for collecting the fees, fines, and commercial taxes owed to the crown as well as for assembling and leading the local military contingent.[13]

Yet how could the imperial government maintain control over a force of some 600 to 700 counts spread out over a vast area? This problem was rendered even more difficult by the fact that it was thought necessary to name local aristocrats with a substantial independent power base to this office, since only such men possessed the standing and authority necessary to keep the peace and enforce legal judgments.[14] One answer has already been hinted at above: the Carolingians made use of the institutionalized, hierarchically structured, Empire-wide organization of the Church to oversee the activities of the counts. Not only were

---

[13] Ganshof, "Charlemagne et les Institutions," pp. 373, 378–379, 382; idem, "Charlemagne et l'Administration de la Justice dans la Monarchie Franque," in: Beumann, *Karl der Grosse*, pp. 394–419, here at pp. 397–405; Janet Nelson, "Dispute Settlement in Carolingian West Francia," in: Wendy Davies and Paul Fouracre (eds.), *The Settlement of Disputes in Early Modern Europe* (Cambridge: Cambridge University Press, 1986), pp. 45–64; McKitterick, *Frankish Kingdoms*, pp. 86–93, 97; Jean-Louis Harouel, Jean Barbey, Eric Bournzel, Jacqueline Thibaut-Payen, *Histoire des Institutions de l'Époque Franque à la Révolution*, 3rd ed. (Paris: Presses Universitaires de France, 1990), pp. 64–71; Jean Dunbabin, *France in the Making 843–1180* (Oxford: Oxford University Press, 1985), pp. 6–8.

[14] Harouel et al., *Histoire*, p. 64; McKitterick, *Frankish Kingdoms*, pp. 87–88; Werner, "Missus – Marchio – Comes," pp. 138–141.

bishops assigned the task of monitoring their local counts, but after 802 Charlemagne began regularly to employ archbishops as *missi domi-nici*, royal agents armed with plenipotentiary powers sent out to tour a given group of counties and conduct inquiries, hear complaints, and try cases.[15]

The Carolingians even went so far as to employ the Church as an alternative source of military manpower, requiring that abbots and later bishops equip and maintain a certain number of fighters, and that the former provide substantial quantities of provisions and transport for military purposes.[16] Unlike the other Germanic rulers, they also broke with the Roman practice of employing only laymen in the central admin-istration. Central government had now come to be coextensive with the royal household, with the leading household officials doubling as admin-istrative chiefs: the count of the palace (head of the royal household) as chief officer of the royal court of justice, the chamberlain (head of the queen's household) as royal treasurer, the seneschal and wine steward (in charge of the palace kitchens and table) as overseers of the royal domain, and the marshall and constable (heads of the palace stables) as commanders of the royal guard. While lay aristocrats continued to occupy these positions, the new offices of chancellor (responsible for written royal communications of all types) and archchaplain (chief advisor on ecclesiastical matters) were filled by churchmen, and they were assisted by a sizable staff consisting entirely of other clerics.[17]

In a further significant shift from the past, the central government had become increasingly peripatetic, constantly moving between a series of royal palaces and monasteries located in the Rhine, Meuse, Oise, and Aisne valleys of northern Gaul, yet another sign of the slow triumph of the countryside over the city during the course of the 8th and 9th centuries.[18]

The near total integration of the Church into the state apparatus as a kind of shadow administration was a creative response to the prob-lems of control which the Carolingians faced thanks to the size of their empire, the limitations of contemporary communication, and the specter of aristocratic power. They supplemented it, however, with another answer that could not have been more different: the extensive use of

[15] Werner, "Missus – Marchio – Comes," pp. 112–121; Kaiser, "Königtum und Bischof-sherrschaft," pp. 104–106; Ganshof, "Charlemagne et les Institutions," pp. 366–370; McKitterick, *Frankish Kingdoms*, pp. 93–97.

[16] Harouel et al., *Histoire*, pp. 66–67; Philippe Contamine (ed.), *Histoire Militaire de la France I: Des Origines à 1715* (Paris: Presses Universitaires de France, 1992), p. 28.

[17] Werner, "Missus – Marchio – Comes," pp. 117–118, 153–154; McKitterick, *Frankish Kingdoms*, pp. 78–85; Ganshof, "Charlemagne et les Institutions," pp. 361–363; Harouel et al., *Histoire*, pp. 63–64.

[18] Werner, "Missus – Marchio – Comes," pp. 110–111.

novel personal ties designed to bind the Empire's political elite as tightly as possible to the person of the monarch. While ties of friendship and patronage/clientage were the lifeblood of Roman politics, and the barbarian kings had always surrounded themselves with a band of retainers (their *antrustiones*) whom they housed and fed, the Carolingians began to deploy personalist methods of rule on a new scale when Charles Martel, Pippin the Short, and Carloman provided their supporters with conditional grants of land taken from the Church (benefices) in return for sworn promises of fidelity and service (vassalage).[19]

The use of vassalage and its linkage with benefices was extended in a number of directions under Charlemagne and his successors. First, the former created a special category of royal vassals or *vassi dominici* who were settled on benefice lands scattered throughout the Empire. These *vassi*, thanks to their direct personal connection with the ruler, were employed as yet another "organ of control," monitoring the activities of both counts and bishops and carrying out special tasks while also forming a highly reliable nucleus within the royal army. At the same time, Charlemagne continued his father's practice of binding the counts to him personally through ties of vassalage, simultaneously converting into a benefice the royal or ecclesiastical lands attached to the office for the material support of its holder. In this way, personalist ties came to affect not merely the officeholder as an individual – as such ties had in Rome, where officials were often friends or clients of other members of the ruling elite – but the office itself, subverting its impersonal character in the interest of greater control over the behavior of its occupant. Charlemagne likewise encouraged counts, bishops, and abbots to create their own vassals as a means of fulfilling their military obligations towards the Crown, thereby further blurring the line between private and public within the Frankish state.[20]

However intricate the organizational methods which the Carolingians employed to buttress their rule, in the world of the 8th and 9th centuries, wealth remained a vital prerequisite for political power. The "golden age" of the Carolingians, from the early 700s through the early 800s, in fact corresponded with a period in which the ruling family enjoyed a substantial flow of income from two sources. The first of these, recently uncovered by archaeologists, was a profitable trade with Anglo-Saxon England and Scandinavia and, through them, with the

[19] François Louis Ganshof, *Qu'est-ce que la Féodalité?*, 5th ed. (Paris: Tallandier, 1982), pp. 37–42; Werner, *Histoire*, pp. 345–346; Heinrich Mitteis and Heinz Lieberich, *Deutsche Rechtsgeschichte*, 19th ed. (Munich: Beck, 1992) p. 83.

[20] Ganshof, *Qu'est-ce que la Féodalité?*, pp. 43–102; idem, "Charlemagne et les Institutions," pp. 373–374, 388–390; Werner, "Missus – Marchio – Comes," pp. 138–147; James, *Origins*, pp. 163–165; Harouel et al., *Histoire*, pp. 60–61.

Arab Near East. This trade, which centered on the tightly controlled royal emporia of Dorestad and Quentovic, furnished the royal house, the Church and members, and the aristocracy with luxury goods as well as providing the silver which allowed Charlemagne to introduce a large-scale reform of the coinage.[21]

An even more substantial source of wealth and, ultimately, of political cohesion was provided by the nearly annual military expeditions which the Carolingians undertook throughout the 8th century. Given the habitual success of the Franks on the battlefield, these expeditions produced substantial quantities of loot that was shared out between the monarch and the *vassi dominici*, counts, bishops, abbots, and their vassals who formed the bulk of the Carolingian army. The fruits of plunder in turn helped fuel the luxury trade mentioned above, for some booty was exchanged for more exotic fare. In addition, tribute payments from the conquered or from those wishing to avoid hostilities regularly flowed into the royal coffers.[22] Consistent gains from war thus forged a strong community of interest between a warrior aristocracy and their sovereigns, a community reinforced by the practice of holding a general assembly (*placitum generale*) at which the affairs of the realm were discussed just prior to the departure of the army.[23]

If foreign expansion played a crucial role in holding the Carolingian Empire together, then the end of that expansion must have been a precipitating factor in its demise.[24] Frankish military aggression seems to have come to an abrupt halt in the early 800s not because of a lack of success, but because the wealth to be won through conquering the distant lands to the east of the Elbe would not have been sufficient to compensate the Empire's aristocracy for the heavy outlays necessary to participate in a campaign. Having gained everything they profitably could from overseas warfare, the Carolingian elite now turned to domestic competition as a way to increase their power and satisfy the demands of their followers.[25]

The unwillingness of aristocratic fighters to take part in costly military

---

[21] Richard Hodges and David Whitehouse, *Mohammed, Charlemagne and the Birth of Europe* (Ithaca: Cornell University Press, 1983), pp. 81–176.

[22] Timothy Reuter, "Plunder and Tribute in the Carolingian Empire," *Transactions of the Royal Historical Society*, 5th series, vol. 35 (1985), pp. 75–94; idem, "The End of Carolingian Military Expansion," in: Peter Goodman and Roger Collins (eds.), *Charlemagne's Heir* (Oxford: Clarendon, 1990), pp. 391–405. See also: Ganshof, "Charlemagne et les Institutions," p. 379; McKitterick, *Frankish Kingdoms*, p. 78; James, *Origins*, p. 158; Randsborg, *First Millennium*, p. 167.

[23] McKitterick, *Frankish Kingdoms*, pp. 97–98; Ganshof, "Charlemagne et les Institutions," pp. 364–366.

[24] Reuter, "End of Carolingian Military Expansion," passim.

[25] Ibid., pp. 402–405; Collins, *Early Medieval Europe*, pp. 296, 300.

expeditions naturally had a negative impact on royal income, an impact exacerbated by the fact that plunder had also helped fuel the lucrative Carolingian trade with northern Europe. This trade was further damaged beginning in the 820s by political upheaval in Syria, the ultimate source of many of the goods which Scandinavian and Anglo-Saxon traders provided to the Franks.[26] Royal financial (and hence political) weakness and increased aristocratic factionalism in turn combined to provoke a long and destructive civil war, lasting from 829 to 843, over the question of how to provide for the younger sons of Louis the Pious, Charlemagne's sole heir. Louis's original intention, as expressed in the *Ordinatio imperii* of 817, had been to eschew the Frankish practice of royal divisions and pass the Empire on intact to his eldest son Lothar. He explicitly justified this break with tradition (and with the principles of Carolingian charismatic kingship) by employing both Roman and ecclesiastical arguments which saw a unified Empire as the sole guarantor of both peace and the expansion of Christendom.[27] In the end, however, the power of the aristocratic factions backing Louis's younger sons was greater than that of those elites (mainly within the Church) favoring unity. After much fighting, the Empire was divided at Verdun in 843 into the two kingdoms of West Francia (later France) and East Francia (later Germany) with the imperial territory of Lotharingia (which included Italy) between them.[28]

In the end, civil war served only to weaken further the position of the ruling house. Moreover, the king of the new West Francian state, Charles the Bald (840–877), enjoyed little breathing space in which to rebuild his fortunes, for his realm was already struggling to cope with Viking raids which were steadily increasing in intensity. These raids are now believed to be partially rooted in the same decline in Carolingian trade which helped weaken the royal family, for diminishing commercial opportunities seem to have led the Scandinavians, fully apprised of the Franks' domestic difficulties, to attack their erstwhile trading partners.[29] The need to combat this danger, as well as to win aristocratic allegiance more generally, led Charles to encourage the accumulation of counties

---

[26] Hodges and Whitehouse, *Mohammed, Charlemagne,* pp. 160–164, 175.

[27] Egon Boshof, "Einheitsidee und Teilungsprinzip in der Regierungszeit Ludwigs des Frommen," in: Goodman and Collins, *Charlemagne's Heir,* pp. 161–189, here at pp. 177–181.

[28] Boshof, "Einheitsidee," pp. 182–189; McKitterick, *Frankish Kingdoms,* pp. 169–173; Collins, *Early Medieval Europe,* pp. 296–300. On the complex process leading to the emergence of separate French and German identities following the Treaty of Verdun, see most recently: Carlrichard Brühl, *Deutschland-Frankreich: Die Geburt zweier Völker* (Wien: Böhlau, 1990).

[29] Hodges and Whitehouse, *Mohammed, Charlemagne,* pp. 164–168; Contamine, *Histoire Militaire,* pp. 36–42; Collins, *Early Medieval Europe,* pp. 313–326.

in the hands of powerful regional leaders and to acquiesce in the transformation of counties and other benefices into hereditary property,
while at the same time multiplying the grants of immunity, land, and
other privileges bestowed on the Church in order to shore up support
in that quarter. By the late 800s, this policy of politically necessary
largesse had left the Carolingians poor and hence nearly powerless.[30]

Unlike in the late 600s, however, no new all-conquering family arose
to fill the power vacuum, created by the decline of royal power. Rather,
over the course of the next century, ambitious aristocratic families across
West Francia drew on authority and resources derived from a variety of
sources – hereditary counties, benefices, allodial estates, ecclesiastical
and secular immunities, royal privileges, kin and clientage networks –
to carve out regional principalities which varied greatly in size, solidity,
and longevity.[31] One of those families, the Robertians/Capetians of the
Paris region, was in fact to emerge as a serious challenger for the
throne in the late 800s, and to capture it definitively in 987. Yet, while
ties of vassalage and the unifying force of the Church, as well as a
residual prestige associated with the royal office, were sufficient to keep
the idea of a single West Frankish (and later French) kingdom alive,
both the Carolingians of the 9th century and their Capetian successors
exercised no more than a loose suzerainty over the lands beyond the
Île de France.[32] It was from this base that the kingdom of France was
rebuilt, but that process would not begin for another century.

ECONOMIC AND ECCLESIASTICAL RENEWAL AND
THE REBIRTH OF ROYAL POWER IN LATIN EUROPE

While the decline of Carolingian power during the course of the 9th
and 10th centuries seemed at the time to be an unmitigated disaster for
western Christendom, it also released creative forces within the economy
and the Church that since Roman times had been held in check by the
heavy hand of imperial and postimperial government. Though in the
long run these forces would contribute positively to the revival of central authority, in the short run they brought about a further fragmentation of political power among the West's pioneer state-formers. In
Latin Europe, this manifested itself in the rise of the castellans and the

---

[30] McKitterick, *Frankish Kingdoms*, pp. 183–188, 192; James, *Origins*, pp. 175–176; Ganshof,
"L'Immunité," p. 216; Dunbabin, *France*, p. 32.

[31] On the rise of the principalities and their varying internal composition, see: J. Dhondt,
Études sur la Naissance des Principautés Territoriales en France (Bruges: De Tempel, 1948);
Dunbabin, *France*, pp. 27–100, esp. pp. 91–92 (critique of Dhondt); James, *Origins*,
pp. 175–187, 196; Harouel et al., *Histoire*, pp. 91–97.

[32] Dunbabin, *France*, p. 100; James, *Origins*, p. 187.

final destruction of the county community across France and Italy, and the breakup of the Umayyad caliphate in Spain.

By the mid-1100s, however, economic dynamism and ecclesiastical renewal had combined with Carolingian administrative paradigms to bring about a revival of royal power in Latin Europe and the formation of new, large-scale states across the rest of the continent. In an effort to reestablish central control over the fragmented political landscapes which failed dark age statebuilding had bequeathed to them, the new rulers of Latin Europe introduced top-down, nonparticipatory forms of local administration which would have a profound effect on the future development of this region.

Economic Expansion

The period from the mid-900s through the early 1300s was one of unprecedented economic expansion across the West. While it is not possible to quantify this expansion directly, the demographic growth which was its most visible consequence can serve as a good proxy. It is now estimated that between the turn of the millennium and the arrival of the Black Death in the 1340s the population of Europe (including Russia and the Balkans) rose from between 30 and 35 million to about 80 million, more than 40% above the highest estimate for the continent's population at the height of the Roman Empire (56.6 million).[33]

The fact that this expansion continued unbroken for nearly four centuries – whereas the Roman economy could only expand for approximately two hundred years before succumbing to ecological, technological, and socioeconomic forces – indicates that a qualitative break with the ancient world had taken place.[34] Furthermore, while the 14th century did bring the demographic catastrophe of the Black Death, even this setback failed to prevent a renewed economic expansion across the continent during the late 14th and 15th centuries, which made possible a population recovery to about 100 million in the early 1600s and 175 million by 1800. Throughout this time, Latin Europe remained an important center of both economic and demographic growth, with

[33] Carlo Cipolla, *Before the Industrial Revolution*, 2nd ed. (New York: Norton, 1980), p. 150; N. J. G. Pounds, *An Historical Geography of Europe 450BC–AD1330* (Cambridge: Cambridge University Press, 1973), p. 116. The lower range estimate which Pounds cites is only 31.4 million. On the expansion of the European economy that began c. 950, see more generally the classic works by Georges Duby, *Guerriers et Paysans* (Paris: Gallimard, 1973); and Robert Lopez, *The Commercial Revolution of the Middle Ages, 950–1350* (Cambridge: Cambridge University Press, 1976); as well as, more recently, Robert Fossier, *Enfance de l'Europe*, 2nd ed., 2 vols. (Paris: P.U.F., 1989), which contains an exhaustive bibliography.

[34] Randsborg, *First Millennium*, pp. 168–169.

the population of France tripling from 5 to 15 million between c. 1000
and c. 1300 and then rising to between 19 and 21 million by the early
1700s, and that of Italy doubling from 5 to 10 million and then climb-
ing to 13 million over the same period.[35]

The great economic expansion which began in the mid-10th century
had two sides: an agricultural takeoff, propelled forward by the increasing demand which resulted from population growth, and made
possible by widespread land clearance and the introduction of new
technologies (the water mill, heavy plow, horseshoe, collar harness,
three-field system);[36] and the return of long-distance trade, confined at
first to the Mediterranean but later spreading to western and northern
Europe as well. While this trade involved a wide variety of products, at
its core stood the exchange by independent merchants of eastern luxury
goods for western woolen cloth and iron goods manufactured in Flanders, northern Italy, and southern Germany.[37] Common to both of
these spheres of economic activity was the fact that they were organized
increasingly around competitive markets: local and regional markets in
the case of agricultural production and international markets centered
on a continent-wide network of cities – many of them of Roman origin
– in the case of international commerce.[38]

It is generally agreed that the most immediate cause of the early
medieval economic resurgence outlined above was the appearance of
an agricultural surplus during the 900s which permitted both demographic expansion and the return of commerce and exchange. The
exact origins of this surplus, however, remain in some dispute. The
waning of the Norman, Magyar, and Saracen threats during this period
was undoubtedly an important precondition for agricultural recovery,
and it is now thought that a favorable climatic shift may have played a
role in increasing crop yields.[39] Many historians and archaeologists,
however, have come to locate the roots of the qualitative changes in
the western economy which lay behind the 10th-century takeoff in the

[35] Cipolla, *Before the Industrial Revolution*, pp. 4, 150; Peter Kriedte, *Spätfeudalismus und Handelskapital* (Göttingen: Vandenhoeck & Ruprecht, 1980), p. 12.

[36] For the impact of new technology on what Lynn White calls "the agricultural revolu-
tion of the early middle ages," see his: *Medieval Technology and Social Change* (Oxford:
Clarendon, 1962), pp. 39–78; also: Duby, *Guerriers*, pp. 205–236; Lopez, *Commercial
Revolution*, pp. 27–55; Fossier, *Enfance*, pp. 615–665.

[37] Lopez, *Commercial Revolution*, pp. 63–122, 130–137; idem, "The Trade of Medieval
Europe: The South"; and M. M. Postan, "The Trade of Medieval Europe: the North,"
both in: M. M. Postan and Edward Miller (eds.), *The Cambridge Economic History of
Europe. Volume II: Trade and Industry in the Middle Ages*, 2nd ed. (Cambridge: Cambridge University Press, 1987), pp. 168–401; Fossier, *Enfance*, pp. 739–767.

[38] Fossier, *Enfance*, pp. 1066–1067; Randsborg, *First Millennium*, p. 167; Richard Hodges,
Dark Age Economics (London: Duckworth, 1982), pp. 196–197.

[39] Fossier, *Enfance*, pp. 1070–1072.

political sphere: more specifically, in the disappearance of centralized authority across East and West Francia, Italy, and northeastern Spain ushered in by Carolingian decline. For, it is argued, the demise of the Carolingian state also brought with it the end of an economic order built around pillage, conspicuous consumption, and gift exchange where much energy was expended in order to supply the households of the royal family and the great magnates and to provide resources for costly military campaigns. While it is true that Charlemagne did attempt to encourage regional trade and production, this only served to increase the centrifugal tendencies already present within his empire.[40]

Under these circumstances, the collapse of central authority permitted the economy to establish, perhaps for the first time, a substantial measure of autonomy vis-à-vis the political order.[41] The decline of the royal court obviated the need for costly display and gift giving, and the end of overseas military expeditions freed up that part of the surplus from their estates that elites had used to equip and maintain themselves during the long campaigning season. This may have been especially important for the most productive agricultural units of the period: the monastic estates which earlier had been forced to shoulder a substantial portion of royal military expenses. Indeed, Fossier, drawing on Duby and Werner, has argued that the spark which set off self-sustaining agricultural expansion came from just such estates.[42] More generally, the rise of new regional and especially local centers of power in place of the single focal point provided by the royal court encouraged the parallel emergence of regional and local markets.[43]

The Rise of the Castellans

It is at this point that the post-Carolingian transformation of the western economy becomes inextricably intertwined with another phenomenon: the rise of the castellans. Beginning in the last decades of the 10th century, aristocrats across France, Italy, and parts of Iberia began to employ the surpluses generated by their estates to build castles from which they could impose their will not only upon their own peasants but also upon all other inhabitants of the district, whether free or unfree. This development marked the final destruction of the county

---

[40] Hodges, *Dark Age Economics*, pp. 153–157, 160, 188–189, 196–197; Randsborg, *First Millennium*, pp. 167–168, 181; Guy Bois, *La Mutation de l'An Mil* (Paris: Fayard, 1989), pp. 246–247.

[41] Bois, *Mutation*, pp. 205–206, 246–258.

[42] Fossier, *Enfance*, p. 1071.

[43] Hodges, *Dark Age Economics*, pp. 196–197; Randsborg, *First Millennium*, pp. 167–168, 181; Bois, *Mutation*, pp. 136–137, 140.

throughout Latin Europe, as rurally based political communities were
broken up into castellanies or "bannal lordships" in which royal powers
of command (the *bannum* or *bannus*) along with the judicial, military,
and fiscal prerogatives they implied now rested with hundreds, if not
thousands, of local strongmen. In this case, public powers were appropriated not from the king directly, but rather from the regional princes
(counts and dukes) upon whom authority had devolved between the
mid-9th and mid-10th centuries.[44]

While for the local population the immediate effects of this appropriation must have been quite negative, given the near-despotic powers
possessed by the castellans and their tendency to fight among themselves for control of more territory, the overall consequences for the
economy seem to have been positive. This was so both because local
lords encouraged land clearance and created protected markets in the
vicinity of their castles and because the (formerly public) taxes, tolls,
judicial and market fees, and other duties which they imposed upon
their subjects forced the latter to use every available means to increase
their output.[45] The common subjugation of all of the local population
to a single lord also encouraged a convergence in status among peasants which dealt a final blow to the rural slavery which, recent research
has shown, persisted throughout Latin Europe for far longer than was
previously believed. For this reason, some observers now see the rise of
the castellans and the local social, economic, and topographic changes
which they provoked as marking the death of the ancient economy and
the birth of its medieval successor in rural Latin Europe.[46]

If the disappearance of effective central authority helped create the
conditions for economic and social transformation in the countryside,
this was even more true in the region's urban areas. Many Roman cities
in Italy and southern France had survived the dark ages intact, though

---

[44] Georges Duby, *La Société aux XIe et XIIe Siècles dans la Région Mâconnaise* (Paris:
S.E.V.P.E.N., 1971), pp. 137–190; idem, *L'Économie Rurale et la Vie des Campagnes dans
l'Occident Médiéval*, 2 vols. (Paris: Flammarion, 1977), vol. II, pp. 84–87; Jean-Pierre
Poly and Eric Bournazel, *La Mutation Féodale* (Paris: Presses Universitaires de France,
1980), pp. 59–103; Fossier, *Enfance*, pp. 364–409; James, *Origins*, pp. 192–196;
Dunbabin, *France*, pp. 143–150. This process seems to have begun even earlier in Italy
(early 900s) and Castile ("land of castles" – 800s), although stone castles did not come
to the latter until the late 1000s. See: Chris Wickham, *Early Medieval Italy* (London:
Macmillan, 1981), pp. 97–98, 172–174; and José Angel García de Cortázar, *Historia
de España Alfaguara II: La Época Medieval*, 9th ed. (Madrid: Alianza, 1983), pp. 130,
158. In Catalonia ("land of castellans"), a former Carolingian territory, bannal lordship appeared suddenly and spread rapidly between 1017 and 1035. See: Thomas
Bisson, *The Medieval Crown of Aragon* (Oxford: Clarendon, 1986), pp. 24–25.

[45] Duby, *L'Économie*, vol. II, pp. 87–89; idem, *La Société*, pp. 254–262, 280–285; Fossier,
Enfance, pp. 409–422; Dunbabin, *France*, pp. 146–150.

[46] Bois, *Mutation*, pp. 243–258 and passim; Duby, *L'Économie*, vol. II, p. 89; idem, *La
Société*, pp. 201–212.

reduced in size and shorn of much of their dependent territory. With the decline of the Carolingians and (in Italy) of the Byzantines, these cities were able to gain a large measure of political autonomy, often first under the leadership of the local bishop and later, beginning in the late 11th and 12th centuries, as self-governing communes. They then made use of this autonomy to free themselves from the constraints previously imposed by the state and reintroduce long-distance trade into Europe by reestablishing commercial links both with the wider Mediterranean world and with northern Europe. There they would soon be joined as trading partners by the new towns and cities founded by French territorial princes and the Anglo-Saxon and Scandinavian kings.[47]

Ecclesiastical Renewal

The profound impact which the weakening of centralized power had upon the economy of Latin Europe was nearly matched by its effect upon the Church. During the course of the late 800s and early 900s, regional rulers across France, Carolingian Italy, and northeasten Iberia appropriated not only regalian rights, but also imperial authority over bishoprics and abbeys within their spheres of influence. Later, castellans would do the same with local parishes. Lay aristocratic control brought with it an upsurge in a whole range of abuses: the buying and selling of Church offices (simony), the appointment of laymen to ecclesiastical positions, and the outright patrimonialization of Church lands. Moreover, as the power of the territorial princes itself went into decline beginning in the late 900s, the Church could not remain aloof from the increasingly uncontrolled violence spreading around it.[48]

While the loss of state protection and tutelage in the wake of Carolingian decline may have exposed the Church to attacks by lay aristocrats seeking to appropriate ecclesiastical wealth and influence, it also granted to that organization a new freedom seized upon by reformers to promote innovative ideas which would have profound effects on the future course of statebuilding in Latin Europe and in the West more generally. One of these was the tripartite theory of society expounded

---

[47]   Edith Ennen, *Die Europäische Stadt des Mittelalters*, 3rd ed. (Göttingen: Vandenhoeck & Ruprecht, 1979), pp. 83–89, 122–143; Rosemary Morris, "Northern Europe Invades the Mediterranean, 900–1200," in: George Holmes (ed.), *The Oxford Illustrated History of Medieval Europe* (Oxford: Oxford University Press, 1988), pp. 175–234, here at pp. 223–233; Fossier, *Enfance*, pp. 751–757; Wickham, *Early Medieval Italy*, pp. 188–193; Pounds, *Historical Geography*, pp. 263–267, 302–305.

[48]   Colin Morris, *The Papal Monarchy: The Western Church from 1050 to 1250* (Oxford: Clarendon, 1989), pp. 23–28; Georges Duby, *Le Moyen Âge 987–1460* (Paris: Hachette, 1987), pp. 157–178; Harouel et al., *Histoire*, p. 136; James, *Origins*, pp. 196, 206.

between 1027 and 1031 by bishops Gérard de Cambrai and Aldabéron de Laon in response to the discord around them. Drawing on Carolingian ideas whose roots go back perhaps as far as the Indo-Europeans, they argued that society was naturally divided into three functionally determined and hierarchically organized "orders" – those who pray, those who fight to protect those who pray, and those who must labor to support prayers and fighters alike – and that disorder arose when one group sought to usurp the divinely ordained place or duties of another.[49]

This tripartite vision had an enormous impact throughout the former Carolingian territories and in other parts of Latin Europe as well because it complemented and further encouraged three social trends already under way: the efforts of reform-minded churchmen to define the clergy as a separate (and superior) group in opposition to the lay aristocracy: the fusion of aristocrats and lesser fighting men (*milites*) into a single class of nobles as many of the latter seized local power as castellans and as the rest of society came to blame disorder on armed men regardless of their rank; and the disappearance of slavery and its replacement by a class of peasant cultivators united by their common subjugation to bannal lords.[50] This vision would continue to influence both social reality and its portrayal in thought right up until the French Revolution, and would be the intellectual inspiration behind the future tricurial organization of representative assemblies in Latin Europe and Germany.

If Gérard and Aldabéron were the theoreticians of an ecclesiastically led hierarchy which stood in sharp contrast to conditions in the world around them, then the great monastery of Cluny, founded in 909 under the direct patronage of Rome, was its physical incarnation. The abbey combined a persistent criticism of Church abuses and an emphasis on renewed spirituality with an attempt, ultimately successful (1024), to free itself from the control of local bishops and organize its extensive network of daughter houses stretching from southern France to Spain into an independent, hierarchically structured organization which it alone controlled. The ideas and practical example of Cluny were a direct source of inspiration to the group of papal reformers who, beginning in 1046, sought to renew the Church by separating it from lay influence, a program that would lead directly to the Investiture Conflict and the creation of an autonomous ecclesiastical hierarchy answerable

---

[49] Georges Duby, *Les Trois Ordres ou l'Imaginaire du Féodalisme* (Paris: Gallimard, 1978), pp. 77–81 and passim; Fossier, *Enfance*, pp. 884–887; Harouel et al., *Histoire*, p. 141.

[50] Jean-François Lemarignier, *La France Médiévale: Institutions et Société* (Paris: Armand Colin, 1970), pp. 163–168; Harouel et al., *Histoire*, pp. 140–141; Dunbabin, *France*, p. 154.

to Rome covering all of western Christendom.[51] A central role in building that hierarchy was played by the ever-expanding law of the Church, the canon law, which was largely derived from Roman law (*ecclesia vivit iure Romano* – "the Church lives according to Roman law"). It was in fact the papal reform movement which now is believed to have been responsible for the rediscovery during the late 11th century of the "pure," Justinian version of Roman law (as opposed to the "vulgar" form which had lived on in Latin Europe).[52] As we shall see, revived Roman law, canon law, and the administrative model furnished by the new ecclesiastical hierarchy would all provide invaluable assistance over the coming centuries to secular rulers attempting to build up their own states.

State Re-Formation in Latin Europe

Beginning in the mid-11th century, changes in the economy, society, and the Church sparked by Carolingian decline came together to permit the first glimmerings of a revival of royal power in France. In 987, the Robertians/Capetians had finally supplanted their rivals on the French throne, but their effective authority was limited to the area around Paris and Orléans. While the economic takeoff of the late 10th century initially strengthened the position of castellans in the royal demesne just as it had elsewhere, in the long run it benefited the Capetians. This was so for two reasons. The family, thanks to the primogeniture they had introduced in the mid-900s, still possessed substantial estates in the fertile Seine valley which were well positioned to supply the rising food needs of neighboring Flanders, then undergoing a process of rapid urbanization linked to the explosive growth of commerce and the cloth industry in the region. By 1044, Henry I (1031–1060) was strong enough to win a first victory against his castellans, though it would not be until the reign of his grandson Louis VI (1108–1137) that the power of the latter was finally broken and direct control over all of the demesne reestablished.[53]

The other pillar of the royal revival, in addition to the growing material

---

[51] Jean-François Lemarignier, "Structures Monastiques et Structures Politiques dans la France de la Fin du Xe Siècle et des Débuts du XIe Siècle," in: *Il Monachesimo nell'Alto Medioevo e la Formazione della Civiltà Occidentale* (= *Settimane di Studio del Centro Italiano di Studi sull'Alto Medioevo*, IV) (Spoleto: Presso la Sede del Centro, 1957), pp. 357–400; Marcel Pacaut, "Structures Monastiques, Société, et Église en Occident aux XIe et XIIe Siècles," *Cahiers d'Histoire*, vol. 20, no. 2 (1975), pp. 119–136; Harouel et al., *Histoire*, pp. 135–137; Morris, *Papal Monarchy*, pp. 64–68, 80 and passim.

[52] Morris, *Papal Monarchy*, pp. 212, 400–403, 532–533, 575–577; Robert Feenstra, "Law," in: Richard Jenkyns (ed.), *The Legacy of Rome: A New Appraisal* (Oxford: Oxford University Press, 1992), pp. 399–420, here at pp. 402–408, 410.

[53] Dunbabin, *France*, pp. 105–106, 162–164, 258.

wealth of the Capetians, was their alliance with the Church of northern France, over which they continued to exercise an important measure of influence. Since the 10th century, many ecclesiastics had hoped for the return of central state authority in order to free the Church from the clutches of the lay aristocracy and protect it from future depredations, and it was with ecclesiastical backing that the last of the Carolingians had been removed from the throne in 987. Thereafter, leading church-men worked hard to legitimize the new dynasty by continuing the prac-tice of episcopal anointment first introduced in 751 and by portraying the Capetians as worthy successors of Charlemagne. For their part, the royal family complemented these efforts by adopting the Carolingian name "Louis" in place of the traditional Capetian "Hugh" or "Robert" and revitalizing the Carolingian conceptions of kingship with elements borrowed from the Cluniac reformers. This early support for ecclesias-tical renewal, which of course ultimately flowed from royal weakness, permitted the Capetians to adapt quickly to the new, post-Gregorian Church of the late 11th and 12th century, in striking contrast to their counterparts in Germany, whose power was to be fatally undermined by the Investiture Conflict.[54]

While the Capetians had made substantial progress in subjugating their demesne by the early 1100s, it was the Benedictine abbot Suger, who was principal adviser to Louis VI and Louis VII between 1122 and 1151, who would provide them with the ideological means to begin to win back the rest of France. This was the theory of feudal monarchy, inspired by ideas derived from Cluny and the Gregorian reforms, which maintained that the lands held by all of the kingdom's lords could be arranged into a hierarchy with the king of France, holding his lands of St. Denis, at its head. This vision, which complemented the equally hierarchical tripartite theory of Gérard and Aldabéron, permitted the Capetians to turn to their advantage the one set of ties which still bound the great territorial princes to them, the ties of vassalage which reached back into the Carolingian era.[55] They did this by clarifying and codifying the rules governing fiefs and vassal relationships and then using these rules when favorable opportunities arose (death of a fief-holder without heir, failure to perform certain duties punishable by revocation of fief) in order to win back appropriated benefices or at least exercise greater influence over their holders. The princes them-selves were willing to accept this new system of feudal law with its

[54] Ibid., pp. 122, 134–136, 157–160, 165–169; Harouel et al., *Histoire*, pp. 95–97, 197–198, 206–207, 211.
[55] Poly and Bournazel, *Mutation Féodale*, pp. 298–305; Duby, *Moyen Âge*, pp. 225–229; Harouel et al., *Histoire*, pp. 215–216; Dunbabin, *France*, pp. 256–259.

emphasis on hierarchy because they themselves could employ it against their opponents the castellans, who had seized local power from them during the late 900s and early 1000s.

The pattern of state re-formation found in France from the mid-11th century onward was thus one in which the Capetians, operating from an increasingly wealthy, geographically compact base in the Île de France, slowly extended their power in roughly concentric circles over a wider and wider area of France using the legal and ideological means furnished by Suger and the Church, backed when necessary by the force of arms. In so doing, they also enjoyed advantages inherent in the structural situation in which they found themselves. Though they began their quest to reestablish royal power from a position of weakness, they were not confronted by a unified block of princely opponents; rather, France's regional rulers were busy fighting with local castellans, with newly prosperous cities seeking freedom from their overlords, and with each other in an effort to consolidate and expand their respective territories. This situation of many-sided competition was broadly favorable to the monarchy, for it meant that although the crown's military and judicial resources were initially quite limited, they often held the balance of power between political rivals outside the royal demesne, a fact which the Capetians could and did use to further their own ends.

The process of state re-formation which occurred during this period in the other areas of Latin Europe exhibits interesting parallels with the French experience. In both Iberia and southern Italy (the area of the peninsula beyond the borders of the new, German-led Empire), rulers operating from geographically compact bases slowly expanded their realms outward through a selective use of military power and the strategic exploitation of rivalries among the competing territorial princes who were their neighbors. In Iberia, it was the disintegration of the once-powerful Umayyad caliphate into 23 regional states (*taifas*) between 1008 and 1031 which created new opportunities for the Christian rulers of León, Castile, Aragon, Catalonia, and Navarre ensconced in their northern strongholds. Over the next four centuries, imbued with a crusading spirit inspired by Cluniac and Gregorian ideas, they would advance southward against a much wealthier Muslim civilization using a mixture of warfare and diplomatic maneuvering designed to exacerbate disunity among their opponents.[56] However, the Church, the nobility, and the military orders specially created to fight the Muslims took advantage of the central role they played in the *reconquista* to win substantial rights of immunity from their rulers with respect to the

---

[56] Collins, *Early Medieval Spain*, pp. 266–269; Angus MacKay, *Spain in the Middle Ages* (London: Macmillan, 1977), pp. 15–35 and passim.

lands they acquired in conquered territory, thereby creating a fragmented political landscape of interspersed "public" (i.e., royal) and private territories within the new, much enlarged Christian kingdoms.[57]

In southern Italy, widespread castle building and the accompanying rise of local lordship during the course of the 900s had further fragmented political power in a region already divided between Lombard principalities and isolated Byzantine enclaves, and threatened since the turn of the 10th century by a Muslim-controlled Sicily. Beginning in about 999, Norman fighters began arriving in southern Italy as mercenaries and soon began to take advantage of the political confusion around them to carve out independent territories of their own. In 1059, the reforming pope Nicholas II granted Apulia and Calabria to the most powerful Norman clan, the Hautevilles, as a base from which to retake Sicily, a task which they had accomplished by 1072. In 1130, the other Norman lords agreed, at the urging of the anti-Pope Anacletus II, to become the vassals of Roger II of Hauteville and recognize him as king of Sicily and all southern Italy up to the papal territories. Yet within this new kingdom, power in many localities would remain in the hands of the descendants of those Norman fighters who had first conquered them.[58]

By the mid-12th century, seven states of substantial size had emerged in that part of Latin Europe outside the boundaries of the Empire: France, Castile-León, Aragon-Catalonia, Navarre, Portugal, Almohad al-Andalus, and Sicily, to which could be added the nearly independent French royal fiefs of Normandy and Flanders. Quite surprisingly, given the cultural and economic differences which had emerged in this area over the previous several centuries, the nascent royal administrative infrastructures of the Christian kingdoms were quite similar to one another, a reflection both of the lingering effects of dark age state formation and the lasting impact of Roman administrative models as mediated through the Carolingian Empire.[59] Thus central government in all of these states was in the hands of a still largely itinerant king, his noble and ecclesiastical advisers, and some combination of the traditional

[57] García de Cortázar, *Época Medieval*, pp. 217–219, 227–229, 279–280, 292–294; Richard Konetzke, "Territoriale Grundherrschaft und Landesherrschaft im spanischen Spätmittelalter. Ein Forschungsproblem zur Geschichte des spanischen Partikularismus," in: *Histoire Économique du Monde Méditerranéan 1450–1650. Mélanges en l'Honneur de Fernand Braudel* (Toulouse: Privat Éditeur, 1973), pp. 299–310.

[58] Wickham, *Early Medieval Italy*, pp. 162–167; Donald Matthew, *The Norman Kingdom of Sicily* (Cambridge: Cambridge University Press, 1992), pp. 9–37; Malcolm Barber, *The Two Cities: Medieval Europe 1050–1320* (London: Routledge, 1992), pp. 225–229; Morris, *Papal Monarchy* (Oxford: Clarendon, 1989), pp. 135–136, 139–143.

[59] On the diffusion of a common Carolingian administrative model across northwestern Europe during the 10th and 11th centuries, see: Bryce Lyon and A. E. Verhulst, *Medieval Finance: A Comparison of Financial Institutions in Northwestern Europe* (Providence: Brown University Press, 1967), pp. 82–83 and passim.

(Carolingian) household officers (count of the palace, chamberlain, seneschal, wine steward, marshall, constable, and sometimes a chancellor), all members of the higher nobility who soon succeeded in making these positions hereditary.[60]

The royal will in areas not under the control of regional and local lords was imposed from the center through an all-purpose official called the *prévot* in France, the viscount in Normandy, the castellan in Flanders, the baillif (*baiulus*) in Catalonia and Sicily, and the *merino/meirinho* in Castile-León, Aragon, Navarre, and Portugal. The job of this official was to collect and disburse income from royal estates and regalian dues, mete out justice, and organize local defense within an ill-defined area often pockmarked with immune or seigneurial lands. He did this without substantial formal assistance from the local free male population, thus establishing the pattern of top-down, administrative local government which would characterize this region to the end of the early modern period and beyond.

Nearly as soon as this position was created, its incumbents, although men of lesser standing, also attempted to interpret it as a fief and convert it into hereditary family property. The almost universal response across Latin Europe during the 11th century was to "farm" out these offices by auctioning them annually or semiannually to the highest bidder.[61] The problem of appropriation had made its first appearance in the new state structures of the post-millennial West.

EARLY GEOPOLITICAL COMPETITION, REPRESENTATIVE
ASSEMBLIES, AND THE CREATION OF SYSTEMS OF
NATIONAL TAXATION

The widespread state formation and re-formation of the 11th and 12th centuries transformed Europe into a world of competing polities which

---

[60] Ferdinand Lot and Robert Fawtier, *Histoire des Institutions Françaises au Moyen Âge*, 3 vols. (Paris: Presses Universitaires de France, 1957–1962), vol. II, pp. 48–58, 65; ibid., vol. I, pp. 10, 379–384; Harouel et al., *Histoire*, pp. 202–203; Dunbabin, *France*, pp. 212, 298; Luís de Valdeavellano, *Curso de Historia de las Instituciones Españoles. De los Orígenes al Final de la Edad Media*, 3rd ed. (Madrid: Revista de Occidente, 1973), pp. 488–495; António Manuel Hespanha, *História das Instituições: Épocas Medieval e Moderna* (Coimbra: Livraria Almedina, 1982), pp. 147–149; H. V. Livermore, *A History of Portugal* (Cambridge: Cambridge University Press, 1947), pp. 90–91. The central government of Sicily during this period was somewhat more sophisticated and influenced by Arab and Byzantine as well as Norman administrative practices. See: Matthew, *Norman Kingdom*, pp. 208–228.

[61] Lot and Fawtier, *Histoire*, vol. II, pp. 141–144; Harouel, *Histoire*, pp. 235–236; Valdeavellano, *Curso de Historia*, pp. 503–504; Bernard Reilly, *The Kingdom of León-Castilla under Queen Urraca 1109–1126* (Princeton: Princeton University Press, 1982), pp. 301–313; Ludwig Klüpfel, *Verwaltungsgeschichte des Königreichs Aragon zu Ende des 13. Jahrhunderts* (Stuttgart: Kohlhammer, 1915), pp. 72–90; Hespanha, *História*, pp. 151–154; Matthew, *Norman Kingdom*, pp. 242–245.

more often than not settled their differences through warfare. Yet intense geopolitical competition and sustained inter-state conflict did not arrive in all parts of the continent at the same time. Not surprisingly, such pressures first affected the populous and prosperous western and southern half of the continent (Latin Europe and England), leading monarchs there from the late 1100s to build larger, more specialized organs of central and local administration staffed by full-time officials.

Over the course of the next century, as the costs of war exhausted traditional revenue sources, the increasingly assertive and ambitious rulers of France, the Iberian states, and Sicily were forced to call national representative assemblies into being, largely in order to seek their financial assistance. The organization of these assemblies into (most often) three *curiae*, each representing a single socially and legally privileged group, was a result both of the extremely fragmented local political landscape inherited by all of these states from their dark age predecessors, which rendered territorially based representation difficult; and of the influence of the "three order" theory of society developed by French churchmen in the wake of the Carolingian collapse. Once in place, these assemblies granted new taxes to meet the mounting costs of war, taxes which brought in their wake a substantial enlargement of the state and its capacities.

The Early Onset of Sustained Geopolitical Competition

As the rulers of 12th-century Latin Europe struggled to consolidate and expand their governing capacities in the face of entrenched regional elites, they were simultaneously confronted with a new set of challenges arising from Europe's postmillennial transformation into a multistate world. Nowhere was this development felt more keenly then in France, where Henry I's conquest of Normandy in 1106 and the ascension of the Angevin Henry II to the English throne in 1154 left England with territories in France larger than those of the French royal demesne itself. The ensuing struggle between the two kingdoms was to ebb and flow for more than three centuries, with the French king Philip Augustus capturing Normandy, Anjou, Maine, Touraine, and Brittany from the English between 1204 and 1206 and then successfully defending these conquests at Bouvines in 1214; Henry III twice invading France in the 1230s and 1240s in an unsuccessful attempt to win back what his father had lost; and hostilities resuming in the 1290s over English possession of Gascony and culminating in the Hundred Years War of 1337–1453, which was only brought to an end by the virtual elimination of the English presence in France.

In addition to these endemic tensions with England, France also fought a series of wars beginning in the 1180s with its powerful quasi-independent fief, Flanders, which took part in much of the Hundred Years War as an English ally. From the early 1200s onward, France's southward expansion also brought it increasingly into conflict with the crown of Aragon, and relations between the two states were exacerbated by the Aragonese seizure of Sicily in 1282 in the wake of a revolt against Charles of Anjou, the uncle of the French king, who had become the ruler of the southern Italian state in 1266.

Similar geopolitical pressures were a constant in the other states of Latin Europe as well. The conquest by the Almoravids of all of the *taifa* states by 1110 and the integration of these states into a single realm confronted the newly expanded Christian kingdoms with a formidable and united enemy, and this danger was in no way diminished by the replacement of the Almoravids with first the Almohads and then the Nasrids at the head of al-Andalus. As a result, the prospect of a quick reconquest of the peninsula, which had seemed possible during the 11th century, soon gave way to a state of continuous warfare marked by Christian surges and reversals lasting until the fall of Granada in 1492.

The Norman kingdom of Sicily also faced hostility from both the papacy (which, despite its earlier role in encouraging their intervention, now saw the Normans as dangerous rivals for power in Italy) and the Byzantines, anxious to win back their lost territories in the south of the peninsula. The Sicilian state was fully integrated into European power politics with the ascension of the German Hohenstaufen emperors Henry VI (1194–1197) and Frederick II (1197–1250) to the Sicilian throne, which embroiled the kingdom in a series of large-scale conflicts that only ended with the defeat of the last Hohenstaufen by Charles of Anjou at Tagliacozza in 1268. As mentioned above, the division of the kingdom in 1282 into two rival states, Aragonese Sicily and Angevin Naples, ensured permanent conflict until the conquest of the latter by Alfonso V of Aragon in 1442–1443. In all of these cases, the constant threat of war arising from long-standing, unresolved conflicts with neighboring states which had manifested themselves as early as the 12th century was as great a spur to statebuilding as warfare itself, which was often intermittent.

The situation was very different in those parts of western Christendom to the north and east of Latin Europe and England, where sustained geopolitical rivalries did not arrive until the 15th and 16th centuries. The Empire, while still an important international actor, was in the process of disintegrating during the 1100s and 1200s in the wake of the Investiture Crisis and the prolonged civil wars which it generated. Except in northern Italy, however, it was not until the late 1300s and 1400s that it would be replaced as an effective political unit by smaller territorial states which would soon be enmeshed in conflicts of their own.

Further to the east, Poland had become a kingdom in 1076 thanks to the intervention of Pope Gregory VII, but the country was divided into a series of duchies in 1138 and would not be fully reunited again until 1320. Aside from an episodic conflict with the Teutonic Order in Prussia, it would not be affected by sustained geopolitical pressure until the rise of Sweden and Russia in the late 1500s. Hungary, a kingdom since the year 1000, managed to remain united despite a serious civil war in the 1290s, but until the Turkish threat appeared at the turn of the 15th century the main military danger to the new polity came not from other states, but from nomadic invaders from the east – the Mongols and the Kumans. Meanwhile in Scandinavia, the West's most isolated and underdeveloped region, the Christian kingdoms of Denmark, Norway, and Sweden emerged over the course of the 11th century, but all had great difficulty consolidating themselves and were plagued by nearly incessant internal strife throughout the remainder of the middle ages. It was only after 1500 that they began to compete regularly with one another and with neighboring states in Germany and the Baltic.

The Rise of Paid Warfare

The growing frequency of sustained inter-state conflict in the West, confined, as we have seen, almost exclusively to England and Latin Europe during the 12th and 13th centuries, helped in its turn to usher in a fundamental change in the way wars were fought that would have a profound effect on the future course of European statebuilding. This was the steady decline in various "feudal" forms of unpaid military service and their replacement by paid troops as the preferred basis for military organization. It is generally agreed that this transformation was essentially completed by the late 1200s.[62]

It would be a mistake to view European warfare prior to the 1100s as built *exclusively* around mounted knights performing feudal service. As John Beeler has said, "It would be difficult, if not impossible, to cite a battle between armies composed entirely of feudal troops."[63] The infantry, often drawn from urban militias, played a greater role during this period than is generally acknowledged, and in Spain cavalry service

---

[62]   Ferdinand Lot, *L'Art Militaire et les Armées au Moyen Âge* (Paris: Payot, 1946), vol. II, pp. 423–425; John Beeler, *Warfare in Feudal Europe 730–1200* (Ithaca: Cornell University Press, 1971), pp. 58–59; Philippe Contamine, *La Guerre au Moyen Âge* (Paris: Presses Universitaires de France, 1980), pp. 192ff.

[63]   Beeler, *Warfare,* p. 248.

was frequently performed by non-nobles. In addition, mercenary knights and specialist soldiers like crossbowmen were used to supplement or replace feudal levies as early as the 1000s. Mercenaries played a significant role, for example, in the Norman army of William the Conqueror which defeated the English at Hastings.[64]

Nevertheless, it is fair to say that until the 12th century, troops of various kinds performing unpaid service still comprised the core of all western European armies. The reasons why what could be called "military feudalism" fell into crisis over the course of the 1100s are complex and need not be explored here. In short, this crisis had two components: a decline in the number of militarily competent persons subject to feudal service of one kind or another, and the unwillingness of those obliged to serve to do so without pay. As a result, it became desirable from the 12th century onward both to supplement feudal levies with mercenary contingents and to provide some form of pay, though not necessarily full wages, to those serving in fulfillment of an obligation.[65]

It was the English and the Italians who almost simultaneously hit upon a more durable and effective way of organizing for war. During the 1270s and 1280s, while engaged in a struggle with the Welsh, Edward I entered into contracts (called indentures) with a number of English nobles which required the latter to furnish the king with a certain number of mounted troops to serve for fixed money wages under conditions specified in the contract.[66] At about the same time, the communes of Italy began drawing up similar contracts (there called *condotte*) with both native and, somewhat later, foreign military enterprisers to supply them with contingents of paid troops. In both cases the contractor himself, called respectively a captain or *condottiere*, would also lead into battle the "company" he had recruited. In Italy, troops raised by *condottieri* would form the core of both the northern communal armies and those of the southern kingdoms from the 14th century onward.[67]

---

[64] Herbert Grundmann, "Rotten und Brabanzonen: Söldnerheere im 12. Jahrhundert," *Deutsches Archiv für die Geschichte des Mittelalters*, vol. V, 1941–2, pp. 418–492. On the English case, J. O. Prestwich, "War and Finance in the Anglo-Norman State," *Transactions of the Royal Historical Society*, 5th series, vol. 4, 1954, pp. 19–54.

[65] Contamine, *La Guerre*, pp. 192–207.

[66] A. E. Prince, "The Indenture System under Edward III," *Historical Essays in Honour of James Tait*, eds. J. G. Edwards et al. (Manchester: n.p., 1933), pp. 283–297, here at p. 285; N. B. Lewis, "An Early Indenture of Military Service, 27 July 1287," *Bulletin of the Institute of Historical Research*, vol. 13, no. 38 (November 1935), pp. 85–89.

[67] Daniel Waley, "Le Origini della Condotta nel Duecento e le Compagnie di Ventura," *Rivista Storica Italiana*, vol. 88, no. 3 (1976), pp. 531–538; idem, "The Army of the Florentine Republic from the Twelfth to the Fourteenth Century," in: Nicolai Rubinstein (ed.), *Florentine Studies* (London: Faber and Faber, 1968), pp. 70–108; Michael Mallett, *Mercenaries and Their Masters* (London: The Bodley Head, 1974), esp. pp. 10–50; Alan Ryder, *The Kingdom of Naples under Alfonso the Magnanimous* (Oxford: Clarendon, 1976), pp. 262–279.

By the early 1300s, the English indenture system had also been perfected and expanded. There can be little doubt that the greater efficiency of his contract army was an important factor in persuading England's Edward III in 1337 to start the Hundred Years War against a state (France) that was between three and four times larger than his own realm. Throughout that conflict, scores of captains, from great nobles to simple knights, recruited mixed companies of cavalry and infantry (archers), often making intensive use of subcontracting in order to raise the number of men they had agreed to provide.[68]

Despite the successes which their new military system brought the English prior to 1337, their rivals the French had been reluctant to adopt it. During the 1200s and early 1300s, French kings continued to raise troops by appeals to feudal obligation while simultaneously offering regular pay as an added incentive. After brilliant English victories like the one at Crécy (1346), however, their opponents saw the writing on the wall. By the 1350s, the core of the French army was also a contract force, recruited through a variant of the indenture called the *lettre de retenue*.[69] The Castilians, now themselves embroiled in the Hundred Years War, soon followed suit by introducing the *acostamiento*. This was an arrangement whereby the king agreed to pay a fixed stipend to a group of nobles to raise military units and maintain them in a state of constant battle-readiness. Meanwhile, as early as the 1280s the crown of Aragon possessed a special kind of paid light infantry, the *almogavers*, which had been used to defeat the forces of Charles of Anjou during the Sicilian Vespers and thereafter formed the basis of the Catalan Company which ravaged the eastern Mediterranean during the early 1300s.[70]

By the 14th century, then, a contract system had come to replace military feudalism as the basis for military organization across western

[68] M. R. Powicke, "Lancastrian Captains," in: T. A. Sandquist and M. R. Powicke (eds.), *Essays in Medieval History Presented to Bertie Wilkinson* (Toronto: University of Toronto Press, 1969), pp. 371–382; Anthony Goodman, "The Military Subcontracts of Sir Hugh Hastings, 1380," *English Historical Review*, vol. 95, no. 374 (January 1980), pp. 114–120.

[69] Lot, *L'Art Militaire*, vol. II, pp. 423–424; Contamine, *La Guerre*, pp. 197–8, 279. Details of the French contract system, which was almost identical to that used in England, are provided in Contamine's *Guerre, État, et Société à la Fin du Moyen Âge: Études sur les Armées des Rois de France 1337–1494* (Paris: Mouton, 1972), pp. 56–62.

[70] Miguel Ángel Ladero Quesada, *Castilla y la Conquista del Reino de Granada* (Valladolid: Universidad de Valladolid, 1967), pp. 111–112; García de Cortázar, *Época Medieval*, pp. 458–459; J. N. Hillgarth, *The Spanish Kingdoms 1250–1516*, 2 vols. (Oxford: Clarendon, 1976), vol. I, pp. 241–242, 253–255; Claude Carrère, "Aux Origines des Grandes Compagnies: La Compagnie Catalane de 1302," in: Centre d'Histoire Militaire et d'Études de Défense Nationale de Montpellier, *Recrutement, Mentalités, Sociétés* (Montpellier: Université Paul Valéry, n.d.), pp. 1–7.

and southern Europe. Such a system enjoyed several advantages over its predecessor. Because service was both paid and voluntary, it was now possible to enlist native "soldiers" (i.e., "pay-takers") willing to fight anywhere for an unlimited length of time, whereas the feudal obligations of a knight were limited to 40 days of service within his own kingdom. In addition, the prospect of both money wages and a share of the spoils that victories in large-scale warfare might bring rendered the profession of arms more attractive to the lower nobility and common people alike. Finally, the ready-made hierarchy of contractor-led companies, each comprising a number of smaller units headed by subcontractors, provided the army with an internal cohesiveness lacking in the feudal levies.

All of these factors came together to produce 14th- and 15th-century field armies which were much larger, better organized, and together for much longer periods of time than those of the early 13th century. Thus while the French army that defeated their English, Flemish, and German opponents at Bouvines in 1214 had numbered only 7,500 combatants, their successors of the 1330s and 1340s were more than 30,000 strong, and the English army which besieged Calais in 1346–7 was just as large.[71]

Yet despite these gains, the contract system contained within it a number of dangers from the point of view of central governments. First, many (though by no means all) of the companies raised in England, France, and Iberia (though not Italy) were under the direct control of magnates, thus providing the latter with a trained military force which could be used against the central authorities. This fact undoubtedly contributed to the high incidence of civil war in all three areas during the 1300s and 1400s. Second, units raised by professional soldiers could become a problem when peace was concluded. Unemployed French and English companies ravaged the French countryside, holding towns and regions to ransom, after the Peace of Brétigny in 1360, and the phenomenon was repeated in both the 1390s and 1440s.[72]

Finally, the construction of an army on the basis of contracts opened up the possibility of a wide range of abuses even among units firmly loyal to the sovereign. The system was attractive to both contractors and subcontractors alike because it turned war into a moneymaking venture. Quite aside from the windfalls of victory, those who raised troops received a guaranteed profit derived from the difference between the sum paid to them by their employer and the total amount spent by

[71] Contamine, *Histoire*, p. 81; idem, *Guerre, État*, pp. 71–73.

[72] During the 1370s, the defense of Florence lay in the hands of a large company of English veterans of the Hundred Years War led by Sir John Hawkwood (known as "Giovanni Acuto" in Italy). On the role of mercenary companies in 14th-century Italian warfare, see Mallett, *Mercenaries*, pp. 25–50.

them on wages for their men. The captain could thus come to see his company primarily as a source of income, an investment like a piece of land or a house. He could attempt to increase his profit margin by any number of ruses – for example, by falsifying the number of men under his command, or by demanding extra funds for supplies and equipment and then not providing them – all of which would be detrimental to the discipline and military effectiveness of his unit.

Hence we find at the heart of the new-style royal armies of the 14th century a situation which we will encounter over and over again in our analysis of ancien régime Europe. In order to meet the pressing demands of war, the king must call upon the services of private groups in society who control resources he needs – whether military expertise, administrative skills, or money. To entice such groups into his pay, however, he must hold out the prospect of personal gain either of a direct financial nature or in the form of heightened social prestige or influence. In such institutions as the contract company, the tax farm, or the venal office there is always a fundamental conflict between the central government's interest in military or administrative efficiency and the captain, farmer, or officeholder's interest in personal profit. Although both interests are "rational" on their own terms, we can say that the first is the source of a drive towards "rationalization" in the Weberian sense, while the second is the source of a tendency towards "irrationalization," or the expansion of private at the expense of public interests, always present within the medieval and early modern state.

Rulers of the 14th century were well aware of the potential for abuse inherent in military contracting, and right from the start they tried to counter it through a series of administrative checks. The most important of these was the muster system first introduced into both the French and English armies during the Hundred Years War and regularly in use in Italy during the same period.[73] It remained a feature of all European armed forces until the 19th century. The essential idea behind the muster system was that the state should only disburse pay to captains (or, later, colonels) after the condition of their respective units had been ascertained by outside officials. Though raised under contract, companies were subject to regular inspections by government mustermasters, who (in theory at least) had to certify that they were up to strength and fully equipped before the treasurers-at-war could release funds to them. As in many other areas, the effectiveness of this method of control depended on both the willingness of the higher reaches of

---

[73] On mustering, see Contamine, *Guerre, État*, pp. 86–94; Richard Newhall, *Muster and Review* (Cambridge: Harvard University Press, 1940); Mallett, *Mercenaries*, pp. 99, 131–132.

military administration to root out "abuses," and on the quality of the officials employed to do the mustering.

The efficiency of the muster system also depended critically on a state's ability to pay its troops with some degree of regularity. With the advent of paid troops and sustained warfare, governments now had to find large sums of cash on a monthly basis for extended periods of time. Failure to meet these obligations could lead either to mutiny or non-cooperation on the part of the army, or expose a state to pressure from its military commanders. The latter might agree to advance personal funds to their troops themselves, but in return would expect the authorities to turn a blind eye to various common forms of corruption like false musters. Throughout the medieval and early modern period, then, honesty and efficiency in military organization was heavily dependent not only on the presence of administrative barriers to "irrationalization," but also on the effectiveness of a state's fiscal apparatus.

Administrative Expansion

The rise in geopolitical competition across Latin Europe during the 1100s and the changes in military organization which accompanied it had an immediate impact on state development in that region. External pressure and the mounting financial burdens lent new urgency to the task of extending royal power over regional and local lords as well as creating strong incentives for the efficient administration of royal financial resources. These new imperatives had a number of institutional consequences common to nearly all of the states under consideration.[74] In the first instance, France, Flanders, Normandy, Catalonia-Aragon-Valencia, and Sicily all introduced a new class of itinerant, regional justices during this period (called, respectively, *baillis/sénéchaux*, *baillis*, justices, vicars/justices, and justiciars) whose task it was to consolidate higher royal jurisdiction over much larger areas, collect a number of regalian dues, and ensure honesty and efficiency among the local *prévots* or their equivalents.[75] The original inspiration for this new official, who was soon to become sedentary, seems to have been the Normans, who perhaps modelled it on the Carolingian *missi*.

This expansion of royal jurisdiction was spurred on both by the simultaneous growth of competing princely and ecclesiastical courts and by the

---

[74] On the nature of these changes in general, see: C. Warren Hollister and John Baldwin, "The Rise of Administrative Kingship: Henry I and Philip Augustus," *American Historical Review*, vol. 83, no. 4 (October 1978), pp. 867–905.

[75] Lot and Fawtier, *Histoire*, vol. I, pp. 29–30, 398, 403–406; vol. II, pp. 144–158; Klüpfel, *Verwaltungsgeschichte*, pp. 72–90; Bisson, *Medieval Crown*, p. 82; Matthew, *Norman Kingdom*, pp. 248–253.

desire to increase revenues, for judicial fees were a very lucrative source of income throughout the middle ages.[76] This emphasis on asserting jurisdictional rights and extracting higher revenues at the regional and local level led of necessity to a larger and ever more sophisticated central government. It was during the late 12th and 13th centuries that specialized writing offices, central courts, and treasuries emerged almost simultaneously in France, Flanders, Normandy, Sicily, and the Iberian kingdoms to handle the steady rise in both judicial business and royal income flowing in the direction of an increasingly sedentary royal court.[77]

Representative Assemblies and Permanent Systems of Taxation

Yet as early as the mid-1200s, the higher levels of revenue which rulers had been able to obtain through judicial expansion and a more thorough exploitation of regalian rights and resources were proving ever more inadequate in the face of incessant geopolitical rivalries coupled with an unstoppable trend towards the use of paid troops. Rulers across Latin Europe responded to these military and financial pressures by creating national representative assemblies in order to provide support, ideological and above all financial, for their chosen foreign policies. What is most striking about these assemblies, which first appeared sporadically in the Iberian kingdoms and Sicily in the late 1100s and early 1200s and became fully institutionalized across the region during the period 1250–1350, is their common organizational structure. Despite the substantial differences among them in size, geopolitical location, and economic structure, France, Flanders, León-Castile, Catalonia, Valencia, Portugal, Piedmont, Naples, and Sicily all came to possess representative bodies which were divided into three estates or *curiae* representing respectively the clergy, the nobility, and the towns of the royal demesne, all of which deliberated and voted separately. Even more surprisingly, assemblies of this type were also to be found in nearly all the German territorial states, which would seem to have shared little with their Latin neighbors, but not in other western polities like England, Poland, and Hungary.[78]

[76] Harouel et al., *Histoire*, pp. 245–247; Morris, *Papal Monarchy*, p. 233; Elizabeth Hallam, *Capetian France 987–1328* (London: Longman, 1980), pp. 165, 242–243.

[77] Hollister and Baldwin, "Rise of Administrative Kingship," pp. 892–897; Harouel et al., *Histoire*, pp. 223–234; Lot and Fawtier, *Histoire*, vol. I, pp. 28, 381–389; Valdeavellano, *Curso de Historia*, pp. 496–497, 561–563, 569–570, 590–592, 594–595; García de Cortázar, *Época Medieval*, pp. 312–313; Matthew, *Norman Kingdom*, pp. 209–228.

[78] C. H. McIlwain, "Medieval Estates," in: J. R. Tanner, C. W. Previté-Orton, and Z. N. Brooke (eds.), *The Cambridge Medieval History. Volume VII: Decline of Empire and Papacy* (Cambridge: Cambridge University Press, 1968), pp. 664–715, esp. p. 700; Evelyn

The most parsimonious explanation for the observed distribution of estate-type assemblies is that they are the result of the one feature shared by the states of both Latin Europe and Germany: the common experience of unsuccessful, large-scale state formation during the so-called dark ages and the consequences which this had for the pattern of local government established in the new generation of polities founded or re-founded after 1000. The collapse of Visigothic, Umayyad, Carolingian, and, last of all, Ottonian-Salian power left Latin Europe and Germany with a fragmented local political landscape and a powerful conceptual construct – the tripartite social theory of Gérard de Cambrai and Aldabéron de Laon – which was both a product of that fragmentation and an attempt to overcome it. Given the lack of territorially integrated local communities like the Roman *civitas* or the Carolingian county in either Latin Europe or Germany, it must have seemed an easier proposition to create functionally rather than territorially based assemblies. Gérard and Aldabéron's tripartite vision provided the perfect ideological blueprint for such an assembly since it explicitly encouraged the solidaristic self-organization of three groups – the clergy, nobles, and burghers – whose privileges were under threat from royal attempts at centralization. The tools to make estate- or order-based assemblies a workable reality were then furnished by Roman and canon law, which by the mid-1200s had developed the institution of the proctorial mandate, thereby making possible the effective representation of larger groups or corporate bodies by delegates armed with *plena potestas* or full powers of decision.[79]

It was these new representative institutions which, through the revenue they granted to help meet the mounting costs of war, laid the groundwork for permanent systems of national taxation and the transition from what Schumpeter called the "domain state" to the "tax state."[80]

Procter, *Curia and Cortes in León and Castile 1072–1295* (Cambridge: Cambridge University Press, 1980), pp. 2, 254–267; Joseph O'Callaghan, *The Cortes of Castile-León 1188–1350* (Philadelphia: University of Pennsylvania Press, 1989), pp. 2, 41–42, 48–59, 193–195; MacKay, *Spain*, pp. 101, 114–115; Joaquim Veríssimo Serrão, *História de Portugal. Volume I: Estado, Patria e Nacão (1080–1415)*, 3rd ed. (Lisboa: Editorial Verbo, 1979), pp. 154–183; Antonio Marongiu, *Medieval Parliaments: A Comparative Study* (London: Eyre and Spottiswoode, 1968), pp. 46, 49, 54, 109–117, 148–162, 196–204; Lot and Fawtier, *Histoire*, vol. I, p. 377; Harouel, *Histoire*, pp. 372–376. For a more detailed analysis of representative assemblies in England, Poland and Hungary, and Germany, with full references, see Chapters 4, 5, and 6 below.

[79] Gaines Post, "Roman Law and Early Representation in Spain and Italy, 1150–1250," and "*Plena Potestas* and Consent in Medieval Assemblies," both in: idem, *Studies in Medieval Legal Thought* (Princeton: Princeton University Press, 1964), pp. 61–90, 91–162; O'Callaghan, *Cortes*, pp. 14–15, 194.

[80] Joseph Schumpeter, "Die Krise des Steuerstaates," in: idem, *Aufsätze zur Soziologie* (Tübingen: J. C. B. Mohr, 1953), pp. 1–71, here at pp. 6–17.

The intimate connection between warfare and the birth of these assemblies is underscored by the fact that they first made their appearance on the Iberian peninsula, where conflict between Christians and Moors was endemic until the Reconquest was completed in 1492. By 1188, a Cortes of three estates was present in León, and similar institutions were soon created in Castile (1217 – separated from León between 1157 and 1252), Catalonia (1218), Aragon (1247), Portugal (1254), and Valencia (1283).[81] In the early 1200s, the Estates of Catalonia and Aragon were already granting two direct taxes, the *bovatge* and *monedatge*, on a regular basis to their sovereign, and the Portuguese Cortes of 1254 and 1261 agreed to a similar tax, the *monetagio*, in return for royal promises to end the use of coinage debasements as a way of raising funds.[82]

In Castile, the first steps towards a system of royal revenue not based principally on regalian rights and resources came during the reign of Alfonso X (1252–1284).[83] During the 1260s, a powerful new dynasty, the Marinids, established themselves in Morocco, and began to provide substantial military aid to the embattled kingdom of Granada and to the Moors living in Spanish-held territory. Castile was hence forced into a new round of wars which lasted well into the 1300s.[84] To pay for these wars, the Cortes of 1268 granted customs duties on both imports and exports which gradually became permanent during the late 1200s. The following year, a special war subsidy (*servicio*) was voted for one year. This tax could not be levied without the consent of the Cortes, but it was renewed innumerable times over the next century in aid of the war effort.[85]

During the 1340s, as the war with the Marinids was entering its final phase, two other important sources of revenue were added to the resources of the Castilian crown. From 1340 onward, the government collected in perpetuity a tax on the clergy, the *tercias reales*, which the Pope had granted occasionally since 1247. Most important of all, in 1342 the Cortes voted Alfonso XI a national sales tax, the *alcabala*, to

---

[81] Valdeavallano, *Curso de Historia*, pp. 465–466; MacKay, *Spain*, pp. 103, 114–115; O'Callaghan, *Cortes*, p. 16; Livermore, *History*, p. 139. More generally, see A. R. Myers, "The Parliaments of Europe in the Age of the Estates," *History*, vol. 60, no. 198 (February 1975), pp. 11–27.

[82] Bisson, *Medieval Crown*, pp. 54–56, 60–61; Valdeavellano, *Curso*, p. 609; Livermore, *History*, pp. 141–142; Veríssimo Serrão, *Historia*, pp. 157–160.

[83] Miguel Ángel Ladero Quesada, "Ingreso, Gasto y Política Fiscal de la Corona de Castilla. Desde Alfonso X a Enrique III (1252–1406)," in: idem, *El Siglo XV en Castilla* (Barcelona: Editorial Ariel, 1982), pp. 13–57, here at p. 14. For what follows, see Ladero Quesada's detailed discussion, pp. 13–39.

[84] MacKay, *Spain*, pp. 64–65.

[85] Ladero Quesada, "Ingreso, Gasto," pp. 26–27, 18–19.

cover the cost of the siege of Algeciras. This grant was reconfirmed many times in the 1370s and 1380s, during the period of Castilian involvement in the Hundred Years War, and became permanent, under circumstances that remain obscure, between 1393 and 1406.[86] Between 1268 and 1300s, then, collaboration between king and Cortes had created a system of national taxation in Castile, the four pillars of which – customs, parliamentary subsidies, sales tax, and tax on the clergy – provided the core of royal revenue for the next three centuries.

The development of taxation in southern Italy was much less closely connected to the rise of representative institutions than it had been in Iberia or would be in France. Since 1194, Hohenstaufen emperors had ruled the kingdom of Sicily, and the emperor Frederick II (1197–1250) went farther than any medieval ruler in using the revived Roman law in an attempt to regain in the fields of legislation and taxation the imperial prerogative enjoyed by Justinian and his predecessors. Southern Italy was fertile ground for such an attempt, because much of it had remained in Byzantine hands until the Arab incursions of the 9th century. It is hardly surprising, then, that in 1235 Frederick, requiring massive funds to continue his struggle against his enemies in Italy and Germany, imposed without consultation a permanent general property tax (the *collecta*) upon his subjects, permitting no exemptions for either the clergy or the nobility. This tax continued to be collected under his Angevin successors, though by the late 1200s they also had begun to convoke meetings of their Estates which sometimes granted additional extraordinary revenues. In Sicily, the *collecta* was only imposed in emergencies after 1282, and the tricurial national assembly came to play a greater role under the Aragonese, regularly voting extra grants for military purposes.[87]

The emergence of an orderly tax system in France lagged behind developments in Iberia and southern Italy. Beginning in 1285, Philip the Fair (1285–1314) was confronted by military pressures similar to those facing his contemporary Edward I. After leading a disastrous invasion of Aragon (1285) and fighting the English in Gascony (1294–7), he remained embroiled in a costly struggle with the Flemish which lasted until 1305. To finance these wars, however, Philip preferred to exploit other options instead of turning to general assemblies for grants

[86] Ibid., pp. 32, 45–47; Salvador de Moxó, *La Alcabala* (Madrid: Consejo Superior de Investigaciones Científicas, 1963), pp. 18–25, 27–30.

[87] Matthew, *Norman Kingdom*, pp. 316–317, 323–324, 329, 336, 342–348; Barber, *Two Cities*, pp. 244–250; Marongiu, *Medieval Parliaments*, pp. 114–115, 149–154, 157–162; Emile Léonard, *Les Angevins de Naples* (Paris: Presses Universitaires de France, 1954), pp. 84, 281–282; Denis Mack Smith, *A History of Sicily* (New York: Dorset, 1988), pp. 57, 61, 70, 79, 96.

of new revenues. First and foremost, he pressured the Church into granting him taxes (tenths or annates) on an almost annual basis. This policy led to a direct confrontation with Pope Boniface VIII, and in order to obtain broad support in this struggle Philip convoked the first-ever meeting of the Estates General in 1302. Second, he imposed general property taxes without broad consultation or consent, first on the south (1294) and then on the rest of the country (from 1295). Finally, various wealthy but marginal groups such as the Templars, Jews, Italians, and other foreign merchants were made to pay heavily.[88]

The government soon learned that such an approach was ultimately counterproductive. Whatever the legal justification for levying taxes without consent, the practical results, at least during this period, were a serious conflict with the Pope, resistance to collection and hence disappointing tax returns, and finally open revolt (1314).[89] Philip's son Philip V seems to have drawn the logical conclusion from this experience, and he called together Estates General in 1320 and 1321, but the latter proved reluctant to grant him taxes in peacetime, and the experiment was not repeated.[90] France had to wait another 25 years until the desperate conditions of the Hundred Years War allowed representative assemblies a regular part in the governing process. These assemblies then played a central role in creating a new public tax system over the course of the next century.

Estates General were convened in 1343, 1346, and 1347, and the Estates of northern and central France (Estates of Langue doil) in 1351 and 1355–6 to approve taxes for national defense. At the same time, a two-tiered system of assemblies was emerging, with regional and local estates meeting frequently to decide on the manner in which funds voted by the Estates General should be raised. This development was encouraged by King Jean II (1350–1364), who saw representative institutions as a means to build consensus and support for the war effort.[91] But on September 19, 1356, the king was captured at the battle of Poitiers, and he was released in 1360 only after the French had agreed to a huge ransom.

King Jean did not need to seek the approval of the Estates in order to collect the funds required for his ransom, since according to feudal law all subjects were obliged to contribute towards the release of their

[88] Joseph Strayer and Charles Taylor, *Studies in Early French Taxation* (Cambridge: Harvard University Press, 1939), pp. 7–19, 95–96; Lot and Fawtier, *Histoire*, vol. II, pp. 550–552; Harouel et al., *Histoire*, p. 373.

[89] Ibid., pp. 9–11, 23, 49ff.

[90] John Bell Henneman, *Royal Taxation in Fourteenth Century France: The Development of War Financing 1322–1356* (Princeton: Princeton University Press, 1971), pp. 32–35.

[91] Ibid., pp. 230–231, 243, 252.

captured sovereign. In December 1360, Jean imposed by ordinance a general sales tax and a tax on wine (henceforth collectively known as the *aides*), as well as a tax on salt (the *gabelle*).[92] An Estates General meeting in 1363 tacitly condoned these indirect taxes and approved a substantial hearth tax (*fouage*) to fund the suppression of roving bands of discharged soldiers who were terrorizing the country. No time limit was placed on this tax.[93]

Throughout the 1360s and 1370s, the *fouages*, *aides*, and *gabelles* continued to be collected without public protest. There existed a well-established medieval principle, rooted in Roman and canon law, that taxes could be levied so long as there was "evident necessity," i.e., the safety of the country was in danger.[94] This certainly was the case in France during this period, and the general view among the politically influential seemed to be that once the Estates had voted taxes for defense, they could remain in force as long as the danger persisted, but no longer. Charles V underscored this point by canceling the *fouage* on his deathbed in 1380, and the indirect taxes were abolished in 1381.

The grave crisis which followed the new English invasion of 1415 and the defeat at Agincourt brought the revival of both the Estates General/Estates of Langue doil and permanent taxation. The former were summoned almost annually in the 1420s, and several times in the 1430s. In 1435, the Estates of Langue d'oil reestablished the *aides* and *gabelles* of 1360 for four years and, after this grant was reapproved in 1436, they were levied without further consultation until the end of the ancien régime. In 1439, the same body approved a general *taille*, the direct tax that was the successor of the *fouage*, for one year to support a standing army. As such an army remained in existence, in the form of the *compagnies d'ordonnance*, even after the defeat of the English in 1453, the *taille* continued to be collected.[95] Building on the groundwork laid in the 1360s, the Estates of the 1430s had, in response to the pressures of war, introduced a series of permanent direct and indirect taxes which provided the French crown with a good portion of its revenues for the next three and a half centuries.

Throughout Latin Europe, systems of public (as opposed to regalian, feudal, or demesnial) revenue were created in roughly the same manner, and for roughly the same reasons, between 1250 and 1450. In Iberia, France, and even Naples and Sicily national representative bodies, called

[92] John Bell Henneman, *Royal Taxation in Fourteenth Century France: The Captivity and Ransom of John II 1356–1370* (Philadelphia: American Philosophical Society, 1976), pp. 117–119.
[93] Ibid., pp. 226–228.
[94] Henneman, *Royal Taxation . . . 1322–1356*, pp. 22–24.
[95] Henneman, *Royal Taxation . . . 1356–1370*, pp. 309–310.

into being to provide support for military and foreign policy initiatives, voluntarily imposed taxes on the entire realm to help finance the new, paid armies. In discussing this development, historians have traditionally emphasized the varying degrees to which Estates in different nations retained legal control over taxation. While this issue is certainly of great importance, it has distracted attention away from a more obvious point: the needs of war had given birth across Latin Europe to a unique institution which, whatever its exact legal prerogatives, could be put to many uses by creative rulers.

Jean II and Charles VII of France understood this. Although both could have invoked the national emergency caused by an English invasion to levy taxes at will, they attempted instead to foster the growth of representative institutions. In addition to the financial assistance such bodies provided, the discussions and debates which went on within them helped create a consensus around the government's military policies, which in turn facilitated both army recruitment and tax collection. Finally, as we shall see below, the representative institutions of the 1300s and 1400s felt it their duty to expose and condemn the growing power of financiers and officeholders within the king's administration and press for reforms that might bolster national defense. Yet the structural weaknesses inherent in these assemblies would both prevent them from developing their full potential and tempt rulers to sweeping them aside, a course of action that would only serve to strengthen the tendencies towards the widespread appropriation of state functions already present within the growing state apparatuses of late medieval Latin Europe.

THE IMPACT OF WAR AND TAXES ON FINANCE AND ADMINISTRATION: THE BEGINNINGS OF PATRIMONIAL ABSOLUTISM

As argued above, the existence of a competitive, multistate environment in Latin Europe since the 1100s ushered in a whole series of interlocking changes in the polities of that area: the expansion and specialization of judicial, financial, and administrative infrastructures; the development of more effective, but also more costly, forms of military organization; and the creation of tricurial assemblies which provided the revenue base to sustain continuous statebuidling. The steady growth of the state, and its increasing reliance on paid troops, rendered it ever more dependent on the small and exclusive group of individuals who at this early date possessed the scarce resources which rulers so desperately needed: financiers and skilled administrators. This dependence would, under conditions of sustained warfare, permit such groups to begin to establish extensive control over a range of key state functions, a trend that would only intensify as kings sought to use revived Roman conceptions of "imperial" rulership to push aside critical Estates and concentrate ever more decisionmaking power in their own hands.

Finance

While the taxes voted by representative assemblies in the later middle ages provided, in the long run, an adequate financial foundation for extended conflicts using paid troops, they could do little to meet the pressing need for ready money (i.e., cash) felt by governments at war. This was so because taxes in the 1300s and 1400s (and for many centuries thereafter) flowed in at a very slow and irregular rate. The problem, then, which all states increasingly faced was how to find the short-term credit capable of bridging the gap between immediate cash expenditures and future tax receipts. During the period under discussion, the states of Latin Europe each developed their own solution to this problem, solutions that were in turn closely linked to the way revenue was collected. What these solutions had in common, however, was that they all ceded substantial influence over still-fragile fiscal infrastructures to powerful financiers with access to ready cash.

In Castile, the reign of Alfonso XI (1312–1350) saw the replacement of direct collection by the farming of nearly all crown revenues, including the customs, *tercias*, and *alcabala*.[96] Farms were let at public auctions supervised by central government officials. The farmers would agree to pay a fixed cash rent to the government at set intervals in return for the right to collect a particular tax directly from the general public. During the 15th century, farms of the *tercias* and *alcabala* covering the entire country were given out to powerful financial syndicates of native businessmen, who in turn divided the farms up and distributed them to subfarmers.[97]

The potential abuses inherent in a credit system which turned the collection of the state's entire income over to private business were compounded by the tendency of Juan II (1406–1454) and his successors to name farmers to the post of royal receiver (*recaudador*) as well. This meant that they were charged with distributing salaries and pensions

---

[96] Miguel Ángel Ladero Quesada, "Los Judíos Castellanos del Siglo XV en el Arrendamiento de Impuestos Reales," in: idem, *El Siglo XV*, pp. 143–167, here at 150. A detailed description of the Castilian farming system can be found in idem, *La Hacienda Real de Castilla en el Siglo XV* (Tenerife: Universidad de La Laguna, 1973), pp. 22–30.

[97] Ibid., pp. 26–27.

assigned on specific revenues, which placed them in a position to extort compensation from recipients in return for timely payment.[98]

Tax farming was widely employed within both the crown of Aragon and in Sicily throughout this period.[99] Aragon also made use of a method for raising cash which would later be taken to extreme lengths in France: "inside" credit.[100] This was a practice whereby government officials would help the crown out of financial difficulties by advancing it money. In a more sophisticated version of this expedient, already foreshadowed in Aragon, financiers could be placed directly into positions in the fiscal bureaucracy with the understanding that they would make regular cash advances.[101] The government of Naples also employed the banking facilities provided first by Florentines and later by native Neapolitans as an additional source of short-term credit.[102]

Revenue farming played an important role in the finances of the French crown as well, though not to the same extent as in the Iberian kingdoms and Sicily. Many revenues of the royal domain and the *aides* of 1360 were farmed, but both the *gabelles* and the *fouages/tailles* were levied directly by new groups of royal officials, respectively the *grenetiers* and *élus*. As the name implies, the latter were initially named by the Estates General, but by 1360 had come under royal control.[103]

The establishment of a system of national taxation in France thus brought with it the creation of an army of new revenue officers – the *grenetiers* and *élus*, their assistants, and the *généraux de finance* and *trésoriers* who supervised them. It was primarily to these and other officials, rather than to bankers or large-scale tax farmers, that the French governments of the late middle ages turned for loans and advances. This use of "inside" credit was already prominent under Philip the Fair, and became even more significant during the Hundred Years War.[104]

While in future centuries the French crown was to use every possible

---

[98] Miguel Ángel Ladero Quesada, "Instituciones Fiscales y Realidad Social en el Siglo XV Castellano," in: idem, *El Siglo XV*, pp. 58–87, here at 86–87.

[99] Matthew, *Norman Kingdom*, p. 234; Mack Smith, *Medieval Italy*, p. 80; Joseph O'Callaghan, *A History of Medieval Spain* (Ithaca: Cornell University Press, 1975), p. 455; Winfried Küchler, *Die Finanzen der Krone Aragon während des 15. Jahrhunderts (Alfons V. und Johann II.)* (Münster: Aschendorffsche Verlagsbuchhandlung, 1983), pp. 37–62.

[100] This evocative term is Martin Wolfe's. See his *The Fiscal System of Renaissance France* (New Haven: Yale University Press, 1972), pp. 64–66.

[101] Wolfe, *Fiscal System*, pp. 64–65; Klüpfel, *Verwaltungsgeschichte*, pp. 174–176.

[102] Léonard, *Angevins de Naples*, pp. 281–282; Ryder, *Kingdom of Naples*, pp. 182–189.

[103] Lot and Fawtier, *Histoire*, vol. II, p. 275.

[104] Joseph Strayer, *The Reign of Philip the Fair* (Princeton: Princeton University Press, 1980), p. 151; E. B. Fryde and M. M. Fryde, "Public Credit, with Special Reference to North-Western Europe," in: M. M. Postan, E. E. Rich, and Edward Miller (eds.), *The Cambridge Economic History of Europe. Volume III: Economic Organization and Policies in the Middle Ages* (Cambridge: Cambridge University Press, 1963), pp. 430–553, here at pp. 478–484.

means of raising cash, the central importance of government officials
to the short-term credit system had far-reaching consequences. While
it placed officeholders at the mercy of state demands for funds, it also
gave the former great leverage over their employers, leverage which
was used to solidify the hold of officials over their offices (see below).
By the late 1300s, finance and administration in France were already
entwined in a unique, and potentially fateful, manner.

Administration

The addition of tax collectors, muster-masters, and treasurers-at-war to
the permanent corpus of government officials was but one of the many
ways that developments in the military sphere affected the administrative side of the western European state from the 1100s onward. Larger
armies and nearly annual campaigns created additional demands at
both the local level – where provisions had to be collected and billets
arranged for passing companies – and the very pinnacle of the government, from which the mountain of written documents pertaining to the
raising of troops and revenue emanated.

The inevitable result of these pressures was an increase in the numbers
of permanent officials at both the national and local levels engaged in
purely clerical and administrative tasks. Examples of this include the
expansion across the region of chanceries and secretariats with their
growing contingents of royal clerks and notaries. To these pure administrators must be added the revenue officers mentioned above: customs
collectors, controllers, and tronagers, *élus*, *grenetiers*, and their staffs. In
their wake came specialized organs of central financial administration
and adjudication which in France took the form of the *chambre de compte*,
cour des aides, and *cour du trésor*.[105] In Castile, an institution similar to the
English Exchequer, the *contaduría mayor de hacienda*, was created during
the reign of Alfonso XI (1312–1350).[106]

It is beyond dispute, then, that the rulers of Latin Europe responded
to the heightened pressures of war by increasing greatly their corps of
permanent state officials. The real issue, however, is what *kind* of administration this produced. To answer this question, we must first examine
the two models of office and officeholding available to rulers and administrators during the all-important 12th, 13th, and 14th centuries when
state apparatuses across this region took on their basic form.

The first of these was the feudal model of office as *feudum* or fief. The
fief was a source of maintenance, usually (but not exclusively) in the

---

[105] Lot and Fawtier, *Histoire*, vol. II, pp. 240–244, 247–250, 279–284.
[106] Ladero Quesada, *La Hacienda Real*, p. 18.

form of land granted as a sign of particular favor by a king or other lord to one of his subjects. The grantee received property rights over the source of maintenance, often including the right to pass it on to his heirs, in return for the performance of certain duties, such as military service.[107] We have already seen how under the influence of this model the traditional household offices of the postmillennial kingdoms were quickly rendered hereditary, and how the first generation of royal officials, the *prévots* and their equivalents, had attempted to appropriate their positions by reinterpreting them as hereditary fiefs, just as the Carolingian counts had done many centuries earlier. Governments across Latin Europe responded to this last threat by farming out the *prévotés* at regular intervals to the highest bidder, an effective but ultimately costly way of preventing their full patrimonialization.[108] At the same time, they chose to make extensive use of ecclesiastics, who both had extensive clerical skills and were immune from feudal temptations, in their rapidly expanding central staffs.

Yet this decision would also have fateful long-term consequences, because it was precisely during this period (1100s/1200s) that the Church was perfecting its own alternative model of office, one that would create almost equally enticing possibilities for appropriation. This was the ecclesiastical benefice, originally a source of income provided to a cleric performing certain duties. Over the course of the 13th century, the rights and privileges enjoyed by benefice-holders were codified in canon law. First, benefices were granted for life, and the holder could be removed only for serious offenses through judicial proceedings. Second, the holder was permitted to resign his benefice and name his own successor as long as he did not die within 20 (later 40) days of doing so (i.e., no death-bed resignations). This was known as *resignatio in favorem tertii*. The implicit purpose of this privilege was to facilitate the retirement of the benefice-holder by permitting him to (in effect) sell his office to a third party for a lump sum of money which would then serve as a kind of pension.

Third, the Pope reserved the right to issue "expectancies," i.e., promises to name an applicant to the next available benefice which might open up due, for example, to the death of the previous holder. In practice, such expectancies were only granted in return for a payment.

---

[107] José María García Marín, *El Oficio Público en Castilla durante la Baja Edad Media* (Seville: University of Seville, 1974), pp. 27–33; Christopher Stocker, "Office as Maintenance in Renaissance France," *Canadian Journal of History*, vol. 6, no. 1 (March 1971), pp. 21–43.

[108] Lot and Fawtier, *Histoire*, vol. I, p. 18; vol. II, p. 142; Harouel et al., *Histoire*, pp. 235–236; Lyon and Verhulst, *Medieval Finance*, pp. 95–96; Matthew, *Norman Kingdom*, p. 244; Klüpfel, *Verwaltungsgeschichte*, pp. 78, 89.

Finally, the Pope had the power to excuse the holder from the requirement that he perform the duties of his office in person and instead
allow him to appoint a deputy. This made it possible for one person, as
long as he secured permission from the Curia, to hold a number of
benefices simultaneously (pluralism).[109] As will be shown below, secular
offices throughout western Europe came to acquire all these attributes
beginning in the 1300s.

It might at first glance seem that the full-fledged benefice system would
have ruinous consequences for efficient Church organization, but the
effects of practices like *resignatio in favorem* and pluralism were tempered
by two factors. In canon law and, quite often, in ecclesiastical practice,
an official's source of income (the *beneficium* proper) was separated from
the administrative duties he performed (the *officium*). Just because one
had the right to nominate a successor to one's *benefice* did not mean
that one could determine who would occupy one's *office*. The Church
still had the ability to fill offices according to some criteria of suitability.

A second factor that must be kept in mind is that clerics for the most
part possessed no children for whom they had to provide. Though
nepotism (in the literal sense) was certainly a problem in the Church,
the lack of overriding family concerns among churchmen helped limit
(at least in theory) the possibilities presented by *resignatio* and pluralism for ensconcing clan members throughout the ecclesiastical administration. Both these restraining factors were to be absent when the
rights and privileges attached to benefices were transferred to purely
secular offices held by laymen, as was soon to happen.

That canon law notions of the benefice would come to be applied to
secular offices is understandable, given the dominant role played by
clerics in 13th-century European governments. Thus in 13th-century
France, all chancery officials, as well as all of the clerks of the royal
council charged with verifying financial accounts, were ecclesiastics;
and the chanceries of León, Castile, and Aragon were all closely tied to
the Church in the high middle ages.[110] These clerics usually held their

[109] Franz Gillmann, *Die Resignation der Benefizien* (Mainz: Verlag von Franz Kirchheim,
1901), pp. 132–153; García Marín, *El Oficio Público*, pp. 22–27; Brigide Schwarz,
"Aemterkäuflichkeit, eine Institution des Absolutismus und ihre mittelalterlichen Wurzeln," in: *Staat und Gesellschaft in Mittelalter und Früher Neuzeit: Gedankschrift für Joachim
Leuschner* (Göttingen: Vandenhoeck & Ruprecht, 1983), pp. 176–196, drawing on her
earlier, more detailed study *Die Organisation Kurialer Schreiberkollegien von ihrer Enstehung
bis zur Mitte des 15. Jahrhunderts* (Tübingen: Max Niemeyer, 1972). François Olivier-
Martin first noticed the influence of canon law concepts and papal practices on 14th-
century French administration in his "La Nomination aux Offices Royaux au XIVe
Siècle et d'après les Pratiques de la Chancellerie," *Mélanges Paul Fournier* (Paris: Recueil
Sirey, 1929), pp. 487–501.
[110] Lot and Fawtier, *Histoire*, vol. II, pp. 87, 198; Valdeavellano, *Curso de Historia*, pp. 497–
498.

offices at pleasure tenure (i.e., their holders could be dismissed at any time) and carried with them no or only very minimal salaries. This was possible because cleric-administrators also held one or more ecclesiastical benefices at life tenure, which provided them with a source of both income and security. In effect, their position was the same as that of other benefice-holders, except that their *officium* lay in the royal government.

As we have seen, the 14th century brought a great upsurge in war and the administrative expansion that accompanied it. At the same time, laymen began to enter offices previously reserved for clerics. This process seems to have begun earliest in France under Philip the Fair – an undoubted reflection of the tense relations between Church and state that obtained during that reign – but it soon spread to the rest of Latin Europe.[111] The period 1300–1450 thus saw both a major expansion in the number of permanent administrative positions found within the western monarchies, and an influx of laymen to fill those positions. Since this new breed of officials did not hold benefices, salaries and/or fees collected directly from the public had to be made available to them, thereby transforming the office itself into a source of income. At first, government positions were granted to laymen on the same terms as they had been granted to clerics, i.e., at pleasure. But this arrangement was clearly disadvantageous to the new administrators. With no benefices on which to fall back, both their income and social status, and that of their family, might well depend entirely on their official position.[112] Dismissal could spell ruin.

Lay officeholders responded to this predicament by reinterpreting their secular offices as benefices, and seeking to gain the same advantages for themselves as those enjoyed by benefice-holders. The identification of secular office and benefice must have seemed a logical one to officials, many of whom had some training in canon law, since offices now had a source of income (salary and/or fees) attached to them. If a lay administrator could win life tenure, the right of *resignatio in favorem*, and the privilege of appointing a deputy, his own future would be secure and the status gains of his family safeguarded, since the right of *resignatio* could be used either to sell the office for a large sum or to name a son, son-in-law, or nephew as successor.

Officeholders made steady progress in realizing these goals throughout the 14th and 15th centuries. This process is most extensively documented

[111] Lot and Fawtier, *Histoire*, vol. I, p. 87; Strayer, *Philip the Fair*, pp. 44–46; Francisco Tomás y Valiente, "Origen Bajomedieval de la Patrimonialización y la Enajenación de Oficios Públicos en Castilla, "*Actas del I Symposium de Historia de la Administración* (Madrid: Instituto de Estudios Administrativos, 1970), pp. 125–159.

[112] J. C. Sainty, "The Tenure of Offices in the Exchequer," *English Historical Review*, vol. 80, no. 316 (July 1965), pp. 449–475, here at p. 453.

in the case of France. In the early 1300s, de facto life tenure, the appointment of deputies, and the private traffic in offices linked to *resignationes in favorem* were already common among local government officials.[113] These practices apparently spread to the most important financial and legal offices in the latter half of the century.[114] By the late 1300s the Parlement of Paris had begun to defend the principle that officeholders could only be removed against their will for serious offenses proven in court.[115] By the 1400s, pluralism and nonresidence had also become common.[116] The program of the *officiers*, then, had been realized and the administration of 15th-century France, whether central or local, judicial or financial, was dotted with clans and dynasties of officials who treated their offices as their own property.[117]

The same pattern appears again in Castile, though with a somewhat different chronology. Complaints about nonresidence and the appointment of substitutes were first heard in the Cortes as early as 1297, and the same body requested in 1327 that the king eliminate pluralism.[118] The widespread introduction of life tenure and traffic in offices through *resignatio in favorem* does not appear to have come until the reign of Enrique II (1369–79). At this time Castile had become embroiled in the war between England and France, and Enrique had come to the throne with the support of the latter after murdering his half-brother. He spent his short reign attempting to defend his gains against the English, their Portuguese allies, and his opponents at home. Through favorable concessions to his officials and to nobles who used their offices as a source of profit, the king attempted to shore up his basis of political support in the face of such pressures.[119]

By the late 1300s, then, principles associated with the benefice had been applied to secular offices in Castile as well.[120] This pattern continued

[113] Martin, "La Nomination . . . ," pp. 495, 497, 498.
[114] Kuno Böse, "Die Aemterkäuflichkeit in Frankreich vom 14. bis 16. Jahrhundert," in: Ilja Mieck (ed.), *Aemterhandel im Spätmittelalter und im 16. Jahrhundert* (Berlin: Colloquium Verlag, 1984), pp. 83–111, here p. 92; Bernard Guenée, *Tribunaux et Gens de Justice dans le Baillage de Senlis à la Fin du Moyen Âge* (Strasbourg: University of Strasbourg, 1963), pp. 169–170, 172. The so-called Cabochian Ordonnance of 1413 cites a long list of offices, both high and low, in which *resignatio in favorem* is common; cited in Martin Göhring, *Die Aemterkäuflichkeit im Ancien Regime* (Berlin: Verlag Dr. Emil Ebering, 1938), p. 25.
[115] Françoise Autrand, "Office et Officiers Royaux en France sous Charles VI," *Revue Historique*, vol. 93, no. 242 (October–December 1969), pp. 285–338, here p. 331.
[116] Gustave Dupont-Ferrier, *Les Officiers Royaux des Baillages et Sénéchaussees et les Institutions Monarchiques Locales en France à la Fin du Moyen Age* (Paris: Bouillon, 1902), pp. 771, 779.
[117] Several examples of such dynasties are cited in P. S. Lewis, *Late Medieval France* (London: Macmillan, 1968), pp. 149–152.
[118] Tomás y Valiente, "Origen Bajomedieval," pp. 144, 150.
[119] Ibid., p. 132.   [120] García Marín, *El Oficio Público*, p. 149.

during the reigns of Juan II (1406–1454) and Enrique IV (1454–1474), which were also rent by civil strife and war with Aragon. These kings even went so far as to make grants of hereditary tenure and to allow office-holders to farm their offices, a practice which inevitably led to relentless exploitation of the public by the farmers.[121] When the Cortes asked Enrique IV to put an end to these iniquities, he frankly replied: "but you know that . . . I am constrained by the unavoidable necessity which presses upon me in these times to defend my royal person and to attract the gentlemen of my kingdom to serve me. . . ."[122] An almost identical pattern of development can be found during this period within the crown of Aragon and at the papal curia, as well as in Flanders, Portugal, and Sicily.[123]

Thus officials across Latin Europe, aided by various legal principles, made great headway during the 1300s and 1400s in "patrimonializing" their offices, i.e., in converting them into something like private property. Clearly a progressive loss of control over the means of administration could not have been in the interest of late medieval rulers, and was bound in the long run to undermine the military effectiveness of their states. Why then did they acquiesce to this trend?

There were two major reasons for so doing. First, the pressures of war lent royal officials extra bargaining power. They most often possessed either special administrative skills, money, or influence over important groups or individuals, all of which were needed by governments attempting to fight wars successfully. This necessity was especially strong when the state either borrowed directly from officials, or encouraged them to cover various expenses out of their own pockets. Under such conditions, how could demands for greater job security or the right to bring one's relatives into royal service be resisted?

Second, these new arrangements *did* contain certain advantages for rulers.[124] The traffic in offices provided officials with funds with which to retire, thereby relieving the treasury of the burden of pensions. This fact, combined with the 20/40 day clause, created a strong incentive for old or infirm officeholders to resign and turn their positions over to younger persons. Also, the institution of *resignatio* brought with it numerous opportunities for royal gain, for fees could be extracted for

---

[121] Tomás y Valiente, "El Origen Bajomedieval," pp. 142, 145–147, 152, 155.

[122] Quoted in García Marín, *El Oficio Público*, pp. 144–145.

[123] Winfried Küchler, "Aemterkäuflichkeit in den Ländern der Krone Aragons," in: Johannes Vincke (ed.), *Gesammelte Aufsätze zur Kulturgeschichte Spaniens* (Münster: Aschendorffsche Verlagsbuchhandlung, 1973), pp. 1–26; Brigide Schwarz, "Die Entstehung der Aemterkäuflichkeit an der Römischen Kurie," in: Mieck, *Aemterhändel*, pp. 61–65; Michael Erbe, "Aspekte des Aemterhandels in den Niederlanden im späten Mittelalter und in der Frühen Neuzeit," in: Mieck, *Aemterhandel*, pp. 112–131; Hespanha, *História*, pp. 384–393; Mack Smith, *Medieval Sicily*, p. 97.

[124] Gillmann, *Resignation*, p. 137.

the confirmation of the resignation and the waiving of the 20/40-day clause as well as through the sale of expectancies. Finally, the appropriation of office by lay officials at least kept them free from the influence of the territorial princes and the Church, the two domestic statebuilding rivals of Latin Europe's rulers.

Representative Assemblies and the Threat of Appropriation

A rich panoply of innovations in military organization, finance, and administration thus arose in Latin Europe between the late 1100s and 1450, most often in direct or indirect response to geopolitical pressures. While many of these innovations moved the polities under consideration towards a pattern of governance that was more public than private, they also contained within them another tendency which became more powerful as the 1300s and 1400s progressed: the tendency towards the appropriation of state functions and powers by private groups and individuals. Could this trend have been stopped, or at least limited? A closer look at the actions and attitudes of the Estates created during this period might suggest an answer.

The principal forms of appropriation identified above were the conversion of military units into sources of private profit, control of revenue collection and disbursement by private businessmen, dependence on officeholders as a source of government credit, and the appropriation of the means of administration by officials. The representative institutions of several states in Latin Europe were aware of all of these phenomena and condemned them as detrimental to the defense of their nations and the happiness of their peoples. They repeatedly called for, and on several occasions during the 1300s and 1400s actually implemented, reforms designed to curb these abuses.

Though the Castilian Cortes of the mid-1400s had not attained the institutional solidity of its English counterpart, it had amassed a record of intervention in administrative and financial affairs that was nearly as exhaustive. The Castilian representatives of the 14th and 15th centuries subjected all of the tendencies towards appropriation discussed above to repeated criticism, and attempted to eliminate them both by statute and through public promises extracted from various monarchs as the price of new taxes.

Tomás y Valiente has determined that the private sale and/or farming of offices was the object of either condemnation or prohibitive legislation in at least 16 Corteses between 1297 and 1455, while the appointment of deputies and nonresidence were attacked 15 times.[125]

---

[125] Tomás y Valiente, "Origen Bajomedieval," pp. 146, 144.

The Castilian Estates also repeatedly insisted throughout the 1300s that the government open its accounts to outside scrutiny, and on one of these occasions, in 1329, the Cortes forced the removal of the Lord Treasurer as a result of the abuses it had uncovered. In 1385 and again in 1425, commissions were named by that body to receive and disburse the revenues which it had voted.[126]

The Cortes's anger at a whole range of practices present within the Castilian state reached a crescendo during the latter part of the reign of Juan II (1406–1454) and that of his brother Enrique IV (1454–1474), a period of war with Aragon and civil war. Pluralism in municipal offices was forbidden in 1432 and 1436, the granting of "expectancies" restricted in 1442, and the exchange of money in cases of *resignatio in favorem* forbidden by law in 1447. In 1451, 1469, and again in 1473, the king was forced to promise that he would revoke all grants of offices or pensions made for life.[127]

Yet the very frequency of such actions implies that the Cortes enjoyed only intermittent success in its quite tenacious battle against financial irregularities, the patrimonialization of office, and abuses of royal patronage. There are many reasons why, as we shall see in Chapter 4, the English Parliament was somewhat more effective in this area than its Castilian counterpart, the most important of which were the greater structural cohesion of the English body and its more frequent meetings during this period. Despite this fact, it is clear that by the mid-1400s, the Cortes had established a long record of both generous financial grants in time of war and of vigilant opposition to mismanagement and corruption within royal government.

The same claim can also be made, with some qualifications, for the French Estates.[128] An examination of their record during the Hundred Years War reveals them to have been invaluable collaborators in the fight against the English. As indicated earlier, they played a crucial role in creating the system of national taxation in France that ultimately financed the war effort. In addition, the French Estates, like those in England and Castile, attempted to use the financial leverage they possessed to promote greater honesty and efficiency within royal government.

The meetings of the Estates General or the Estates of Langue doil fall into two clusters, one during the first phase of the struggle with

---

[126] Wladimiro Piskorski, *Las Cortes de Castilla en el Período de Tránsito de la Edad Media a la Moderna 1188–1520* (Barcelona: El Albir, 1977), pp. 168–170.

[127] Tomás y Valiente, "Origen Bajomedieval," pp. 154, 156, 159, 142–143; García Marín, *El Oficio Público*, p. 342.

[128] "The Estates" or "the French Estates" will be employed as a collective term referring to both the Estates General of all of France and the Estates of Languedoil, a body made up of representatives from all of France except Languedoc.

England (1343–1381), and a second during the reign of Charles VII (1422–1461). At the war's first Estates General, in 1343, the deputies seemed content simply to vote substantial subsidies to support the fight against the English. By 1346, however, there were already calls for an end to state manipulation of the coinage, and the Estates of 1348 forced, in return for the taxes which it voted, both the removal of the Lord Chancellor and a reform of the currency.[129]

Jean II's ascension to the throne in 1350 ushered in a period of more intense cooperation with the Estates, culminating in the great assemblies of 1355–1357. The Estates of Langue doil, meeting in 1355, passed an ordinance outlawing a number of abuses associated with royal officeholders (traffic in state debt, participation in commercial transactions, seizures of private property without compensation, non-residence) and instituting Estate supervision of army musters to avoid fraud. In addition, the *aides* voted were to be collected by officials appointed by the Estates (the *élus*).[130] After a further meeting in March 1356, a new ordinance was passed forbidding the traffic in offices and pluralism.[131]

The defeat and capture of Jean II at Poitiers in September 1356 provided the Estates with a great opportunity. In October 1356, they presented Jean's son, the teenage dauphin Charles, with a plan for thoroughgoing fiscal and administrative reform which the latter accepted in February 1357 in return for a generous vote of supply. These reforms, which passed into law as the Grand Ordinance, included the removal from office of 22 leading ministers and financial officials, supervision by the Estates of the currency, and the appointment of nine *enquêteurs-reformateurs* empowered to investigate the conduct of all royal office-holders and remove those found guilty of corruption, incompetence, or abuses of power.[132] All these provisions were implemented and had begun to take hold when the Estates became embroiled in a nascent civil war between partisans of the dauphin and of the king of Navarre, which led to an uprising in Paris in February 1358 and its bloody suppression by the dauphin later in the year. At a meeting of the Estates of Languedoil called in May 1359, the work of 1355–57 was officially repudiated.[133]

[129] Henneman, *Royal Taxation . . . 1322–1356*, pp. 172–173, 196, 229–230; Raymond Cazelles, *La Société Politique et la Crise de la Royauté sous Philippe de Valois* (Paris: Librairie d'Argences, 1958), pp. 219, 224.

[130] Raymond Cazelles, *Société Politique, Noblesse et Couronne sous Jean le Bon et Charles V* (Geneva: Droz, 1982), pp. 203–205; Contamine, *Guerre, État*, p. 87.

[131] Roland Mousnier, *La Vénalité des Offices sous Henri IV et Louis XIII*, 2nd ed. (Paris: P.U.F., 1971), p. 18.

[132] Henneman, *Royal Taxation . . . 1356–1370*, pp. 25–57.

[133] Jean Kubler, *L'Origine de la Perpétuité des Offices Royaux* (Nancy: Université de Nancy, 1958), p. 99.

Yet the Grand Ordinance, with its concern for "honest, economical, and efficient government,"[134] lived on in the minds of many Frenchmen as a potent remedy for all the ills which they continued to suffer at the hands of officeholders and financiers. Two assemblies representing Langue doil held in 1367 persuaded Charles (now Charles V) to name *enquêteurs-reformateurs* once again to investigate the actions of royal officials.[135] More importantly, many features of the Grand Ordinance reappeared in the Cabochian Ordinance of 1413, a document of 258 articles containing the most comprehensive and detailed plans for government reform ever drawn up in medieval France. The University of Paris had drafted this ordinance during the Estates General of 1413, and a rebellious mob forced the king to accept it in May 1413. The Cabochian Ordinance expressly forbade all sale or traffic in offices, as well as pluralism, nonresidence, and the appointment of deputies. In addition, an attempt was made to bring order and rationality to the kingdom's financial administration by creating a clear hierarchy of institutions organized under the *chambre de compte*.[136] Yet once again, as in 1357–8, royal repression cut short another attempt to end the deepening pattern of "irrationalization" within the French state, a pattern that certainly contributed to the country's collapse before the armies of Henry V between 1415 and 1421.

In 1421, Charles VII took over effective control of a dismembered kingdom from his insane father, and initiated a new policy of intensive cooperation with central assemblies that culminated, 30 years later, in the total defeat of the English. Between 1369 and 1421, only two meetings of the Estates had taken place (1380–1 and 1413); now, they were convoked 27 times in as many years.[137] Year after year, the Estates voted generous subsidies to be used against both the English and the "free companies" of soldiers that plagued much of France. In return, they demanded an end to currency manipulation and real administrative reform. Charles VII kept his end of the bargain, reorganizing and rationalizing many areas of the state including, most importantly, financial administration, between 1433 and 1452.[138] A new permanent military force, the *compagnies d'ordonnance*, was created, and by an ordinance

---

[134] Henneman, *Royal Taxation . . . 1356–1370*, p. 46.
[135] Henneman, *Royal Taxation . . . 1356–1370*, pp. 243–244.
[136] Georges Picot, *Histoire des Etats Généraux*, 2nd ed. (Paris: Hachette, 1888), vol. I, pp. 268–270.
[137] J. Russell Major, *Representative Institutions in Renaissance France, 1421–1559* (Madison: University of Wisconsin Press, 1960), p. 151. The figures refer to meetings of the Estates General and of the Estates of Languedoil for the unoccupied territories. Several of these meetings remain rather shadowy.
[138] James Collins, *The Fiscal Limits of Absolutism* (Berkeley: University of California Press, 1988), pp. 28–29.

of 1439, the Estates outlawed the private recruitment of troops and seigneurial *tailles*, in effect creating a royal monopoly of both coercion and taxation. French statesmen and historians were often to forget during the coming centuries that it was precisely during the ancien régime's most intense period of "constitutionalism" that France won its greatest military victories.

Yet in retrospect this period in French history turns out to have been an aberration, not a harbinger of things to come. After 1453, as the next chapter will show, French rulers had little use for the Estates General. What is more, this outcome in France was in keeping with an overall trend throughout Latin Europe which saw a progressive decline, and eventual elimination, of most of the Estates. Two factors can explain this broad pattern of development. First, from as early as the 1200s the region's monarchs were busy employing both the revived Roman law and the (heavily Roman) canon law to assert their prerogatives in the fields of diplomacy, military affairs, legislation, and even taxation.[139] Revived Roman and canon law carried greater weight in Latin Europe because they were congruent with other legal traditions – the legacies of the Carolingians, Visigoths, Lombards, and Byzantines, as well as "vulgar" Roman law – which had made the imperial past a living presence in this area.

Second, despite the examples of trenchant criticism and vigorous action cited above, the estate-based assemblies were plagued by basic structural weaknesses, weaknesses which prevented these assemblies from blocking the "reception" of Roman law in the way that the English, Polish, and Hungarian parliaments were to do. The individual estates for the most part saw themselves as defenders of group privileges, and this attitude had unfortunate consequences. In some cases, such as those of Castile and Naples, it led particular orders to abandon the assemblies altogether and instead treat with the ruler directly, thereby isolating the remaining estates. In the other cases, the *curiae* often squabbled, showing little solidarity either among themselves or within their ranks. Furthermore, the representative base of the all-important third estate was often extremely narrow, since it did not include all towns, but only a select few from the royal demesne whose procurators were, due to their small number, open to direct manipulation by the sovereign. Had rulers been interested in working together with their Estates, these structural deficiencies could perhaps have been overcome, but

---

[139] Harouel et al., *Histoire*, pp. 241–243, 287–288; O'Callaghan, *Cortes*, pp. 127–129, 199; MacKay, *Spain*, pp. 99–100, 121, 133, 138–140, 154–155; Matthew, *Norman Kingdom*, pp. 342–343; Léonard, *Angevins de Naples*, p. 271; Marongiu, *Medieval Parliaments*, pp. 148–150.

except in moments of extreme crisis such an attitude seems to have been foreign to the princely mind.[140]

As a result of these factors, only the Estates of Aragon among the assemblies of Latin Europe had retained powers of co-legislation by the end of the middle ages, and even the power to grant extraordinary taxation had already been severely undermined in France, Naples, and Portugal. Over the coming centuries, the remaining prerogatives of the Estates of this region would continue to be eroded, leaving the polities there with no structural or institutional counterweight to tendencies towards appropriation. Furthermore, the next round of warfare would strengthen still further the hand of military enterprisers, tax farmers, financier-officeholders, and patrimonial officials.

CONCLUSION

The Late Roman Empire, Latin Europe's illustrious ancestor, was a sophisticated, highly institutionalized, caesaro-papist polity which rested upon a constrained, nondynamic market economy. The Germanic leaders of the 5th and 6th centuries inherited many valuable remnants of the institutionalized imperial state and used them to form very large, and quite durable, kingdoms of their own. As the Roman social and political infrastructure which provided the framework for these polities melted away, so too did public authority, releasing in its wake the forces of aristocratic power which the *imperium Romanum* had always been able to hold in check.

Yet, as I have argued, the decline of centralized states across much of this region during the early middle ages also brought a new dynamism to both the economy and the Church, which meant that attempts to reconstruct state authority would have to contend not only with an obstreperous aristocracy, but also, for perhaps the first time in history, with a growing economy based on competitive markets and an independent-minded religious hierarchy. While the original locus of these radical changes in the material and spiritual realms lay in the lands of the former Carolingian Empire, they could not help but affect the rest of the continent as well. The most immediate ways in which they did this was by assisting in the slow revival of public authority in Latin Europe and by facilitating the formation of new states across the rest of the West.

---

[140] Marongiu, *Medieval Parliaments*, pp. 151, 154, 236–242; A. R. Myers, *Parliaments and Estates in Europe to 1789* (London: Thames & Hudson, 1975), p. 62; H. G. Koenigsberger, "The Parliament of Piedmont during the Renaissance, 1460–1560," in: idem, *Estates and Revolutions* (Ithaca: Cornell University Press, 1971), pp. 19–79, here at 21, 68–69; Lot and Fawtier, *Histoire*, vol. II, pp. 574–575; O'Callaghan, *Cortes*, pp. 42, 77, 128–129, 203; Mack Smith, *Medieval Sicily*, p. 90.

Postmillennial, multistate Europe was at once bound together by the cultural hegemony of a reformed, supranational Church and the expanding embrace of regional and international markets, and pulled apart by the explosive forces of geopolitical competition. The early arrival of these forces in the highly developed western and southern regions of the continent quickly transformed the kingdoms of Latin Europe, already both blessed and cursed with the legacy of dark age state formation, into statebuilding pioneers, but in the long run they were to pay a heavy price for their precocity.

The fact that the rulers of these kingdoms were required to counter sustained external threats before they had succeeded in bringing their great fief-holders – the territorial princes – fully under control left these rulers in a weak position vis-à-vis the small groups with the military expertise, ready cash, and administrative know-how necessary for rapid state expansion, thereby rendering such essential state functions vulnerable to appropriation. While Latin Europe's monarchs could have worked closely with their Estates to counter these foreign and domestic threats to still-fragile public authority, they chose instead to draw on neo-Roman political and legal traditions to centralize power in their own hands. As we shall see in the next chapter, this course of action would, under conditions of large-scale war, allow tendencies toward appropriation to triumph.

Chapter 3

THE TRIUMPH OF PATRIMONIAL ABSOLUTISM AND THE FAILURE OF REFORM IN LATIN EUROPE, c. 1500–1789

It was during the century and a half between the French invasion of Italy in 1494 and the Peace of the Pyrenees in 1659 that both absolutism and the appropriation of core state functions by private groups and individuals became firmly entrenched across a Latin Europe now dominated by two polities: France and a Spanish Empire which included most of the Iberian and Italian peninsulas as well as the Low Countries. Rather than pursue their geopolitical goals in collaboration with (structurally weak) representative assemblies, the rulers of these states chose instead to use the considerable prerogative powers they had built up in the centuries-long battle against their territorial lords and against the domestic influence of the papacy to undermine or entirely eliminate those institutions. They then exploited the enhanced freedom of maneuver gained thereby to engage in an almost constant round of large-scale warfare.

Intense geopolitical pressure, far from furthering modernizing reforms in the interest of greater battlefield effectiveness, in fact led these states to make more extensive use of the kinds of appropriation-prone administrative and financial practices first introduced during the middle ages, despite the fact that more modern (and efficient) alternatives had been developed in the interim. By the mid-1600s, proprietary office-holding had become the norm in France, Spain, the southern Netherlands, Milan, Naples/Sicily (all Spanish possessions), Portugal, Savoy, Tuscany, and the papal curia. In addition, private financiers controlled most forms of revenue collection and short- and long-term borrowing in all of these states.

By the late 17th century, the internal contradictions of patrimonial absolutism had forced Spain and its Italian dependencies and allies out of the first rank of European powers. While the decrease in geopolitical pressures that resulted from reduced ambitions left some room for reform efforts, none of these initiatives produced fundamental changes in either the pattern of government or state infrastructures on either peninsula. By contrast, the France of Louis XIV was able to maintain its place among the great powers by introducing "reforms" which merely further institutionalized venal officeholding and the country's unique system of "inside" credit. When, during the course of the 18th century, the growing threat from Britain and an ever-worsening fiscal crisis combined to produce the first serious attempts at fundamental institutional change, these attempts were repeatedly blocked by a shifting alliance of aristocratic favorites, proprietary officeholders, and financiers with strong vested interests in the old system. In the end, it was the structural inability of absolutist France to reform itself that led to the opening of the political system in 1787–89 and a revolution which brought an end to patrimonial absolutism not only in that country, but across Latin Europe more generally.

WAR AND THE TRIUMPH OF PATRIMONIAL ABSOLUTISM IN FRANCE, 1494–1659

Of all the major western powers, France was the country in which national representative institutions were weakest and practices favoring appropriation the most deeply entrenched by the close of the middle ages. Despite the important role played by the Estates General in bringing the Hundred Years War to a successful conclusion, French monarchs stubbornly ignored this institution after 1484. In the absence of any organized body willing and able to push developments in a different direction, the intense military pressures faced by France after its invasion of Italy in 1494 inevitably led to a massive increase in the role played by private finance, proprietary officeholding, and military entrepreneurship within the French state apparatus. It was thus during the period of the Italian wars that many of the features that would characterize the ancien régime down to 1789 were first introduced. While in the short and even medium term this mounting "irrationalization" – the steady expansion of private at the expense of public interests within France's administrative, financial, and military infrastructure – may not have impaired the country's battlefield effectiveness, in the long term it helped generate the repeated crises which racked the French polity from the First Civil War in 1562–3 through the Fronde in 1648–53.

Decline of the Estates General After 1440

There can be little doubt that bringing together a national assembly in a country as large and diverse as France was a difficult and often unpopular undertaking. Delegates had to travel long distances at considerable

expense, and provincial loyalties – as well as the jealous defense of
privileges that had resulted from tricurial divison – impeded effective
cooperation. The decision to introduce a degree of "territoriality" into
the Estates General of 1484 by requiring each of the three orders in
every *baillage* to select (through indirect means in the case of the Third
Estate) one deputy to represent them seems only to have strengthened
these provincial loyalties, thereby adding a new set of regional divisions
to the pre-existing institutionalized tension among the orders.[1]

If the government had hoped to render the Estates more effective
and cohesive by introducing territorially based elections, they could
only have succeeded in this had the order principle been abandoned
entirely and the selection of those deputies been linked not to the
baillage – an administrative subdivision of no broader significance to the
populace or local elites – but rather to a meaningful, consolidated unit
of local government. As we have seen, however, no such unit existed in
either medieval or early modern France. The country's local political
landscape remained, even after the incorporation of the great fiefs,
riddled by seigneurial and ecclesiastical jurisdictions, a legacy of precocious state formation. To these the medieval effort to restore royal
authority had added a welter of administrative circumscriptions (the
baillages/sénéchaussées, élections, généralités, gouvernements), each with its own
disparate boundaries.

Nevertheless, there is good evidence that despite its structural deficiencies, the Estates General did represent – and was perceived to
constitute – a real threat to venal administrators and financiers. Not
only were the Estates identified in the popular imagination of the time
with the much more powerful English Parliament, but Russell Major,
drawing on the testimony of Philippe de Commynes, argues that it was
hostility towards that body on the part of Charles VII's ministers that
led the king after 1440 to abandon his policy of frequent convoca-
tions.[2] At the Estates General of 1484, for example, the deputies drew
up a detailed program of government reform, including demands for
the abolition of the traffic in offices and other administrative "abuses,"
a more equitable distribution of the tax burden, and the removal of most
of the officials concerned with revenue collection, who were condemned

---

[1] P. S. Lewis, "The Failure of the French Medieval Estates," in: idem, *Essays in Late
Medieval French History* (London: Hambledon, 1985), pp. 105–126, here at 110–115;
idem, *Late Medieval France* (London: Macmillan, 1968), pp. 359–372; Jean-François
Lemarignier, *La France Médiévale: Institutions et Société* (Paris: Armand Colin, 1970), pp.
335–336.

[2] Ferdinand Lot and Robert Fawtier, *Histoire des Institutions de la France au Moyen Âge*
(Paris: Presses Universitaires de France, 1958), vol. II, p. 575; J. Russell Major, *Repre-
sentative Institutions in Renaissance France 1421–1559* (Madison: University of Wisconsin
Press, 1960), p. 36.

as corrupt and exploitative.[3] Just as significantly, the Estates succeeded in forcing the leading royal financial officials, the *généraux des finances*, to open their accounts to the assembly. To secure their demands, the Estates pressed for the entry of several of their number into the royal council, and extracted a promise that they would be convoked again in two years' time.

Yet two years later, the assembly was not recalled. Indeed, a full, working Estates General was not to meet again until 1560. From 1494 onward, successive French monarchs were determined to pursue their foreign policy goals free from any possible constraints that might be imposed by an assembly of the entire kingdom. That they were free to do this was a result of the fact that, as shown in the previous chapter, their predecessors had responded to competition from the great feudatories and the papacy by using Roman law arguments about the duty of rulers to defend to realm and maintain its unity in order to command, legislate, and tax without seeking the approval of any earthly body or institution. After having battled for over three centuries to achieve a de jure and de facto sovereignty vis-à-vis foreign and domestic rivals, by the late 1400s the kings of France were not prepared to share that sovereignty with the Estates General or any other representative body. The most comprehensive theoretical statement of royal sovereignty was provided somewhat later by Jean Bodin, who in his *Six Books of the Republic* (1576) did not hesitate to ascribe full imperial powers to the French king: he was the font and source of all temporal law but at the same time *legibus solutus*, not bound himself by any laws save those of God and of the royal succession.[4]

In practice, this decision to dispense with the advice and cooperation of a national representative assembly led to nearly half a century of costly warfare, much of it waged over territory in distant Italy. The attempt on the part of the government to fight a large-scale war without the consent or cooperation of the broader political nation could not but strengthen the hand of all those who wished to exploit the French state for their own purposes. From 1494 to 1559, all the most problem-

---

[3] Georges Picot, *Histoire des États Généraux*, 2nd ed. (Paris: Hachette, 1888), vol. II, pp. 28–39, 67–96. See also the extended discussion in Major, *Representative Institutions*, pp. 60–116.

[4] On Bodin, see most recently: Julian Franklin, "Sovereignty and the Mixed Constitution: Bodin and His Critics," in: J. H. Burns (ed.), *The Cambridge History of Political Thought 1450–1700* (Cambridge: Cambridge University Press, 1991), pp. 298–328, here at pp. 307–309; also: Dieter Wyduckel, *Princeps Legibus Solutus* (Berlin: Duncker & Humblot, 1979), pp. 13, 16, 32–33, 100, 151–152, 165 and passim; Jean-Louis Harouel, Jean Barbey, Eric Bournazel, and Jacqueline Thibaut-Payen, *Histoire des Institutions de l'Époque Franque à la Révolution*, 3rd ed. (Paris: Presses Universitaires de France, 1990), pp. 289–297.

atic practices of the late medieval period – the patrimonialization of officeholding, the increasing dominance of financiers within the state, and military entrepreneurship – were legitimated, institutionalized, and actively encouraged by a political leadership obsessed above all with putting troops in the field for just one more campaigning season. It is interesting to note in this context that while Bodin argued that the French king was not *required* to seek the approval of the Estates before legislating, raising taxes, or making other weighty decisions, the *prudent* ruler would do this anyway.[5] Needless to say, Bodin's advice went largely unheeded after 1576.

The Struggle with Spain, 1494–1559

The origin of France's Italian wars is to be found in the decision of the young Charles VIII, confident of French military power following victories over the English and Burgundians, to pursue an extremely dubious claim to the throne of Naples.[6] This inevitably led to a direct confrontation with Spain, newly united under one crown, which already possessed extensive interests in Italy. Between 1494 and 1517, the two powers battled for control of the rich peninsula, with the French finally succeeding in establishing a foothold in Milan. When, after 1519, sovereignty over the Netherlands and the Holy Roman Empire also fell into the hands of the Spanish heir Charles V of Habsburg, the struggle with Spain became a contest for hegemony in western Europe as a whole that was to last until 1559 and the Peace of Cateau-Cambrésis.

Between a quarter and a third of the French armies which fought against the Habsburgs were composed of cavalry, and the core of the cavalry was provided by the *compagnies d'ordonnance*, a permanent military force established in 1445 by Charles VII. In peacetime, they were distributed among the various provinces of France where they were controlled and commanded by the local royal governor, almost always a member of a prominent magnate family. The governor was free to fill the ranks of the prestigious *compagnies* with representatives of the most important local clans and factions, thus solidifying his basis of support in the province.[7] The significance of the various royal governors was further enhanced in wartime by their ability to direct some of the benefits which flowed from an expanding war machine to clients in

[5]   Franklin, "Sovereignty and the Mixed Constitution," p. 308.
[6]   Yvonne Labande-Mailfert argues that this decision was entirely Charles's, and in fact met with widespread opposition among French political elites. See her *Charles VIII et son Milieu* (Paris: Klincksieck, 1975), pp. 196, 224–226.
[7]   Robert Harding, *Anatomy of a Power Elite: The Provincial Governors of Early Modern France* (New Haven: Yale University Press, 1978), pp. 21ff.

their home provinces. The added power which the Italian wars brought to magnate-governors was to have ominous consequences for France after 1559.

In contrast to the *compagnies d'ordonnances*, the infantry of the French army was raised mainly through contracts with Swiss or German mercenary captains. This practice had begun in the early 1480s, when Louis XI had first employed 6,000 Swiss.[8] In 1505, Louis XII contracted with six French gentlemen to create a number of native infantry units modeled on those of the Swiss and Germans, but mercenary forces retained a dominant position within the royal army right down to 1558, when they still supplied 21,000 men out of a total infantry contingent of about 40,000.[9]

The total number of men whom the French king strove to keep under arms increased during the course of the early 16th century as the theater of operations was extended from Italy to Germany and the southern Netherlands. The Italian invasion force of 1494 numbered no more than 20,000 combatants, and was thus smaller than many of the armies assembled during the Hundred Years War. By the 1500s, however, average army size seems to have risen to about 30,000, though forces of over 40,000 could be raised for exceptional occasions like the renewed assault on Milan in 1515 or the defense of Provence in 1536. During the last campaign of the war in 1558, Henry II was able to field an army of close to 50,000.[10]

The cost and duration of this and many subsequent early modern conflicts was the result of important recent changes in military technology. The perfecting of artillery capable of breaching castle walls and the development of new infantry tactics during the course of the 1400s had held out the possibility that conflicts might once again be decided by a single decisive battle, as they had before the appearance of the stone castle beginning in the 12th century. But these hopes were dashed when a revolutionary new system of urban fortification built around the bastion was invented in early 16th-century Italy. The spread of bastion defenses across western Europe rendered many cities impregnable to anything except lengthy sieges by massed infantry.[11] For the next several centuries, combatants were required to carry out long and arduous campaigns to reduce their opponents' strategic strongholds one by one.

---

[8] Pierre-Roger Gaussin, *Louis XI: Roi Méconnu* (Paris: Librairie Nizet, 1976), p. 193.
[9] Gaston Zeller, *Les Institutions de la France au XVIᵉ Siècle* (Paris: P.U.F., 1948), p. 303; Ferdinand Lot, *Recherches sur les Éffectifs des Armées Françaises des Guerres d'Italie aux Guerres de Religion 1494–1562* (Paris: S.E.V.P.E.N., 1962), p. 184.
[10] Lot, *Recherches*, pp. 21, 41, 56, 65, 70, 132, 186.
[11] These changes are the subject of Geoffrey Parker's *The Military Revolution* (Cambridge: Cambridge University Press, 1988).

As the cost of such operations reached new heights, conflicts could drag on indefinitely with little prospect of outright military victory.

The huge sums of money now required to maintain larger armies for greater lengths of time also had to flow with some regularity, for German and Swiss military enterprisers were more than willing to switch sides or go home if not paid. The most obvious way to meet the added costs of war was through tax increases. Since the mid-15th century at the very latest, French monarchs had established their de facto right to alter the level of taxation without consulting either the Estates General or any other national representative body. Yet in practice this did not mean that a French king could simply raise taxes at will. By failing to gain prior approval for new impositions, the monarch always ran the risk of encountering passive or even active resistance from taxpayers which in the end might cost the government more money than it had hoped to gain through the tax. Thus while the decision to dispense with the Estates from the late 1400s onward may have brought greater foreign policy freedom for French kings, it also forced them to look increasingly to nontax revenues as a way of paying for their projects, which in turn had grave consequences for the future institutional development of the French state.

War and Finance, 1494–1559

This point can be illustrated through a brief look at financial policy during the Italian wars. Despite the general rise in prices which occurred over these decades, *taille* revenues could only be increased from 2.1 million livres per annum in 1497 to an average of 5.8 million livres p.a. in the 1550s. Thanks to the faster rise in revenues from indirect taxes, partly an automatic consequence of both inflation and economic growth, total tax revenues increased from about 3.5 million livres to about 12 million livres over the same period.[12] Yet even this figure could not be reached without major revolts in 1542 and 1548 over attempts to raise the *gabelle*.[13]

---

[12]   J.-J. Clamageran, *Histoire de l'Impôt en France* (Paris: Guillaumin, 1868), vol. II, pp. 84, 139, 146. Research by L. Scott Van Doren on the Dauphiné has, however, discovered that a certain amount of tax revenue was levied for military purposes at a local level which does not appear in the financial records of the central government. Whatever the extent of such levies in other provinces, it remains beyond dispute that taxes were never able to cover the costs of war during this period. See Llewain Scott Van Doren, "War Taxation, Institutional Change, and Social Conflict in Provincial France – The Royal *Taille* in Dauphiné, 1494–1559," *Proceedings of the American Philosophical Society*, vol. 121, no. 1 (February 1977), pp. 70–96.

[13]   On these revolts, see: R. J. Knecht, *Francis I* (Cambridge: Cambridge University Press, 1982), pp. 384–389.

During the early part of the Italian wars, until about 1515, the amount of money which the Crown had to raise above and beyond ordinary tax and demesne revenue was relatively small, about 250,000 livres a year compared to total expenditure of 4 million livres. As the wars progressed, however, the gap between tax and demesne income on the one hand and total needs on the other grew. This gap reached an average of 1.5 million livres a year under Francis I (1515–1547) and more than 4 million a year under his son, Henry II (1547–1559), amounting to 20% and 25% of ordinary revenue respectively.[14] Clearly these rulers would have to raise large amounts of money by extraordinary means if they wished to continue their pursuit of glory and conquest.

The financial difficulties of Francis I and Henry II were further complicated by a problem faced by all late medieval and early modern governments, namely, the need to convert tax revenues into ready cash which could be used to pay troops during the six- to eight-month campaigning season. The French monarchs sought to solve both of these problems simultaneously by borrowing. The great commercial city of Lyons, then at the height of its power, offered them an ideal location to do so. Four times a year, fairs were held at Lyons at which merchants and banking houses from Italy, Switzerland, southern Germany, and France settled their accounts with one another. From the 1520s onward the French Crown began to borrow ever larger sums of money at Lyons.[15] During the 1540s, between 300,000 and 500,000 livres were raised annually. Almost all of these loans took the form of short-term, floating debt at interest rates of 12–16% per annum. Repayment of the principal was due in 3 months, at the time of the next fair, but it was almost always rolled over.[16]

As the struggle between Henry II and Charles V grew into an all-out confrontation in the 1550s, the pace of borrowing quickened. Because principal repayment was constantly deferred, the French Crown had accumulated a debt of 4.9 million livres by 1555, and the government's credit was in decline as investor skepticism mounted over its ability to repay such a sum. The Crown responded by presenting a brilliant scheme to guarantee repayment. Over 3.5 million livres of the outstanding debt would be incorporated into a kind of financial association, the *Grand Parti*, which would then advance the government another 1.6 million

---

[14] Clamageran, *Histoire*, vol. II, pp. 130–131, 146.
[15] The two principal sources on the Lyons money market in the 16th century and French royal borrowing there are: Richard Ehrenberg, *Das Zeitalter der Fugger* (Hildesheim: Georg Olms, 1963), vol. II, pp. 69–107, 159–169; and Roger Doucet, "Le Grand Parti de Lyons au XVIᵉ Siècle," *Revue Historique*, vol. 171, no. 3 (May–June 1933), pp. 473–513; vol. 172, no. 1 (July–August 1933), pp. 1–41.
[16] Doucet, "Le Grand Parti," pp. 478–479, 487–489.

livres. The government in turn would pay the company 5% of the outstanding capital 4 times per year, 4% of which would cover interest, and 1% repayment of the principal. In this way, the state would be able to extinguish all of its short-term debt in 10 years.[17]

The originality and far-sightedness of this plan, which apparently had been worked out with the help of Italian bankers, is striking. An institution had been created which was designed to attract both international capital and the savings of thousands of small domestic investors, and which would have been capable of supplying both the short- and long-term credit needs of the French Crown in a regular and orderly manner (albeit at a high rate of interest, though this would have come down over time). Yet the absolutist French regime proved unable, given the pressures of war, to live up to its end of the bargain. From November 1557 onward, the Crown could no longer meet its obligations in full, and in 1559 interest and principal payments to the *Grand Parti* were suspended altogether, leaving behind a debt that had swollen in the interim to 11.7 million livres and that was to be virtually ignored for the next 40 years.[18] It would not be an exaggeration to claim that the reputation of the French monarchy among both foreign and small domestic investors never really recovered from this episode. The chance to build a system of public finance in France had been destroyed by the irresponsibility of the French monarchy, and in the future the government would have to look to other sources for both cash and additional revenue.

At the same time as Francis I was just beginning to develop his relationship with the bankers of Lyons, he was experimenting with another form of borrowing which would prove of great significance in the history of the ancien régime, the sale of *rentes*. The *rente* was a credit instrument developed in western Europe during the middle ages and designed to avoid the canonical strictures against usury.[19] In return for a lump sum payment, a borrower would sign over to a lender the rights to an income stream from some type of property like a piece of land or a building. The lump sum (the "capital" generated by the *rente*) would typically equal between 10 and 20 times the annual value of the alienated income source, which implied an interest payment of 5–10%. In 1425 and again in 1455, the Pope explicitly approved this form of lending, provided that the borrower possessed the right to buy back his alienated property by returning the lump sum he had initially received from the lender.[20]

---

[17]   Ibid., pp. 490–498.   [18]   Ibid., vol. 172, no. 1, p. 9.

[19]   On the origins of *rentes* and their use by both the private and public sectors during the 16th century, see: Bernard Schnapper, *Les Rentes au XVIe Siècle: Histoire d'un Instrument de Crédit* (Paris: S.E.V.P.E.N., 1957).

[20]   Ibid., p. 45.

Although the creation of *rentes* had long been used by private individuals as a means of raising cash, it was only in 1522 that Francis I, still reeling from the defeat suffered against the forces of Charles V at Bicocca, decided to use it to improve his own finances. Francis proposed to raise 200,000 livres in cash by selling *rentes* up to that value at denier 12, or 8.33% interest. Aware that the confidence of the public in the Crown's creditworthiness was relatively low, the king agreed to transfer the revenues from which the interest would be paid (various indirect taxes) to the municipal government of Paris, which would be responsible for administering the new *rentes*. Hence these *rentes* acquired the name *rentes sur l'Hôtel de Ville de Paris*.[21]

The *rentes* clearly had both advantages and disadvantages as a means of raising money. On the one hand, *rentes* agreements were superior to the loans contracted in Lyons in the sense that the government was not under pressure to begin repayment of the principal immediately. Thus, for an annual interest payment of, in the case of the 1522 issue, 16,666 livres, the Crown would benefit from a one-time increase in revenue of 200,000 livres without having to set aside extra funds for amortization. On the other hand, if the government proved unable ever to reimburse the 200,000 livres, it would be doomed to pay in perpetuity the 16,666 livres in interest. Another way of putting this is that until reimbursement, the Crown had in fact permanently alienated the revenue source against which the interest payments were guaranteed.

Despite the success of the 1522 sale, Francis made sparing use of *rentes* in future years, raising only 750,000 livres through this means. Under Henry II, however, the figure quickly rose to nearly 7 million livres.[22] What is striking about the sale of *rentes* during this period, however, is *who* purchased them. Despite the precautions taken by the state to bolster its credibility, the general public seems to have avoided them right from the beginning. Studies of the sales of 1553 and 1554 reveal that the buyers were overwhelmingly persons whose interests and future were closely tied to the state – royal officeholders and members of the higher nobility.[23]

Future government actions confirmed the wary attitude towards the *rentes* of those without inside connections. When in the 1560s, after the bankruptcy of 1559, new *rentes* became difficult to sell, the Crown tried

[21] Paul Cauwès, "Les Commencements du Crédit Public en France: Les Rentes sur l'Hôtel de Ville au XVIᵉ Siècle," *Revue d'Economie Politique*, vol. 9, no. 2 (February 1895), pp. 97–123; vol. 9, no. 10–11 (October-November 1895), pp. 825–865; vol. 10, no. 5 (May 1896), pp. 407–479; here at 112–113.

[22] Schnapper, *Les Rentes* p. 173. Cauwès, "Les Commencements," pp. 826, 836, provides somewhat higher figures of 950,000 livres and 7.2–7.3 million livres respectively.

[23] Schnapper, *Les Rentes*, pp. 160–161, 172.

to force them on the public through legal means. And after 1571, the inevitable happened: in spite of all the safeguards built into the *rentes* contracts, interest payments became irregular.[24] This was just the start of a long series of abuses perpetrated by the French Crown on its *rentiers* over the next two centuries: arbitrary cuts in the rate of interest, reductions in capital, nonpayment of interest, forced purchases of new *rentes*. What is more surprising than these practices, which were typical of the way the French monarchy treated all its creditors, was the loyalty shown by officeholders toward this form of investment. *Rentes* were just another one of the ties forged during the Italian wars which bound the French political class and their monarch together in a "community of fate" from which neither (in the end) were to escape.

War and Proprietary Officeholding, 1494–1559

The other tie forged, or at least acknowledged and strengthened, during this period was the one created by proprietary officeholding. As mentioned in Chapter 2, de facto life tenure and private payments for offices linked to the right of *resignatio in favorem* had become well entrenched within the French administrative system by the 1400s, yet the legal status of such practices was precarious. Repeatedly throughout the 15th century, most often under pressure from the Estates General, the French Crown had passed ordinances outlawing the traffic in offices, the most recent of which dated from 1493.[25]

Not only were such laws disregarded, but as the fiscal pressures generated by the struggle with Spain mounted, the government itself began to look for a way to profit more fully from the private demand for offices. While in the past the Crown had received payments in return for the confirmation of *resignationes*, it now took the decisive step of openly selling positions that had fallen vacant and of creating new offices expressly in order to sell them for a profit. Louis XII initiated a small number of public sales in 1512–3, but Francis I began the practice in earnest with the creation of 20 new positions in the Parlement of Paris in 1522.[26] Thereafter, offices were created and sold at an ever more rapid pace in all areas of the state: 42 more positions were added to the Parlement of Paris, 37 to that of Bordeaux, and 59 to that of

---

[24] Ibid., pp. 156, 169–171.

[25] Martin Göhring, *Die Aemterkäuflichkeit im Ancien Régime* (Berlin: Verlag Dr. Emil Ebering, 1938), pp. 29–30.

[26] For the backround and details of this operation, see: Christopher Stocker, "Public and Private Enterprise in the Administration of a Renaissance Monarchy: The First Sales of Offices in the Parlement of Paris (1512–1524)," *Sixteenth Century Journal*, vol. 9, no. 2 (July 1978), pp. 4–29.

Toulouse, while the number of local financial and judicial officials was multiplied with apparent ease. In 1552, Francis I's son Henry II set up an entirely new system of courts, the *présidiaux*, in order to generate new offices, and in 1554 he introduced the *alternatif*, the practice of sharing an office between two holders.[27]

The kings of France thereby aided and abetted a trend towards the appropriation of public functions which had been under way for several centuries due to the precocious onset of sustained geopolitical pressure in France and Latin Europe more generally. In 1534, the government indirectly legalized the private traffic in offices by declaring that only sales which occurred less than 40 days before the death of the holder were void, in which case the office in question would revert to the Crown. This regulation was also designed to increase royal profits from the office trade both through the resale of forfeited positions and through the sale of reversions or *survivances*, which could be purchased as a kind of insurance policy against the sudden death of the officeholder.

Whatever the magnitude of the profits earned by the Crown from the sale of offices down to 1559 – and there is a maddening lack of conclusive evidence on this matter[28] – there can be no doubt that such sales had a profound impact on French state structure, especially in conjunction with the important changes introduced into the country's financial administration between 1523 and 1552. Over the course of these decades, partly in response to the administrative pressures of war, but also partly as an excuse to create new positions, the old system of financial administration was expanded and systematized.

At the heart of the new system lay the distinction between *officiers de finance*, *comptables*, and *ordonnateurs*.[29] The *officiers de finance*, called *trésoriers de France* at the regional level and *élus* at the local level, were *venal* administrator-magistrates (i.e., administrator-magistrates who had purchased their offices) responsible for apportioning the *taille*, supervising revenue collection, and judging legal disputes involving financial matters. The *comptables* were venal accountants like the receivers (local),

[27] Roland Mousnier, *La Vénalité des Offices sous Henri IV et Louis XIII*, 2nd ed. (Paris: P.U.F., 1971), pp. 41, 43; Roger Doucet, *Les Institutions de la France au XVIᵉ Siècle* (Paris: Picard, 1948), vol. I, pp. 411–412.

[28] Mousnier (*La Vénalité*, p. 68) cites a contemporary Venetian observer who claimed that this source brought in 900,000 livres per annum during the reign of Francis I, while J. H. M. Salmon argues that revenues from the sale of offices were running at 1.5 million livres a year in 1547 [*Society in Crisis: France in the Sixteenth Century* (London: Methuen, 1979), p. 76]. Yet Frederic Baumgartner, invoking estimates of the Estates General of 1560, states that total sales brought in an average of only about 300,000 livres a year during the reign of Henry II, a time of large new creations [*Henry II* (Durham, N.C.: Duke University Press, 1988), p. 90].

[29] Richard Bonney provides a brief but lucid overview of this complex system in his work *The King's Debts* (Oxford: Clarendon, 1981), pp. 1–21.

receivers-general (regional), or one of the countless treasurers like the *trésoriers de l'extraordinaire de la guerre* (war treasurers) who were respons-ible for collecting and disbursing tax revenue. They took their orders from the *ordonnateurs*, central directors like the *surintendant* and *intendants des finances*, who coordinated the whole system from Paris.

The administrative framework just described, which was in place by 1556, remained essentially unaltered down to the Revolution, with the exception, of course, of the unending multiplication of most of the offices involved.[30] The administrative result of the wars of the early 16th century, then, was the creation of a curious hybrid: a centralized, sym-metrically constructed apparatus staffed by officials who treated their positions as heritable, saleable property. Because officeholders now possessed a "proprietary" interest in the French state, they could be pressured into providing the funds necessary for its survival. They thus formed, as the experiment with *rentes* had shown, a "captive" source of credit which could partially replace – or at least so it was hoped – the outside investors too wary to lend to the Crown. The progressive intro-duction of moneylenders into the body of the state itself over the course of the next century, an innovation which converted venal accountants (the *comptables*) into venal officeholder-financiers, completed the crea-tion of a system of "inside" credit[31] rendered necessary by the loss of public confidence in royal finances after the failure of the *Grand Parti* and the suspension of regular interest payments on *rentes*.

The Wars of Religion and Deepening Patrimonialism

While religious differences were a primary cause of the civil strife which racked France for nearly 40 years following the Peace of Cateau-Cambrésis in 1559, the changes which the French state had undergone during the previous period of warfare played their part as well. As mentioned earlier, war had strengthened the position of the great magnate governors in their role as both military leaders and as patrons and influence brokers. The French bankruptcy of 1557–9 and the sub-sequent peace thus acted as a double threat to the magnates' power. Not only were the armed forces to be partially demobilized, but the flow of patronage from Paris to the provinces, which the governors had used to build regional alliances and satisfy their supporters, came to an abrupt halt for lack of funds. It was in response to this double threat,

---

[30] The number of *trésoriers de France*, for example, was increased from 16 in 1552 to 457 (!) in 1648. Jean-Paul Charmeil, *Les Trésoriers de France à l'Époque de la Fronde* (Paris: Picard, 1964), p. 16.
[31] The term is Martin Wolfe's, *The Fiscal System of Renaissance France* (New Haven: Yale University Press, 1972), p. 64.

as Robert Harding has shown, that governors turned to the nascent religious parties in their regions as new power bases.[32]

The religious wars themselves had a somewhat contradictory impact on French state development. On the one hand, the French Crown and royal army were active participants in the civil wars, engaged first in fighting the Huguenots, and then the Catholic Ligue. This military activity generated substantial financial pressures at a time when ordinary tax and demesne revenues were severely compromised by the division of the country into rival spheres of influence. The monarchy thus attempted to meet these pressures through an intensified use of the "extraordinary" measures (sale of offices, creation of *rentes*) first employed during the Italian wars, as well as through an expansion of revenue farming.

In this way, the religious wars served to confirm and accelerate the "irrationalization" of the state which had made such progress over the previous half-century. At the same time, however, civil strife forced successive rulers once again to revive the Estates General, in the hopes that it might help the country out of its severe internal crisis. The resuscitation of this body in turn created better prospects for a radical reform of the French state than had existed at any time since the 15th century, prospects that were never to be realized.

The efforts by the French Crown after 1560 to use officeholding and *rentes* as a means of raising money quickly dwarfed any earlier attempts in that direction. During the 1560s, the practice of dividing offices into two parts was extended to more positions including, in 1570, all *comptables* (receivers, treasurers, paymasters). Once again, scores of new members were added to the sovereign courts. As a result, the revenues from such sales came to make up between 10% and 15% of total royal revenue between 1560 and 1576.[33] Under Henry III (1574–1589), the Crown began to turn activities like selling fish or livestock into venal offices.[34] By the end of the century, the number of venal officeholders in France stood at 11,000, compared with the 4,041 officials that Mousnier and his associates have counted for 1515.[35]

A glance at the creation of new *rentes* during this period tells a similar story. While 7.6 million livres were raised between 1522 and 1559

---

[32] Harding, *Anatomy*, pp. 46ff.   [33] Wolfe, *Fiscal System*, pp. 130–131.
[34] Mousnier, *La Vénalité*, p. 42.
[35] The estimate of 11,000 is by Wolfe, *The Fiscal System*, pp. 133–134. Mousnier's figure can be found in: Roland Mousnier et al., *Le Conseil du Roi de Louis XII à la Révolution* (Paris: P.U.F., 1970), p. 18. These two results point to a doubling of the number of offices since the reign of Louis XII, a relatively believable conclusion given the fact that the number of positions in the Parlement of Paris also doubled over the same period to over 200 (Göhring, *Die Aemterkäuflichkeit*, pp. 54–55).

through the sale of *rentes*, this figure rose to 37 million livres between 1560 and 1586.[36] Thus, if *rentes* proved to be only limited instruments of public credit before 1559, their importance increased dramatically thereafter. At first the Crown tried to counter growing antipathy towards this form of investment, even among royal officials, by forcing the latter to purchase *rentes* against their will. Then, from 1572 onwards, the government took to selling large quantities of *rentes* directly to *partisans* (financiers) for cash at prices far below their face value.[37] At the same time, the payment of interest on outstanding *rentes* became ever more irregular. By 1585, over 4 million livres owed in interest was past due, and payments to most *rentiers* stopped altogether after 1586.[38]

The role of *partisans* in the sale of *rentes* reflected the growing importance of this group in all areas of French government finance after 1559. The collapse of the *Grand Parti* and the growing inability of *rentes* to attract broadly based investment led the Crown to search for other sources of credit. It found one such source in the professional financiers who were willing to advance the government cash on the security of various existing forms of state revenue or of some new form of imposition. While both financial officials and outside financiers had regularly advanced the government funds from the late medieval period onward, they had been overtaken in this function by the rise of the Lyons credit market. With its demise, they soon returned to prominence.[39]

In order to attract ever larger advances from financiers, the French Crown began to abandon the traditional pattern of small, local revenue farms and move towards large farms leased for long periods of time. Thus in 1578, the salt tax levies for almost all of northern France were consolidated into a single farm, the *grandes gabelles*, and in 1584 a number of important customs duties were brought together into the *cinq grosses fermes*, both prominent institutions of the ancien régime. Even nontax revenues were put to farm. In addition to the subcontracting of *rentes* sales mentioned above, the sale of offices in the Parlement of Paris was farmed in 1575.[40] During the late 1500s, the financiers

---

[36] Schnapper, *Les Rentes*, p. 173.

[37] Wolfe, *The Fiscal System*, p. 115; Schnapper, *Les Rentes*, pp. 156–157. *Partisan* and *traitant* were general terms used during the ancien régime to designate financiers involved in government activities. *Traitant* comes from *traité*, a contract to collect a certain tax or revenue in return for a lump sum payment. *Partisan* is derived from *partido*, the Italian term for a loan agreement with a ruler. Despite their different origins, the terms seem to have been used interchangeably.

[38] Bonney, *The King's Debts*, pp. 26, 46, 57.

[39] Françoise Ba;ard, *Le Monde des Financiers au XVIIe Siècle* (Paris: Flammarion, 1988), p. 15.

[40] Zeller, *Les Institutions*, p. 278; Doucet, *Les Institutions*, vol. I, p. 414; vol. II, pp. 582–583, 594.

involved in these transactions were still primarily foreigners, mainly Italians with ties to the queen mother, Catherine de Medicis, working outside the official financial administration, a situation which placed them in a politically vulnerable position. One of the great "accomplishments" of the next century was to be the elimination of the Italians and the full integration of native financiers into the royal financial apparatus itself, where they would join the older corps of venal officeholders in an alliance capable of blocking any attempts radically to reform the French polity.

Yet this had not yet come to pass by the late 16th century. The very depth of the crisis gripping the country during this period created one of the last opportunities during the ancien régime for major changes in the character of French politics. Since the 1560s, disquiet over contemporary developments within the French state had become entangled with religious differences. Not only the Huguenots, but more importantly the extreme Catholics of the Ligue, had revealed themselves as fierce opponents of both venality and of the *partisans*, and as advocates of an institutionalized Estates General. The explanation for this was the presence within the Ligue ranks not only of many nobles, who saw the patrimonialization of office as a threat to their patronage power, but more importantly of many members of that portion of the bourgeoisie without any ties to the state, the so-called *bourgeoisie secondaire*.[41]

When the dire state of his finances forced Henry III to convoke the Estates General in 1576 and again in 1588, these assemblies were dominated by adherents of the Ligue. Not surprisingly, then, the Estates on both occasions proposed a package of reforms reminiscent of those of the 15th century, including the replacement of an officeholding system based on venality with one based on the election of officials, the removal of *partisans* and *traitants* from the financial administration and their prosecution, and more frequent meetings of the Estates itself.[42] Many of these demands, including the abolition of venality, *resignatio in favorem*, reversions, and countless superfluous offices, were in fact incorporated by Henry into the Ordinance of Blois of 1579,[43] but they remained a dead letter, not least because royal officeholders and financiers were among the king's strongest supporters. Following his assassination in 1589, they transferred that support to his successor, Henry IV.

[41] Roland Mousnier, *L'Assassinat d'Henri IV* (Paris: Gallimard, 1964), pp. 185–187; Johannes Willms, *Die Politik der Officiers Royaux auf den États Généraux 1576–1614* (Heidelberg: n.p., 1975), p. 178 and passim.
[42] Picot, *Histoire*, vol. III, pp. 92–93, 181–183, 283–284, 394, 416.
[43] Ibid., pp. 354–360.

Henry IV, Sully, and the "Rationalization" of "Irrationalization"

By the 1580s it was clear, then, that the outcome of the civil war would determine the fate of structural reform in France. The defeat of the Ligue could only mean one thing. In the words of Roland Mousnier, "The victory of Henry IV was the victory of the officeholders."[44] Seen in this light, the policies of the new king and his minister Sully become readily comprehensible. Henry, who could never have succeeded in claiming his throne against the combined forces of the Ligue and its Spanish allies without the support of *officiers* and *partisans*, had no desire to turn on them after 1598.

At the same time, however, Henry was determined to restore the power and military effectiveness of the monarchy, which were both undercut by the patrimonialization of finance and administration. The solution to this dilemma, worked out by the king and his chief minister Sully, was one that would be copied 60 years later in similar circumstances by Louis XIV and Colbert: a "rationalization" of "irrationalization." Sully would introduce reforms aimed not at changing the basic character of the French state, but rather at making it run more efficiently within the constraints imposed by proprietary officeholding and private finance.

The essence of Sully's approach is captured in his most famous reform, the introduction of the *paulette* in 1604.[45] This measure provided officeholders with what they had most desired since 1534: protection from the provisions of the 40-day clause. By paying an "insurance premium" of 1/60th the value of their office to the Crown each year, an officeholder would be permitted to resign his office in favor of anyone of his choosing at any time, even on his deathbed. The heritability of offices was now ensured, which eliminated one of the primary complaints of the *officiers*. At the same time, the Crown would be ensured a steady return from venality without the negative consequences entailed in the wholesale creation of new positions. In fact, income from the *paulette* and other office taxes accounted for 12% of ordinary government revenue between 1605 and 1609.[46]

Bringing order to the system of proprietary officeholding was, then, one of the central planks of Sully's "reform" policy. The other two both aimed at securing a reliable supply of credit for the Crown. First, Sully initiated special judicial proceedings, or *chambres de justice*, against the

[44] Mousnier, *L'Assassinat*, p. 188.
[45] On the *paulette*, see Mousnier, *La Vénalité*, pp. 232ff.; idem, *L'Assassinat*, pp. 188–190; Bonney, *King's Debts*, p. 61.
[46] Bonney, *King's Debts*, p. 62.

financiers in 1597, 1601, 1605, and 1607. These tribunals were not, as they might first appear, a betrayal of the king's supporters; on the contrary, they offered Sully the opportunity to strengthen the position of the interconnected group of *partisans* and *traitants* he favored by selectively pursuing those whose loyalty was in question.[47] Characteristically, the task of collecting the fines levied during these trials was farmed. Finally, in 1604, Sully sought to restore some measure of attractiveness to government *rentes* by resuming interest payments which had been suspended 19 years earlier. Though he would not honor claims for arrears, he did attempt to ensure that interest was paid punctually in the future.

Henry IV's victory in the wars of religion had thus permitted a "refounding" of the French state based upon an alliance between the Crown, venal officeholders, and financiers. It was hoped that the co-operation of those most committed, both materially and ideologically, to the cause of royal absolutism would permit the French state in the future to meet the demands of large-scale warfare without seeking the assistance of the Estates General, while at the same time maintaining a united front against the magnates, still intent on building their own power at the expense of that of the king.

Renewed Warfare and Its Consequences

Such hopes proved to be illusory, however, for they failed to take account of the fundamental limits which absolutism placed on long-term military effectiveness, limits rendered even more definitive in France by the triumph of proprietary officeholding. The lack of broad-based consent for taxation, as well as its highly unequal and frequently irrational incidence, meant that the French government could never raise tax levels high enough to cover the actual cost of major wars. Yet the tax system could never really be reformed without disturbing the very socio-political pillars – the society of orders, feudal privileges, the special rights of the Church – upon which absolutism stood precariously balanced. Where then were the extra funds needed to protect France's geopolitical interests to come from? The installation of a huge corps of permanent, venal officials by the late 1500s was a solution. The *officiers*, now "co-proprietors" of the state, would have to pay.

However, such exploitation of officeholders by the government for revenue-raising purposes was ultimately a self-destructive strategy, for it undermined that alliance of Crown, *officiers*, and financiers which, as farsighted statesmen like Sully and Colbert both realized, represented

---

[47] Bonney, *King's Debts*, p. 64; Wolfe, *Fiscal System*, pp. 234–235.

the best hope for the regime's survival. Yet the only alternative to exploitation was peace, and peace was something that, given the country's geopolitical situation, no French government could maintain for long.

The contradictions present within the French state rebuilt by Henry IV and Sully became all too evident as soon as it once again became enmeshed in international conflict. The Thirty Years War had begun in 1618, and France could not remain uninvolved for long. Between 1628, when war broke out with Spain in northern Italy, and 1659, France was to be at peace for only four years (1631–5). From 1635 onward it was at war with Spain and (until 1648) with the Empire as well, a repeat of the situation before 1559. A new struggle for hegemony in western Europe had begun.

Almost from the start of this renewed conflict with the Habsburgs, the French government found itself in desperate financial straits. The principal reason for this was that, unlike in 1494, the Crown began this series of wars with a heavy burden of debt accumulated over the prior century. In 1627, before the start of major hostilities, 56% of state revenues were already absorbed by debt service in the form of interest to *rentiers* and *gages* (salaries) paid to officeholders.[48] Where was money for a new war to come from?

It was to come, at least initially, from a series of financial sleights of hand which aimed at deriving the maximum possible ready cash from tax increases. For example, the *taille* for a given year would be raised by, say, 2 million livres. Then, *rentes* or something like them would be created with the 2 million livres serving as a source for future interest payments. The capital value of the instruments emitted, whether *rentes*, new offices, or permanent salary increases (*augmentation de gages*), would ideally be between 10 and 15 times the amount of annual interest payments. In this way, a 2 million livres tax increase would produce a one-time gain of 20–30 million livres for the government. But the latter could not wait for the *rentes* or new offices to be sold, and so it almost always farmed their sale to a *partisan* for a cash payment equal to 75–80% of the capital value of the *rentes* or offices in question. Thus through a complex series of maneuvers, the Crown could expect to obtain, by merely decreeing a *taille* increase of 2 million livres, an almost immediate payment of 15–24 million livres from the financiers.

It is not hard to understand why this manner of proceeding looked irresistible to a French government locked in battle with a deadly rival. But it was also an approach to finances that would never have been tolerated had the Crown's actions been subject to outside scrutiny, for it amounted to an extreme case of liquidating assets for short-term

---

[48]   Bonney, *King's Debts*, pp. 133–134.

gain. It was a recipe for financial as well as political disaster. Yet for a time it worked. Between 1627 and 1634, direct taxes were increased by 65%, from 20.7 to 34.2 million livres.[49] At the same time, hundreds of new offices were created and large forced purchases of *rentes* and *augmentation de gages* extorted from officeholders as the price for the renewal of the *paulette* in 1630.[50] In addition, 73.2 million livres were raised through the sale to revenue officials of *droits aliénés*, the right to retain a certain portion of tax receipts they collected.[51]

In 1634–5, this entire delicate edifice came crashing down. Having alienated too much revenue, the government simply decided to take it back. The sales of *droits aliénés* were annulled, and their holders compensated with *rentes* of much lower value. With a single stroke, the Crown removed any incentive that the giant *taille* bureaucracy might have had to collect taxes efficiently. To supervise these recalcitrant officials, the government made increasing use of *intendants*, venal officeholders with seats in the Parlement of Paris who were detached from that court and sent to the provinces as plenipotentiaries of the executive armed with broad judicial and administrative powers.[52] To the sullen noncompliance of *trésoriers* and *élus*, however, was soon added the open hostility of the common people, who were unwilling to countenance any more tax increases. Despite the use of the army in putting down rebellious peasants, the government for the remainder of the war was unable to increase tax receipts above the levels of the early 1630s.[53]

Throughout the late 1630s and 1640s, the Crown was thus forced to fight two battles: one against the Habsburgs in Germany, Italy, and the Netherlands, and the other against its own subjects, common people as well as elites, at home. In addition to the measures used to collect taxes in the face of frequent uprisings, the government brought ever greater pressure to bear on officeholders to register new tax edicts and to advance the state more money even as payments of both *rentes* interest and *gages* were falling hopelessly in arrears. What is surprising is not that the *officiers* finally revolted in 1648, when Mazarin threatened once again not to renew the *paulette*, but that they had tolerated the Crown's extortions for so long.

Needless to say, both the parlous state of French finances and the

---

[49] James Collins, *Fiscal Limits of Absolutism: Direct Taxation in Early Seventeenth Century France* (Berkeley: University of California Press, 1988), p. 233. These figures refer to direct taxes from the *pays d'élection* only.
[50] Göhring, *Aemterkäuflichkeit*, pp. 115–119; Mousnier, *La Vénalité*, pp. 292ff.
[51] Collins, *Fiscal Limits*, p. 233.
[52] On the origins and activities of the *intendants* during this period, see the seminal work of Richard Bonney, *Political Change in France under Richelieu and Mazarin 1624–1661* (Oxford: Oxford University Press, 1978).
[53] Collins, *Fiscal Limits*, pp. 100–101, 200–201, 218–220.

endemic conflict between government and administration had grave consequences for France's military effectiveness. With insufficient cash available to pay its troops, the state took to treating its army officers in the same way it treated civilian officials. While nearly all captains and colonels in the French army had paid for their units, these purchases did not enjoy the same legal protections as the purchase of an office. By threatening to disband a given company or regiment, the government could thus force an officer to maintain his troops using his own funds.[54] This only encouraged commanders to attempt to pocket as much as they could for themselves when pay finally did arrive. In addition, it drove many soldiers to desert. A recent study of the real, as opposed to paper, strength of the French army has revealed an average company size of only 21 men (nominal strength: 50–70) between 1641 and 1647.[55] In the final analysis, it was only the even greater weakness of their Spanish opponents that saved the French from certain defeat during this period. The favorable peace terms of 1659 owe more to Cromwell's timely intervention than to any achievement by the French army.

While the rebel officeholders, nobles, and soldiers were never quite able to seize control of the French state during the Fronde which began in 1648, perhaps this was because there was little state left to seize. As in the late 1550s, a French state hollowed out from within by appropriation had again collapsed under the pressures of extended warfare. The contradictions inherent in this form of absolutism, contradictions between the geopolitical ambitions of rulers and their long-term capacity to mobilize resources using institutional arrangements and methods introduced during the early days of statebuilding, had proven impossible to overcome under the leadership of the cardinal-ministers Richelieu and Mazarin.

PATRIMONIAL ABSOLUTISM IN IBERIA AND ITALY, 1492–1789

As in France, the period between the last decade of the 15th century and the Peace of the Pyrenees in 1659 saw the triumph, though in a somewhat milder form, of both royal absolutism and appropriationist forces throughout the rest of a Latin Europe now dominated by Spain. Spain's monarchs had, by the close of the middle ages, accumulated substantial imperial powers due to their long struggle to defeat the Moors and to

---

[54] D. A. Parrott, "The Administration of the French Army during the Ministry of Cardinal Richelieu," unpublished Oxford D.Phil. thesis, 1985, pp. 184–186, 194ff.

[55] Bernhard Kroener, *Les Routes et les Étapes* (Münster: Aschendorff, 1980), pp. 4, 177.

control territories fractured by the vast immune estates of the nobility, the Church, and the military orders. Like their French rivals, the Spanish monarchs used these powers to legislate throughout most of their extended realm without seeking the approval of local Estates. In Castile, by far the most important component of the Spanish Empire, the Cortes had retained the right to approve new taxes, but successive monarchs from Charles V (1516–1556/8) onward succeeded in undermining both the independence and representativeness of that body and with it any wider influence the assembly might have had over foreign policy.

Unconstrained by effective representative institutions, the Habsburg rulers of Spain were free to pursue geopolitical goals which embroiled them for over a century and a half in an almost endless series of large-scale conflicts, several of which (the Eighty Years War with the Dutch, 1567–1648, and Spanish involvement in the Thirty Years War, 1618–1648) were of questionable strategic relevance to the Iberian lands at the heart of the Empire. Without the cooperation of the wider nation it proved impossible, just as in France, to generate sufficient tax revenue to pay for these wars, and the highly regressive tax structure that was a hallmark of absolutist regimes everywhere inflicted serious damage on the Spanish economy. Furthermore, chronic lack of money played into the hands of those seeking to appropriate public power for their own private ends, and by the mid-17th century most core state functions in both the Iberian and Italian territories of the Empire were in the hands of proprietary officeholders, financiers, military enterprisers, and the noble owners of private jurisdictions and immunities.

The loss of great power status after 1659 in the wake of complete economic and financial exhaustion brought with it not a move away from the absolutism that had led the country to the brink of collapse, but rather its intensification as, after 1714, the new Bourbon ruling house sought to regain some of Spain's past glory. Driven by these ambitions, and in an effort to improve the country's military effectiveness, the Bourbons did introduce reforms aimed at modernizing the structure of the state apparatus. Most of these reforms, however, failed in the face of fierce opposition from vested interests – the common fate of efforts at political reform throughout Latin Europe during this period. As in France, the end of patrimonial absolutism would only come throughout the rest of this region with the political upheavals of the period 1789–1815.

War, Taxation, and the Castilian Cortes

By the mid-1500s, the king of France's principal opponents, the Habsburg rulers of Spain, had become the masters of most of the rest of Latin Europe. In 1492, Ferdinand and Isabella, whose marriage had united Castile, Aragon, and Aragonese-ruled Naples and Sicily under one crown, finally completed the *reconquista* by overrunning the kingdom of Granada just as Columbus was about to discover America. The union four years later of the royal couple's daughter Juana and Philip of Habsburg eventually secured the wealthy Netherlands for Spain, though the northern half would be definitively lost to the Dutch rebels after 1607. Navarre was taken over in 1512, and Milan and Portugal passed into Spanish hands in 1540 and 1580 respectively, though the latter was to regain its independence in 1641. Finally, Ferdinand and Isabella's grandson Charles V inherited the Habsburg lands in central Europe and held the office of Holy Roman Emperor from 1519 to 1558, though thereafter his central European territories were passed on to what would become the separate Austrian branch of the family.

As noted earlier, Charles VIII's invasion of Italy in 1494 in pursuit of a French claim to the throne of Naples brought France into a protracted conflict with the Spanish rulers of that kingdom. The conflict was to continue (with some interruptions) until the Peace of Cateau-Cambrésis in 1559. At first, Charles's opponents Ferdinand and Isabella sought to involve the Cortes of Castile in the war effort, calling together that body 12 times between 1498 and 1516. This action was largely voluntary, since the Cortes had by this time lost all powers of co-legislation and the monarchs had been able to levy taxes on numerous occasions without its consent during the 1480s and 1490s.[56] However, following the so-called *communero* revolt of 1520–1521 directed against his rule, their grandson and successor Charles V would initiate a more subtle policy of preserving that institution for fiscal purposes while simultaneously eliminating it as a source of potential opposition to his ambitious foreign policy.

What Charles attempted to do, in effect, was subvert the independence of the Cortes by providing strong incentives for cooperation with the government's military projects. This approach was made possible by the structural transformation which the Cortes was undergoing during the course of the 15th and early 16th centuries. The organization of this and other curial-type representative institutions around separate social orders made it possible for monarchs here and elsewhere to confirm the privileges of individual estates bilaterally, thereby obviating the need to involve them in any further plenary meetings of the assembly. This is the strategy which successive Castilian monarchs pursued after 1480, vis-à-vis the nobility and clergy. Their privileges guaranteed

---

[56] Henry Kamen, *Spain 1469–1714: A Society in Conflict* (London: Longman, 1983), pp. 31–32.

they were called to just two more Cortes (1527 and 1538) and then to no more. Furthermore, after the 14th century, many towns and cities had passed from direct royal control into the hands of the nobility, clergy, and military orders. This fact, combined with the government practice of inviting as few towns as possible to the Cortes in order to increase manageability, diminished the number of municipalities represented in that body from over 100 in the early 14th century to only 18 at the close of the 15th century.[57]

As a result of these developments, the Castilian Estates were reduced by the second half of Charles V's reign to a single chamber of only 36 deputies or *procuradores*, two each chosen from among the ruling oligarchies of the 18 remaining "Cortes" cities. These cities were of central importance to the functioning of the Castilian state because their officials were also responsible for administering the scattered royal lands – i.e., those not under the "private" jurisdiction of the nobility, the Church, or the military orders – in the extensive hinterlands surrounding them.[58]

Charles was to employ a number of methods to convert the *procuradores* into loyal supporters of the government. Perhaps most importantly, he left the existing urban oligarchs in place, despite the fact that many had participated in the *comunero* movement. The king also created a new order of "stewards and gentlemen" drawn in part from this group and paid its members handsome pensions from the royal treasury.[59] In addition, two laws approved by Charles at the Cortes of Valladolid in 1523 reassured the oligarchs as to the future security of their tenure in municipal offices. First, while the sale or traffic in royal judgeships was forbidden, the same stricture was not extended to local government positions. Second, the government stated that any future sales of such municipal offices would not affect the right of current officeholders to dispose of their charges through *resignationes in favorem*.[60] Through these two acts, Charles and the Cortes together had reaffirmed the legality of proprietary officeholding within the municipalities and other areas of state administration outside of the judiciary. Finally, steps were taken to

---

[57] Wladimiro Piskorski, *Las Cortes de Castilla en el Período de Tránsito de la Edad Media a la Moderna 1188–1520* (Barcelona: El Abrir, 1977), pp. 16–19, 28–43; Kamen, *Spain*, p. 84.

[58] J. H. Elliott, *Imperial Spain 1469–1714* (New York: St. Martin's Press, 1964), pp. 81–85; Stephen Haliczer, *The Comuneros of Castile* (Madison: University of Wisconsin Press, 1981), pp. 115–121.

[59] Ibid., pp. 212, 218.

[60] Francisco Tomás y Valiente, "Les Ventes des Offices Publics en Castille aux XVIIᵉ et XVIIIᵉ Siècles," in: Klaus Malettke (ed.), *Aemterkäuflichkeit: Aspekte Sozialer Mobilität im Europäischen Vergleich (17. und 18. Jahrhundert)* (Berlin: Colloquium Verlag, 1980), pp. 89–121, here at 102; Antonio Domínguez Ortíz, "La Venta de Cargos y Oficios Públicos en Castilla y sus Consecuncias Economicas y Sociales," in: idem, *Instituciones y Sociedad en la España de los Austrias* (Barcelona: Ariel, 1985), pp. 146–183, here at p. 151.

influence the 36 members of the Cortes directly. The Crown undertook henceforth to pay them regular salaries and, from the later part of the century onwards, generous expenses (*ayudas de costa*) as well. Also, requests for royal favor, whether in the form of money grants or appointments, were viewed in a positive light by the government. Of 107 such requests made at the Cortes of 1537, all but 7 were met.[61]

Yet the compromise between Crown and Cortes touched on matters far more significant for the Spanish state as a whole than honors and gratuities. The late 15th and early 16th centuries had seen a running battle between the government and the principal cities over the central issue of revenue collection. During much of the later middle ages, Castile's most important tax, a sales tax called the *alcabala* which accounted for between 70% and 80% of total ordinary revenues, had been farmed by the central authorities.[62] The municipalities had long opposed this procedure and would have preferred instead an arrangement whereby the Cortes would agree to pay the Crown a fixed sum of money in regular installments apportioned among the 18 city-regions, each of which would then be free to collect the funds voted in any way it chose. This alternative system, known in Spanish as *encabezamiento*, was first introduced in some areas by Isabella in 1495 and gradually extended to much of the country by 1519. In that year, Charles announced that his pressing financial needs had led him to decide to end the *encabezamiento* system and return to tax farming. This policy change was a major cause of the *comunero* revolt.[63]

Following the end of the uprising, Charles agreed to restore *encabezamiento*, and indeed to extend it to include another important tax, the *tercia* or levy on clerical tenths. The system was reintroduced in stages after 1523, and was extended to the entire kingdom by an act of the Cortes in 1534. At the same time, the *Diputación*, a standing two- (later three-) man committee of the Cortes, was charged with overseeing the *encabezamiento*, in preference to royal officials.[64] Because the *servicios* or direct taxes voted by the Cortes were already collected by the municipalities, this meant that Castilian financial administration was completely in the hands of the proprietary officeholders of the country's 18 city-regions and the tax farmers who continued to collect a

---

[61] Francisco Tomás y Valiente, "La Diputación de las Cortes de Castilla (1515–1601)," in: idem, *Gobierno e Instituciones en la España del Antiguo Régimen* (Madrid: Alianza, 1982), pp. 37–150, here at p. 55; I. A. A. Thompson, "Crown and Cortes in Castile, 1590–1665," *Parliaments, Estates and Representation*, vol. 2, no. 1 (June 1982), pp. 29–45, here at p. 37; Haliczer, *The Comuneros*, p. 227.

[62] Miguel Ángel Ladero Quesada, *España en 1492* (Madrid: Hernando, 1978), pp. 120, 122.

[63] Haliczer, *The Comuneros*, pp. 158–159.

[64] Tomás y Valiente, "La Diputación," p. 58.

variety of indirect taxes and tolls. This state of affairs was reinforced after 1590 when a permanent commission of the Cortes was placed in charge of the *millones*, a new and very large tax voted by that body and collected once again at the municipal level.[65]

This far-reaching appropriation of important central government powers brought significant benefits, both direct and indirect, to urban elites and *procuradores* alike. The latter not only received a special lump sum payment each time they voted a *servicio*, but also were allowed to retain 1.5% of all revenues derived from both *servicios* amd *millones*. In addition, representatives lucky enough to be chosen for the *Diputación* were entitled to a very high salary and a generous grant for expenses drawn from the *alcabala* and *tercias* revenues.[66]

The oligarchs of the Cortes cities gained in a substantial, but less easily quantifiable, way from this system as well. Because they now possessed wide powers to determine the distribution and incidence of taxation within both their own towns and the regions subject to them, they were in a position to structure the tax system in a way that was most beneficial to themselves. In practice, this meant raising most funds through indirect taxes such as *sisas* or impositions on various basic food items, which were used by most cities to meet their *millones* obligations. Such taxes, of course, fell much more heavily on the poor than they did on the well-to-do. When this is considered together with the fact that as *hidalgos*, or gentlemen, the members of town councils already enjoyed various tax exemptions, it is clear that the new system of financial administration allowed urban elites largely to insulate themselves from the effects of tax increases by shifting the burden onto the *pechero* or common taxpayer, who had no voice in the governance of early modern Castile.[67]

The Crown expected a very specific quid pro quo for all the advantages which the *procuradores* and their backers gained from the new fiscal arrangements: generous financial support for the monarchy's foreign policy, which in practical terms meant its wars.[68] For despite the

---

[65] The *millones*, as Charles Jago points out, was not so much a tax as a tax agreement in which the Cortes undertook to raise several million ducats (hence the name) for the Crown. The way in which this was to be done was left to the discretion of each of the municipal governments of the Cortes cities. See Charles Jago, "Habsburg Absolutism and the Cortes of Castile," *American Historical Review*, vol. 86, no. 2 (April 1981), pp. 307–326, here at p. 312.

[66] Thompson, "Crown and Cortes," pp. 31, 37–38; Tomás y Valiente, "La Diputación," pp. 123–126.

[67] Jago, "Habsburg Absolutism," pp. 312–316; Antonio Domínguez Ortíz, "La Desigualdad Contributiva en Castilla durante el Siglo XVII," in: idem, *Instituciones y Sociedad*, pp. 97–145, here at 98–102.

[68] Ramón Carande, *Carlos V y sus Banqueros* (Madrid: Sociedad de Estudios y Publicaciones, 1949), vol. II, pp. 514–517.

wealth of the Indies, the Spanish Habsburgs were incapable of meeting the cost of large-scale conflicts without extra taxes voted by the Castilian Cortes. Whereas only a few years earlier the Cortes had led a national revolt against the costly foreign entanglements of Charles V, from the 1520s onwards they loyally voted ever larger sums in taxes for the emperor's wars and those of his successors.

Since the new financial system shielded the members of the Cortes, as well as their families and friends, from the adverse consequences of their actions, this must have been a bargain that was not too difficult to keep, especially since the *procuradores*'s private income was directly linked to how much revenue they voted. The post-*comunero* settlement thus created a structural situation in which the overblown obsession of the Spanish monarchs with *reputación* and the private interests of the Cortes reinforced each other in such a way as to keep Spain almost continually at war between 1521 and 1659.

War and Spanish Finances

To understand just why the fiscal support of the Castilian Cortes was so crucial for the Crown we must briefly examine the broader structure of Spanish military finance. The latter was constructed upon the twin pillars of the *juro* and the *asiento*. The *juro* was basically the Castilian equivalent of the French *rente*. As the pressures of the Italian wars mounted, the Spanish government turned increasingly, just as the French had done, to the sale of *juros* as a way of generating large, one-time gains from the alienation, often permanent, of various revenue sources.[69]

In 1522, the annual interest charge for *juros* was already consuming 36.6% of the Crown's total ordinary revenue. By 1560, at the end of the first major conflict with France, they had reached 103.9% of ordinary revenue and, despite efforts to retire some of the debt, still stood at 96.5% in 1598 after 30 years of war with the Dutch.[70] In practical terms this meant that from the mid-1500s onward the income from nearly all of the Crown's most reliable and predictable sources, such as the *alcabala*, was no longer available because it had been pledged to *juro* holders.

---

[69] Álvaro Castillo, "Dette Flottante et Dette Consolidée en Espagne de 1557 à 1600," *Annales*, vol. 18, no. 4 (July–August 1963), pp. 745–759, here at p. 753.

[70] Álvaro Castillo, "Los Juros de Castilla: Apogeo y Fin de un Instrumento de Crédito," *Hispania*, vol. 23, no. 89 (1963), pp. 43–70, here at pp. 51–52. See also Modesto Ulloa, *La Hacienda Real de Castilla en el Reinado de Felipe II*, 3rd ed. (Madrid: Fundación Universitaria Española, 1986), pp. 129–132, 827–829, which cites a somewhat lower figure for 1598 of 84%.

The money raised through *juro* sales was earmarked in its entirety for the repayment of the *asientistas*, financiers who had signed an *asiento* with the Crown. The *asiento* was an agreement to pay a certain sum in cash at a certain time at some location outside Spain, for example Flanders or Italy. The government then agreed to reimburse the *asientista* in Castile with interest at a later date.[71] The *asiento* thus combined elements of a short-term loan and a foreign exchange operation. Such an approach was necessary because the monarchy constantly maintained large numbers of troops overseas who had to be paid regularly in foreign currency. The price paid by the Crown for this service, which was provided by Spanish, German, *marrano* (Portuguese Jewish), and – above all – Genoese financiers, was high. Although the nominal interest rate on *asientos* was 12% per annum, the government sometimes had to pay over 30% interest to meet its obligations to the army, as it did during the 1550s.[72]

The form of repayment most desired by the *asientistas* was of course the gold and silver of the Indies. During the reign of Charles V, receipts from this source remained modest, reaching between 200,000 and 300,000 ducats per year in the 1530s and 1540s and 871,000 in the early 1550s. On the other hand, the amounts that had to be repaid annually on *asientos* averaged 1.2 million ducats and 2.5 million ducats respectively.[73] Even when the level of remittances flowing to the royal treasury was at its height in the 1580s and 1590s, they averaged only about 2.2 million ducats per year, at a time when the *asientos* contracted for often ran between 4 and 6 million ducats.[74] During the 1600s, there was a return to the situation that had obtained under Charles V, with remittances falling to an average level of about 1.5 million ducats and annual *asientos* running at between 5 and 10 times this amount.[75]

With ordinary income encumbered by the burden of *juro* interest, and the wealth of the Indies insufficient, the Spanish government clearly needed to rely on extraordinary revenues of some kind if it wished to continue to pursue the aggressive foreign policy inaugurated under Charles V. This is precisely why the new impositions voted by the Cortes were so significant for the government, and became ever more so as remittances from the Indies declined and the costs of great power obligations escalated with the start of the Thirty Years War in 1618. By

---

[71] Ehrenberg, *Das Zeitalter*, vol. II, pp. 185, 222ff.
[72] Antonio Domínguez Ortíz, *Política y Hacienda de Felipe IV* (Madrid: Pegaso, 1983), p. 92; Carande, *Carlos V*, vol. III, p. 20 and passim.
[73] Carande, *Carlos V*, vol. I, 2nd ed., p. 240; Miguel Artola, *La Hacienda del Antiguo Regimen* (Madrid: Alianza, 1982), pp. 86–87.
[74] Ulloa, *La Hacienda Real*, pp. 697, 810, 816.
[75] Domínguez Ortíz, *Política y Hacienda*, p. 266.

the 1620s, 30% of the Crown's annual disposable income was coming from the *millones* alone, and the power to renew both the *alcabala* and other *servicios* lay in the Cortes' hands as well.[76]

Yet the Cortes never used its considerable powers, as it had before 1521, to stop a costly foreign policy. Many facets of this foreign policy were both irrational and damaging to the national interest, such as the obstinate, 80-year struggle with the Dutch or the heavy involvement in central Europe, an area of no geopolitical or economic significance for Spain. At the same time, however, the thoroughly unrepresentative character of the Cortes rendered it incapable of actually raising through taxes the money required for the Crown's wars. Because of self-interested antipathy to property taxes, both the assembly and the municipalities insisted on piling tax after tax upon basic articles of consumption, an approach which over the course of a century and a half seriously damaged the Castilian economy without in the end ever providing enough money fully to meet the country's military needs. From the late 1500s onwards, these needs could only be met through recourse to a whole range of expedients, two of which – the sale of offices and the sale of *señoríos* – had particularly damaging consequences for the long-term development of the Spanish state.

The Sale of Offices and Full Patrimonialization

As one might expect, the sale of offices, which began in earnest in the 1560s and reached its apogee during the reign of Philip IV (1621–1665), took place for the most part within the sphere of municipal government which, as we have seen, doubled as a kind of royal territorial administration within Castile.[77] The Crown not only sold a range of treasurerships and receiverships which, though formerly part of the central fiscal apparatus, had in practice become part of the large city-controlled financial administration;[78] it also created additional municipal councillorships in the leading cities and put them up for sale. There can be no doubt that these actions further solidified the hold of proprietary officeholders over Castile's city-regions. At the same time, judging by early 18th-century results, these sales seem to have fostered a greater unity among the elites of Castile's cities by allowing all patrician families to be represented on the local council, whereas in the 15th

---

[76] Jago, "Habsburg Absolutism," p. 317.
[77] Tomás y Valiente, "Les Ventes," pp. 103ff.; Domínguez Ortíz, "La Venta de Cargos," pp. 176–177.
[78] Ulloa, *Hacienda Real*, p. 655.

and early 16th centuries, rival clans had fought fiercely for control of such institutions.[79]

It has been estimated that the massive sales of municipal offices and other administrative positions of the late 1500s and 1600s had by 1650 created 30,000 proprietary officeholders in Castile alone; since its population at that time numbered about 5 million, this meant that there was essentially one officeholder for every 166 inhabitants. This was over *twice* the number of proprietary officeholders per capita found in France, which in 1665 possessed 46,047 *officiers* out of a total population of 17.5 million, or one for every 380 inhabitants.[80]

A practice as damaging in the long run for the cause of statebuilding in Spain as the sale of municipal and financial offices was the transfer of whole villages and towns to private, seigneurial jurisdictions (*señoríos*). In the late 1500s, only about 30% of the territory of Castile was under direct royal authority.[81] The rest of the land formed part of *señoríos*, which gave the lord broad legal and administrative powers over his area and left his subjects only the right of final appeal to the royal courts. While the Church and the military orders controlled some *señoríos*, most were in the hands of the nobility, which had strengthened its position in the 16th century when the Crown, with papal authorization, had sold off a certain amount of Church land to raise money.[82]

This trend was reinforced during the reign of Philip IV when, under the pressures of war, the Crown took to selling a considerable number of towns and villages to private individuals. In all, Domínguez Ortíz has estimated that about 230,000 Castilians were put up for sale during this decade, though some avoided their transfer to a *señor* by raising the purchase price themselves.[83] Although this alienation of legal authority was egregious enough in itself from the point of view of state development, it was aggravated in many cases by the practice of selling the right to collect *alcabalas* and other taxes to the new lord as well, decreasing thereby the Crown's revenue base. As in France, the actual business of marketing both lands and offices was turned over to financiers, in

---

[79] Haliczer, *The Comuneros*, pp. 120–121; Joachim Böer, "Aspekte der Aemterkäuflichkeit in Vallodolid (Altkastilien) im 18. Jahrhundert: Das Beispiel der *Regidores*," in: Malettke *Aemterkäuflichkeit*, pp. 122–124, here at 122–123.

[80] Domínguez Ortíz, "La Venta de Cargos," p. 176; John Lynch, *Spain under the Habsburgs*, 2nd ed., 2 vols. (New York: New York University Press, 1981), vol. II, p. 136; Roland Mousnier, *Le Conseil du Roi de Louis XII à la Révolution*, 2nd ed. (Paris: P.U.F., 1971), p. 20.

[81] I. A. A. Thompson, *War and Government in Habsburg Spain 1560–1620* (London: Athlone, 1976), p. 65.

[82] Antonio Domínguez Ortíz, "Ventas y Exenciones de Lugares durante el Reinado de Felipe IV," in: idem, *Instituciones y Sociedad*, pp. 56–96, here at pp. 56–57.

[83] Ibid., p. 62. Also Lynch, *Spain*, vol. II, pp. 2–3.

this case to members of the powerful clans of Genoese who were the principal *asientistas* to the Spanish Crown from 1559 until 1627, and then again in the 1640s and 1650s.[84]

Finally, the steady growth in the institutional strength of municipal elites, territorial nobles, and financiers under the impact of war, and the continuing fiscal difficulties of the Crown, allowed these groups to gain an ever greater hold over the armed forces, thus undermining the institution that had once been the most modern and forward-looking in the Spanish state. During the mid-1500s, at a time when military entrepreneurship was expanding throughout the West, the Spanish were building a highly effective army administered directly by royal officials and recruited by captains at the state's expense.[85]

All of this changed, however, from the late 1500s onward. Increasingly, captains were forced to advance money from their own pockets to pay their troops, and the "company economy" began to make its appearance. The government gave in with ever greater frequency to the requests of territorial lords to raise troops and thus convert themselves into military entrepreneurs. Coastal towns and regions also agreed to build and outfit ships for the royal fleet on the condition that the ships in question could form regional squadrons under their own commanders. Lastly, the direct administration of provisioning and weapons production, another Spanish peculiarity, was abandoned and these activities turned over to the ubiquitous Genoese financiers.[86] By the 1630s and 1640s, then, the Spanish government had as little, and perhaps even less, control over its armed forces as did their French rivals, a startling contrast to the situation a century before and a striking commentary on the effects of sustained warfare on state development under conditions of absolutism.

By the time the Peace of the Pyrenees was finally concluded, then, continuous warfare under conditions of absolutism had allowed the appropriationist tendencies first implanted within the Castilian state in the wake of early geopolitical competition to come to full fruition, leaving much of that country's administrative, financial, and military infrastructure in the hands of proprietary officeholders, financiers, and

---

[84] Domínquez Ortíz, "Ventas y Exenciones," pp. 60, 65; idem, *Politica y Hacienda,* p. 104. On the Genoese more generally, see: Felipe Ruíz Martín, "Los Hombres de Negocios Genoveses de España durante el Siglo XVI," in: Hermann Kellenbenz (ed.), *Fremde Kaufleute auf der Iberischen Halbinsel* (Cologne: Böhlau, 1970), pp. 84–99.

[85] The classic work on the administration of the Spanish army at the height of its powers is Geoffrey Parker, *The Army of Flanders and the Spanish Road 1567–1659* (Cambridge: Cambridge University Press, 1972). See also the detailed study of René Quatrefages, *Los Tercios Españoles (1567–77)* (Madrid: Fundación Universitaria Española, 1979).

[86] Thompson, *War and Government,* pp. 99, 111–112, 121, 151, 198ff., 231–233, 254–255, 278.

military enterprisers and many of its inhabitants under the private jurisdiction of the nobility, the Church, and the military orders. Far from
promoting centralization and modern bureaucratization, as it would
for some states affected later than Castile by the onset of geopolitical
competition, war had acted here as a stimulus to administrative fragmentation and privatization.[87] The steady appropriation of state power
by narrow social groups in turn opened the way for a relentless fiscal
exploitation of the Castilian populace which in the end destroyed the
country's economy and helped drive the Spanish Empire from the ranks
of the great powers after 1659.

The Progress of Patrimonial Absolutism Outside Castile

Developments in the other lands under the Spanish Crown followed a
pattern broadly similar to that in Castile during this period. The right
of monarchs to legislate without the approval of the Estates had long
been established in Naples and Sicily, but Habsburg viceroys regularly
called together the assemblies of both kingdoms once every two to
three years in order to vote extraordinary taxes in support of the on-
going war effort. As in Castile, this step was taken more out of a calculated desire to build support for royal policy than out of necessity. This
is shown by the fact that after disputes over taxes with the Neapolitan
Estates in 1639 and 1642, that body was never convoked again, though
taxes continued to be collected nonetheless. The more cooperative
Sicilian Estates, however, continued to meet every three years.[88] In the
southern Netherlands the Estates General met regularly to vote new taxes
prior to the revolt, but were only convened twice (1598 and 1632) after
the territory's reconquest by the duke of Parma in 1579.[89]

The situation was somewhat different within the Crown of Aragon,
where the Estates did retain powers of both taxation and co-legislation.
The Habsburgs responded to this obstacle by largely ignoring this poor
and sparsely populated area, since it could in any case contribute little to
defray the costs of war. Charles V (1516–1556/8) convoked just six meetings with the assemblies of Aragon, Catalonia, and Valencia, his son Philip

---

[87] This "revisionist" interpretation of early modern Spain was first formulated, though
with a rather different emphasis, in I. A. A. Thompson's often-overlooked work *War
and Government in Habsburg Spain 1560–1620*.

[88] Antonio Marongiu, *Il Parlamento in Italia nel Medio Evo e nell'Età Moderna* (Milano:
Giuffrè, 1962), pp. 335–338, 344, 402, 429–447; H. G. Koenigsberger, "The Parlia-
ment of Sicily and the Spanish Empire," in: idem, *Estates and Revolutions* (Ithaca:
Cornell University Press, 1971), pp. 80–93.

[89] A. R. Myers, *Parliaments and Estates in Europe to 1789* (London: Thames and Hudson,
1975), pp. 79, 127–128.

II (1556–1598) two, and Philip III (1598–1621) and Philip IV (1621–1665) together only four. When Aragon revolted against Castilian rule in 1591–1592, the rebellion was put down by force and in its aftermath the legislative and judicial powers of the Cortes substantially reduced.[90]

The overall decline between 1494 and 1659 in the significance of Estates throughout Iberia and Italy was not simply a result of Spanish policy, but rather the result of structural features of the tricurial assemblies common to all of Latin Europe. This is shown by the cases of Portugal and Savoy, where the loss of power on the part of the Estates was even more precipitous than in the territories under continuous Spanish dominion. By the end of the 15th century, the Portuguese Cortes had also lost its legislative powers, and it met only seven times between 1495 and 1557 and another six times between 1562 and 1645 in order to approve new taxes, a pattern which Livermore ascribes to the heightened power of the sovereign based on the reception of Roman law.[91] The Estates of Piedmont, the most important representative body within the duchy of Savoy, met regularly until the country came under French control in 1536. After Emmanuel Philibert won back his state in 1559, he called together the Estates once (1560) and then did away with them altogether.[92]

The appropriation of core state functions through proprietary officeholding and financial and military subcontracting also intensified during this period in both the Spanish and non-Spanish areas of Italy and Iberia outside of Castile. As shown in Chapter 2, proprietary officeholding and the private traffic in offices linked to *resignaciones* had arisen across this region during the middle ages as a result of the precocious statebuilding efforts undertaken by rulers in response to early, sustained geopolitical pressure. Beginning in the 1500s, however, the Spanish authorities gave further scope to appropriationist tendencies by introducing the systematic creation and sale of offices as a revenue-raising device not only in Castile, but also in Catalonia, Navarre, Valencia, Naples, Sicily, and Portugal – and even in the American colonies.[93]

---

[90] Elliott, *Imperial Spain*, pp. 193, 249, 277, 298, 326, 333; Lynch, *Spain*, vol. I, pp. 9–10, 47–48, 209–210; Koenigsberger, "Parliament of Sicily," p. 91; Juan Beneyto, "Les Cortes d'Espagne du XVIᵉ au XIXᵉ Siècle," in: *Receuils de la Société Jean Bodin, XXIV: Gouvernés et Gouvernants, Troisième Partie: Bas Moyen Age et Temps Modernes (I)* (Bruxelles: Editions de la Librairie Encyclopédique, 1966), pp. 461–481, here at pp. 469–470.

[91] H. V. Livermore, *A History of Portugal* (Cambridge: Cambridge University Press, 1947), pp. 223, 252, 263–264, 277, 281, 291–292.

[92] Marongiu, *Medieval Parliaments*, pp. 199, 204–205; Koenigsberger, "Parliament of Piedmont," pp. 67–79.

[93] K. W. Swart, *Sale of Offices in the 17th Century* (Utrecht: HES Publishers, 1980), pp. 40–44, 87–88; James Casey, *The Kingdom of Valencia in the Seventeenth Century* (Cambridge: Cambridge University Press, 1979), pp. 186–188; Roberto Mantelli, *Burocrazia e Finanze*

Venice and the Papacy also publicly sold offices – indeed, they may have inspired the practice in France and Castile – as did Savoy.[94] While public sales rarely took hold in Milan, the southern Netherlands, or Tuscany, proprietary officeholding and with it the private traffic in offices grew stronger during this period, and in the first two territories as well as in Naples and Portugal offices were frequently farmed out by their owners.[95] The more typical form of farming – tax farming – was universally employed through Latin Europe as a way of raising ready cash, though this was achieved at the heavy price of turning over direct control of revenue collection to private businessmen.[96] Only Savoy, culturally close

Pubbliche nel Regno di Napoli a Metà del Cinquecento (Napoli: Lucio Pironti, 1981), pp. 91–128; Vittor Ivo Comparato, *Uffici e Società a Napoli (1600–1647)* (Firenze: Leo Olschki, 1974), pp. 39–71; Antonio Calabria, *The Cost of Empire* (Cambridge: Cambridge University Press, 1991), p. 47; Denis Mack Smith, *A History of Sicily* (New York: Dorset Press, 1988), pp. 118–119, 245; H. G. Koenigsberger, *The Practice of Empire* (Ithaca: Cornell University Press, 1969), pp. 136–139; António Manuel Hespanha, *Vísperas del Leviatán: Institutiones y Poder Político (Portugal, Siglo XVII)* (Madrid: Taurus, 1989), pp. 420, 424–429; idem, *História das Instituições* (Coimbra: Livraria Almedina, 1982), pp. 389–393; Reinhard Liehr, "Aemterkäuflichkeit und Aemterhandel im kolonialen Hispanoamerika," in: Mieck (ed.), *Aemterhandel*, pp. 159–180.

94 Swart, *Sale of Offices*, pp. 84–86; Roland Mousnier, "Le Trafic des Offices à Venise," *Révue Historique du Droit Français et Étranger*, vol. 30, no. 4 (1952), pp. 552–565; R. Burr Litchfield, *The Emergence of a Bureaucracy: Florentine Patricians 1530–1790* (Princeton: Princeton University Press, 1986), pp. 177–178; Wolfgang Reinhard, "Aemterhandel in Rom zwischen 1534 und 1621," in: Ilja Mieck (ed.), *Aemterhandel*, pp. 42–60; Brigide Schwarz, "Die Entstehung der Aemterkäuflichkeit an der Römischen Kurie," in: ibid., pp. 61–65; Peter Partner, *The Pope's Men* (Oxford: Clarendon, 1990), pp. 12–17, 28–31, 197–202; Enrico Stumpo, *Finanza e Stato Moderno nel Piemonte del Seicento* (Roma: Istituto Storico Italiano, 1979), pp. 156–185, 226–235; Geoffrey Symcox, *Victor Amadeus II: Absolutism in the Savoyard State 1675–1730* (Berkeley: California University Press, 1983), pp. 62–63, 246.

95 Federico Chabod, "Stipendi Nominali e Busta Paga Effettiva dei Funzionari dell'Amministrazione Milanese alla Fine del Cinquecento," in: idem, *Carlo V e il suo Impero* (Torino: Einaudi, 1983), pp. 281–450, here at pp. 346–355; idem, "Usi e Abusi nell'Amministrazione dello Stato di Milano a mezzo il Cinquecento," in: ibid., pp. 451–521; Alessandro Visconti, *La Pubblica Amministrazione nello Stato Milanese durante il Predominio Straniero (1541–1796)* (Roma: Athenaeum, 1913), pp. 53–55, 244–245; Swart, *Sale of Offices*, pp. 78–81; Michael Erbe, "Aspekte des Aemterhandels in den Niederlanden im späten Mittelalter und in der Frühen Neuzeit," in: Mieck (ed.), *Aemterhandel*, pp. 112–131, here at pp. 121–131; Litchfield, *Emergence*, pp. 178–181; Comparato, *Uffici e Società*, p. 140; Hespanha, *Vísperas*, p. 429.

96 Casey, *Kingdom of Valencia*, pp. 82–83; Mantelli, *Burocrazia*, p. 229; Calabria, *Cost of Empire*, pp. 44–45; Mack Smith, *History*, p. 274; Erbe, "Aspekte des Aemterhandels," p. 130; Hespanha, *Vísperas*, pp. 113–114; Litchfield, *Emergence*, pp. 53, 271–272; Stuart Woolf, *A History of Italy 1700–1860* (London: Methuen, 1979), pp. 72–73, 145.
    Jean-Claude Wacquet has recently highlighted the way that 17th- and 18th-century Florentine elites enriched themselves through the appropriation of public debt funds. See: Jean-Claude Wacquet, "Note sur les Caractères Originaux du Système Financier Toscan sous les Médicis," in: Jean-Philippe Genet and Michel Le Mené (eds.), *Genèse de l'État Moderne: Prélèvement et Redistribution* (Paris: Éditions du C.N.R.S., 1987), pp. 111–114; and his *De la Corruption: Morale et Pouvoir à Florence aux XVIIe et XVIIIe Siècle* (Paris: Fayard, 1984).

to France, seems to have complemented farming with the Gallic system of "inside" credit.[97]

As geopolitical pressures on the governments of the Iberian and Italian peninsulas diminished after 1659, state development there came to be dominated by two broad trends. On the one hand, with the advent of peace throughout much of the region those representative bodies that still clung to life became dispensable. Thus, during this period rulers nearly everwhere finally moved to do away with their Estates or reduce them to purely ceremonial functions. Those of Savoy, the southern Netherlands, and Naples had already breathed their last in 1560, 1632, and 1642 respectively, and the last working session of the Castilian Cortes ended in 1665. While four meetings of the Portuguese Cortes were held during the late 1600s, they were simply for the purpose of swearing oaths or discussing dynastic questions. After 1697, the assembly was never again convoked.[98] Finally, the arrival of the new Bourbon dynasty in Spain also meant the end for the Estates of the Crown of Aragon. The Cortes of Aragon and Valencia were abolished in 1707 and that of Catalonia in 1716, and thereafter the whole region lost its special status and was simply merged with Castile.[99] For the remainder of the century until 1789, only one national representative assembly of any significance remained in all of Latin Europe: the *parlamento* of Sicily, and its powers were limited to approving new taxes. Absolutism had triumphed more thoroughly here than anywhere else in western Christendom.

On the other hand, reformers made numerous attempts, especially from the 1750s onward, to begin to win back direct control over state powers and functions that had been lost to private groups and individuals over many centuries. These attempts were motivated both by the traditional desire to increase military effectiveness through financial solvency and by the growing influence of Enlightenment ideas. While reformers in a few states (Lombardy, Tuscany, in part Spain) were able to replace tax farming with direct collection, their ability to alter the basic *character* of state infrastructures across this region was very limited, for court rivals could (and most often did) ally with the vast army of officeholders, financiers, and other privilege holders – who stood to lose from modernizing reforms – to drive overambitious ministers like Ensenada from power.[100]

---

[97] Stumpo, *Finanza e Stato*, pp. 109, 187–188.

[98] Jago, "Habsburg Absolutism," pp. 325–326; Livermore, *History*, pp. 340–341.

[99] John Lynch, *Bourbon Spain 1700–1808* (Oxford: Basil Blackwell, 1989), pp. 62–66, 106–107.

[100] Woolf, *History*, pp. 70–74, 98–107, 144–146, 148–151; Lynch, *Bourbon Spain*, pp. 91–92, 102–104, 168–186, 192, 249–250, 296, 374.

Only when a ruler himself took an active role in the reform process, as in Tuscany under Archduke Leopold or Lombardy under Joseph II, was it possible to replace proprietary officeholding with something closer to a proto-modern bureaucracy.[101] In all the other states of Latin Europe, efforts at administrative and financial reform failed in the face of tenacious opposition from vested interests – and nowhere more spectacularly than in France, where the destruction of the ancien régime and its many ramifications finally created the requisite conditions to sweep away patrimonial absolutism.[102]

THE "REFORM" OF PATRIMONIAL ABSOLUTISM UNDER COLBERT AND LOUIS XIV, 1660–1714

With the signing of the Peace of the Pyrenees in 1659, France finally emerged from the period of unceasing conflict, both foreign and domestic, that had begun in 1628. The experience of the Fronde (1648–53), as well as the financial and military disasters which preceded and followed it, had shown that the French state was in urgent need of reform if it wished to remain among the great powers, rather than to share the fate of its erstwhile enemy Spain. The pressures of war had once again undermined the complex alliance of proprietary officeholders, financiers, and magnates which Henry IV and Sully had only just patched together in the aftermath of the Wars of Religion.

Yet what kind of "reform" was really possible in the absolutist France of Louis XIV? Following the death of Cardinal Mazarin, Jean-Baptiste Colbert was soon to become the young monarch's most important minister. Colbert was genuinely concerned about the future of his country, but like all early modern statesmen he was even more concerned about the future of his own family. Answerable to no one but the king, and enjoying his full support, Colbert was free to combine the goals of national revival and family aggrandizement.

And France's fortunes did indeed improve substantially after 1660 when compared to the 1630s or 1640s. Both traditional historiography and the statebuilding literature have tended to attribute this to the introduction of new, bureaucratic procedures into the moribund corpus

---

[101] Litchfield, *Emergence*, pp. 283–337; Woolf, *History*, p. 128.
[102] Swart, *Sale of Offices*, pp. 39–40, 81, 88–89; Partner, *Pope's Men*, p. 215; Amedeo Sorge, "La Venalità degli Uffici nel Regno di Napoli: Un Tentativo di Reforma nel Primo Decennio Borbonico," in: Mario Di Pinto (ed.), *I Borbone di Napoli e i Borbone di Spagna*, 2 vols. (Napoli: Guida Editori, 1985), vol, I, pp. 291–304; Miguel Artola, *Historia de España Alfaguara V: La Burguesía Revolutionaria (1808–1874)* (Madrid: Alianza Universidad, 1973), pp. 29–37, 286 and passim.

of the ancien régime. Such a view overlooks the fact that it is possible to "rationalize" patrimonial states in a way that pushes them not towards, but further away from more modern forms of state organization. I have deemed this process the "rationalization" of "irrationalization." I argue in this section that through the single-minded pursuit of his own private interests, Colbert did succeed in bringing a higher degree of order and efficiency to key areas of the French polity. But it was rampant nepotism and the intensified use of patronage/clientage, and not modern organizational methods, that allowed the French financial system and armed forces to function more effectively in the 1660s and 1670s. In many respects, Colbert's methods of rule bear a curious resemblance to those of the early Carolingians: like them, he employed a network of personal ties as a means of gaining some control over entrenched elites who had already appropriated substantial state powers. As with the Carolingians, this pattern of rule was to prove unstable and, in the end, self-destructive.

The nearly 20 years of war which began in 1688 soon exposed the structural limitations inherent within Colbert's "reforms." Unable, given the confines of an absolutist political system, to mobilize sufficient resources to wage sustained warfare on several fronts, the government was forced to fall back upon the old expedient of *affaires extraordinaires* which Colbert had sought to render unnecessary. This episode illustrates in the clearest possible terms the practical meaning of "path-dependent development," as institutional choices made far in the past acted to constrain severely the freedom of maneuver of France's leaders even under conditions of the most dire military threat. The disasters of the War of the Spanish Succession demonstrated clearly enough that ancien régime France as then constituted would never be able to keep pace with a Britain now poised to reap all the geopolitical benefits of authentically modernizing institutional change.

The "Reforms" of Colbert

Rather than appoint a new, all-powerful chief minister following the death of Cardinal Mazarin in March 1661, the young king Louis XIV decided to play that role himself while entrusting the day-to-day business of government to Mazarin's three top officials: Michel Le Tellier, the secretary of war; Hugues de Lionne, the foreign secretary; and Nicolas Fouquet, the *surintendant des finances*. A relative and protégé of Le Tellier's, Jean-Baptiste Colbert, was also named to assist Fouquet as an *intendant des finances*.

Within six months Colbert, with the support of Le Tellier and Lionne, had carried out a spectacular coup.[103] Colbert had secretly persuaded Louis to turn on Fouquet and place the direction of financial affairs in his own hands. In September, Fouquet was arrested, and in November a *chambre de justice* (special trial) of over 400 financiers and *traitants* organized. The stated goal of this massive judicial process, which lasted for four years, was to expose the mismanagement and peculation present within the country's finances over the past 25 years and punish those responsible. The "reforms" of Colbert had begun.

In order to understand properly the aims of Colbert's policies, as well as the methods he employed to implement them, we must first examine briefly his own background and previous activities. The Colberts were an extremely prominent local family in Rheims. Although they had made their fortune in commerce, they also had strong ties to the world of the law (and hence venal office) and government finance. Colbert's grandfather had been both a judicial officer and a farmer of the salt tax, the *gabelle*. His father was a draper and local tax farmer in Rheims who had purchased the important office of receiver and payer of the *rentes* and established himself in Paris.[104]

Colbert's own training was much in keeping with his milieu. After university studies and an apprenticeship to a banker in Lyons, he first became an assistant to the treasurer of the *parties casuelles* (the department charged with selling offices), and then purchased the office of *commissaires de guerre* (war commissary), where he served under Le Tellier, a cousin by marriage of Colbert. Finally, with the former's assistance, Colbert was chosen by Mazarin in 1651 to administer the cardinal's personal finances.[105] Far from being a "new man," Colbert had close ties of both interest and affection to the elite world of government finance and higher administration. His career had been furthered by the influence of his uncle Pussort, his cousin Colbert de St. Pouange, and the latter's brother-in-law Le Tellier, and he had cultivated the patronage of Mazarin.

It was Colbert's activities while in the service of Mazarin that provide the immediate background for the "coup" of September 1661. During the last few years of his life, the cardinal had amassed, with Colbert's assistance, what was probably the largest private fortune in the history of the ancien régime. Whereas in 1658, Mazarin's assets amounted to

[103] Bonney, *King's Debts*, pp. 264–265.
[104] Jean Bérenger, "Charles Colbert, Marquis de Croissy," in: Mousnier, *Le Conseil*, pp. 153–174, here at pp. 153–154; René Pillorget, "Henri Pussort, Oncle de Colbert (1615–1697)," in: ibid., pp. 255–274, here at p. 257; Daniel Dessert and Jean-Louis Journet, "Le Lobby Colbert: Un Royaume, ou une Affaire de Famille?" in: *Annales*, vol. 30, no. 6 (November-December 1975), pp. 1303–1336, here at 1304–1305.
[105] Pillorget, "Henri Pussort," pp. 261–262; Dessert, "Le Lobby Colbert," pp. 1304–1306.

8 million livres, already a vast sum, they had grown to over 35 million livres at the time of his death. Even more egregious was the fact that almost 9 million of this was in coin, hoarded during a period when France and her armies were suffering from severe shortages of cash. The cardinal had clearly used all the power at his disposal to subvert the finances of the French monarchy to his own advantage.[106]

Neither Louis nor Colbert wished this startling secret to become known, so Colbert conceived of a plan that would both divert attention from Mazarin's past and remove a dangerous rival. He would blame all of France's financial ills of the past 25 years on the thieveries of the financiers, with Fouquet at their head. The public persecution of an unpopular group would both help bolster the Crown's sagging legitimacy and create a unique opportunity to bring about major changes within the financial system from which Colbert and his allies could profit.[107] Having obtained the approval of Louis and Le Tellier for his scheme, Colbert was free to take over the direction of French finances himself and set the *chambre de justice* of 1661–1665 in motion.

One of the most tangible and immediate effects of this trial was that it allowed the French government to default painlessly on many of its obligations, for the army of arrested financiers were owed substantial sums by the Crown. In addition to this write-off of old debt, the state coffers were filled with the huge fines, many of them payable in cash, levied against the financiers. These fines initially amounted to about 157 million livres, a sum nearly twice as great as total French government expenditure in 1665.[108] It was the *chambre* that permitted Colbert the luxury of reducing simultaneously both direct taxes (the *taille*) and the state debt.

Yet for Colbert, the *chambre* was more than just a convenient means of improving the government's financial position. It offered a unique opportunity to transform the financial system itself. The most intractable problem faced by the French monarchy over the past century or more had been its inability to raise sufficient amounts of short-term credit in an orderly and consistent manner. England had experienced similar difficulties earlier in the century, and the Restoration government was about to overcome them through the creation of a new

---

[106] Daniel Dessert, *Fouquet* (Paris: Fayard, 1987), pp. 206–225, 237. To put these figures in some perspective, total French central government expenditure amounted to about 65 million livres in 1662, and the total money stock of France in the early 1680s was only 500 million livres. Hence Mazarin had succeeded in squirreling away about 2% of the entire French money supply. Bonney, *The King's Debts*, p. 325; Herbert Luethy, *La Banque Protestante en France* (Paris: S.E.V.P.E.N., 1959), vol. I, p. 96.

[107] Dessert, *Fouquet*, pp. 225–239.   [108] Bonney, *King's Debts*, pp. 266, 325.

financial instrument, the Treasury Order, a negotiable, interest-bearing bond sold to the general public at the Exchequer for cash. Repayment was legally guaranteed by an act of Parliament.

Neither Colbert nor his master had any interest in pursuing this kind of solution, for it would have required the revival of representative institutions in France capable of convincing a wider public that their investments were secure.[109] Instead, Colbert's actions indicate that he had conceived of another way to address the cash problem which would render France more solvent (and hence stronger militarily), while at the same time enhancing his own personal power and that of his family. His idea was to make much better use of the credit potential to be found within the French government apparatus itself. If all those with a long-term commitment to the survival of the state as then constituted – officeholders, higher nobles, churchmen, contractors, tax farmers – could be persuaded to invest more generously in its future, perhaps the country could meet its external challenges without an uncontrolled return to *affaires extraordinaires* and other divisive expedients.

A key role in such a plan would have to be played by the *officiers comptables*, those venal accountants such as the receivers general, the local receivers of the *taille*, or the war treasurers who were responsible for actually collecting and/or disbursing cash. They had frequently acted as government lenders in the past, advancing ready money at interest in anticipation of tax receipts, but their potential had not yet been fully realized. By imposing heavy fines through the *chambre*, Colbert was able to force many of the old *comptables* to sell their places and make way for his own men. Sometimes the latter were relatives engaged in finance, and sometimes financiers who had sought the minister's protection. In this way, Colbert implanted a network of well-connected money-lenders personally loyal to him at the very heart of the French financial apparatus.[110]

How could a *comptable* such as a receiver general gather together the large quantities of coin which the state sought? He could of course make use of his own wealth, but this would be in no way sufficient. Alternatively, as a member of a large, well organized group like "le lobby Colbert,"[111] he could draw on the resources of hundreds of individuals linked together by ties of parentage, patronage/clientage, or partnership, many of whom might not be directly involved in government lending.

---

[109] In France, as in England as well, the king could not be sued in court to recover debts. Hence the significance of parliamentary guarantees enshrined in statutes.

[110] Daniel Dessert, *Argent, Pouvoir et Société au Grand Siècle* (Paris: Fayard, 1984), pp. 202–203, 329–332; Dessert and Journet, "Le Lobby Colbert," pp. 308–310.

[111] Dessert and Journet, "Le Lobby Colbert," op. cit.

Yet the Colbert network did not represent the greatest potential source
of funds. This was to be found among the chateaux of France's great
nobles. Every year their vast estates produced substantial amounts of
cash, not all of which could be spent on conspicuous consumption.
Many of the financiers associated with Colbert already possessed some
links to the higher nobility through their activities as private financial
advisors and managers of large estates. Now, as receivers or treasurers,
they were in an excellent position to attract discreet aristocratic investments. By using the *comptables* as intermediaries, image-sensitive nobles
could enjoy the profits to be made in government finance without
publicly associating with *sales traitants*. Furthermore, the knowledge that
Colbert would ultimately stand surety for all those in his "lobby" provided an extra measure of security for those nervous about investing.
Behind the financiers now ensconced within the French state, then,
there stood the combined wealth of the country's greatest families,
beginning with the heirs of Richelieu and Mazarin.[112]

In addition to the *comptables*, the farmers of the indirect taxes constituted a second source of short-term credit with vast potential. In order
to exploit this potential, Colbert not only installed his own people in
the farms, but also sought to combine them into larger, more efficient
units that would be more attractive as objects of investment.[113] In 1664,
the *gabelle* (salt tax) and the national import-export duties were brought
together in one farm, to be joined in 1668 by the *aides* (sales taxes) and
the *cinq grosses fermes* (a set of internal tolls). The total lease of this
combined farm was substantially greater than that of its separate predecessor farms. Finally, in 1680, the farms of the royal demesne were
added to form an organization responsible for nearly all of the kingdom's indirect taxes. This was the General Farms (*fermes générales*) that
were to persist until the Revolution.[114] As expected, these new, concentrated farms were to attract substantial elite investment.[115]

Colbert's administration of the provinces exhibits much the same
logic as his actions in other spheres of government. Of course, his
scope for direct control in this area was somewhat limited by the fact
that the vast majority of local financial and judicial officials (the *trésoriers
de France*, *élus*, regional *parlementaires*, *juges de présidiaux*, and many more)
were proprietary officeholders. Also, there were the magnates to contend
with, whose families had long ago appropriated all of the significant

---

[112] Dessert, *Argent, Pouvoir*, pp. 354–355, 362–365.   [113] Ibid., p. 332.
[114] Yves Durand, *Les Fermiers Généraux au XVIIIe Siècle* (Paris: P.U.F., 1971), p. 51; George
Matthews, *The Royal General Farms in Eighteenth Century France* (New York: Columbia
University Press, 1958), pp. 47–50.
[115] Dessert, *Argent, Pouvoir*, pp. 358–361.

regional governorships. Yet Richelieu and Mazarin had bequeathed to Colbert a potent means through which to make his influence in local affairs felt: the person of the *intendant*.[116]

While the position of the *intendants*, as (venal) officials granted special, extraordinary powers revocable by the sovereign at will, is often held up as a great virtue, it was this very characteristic which allowed Colbert to turn provincial administration into yet another family enterprise. Thanks to Mazarin's patronage, three members of the Colbert family were already serving as *intendants* before 1661.[117] After that date, Colbert controlled directly the appointments to all intendancies other than those in the militarily sensitive frontier provinces, which were the domain of Le Tellier. Predictably, he used this power (as did Le Tellier)[118] to fill these posts entirely with family members and clients. Fifteen blood relatives or relations by marriage of the minister served as *intendants* up until his death in 1683.[119] Not without reason, Richard Bonney has called Colbert "the greatest nepotist in appointments to intendancies," and Marshall Turenne is said to have remarked that "M. Colbert was a godfather who never missed an opportunity to set up one of his own."[120] So much for the idea of *intendants* as ambitious young men of obscure background chosen on merit.

What role did Colbert wish these trusted associates to play in the provinces? In the 1630s and 1640s, opposition to the *intendants* had come from the fact that they had often acted solely as the agents of the central government, seeking to impose Paris's will on their *généralité* by force. Despite his high degree of personal control over the revived corps of *intendants*, Colbert did not intend to use them in this way. Instead, they were to be employed as the primary means of bringing about a *rapprochement* between the government and local elites.

The first way in which the *intendants* could do this was by providing information. Between 1663 and 1665, Colbert asked them to furnish

---

[116] It should be emphasized once again that the *intendants* were never the "new men" of legend. They were always chosen from among the *maîtres des requêtes*, a group of high venal magistrates with close family and institutional ties to the sovereign courts and who performed special duties for the king.

[117] Bonney, *Political Change*, p. 89.

[118] For an examination of the way in which Le Tellier used "personalist" methods like those of Colbert to bring order to a French army organized around the private ownership of military units, see: Thomas Ertman, "War and Statebuilding in Early Modern Europe," unpublished Ph.D. dissertation, Department of Sociology, Harvard University, 1990, pp. 257–264.

[119] Charles Engrand, "Clients du Roi. Les Colberts et l'Etat 1661–1715," in: Roland Mousnier (ed.), *Un Nouveau Colbert* (Paris: C.D.U. et SEDES réunis, 1985), pp. 85–97, here at p. 91.

[120] Bonney, *Political Change*, p. 89.

him with a detailed guide to the structure of local power in their area, with full details on family and patron/client ties.[121] He could then use this information to forge local alliances through the judicious use of government patronage, sometimes dispensed through the *intendant* and sometimes directly from Paris. In this way Colbert could, with the help of an *intendant* "on the ground," link a whole array of self-contained, provincial patron/client networks to his own broader, national network.

In Languedoc, for example, Colbert succeeded by the 1670s in breaking down a long-standing division into a pro- and an anti-Paris faction of the local elite. Financial links were forged between the two groups and then the new, composite group was tied to the center through close relations with the local *intendant*. The government-backed Mediterranean-Atlantic canal project also played an important role in this process of vertical and horizontal linkage.[122]

Another key function of the *intendants* also helped to promote elite integration and overall political stability: their involvement in direct tax collection. During the 1630s and 1640s, these officials had often been ordered to collect the *taille* by whatever means were necessary, even if this required calling in the army. This was not to occur after 1661, for Colbert realized that the use of force was counterproductive.[123] Instead, the *intendants* were to confine themselves to supervising the *trésoriers de France* and the *élus* in their task of assessing the *taille*, helping (or forcing) them to come up with an apportionment that balanced a range of competing local interests.

With an outside official present to mediate the contentious *taille* disputes as well as disputes between the local population and the tax farmers, a better flow of revenues to the receivers and receivers-general could be ensured. This in turn encouraged local elites to invest with the *comptables* who, as mentioned above, were most often part of a larger financial network centered on Paris. The case of Languedoc again shows that this possibility was more than just theoretical, as participation by nobles, officeholders, and local financiers in state finance increased markedly after 1660.[124]

While others might have believed that a fundamental and irreversible improvement had occurred in France as a result of his policies, Colbert

---

[121] Roger Mettam, *Power and Faction in Louis XIV's France* (Oxford: Basil Blackwell, 1988), pp. 58, 270; Arlette Lebigre, "Colbert et les Commissaires du Roi," in Mousnier, *Un Nouveau Colbert*, pp. 133–144, here at p. 135.

[122] William Beik, *Absolutism and Society in Seventeenth Century France: State Power and Provincial Aristocracy in Languedoc* (Cambridge: Cambridge University Press, 1985), pp. 241–243, 275–276, 292–297, 311–312.

[123] Mettam, *Power and Faction*, p. 279.

[124] Beik, *Absolutism and Society*, pp. 251, 257–258, 269–270.

was not taken in by his own propaganda. He realized that the pressures of a major war could undo what he had achieved, and so he opposed Louis's plan to invade Holland in 1672. Even Le Tellier counseled restraint,[125] and this conflict wound down substantially after 1673 and did not represent a real strain on French finances or organizational resources. On the whole, Colbert's methods were effective enough to get France through the 1670s and early 1680s with only three sales of *rentes* (1674, 1679, 1680), while income from the *parties casuelles* (sale of offices) dropped to a maximum of 9.6 million livres (1675), compared to over 140 million livres in the late 1630s.[126] The times of *affaires extraordinaires* seemed to be over. But France was soon to face a challenge which would expose all the weaknesses of Colbert's "reforms": prolonged war with England.

The Test of War, 1688–1714

In 1688, Louis plunged his country into a war with Britain and her allies that was to last until 1714, with only a brief respite in 1697–1702. No struggle has ever illustrated more starkly the qualitative difference between bureaucratic constitutionalism and patrimonial absolutism. Though her economy was only about half the size of France's during this period, Britain was able to throw nearly as much money as her rival into the war effort and raised this money with relative ease. By contrast, as the years wore on the French state was forced to resort to ever more extreme and politically counterproductive measures to produce the funds necessary to continue the conflict. As her navy collapsed and her armies suffered defeat after defeat, the limits of Colbert's "reforms" were clearly exposed for all to see.

If the country was to have any hope of sustaining a war that had to be waged on three and even four fronts (Low Countries, Spain, Germany, Italy) and at sea, vast amounts of revenue would be required. Spending during the 1670s had been running at about 128 million livres per annum on average, and this figure had been pushed up to the 148 million livres level between 1680 and 1688, though not without the sale of about 70 million livres in new *rentes* by Colbert's successor Le Peletier.[127]

---

[125] Paul Sonnino, *Louis XIV and the Origins of the Dutch War* (Cambridge: Cambridge University Press, 1988), pp. 6–7.

[126] Albert Hamscher, *The Parlement of Paris after the Fronde 1653–1673* (Pittsburgh: University of Pittsburgh Press, 1976), p. 80; Göhring, *Aemterkäuflichkeit*, p. 170; Bonney, *King's Debts*, p. 312.

[127] Alain Guéry, "Les Finances de la Monarchie Française sous l'Ancien Régime," *Annales*, vol, 33, no. 2 (Mars–Avril 1978), pp. 216–239, here at p. 237, drawing on the figures

Since French national output may have been as high as 2.7 billion livres per year around the turn of the century,[128] there would seem to have been ample room for a substantial increase in government expenditure during the wars. Yet spending could be raised to an average annual level of only 234 million livres between 1689 and 1699, and 278 million between 1702 and 1715, respectively 8.7% and 10.3% of national output, and even this required the most extreme exertions.[129] Britain, by contrast, was able to lift government expenditure from 4.2% of national output (1687) to 11.4% (1690s) and then 14% (1700s) with almost effortless ease, and when she left the war in 1713, her fiscal potential was far from exhausted.[130] The gap between French and British wartime financial performance was to grow with every successive conflict during the 18th century.

It was surely the nature of the French state which lay at the root of its inability to mobilize resources more effectively. A comparison with the way things were done across the Channel will illustrate this clearly. In Britain after 1689, the war effort was a subject of constant debate in Parliament. Such debate allowed a consensus to be formed among the political classes, as well as among the population at large, on war aims and strategy. MPs, permitted for the first time since the Commonwealth to participate directly in the making of military and foreign policy, were in turn willing to vote substantial tax increases to pay for the war, and the general public, kept well informed of developments both in Parliament and on the battlefield, readily paid them.

The situation in France was quite different. The decision to embark on a major European conflict in 1688 (and to renew that conflict in 1702), lay entirely with Louis and a handful of his advisers. The French populace had repeatedly shown in the 1630s and 1640s that there were clear limits to its willingness to pay for foreign adventures and wars of conquest. The king and his ministers had learned this lesson well, and so they made little effort to raise either direct or indirect taxes during

of Mallet. To Guéry's expenditure totals must be added the amounts paid out as *charges*, i.e., the salaries of *officiers* and the interest on *rentes*. Partial figures for *charges* can be found in: Clamageran, *Histoire*, vol. II, p. 616; vol. III, p. 19. For the data on *rentes*, A. Vührer, *Histoire de la Dette Publique en France* (Paris: Berger-Levrault, 1886), p. 116.

[128] James C. Riley, *The Seven Years War and the Old Regime in France* (Princeton: Princeton University Press, 1986), p. 22.

[129] Guéry, "Les Finances," p. 237; Clamageran, *Histoire*, vol. III, pp. 19, 44, 48, 117–119.

[130] Phyllis Deane and W. A. Cole, *British Economic Growth 1688–1959* (Cambridge: Cambridge University Press, 1967), p. 2; B. R. Mitchell and Phyllis Deane, *Abstract of British Historical Statistics* (Cambridge: Cambridge University Press, 1962), p. 389, for data on British national output and government expenditure. It should be noted that national output figures for Britain and (even more) France in the 18th century are highly approximate, though they improve as the century progresses.

the first five years of the war. Both *tailles* and *fermes* revenues were actually lower in 1694 than they had been in 1684.[131] Unable to meet the costs of its ambitions through taxes, the government turned to more dubious, and in the long run equally dangerous, sources of income.

Between 1689 and 1694, three principal means were used to close the yawning gap between regular tax revenue and expenditure, variously estimated at between 54 and 69 million livres per year:[132] the creation of new *rentes*, currency debasement, and *affaires extraordinaires*. *Rentes perpétuelles* with a capital value of 21.6 million livres were sold in 1689, and further *émissions* totaling 62.4 million occurred in 1691, 1692, and 1693.[133] In addition, 1689 saw the first sales, albeit in small quantities, of *rentes viagères* or life annuities, a form of borrowing that would have fatal consequences for the French monarchy in the next century.[134] Thus over 90 million livres were raised through *rentes* during the first five years of the war. In addition, the government earned 60 million livres in profits by twice devaluing (1690 and 1693) the French currency, an ancient practice that, as always, was to have very disruptive economic consequences.[135]

Both these expedients were overshadowed, however, by the income from so-called *affaires extraordinaires*. Each *affaire* entailed a contract (*traité*) between the government and a syndicate of financiers (*traitants*) which granted to the latter the right to raise money in a certain way in return for a cash advance. Between 1689 and 1694, contracts were

---

[131] Clamageran, *Histoire*, vol. III, pp. 8–9.

[132] The lower estimate is based on Guéry, "Les Finances," p. 237, and the higher on Clamageran, *Histoire*, vol. III, p. 21.

[133] Clamageran, *Histoire*, vol. III, p. 26. Philippe Sagnac, in his article "Le Crédit d'Etat et les Banquiers à la Fin du XVII⁰ et au Commencement du XVIII⁰ Siècle," *Revue d'histoire moderne et contemporaine*, vol. 10, no. 4–5 (Juin-Juillet 1908), pp. 257–272, cites figures that are somewhat lower and also less convincing.

[134] As the name implies, interest on *rentes viagères* was not paid in perpetuity, as was the case with the older *rentes perpétuelles*, but only for life. As a result, they carried a rate of interest that was usually twice as high as that of other *rentes*. The catch here is that the lender could make continued payment of interest dependent on the life of anyone he chose. Thus a 50-year-old *parlementaire* could purchase a *rente viagère* of 1,000 livres and designate his 5-year-old grandson as the "life." As long as the *parlementaire* or his heirs could produce proof that the grandson was still alive, they would continue to receive interest payments. While *rentes viagères* possessed the advantage of being self-extinguishing, and thus more favorable to the state in the long run, they could also lead to substantially higher debt charges in the short or medium term unless different rates of interest were paid on "lives" of different ages. Although the French government took this elementary precaution in 1689 and 1693, it was often forced in later years, as a consequence of its poor credit rating, to pay the same interest to all "lives" in order to attract investors. This borrowing strategy ultimately had disastrous consequences, as we shall see. For a clear and concise discussion of *rentes viagères*, see Luethy, *La Banque Protestante*, vol. II, pp. 470–475.

[135] Clamageran, *Histoire*, vol. III, pp. 26–27.

signed totaling about 250 million livres, in return for which the state
was to receive advances of 192 million livres, an interest rate of 23%.
Over 80% of these contracts involved the sale of new offices and the
extraction of forced loans (*augmentation de gages*)[136] from existing officeholders.[137]

In the usual manner, a whole range of new, and unnecessary, offices
was created within all of the sovereign courts, both in Paris and the
provinces, and in the regional and local tribunals like the *bureaux de
finances* and *présidiaux*. In 1692, one of the last nonvenal corners of the
French state – municipal government – was put on the auction block
as the positions of mayor and town councillor were made hereditary
and sold.

Finally, a host of entirely absurd offices were created, including official burial announcer, barrel roller, and wall and room inspector. As the
contrôleur général Pontchartrain is said to have told Louis XIV when
asked how he expected to sell such wares, "Each time that Your Majesty
creates an office, the Lord God creates a fool to buy it." Yet such
purchasers were not complete fools, for though not all offices carried
salaries with them, almost all included the right to collect fees. Furthermore, their holders often gained valuable privileges, such as the acquisition of nobility and exemption from a range of taxes and from the
duty of billetting soldiers.[138]

For those not willing to purchase an office to gain such privileges,
the government also offered them for sale directly. In 1691 and 1692,
countless patents of nobility were sold, and in 1693 and 1694, lifetime
exemptions from the *taille* were offered to the inhabitants of certain
provinces.[139] It is hard to imagine a more desperate or short-sighted
financial policy, as the French state both burdened itself in perpetuity
with heavy payments (interest on *rentes* and *gages*) and sold off sources
of future revenue for small short-term gains. And 11 years of war still
lay ahead.

In 1694, the Estates of Languedoc, the country's most important
remaining representative institution, suggested that only a graduated,

---

[136] An *augmentation* was the payment of an additional capital sum to the government (or,
more precisely, to a *traitant*) by an officeholder, which in turn entitled him to receive
a somewhat higher salary (*gages*) thereafter. Sometimes the purchase of *augmentation*
was voluntary, but most often the *officiers* had no choice in the matter.

[137] Clamageran, *Histoire*, vol. III, p. 23. Bonney, *King's Debts*, p. 316, provides partial
figures that are somewhat lower, but cites the same rate of interest. Precision in all
such matters has been rendered all but impossible by 18th-century fires in the *Cour
des Comptes* and the office of the *contrôleur général* which destroyed the bulk of the
ancien régime's financial documents.

[138] Göhring, *Aemterkäuflichkeit*, pp. 172–181.

[139] Clamageran, *Histoire*, vol. III, p. 25.

universal direct tax of the kind that they had often voted for their own province could solve France's financial problems. Despite the strong resistance of Pontchartrain, a new tax, the *capitation*, was introduced in 1695. The population was divided into 22 categories according to rank, with the highest group asked to pay 2,000 livres and the lowest 1 livre. Despite the promising nature of this tax, the authorities allowed the usual range of special arrangements, reductions, and evasions for those with influence, and the total net return barely reached 18 million livres per annum.[140] The experience of the *capitation* was to be repeated over and over again during the next century, as every attempt to introduce a new, more just direct tax was undermined or discredited by a culture of privilege, influence, and profiteering deeply embedded in the ancien régime.

The financial situation faced by the French government from 1695 until the end of the War of the Spanish Succession in 1714 was indeed desperate. The events surrounding the *capitation* reinforced a lesson previously learned in the 1630s and 1640s: the political structure of France, characterized as it was by pervasive privilege and the absence of a national representative body, simply ruled out the possibility that large-scale warfare might be paid for through broad-based tax increases. The only other option was to force payment from those groups whose own futures depended on the survival of the ancien régime state: the officeholders and financiers. Colbert's policies implied that this could best be done by providing favorable investment conditions and a good measure of security. The pressures of war rendered his successors unwilling to try persuasion: after 1695, they turned increasingly to outright coercion.

The raw numbers for 1695–1715 are frightening enough in themselves: 505.7 million livres in *affaires extraordinaires* (of which 380 million livres actually reached the state), more than 41 alterations in the value of the currency yielding about 70 million livres in profits, and the creation of a mountain of new *rentes* with a capital value of over 1.26 *billion* livres.[141] What these numbers do not reveal is the extent to which the government was willing to use trickery and even force against its potentially most loyal supporters in order to meet its financial needs.

Those at the lower end of the administrative hierarchy were the easiest to exploit. The government often created a host of minor offices which it then threatened to suppress "in the interest of the public" unless the officeholders paid additional sums. In 1702 and 1703, those

---

[140] Marcel Marion, *Histoire Financière de la France depuis 1715* (Paris: Arthur Rousseau, 1914), vol. I, pp. 10–12; Clamageran, *Histoire*, vol. III, pp. 31–41.
[141] Bonney, *King's Debts*, p. 316; Clamageran, *Histoire*, vol. III, pp. 46–47, 107–109.

officiers liable to taxation were offered the opportunity to purchase exemptions from the *taille*, and many did so. Then in 1705, the government promptly canceled all privileges attached to offices worth under 4,000 livres. For an additional fee, of course, these privileges could be bought back.[142]

There was naturally a limit to the benefits that could be gained from such chicanery, for the owners of minor offices were people of modest means. To arrive at the enormous sums which it needed, the government had to take on more powerful groups. As the market in offices dried up, many of the sovereign courts were forced to buy up, or "incorporate," unsold positions themselves. At the same time, the purchase of *augmentations de gages* ceased to be a matter of choice. In 1701, *officiers* were forced to take up 9 million livres in *augmentation* under threat of exclusion from the *paulette*. In the years which followed, intendants were instructed to allow the *traitants* who had farmed the *augmentations* to take legal action against recalcitrant officials. In numerous cases, their property was seized and auctioned off, with the proceeds turned over to the financiers. The most egregious weapon used in this guerrilla war between the government and the *officiers* was the writ of solidarity, which held all members of a judicial or administrative corps legally responsible for the *augmentation* payments of any of its members.[143]

As if these humiliations were not enough, the government also could not resist the temptation to manipulate the *rentes* upon which the material well-being of so many officials depended. In 1701, during the brief period of peace between the two wars, the *contrôleur général* Chamillart unilaterally reduced the interest on the oldest *rentes*, the *rentes sur l'Hôtel de Ville*, from 5.5% to 5%. In 1709, the payment of *rente* interest was suspended and, the following year, the rate of interest on all *rentes* lowered to 5%. In 1713, with over two years of interest outstanding, the *contrôleur général* Desmarets decided to take drastic action. The capital on many categories of *rentes*, especially those purchased since 1689, was forcibly reduced by between 25% and 40%, and the interest rate again lowered to 4%, thereby saving the state 14 million livres in annual payments.[144] There can be little doubt that these actions taken by the government against many of its highest officeholders had a lasting impact. The spirit of trust, mutual respect, and cooperation

---

[142] Göhring, *Aemterkäuflichkeit*, pp. 202, 217–219.

[143] Adolphe Vuitry, *Le Désordre des Finances et les Excès de la Spéculation à la Fin du Règne de Louis XIV et au Commencement du Règne de Louis XV* (Paris: Calman Levy, 1885), pp. 49–50; Göhring, *Aemterkäuflichkeit*, pp. 223–227; Marcel Marion, *Dictionnaire des Institutions de la France aux XVIIᵉ at XVIIIᵉ Siècles* (Paris: Picard, 1984), pp. 29–30.

[144] Sagnac, "Le Crédit de L'Etat," pp. 260–261; Clamageran, *Histoire*, vol. III, pp. 110–111.

which Colbert had sought to foster was now gone, and the traumatic experiences of the war years were to live on forever after in the collective memory of the country's magistrates.

The disappearance of exploitive fiscal measures between 1661 and 1689 seems to have left the *officiers* ill prepared to defend their rights and privileges during the Nine Years War and the War of the Spanish Succession. They were not to repeat this mistake again. Throughout the remaining decades of the ancien régime, the body of officeholders, with the *parlementaires* at their head, strongly resisted any changes that they saw as a threat to their position. Their determined obstructionism and attacks on royal "despotism" were seriously to constrain the government's ability to finance the wars in which France became involved after 1741. And when real reformers were finally given their chance, they found in the *parlements* their most dedicated opponents. During the 1690s and 1700s, the French Crown had indeed one time too many abused those upon whom its future depended.

GEOPOLITICAL PRESSURES, THE FAILURE OF REFORM, AND
THE END OF PATRIMONIAL ABSOLUTISM, 1715–1791

In the decades following the death of Louis XIV in 1715, the French state proved itself incapable of responding effectively to the lessons of the War of the Spanish Sucession. When the military setbacks and financial burdens of the War of the Austrian Sucession (1741–1748) and the Seven Years War (1756–1763) finally gave statesmen with radical ideas their chance, it was already too late. With depressing predictability, the reform attempts of Terray and Maupeou, Turgot and, most importantly, Necker were subverted by court intrigue and the opposition of *parlementaires* and financiers. Enduring structural reform within the confines of absolutism proved to be an impossibility, and the costs of relentless military pressure from a modernized British state eventually drove the French government to countenance political change as a way out of its intractable financial problems.

In the end, the revival of a national representative body in the form of the Estates General/Constituent Assembly allowed the reformers of 1789–1791 to succeed where Terray and Necker had previously failed. An institutional force was now in place which was powerful enough, thanks in part to the pressure of the streets, to defeat the *noblesse d'état* ("state nobility" – Paul Ardascheff)[145] of officeholders, financiers, and *rentiers* which in the past had proved invincible. Within less than two years, the entire character of the French state apparatus was transformed.

---

[145] Paul Ardascheff, *Les Intendents de Province sous Louis XVI* (Paris: Félix Alcan, 1909).

Proprietary officeholding, "inside" credit, and military entrepreneurship were replaced in short order by a salaried professional bureaucracy, a centralized system of direct financial administration, and a nonvenal army and navy.

It was not absolutism, but rather the end of absolutism that brought the modern state to France. The revolution which the Constituent Assembly wrought on the French state apparatus remained unaffected by the many changes of regime between 1792 and 1815, with one fundamental exception. While France's new bureaucratic infrastructure proved strong enough to survive the decline of representative institutions over the next two decades, the same was not true of the fledgling system of public finance inaugurated by the Revolution. Only after 1815, when a representative assembly finally became a permanent part of the French state, could an effective system of public credit similar to that of Britain become a reality.

War and Attempts at Real Reform

From the death of the Regent in 1723 until 1741, France enjoyed a period of almost uninterrupted peace and prosperity. The new chief minister, Cardinal Fleury, took advantage of these favorable circumstances to restore in its entirety the old, Colbertian financial system built around "inside" credit and tax farming. The General Farms were reconstituted and reorganized in 1726, just in time to profit from a new upsurge in growth. As revenue from indirect taxes rose in tandem with economic expansion, the farmers became an ever more important source of short-term, and later, long-term credit for the government.[146] The *comptables* also continued in their role as sources of large advances to the Crown. The *billets* and *rescriptions* issued by farmers and receivers, the only short-term papers to survive Louis XIV's wars with their reputation intact, had now become a normal, and increasingly central, part of the system of government finance. By 1741, France at last possessed a fully articulated and unique system of *private* government finance, in which the fiscal health and immediate financial needs of western Europe's biggest state depended wholly on the credit of a group of independent, largely unsupervised businessmen.[147]

The stage was now set for the final drama of the ancien régime. Despite the long success of both Fleury and his British counterpart

---

[146] Matthews, *Royal General Farms*, pp. 80–81, pp. 248ff.
[147] John Bosher, *French Finances 1770–1795* (Cambridge: Cambridge University Press, 1970), provides a detailed description (pp. 67–111) of the *comptables* and their activities in mid-18th-century France.

Walpole at maintaining peace, it was inevitable, given France's geopolitical position and interests, that France would someday become involved in another series of conflicts with Britain and its allies. When France entered the War of the Austrian Succession in 1741, the government benefited from a higher degree of political and financial maneuverability than it was ever again to enjoy, thanks to nearly 20 years of relative peace and fiscal retrenchment. By the time it was over in 1748, this new conflict had cost the government a colossal 757 million livres, only about half of which could be covered by new taxes.[148] The positive benefits of several decades of fiscal prudence had been entirely squandered on this foreign adventure.

After a respite of barely eight years, France then became embroiled in one of the West's first truly global struggles, the Seven Years War. This conflict, fought in Europe, India, and North America, cost between 1.1 and 1.3 billion livres, or nearly 50% more than the previous one.[149] This time, when the Crown moved to double and triple the hated *vingtième* to help pay for the war, the *parlements*, now joined by the *cour des aides* and *cour des comptes*, were ready. Remonstrance followed remonstrance and, despite the great threat to the kingdom posed by repeated British victories, the king could only force registration of tax increases with the help of *lits de justice*.[150] As a result, taxes could cover barely 29% of the war's costs, leaving some 64% to be made up by the same range of loans employed during the previous war.[151]

The inevitable consequence of such heavy borrowing, especially when much of it took the form of self-amortizing loans, was to increase the state's annual burden of debt charges nearly two and a half times in less than 15 years, from 85 million livres in 1753 to 196 million in the late 1760s.[152] This last figure was more than 26 million livres higher than the total of *all* the French Crown's net revenues in 1769. As a result, by the end of that year all tax receipts for 1770 and a portion of those for 1770 had already been anticipated. France stood once again on the verge of bankruptcy.[153]

The severe fiscal crisis which now confronted Louis XVs government was only the most tangible manifestation of a much deeper, structural

---

[148] Michel Morineau, "Budget de l'Etat et gestion des finances royales en France au dix-huitième siècle," *Revue Historique*, vol. 264, no. 536 (Octobre–Décembre 1980), pp. 289–336, here at 304–305.

[149] The lower figure is Morineau's, "Budgets de l'Etat," p. 307; the higher, Riley's *Seven Years War*, pp. 140–141.

[150] Jean Égret, *Louis XV et l'Opposition Parlementaire* (Paris: Armand Colin, 1970), pp. 76–79, 103–110; Riley, *Seven Years War*, pp. 143, 210–213.

[151] Ibid., p. 142; Clamageran, *Histoire*, vol. III, pp. 331–333, 355–356, 369.

[152] Riley, *Seven Years War*, pp. 178, 184.

[153] Marion, *Histoire Financière*, vol. I, pp. 245–246.

crisis of the French state. As the 18th century wore on it became increasingly clear that France's patrimonial administrative, financial, and military infrastructure was incapable, even in its "rationalized," Colbertian incarnation, of standing up over the long term to the military challenge posed by a modernizing British state. While the French armed forces might on occasion, thanks to talented leadership, acquit themselves well, the cumulative fiscal burden of large-scale conflict was crushing the ancien régime beneath it.

It was the very nature of patrimonial absolutism itself which rendered France incapable, despite its great aggregrate wealth and population, of meeting the costs of great power status. The system of patrimonial absolutism debilitated the country in three closely related ways. First, the high degree of autonomy enjoyed by proprietary officeholders in the prinicipal ministries, as well as the special position of the court, placed sharp limits on the ability of a *contrôleur général* to reduce absolute levels of government spending, even if he sincerely desired to do so. Under ordinary circumstances he did not of course desire to do so, for state expenditure was an invaluable weapon in the influence-driven politics of the ancien régime.

Second, if proprietary officeholding combined with patron-client relationships left little room for budget cuts, the political influence enjoyed by the *noblesse d'état* and other privileged groups rendered an expansion of the tax base, the other logical response to increased fiscal demands, all but impossible. Following the severe abuse of officeholders which had occurred under Louis XIV, the *parlementaires* of the late 18th century were determined to protect their social status by doggedly resisting any and every tax reform or permanent tax increase. If France wished to continue to challenge Britain on land and at sea, others would have to pay the bill.

Finally, the ancien régime's combined system of revenue collection and short-term finance, built around the twin institutions of "inside" credit and tax farming, meant that the government was not even capable of fully exploiting the inequitable and irrational tax base it did possess. The collection process itself was inefficient and riddled with corruption, but that was the least of the state's problems. During the 1770s, over *40%* of the revenues actually declared by farmers and *comptables* had to be given back to them in the form of interest and reimbursement for expenses. In 1773, for example, the total net government revenue on gross tax receipts of 375 million livres was only 215 million livres.[154]

---

[154] Eugene White, "Was There a Solution to the Ancien Régime's Financial Dilemma?" *Journal of Economic History*, vol. 49, no. 3 (September 1989), pp. 545–568, here at pp. 550, 552.

Over the previous century and a half, geopolitical pressures had combined with financial crisis to produce several attempts – most notably those of Sully and Colbert – to "reform" the French state. After 1770, the double shock of military defeat and severe fiscal crisis created an atmosphere conducive to radical action. Three successive ministries – those of Terray and Maupeou, Turgot, and Necker – dared for the first time to attack the private control of state functions directly in order to save the country from financial ruin. In the end, all three were defeated and their achievements reversed. This demonstrated in an unequivocal fashion that without firm institutional support from outside the central executive, partisans of modernizing reform would never overcome those vested interests supporting patrimonial absolutism, no matter how dire the straits in which France found itself.

When the ministerial team of Terray (*contrôleur général*) and Maupeou took effective control of the government in late 1769, France was on the verge of financial collapse. Terray's initial response to this situation was all too familiar: repayment of capital on various loans was stopped, interest on *rentes* was forcibly reduced and, most drastic of all, payment was suspended on the promissory notes issued by the receivers general and the farmers general.[155]

But this time, the government attempted to do more than just declare a partial bankruptcy. When a conflict between the Crown and the Parlement of Paris over a long-running political case came to a head in late 1770, one of Maupeou's advisors urged him to seize the opportunity and eliminate the powerful judiciary body, for decades the major impediment to tax reform. Maupeou did just this, replacing the *parlements* of both Paris and the provinces with a new system of superior courts staffed by salaried, nonvenal magistrates. The ancient tax court, the *cour des aides*, was done away with altogether.[156] This "coup" was certainly the most stunning blow dealt to the *noblesse d'état* during the life of the ancien régime, for the sovereign courts had always been the most eloquent defenders of patrimonial interests. They also stood at the center of a complex alliance system linking financial, military, and administrative elites. Terray responded by declaring a portion of the *vingtième*, France's most equitable tax, permanent, while at the same time attempting to ensure a more accurate valuation of the property on which it was based.[157]

---

[155] Marion, *Histoire Financière*, vol. I, pp. 251–256. The most famous victim of this suspension of payments on *rescriptions* and *billets* was Voltaire, who claimed to have lost 200,000 livres thereby.

[156] Durand Echeverria, *The Maupeou Revolution* (Baton Rouge: Louisiana State University Press, 1985), pp. 15–19; William Doyle, *The Parlement of Bordeaux and the End of the Old Régime 1771–1790* (London: Ernest Benn, 1974), pp. 146–147.

[157] Marion, *Histoire Financière*, vol. I, pp. 264–271.

Yet from the moment the *parlements* were abolished in 1771, the *noblesse d'état* orchestrated a fierce campaign against the measure, accusing the ministry of harboring designs to impose despotism on France. When Louis XV suddenly died in 1774, opponents of Terray and Maupeou within the court were able to use this public pressure to persuade the new king, the ill-fated Louis XVI, to restore the old sovereign courts with all their rights and privileges intact.[158] This episode illustrates in a striking manner that real tax reform was politically impossible under absolutism.

With the return of the *parlements* in 1774, the prospects for large-scale, permanent tax increases as a solution to France's financial problems once again receded. Ironically, by closing off this particular escape route the proprietary officeholders and their allies simply encouraged even more radical attempts at structural reform. For Terray's replacement as *contrôleur général* was none other than the economist Turgot, whom the court faction around Maurepas had recruited for its ministerial "team." Turgot's answer to the country's fiscal problems is well known: increase economic growth, and hence government revenue, by removing counterproductive restrictions on trade and noisome feudal privileges. To ensure that the fisc would in fact benefit from economic expansion, improvements in the system of revenue collection would also be needed. Finally, the elimination of wasteful and extravagant spending would free up funds which could then be used for debt reduction.[159]

During his brief tenure in office, Turgot was able to put much of his "minimum program" into practice. The grain trade was freed in 1774, the unnecessary office of alternative receiver of the *taille* abolished, and closer government control over the farmers general introduced. There is evidence that the abolition of the general farm was an important long-term goal of Turgot, but that he was constrained from realizing this goal by the large sums which the Crown still owed to the farmers.[160] In addition, Turgot does seem to have been able to achieve a small surplus on the ordinary budget through his cost-cutting measures, though he was undoubtedly helped in this by the fact that the new war minister, St. Germain, had just embarked on an economy drive of his own.[161]

In 1776, Turgot attempted to proceed with a second stage of more radical economic and social reforms, proposing to abolish the guilds,

---

[158] Echeverria, *Maupeou Revolution*, pp. 28–34.
[159] Ernest Lavisse, *Histoire de la France depuis les Origines jusqu'à la Révolution* (Paris: Hachette, 1911), vol. IX, pt. 1, p. 25; Marion, *Histoire Financière*, vol. I, pp. 280–281.
[160] Matthews, *Royal General Farms*, pp. 256–257.
[161] White, "Was There a Solution," p. 556, cites contemporary sources which claim that Turgot achieved a surplus of 51 million livres in 1775 and 7 million livres in 1776, and then goes on to argue that other evidence lends credence to such assertions.

do away with a range of feudal obligations, and replace the *corvée* with a contribution for road construction to be paid by all, including nobles and members of the clergy. The Parlement of Paris, predictably antagonized by this last measure, refused to register the minister's reforming edicts and placed itself at the head of the general attack on Turgot's program, an attack which had been initiated by financiers angered by his tamperings in the area of revenue collection. This elite pressure was then exploited by the court opponents of the *contrôleur général* and of his ex-patron Maurepas to destroy the former's standing with the king. Turgot further contributed to his own downfall by opposing French intervention in the American war, a policy advocated by the foreign minister, Vergennes, on the grounds that it would bring certain financial ruin.[162] In May 1776, the reformer suffered the same fate as Terray and Maupeou and was dismissed.

By 1776, then, a shifting alliance of rival politicians, courtiers, proprietary officeholders, and financiers had defeated the reform efforts of first Terray and Maupeou and then Turgot, and had largely reversed most of their achievements. As a result, the financial problems of the French monarchy remained unsolved. While economy measures had largely halted the growth of ordinary expenditure after 1770, debt service charges absorbed at least 42%, and probably closer to 50%, of ordinary gross revenue.[163] To this figure must be added the minimum 14–17% of gross revenues retained by the tax farmers and receivers to cover their collection costs.[164]

The Last Hope: Necker

It was in such a fiscal climate that the French government decided to embark upon a policy of intervention in the American Revolution, a policy which led to open warfare with Britain in 1778. If expenditures for military preparation and rearmament are included, this war cost France between 1 and 1.3 billion livres.[165] It is hardly surprising that under the circumstances Louis XVI decided to confide the task of financing this conflict to a prominent Swiss banker, Jacques Necker.[166]

---

[162] Lavisse, *Histoire*, vol. IX, pt. 1, pp. 30–31, 39–41, 46–51; Marion, *Histoire Financière*, vol. I, p. 289.
[163] Morineau, "Budgets de l'Etat," pp. 308–309.
[164] Reilly, *Seven Years War*, pp. 61–62. The 40% difference between gross and net tax revenues cited above (footnote 154) includes both collection costs and interest and principal repaid to farmers and *comptables* for short-term advances made by them to the government.
[165] Morineau, "Budgets de l'Etat," p. 312; Robert Harris, *Necker: Reform Statesman of the Ancien Régime* (Berkeley: University of California Press, 1979), p. 118.
[166] Robert Harris, "French Finances and the American War, 1777–1783," *Journal of Modern History*, vol. 48, no. 2 (June 1976), pp. 233–258, here at p. 243.

Necker's views on war finance were relatively straightforward. He believed that the least economically damaging way to pay for a major conflict was to borrow most of the extraordinary revenue needed, while at the same time setting aside sufficient permanent, *ordinary* revenue to cover the new debt charges generated by this wartime borrowing.[167] This was of course precisely the approach used by France's rival Britain to finance its 18th-century wars. But the key question here was *where* the ordinary revenue needed to pay off the costs of war was to come from, a question rendered all the more urgent in the French case by the fact that existing ordinary revenues were barely capable of meeting past debt charges, let alone new ones. In Britain, Parliament would simply have "funded" the new debt by voting a new tax designed to meet interest payments for a specific loan. This option was of course not available in France. What were the alternatives?

The experiences of Terray and Turgot had already demonstrated that it was politically impossible either to increase permanently the existing level of taxation or to impose new taxes on the privileged. Yet Necker was convinced that there was another way to find the money needed to pay for the loans he was about to solicit: radical administrative reform. If a system of financial administration similar to the one found in Britain could be introduced into France, the permanent savings that would accrue to the government would be substantial.[168] The creation of a single treasury would allow for effective monitoring of state expenditure, leading to the elimination of waste and fraud. The management of short-term credit by such an agency would reduce the costs of borrowing. Finally, the "nationalization" of revenue collection along British lines would raise the percentage of gross tax receipts actually available to the Crown.

The strategy embarked upon by Necker was one fraught with risks: if his reforms failed to produce the necessary savings, the government would be left with a mountain of new financial obligations which it would be unable to meet. Yet with an audacity that only someone from outside the charmed circle of the political elite could muster, Necker set out to transform some of the most basic features of the French state apparatus. His reforms touched upon four basic areas of financial administration: revenue collection, revenue disbursement, short-term credit, and overall coordination and control of state finances.[169]

---

[167] Luethy, *La Banque Protestante*, vol. II, p. 468; also White, "Was There a Solution," p. 558.

[168] Harris, "French Finances," pp. 243–244; idem, *Necker*, pp. 123–124.

[169] Unless otherwise noted, this discussion of Necker's reforms is based upon the pioneering work on this subject, John Bosher's *French Finances*, pp. 142–165. A shorter account of Necker's reforming plans and their implementation can also be found in

As stated earlier, at the center of the ancien régime's financial system as it developed after 1648 stood a small and closely knit group of officeholder-financiers or *comptables*. As receivers they were the key figures in the collection of a good portion of the Crown's revenue, as treasurers and "payers" they were in charge of spending that revenue, and in both roles they provided the government with much of its short-term credit, advancing funds on future tax receipts or meeting the demands of creditors on the king's behalf when the latter lacked sufficient cash resources.[170] In order to make such advances to the Crown, the *comptables* themselves had to borrow from the wider public, and their ability to do so was based on their personal credit and that of the clan or financial network with which they were associated. In the crucial sphere of short-term finance, then, there was really no such thing as public credit under the ancien régime, only the collective private credit of several hundred financiers which the government was permitted to use, but at a very high price.[171]

In order to undermine this system, Necker took several crucial steps. First, he sought to break the power of the treasurer-financiers by eliminating nearly 500 such positions and transforming the remaining treasurers, one for every major department, from independent officeholder-financiers into salaried officials directly answerable to the *contrôleur général*.[172] In addition, he eliminated the 48 receivers general, probably France's most powerful financiers, and placed the collection of direct taxes under a *régie* headed by 12 salaried government commissioners, who now administered a single consolidated revenue fund, the *recette général*, rather than the 24 separate *caisses* of the old receivers.[173] Necker also reorganized the collection of a range of minor royal revenues and

the same author's "Jacques Necker et l'État Moderne," *Report of the Canadian Historical Association*, 1963, pp. 162–175.

[170] The farmers general played a role within the French financial system similar to that played by the receivers general of the *taille*, but their legal status was somewhat different since they acted together as a company, rather than as independent officeholders administering a single tax or spending fund (a *caisse*), as was the case with the *comptables*.

[171] Bosher, *French Finances*, pp. 6, 100.

[172] Bosher, *French Finances*, pp. 148–150; Henri Legohérel, *Les Trésoriers de la Marine (1517–1788)* (Paris: Editions Cujas, 1965), pp. 338–339. Necker's actual title was not *contrôleur général* but first "director of the royal treasury," and then (from June 1777) "director general of finances," though he was in fact in charge of the *contrôleur général*'s office. It was Necker's Protestant faith that precluded him from receiving the more illustrious title. See Harris, *Necker*, pp. 104–105.

[173] Bosher, *French Finances*, pp. 161–162. A *régie* was a method of revenue collection midway between direct administration and a tax farm. Though the collection process itself was directed by a board of salaried commissioners, those commissioners received extra premiums from the government if the total revenue collected exceeded a given target figure. See ibid., pp. 157–158 and Harris, *Necker*, pp. 139–140; also Marion, *Dictionnaire*, p. 477.

of the income from the royal demesne, both of which had previously been farmed, into two other *régies*, while at the same time abolishing 506 superfluous offices responsible for demesne administration.[174]

Yet if this replacement of proprietary *comptables* by salaried officials in the areas of revenue disbursement and collection was to be truly effective, it would have to be accompanied by measures to transform the *contrôleur général*'s office into an effective agency of oversight and coordination. Prior to the advent of Necker, this office was largely incapable of performing such functions, for its six departments were each the private domain of a venal *intendant de finance* who hired, fired, and paid his own employees and acted independently of the *contrôleur général*. In 1777, Necker suppressed the *intendants* and restaffed their departments with government employees operating under a senior civil servant, a *premier commis*, who was in turn answerable to the *contrôleur général*.[175]

Necker then proceeded to make use of this new bureaucratic instrument, a kind of embryonic French Treasury, for three purposes. First, he demanded regular monthly statements of their accounts from all treasurers and receivers. This allowed the *contrôleur général* for the first time to construct, on a regular basis, an accurate picture of the overall state of French finances. Armed with this information, he could direct the flow of funds from the various revenue treasuries (still unconsolidated) to the departmental paymasters in the most efficient manner possible, thus preventing the *comptables* from making speculative use of idle funds and saving the government the cost of unnecessary short-term borrowing.[176]

Second, Necker also attempted to impose some degree of central control over the credit operations of both the departmental treasurers and the new *régies* by requiring them to seek the approval of his office before issuing promissory notes or other credit instruments and by declaring that henceforth all such notes would be backed by the Crown, not just by the personal credit of the *comptable* in question. In this way, Necker sought to take the first step towards centralizing all short-term credit required by the government in the hands of a single treasury, and removing it from the purview of individual financiers ensconced within the French financial administration.[177]

Third, Necker made use of his enhanced institutional position and capacities in order to eliminate unnecessary or wasteful spending and thus free up funds to meet interest payments. Since it was impossible

[174] Bosher, *French Finances*, pp. 157–160; Harris, *Necker*, pp. 140–142.
[175] Bosher, "Jacques Necker," pp. 165–166; Harris, *Necker*, pp. 104–105.
[176] Bosher, "Jacques Necker," pp. 168–169; idem, *French Finances*, pp. 153–155; Harris, *Necker*, pp. 112–116.
[177] Bosher, *French Finances*, p. 155; Legohérel, *Les Trésoriers*, p. 339.

to impose greater financial discipline on the military during wartime, the areas that Necker chose to attack were also among the most politically sensitive: the expenses of the royal family and the pensions paid by the Crown to powerful individuals. Through administrative centralization and stubborn persistence, the latter were reduced from an average annual level of 35.2 million livres in the late 1770s to 28 million livres in 1781. In addition, 2 to 2.5 million livres were eliminated from the budget for the royal household, mainly by focusing on the spending of lesser members of the royal family.[178]

The fundamental question here, however, is whether Necker actually succeeded in producing sufficient savings to cover the long-term costs of financing the American War. Though the truth is always difficult to determine with absolute certainty in matters of ancien régime finance, the latest research supports Necker's own assertions, made after his dismissal, that he did in fact do so.[179] In a memorial written in April 1787, he purported to show that his structural reforms had freed up a total of 84.5 million livres through a combination of expenditure reductions and increases in net revenue. It was these "ameliorations" that had allowed the ordinary budget deficit to be reduced from 23–24 million livres in 1776 to 5.5 million in 1778, to zero in 1779, and finally to a surplus of 2.9 million livres in 1781 despite the new debt charges which the war had generated.[180]

This accomplishment was all the more remarkable considering the high price which the French Crown had to pay for long-term credit during the American War. By 1776, investors were no longer willing to purchase the traditional *rentes perpétuelles* at 4% interest, as the failure of a loan issue launched by Terray in 1770 clearly showed. As a result, Necker was only able to attract the 530 million livres in long-term loans which he raised to finance the war by selling self-amortizing *rentes viagères* and lottery loans which cost the government between 8 and 11% a year in debt charges.[181] James Riley has calculated that France was paying an average interest rate of 8.7% on long-term loans during the American War at a time was Britain was borrowing even larger sums at between 3.7 and 4.9%.[182]

[178] Harris, *Necker*, pp. 107–109, 153; idem, "French Finances," p. 245.
[179] Necker is supported by Harris ["Necker's *Compte Rendu* of 1781: A Reconsideration," *Journal of Modern History*, vol. 42, no. 2 (June 1970), pp. 161–183, and idem, "French Finances," p. 246] and by White ["Was There a Solution," pp. 553, 559], against the attacks of older authorities like Marion, *Histoire Financière*, vol. I, pp. 332–335.
[180] Harris, *Necker*, pp. 153–159, which contains a complete list of all "ameliorations"; idem, "French Finances," pp. 244–245; White, "Was There a Solution," p. 553.
[181] Luethy, *La Banque Protestante*, vol. II, pp. 468–472; Harris, *Necker*, pp. 124–136.
[182] James Riley, *International Government Finance and the Amsterdam Capital Market 1740–1815* (Cambridge: Cambridge University Press, 1980), pp. 110–111, 125.

It seems reasonable to agree with Eugene White, then, that if Necker had been permitted to stay in office and at the very least defend the reforms he had already introduced, France would have been able to avoid the great financial crisis of 1786–1789.[183] But the point here is that under conditions of patrimonial absolutism Necker could not remain in office and his reforms could not succeed. No institutional counterweight existed to the powerful elite groups, hurt by his reforms, who intrigued to have him removed. By 1781, a coalition of financiers, proprietary officceholders, and disgruntled members of the royal family had formed an opposition group which was powerful enough to remove him *despite* the tangible increase in French financial (and hence military) capacities which he had achieved.[184]

Over the next six years, Necker's successors Joly de Fleury, D'Ormesson, and Calonne proceeded to reverse nearly all of the Swiss banker's reforms. Many of the old offices of treasurer and *payeur* were recreated and sold to leading financiers; the *recette générale* was dissolved and control over direct tax collection returned to the 48 receivers-general; dominance over the departments of the *contrôle général* was restored to the resuscitated *intendants de finance*; and all *comptables* were given the freedom once more to manage their *caisses* and issue credit as they sought fit.[185] Proprietary officeholding and "inside" credit had triumphed once again and, almost overnight, France found herself back in the 1760s.

This time, however, the situation was far worse than it had been in the aftermath of the Seven Years War, for the reversal of Necker's reforms also meant the evaporation of his "ameliorations," the resources designated to meet the costs of the American War loans. The result was a rapid deterioration of the state of the ordinary budget. In 1782, that budget had been in surplus, but by the end of the war in 1783, it already was in deficit. Under Calonne, these deficits grew larger every year, exceeding 85 million livres in 1786, a direct result of both the return to the old financial system and of what Marion has termed Calonne's "prodigality" in the disbursement of royal gifts and pensions to the powerful.[186] In the financial sphere at least, absolutist France was about to reach the end of the line. After one last attempt at radical reform under Loménie de Brienne was defeated by an unlikely alliance of *parlementaires* and financiers opposed to any fundamental change and *patriotes* and *nationaux* who claimed that political liberalization was a prerequisite for lasting reform, the state fell into de facto bankruptcy

---

[183] White, "Was There a Solution," passim.
[184] Harris, *Necker*, pp. 193, 197–198, 237–240; Bosher, *French Finances*, pp. 165–173.
[185] Bosher, *French Finances*, pp. 36, 166, 180–182. Legohérel, *Les Trésoriers*, pp. 343–347.
[186] White, "Was There a Solution," pp. 550–551, 562; Marion, *Histoire Financière*, vol. I, pp. 359–360.

by the summer of 1788. Only under these circumstances could Louis XVI finally be persuaded to convoke a meeting of the Estates General for May 1, 1789.[187]

The Return of Representative Institutions and Successful Reform

Almost from the moment they reconstituted themselves as first the National Assembly and then the National Constituent Assembly, the members of the Estates General set out with alacrity to realize the sweeping modernization of the old régime's administrative and financial structure that had been demanded in so many *cahiers de doléances*. With one of its first and most famous acts the Assembly destroyed with one blow the very foundations of patrimonial absolutism and initiated the process that Theda Skocpol has termed "the birth of the 'modern state edifice' in France."[188] For its decree of August 11, 1789, not only swept away a whole range of feudal practices, but also abolished proprietary officeholding and the entire system of social and legal inequality based on the existence of three estates, each with their own rights and privileges.[189] While proprietary officeholding had of course stood at the heart of the old state apparatus, the persistence of a society of orders had also acted as a powerful impediment to administrative modernization by undermining all attempts to build organizational hierarchies based solely on function.[190]

With the central pillars of patrimonial absolutism now removed, the men of the Assembly, as represented above all in its constitutional, tax, and finance committees, could set about constructing a new state apparatus. They were guided in this task by three principal sets of concerns, which were to inform all of the structural reforms of the coming years. First, the new administrative organs were to be manned by salaried, professional officials selected for their abilities irrespective of social origin or family connections. Second, this new corps of civil servants was to be organized in the most efficient and rational way possible so that the entire public administration functioned like a well-oiled machine.[191]

---

[187] John Bosher, *The French Revolution* (New York: Norton, 1988), pp. 111–112, 114–116, 120; William Doyle, *Origins of the French Revolution*, 2nd ed. (Oxford: Oxford University Press, 1988), pp. 109–110, 112–114.

[188] Theda Skocpol, *States and Social Revolutions* (Cambridge: Cambridge University Press, 1979), pp. 174–205, especially pp. 179, 198–202.

[189] Doyle, *Origins*, pp. 207, 209.

[190] It was Weber who first identified status leveling as a prerequisite for the development of modern (as opposed to patrimonial) bureaucracy. See Max Weber, *Economy and Society* (Berkeley: University of California Press, 1978), pp. 983–984, 1002, 1081. See also Bosher, *French Finances*, pp. 282–283; and idem, *French Revolution*, pp. 248–249.

[191] Bosher, *French Revolution*, pp. 246–248.

Finally, the revolutionaries were obsessed with the danger posed to
the new bureaucratic order posed by "corruption." They saw this threat
of corruption as emanating from two distinct directions. On the one
hand, individuals or larger groups might exploit their positions for
private gain, an endemic phenomenom under the ancien régime. On
the other hand, the central executive might try to use the powers vested
within it to undermine the independence and impartiality of public
servants for its own political ends, as the French believed was common
in Britain. The Assembly and its successors looked to strict legislative
oversight of administration and finance and the aggressive application
of public scrutiny as effective defenses against both dangers.[192]

Over the course of the next two years, these concerns helped guide
the Assembly in the immense task of building a modern state apparatus
in place of the old patrimonial one. Unfortunately, only a brief summary of this remarkable process can be presented here. Its principal
features, in addition to the move from a proprietary to a salaried,
nonproprietary bureaucracy mentioned above, were: the introduction
of a new, equitable system of direct and indirect taxation and tax collection (August 1789–March 1791); the centralization and nationalization of short-term government credit (December 1789–September
1790); the creation of a uniform framework for regional administration built around 83 *départements* (January 1790); the separation of
royal from public finances through the inauguration of a civil list (June
1790); the founding of a national treasury with control over both receipts and expenditures (March 1791); and finally, the reorganization
of the executive around a cabinet and six ministries (April 1791).[193]

Of all of these reforms, those pertaining to financial administration
were of special significance, given the experience of the ancien régime
in this area. On the one hand, the tax and finance committees of the
Assembly, working together with Bertrand Dufresne, a former *premier
commis* under Necker, set about the task of creating a single central
treasury into which all revenues would flow and from which all expenses would be paid. This was largely accomplished by March 1791,
but the task of eliminating all former *comptables* dragged on until 1796,
when the *payeurs des rentes* were finally dismissed.[194]

Yet the public treasury thus created was not really the equivalent of
the British Treasury. Fearful of the political consequences of such a

---

[192] Bosher, *French Finances*, pp. 228–229, 309–312; Clive Church, *Revolution and Red Tape:
The French Ministerial Bureaucracy 1770–1850* (Oxford: Clarendon, 1981), pp. 50–51.
[193] The best short overview of these reforms can be found in: Hans Haussherr, *Verwaltungseinheit und Ressorttrennung* (Berlin: Akademie Verlag, 1953), pp. 172–185, and
Bosher, *French Revolution*, pp. 251–266. Bosher, *French Finances*, pp. 215–275, and
Marion, *Histoire Financière*, vol. II provide more detailed accounts.
[194] Bosher, *French Finances*, pp. 220–224.

concentration of financial power, the Assembly had divided responsibility for fiscal matters between the *trésor* and a ministry of public contributions charged with managing the new public tax and customs services. While the latter was clearly to be part of the executive, the former was to be a nonpolitical, purely technical agency, managed by an official or officials named by the executive but closely watched by both a standing committee of the legislature and an independent bureau of accounts, which had been created in September 1791 to replace the old *cour des comptes*. All of these safeguards were designed to ensure that public finances would be managed for the public good, rather than for party-political or private ends, and the independence of the treasury was largely preserved until the advent of Napoleon.[195]

Indeed, it was the return to a new kind of absolutism under Napoleon, not the radicalization of 1792–1795, that posed the greatest threat to the achievements of the revolution in the sphere of state organization. Quite surprisingly, the period of intense revolutionary mobilization had played a positive role in consolidating the state apparatus constructed between 1787 and 1791. Despite the political upheavals of the Terror, the structure of administration and finance remained little changed. At the same time, the intense pressures of war, when combined with the oversight and vigilance exercised by the Convention and its committees, furthered the development of formalized lines of command and written operating procedures within a bureaucracy that was expanding by leaps and bounds. Such pressures also led to the creation of an entirely new kind of army based upon universal military service.[196]

With the return to monocratic government after 1800, however, war had a markedly different effect upon the French state. The independence of the treasury was undermined and the position of minister downgraded to the old role of executor of the monarch's will. More ominously still, Napoleon chose to meet the vast costs of his far-flung wars not by rebuilding the system of public credit, admittedly shaken by *assignat* inflation, but rather by turning once again to the financiers and contractors whom the revolutionaries had driven from the public sphere.[197] It was only Waterloo and the return to a system of government with surprising parallels to that of 1791 which put an end to this creeping reappropriation of the French state and allowed the modernizing reforms of the Assembly to be permanently institutionalized.[198]

---

[195] Ibid., pp. 224–230, 244, 247–252; Haussherr, *Verwaltungseinheit*, pp. 176–181.
[196] Church, *Revolution*, pp. 69–74, 94–99, 311.
[197] Haussherr, *Verwaltungseinheit*, pp. 186–187; Bosher, *French Finances*, pp. 315–316; Michel Bruguière, *Gestionnaires et Profiteurs de la Révolution* (Paris: Olivier Orban, 1986), pp. 146–155.
[198] Haussherr, *Verwaltungseinheit*, p. 188.

CONCLUSION

As presented in this and the previous chapter, the picture of state development in Latin Europe during the medieval and early modern periods is quite different from the one found in the standard state-building literature. While war and geopolitical pressures more generally may have fostered the expansion of states in this area in terms of absolute size, it certainly encouraged neither rationalization in the Weberian sense nor the creation of proto-modern institutions. Such institutions arose in Latin Europe not as a result of a slow, evolutionary process of innovation, reform, and refinement under conditions of international competition, but rather in the wake of violent political upheaval or (in the case of most Latin countries other than France) foreign conquest and occupation.

What was in fact "rationalized" and "reformed" over the many centuries from the 1200s onward was a patrimonial state form wholly different in its logic and organizing principles from the rational-bureaucratic state of 19th-century Europe. Under patrimonial absolutism, the pursuit of private interest and advantage was not structured so as to produce something approaching collectively positive outcomes in the political sphere. Rather, the pursuit of private interests was fundamentally at odds with attempts to rebuild the kind of *public* institutions and authority based on an institutionalized distinction between the public and the private – between the office and the officeholder, state and private finances and property, national armed forces and private security services, and public justice and the exercise of naked domination by the powerful and influential – that had been present at least in embryo under the Roman Empire and, albeit in diluted form, for several centuries after its demise. The Roman state, like many states today, may have been corrupt, meaning that private interests may have subverted the prescribed operation of public institutions. However, such corruption must be sharply distinguished from a set of practices which converted public or proto-public offices into permanently private property, thereby subverting not the norms of behavior thought proper for a public official, but the very notion of a public official itself. Likewise, the current practice of privatizing certain basic services as a way of bringing greater efficiency to a huge state apparatus organized along rational-legal lines has nothing in common with privatizing state revenue collection or national defense as a *substitute* for building such an apparatus.

As we have seen, such "appropriating" practices came to be embedded across Latin Europe because at the time they were first introduced (1200s–1400s), they represented the most effective way available of solving the massive administrative, financial, and military problems that the rulers of this region so precociously confronted because of the early onset of sustained geopolitical competition. Once in place, these practices proved relatively successful, at least in the short and medium term, in increasing and maintaining military capacities. Any attempt to replace them would have involved the politically costly task of overcoming the resistance of vested interests that only grew stronger as war swelled the ranks of proprietary officeholders and rendered the state increasingly dependent on the financiers. It is hardly surprising, then, that under constant pressure to put armies in the field (and navies to sea), monarchs and their ministers consistently chose to try to "rationalize" what Weber would call patrimonialist institutions, rather than replace them altogether, even if this replacement would in the end have resulted in tremendous efficiency gains.

Was the triumph of appropriation inevitable, given the early onset of geopolitical competition and large-scale statebuilding in Latin Europe? No, as the case of England will show. There, the presence of a quasi-permanent, national representative body standing outside the central government eventually forced the latter to replace "patrimonial" arrangements with "public" ones in the interest of national defense. As shown earlier, the representative institutions of medieval Latin Europe also exhibited a consistent and well-documented opposition to proprietary officeholding and financial subcontracting.

Yet the Estates of Latin Europe were never able to play the role that the English Parliament did. They were unable to do so, I have argued, because they were burdened by the legacy of the early appearance (500s–600s) and subsequent disintegration of large-scale states built upon a well-preserved Roman sociopolitical infrastructure. The failure of dark age statebuilding across Latin Europe meant that the new kingdoms which arose in this area after the turn of the millennium were encumbered with fragmented local political landscapes which led resident ecclesiastical, noble, and urban elites to organize themselves along status, rather than geographic, lines. As a result, the national representative assemblies which the region's rulers called into being between the 12th and 14th centuries were not the robust, territorially based bodies found in England, Poland, and Hungary, but rather structurally weaker, status-based Estates which ultimately proved unable to resist the steady advance of royal power. After Latin Europe's aggressive monarchs had first undermined and then abolished their Estates over the course of the 16th and 17th centuries, there was nothing to stop the forward march of "irrationalization" fueled by constant warfare so graphically embodied in the case of ancien régime France. The British case will show, however, that even for early statebuilders an alternative route to institutional modernization did indeed exist.

Chapter 4

BUREAUCRATIC CONSTITUTIONALISM
IN BRITAIN

It would be difficult to find a greater contrast than that between the patrimonial absolutism of 18th-century France and its Latin neighbors and the bureaucratic constitutionalism of France's great geopolitical rival, Britain.[1] The absolutist rulers of Latin Europe could legislate, tax, and conduct foreign policy as they saw fit, unconstrained by national representative assemblies; whereas in Britain, the monarch, though still influential, had lost many of his effective powers to a Parliament without whose approval no new laws could be passed, revenue raised, or wars begun. State infrastructures in Latin Europe were built around proprietary officeholding, "inside" credit, and tax farming; while Britain possessed a set of core administrative, financial, and military departments numbering close to 10,000 employees[2] organized along modern bureaucratic lines, and an entirely market-based system of public finance. Finally, Latin Europe's confused patchwork of local administrative districts overseen by competing proprietary officials constrasts sharply with an orderly pattern of 52 English and Welsh and 33 Scottish counties enjoying a substantial degree of self-government.

Certain similarities can of course be found between these two disparate state types, most notably the survival within Britain of isolated pockets of proprietary officeholding within the Exchequer and the royal household. Yet on the whole, the two types do seem to represent polar opposites within the world of early modern Europe. This is all the more remarkable given that England shared many common historical experiences with the countries of Latin Europe. Like them it had been part of the Roman Empire, and during the Anglo-Saxon period had maintained significant cultural ties with the Carolingian realm. Furthermore, England was conquered and ruled for many centuries by a French nobility with substantial possessions and interests on the other side of the Channel.

---

[1] Although the "British" state was created in 1707 by the union of England and Wales with Scotland, for simplicity's sake I will use this term only to refer to the post-1714 period.

[2] John Brewer, *The Sinews of Power* (London: Unwin Hyman, 1989), p. 66.

What accounts for this unexpectedly divergent outcome to the process of medieval and early modern political development in these two regions? As argued in Chapter 1, the answer lies in the fact that the states of Latin Europe were built atop the ruins of that region's failed dark age polities (the Carolingian, Umayyad, and Byzantine empires), which left them with a highly fragmented local political landscape. Such a landscape forced statebuilding rulers attempting to integrate their domains to send out multi-purpose royal officials from the center in order to reassert royal prerogatives in a nonparticipatory manner vis-à-vis powerful local lords, churchmen, and municipalities. Within the British isles, by contrast, no such large-scale, neo-Roman state had ever arisen. The new English kingdom was thus constructed upon "virgin territory," unencumbered by the legacy of unsuccessful dark age statebuilding. The most tangible consequence of this very different pattern of state formation was the presence in England (and later in Scotland) of territorially integrated local government built around the participatory political communities of the shire and hundred. The shires would in turn be reinforced and their competences extended by the Norman and Angevin conquerors, who came to view these communities not as obstacles to, but as effective instruments of, centralized royal control.

The arrival of the Normans and the Angevins, with their extensive holdings on the continent, soon plunged England into a pattern of conflict with its neighbor France (and with Scotland) that would persist for many centuries to come. The early onset of sustained geopolitical competion, which affected both England and the polities of Latin Europe, provoked the construction, as early as the 1100s, of specialized organs of administration, finance, and justice (Chancery, Exchequer, central law courts). Shortly thereafter, during the course of the 1200s, the rising cost of warfare also led (as on the continent) to the emergence of a national representative assembly, the English Parliament. Unlike the Estates of Latin Europe, however, this body was not organized into three *curiae*, each representing a distinct social order. Rather, the English Parliament consisted of one chamber containing both the peers and leading churchmen of the realm, and a second consisting of the chosen representatives of both the shire communities and the towns.

While the divergent circumstances surrounding state formation in England and in Latin Europe may have resulted in the appearance in the two regions of very different kinds of representative assemblies, the common experience of early geopolitical competition, and the early state expansion that resulted therefrom, meant that the island kingdom was condemned to make use of the same appropriation-prone institutions (proprietary officeholding, tax farming, "inside" credit, military entrepreneurship) that would come to dominate the state apparatus in

France, Iberia, and Italy. Yet the presence at the heart of the English polity of a stronger, territorially based Parliament largely hostile to these institutions helped check their growth somewhat during the 1300s and early 1400s. With the end of the Hundred Years War in 1453, however, parliamentary meetings became shorter and less frequent. As a result, patrimonial practices became ever more entrenched under the rule of the Tudors and early Stuarts. Indeed, the ubiquity of such practices, and the repeated financial crises they helped provoke, proved to be an important factor in sparking off the English civil war in 1641–1642.

While parliamentary victory in that conflict brought with it the first steps towards the replacement of both proprietary officeholding and tax farming, these changes were largely reversed at the Restoration. However, regular, nearly annual meetings of a newly self-confident Parliament after 1660 transformed that body into a third key independent variable determining the path of English development by allowing it to lend decisive support to reformers within the central government. These reformers, responding to renewed geopolitical pressures, moved to break the predominance of appropriation-prone institutions and methods in order to build a revitalized, nonproprietary fiscal-military apparatus and a market-based system of public finance capable of withstanding the tremendous military and political challenges of the period 1688 to 1714. It was this newly bureaucratic and irreversibly parliamentary British state which, through its seemingly limitless ability to mobilize resources for war, drove its rival, ancien régime France, inexorably towards bankruptcy and revolution over the course of the 18th century.

UNENCUMBERED STATE FORMATION, EARLY GEOPOLITICAL
PRESSURE, AND A PRECOCIOUS ATTEMPT AT SHARED RULE,
C. 400–1453

During the centuries in which the great realms of the Visigoths, Umayyads, Lombards, and Franks held sway in Latin Europe, the former Roman province of Britain was divided into numerous small-scale kingdoms linked only by the common Church which had first brought Christianity to the Angles, Saxons, and Jutes during the course of the 7th century. Yet the most enterprising Anglo-Saxon rulers, those of Wessex, turned this backwardness to their advantage by borrowing the latest "technologies of rule" from their more advanced Carolingian neighbors and using them, during the course of a century-long struggle with the Scandinavians of the Danelaw, to unify the country under their aegis (954). In completing this historic enterprise, the West Saxon kings benefited from the "advantage of the latecomer," for they were able to build their new realm around rurally based local political communities (the shires and hundreds) at precisely the moment (the late 900s) when just such communities were disintegrating in the older Carolingian polity. Furthermore, at a time when the first stirrings of economic expansion based on competitive markets were undermining the last remnants of public authority across Latin Europe, the West Saxon monarchs were enjoying the profits of a state-led program of market encouragement and deregulation.

The Norman conquest of a recently united England soon involved that country in a series of conflicts with France that were to persist, on and off, until 1453 and were to transform England into a statebuilding pioneer. It was during the greatest of these conflicts, the Hundred Years War, that the distinctive English pattern of "shared rule" between a strong, sophisticated central government and self-confident shire communities represented in Parliament made its first, precocious appearance. These shire communities, through their chosen delegates, successively claimed the right not only to approve new taxes, but also to participate in any modification of the "common law" which they had helped to create in the shire and hundred courts. At the same time, the protracted struggle against France also led to a massive increase in the use of appropriation-prone administrative, financial, and military methods which, despite persistent opposition from the nascent House of Commons, were to become ever more entrenched over the next several centuries.

Foundations of Participatory Local Government

Like its neighbors in Latin Europe, Britain had been part of the Roman Empire. Yet this outlying province, poorer and even more weakly urbanized than northern Gaul, was among the first areas in the West to be abandoned by the imperial government. Following the destruction of the British garrison during the usurper Constantine III's struggle for power (407–411), the authorities in Ravenna were unable to send any fresh troops to defend the island. Several decades later, a savage civil war broke out between the remaining Romano-British elites and Saxon federates who had earlier settled in the southeast of the country. This civil war ended with the complete destruction of the remaining Roman sociopolitical infrastructure throughout the province. By the late 400s, *civitates*, villas, spoken Latin and Christianity had all virtually disappeared, and with them the possibility of constructing a single, large-scale, post-Roman successor state in Britain like those that were about to arise in Italy, Spain, and Gaul.[3]

Into the vacuum created by the end of Roman life and rule in this

---

[3] J. N. L. Myres, *The English Settlements* (Oxford: Clarendon, 1986), pp. 202–219; Richard Hodges, *The Anglo-Saxon Achievement* (London: Duckworth, 1989), p. 186; D. J. V. Fisher, *The Anglo-Saxon Age c. 400–1042* (London: Longman, 1973), pp. 5–7.

erstwhile province came a wave of Germanic invaders who brought with them their own language, customs, and forms of social organization. Like the remaining Celtic population, which was concentrated in the western and northern periphery of Britain, these new settlers created a number of small-scale polities over the course of the late 400s and 500s. As a result, the island may have numbered as many as 30 distinct political units in the early 7th century, though the traditional "heptarchy" (seven kingdoms) of Essex, Sussex, Wessex (Saxons), Kent (Jutes), and East Anglia, Mercia, and Northumbria (Angles) already dominated much of the area that would later become England. Initially, these polities were pagan, for Christianity was only introduced following the outside initiative of Pope Gregory the Great, who in 597 sent the monk Augustine on a mission to Kent. Because the impetus for this mission came from Rome, it was possible over the course of the next century to construct a single, relatively independent English Church embracing all of the heptarchy. Once in place, that Church would play a decisive role in creating a sense of cultural unity among the Anglo-Saxon peoples, thus paving the way for their eventual political unification.[4]

Although first the Northumbrians and later the Mercians were able to establish a kind of hegemony over the other Anglo-Saxon realms during the 600s and 700s, the real drive to create a single English kingdom of the kind promoted by the Church only began after the Viking invasion and settlement of the 9th century. The first raids on Britain took place in the 830s, and in 865 a large Viking army arrived in East Anglia and succeeded in subjugating most of the country before the West Saxon king Alfred stopped its advance at Edington in 878. Wessex, then, would be the base from which the slow reconquest of the Danelaw (Scandinavian-controlled East Anglia, East Mercia, Northumbria) would proceed, a process brought to a preliminary conclusion when Alfred's grandson Eadred won the Norwegian kingdom of York from Eric Bloodaxe in 954.[5] It was during the course of this conflict that, under West Saxon leadership, a single polity was formed. In this as in many other ways, developments in late-forming England were distinctly out of phase with those in Latin Europe. Whereas Viking incursions helped tear the Carolingian Empire apart, across the channel they provided the stimulus necessary to bring the Anglo-Saxons together.[6]

---

[4]   Fisher, *Anglo-Saxon Age*, pp. 108–113; Hodges, *Anglo-Saxon Achievement*, p. 191; Roger Collins, *Early Medieval Europe 300–1000* (New York: St. Martin's, 1991), pp. 162–174; H. R. Loyn, *The Governance of Anglo-Saxon England 500–1087* (London: Edward Arnold, 1984), pp. 5, 60.
[5]   Fisher, *Anglo-Saxon Age*, pp. 236–249; Collins, *Early Medieval Europe*, pp. 326–332.
[6]   Malcolm Barber, *The Two Cities: Medieval Europe 1050–1320* (London: Routledge, 1992), p. 309.

A further irony here is that the West Saxon kings probably could never have accomplished this task without "technical assistance" from the Carolingians. Wessex already contained shires as early as the 700s, but John Campbell has recently argued – though his views are still a matter of some controversy – that it was the influence of the Carolingian county which allowed these vaguely defined districts to be transformed into effective units of local government during the course of the 800s and early 900s.[7] As the West Saxons extended their control first over the rest of southern England and then over the Danelaw, shires (and their subdivisions, hundreds) were systematically introduced, often centered around a royal fortification. As a result, the whole country up to the Tees and Mersey rivers was covered with such districts by the late 900s.[8]

Like the county, the shire was initially headed by an influential nobleman, the ealdorman, appointed by the king and answerable directly to him. This English cousin of the count, who was sometimes assisted by the local bishop, was responsible for calling out and commanding the shire levy, overseeing the collection of royal revenues and, most important of all, presiding over the twice annual meetings of the local freemen at which pressing problems were discussed, taxes assessed, disputes settled, and serious criminal cases tried in the shire court. Royal orders were transmitted to the shires by means of writs, vernacular-language documents prepared at court and authenticated with the king's seal and designed to be read out to the shire assembly. In a notable advance over the Carolingians, the Anglo-Saxon king Aethelred (978–1016) came increasingly to replace the ealdorman as head of the shire with a humbler royal official, the sheriff (shire-reeve), thereby diminishing the danger that the shire might fall victim to aristocratic appropriation of the kind so common in Latin Europe.[9]

As mentioned above, both shire and county were subdivided into smaller units called "hundreds" (a literal translation of the Carolingian *centenae*) whose free inhabitants were responsible for apprehending criminals, deciding lesser criminal and civil cases in the hundred court (held every four weeks), collecting taxes, and in general meeting the

[7] For the new thinking on the influence of Carolingian practices upon Anglo-Saxon government, see the seminal articles by James Campbell, "Observations on English Government from the Tenth to the Twelfth Centuries," and: "The Significance of the Anglo-Norman State in the Administrative History of Western Europe," both in: idem, *Essays in Anglo-Saxon History* (London: Hambledon Press, 1986), pp. 155–170, 171–189.

[8] Loyn, *Governance*, pp. 53–56, 135–137; F. M. Stenton, *Anglo-Saxon England*, 3rd ed. (Oxford: Clarendon, 1971), p. 294; Fisher, *Anglo-Saxon Age*, pp. 255–257.

[9] Loyn, *Governance*, pp. 67–68, 113–117, 133–140; Stenton, *Anglo-Saxon England*, pp. 297–299, 548–550; Fisher, *Anglo-Saxon Age*, pp. 258–260, 310.

military and fiscal obligations imposed upon them by the shire or the central authorities. Boroughs, nearly all of which were royal, were organized in a similar way to hundreds, complete with their own local courts.[10] Local government, first in Wessex and latter in the whole of a united England, was a collaborative venture involving royal officials, local notables, and the entire free (male) population of the shire, hundred, or borough acting in accordance with royal directives and legislation as well as the "folk law" preserved in the collective memory of the area.

Central government also exhibited clear signs of Frankish influence. West Saxon monarchs from Alfred (871–899) onward, building on the Carolingian models borrowed from the late 8th-century Mercian kings, adopted an explicitly theocratic model of rulership symbolized by the ceremony of anointment which Charlemagne's father Pippin had first undergone in 751.[11] The council (witan or *curia regis*) was similarly the principal forum for royal decisionmaking. Like the Carolingians, the kings of Wessex promulgated legislation (including extensive written law codes like that of Alfred) and enacted other solemn business at enlarged versions of this council (the witangemot) which included the ecclesiastical and lay magnates and important officials of the realm. Their households consisted of the same traditional officials (stewards, butlers, chamberlains) assisted by a clerical writing office, and a group of personal retainers with more than a passing resemblance to the *vassi dominici* (here known as king's thegns) made up the backbone of their armies.[12] Finally, Carolingian methods of land tax assessment and collection by shires and hundreds were used beginning in 991 to raise the huge sums of money, the Danegeld, needed to buy off a new wave of Viking raiders.[13]

The fact that Anglo-Saxon kings were able to raise impressive amounts of revenue in coin during the late 10th and 11th centuries was the direct consequence of a state-led program of economic development using imported methods and technologies which the West Saxon kings initiated beginning in the late 800s. During the 700s and early 800s,

[10] Loyn, *Governance*, pp. 140–154; Fisher, *Anglo-Saxon Age*, p. 258; Campbell, "Observations on English Government," pp. 159, 161–162; idem, "Significance of the Anglo-Norman State," p. 182.

[11] Hodges, *Anglo-Saxon Achievement*, pp. 117, 121–131, 142, 152, 193–195; Loyn, *Governance*, pp. 63, 85–90; Fisher, *Anglo-Saxon Age*, pp. 227–234, 280.

[12] Loyn, *Governance*, pp. 95–107, 165–166; Fisher, *Anglo-Saxon Age*, pp. 252–254, 260–265; Bryce Lyon and A. E. Verhulst, *Medieval Finance: A Comparison of Financial Institutions in Northwestern Europe* (Providence: Brown University Press, 1967), pp. 53, 79, 82.

[13] Campbell, "Observations on English Government," pp. 159–160; idem, "Significance of the Anglo-Norman State," pp. 179–180, 183–184; Loyn, *Governance*, pp. 120–121, 139; Fisher, *Anglo-Saxon Age*, pp. 257–258, 306; Stenton, *Anglo-Saxon England*, pp. 376, 412–413.

the rulers of Mercia, Wessex, and the smaller polities of the heptarchy had imitated the Franks and encouraged commercial contacts with the continent through tightly regulated monopoly emporia like Hamwic and Ipswich. Like their Frankish counterparts Dorestad and Quentovic, however, these towns had suffered from the marked decline in northern European trade which began in the 820s (see Chapter 2).[14]

Faced with limited possibilities for profit through international commerce and in need of money to pursue the war against the Scandinavians, Alfred and his successors chose to stimulate their domestic economy through a massive program of urban expansion. At the same time, a currency reform modeled on those of Charlemagne was carried out. Its aim was to produce enough coins of sufficiently small denomination so that money could once again be used as the normal medium of exchange. In addition, a number of Carolingian craft innovations (single-flue kiln, pottery kick-wheel, warp-weighted loom, carbonized steel) were introduced into the country and urban-based craft production encouraged.[15] As a result of these policies, during the course of the 10th century "[t]he monopolistic market systems and periodic fairs of Middle Saxon England were largely replaced by a hierarchy of ranked, competitive market-places."[16] The Danes of the north, perhaps driven by the need to keep up with their Anglo-Saxon rivals, seem to have adopted a similar set of policies, liberally imitating both the West Saxons and the Franks in matters of town building, monetary policy, and craft technology. The growth of towns and trade in both parts of England also helped reinforce a pattern of agricultural and demographic expansion already underway by 900, half a century before the economic recovery in Latin Europe began.[17]

It was this Anglo-Saxon state, slowly constructed – in a land now free from Roman influence – around the interaction between a strong central government and the consolidated local political communities of the shires, that William the Conqueror inherited in 1066. The Normans, whose own polity was similarly organized along neo-Carolingian lines, were familiar with the operation of shires and hundreds through their own counties and *centenae*.[18] They quickly moved to consolidate their hold over these cornerstones of the old English polity by appointing

[14] Hodges, *Anglo-Saxon Achievement*, pp. 76–104, 119, 133–135, 192–194.
[15] Hodges, *Anglo-Saxon Achievement*, pp. 141–142, 155–165, 200; Campbell, "Observations on English Government," pp. 155–158, 160–161; Loyn, *Governance*, pp. 122–126.
[16] Hodges, *Anglo-Saxon Achievement*, p. 166. Hodges has gone so far as to call this development "the first English industrial revolution."
[17] Ibid., pp. 156–162, 166–168, 176–178.
[18] Indeed, they called the shires "counties" and both names have been used interchangeably ever since.

their own men as sheriffs and building imposing royal castles at the center of every shire from which these officials could exercise their authority. Yet, as surprising as this may seem, the participatory pattern of shire and hundred political life that had developed under the Anglo-Saxons continued after 1066 with little or no alteration. Even the difficulties caused by the arrival of an alien warrior elite were soon overcome by the intermarriage of prominent local Norman and English families. Indeed, over the next two centuries the cooperation of Norman/Angevin elites and the (free) English population in shire and hundred courts would help to forge a "common law" of conqueror and conquered that would set England apart even more firmly from its continental neighbors.[19]

Geopolitical Competition and the Growth of the State Apparatus

The advent of the Normans and their Angevin successors to the throne of this powerful, centralized Anglo-Saxon polity plunged England of necessity into a state of endemic conflict with the Capetian kings of France, for the extensive holdings of the Norman and Angevin rulers in Normandy, Anjou, and Aquitaine represented a mortal threat to a French kingdom which was only just beginning to recover from the decline of the past 200 years. Sustained geopolitical pressure in turn led to a remarkable expansion and internal differentiation of the English state's administrative, financial, and judicial infrastructure over the course of the 1100s and 1200s. Thus one of the West's newest states was also among the first to embark upon a qualitatively and quantitatively new phase in political development under the influence of foreign entanglements.

The driving force behind these statebuilding innovations was the need for money to support both the knights raised on the basis of feudal obligations and the mercenaries whom the Norman kings regularly employed from the Conquest onward. The easiest way to increase government revenues was through more effective and capable administration of the very considerable sources of royal revenue: income from the king's demesnes, feudal incidences (impositions that could be demanded under certain circumstances from royal vassals), and judicial fees. During the reigns of Henry I (1100–1135), who conquered Normandy from

---

[19] Stenton, *Anglo-Saxon England*, pp. 683–687; Loyn, *Governance*, pp. 176, 195–197; N. J. G. Pounds, *The Medieval Castle in England and Wales* (Cambridge: Cambridge University Press, 1990), pp. 6–11, 57–59; W. L. Warren, *The Governance of Norman and Angevin England 1086–1272* (London: Edward Arnold, 1987), pp. 25–27, 30–31; R. C. van Caenegem, *The Birth of the English Common Law*, 2nd ed. (Cambridge: Cambridge University Press, 1988), pp. 5, 13–15, 85–110.

his brother Robert in 1106 and remained heavily involved in continental politics thereafter, and his grandson Henry II (1154–1189), ruler of England, Normandy, Anjou, and Aquitaine, a large-scale reorganization of the English state took place in the interest of heightened efficiency. Following the Conquest, the Anglo-Saxon writing office was upgraded to the status of a chancery, overseen by a chancellor who was usually an important bishop. Over the course of the 12th century this administrative nerve center, responsible for drawing up royal writs and charters, took on an ever larger staff of trained clerics and developed procedures that allowed it to function smoothly without direct supervision from its frequently absent head. By about 1200, the chancery had become a sedentary department, permanently lodged with its ever-expanding archives at Westminster.[20]

It was over this same period that England came to acquire a specialized treasury, the Exchequer, separated from a still-itinerant royal household. Even before the Conquest, income in coin had been deposited in Winchester, and Henry I appointed a treasurer to oversee these funds. More importantly still, from about 1110 this treasurer, aided by a number of prominent household officials, began to audit on a regular basis the accounts of the sheriffs who were charged with collecting most of the royal revenues in the shires. The results of such audits were recorded for reference purposes in documents known as pipe rolls. It was from these beginnings that the Exchequer arose, and the business of guarding, disbursing, accounting for, and settling disputes over royal revenue became concentrated in a single office. By the end of the 12th century, it had become a permanent department that was at once the royal treasury and accounting bureau as well as a financial court staffed by a fixed corps of justices.[21]

Whatever improvements were made at the center, the key to the effective operation of English government lay in the shires, or counties as they were now known under the Normans and Angevins. To monitor the activities of the sheriff and ensure that justice was done in shire and hundred courts, Henry I revived the old Carolingian institution of the *missi*. This involved sending itinerant royal justices into the countryside to conduct trials and hold inquiries into local complaints and inequities

---

[20] C. Warren Hollister and John Baldwin, "The Rise of Administrative Kingship: Henry I and Philip Augustus," *American Historical Review*, vol. 83, no. 4 (October 1978), pp. 867–905, here at pp. 871–873, 881; Warren, *Governance*, pp. 145, 187–189.

[21] Hollister and Baldwin, "Rise of Administrative Kingship," pp. 877–881; Warren, *Governance*, pp. 82–83, 128–129, 185–186. The sophisticated workings of the medieval English Exchequer are described in a dialogue written about 1179 by a former treasurer: Richard FitzNigel, *Dialogus de Scaccario*, ed. Charles Johnson (Oxford: Oxford University Press, 1983). The term "exchequer" is derived from the checkered cloth used during audits as a kind of abacus.

assisted by panels of sworn witnesses (juries). This system of "justices in eyre," or circuit judges, was discontinued after Henry I's death, but was permanently restored by his grandson Henry II after 1166 and aggressively employed during his reign to root out corrupt or abusive sheriffs. The pattern of local government as a collaborative venture between traveling royal officials, sheriffs and their assistants, and local men serving either as elected officials (coroners) or as members of temporary commissions (juries) was to persist until the 19th century. Increasingly, however, the duties of sheriffs came to be taken over by justices of the peace, panels of local notables appointed by the Crown for limited terms of office. Meanwhile in Westminster, a separate body of justices hearing civil suits was beginning to transform itself into the Court of Common Pleas, a process that would be completed after 1215.[22]

While it is no longer possible to measure with any accuracy the revenue gains that flowed from these reforms, they must have been substantial. The reforms resulted not only in a much higher level of scrutiny and control of the all-important sheriffs, but also in a marked expansion of royal justice, which was highly profitable.[23] Yet with the advent of Philip Augustus to the throne of France in 1188, and the heightened conflict between the two countries that soon followed as a result of the latter's more aggressively anti-English policies, ordinary sources of royal income soon proved to be inadequate. Between 1194 and 1214, Henry II's sons Richard I and John were forced to resort to an increasingly unpopular series of measures, including the frequent imposition of scutage (a fine on those owing knight's service) and tallage (taxes imposed on the royal demesne), the use of judicial eyres as a revenue-raising device, the harsh enforcement of the forest laws, and the abuse of a range of feudal privileges in order to raise the funds needed to finance costly campaigns against the French monarch. The final defeat of the English and their German and Flemish allies at Bouvines in 1214 led to a revolt of John's barons against these practices, and the imposition on the king of Magna Carta the following year.[24]

---

[22] Hollister and Baldwin, "Rise of Administrative Kingship," pp. 882–887; Warren, *Governance*, pp. 133–140; Barber, *Two Cities*, pp. 324.

[23] Warren, *Governance*, p. 159. During the 1240s, a period for which accurate figures are available, judicial receipts provided about 20% of the king's cash income in years when a general eyre or judicial visitation to the counties was underway. See: Robert Stacey, *Politics, Policy and Finance under Henry III 1216–1245* (New Haven: Yale University Press, 1987), pp. 206, 213–215.

[24] Warren, *Governance*, pp. 144–169; G. L. Harriss, *King, Parliament, and Public Finance in Medieval England to 1369* (Oxford: Clarendon, 1975), pp. 7–17. On the background to Magna Carta and its contents, see the new edition of J. C. Holt's classic work: *Magna Carta*, 2nd ed. (Cambridge: Cambridge University Press, 1992).

The Emergence of Parliament

Magna Carta, while setting limits on the kinds of royal exactions just mentioned, also recognized that the king might levy extraordinary taxes (*auxilia* or aids) on all of his subjects in cases of "urgent necessity," provided he received the consent of the "common counsel of the realm," which was explicitly defined as the lay and ecclesiastical tenants-in-chief or magnates assembled in the *magnum concilium* or grand council. Throughout the long reign of Henry III (1216–1272), this body was accepted as speaking for the "community of the realm" (*communitas regni*) as a whole. It felt free not only to grant several aids (1225, 1232, 1237) in order that the king might pursue his quarrels with the French, but also to turn down many of his requests for money (1242, 1244, 1248, 1253, 1257, 1258) when it concluded that Henry's foreign policy was not in the interest of the country as a whole.[25]

By the mid-1200s, however, the grand council had begun to lose its exclusive right to interpret the will of the broader community of free men. As early as 1254, Henry had asked the shires to send two "knights" each to a discussion of a new aid in order to supplement the members of the council. Representatives of both the counties and the boroughs were also summoned on several occasions during the 1270s and 1280s by Henry's son and successor Edward I (1272–1307). From the 1290s onward, as Edward became involved in wars with the Welsh, Scots, and French using contract troops (see Chapter 2), he began to summon two (elected) representatives with full proctorial powers from every shire and borough to meetings, now regularly called Parliaments, in order to vote him the ever heavier taxes needed to finance his military campaigns.[26] By the 1330s, prior to the outbreak of the Hundred Years War, the internal makeup of Parliament had become relatively fixed, with the lay (between 40 and 100) and ecclesiastical (c. 50) magnates of the old grand council now sitting as the House of Lords, and the shire (74) and borough (c. 150) members grouped together as the House of Commons.[27]

The emergence of this form of national representative institution in medieval England, rather than a tricurial assembly of estates, was a

[25] Holt, *Magna Carta*, p. 454 (text of Magna Carta); Warren, *Governance*, pp. 192–193; Harriss, *King, Parliament*, pp. 25–39; Sir Frederick Pollock and Frederick William Maitland, *The History of English Law before the Time of Edward I*, 2nd ed. (Cambridge: Cambridge University Press, 1968), vol. I, pp. 349–350.

[26] A. L. Brown, *The Governance of Late Medieval England 1272–1461* (London: Edward Arnold, 1989), pp. 156–157, 161–169; Harriss, *King, Parliament*, pp. 41–45.

[27] Brown, *Governance*, pp. 169, 173–174, 178–179, 182–183, 188, 202.

direct consequence of the preexisting pattern of local government found there. It was the survival into the 13th century of "communities of the shires" with their roots in the later dark ages, and the interaction between the central government and the local population of free men which took place within them, that paved the way for the kind of national-level cooperation between the Crown and the country at large that became institutionalized in Parliament. For the existence of local bodies heavily involved in judicial, administrative, and financial affairs through the activities of grand juries and shire and hundred courts made it impossible for the grand council to uphold for long the claim that it alone spoke for the community of the realm. That community was in one sense nothing more than the sum of the self-governing counties and boroughs.[28]

Given the regular involvement of many members of Parliament in the interpretation and application of the law through their membership in shire, hundred, and borough courts, it is hardly surprising that that body came to acquire a right of co-legislation in addition to its veto power over new taxation. Less influenced by Roman traditions, rulers in 13th-century England viewed the law as the custom of the community, not as a body of (manmade) rules promulgated by the emperor or king for the public good. That law, the result of the fusion of Norman and Anglo-Saxon legal traditions over the course of the previous two and a half centuries, could only be changed with the common counsel of the community – which, as in matters of taxation, initially meant the consent of the *magnum concilium*. Thus when Parliament took over the function of common counsel during the late 1200s and early 1300s, it acquired a role in the process of legislation as well. By the mid-1300s, it was universally accepted both that new statutes could alter the Common Law and that those statutes could only be promulgated with the consent of Parliament.[29]

Unencumbered state formation thus played a decisive role in shaping both the structure and the prerogatives of England's national representative assembly. Because the country was left without a functioning Roman infrastructure after the imperial withdrawal, the rapid formation of a large-scale successor state covering the former province of Britain was impossible, and so the waves of Germanic invaders had to construct a new polity from the bottom up, a process only completed in the late

[28] This is the principal point of Helen Maud Cam's famous essay, "The Theory and Practice of Representation in Medieval England," in: E. B. Fryde and Edward Miller (eds.), *Historical Studies of the English Parliament. Volume I: Origins to 1399* (Cambridge: Cambridge University Press, 1970), pp. 262–278, esp. pp. 273–278; also Warren, *Governance*, pp. 31, 229.

[29] Brown, *Governance*, pp. 218–224.

900s. As a result, triumphant West Saxon rulers could introduce Carolingian-inspired shires and hundreds at a time and under circumstances that favored their long-term survival. That survival in turn meant that when a parliament was created in the late 13th century, it would be built around the representatives of territorially integrated, self-governing local political communities rather than separate privileged estates. In addition, because English monarchs did not benefit from a Roman inheritance which invested rulers with nearly limitless powers, they found themselves ill-equipped to resist pressures towards "shared rule," at least in the areas of taxation and legislation, with those representing the community of the realm.

Permanent Taxation and Finance

Even before a pattern of shared rule had been fully institutionalized, Parliament was already making an important contribution toward the creation of a system of permanent national taxation as it attempted to finance Edward I's costly foreign policy. The first step in this direction was the unrestricted grant of an export duty on wool in 1275 in order to help defray the expenses of that monarch's crusade of 1270–1274. In 1303, this legislation was supplemented by an agreement with the foreign merchants operating in England to impose special duties on wine and cloth imports and a general levy on all other imports and exports.[30] The "new customs" of 1303 were introduced during a period of feverish military activity which had begun in 1294, when Edward I became embroiled successively in wars in Gascony, Wales, Flanders, and Scotland. To meet the massive costs of these conflicts, Edward turned to Parliament. Whereas the latter had voted only three property taxes (subsidies) between 1275 and 1290, six were granted over the next 16 years, and at higher rates.[31] Eleven more subsidies were voted between

---

[30]   Michael Prestwich, *Edward I* (Berkeley: University of California Press, 1988), pp. 99–100, 530; Norman S. B. Gras, *The Early English Customs System* (Cambridge: Harvard University Press, 1918), pp. 59–71. The customs of 1275 and 1303 became part of the hereditary revenue of the Crown at the rates fixed at that time, and hence declined in value over time. By the late 1300s, after a long struggle, Parliament won the right to control indirect taxation. See F. W. Maitland, *The Constitutional History of England* (Cambridge: Cambridge University Press, 1908), p. 180. Customs duties voted thereafter were granted either for the life of the sovereign in question or for a term of years. See Frederick C. Dietz, *English Government Finance 1485–1558* (New York: Barnes and Noble, 1964), pp. 11–12.
[31]   Richard Kaeuper, *War, Justice and Public Order: England and France in the Later Middle Ages* (Oxford: Clarendon, 1988), pp. 35–36; James Field Willard, *Parliamentary Taxes on Personal Property 1290 to 1334* (Cambridge: Medieval Academy of America, 1934), p. 9.

1307 and 1337.[32] Once war with France began in earnest in 1337, it was the customs revenues mentioned above and annual property taxes, voted time and again by Parliament, which provided the vast sums that this struggle consumed down to 1453.

As argued in Chapter 2, however, winning consent to new taxes was only half the battle, for a reliable source of short-term credit had to be found capable of converting this revenue into large amounts of ready cash. In England as in Latin Europe, the lack of developed credit markets in the 13th and 14th centuries forced the government there to rely above all on a small group of financiers with access to ready money in order to meet their credit needs. E. B. Fryde has traced the origins of the credit system which the first three Edwards employed to the year 1254, when the Pope encouraged Henry III to attempt a conquest of Sicily and offered the services of his Italian bankers to aid him. When his son Edward I came to the throne in 1274, he decided to look to the Italian merchant firms established in England as a source of credit to help underwrite his own military ambitions.[33] In 1275, as mentioned above, Parliament granted an export duty on wool, thus creating a rich new source of long-term income. Edward simultaneously appointed the Riccardi company of Lucca as his royal banker. The company was to make cash payments when the king directed them to do so. As security, they were assigned the receipts of the new customs.[34]

It is important to note that the Riccardi did not officially "farm" the customs. Royal collectors in each port were supposed to inspect wool exports and assess them for duty. The Italians were, however, permitted a role in choosing these collectors. In addition, their attorneys were allowed to receive the revenues assigned to them directly from the hands of the collectors.[35] This arrangement worked well for nearly 20 years, with the Riccardi providing Edward with a large and steady stream of cash to pay for the contract troops which conquered Wales.

The company's credit was irreparably damaged by the disruptions in trade associated with the outbreak of the war with France in 1294, and the king unceremoniously jettisoned them. Though the Riccardi were gone, the credit system which they had helped create lived on. Other

[32]   G. L. Harriss, "War and the Emergence of the English Parliament 1297–1360," *Journal of Medieval History*, vol. 2, no. 1 (March 1976), pp. 35–36, here at p. 37.
[33]   E. B. Fryde and M. M. Fryde, "Public Credit with Special Reference to North-Western Europe," *Cambridge Economic History of Europe* (Cambridge: Cambridge University Press, 1963), vol. III, pp. 430–553, here at p. 454.
[34]   Richard Kaeuper, *Bankers to the Crown: The Riccardi of Lucca and Edward I* (Princeton: Princeton University Press, 1973), pp. 82–85.
[35]   Ibid., pp. 148–150.

Italian bankers – first the Frescobaldi (1299–1311), then the Bardi (1312–1346) – took their place, advancing large sums on customs revenues now strengthened by the new duties of 1303. The apogee of this system was reached under Edward III, when the latter financed his invasion of France in 1337 through huge cash loans provided by the Bardi, the Peruzzi, and a group of English merchants headed by William de la Pole.[36] Though these advances were backed by the customs, the profits of the wool trade, and parliamentary subsidies, Edward III proved unable (or unwilling) to repay them: he reneged on loans and interest totaling over 180,000 pounds, thus helping to drive both the Bardi and Peruzzi into bankruptcy by 1346.[37] The king was able to continue borrowing from English merchants and financiers for a few years more, but by 1353 they were ruined as well.

This precocious, and in the end disastrous, English solution to the problem of short-term credit had several key features. First, revenue collection remained largely separated from borrowing. The customs service was staffed by a small number of royal officials, and direct taxes were gathered by ad hoc collectors named by the Crown but drawn from the freemen of the shires.[38] Second, repayment of the loans provided by the Italian and English financiers depended entirely on the goodwill of the reigning monarch. By repeatedly failing to honor its obligations, the government not only helped destroy all possible sources of large-scale credit, but also, for a very long time to come, soured the desire of both foreign and domestic businessmen to lend to the English government. In the late 14th and 15th centuries, the Crown had to make great efforts to coax small advances out of a much wider spectrum of its citizenry.[39] Thus, ironically, it was the excesses of early English credit policy which in the end prevented financiers from gaining a permanent foothold within the kingdom's financial and administrative apparatus before the early 17th century.

Pressures Toward Patrimonialism

As indicated above, the expansion of the English polity's fiscal capacities beginning in the 1100s went hand in hand with a vast increase in the number of officials it employed, especially in the ever more specialized central administration. As in Latin Europe, the predominance of feudal and ecclesiastical models of officeholding during this period of initial state expansion in England helped to create a complementary

---

[36] Fryde, "Public Credit," pp. 459–460; Kaeuper, *War, Justice*, pp. 54–55.
[37] Fryde, "Public Credit," p. 460.   [38] Willard, *Parliamentary Taxes*, pp. 33–45.
[39] Fryde, "Public Credit," pp. 463–469.

appropriationist threat to the one posed by the Italian and English financiers mentioned above. This threat manifested itself initially, as in France, in attempts by ealdormen and then sheriffs to make their positions hereditary, and was countered first by applying the farm system to shire revenues, then by employing itinerant justices as a check on the activities of sheriffs, and finally by transferring many of the powers of that official to "amateur" justices of the peace who acted collectively and whose tenure in office was strictly limited. Similarly, direct tax collection, a point of entry for officeholder-financiers in France, was consistently consigned to commissions of local freemen formed in the shires and hundreds.[40]

While appropriationist tendencies at the level of the counties could thus be held partially in check by the participatory character of English local government, they proved much more difficult to combat at the center. As in Latin Europe, most of the new positions created within the central administration after the 12th century – and all of those within the two leading departments, Chancery and the Exchequer – were filled by clerics. These offices were held at pleasure tenure (i.e., their holders could be dismissed at any time) and carried with them no or only very minimal salaries. This was possible because these cleric-administrators were also in possession of one or more ecclesiastical benefices at life tenure, which provided them with a source of both income and security.[41] Although many clerics were removed from their posts during Edward III's purges of 1340 and 1371, a large-scale switch from ecclesiastical to lay administrators seems to have come only in the first half of the 15th century.[42]

Yet in contrast to the situation among the polities of Latin Europe, which also engaged in large-scale statebuilding during this period in response to geopolitical pressures, in England it was to be feudal law, and only secondarily the canon law of benefices, that would provide the framework for the pattern of proprietary officeholding which emerged in the late middle ages. The real starting point for the English law of

---

[40] Fisher, *Anglo-Saxon Age*, p. 259; Lyon and Verhulst, *Medieval Finance*, pp. 58–59, 95; Brown, *Governance*, pp. 71–73, 122–128.

[41] T. F. Tout, "The English Civil Service in the Fourteenth Century," *The Collected Papers of Thomas Frederick Tout* (Manchester: Manchester University Press, 1934), vol. III, pp. 191–221, here at 199–201.

[42] Tout, "The English Civil Service," p. 211; Robin Storey, "England: Aemterhandel im 15. und 16. Jahrhundert" [in English], in: *Aemterhandel im Spätmittelalter und im 16. Jahrhundert*, ed. Ilja Mieck (Berlin: Colloquium Verlag, 1984), pp. 186–207, here at 200; J. C. Sainty, "The Tenure of Office in the Exchequer," *English Historical Review*, vol. 80, no. 316 (July 1965), pp. 449–475, here at pp. 451–452.

offices that was to hold sway for the next 500 years was a clause in the Second Statute of Westminster issued in 1285.[43] During the course of the 1200s, English lawyers had been influenced by the tendency in canon law to extend rights to "incorporeal things," such as the right of a lord to appoint the priest of a particular church (advowson).[44] In the statute of 1285, this logic was then extended to certain kinds of offices, but with a distinctly English twist. It in effect stated that offices held in fee (i.e., hereditary offices) were to be regarded, legally speaking, exactly as if they were freehold land. While important, this change in itself had few administrative consequences, since hereditary offices were few and were of a lowly character (mainly the wardenship of parks, woods, and the like).

This statute took on added significance, however, once laymen entered English government service in large numbers after 1400. These laymen soon succeeded in having their tenures converted from "at pleasure" to "life," often coupled with the right to execute the duties of the office by deputy.[45] Once they had secured life tenure, officeholders attempted to claim, drawing on the statute of 1285, that their offices were freehold property.[46] As soon as this interpretation gained general acceptance, as it seems to have done by the end of the 15th century, an official holding at life tenure could legally claim compensation from a successor if he resigned his office voluntarily.

Thus a common law doctrine peculiar to England, though inspired in part by canon law, provided the same kind of justification for the patrimonialization of office that the canon law of benefices and the institution of *resignatio in favorem* had offered in Latin Europe. Yet English practices differed from those of its neighbors in two significant ways. First, though the freehold interpretation allowed an official effectively to sell his office, it did not allow him full freedom to name his replacement. Once a transaction had been agreed upon, the purchaser still had to obtain the approval of the king (or of whomever possessed

---

[43] Pollock and Maitland, *The History*, vol. II, p. 135.

[44] W. S. Holdsworth, *A History of English Law*, 7th ed. (London: Methuen, 1956), vol. III, pp. 98, 139–142.

[45] Sainty, "The Tenure of Office," pp. 451–453.

[46] This is so because the commom law makes no distinction between property held in fee and property held at life tenure, except for the fact that the former can be bequeathed to one's heirs while the latter cannot. Both types of property are considered freeholds and in every other way are legally identical. Thus at common law both hereditary tenure in fee and life tenure are considered freeholds, unlike tenure at will or tenure for a term of years. The fundamental distinction at common law is not between heritable and nonheritable property, but between freeholds and property held only for a term of years or at will. See Pollock and Maitland, *The History*, vol. I, pp. 356–358, 370.

the gift of the office)[47] before the sale could go forward. Obtaining such approval often involved another, though this time unofficial, payment. This meant that in theory at least, the king retained greater control over personnel policy than was the case in France or Spain, though this advantage was undercut by the fact that English monarchs had already relinquished the right of appointment to many positions within their administrations to powerful nobles.

A second peculiarity of the pattern of officeholding in England also flowed from the common law doctrine of incorporeals. If an office at life tenure or, more specifically, the fees and emoluments attached to it, was freehold property, then it followed that any attempt to increase the number of officials performing the same task amounted to a deprivation of property without due process, for some of the fees which had previously gone to the older officeholders would now be appropriated by their new colleagues. This admittedly extreme extension of the freehold concept of office was in fact upheld by the Court of Common Pleas in *Cavendish's Case* (1587),[48] though it seems to have been current for some time before. In practical terms, this decision provided added legal backing to proprietary officeholding but at the same time severely limited the Crown's freedom to multiply the number of existing offices (though not to create entirely new ones), a favorite practice of both the French and Spanish kings throughout the 16th and 17th centuries.

Parliamentary Opposition to the Patrimonialist Threat

As might be expected, the English Parliament, and especially the House of Commons, took a dim view of the appropriation-prone methods and institutions which their sovereigns needed to employ in order to realize their geopolitical ambitions. As early as 1298, parliamentary criticism of the corrupt and extortionate manner in which Edward I's officials were collecting taxes and gathering supplies for the king's campaigns in Wales, Scotland, Gascony, and Flanders led to the creation of a commission of inquiry and ultimately to several dismissals and arrests.[49] In 1301 and again in 1307, members of Parliament accused Bishop

---

[47]   In the earlier centuries of the middle ages, the English kings had been less vigilant than their continental counterparts in protecting their exclusive right to name officials. Hence the right of appointment to many mid- and lower-level offices had passed (by tradition or grant) to some higher officeholder such as the Lord Chancellor, Chief Justice of the King's Bench or Court of Common Pleas, or Lord Treasurer. This official was then said to have the appointment of a given office "in his gift."

[48]   Holdsworth, *A History*, pp. 257, 260–261.

[49]   Prestwich, *Edward I*, pp. 427–432.

Walter Langton, the Lord Treasurer, of corruption, simony, pluralism, and interfering in the course of justice.[50]

This first wave of parliamentary attacks on the Crown's financial and administrative practices culminated in the Ordinances of 1311, an act containing a comprehensive program of government reform. The Ordinances sharply criticized the role played by the Frescobaldi in the king's finances, and demanded the replacement of a whole range of officeholders. In addition, the act stated that all revenues should be paid into the Exchequer, Parliaments held once or even twice a year, and complaints by the public against royal officials brought directly to that body. While the Frescobaldi fled England and many changes in personnel were in fact made in the wake of the Ordinances, they were repealed by Edward II in 1322.[51] Nevertheless, they remained a powerful source of inspiration and precedent for generations of parliamentary reformers to come, as the frequent references to them throughout the 1300s and early 1400s attest.

Edward III had apparently learned the lessons of his father's and grandfather's reigns, and sought from the beginning to establish a working partnership with Parliament in pursuit of his claim to the French throne.[52] While the assemblies that were to meet almost annually[53] until the death of Henry V in 1422 were on the whole generous in granting taxes for the war, their scrutiny of the way these taxes were spent and the kingdom administered grew ever sharper as the conflict with France dragged on. During the 1340s, Parliament consistently criticized the manner in which the nation's finances were managed. In 1340 and again in 1341, Parliament demanded and won the right to inspect the accounts of the king's principal bankers, the Bardi and William de la Pole.[54] In 1343, officials holding their position in fee (i.e., as heritable property), for life, or for a term of years were held responsible for the abuses occurring in customs collection.[55] Parliament also attacked the

---

[50] Ibid., pp. 546–550.
[51] J. O. Prestwich, *The Three Edwards* (London: Methuen, 1980), pp. 82–85; May McKisack, *The Fourteenth Century 1307–1399* (Oxford: Clarendon, 1959), pp. 14–22; G. L. Harriss, "The Formation of Parliament 1272–1377," in: R. G. Davies and J. H. Denton (eds.), *The English Parliament in the Middle Ages* (Manchester: Manchester University Press, 1981), pp. 29–60, here at 35–36.
[52] E. B. Fryde, "Parliament and the French War, 1336–40," in: E. B. Fryde and Edward Miller (eds.), *Historical Studies of the English Parliament* (Cambridge: Cambridge University Press, 1970), vol. I, pp. 242–261, here at p. 243.
[53] During the period 1327 to 1377, for example, there were only nine years in which neither a Parliament nor a representative council met. See: W. M. Ormrod, *The Reign of Edward III* (New Haven: Yale University Press, 1990), pp. 208–209.
[54] Harriss, *King, Parliament*, pp. 261–263, 442.
[55] Robert Baker, "The English Customs Service 1307–1343: A Study of Medieval Administration," *Transactions of the American Philosophical Society*, New Series, vol. 51, pt. 6 (October 1961), pp. 3–76, here at p. 46.

activities of the English financiers to whom the customs had been formally farmed in 1345, and imposed conditions on the king's dealings with them as a condition for a new grant of taxes in 1348.[56]

In the 1370s, as Edward III's health declined, abuses of patronage and profiteering began to creep into many spheres of royal government. The so-called Good Parliament of 1376 took the lead in combating these trends, impeaching ten officials of the royal household and financiers accused of various malpractices.[57] In a petition presented to the Commons in that year, annual Parliaments were explicitly identified as the remedy for misgovernment and corruption.[58]

During the reigns of both Richard II (1377–1399), Edward's unpopular grandson, and his deposer Henry IV (1399–1413), Parliament extended its role as an agency of administrative and financial oversight even further. Beginning in 1379, the Commons created a series of "commissions of reform" invested with wide latitude to identify and remove incompetent or spendthrift officials, correct mismanagement, and recommend economies within the royal household. Such commissions were active in 1379, 1381, 1386–7, 1387–9, and 1406–10.[59] At the same time, Parliament both investigated and sought to eliminate the traffic in offices at the English court by specifically forbidding "brocage" (brokerage or influence-peddling) in rules drawn up to guide the royal council in 1406.[60]

Parallel to these efforts, Parliament attempted to expand its scrutiny of royal finances by appointing special war treasurers to receive and disburse the funds voted to finance the conflict in France. Such treasurers were to present their accounts directly to the House of Commons, a requirement that reflected a realistic assessment of the ability of the Exchequer, with its ponderous accounting procedures, to act as an effective organ of control. War treasurers were named almost annually between 1377 and 1390, and again between 1404 and 1406.[61]

By the early 1400s, then, English monarchs had worked closely with Parliament for more than a century to build a broad-based consensus

[56] E. B. Fryde, "The English Farmers of the Customs, 1343–1351," *Transactions of the Royal Historical Society*, 5th series, vol. IX (1959), pp. 1–17; Harriss, *King, Parliament*, pp. 326–327; Frederic Richard Barnes, "The Taxation of Wool, 1327–1348," in: George Unwin (ed.), *Finance and Trade under Edward III* (Manchester: Manchester University Press, 1918), pp. 137–177, here at pp. 174–177.

[57] Chris Given-Wilson, *The Royal Household and the King's Affinity* (New Haven: Yale University Press, 1986), pp. 146–154.

[58] A. L. Brown, "Parliament, c. 1377–1422," in: Davies and Denton, *The English Parliament*, pp. 109–140, here at p. 111.

[59] Given-Wilson, *The Royal Household*, pp. 117–121.

[60] Charles Plummer, notes to his edition of Sir John Fortescue, *The Governance of England* (Oxford: Oxford University Press, 1885), pp. 336–337.

[61] Given-Wilson, *The Royal Household*, pp. 123–130.

around, and raise the funds necessary for, their military enterprises. As a result of this interaction, Parliament had come to occupy an important role as an agency of administrative and financial oversight and a source of reforms aimed at securing what at the time was called "bone governance." This was an ideal that clearly included, in the view of G. L. Harriss, modern conceptions of efficiency and probity in the interest both of the greatest possible military effectiveness and the lowest possible level of taxation.[62] The great victories of Henry V's armies certainly owed something to Parliament's success in holding in check "appropriationist" tendencies present within the English state. Though Parliament was soon to suffer, as were other state institutions, under the dual impact of military defeat and the fratricidal Wars of Roses, the 1300s and 1400s left a legacy which could be drawn on for centuries to come.

Like its counterparts in Latin Europe, the English state grew tremendously in both size and sophistication between the 12th and 15th centuries. Central government, once the domain of a handful of household officials assisted by a small number of clerics, now consisted of a chancery, a treasury that also doubled as accounting office and financial court, and two central law courts – in addition to a still-extensive royal household and a royal council in which the direction of government policy was decided. A mixed army of feudal levies and mercenaries had given way to one built exclusively around paid, professional troops, and this force was financed by a permanent system of indirect taxation supplemented when needed by direct taxes on property. A substantial corps of royal officials – sheriffs, itinerant judges, customs officers, muster-masters – carried government policy into the country at large, and many of these officials, together with their colleagues within the central administration, had already acquired proprietary rights over their offices.

These features of England's state apparatus at the close of the middle ages were broadly shared by those of France, Spain, Portugal, and the Italian principalities. This is hardly surprising, since they flowed from a common cause: the early impact upon all of these polities of competition, most often of a military character, with other states. The intense interaction among the polities of Latin Europe as well as between France and England had led to the construction of similar institutions using similar methods over a similar span of time. Yet in one key respect, England was very different from its neighbors: untroubled by the entrenched

---

[62] G. L. Harriss, "The Management of Parliament," in: idem (ed.), *Henry V: The Practice of Kingship* (Oxford: Oxford University Press, 1985), pp. 141–142.

power of local elites "inherited" from previous, failed attempts at large-scale statebuilding, the Anglo-Saxon kings and their Norman successors could nurture a participatory form of local government based on the county and borough and symbolized by the institution of the jury, rather than relying entirely on royal officials to enforce their will out in the country at large.

The development of participatory local government in England led to the emergence of a territorially based national representative assembly very different from the curially organized Estates found across the Channel. Both the national Parliament and the shire, hundred, and borough courts in the localities represented an important source of opposition to the appropriating tendencies found within England's new administrative, financial, and military infrastructure. Over the coming centuries these two tendencies – the patrimonial and the "communitarian," with their respective roots in early statebuilding and "unencumbered" state formation – would battle one another to determine the ultimate character of the English state.

DEEPENING PATRIMONIALISM AND
ITS TEMPORARY DEMISE, 1453–1659

Unlike its neighbors in Latin Europe, England engaged in little large-scale warfare during the 16th and early 17th century. Yet this development was a double-edged sword. On the one hand, it meant that those who normally sought to exploit the pressures of war to advance their own appropriating interests enjoyed fewer opportunities to do so. Yet on the other hand, the absence of financial pressures generated by constant conflict led to a relative decline in the position of Parliament, as the frequent meetings of earlier centuries called in order to vote new taxes were now no longer necessary. In the absence of effective parliamentary oversight, proprietary officeholders were able to consolidate their position and financiers to gain a new foothold within the English state apparatus.

The strengthening during the Tudor and early Stuart periods of patrimonialist tendencies with their roots in previous centuries contributed to a persistent financial crisis which gripped the English state after 1603. At the same time, the growing aura of "corruption" which came to surround the courts of James I and Charles I only served to exacerbate tensions between the Crown and much of the political nation already present due to differences over religion. With Parliament's return to the political scene in 1624–1629 and again in 1640–1641 in the wake of renewed external warfare, these tensions soon exploded into civil war. While Parliament's victory over the king brought with it a sustained attack on patrimonial practices and institutions, the failure of both the Commonwealth and Protectorate regimes to win over the all-important elites of the self-governing counties and boroughs had led by 1660 to the restoration of the monarchy and the reversal of most of these structural reforms.

Deepening Patrimonialism

Three important structural changes of the late 15th century fueled the transformation which was to take place in the character of English administration and finance over the coming century and a half. First, the power of the great magnates with their regional strongholds and private armies was broken during the Wars of the Roses and their after-math. From the time of Henry VII onward, the country's nobles made the court the focus of their political activity, forming themselves into factions which competed with one another for the attention of the sovereign and for the control of various forms of patronage at his or her disposal.[63]

Second, the replacement of the clergy with laymen within the royal administration, a process which had begun in halting fashion during the late 1300s and early 1400s, now picked up speed. The advent of lay officials normally brought with it a host of new practices – including the attempts to convert "at pleasure" to life tenure, increases in fees charged to the public, requests for reversions, and pluralism – as the new admin-istrators sought to build a secure social and economic future for their families around their offices, much as one would do around a landed estate. Moreover, once life tenure had been secured, the office became proprietary and hence a marketable item for which payment could be demanded at the time of one's retirement.[64] This second set of changes tended to feed into the first one mentioned above, for an alteration in tenure, the grant of a reversion (to assure, for example, that one's son would acquire the office), or the transfer of the position to a third party often required at least formal royal approval, something that could not be obtained without the intercession of a patron at court (and the payment of a gratuity).

Finally, a third structural change that permitted the other two to continue apace was the decline in the position of Parliament in the period after the Hundred Years War. As mentioned earlier, Parliament

---

[63] David Starkey, "From Feud to Faction," *History Today*, vol. 32, no. 11 (November 1982), pp. 16–22. Starkey relates (p. 16) that the first recorded use of the term "faction" in English occurred in 1509.

[64] Sainty, "The Tenure of Office," pp. 452–454.

had become a nearly equal partner in government during the great struggle with France, meeting almost annually by the late 1300s to vote funds for the war.[65] The assembly actively sought to maintain a high level of efficiency and honesty among the king's servants, employing to that end procedures such as impeachment, the creation of reforming commissions, and the appointment of its own officials. This precocious pattern of interaction between Parliament and the central executive, prefiguring in some respects the politics of the 1690s, was disrupted by the disorder and strife of the reign of Henry VI and of the civil wars which followed it.

At the same time, England's withdrawal from European politics after its defeat in France meant that even when order was restored after 1485, there was little need to call Parliament with any regularity. It is hardly surprising then, that in the first 20 years of his reign, Henry VIII called only four Parliaments. When the assembly did begin to meet with greater frequency from 1529 onward, it was occupied mainly with weighty religious issues, as it was to be for a long time to come. Under such conditions, it proved very difficult for Parliament to exercise the kind of administrative oversight that had been possible earlier.

As a result of the interaction of the three factors discussed above, the pattern of English central government in the second half of the 1500s was quite different than it had been a century and a half earlier. Nearly all the significant administrative positions, with the exception of the great offices of state, were now held by lay proprietary officeholders who collected the bulk of their income in the form of fees and gratuities. Pluralism, the appointment of deputies, and the granting of reversions were all common, as was the traffic in offices among private individuals.[66]

Appointments to office and other royal favors were all obtained through patronage, and in the 1560s and 1570s such patronage was largely in the hands of two individuals, Lord Burghley and the Earl of Leicester. Each of them formed large patron-client groups which extended from the court into the Church, central government, and the counties. This high degree of centralization in the exercise of patronage, as well as the relatively cooperative relationship enjoyed by Burghley

---

[65] Brown, "Parliament c. 1377–1422," p. 110.

[66] J. C. Sainty, "A Reform of the Tenure of Office during the Reign of Charles II," *Bulletin of the Institute of Historical Research*, vol. 41, no. 104 (November 1968), pp. 150–171, here at p. 152; Penry Williams, *The Tudor Polity* (Oxford: Clarendon, 1978), pp. 82–99; J. D. Alsop, "Government, Finance and the Community of the Exchequer," in: Christopher Haigh (ed.), *The Reign of Elizabeth I* (London: Macmillan, 1984), pp. 101–123, here at pp. 106–107, 111, 123.

and Leicester, help to bring a high degree of order to the competition for place which dominated the English court.[67]

Late 16th-century England is comparable to the France or Castile of this period in that the same range of patrimonial practices was firmly rooted within the royal administration. Indeed, if one looks only at central government, England fares worse than Castile, most of whose leading officials still held at-pleasure tenure. It would be inaccurate to claim, for example, that the sale of offices did not occur in England. Not only was a lively traffic in places among private individuals the norm, but money payments were almost always required in order to obtain an appointment, though such payments benefited private patrons, not the Exchequer. It is true that the Crown did not create new offices expressly for public sale, as in other countries. In a sense, however, this was an expression of the strength of proprietary officeholding in England, not its weakness. In England (as in contemporary Milan and post-1641 Portugal), officials were able successfully to defend the position that the multiplication of existing offices would represent an infringement on the property rights of existing holders (*Cavendish's Case*, 1587).[68]

The Crown had made various attempts during the 1500s to alter the prevailing pattern of administrative development, though again due to the absence of war and thus of the incentives it would have created for military effectiveness, none of these attempts was sustained. The creation during the 1530s by Henry VIII and his minister Thomas Cromwell of a whole series of new revenue boards staffed by nonproprietary officials did represent a serious challenge to the Exchequer, that bastion of proprietary officeholding.[69] Yet by 1554 the most important of these bodies, the Court of Augmentation, the Court of First Fruits and Tenths, and the Office of General Surveyors, had all been incorporated into the Exchequer, thereby reestablishing its preeminence within the English financial administration. For the next century, the department

---

[67] The classic pieces on the Elizabethan patronage system are: J. E. Neale, "The Elizabethan Political Scene," in: idem, *Essays in Elizabethan History* (London: Macmillan, 1958), pp. 59–84; and Wallace MacCaffrey, "Place and Patronage in Elizabethan Politics," in: S. T. Bindoff, J. Hurstfield, and C. H. Williams (eds.), *Elizabethan Government and Society: Essays Presented to Sir John Neale* (London: Athlone, 1961), pp. 95–126. Simon Adams, "Faction, Clientage and Party: English Politics, 1550–1603," *History Today*, vol. 32, no. 12 (December 1982), pp. 33–39, provides a convincing corrective (pp. 36–37) to Neale's claim that Burghley and Leicester and their respective followers acted like two rival factions.

[68] Holdsworth, *A History*, vol. I, pp. 257, 260–261.

[69] This is one of the central concerns of G. R. Elton, *The Tudor Revolution in Government* (Cambridge: Cambridge University Press, 1953). But see the revisionist essays in Christopher Coleman and David Starkey (eds.), *Revolution Reassessed: Revisions in the History of Tudor Government and Administration* (Oxford: Clarendon, 1986).

was to remain a bastion of extreme conservatism, racked by numerous financial scandals.[70]

Although Parliament did not meet regularly enough during this period to act as a running check on the activities of royal officials, it did repeatedly seek to combat tendencies towards appropriation with legislation, the most powerful weapon it possessed. In 1552, Parliament passed a statute expressly forbidding the traffic in offices.[71] In 1563 and 1586 bills were approved which attacked the corrupt practices of purveyors, and in 1589 bills aimed at reforming both purveyance and the Exchequer carried. The queen, however, vetoed all of these measures, believing them to be cases of parliamentary meddling in prerogative areas.[72]

Finally, in 1571 a bill was introduced in Parliament which set out to prevent royal receivers from making private use of the queen's money by converting failure to pay over cash balances within two months into a felony (i.e., punishable by death). In this case, Parliament was supported by Burghley, and the bill passed into law, though the penalty was reduced from death to confiscation of the offender's property.[73] Nevertheless, neither the statute of 1552 nor that of 1571 proved capable of preventing the abuses against which they were directed. With Parliament reduced to occasional meetings and both the executive and the courts dominated by proprietary officeholding, this was hardly surprising.

The advent of naval warfare with Spain (1588–1603) did not in itself provide much impetus to the tendencies towards appropriation within the English state, for military costs that could not be met out of ordinary revenue were largely covered by grants from Parliament and by booty captured from the enemy.[74] A number of developments during the 1590s did, however, have ominous implications for the future. The death of Leicester in 1587 and the appearance of Essex as the new royal favorite undermined the orderly patronage regime of the 1570s and 1580s, and led to open competition and conflict between the Essex

---

[70] On the decision to eliminate the revenue courts in 1554; see: James Alsop, "The Revenue Commission of 1552," *The Historical Journal*, vol. 22, no. 3 (1979), pp. 511–533, esp. pp. 530–533. On the character of the Elizabethan Exchequer, see: Christopher Coleman, "Artifice or Accident? The Reorganization of the Exchequer of Receipt c. 1554–1572," in: Coleman and Starkey, *Revolution Reassessed*, pp. 163–198; and G. R. Elton, "The Elizabethan Exchequer: War in the Receipt," in: idem, *Studies in Tudor and Stuart Politics and Government* (Cambridge: Cambridge University Press, 1974), vol. I, pp. 355–388.

[71] G. E. Aylmer, *The King's Servants* (London: Routledge & Kegan Paul, 1974), p. 228.

[72] J. E. Neale, *Elizabeth and Her Parliaments 1584–1601* (London: Jonathan Cape, 1957), pp. 187–188, 207ff.; G. R. Elton, *The Parliament of England 1559–1581* (Cambridge: Cambridge University Press, 1986), p. 125.

[73] Elton, *The Parliament*, pp. 170–174.

[74] W. R. Scott, *The Constitution and Finance of English, Scottish and Irish Joint-Stock Companies to 1720* (Cambridge: Cambridge University Press, 1912), vol. III, pp. 505–507.

and Cecil factions over appointments and rewards.[75] The arrival of James I with his new entourage of favorites and his fabled liberality soon transformed this competition into a patronage free-for-all, as a whole range of courtiers fought for both influence and clients. Meanwhile, the large-scale expansion of English secondary schools and universities was producing a rising number of educated graduates seeking government posts, a factor which only helped fuel the scramble for place.[76]

The pattern of unregulated competition for patronage characteristic of the reign of James I had direct and tangible fiscal consequences. Whereas Elizabeth had managed to run a surplus on ordinary revenue, this turned into a sizable deficit within less than ten years of James's ascension to the throne. The principal reason for this deficit was a huge increase in spending, which included over £40,000 annually in royal household expenditures and £50,000 in fees and annuities paid to individuals. These deficits helped to produce an increase in the royal debt from £100,000 at the death of Elizabeth in 1603 to about £735,000 three years later. Despite periodic bouts of belt-tightening, the Crown proved unable to crawl out from under this pile of debt during James's reign (1603–1625).[77]

The government's financial difficulties, which extended into the reign of Charles I (1625–1649) and were exacerbated by disastrous conflicts with Spain (1624–1630) and France (1627–1630), had two important long-term consequences. First, the Crown turned increasingly to patrimonial practices in an effort to raise the cash needed for high living and, later, war. In 1604, the customs, the monarchy's largest source of ordinary revenue, were put to farm. The farmers soon became the government's primary source of short-term credit, a development that rendered them indispensable and led Charles stubbornly to resist the growing tide of opposition to farming.[78] At the same time, a figure similar to the French officeholder-financier made his first appearance in England. From 1618 onward, the Crown turned to two treasurers, William Russell and Philip Burlamachi, to raise cash on their own account that would then be used to pay troops and meet other expenses.[79]

[75] Adams, "Faction, Clientage," pp. 37–39.

[76] Joel Hurstfield, "Political Corruption in Modern England: The Historian's Problem," in: idem, *Freedom, Corruption and Government in Elizabethan England* (Cambridge: Harvard University Press, 1973), pp. 137–162, here at pp. 155–156.

[77] Robert Ashton, "Deficit Finance in the Reign of James I," *Economic History Review*, 2nd series, vol. 10, no. 1 (August 1957), pp. 15–29, here at pp. 18–19, 21, 23–24.

[78] Robert Ashton, "Revenue Farming under the Early Stuarts," *Economic History Review*, 2nd series, vol. 8, no. 3 (April 1956), pp. 310–322; idem, *The Crown and the Money Market 1603–1640* (Oxford: Clarendon, 1960), p. 83.

[79] Robert Ashton, "The Disbursing Official under the Early Stuarts: The Cases of Sir William Russell and Philip Burlamachi," *Bulletin of the Institute of Historical Research*, vol. 30, no. 82 (November 1957), pp. 162–174.

By the 1620s, then, the "irrationalization" of the English state was proceeding apace. It now possessed an administrative apparatus that was, as Gerald Aylmer has said, totally dominated by the "3 p's" of patronage, patrimony, and purchase.[80] Yet the outcry in Parliament over this course of development was growing ever louder. The Crown responded to parliamentary pressure for reform by creating royal commissions of inquiry. Commissions were appointed to investigate the navy in 1608, 1618, and 1626, the Ordnance in 1618, 1626, 1629, and 1630, and officeholders' fees in 1610, 1623, and 1627. The results of these efforts clearly reveal the character of the English state during this period. Rather than carry out structural reforms, the commissions, which were normally staffed by officeholders themselves, concentrated on accusing individuals who belonged to the wrong faction or lacked the protection of a strong patron of some form of malfeasance. The hapless official was then forced to "compound" with the commissioners, i.e., pay a fine.[81]

By turning royal inquiries into a means of extorting money from unlucky officeholders, the Crown had shown that it was incapable of reforming itself. The failure of these attempts at reform meant that the government missed an opportunity to reverse the loss of legitimacy that increasing appropriation had brought among the political elite in the counties.[82] The absence of thoroughgoing reform also translated into chronic financial difficulties for the Crown. Both these factors helped set the stage for the crisis of 1640–1642, for it was financial pressures that ultimately defeated Charles's efforts to rule without Parliament after 1629.[83]

The course of development taken by the Tudor and early Stuart polity shows quite clearly that tendencies towards appropriation were nearly as strong in England as they were in Latin Europe, a result which implies that such tendencies were the consequence of precocious statebuilding provoked by an early exposure to sustained geopolitical pressures. By the reign of Charles I, the English state had become a kind of parasite, extracting resources from the productive sectors of the nation and redistributing them among a small political class with access to power, offices, and contracts.

At the same time, Parliament proved unable to check these tendencies

---

[80] Aylmer, *The King's Servants*, p. 89. This work provides an extremely detailed portrait of the administrative system of early Stuart England.

[81] G. E. Aylmer, "Attempts at Administrative Reform, 1625–1640," *English Historical Review*, vol. 72, no. 283 (April 1957), pp. 229–259; idem, "Charles I's Commission on Fees, 1627–1640," *Bulletin of the Institute for Historical Research*, vol. 31, no. 83 (May 1958), pp. 58–67.

[82] Linda Levy Peck, "Corruption at the Court of James I: The Undermining of Legitimacy," in: Barbara C. Malament (ed.), *After the Reformation: Essays in Honor of J. H. Hexter* (Philadelphia: University of Pennsylvania Press, 1980), pp. 75–90.

[83] Aylmer, "Attempts . . . ," p. 258.

in an effective manner through either statutes or royal commissions of inquiry which it did not control. The reasons for these failures lay in the infrequency of parliamentary sessions during the 16th and early 17th century. When that body had met on a more regular basis for extended periods of time during the Hundred Years War, it accomplished this task with far greater success. Only with the institutionalization of Parliament during the Commonwealth and later, after the Restoration, would it be possible to carry out the thoroughgoing structural transformation of the English state that the assemblies of the early 1600s had sought but had been unable to impose on a recalcitrant Crown and its officials.

Effects of the Civil War

The Civil War and its aftermath brought a swift end to many of the more egregious features of early Stuart government. By breaking up the old national patronage networks centered on the Court, it removed a key structural underpinning of the parasitical state which had flourished before 1642. Yet the alternatives provided by successive revolutionary governments proved to be both administratively and politically unstable, and hence held out no long-term solution to the problems of English state development. Nevertheless, many of the changes introduced during the Civil War and Interregnum had ramifications which reached far into the Restoration period.

Most importantly, the domestic conflicts of the 1640s and 1650s brought the techniques of modern land warfare to England. Both sides drew on the expertise of Britons who had served on the continent to construct regional armies organized around companies and regiments and supported, in the manner of the Swedish forces in Germany, by local taxes and "contributions."[84] With the creation of the New Model Army in 1645, England acquired one of Europe's first, and most up-to-date, directly administered standing armies.[85] This force was partially financed by a new kind of tax, the excise on domestic commodities, a kind of impost borrowed from the Dutch.[86]

---

[84] Ronald Hutton, *The Royalist War Effort 1642–1646* (London: Longman, 1982), pp. 22–23, 28–32, 48, 88–94, 105–109; Martyn Bennett, "Contribution and Assessment: Financial Exactions in the English Civil War, 1642–1646," *War and Society*, vol. 4, no. 1 (May 1986), pp. 1–9; Ian Roy, "England Turned Germany? The Aftermath of the Civil War in its European Context," *Transactions of the Royal Historical Society*, vol. 28 (1978), pp. 127–144; Stephen Porter, "The Fire-raid in the English Civil War," *War and Society*, vol. 2, no. 2 (September 1984), pp. 27–40.

[85] C. H. Firth, *Cromwell's Army*, 4th ed. (London: Methuen, 1962), pp. vi, 1, 108–109 and passim.

[86] Edward Hughes, *Studies in Administration and Finance 1558–1825* (Manchester: Manchester University Press, 1934), pp. 118–124.

The Commonwealth and Protectorate also initiated fundamental changes in the character of state administration. Not only did scores of officials associated with the old regime lose their places in the wake of the king's defeat, but the basic parameters of officeholding were altered as well. Life tenure, and with it proprietary rights, was generally eliminated, sale of offices curbed, salaries raised, fee-taking discouraged, and recruitment opened to all with talent. Boards of commissioners were named to run major departments like the Ordnance and Navy Office and supervise customs and excise collection.[87] All of these changes brought noticeable improvements in efficiency, professionalism, and probity, notably in the navy.[88] The victories of Cromwell's armed forces over the Scots, Irish, and Dutch served to establish a link in the minds of government officials and the general public alike between the administrative methods of the Interregnum and military prowess.

Most importantly, the Civil War had profound effects on the character of Parliament. In their new role as both legislature and quasi-executive, the Commons were forced to take an active role in former prerogative areas such as foreign policy. They also sought to monitor closely the workings of state administration by appointing standing committees to oversee major departments.[89] This pattern of supervision and intervention continued, though in less pronounced form, even under the Protectorate.

Although the various revolutionary governments succeeded in substantially increasing the English state's military and administrative capacities, they were unable to solve the perennial problem of finance. Though partly the result of poor organization – ten different treasuries were responsible for revenue collection – and the heavy costs of the Dutch and Spanish wars, the Protectorate's financial difficulties were at base a reflection of its fundamental lack of legitimacy. Given the fact that justices of the peace and other "amateur" officials continued to carry out much of the routine work of administration in the counties, hundreds, and boroughs, resistance to the regime on the part of local political society had an immediate impact on the government's ability to collect taxes, despite the intimidating presence of troops in the shires. Like the Stuarts before him, Cromwell was forced to borrow heavily from London's goldsmith-bankers to stay afloat, but when the regime of his son proved unable to pay even the armed forces – its sole solid base of support – a restoration became inevitable.[90]

[87] G. E. Aylmer, *The State's Servants: The Civil Service of the English Republic 1649–1660* (London: Routledge & Kegan Paul, 1973), pp. 81–83, 115, 326–328, 341–343.
[88] Ibid., pp. 40–41, 156–160, 342; M. Oppenheim, *A History of the Royal Navy and of Merchant Shipping in Relation to the Navy from 1509 to 1660 with an Introduction Treating of the Preceding Period* (London: The Bodley Head, 1896), pp. 324–327, 346–360.
[89] Aylmer, *State's Servants*, pp. 9–17; Oppenheim, *A History*, pp. 346–347.
[90] Maurice Ashley, *Financial and Commercial Policy under the Cromwellian Protectorate*, 2nd ed. (Oxford: Oxford University Press, 1962), pp. 40–45, 100–110; Hughes, *Studies,*

Thus during the Interregnum the combination of an (internal) military threat and regular parliamentary scrutiny eliminated in a remarkably short time patrimonial features of the English state which, though rooted in the middle ages, had grown stronger with the relative decline of Parliament under the Tudors and early Stuarts. Yet the advances made in defense and administration during 1640s and 1650s could not be institutionalized because the revolutionary regimes of the Interregnum were never able to win over the pillars of the English state – the leading men of county and borough society. The experience of those decades showed that even a government equipped with a powerful army and central administration could not impose itself on a country resolutely hostile to its ideological program.

THE RESTORATION AND THE ENGLISH "REVOLUTION IN GOVERNMENT," 1660–1688

When the Protectorate regime collapsed in 1659–1660, it appeared that the chance to reform the English state had been permanently lost. The restoration of the monarchy quickly brought with it a full-fledged return to the patrimonial administrative and financial practices of the 1630s, and England seemed condemned to remain a second-class power, unable to hold her own against the might of Louis XIV's army or the Dutch navy. Yet by the beginning of the next century, a newly formed Great Britain was well on its way to becoming Europe's dominant state as its armed forces inflicted defeat after defeat upon its traditional rival France. These victories on the battlefield and at sea were only possible thanks to a huge, nonproprietary fiscal-military bureaucracy and a highly effective, market-based system of public finance. This new bureaucracy and financial system represented a sharp break with the appropriation-prone administrative and fiscal infrastructure with which the country had been saddled since the late middle ages.

Unlike its neighbors in Latin Europe, England *was* able to overcome the patrimonial consequences of early sustained geopolitical competition and the precocious state expansion it produced. How was this possible? I argue below that the almost continuous presence of Parliament in the period after 1660, under conditions of heightened geopolitical competition, allowed reformers operating from within central government to overcome resistance from vested interests. Parliament thus emerged as a decisive third independent variable in the English case, enabling these reformers to begin to construct the new, nonproprietary state apparatus and public credit system that, after 1689, would permit Britain to become the first global power.

pp. 132–135; Andrew Colby, *Central Government and the Localities: Hampshire 1649–1689* (Cambridge: Cambridge University Press, 1987), pp. 41–51.

The Restoration Settlement and Its Ramifications

Despite the resounding defeat which the Royalists had suffered in the Civil War, Charles was restored to the throne with all traditional prerogative powers intact, rendering him a force to contend with right up until his early death in 1685. The new king appeared to have no firm foreign or domestic policy goals other than the extension of religious toleration to Dissenters and especially to Catholics. His prime personal motivation was a desire to exercise his royal prerogatives with a minimum of interference from either overmighty ministers or Parliament, as well as to pursue his legendary appetite for private pleasures unhindered.[91] Over the years, as the constraints imposed by Parliament began to chafe, Charles's desire grew to free himself from them. Yet this made the king less a potential absolutist in the mold of Louis XIV than a devoted proponent of "old corruption," determined to derive the maximum benefits from office for both himself and his boon companions.

If Charles's fondness for the pattern of antebellum politics derived from his private predilections, that of his principal advisor Clarendon had firmer intellectual roots. The latter saw the Restoration as a mandate to return to the ancient institutions and usages which, he believed, provided the best guarantee for future stability. Clarendon thus favored a complete return to the state as it had existed in 1642.[92] This desire was lent added weight by a horde of former officeholders and holders of reversions (legal promises to grant an office upon the death of the current incumbent) who demanded to have their proprietary rights restored. Furthermore, scores of faithful supporters who had stood by the king during his years in the wilderness had to be rewarded.

In response to these pressures, Charles chose to reverse most of the reforms of the Interregnum. Although the abolition of the Court of Wards and the other prerogative courts was accepted, all the other institutions of central government were revived in their old form. While the higher salaries of the Protectorate were retained, Charles and Clarendon reintroduced the whole panoply of old administrative practices: proprietary officeholding, grants of reversion, traffic in offices, employment of deputies, and fee-taking.[93] The Treasury, Ordnance, and Admiralty

[91] J. R. Jones, *Charles II: Royal Politician* (London: Allen & Unwin, 1987), pp. 2–3, 8, 162–163, 186–187; Ronald Hutton, *The Restoration* (Oxford: Oxford University Press, 1985), pp. 187ff.

[92] Jones, *Charles II*, p. 56; Henry Roseveare, *The Treasury: The Evolution of a British Institution* (New York: Columbia University Press, 1969), p. 54.

[93] Aylmer, *State's Servants*, p. 337; Howard Tomlinson, "Financial and Administrative Developments in England, 1660–88," in: J. R. Jones (ed.), *The Restored Monarchy 1660–1688* (London: Macmillan, 1979), pp. 94–117, here at p. 94; J. C. Sainty, "The Tenure of Offices," pp. 463–465; idem, "A Reform in the Tenure of Offices," pp. 155–156.

were removed from the hands of commissioners and returned to the rule of their traditional officeholders. These decisions encouraged the reappearance of other "traditional" practices like bribery, embezzlement, and influence peddling which had declined under the rule of the Saints.

The Restoration also marked a return to an old familiar pattern on the level of everyday politics. With the Court again liberally dispensing offices and rewards, factions cemented by patron/client relationships soon formed. The most powerful of these, at least initially, was the one surrounding Clarendon (now the Lord Chancellor), and it included the Lord Treasurer, Southampton, and the Lord Lieutenant of Ireland, Ormonde. This group was committed above all to the return of the status quo ante in church and state. Two opposition factions soon appeared, however, one led by Lord Arlington, a crypto-Catholic courtier, and the other by the 2nd Duke of Buckingham, son of James I's favorite.[94] Neither had any firm ideological goals other than a desire for favor and its rewards. Hence right from the start several features of the Restoration seemed to presage a return to the structural problems of the 1620s and 1630s: a monarch who saw politics as a game played for personal gain, a band of fractious courtiers who largely shared this view, and an administrative system whose bad old ways were now to be sanctified with the mantle of "tradition."

The 1660s soon came to resemble the 1630s in the area of government finances as well. At the outset of the Restoration, the Convention Parliament possessed the crucial power to set the level of Charles's life revenue. This body intended to grant the king an income on which he could reasonably (though not extravagantly) live in peacetime. Because of a series of miscalculations on the part of both Parliament and the Court, the taxes voted to provide this income (which included a limited version of the Interregnum excise) generated substantially less revenue than expected. In addition, the legislature failed to set aside sufficient funds to pay off the sizable debts left over from the Protectorate, including a mountain of back pay owed to the armed forces.[95]

By the time the new Cavalier Parliament realized all of this in 1662, it was ill disposed to correct the oversight. The waste and extravagance of the new government, a direct consequence of the revival of antebellum practices mentioned above, had alienated the Commons. As a result, Parliament resisted pressures to augment the king's permanent revenue,

---

[94] Hutton, *The Restoration*, pp. 191–194; Jones, *Charles II*, pp. 63–66, 73, 79.
[95] C. D. Chandaman has finally untangled the mysteries of the Restoration financial settlement in his magisterial *The English Public Revenue 1660–1688* (Oxford: Clarendon, 1975), pp. 196–203.

and instead chose to meet periodic deficits by voting one-time grants, thus maintaining a crucial source of leverage over the Court.[96]

The ramifications of Parliament's decision to limit the king's lifetime income continued to make themselves felt throughout his reign. First and foremost, it meant that regular parliamentary meetings were necessary to vote supplementary grants even if Charles managed to stay out of a war (which he did not). Second, it drove the Crown back into the arms of the financiers in an effort to raise cash. In 1662, the customs and excise were again put to farm in return for large advances. Finally, tight finances made the king more willing to listen to a group of "new men" within the government who advocated thoroughgoing reforms which would render the English state more efficient, more solvent, and more militarily powerful.

It was not only the blatant corruption of the newborn Restoration state which convinced a number of officials in the upper reaches of government that a return to the old ways was a mistake, however. The new international situation in which England found itself from the 1660s onward made reform a matter of national security. On the one hand, the commercial and naval power of the Dutch, backed by the resources of a state which seemed to enjoy an endless wellspring of credit, posed a serious long-term threat to England's economic well-being. The Commonwealth had passed the Navigation Acts in 1651 in an effort to damage the Dutch carrying trade, and in the war that followed the navy had acquitted itself well. Since then, however, English state capacities had declined, whereas the Dutch remained as strong as ever.

The reviving power of France posed an even more serious threat to English security. For almost a century that country had been racked by internal disorder, and England's perennial fear of her neighbor had subsided. But as the 1660s and 1670s progressed, the far-reaching nature of the changes introduced by Louis XIV and Colbert became clear, as did the aggressive character of the French king's foreign policy. Suddenly England found itself facing an expansionist Catholic power nearly four times its size lying just 12 miles off the coast.

These threats convinced a handful of exceptionally talented politicians and administrators within the English government that something had to be done. The most prominent member of this group was undoubtedly Sir George Downing, a nephew of John Winthrop raised in New England. He had served as Cromwell's chief of intelligence and ambassador to the Hague before nimbly switching his allegiance to Charles just before the Restoration. During his years in Holland, Downing had come to know at first hand the challenges posed by the Dutch. As a

<hr />

[96]   Ibid., pp. 203ff.; Hutton, *The Restoration*, pp. 185–190.

Teller of the Exchequer, he was also intimately acquainted with the shortcomings of the traditional English fiscal apparatus. He came to believe that only a radical change in the country's financial system, combined with a return to Interregnum-style administration and a strong navy, would allow England to hold its own against the Dutch.[97]

These views were seconded by an erstwhile employee of Downing at the Exchequer, Samuel Pepys. He had formerly served as private secretary to the head of the Protectorate fleet, Edward Montagu, and was now Clerk of the Acts at the Navy Board.[98] Although the Interregnum experiences of Downing and Pepys certainly shaped their views, it was not only former servants of the republican government who saw the need for change. Sir William Coventry, son of Charles I's Lord Keeper and an ardent royalist, was so strident about reform that he seems to have had no friends other than Pepys and Sir John Duncombe, another "new man."[99]

Aside from their common belief in administrative and financial reform and in a strong military, all of these men were obsessed with the details of bureaucratic organization such as record keeping, minuting, and the proper division of labor among different offices. Indeed, Coventry was ridiculed in a play written by two political rivals for the pride he took in a combination desk and filing cabinet which he had invented.[100]

Though Charles never seems to have had much interest in increasing England's military might, and only backed moves towards rationalization and greater efficiency if they promised to lessen his dependence on Parliament, the reformers did receive the support of two important

[97] Henry Roseveare, "Prejudice and Policy: Sir George Downing as Parliamentary Entrepreneur," in: D. C. Coleman and Peter Mathias (eds.), *Enterprise and History: Essays in Honour of Charles Wilson* (Cambridge: Cambridge University Press, 1984), pp. 135–150, esp. pp. 140–142; idem, *The Treasury*, pp. 59–60; there is one biography of Downing, but it is very weak on his career as a Restoration reformer: John Beresford, *The Godfather of Downing Street* (London: Richard Cobden-Sanderson, 1925).

[98] The principal source on Pepys are his fascinating diaries covering the years 1660 through 1669, now available in a definitive scholarly edition: *The Diary of Samuel Pepys*, Robert Latham and William Matthews (eds.), 11 vols. (London: Bell & Hyman, 1970–83). Arthur Bryant's trilogy on Pepys remains the standard biography: *Samuel Pepys: The Man in the Making* (Cambridge: Cambridge University Press, 1933); *Samuel Pepys: The Years of Peril* (Cambridge: Cambridge University Press, 1935); *Samuel Pepys: The Saviour of the Navy* (Cambridge: Cambridge University Press, 1938).

[99] Edward Hyde, Earl of Clarendon, *The Life of Edward Earl of Clarendon* (Oxford: Clarendon, 1827), vol. II, pp. 200–204; Gilbert Burnet, *History of My Own Time*, edited by Osmund Airy (Oxford: Clarendon, 1897–1900), vol. I, pp. 478–479; Pepys, *Diary*, vol. IX, pp. 40–41.

[100] The play was *The Country Gentleman* (1669) by the Duke of Buckingham and Sir Robert Howard. In it, Coventry is presented as "Sir Cautious Trouble-All" and Duncombe as "Sir Gravity Empty." See Pepys, *Diary*, vol. IX, pp. 445, 471.

figures in the early Restoration government, James Duke of York (the king's brother and future James II) and General George Monck, by that time Duke of Albemarle. James had been given command of the navy in 1660 and hoped to build it into a powerful base of political support by staffing it with loyal and talented officials. To this end he appointed Coventry secretary to the Admiralty and Pepys Clerk of the Acts (secretary to the Navy Board) and consistently encouraged their vigorous efforts at administrative reform.[101]

Meanwhile, the small standing army had been left in the hands of Albemarle, who had made the Restoration possible by bringing the Republic's Scottish army over to the king. Albemarle was a professional soldier of great experience who attempted, with the help of his old Secretary-at-War Sir William Clarke, to retain the advantages of the New Model Army within the small (approximately 6,000-man) permanent force which Parliament had permitted to remain in existence under the euphemistic term "Guards and Garrisons."[102]

While the encouragement which the reformers received from James, Albemarle, and other courtiers was important, it was ultimately the support (often unwitting) of Parliament which allowed major changes to be introduced and later institutionalized. The experiences of the Interregnum had left a deep mark on the collective memory of that body. On the one hand, Parliament had come to see *domestic* military power as the primary threat to its existence. On the other hand, the Civil War had created new precedents for active parliamentary involvement in foreign affairs and the details of domestic administration.

Furthermore, the country gentry who made up the great bulk of the Commons brought with them to Westminster a natural suspicion of a state apparatus which they saw as corrupt and a court which seemed more and more tainted by Catholic and pro-French sympathies. These sentiments drove MPs, whatever their theoretical views on the royal prerogative, to investigate corruption and maladministration and openly to advocate first an anti-Dutch, and then an anti-French and pro-Dutch foreign policy.[103] In this way, Parliament not only strengthened the position of reformers like Pepys and Downing in their battle against "old corruption," but also served to remind Charles of the new geo-political threats facing the nation.

---

[101] Clarendon, *Life*, vol. II, pp. 202, 459–460; Burnet, *A History*, vol. I, p. 298; Pepys, *Diary*, vol. X, p. 207 and passim.

[102] John Childs, *The Army of Charles II* (London: Routledge & Kegan Paul, 1976), pp. 7–9, 90–91, 94–95, 233. Childs's book provides details on all aspects of the Restoration army.

[103] D. T. Witcombe, *Charles II and the Cavalier House of Commons 1663–1674* (Manchester: Manchester University Press, 1966), pp. 13–15, 26, 163–166, 178 and passim.

In the late 17th and 18th centuries, it was certainly possible to field an effective army and even navy without the institutions of a modern, or even proto-modern, state behind them. Indeed, there were three possible organizational responses to the current geopolitical situation available to the English government – complacency, rationalization, or irrationalization. Nevertheless, the existence of a permanent national representative body at the pinnacle of the state created a unique structural situation in Restoration England. Parliament, in effect, provided a strong counterweight to anti-reform forces within the old state apparatus. This enabled reformers to put into practice the most difficult organizational response: the rationalization of a largely patrimonial state infrastructure.

War and the First Round of Permanent Reforms

During the four short years between 1667 and 1671, the first major steps were taken towards the permanent rationalization of the English state. Taking advantage of pressures from Parliament for reform, the group of young administrator-politicians mentioned above established the departmental supremacy of the Treasury, introduced modern organizational routines, attacked proprietary officeholding, and began the long, arduous process of replacing financial cliques with broad-based investment by the general public as the source of short-term government credit.

It was the Second Dutch War (1665–7) which provided the first opportunity for major reform during the Restoration. Coventry and Pepys, with the Duke of York's backing, had been able to introduce important administrative improvements in the navy in the early 1660s, and a Commonwealth-style commission headed by Duncombe had been appointed to run the notoriously corrupt Ordnance Office in 1664.[104] Yet the presence of Clarendon and Lord Treasurer Southampton at the head of government, as well as of many proprietary officeholders within it, had thus far blocked major changes.

James, perhaps deceived by the progress already made within his own department, came to see a successful war against the Dutch as a good way to increase his own prestige and standing at Court. He was seconded by Downing, then English ambassador at the Hague, who was convinced that the Dutch would make commercial concessions under

---

[104] Pepys, *Diary*, vol. VIII, p. 178; H. C. Tomlinson, "Place and Profit: An Examination of the Ordnance Office, 1660–1714," *Transactions of the Royal Historical Society*, 5th series, vol. 25 (1975), pp. 55–75, here at pp. 58–59; idem, *Guns and Government: The Ordnance Office under the Later Stuarts* (London: Royal Historical Society, 1979), p. 16.

the threat of war but would not actually be willing to fight. Although Coventry, equipped with an expert knowledge of both the state of the navy and of government finances, believed that England was not yet in a position to win such a contest, he was overruled, and full-scale conflict broke out in 1665.[105]

Though the war began well for England with a naval victory off Lowestoft, Coventry's fears proved well-founded. Neither England's financial system nor its naval administration were yet capable of standing up to the pressures of sustained warfare, and both deteriorated rapidly over the course of 1666 and 1667. The situation was not helped by the ravages of the plague and fire of London (September 1666). By June of 1667, English defenses had deteriorated to the point where the Dutch were able to sail up the Thames and burn the great naval dockyard at Chatham.

As the military situation grew worse, Parliament directed its wrath at the principal government departments. As early as 1665, the navy's second in command, the Earl of Sandwich, was forced to resign over allegations in the House that he had embezzled prize money (the proceeds from captured Dutch shipping). In September 1666, the Commons demanded to see the navy, naval stores, and Ordnance accounts before appropriating further funds for the war. Finally, after peace was concluded in July 1667 in the wake of the Chatham raid, Parliament launched a sustained series of attacks on various senior naval officials (Carteret, Brouncker, Pett) through its Committee on Miscarriages, which had been created to examine Navy management during the war.[106] Their subsequent removal assured Pepys a dominance in naval administration which was to last, with only one interruption, until 1688.

Ironically, the major political casualty of the war was Clarendon, who had opposed it all along. As his position weakened under the impact of defeat, Arlington and Buckingham, the factional leaders who had long opposed him, saw their chance. Buckingham, who had grown up with the king, already had Charles's ear. But Arlington, not enjoying such advantages, sought to improve his standing by recruiting leading reformers like Coventry and Duncombe and the brilliant young crypto-Catholic politician Sir Thomas Clifford into his entourage.[107] He was

[105] Pepys, *Diary*, vol. V, pp. 107, 111, 212; vol. X, p. 113; Hutton, *The Restoration*, pp. 215–217.
[106] Witcombe, *Charles II*, pp. 37–38, 40, 42–45, 65, 80–81, 88–89, 93–98; Pepys, *Diary*, vol. VIII, pp. 484–485 and passim, and vol. IX passim. A complete listing of the countless references in the diary to investigations by the Commons into the administration of the navy during the Dutch War can be found in ibid., vol. XI, p. 205.
[107] Clarendon, *Life*, vol. II, pp. 204–210, 460; Burnet, *A History*, vol. I, p. 402; Pepys, *Diary*, vol. VIII, pp. 185–186.

thus able to present a strong opposition "team" to the king, ready to step in at any moment to rectify the mismanagement of Clarendon and his friends.

Arlington's great chance came in May 1667 when Lord Treasurer Southampton died. Arlington urged Charles to put the Treasury into commission, and was seconded by James, who had been favorably impressed by the improvements made under the Duncombe-led commission at the Ordnance. Charles consented and appointed Coventry, Duncombe, and Clifford to the new Treasury Board, with Albemarle as figurehead First Lord. Quite fittingly, the Commission chose Downing to be its secretary.[108] Six months later, Clarendon himself was gone, forced to flee after being impeached by the House.

The activities of the Restoration's Second Treasury Commission[109] took place in an atmosphere of steady attacks by Parliament on corruption and inefficiency in government. Mention has already been made to the Committee on Miscarriages, set up in October 1667 to determine why the navy had performed so badly during the Dutch War. Moreover, after more than a year of pressure, the Commons forced the king in December 1667 to accept a Commission of Public Accounts empowered to investigate the fate of the money voted by Parliament to support the conflict.[110] The activities of both of these bodies provided crucial indirect support to the Treasury commissioners in their efforts to alter the basic pattern of English administration and finance. Taken together with the contemporaneous reforms in the navy and Ordnance, the Commission's accomplishments represented the first step on the road to a major and permanent restructuring of the English state apparatus.

The primary goal of the Commission was to establish the Treasury as a kind of "master department" with the power to oversee and regulate central government finance and administration by apportioning revenue and monitoring the expenditures and appointments of the other government departments (Admiralty, Navy Board, Guards and Garrisons, Household, Exchequer, Mint, Works). In addition, it sought to solidify the Crown's finances by closely supervising revenue collection and managing government credit. Although this Treasury program was only fully realized under Godolphin (1702–10), the Second Treasury Commission made an important start. Armed with broad powers granted

---

[108] Clarendon, *Life*, vol. III, pp. 240–245; Pepys, *Diary*, vol. VIII, pp. 229–230, 238. Lord Ashley, the later Lord Shaftesbury, patron of Locke and "founder" of the Whig party, also received a place on the Commission by virtue of his position as Chancellor of the Exchequer, at that time a lifetime, venal post which Ashley himself owned.

[109] The Treasury had briefly been in commission in 1660 before the appointment of Southampton as Lord Treasurer.

[110] Pepys, *Diary*, vol. VIII, pp. 559–560; Witcombe, *Charles II*, pp. 52–53, 76, 79, 90.

to it in a series of Privy Council orders of 1667 and 1668, Downing and his colleagues promulgated fundamental changes in five areas.

First, the Commission set about putting its own house in order by introducing, at Downing's instigation, a precise system of records (warrant books, letter books, minute books) and a set of written procedures for departmental business. The fact that decisions had to be discussed and taken collectively helped encourage this formalization. Second, some measure of control (or at least oversight) over expenditure was instituted by the rule of "specific sanction," which required written Treasury approval for departmental disbursements. In addition, departments were required to send in weekly statements of receipts, spending, and cash balances in order to provide the Treasury with the information necessary for a rational distribution of revenue.[111]

Third, the Commission launched an ambitious scheme to alter fundamentally the existing system of government credit. Because of the slow and irregular rate at which tax receipts were collected in the 17th century, no state could rely on such receipts for its daily expenditures. The problem of how to come up with large amounts of ready cash in advance of taxes was a universal one, and the solution chosen had a profound effect on state structure. As mentioned earlier, the English state had, since the time of James I, come increasingly to rely – as its main source of operating cash – on huge advances from the syndicates of bankers and merchants who farmed the customs, and later the excise. Downing felt strongly that this gave London's goldsmith-bankers too much leverage over the government, and in fact worked to limit the latter's access to funds.[112]

As an alternative, Downing conceived of a plan to borrow running cash directly from the general public, a plan first embodied in the so-called Additional Aid of 1665. This statute was pushed through Parliament by Downing and Coventry against the wishes of Clarendon.[113] According to the Act, money raised through a new tax passed to support the Dutch War would be set aside to pay off loans offered directly to the Exchequer at 6% (the bankers were at that time charging 10%). The lender would receive a numbered receipt called a Treasury Order, and repayment of these loans, guaranteed by parliamentary statute, would occur in strict numerical sequence. Since these Orders were assignable by endorsement, they could also be issued to departmental

---

[111] Roseveare, *The Treasury*, pp. 62–63; idem, *The Treasury 1660–1870: The Foundations of Control* (London: George Allen & Unwin, 1973), pp. 26–28, 31, 111–115; Tomlinson, *Guns and Government*, pp. 36–39.

[112] Roseveare, *The Treasury*, p. 61; idem, *The Treasury 1660–1870*, p. 23.

[113] Clarendon, *Life*, vol. III, pp. 4–26; Pepys, *Diary*, vol. VI, p. 292.

paymasters to be used as a form of payment for goods and services, or sold on the money market to raise cash.[114]

After the success of the Additional Aid of 1665, similar borrowing clauses were inserted in the other new tax bills passed to finance the war. Holders of Treasury Orders drawn on these taxes were legally assured of repayment by acts of Parliament, and could sue the government at common law for their money. In the tight credit conditions which obtained following the end of the war, the Treasury decided to allow Orders to be drawn on the ordinary revenue as well. Yet unlike earlier issues, the only security these new Treasury Orders enjoyed was a "solemn promise" made by the king on June 18, 1667, to the effect that the government would punctually honor all its obligations.[115] As will be seen, this distinction was to have fateful consequences several years later.

Fourth, the new Commission attempted to tackle head-on the massive problem of proprietary officeholding which beset the entire central government. On January 31, 1668, the Treasury obtained by an Order in Council the right to review the terms of all future grants of offices whose incumbents were paid directly from the Exchequer. Armed with this important power, the Commissioners set about changing as many positions as possible from life to "at pleasure" tenure and curbing the sale of reversions. They generally were quite successful at this in all departments except the Exchequer, which vigorously resisted their interference.[116]

Finally, the Treasury moved to gain greater control over revenue collection. In 1671, a syndicate of farmers led by the brewer and financier Sir William Bucknall, which already held the lease to much of the Excise, sought to take over the Customs as well. At first the Commission seemed ready to agree, but when Bucknall tried at the eleventh hour to pressure the Treasury into accepting a less favorable contract, the Board moved decisively to remove him and take over collection itself. The Treasury set up a subsidiary commission to carry out the formidable

---

[114] Roseveare, *The Treasury 1660–1870*, pp. 23–26. For a lucid discussion of the complicated details of the Treasury Order system, see Chandaman, *English Public Revenue*, appendix 1. To gain support for his reform among the investing public, Downing published a pamphlet explaining how the system worked and included in it a facsimile of a Treasury Order: [Sir George Downing], "A State of the Case Between furnishing His Majesty with Money by way of Loan, or by way of Advance of the Tax of any particular Place, upon the Act for the 1,250,000 l. passed at Oxford, October 9, 1665" (London, 1666). An original of the pamphlet is preserved in the Goldsmiths' Library, London; the Kress Collection at the Harvard Business School also possesses a microfilm copy.

[115] Roseveare, *Treasury 1660–1870*, p. 32.

[116] Sainty, "A Reform," pp. 156–160; idem, "The Tenure of Office," pp. 464–466.

task of creating a national network of state customs officials at short notice, and placed Sir George Downing at its head. Downing succeeded in his latest assignment by taking many of the farmers' employees into government service. The English customs were never again to be put to farm.[117]

The Second Treasury Commission had accomplished a great deal since 1667. Treasury supremacy over the other departments had been clearly established, the Board's procedures set standards of organization for others to follow, and a start had been made in solving the deeply rooted problems of administrative practice, credit, and revenue collection which had plagued the English state since the days of the early Stuarts. Parliament recognized these achievements in 1670–1 by voting substantial extraordinary supplies.[118] But by this time the period of reform was nearly at an end.

By the end of 1670, the Commission was only a shadow of its former self. Coventry had been removed by the king in 1669 for challenging Buckingham to a duel after the latter had insulted him in his play *The Country Gentleman*.[119] Albemarle had died in 1670 and Downing had relinquished his post as Treasury Secretary to manage the new Customs Commission. Sir Thomas Clifford, Arlington's young protégé, was now the dominant figure at the Treasury and in the government more generally. In record time, this obscure gentleman from Devon had risen to become one of Charles's closest advisors. After laboring long and hard to implement the Treasury's reform program, he was to deal it a damaging blow by his actions of the next two years.

The reformers of 1667–71 had, with the backing of the Commons, increased the powers of the Treasury and widened the state's borrowing base in order to enhance England's military capabilities in the face of a twofold foreign threat. During most of the next decade, other politicians attempted to use the new capacities concentrated in the Treasury to undermine Parliament's independence. The failure of first Clifford and then Danby in this enterprise set the stage for a new wave of reform after 1679.

Anti-Reformist Efforts

The generous grants of 1670–1 came too late for Charles. Alienated by the Commons's obstreperousness in the wake of the Dutch War, he had begun after 1668 to search for a way to free himself from dependence

---

[117] Chandaman, *English Public Revenue*, pp. 26–29.
[118] J. R. Jones, *Court and Country: England 1658–1714* (Cambridge: Harvard University Press, 1978), pp. 167–168.
[119] Pepys, *Diary*, vol. IX, pp. 466–468, 471–472, 478.

on Parliament. Clifford, strongly seconded by his co-religionists James and Arlington, devised a plan not only to increase the Crown's financial independence, but also promote the cause of Catholicism in England. First, Clifford would use the new strength of the Treasury to dispense bribes and favors to members of Parliament, and to gain extra funds for the government. As early as 1669, a popular pamphlet had already dubbed him the "bribemaster general."[120]

Next, Louis XIV would be approached about providing a large, covert annual subsidy to Charles. The French king was indeed willing to do this in return for English support for his planned invasion of the United Provinces, and for a public declaration by Charles that he had converted to Catholicism. Louis even promised to send troops to help quell any disturbances in England this declaration might provoke. Since the condition of the navy had improved greatly since 1667, Charles had reason to believe that a new war with the Dutch might bring substantial permanent financial gains in the form of higher customs revenues gained from increased commerce, all of which was free from parliamentary control.[121] As a result of these calculations, Charles agreed to Louis's demands, and the infamous Treaty of Dover was signed in 1670.[122] True to his duplicitous nature, the king had voiced great approval for the Treasury Commission's reform program while at the same time secretly pursuing a quite different line of policy.

When the time for Louis's attack on Holland approached in late 1671, Clifford found that despite his efforts to influence Parliament, the government was still laboring under a mountain of debt accumulated from the last war with the Dutch. As a result, no funds were available to outfit the fleet, an absolute prerequisite for participation in any conflict. The solution which Clifford found to this problem was cynical in the extreme. He persuaded Charles to declare on January 2, 1672, that the government would suspend repayment on all Treasury Orders not secured by act of Parliament on specific tax revenues, i.e., all Orders guaranteed by the king's "solemn promise" of 1667. The so-called Stop of the Exchequer destroyed in one fell swoop nearly all of the progress made since Downing's Additional Aid of 1665 in establishing a broad public market for government borrowing. At the same time, however, the Stop showed that not even an irresponsible king could touch the Orders backed by Parliament, and thus conclusively proved that only the latter could provide a firm basis for public credit.[123]

[120] Witcombe, *Charles II*, p. 99; Jones, *Charles II*, pp. 94–95; Burnet, *A History*, vol. I, pp. 553–554.
[121] Jones, *Court and Country*, pp. 169–170.   [122] Idem, *Charles II*, pp. 88–91.
[123] Chandaman, *English Public Revenue*, p. 298; Andrew Browning, "The Stop of the Exchequer," *History*, vol. 14, no. 56 (January 1930), pp. 333–337.

As might have been predicted, Clifford's master plan quickly turned to disaster. Two days after declaring war on the United Provinces on March 13, 1672, Charles suspended the penal laws against Catholics and Dissenters (Declaration of Indulgence), provoking a storm of anger among the Anglican gentry. While the navy did indeed perform quite well, opposition to the war rose as it became clear that Louis XIV was intent on utterly destroying the United Provinces. Sympathy for the Dutch among the English public rose as the former were forced to break their dykes and flood much of the country to prevent the French from capturing Amsterdam.

By the spring of 1673, Charles had been forced to withdraw the Declaration of Indulgence, and in its stead a Test Act was passed forcing officeholders to swear allegiance to the Anglican Church. Rather than take the Test, both Clifford, Lord Treasurer since November 1673, and James (Lord High Admiral) resigned their posts. By the end of the year, many in Parliament were pressing the government not only to make peace with the Dutch (now led by William of Orange, Charles's nephew), but actively to enter the war on their side against the absolutist French.[124]

The events of 1672–3 brought a permanent change to the views of Parliament. Catholic France was now, and was to remain for the next century and a half, the principal enemy, and Holland a valued ally. Suspicion of the king, his brother, and their motives was rising. What had begun as a policy to increase royal independence from Parliament had only served to strengthen that body.

Charles's attempt to widen his room for maneuver with the help of Louis had failed, but he soon found another courtier-politician with a new plan to increase royal autonomy from Parliament. This was Sir Thomas Osborne, an obscure Yorkshire follower of Buckingham and better known to posterity as Lord Danby.[125] As Treasurer of the Navy after 1669, he had gained first-hand experience of the power now concentrated in the Treasury. His plan was to use this power, in the manner of Clifford, to "manage" the Commons, while at the same time placating them with anti-Catholic policies at home and anti-French policies abroad.[126] First Charles had tried to circumvent Parliament by turning to the French for an independent source of income; now,

[124] Witcombe, *Charles II*, pp. 141–142, 146, 164, 166; Keith Feiling, *A History of the Tory Party 1640–1714* (Oxford: Clarendon, 1924), pp. 151–152.

[125] The standard biography of Danby is Andrew Browning's three-volume work *Thomas Osborne Earl of Danby and Duke of Leeds 1632–1712* (Glasgow: Jackson, Son & Co., 1944–1951).

[126] Danby set down his policy goals in a memorandum reprinted in Browning, *Thomas Osborne*, vol. II, p. 63. See also ibid., vol. I, p. 146 and Feiling, *History*, p. 154.

with Danby's help, he would try to subvert it using the newly reformed Treasury.

Danby was appointed Lord Treasurer in June of 1673, and over the next six years he vigorously implemented his "counter-reformation." It had three major elements. First, he sought to repair the credit of the Treasury, heavily damaged by the 1672 Stop of the Exchequer. With investor confidence shaken, he turned away from Downing's Treasury Order system and sought instead to borrow large sums from a single network of financiers, a method then employed in France by Colbert. To this end, Danby appointed Richard Kent, a front man for the financier Sir Stephen Fox, to the post of Receiver-General of the Excise. Fox then used the receipts of the excise as the security against which he advanced the government large and regular sums of his own money and money borrowed from other financiers and wealthy investors.[127] In 17th-century parlance, this was known as an "undertaking," a variant of the system of "inside" credit employed in France. As a method of raising working cash, it was the polar opposite of the Treasury Order system.

Second, Danby employed his new stream of cash to win over members of Parliament for the Court. He made detailed surveys of the Commons in order to identify potential government supporters, and then used his control of revenue liberally to dispense pensions drawn on the excise in order to shore up their loyalty. These grants were supplemented by direct payments from the Treasury's discretionary fund, the "secret service" account.[128] As an adjunct to this policy, Danby abandoned the guidelines of the 1667–71 Commission and began to re-introduce life tenure and the sale of reversions, thereby seeking to gain the favor of the beneficiaries in the House.[129] In time-honored fashion, he also sought to provide as many seats and offices as possible to members of his family and his band of clients from Yorkshire.[130]

Finally, Danby supplemented his bribes with a foreign policy more in keeping with the sentiments of the House. In February 1674, he made peace with the Dutch. In 1677, he backed Pepys's urgent request of the Commons to provide substantial funds to build 30 new ships to counter the growing naval power of France. In November 1677 he arranged the marriage of James's eldest daughter Mary, who had been

---

[127] Christopher Clay, *Public Finance and Private Wealth: The Career of Sir Stephen Fox 1627–1716* (Oxford: Clarendon, 1978), pp. 98–110.

[128] Clayton Roberts, "Party and Patronage in Late Stuart England," in: Stephen Baxter (ed.), *England's Rise to Greatness 1660–1763* (Berkeley: University of California Press, 1983), pp. 185–212, here at pp. 188–189; Browning, *Thomas Osborne*, vol. I, pp. 167–173. Browning has brought together a collection of lists of pensioners and supporters used by Danby in his efforts to manage Parliament in ibid., vol. III, pp. 45–120.

[129] Sainty, "A Reform," pp. 10–162.   [130] Feiling, *History*, p. 165.

raised a Protestant, to William of Orange, and shortly thereafter concluded an anti-French alliance with the United Provinces.

Yet Danby was unable to convince Parliament of the government's
sincerity. Suspicions about Charles's and James's pro-French sympathies
continued to grow. Indeed, Charles had once again been in secret
contact with Louis. Then, in September 1678, a former preacher named
Titus Oates revealed a supposed Catholic plot to murder Charles and
take over the country. In the ensuing hysteria, Danby was swept from
office and the Whigs began to seek to debar the Catholic James from
the succession. The Exclusion Crisis (1679–1681) had begun.[131]

Despite his liberal grants of pensions and offices paid for by new
sources of credit, Danby had been unable successfully to undermine
the independence of Parliament. The resources available to the Treasury in the 1670s were not up to such a project.[132] His one concrete
achievement had been to reverse many of the gains made between
1667 and 1671. But a new change of direction by Charles in the face
of intense parliamentary attacks meant that the legacy of Downing and
his colleagues would soon be revived. Over the next six years, a new
Treasury commission was to reassert that department's supremacy, renew the attack on inefficiency and proprietary officeholding, and greatly
expand the direct state collection of tax revenues.

A Second Reform Offensive

Eleven years earlier, the logic of factional politics had given a small
group of young reformers the chance to put their ideas into practice
and, supported by intensive parliamentary inquiries into administrative
practices, they had achieved a great deal. At the time, Charles did not
seem to have fully realized the benefits that rationalized finance and
administration could bring to him. After the failed attempts first to
bypass Parliament with the help of French subsidies and then to subvert
it with pensions and grants of office, there was little to lose by giving
reform another try. If the king's permanent revenues could be managed with the utmost efficiency and waste rooted out, perhaps the royal
income would prove sufficient to allow the king to live for long periods
without having to come on bended knee to the Commons. Once again,
as in 1667, fierce parliamentary attacks directed at the corruption of
the previous government created the proper atmosphere for a major

---

[131] The details of English domestic and foreign policy between 1677 and 1679 are extremely complex and frequently baffling. Jones provides a cogent summary of them
in his *Charles II*, pp. 121–134.
[132] Roberts, "Party and Patronage," pp. 189–190.

housecleaning. In March of 1679 Charles appointed a third Treasury commission.

In a way, the magnitude of the previous Commission's achievement was reflected in the fact that the king could afford to name nonprofessionals to the new Treasury board. Neither Laurence Hyde nor Sidney Godolphin, the men who were to dominate this Third Commission, possessed any prior financial background. True, they were assisted by Sir John Ernle, who had been Comptroller of Naval Stores, Sir Edward Dering, a former Customs Commissioner, and (after November 1679) by the financier Sir Stephen Fox.[133] But it was the novice Hyde, Clarendon's younger son, who was to be the driving force at the Treasury for the next eight years, and his method was simply to follow to the letter the procedures laid down by his predecessors Coventry, Downing, and Duncombe, and to carry forward the plans they had not been able to realize.

The central aim of the new Treasury team was to bring ordinary revenue and expenditure into balance by ruthlessly rooting out waste both at Court and in the administration, tightening control over departmental spending, and heightening the efficiency of tax collection. In addition, they were determined to put an end once and for all to life tenure and reversions. Finally, public credit was to be restored by paying off the debts built up by Danby's free-spending ways and keeping a more careful watch over departmental borrowing.[134]

The first area which the Commission attacked was the bloated expenditures of the Household, Wardrobe, Chamber, and Privy Purse. Effectively using the atmosphere of extreme crisis generated by the Exclusion Parliaments, Hyde and his colleagues ordered spending in these departments slashed by nearly 60%.[135] Despite the resulting storm of protests and angry attacks on Hyde, the Treasury was able – with the active support of the king – to make its restrictions stick. The obstreperous Parliaments of 1679–81 had hardened Charles's resolve to live within his means no matter what the cost so that he would no longer be dependent on their good will.[136]

Setting similarly low-expenditure targets for the military, and for the navy especially, could prove damaging to national defense if not

---

[133] J. C. Sainty, *Treasury Officials 1660–1870* (London: Athlone, 1972), p. 18; J. M. Collinge, *Navy Board Officials 1660–1870* (London: Institute of Historical Research, 1978), p. 99; Sir Edward Dering, *The Diaries and Papers of Sir Edward Dering Second Baronet 1644 to 1684*, Maurice Bond (ed.) (London: Her Majesty's Stationery Office, 1976), p. 20.

[134] Roseveare, *The Treasury 1660–1870*, pp. 43–44; Chandaman, *English Public Revenue*, pp. 247ff. Dering, *Diaries and Papers*, p. 115.

[135] Chandaman, *English Public Revenue*, pp. 249–250, 253.

[136] Burnet, *History*, vol. II, p. 341.

supported by an intimate knowledge of the services' real needs. Hence
the Commission resolved to obtain far more information from the
Secretary-at-War's office and Navy Board, and subject their activities to
closer scrutiny in order to arrive at reasonable spending limits. The net
result of all of these initiatives, which continued long after the Exclusion Crisis had ended in 1681, was to increase greatly the Treasury's
knowledge of and power over departmental spending.[137]

This control over spending was complemented by a new, more aggressive approach towards the all-important excise farmers. First, in 1680 a
much tougher contract was negotiated to squeeze the last penny from
the farmers. Then, in 1683, the Treasury took over collection itself,
using the 1671 "nationalization" of the customs as a model. As a result
of these reforms, the state's coffers gained maximum benefit from the
upturn in trade of the 1680s. Some of this revenue was then used to
reduce substantially the debt inherited from the 1670s.[138] Finally, the
Commission launched a new assault on life tenure, reversions, and the
traffic in offices, and this time took the war to that citadel of traditional-
ism, the Exchequer.[139]

Thanks to such efforts, the Third Treasury Commission successfully
accomplished what the king had asked of it. Between 1681 and his
death in February 1685, Charles lived "of his own" without once having
to call Parliament. The plans first devised by a handful of patriotic
reformers determined to increase England's military capacity had been
taken up by a group of talented young courtiers obsessed with efficiency as a means of freeing their royal master from the constraints of
regular Parliaments. Had they unwittingly laid the groundwork for
absolutism in their country?

This is doubtful, at least as far as Charles is concerned. By gaining a
certain measure of financial independence from Parliament, the king
had only done what the constitutional theory of the day had argued
he always should do: live within the means of his ordinary revenue
in peacetime. Charles never showed the slightest intention of raising
taxes or of legislating without parliamentary approval. The only way
he could have done so would have been through armed force, and
it was precisely during this period of the late 1670s and early 1680s that
the king allowed conditions in the navy to deteriorate.[140] In addition,

---

[137] Chandaman, *English Public Revenue*, pp. 251–252.
[138] Ibid., pp. 71–76, 254–255; see also Hughes, *Studies*, pp. 155–163.
[139] Sainty, "The Tenure of Offices," pp. 466–467; idem., "A Reform," pp. 162–163.
[140] Charles had chosen to dismiss Pepys from his post as Secretary of the Admiralty at the
height of the Popish Plot hysteria because he was a known intimate of James. Charles
then placed the direction of the navy in the hands of a commission of thoroughly
inexperienced politicians who did substantial damage to the battle-readiness of that

expanding his tiny army seems never to have been a major concern of Charles.[141]

The same cannot be said, however, for his brother James. For him, rational government had always been a means of buttressing military power, hence the loyalty which he inspired in reformers like Pepys, who was certainly no lover of Catholicism. But it was not until his own reign that James was to make clear that this military power was aimed at his own people.

One can legitimately ask, however, how the English state would have developed had Charles not been succeeded by a sovereign determined to impose Catholic absolutism by force of arms, but rather by one simply content to live within his or her resources. The experiences of the Tudor period provide a useful guide here, for by the early 1680s Charles had in fact established a position vis-à-vis Parliament similar to that enjoyed by Henry and Elizabeth. As discussed above, the occasional Parliaments of that earlier period proved unable to prevent the consolidation and spread of patrimonial practices and institutions within the English state, a trend which accelerated rapidly under the early Stuarts.

The roots of these appropriating tendencies can of course be traced back to England's early exposure to sustained geopolitical pressures and the precocious large-scale statebuilding that resulted therefrom. These tendencies were still very much present in the England of the 1680s. They had been held in check by parliamentary pressures after 1660. True, the emergence of a distinctive departmental ethos at the Treasury and the Navy Board (and, to a lesser degree, at the War Office and Ordnance), engendered by established routines and clerical continuity, promised to provide some defense against a return to the situation of the 1630s, but it is very doubtful whether this would have proven enough. An English government of the late 17th century free of both war and Parliaments would soon have lapsed back into its old habits.[142] It was only in the 1700s that a new guarantor of efficiency, the London financial markets, was in a position to act as a partial structural

service during their five-year tenure. See J. R. Tanner, *A Descriptive Catalogue of the Naval Manuscripts in the Pepysian Library at Magdalene College, Cambridge* (London: Naval Records Society, 1903), pp. 57–64.

[141] In 1685, after the loss of Tangier, the core of the English standing army was composed of ten regiments, the same total as in the 1660s if the four Tangier regiments are included. See Childs, *Army*, pp. 233–235.

[142] It goes without saying that had Charles or a like-minded successor become involved in an international conflict after 1681, he or she would have had to recall Parliament in order to obtain the proper funding. And as the experiences of both 1665–7 and 1672–4 show, post-Restoration Parliaments always demanded the right to scrutinize closely the war effort in return for financial support.

equivalent to parliamentary pressure, and a sophisticated political press was emerging which would help in the same task. But neither was yet present in 1685.

During James's brief time on the throne (1685–88), many of the trends present during Charles's last years continued. Hyde, now Lord Rochester, was put in sole charge of the Treasury and he stayed there until January 1687, when his strong Anglicanism led him to break with the king. He was replaced by a commission which included Godolphin, Ernle, and Fox.[143] The policies of the Third Commission were thus extended without major alteration into the new reign. The generous permanent revenue voted James by his ascension Parliament,[144] combined with the usual careful management by the Treasury, obviated the need to convoke any further Parliaments during these three years.

Unlike Charles, James quickly set out to bolster substantially both the army and navy. He had already begun this task during the last two years of his brother's reign, when political conditions finally permitted him to return to Court. He promptly restored Pepys to his place in the Admiralty (1684), and the latter spent the next four years repairing the damage done by Charles's naval amateurs.[145] The most dramatic change, however, occurred in the army. At his ascension, James inherited an English army of 8,865 men. Monmouth's Rebellion provided him with an opportunity to raise this figure to nearly 20,000 by the end of 1685. By the time William landed in 1688, James's army possessed a paper strength of about 35,000.[146] This rapid expansion was effectively managed by another young and talented civil servant, William Blathwayt, who had been named Secretary-at-War in 1683.[147] The Commons' generosity in 1685 and expanding trade were only partly responsible for James's ability to afford a massive military buildup without consulting Parliament. The real credit goes to the Treasury and the economies it imposed through efficient management.[148]

In 1688, James clearly believed that he had a powerful fiscal-military machine at his disposal run by apolitical civil servants willing to carry out his every wish. And indeed when one looks at the cases of Pepys, Blathwayt, Godolphin, and Fox, one can only conclude that he was not entirely wrong in believing this. Staunch Protestants all, they stayed at

---

[143] Sainty, *Treasury Officials*, p. 18.

[144] See Chandaman's lucid discussion of the 1685 settlement and the misconceptions surrounding it in *English Public Revenue*, pp. 256–261.

[145] Tanner, *Descriptive Catalogue*, pp. 65–91.

[146] John Childs, *The Army, James II and the Glorious Revolution* (Manchester: Manchester University Press, 1980), pp. 1–3.

[147] Blathwayt's career is chronicled in: Gertrude Jacobsen, *William Blathwayt: A Late Seventeenth Century English Administrator* (New Haven: Yale University Press, 1932).

[148] Chandaman, *English Public Revenue*, pp. 259–261, 275–276.

their posts until the bitter end, though it is doubtful whether any of them would have actively participated in a campaign to impose Catholicism on the country by force. Where James certainly did miscalculate, however, was in judging the sentiments of his army's leaders. Alienated by the steady replacement of English officers with Irish Catholics, they went over with their troops to the Prince of Orange in considerable numbers, thus ensuring the king's defeat.[149]

That James, unlike his brother, did indeed intend to impose some kind of absolutism on England seems beyond dispute. His large-scale purges in the army and the commissions of the peace, his attempt to pack the 1688 Parliament, and his attacks on the Church of England all point in that direction, as does his well-known admiration for Louis XIV's regime. If William had not intervened, could James have succeeded in his designs? As in the case of Charles, historical analogy perhaps provides an answer.

Between 1649 and 1660, a variety of regimes, unpopular because of their religious sectarianism, ruled England with the help of a powerful army and navy. The Interregnum governments were able to improve the quality of central administration significantly, but only by relying on the assistance of Parliaments which had lost most of their legitimacy in the country as a whole. Moreover, none of these governments proved capable of putting the state's finances on a sound public footing by breaking its dependence on a small circle of City financiers. At base, this was due to the fact that in spite of the presence of armed troops in nearly every county in England, the authorities were unable to extract a sufficient amount of revenue from a hostile population. In this respect they fared little better than the Swedish army in Germany during the Thirty Years War, and it was this fact which ultimately doomed the revolutionary regimes of the 1650s. It is difficult to see how the fate of an even less popular Catholic dictatorship could have been any different.

When James fled England forever in December 1688, he left behind for his successors William and Mary a state apparatus fundamentally different from the one revived by his brother in 1660–2. A hierarchically organized central administration, manned by nonproprietary officials and supervised by an ever-vigilant Treasury, had replaced a disparate jumble of boards and departments staffed by proprietary officeholders and court favorites. Perhaps of even greater significance was the fact that a revolutionary system of public finance, built around efficient, state-controlled revenue collection and an ability to borrow from the general public rather than a handful of financiers, was already in place,

[149] Childs, *The Army, James II*, pp. 139–140, 150–164, 203–205.

albeit in embryonic form. The supreme test now lay before this new English state: sustained, large-scale warfare.

THE CONSOLIDATION OF THE NEW BRITISH STATE AFTER 1689

William had crossed the Channel not primarily to preserve the freedoms of Englishmen, but to save western Europe from Louis XIV. His ascension to the English throne plunged the country into 20 years of war with France (Nine Years War, 1689–1697; War of the Spanish Succession, 1702–1713), separated by only five years of uneasy peace. These were conflicts on a scale unlike anything England had experienced since the Hundred Years War, and they placed the central government under tremendous financial and administrative pressure. The usual result of such pressures among Europe's early statebuilders was, as we have seen in the two previous chapters, an "irrationalization" of the state. As organization broke down and money dried up, the authorities in Latin Europe were usually forced to place themselves in the hands of financiers, contractors, regional magnates, and anyone else with resources in order to stay afloat.

This did not happen in England after 1689. The revival of parliamentary power which was the Glorious Revolution's most significant achievement created conditions under which the reformed administrative system introduced between 1660 and 1688 could be preserved and expanded.[150] While the government made many mistakes during the Nine Years War, ministers and leading civil servants gained valuable experience and learned important lessons which they were to use during the War of the Spanish Succession (1702–13) finally to complete and perfect the fiscal-military system first envisaged by Sir George Downing in the 1660s.

Administrative Demands of Large-Scale Warfare

England's new leaders faced two immediate challenges during the Nine Years War: first, they had to meet the organizational demands of the huge military buildup which a land and sea war against France required; and second, they had to find the ready money to pay for that buildup. The former task proved to be much easier than the latter.

Ironically, it was the exertions of James which provided William with

---

[150] John Brewer has developed this idea with eloquence in his book *The Sinews of Power* (London: Hutchinson, 1989). I have benefited immeasurably from many discussions with Prof. Brewer on this period, although our interpretations differ on a number of points.

the efficient military machine which he was now to turn upon James's new protector Louis XIV. Though William, an experienced officer, took personal charge of the British army, he decided to retain William Blathwayt, the professional administrator who had served as James's Secretary-at-War, as his assistant. Blathwayt had managed the expansion of the army to 35,000 men in 1688, and the procedures he had developed for this proved able to accommodate a further increase to 87,440 in 1696 without excessive difficulty.[151]

From an administrative point of view, a similar situation obtained in the navy. The special commission (headed by Pepys) set up to reverse the navy's decline between 1679 and 1684, and to restore the fleet to top form, had just completed its work when the Revolution broke out. Current scholarship has substantiated Pepys's subsequent claim that he left the navy in excellent condition when he turned it over to James's opponents in December 1688. As a result, one must ascribe the poor state of the fleet in the first years of the war to the inexperience of a "political" Admiralty Board named by William in 1689.[152]

From 1691 on, however, the "professionals" within naval administration began to regain the upper hand: the Navy Board's three leading officers (Haddock, Tippetts, Sotherne) had 57 years of experience between them, and the new Admiralty Secretary named in 1695 (Burchett) had been a protégé of Pepys's in the 1680s.[153] The navy's main problems throughout the war were not organizational, but financial. The regulations laid down before 1688 proved capable of handling an increase in the fleet from 173 ships in that year to 323 in 1697, a truly remarkable expansion.[154]

Parliamentary Oversight

While the administrative personnel at the top of the key government departments changed remarkably little after 1688, the political environment in which they were forced to operate certainly did. The Parliaments

---

[151] Ivor Burton, "The Secretary at War and the Administration of the Army During the War of the Spanish Succession," unpublished Ph.D. dissertation, University of London, 1960, p. 61. This figure includes 65,609 "subject" troops (English, Scots, Irish, and Huguenot refugees) and 21,831 Dutch, German, and Danish troops in British pay. I would like to thank Dr. Ivor Burton for his kind permission to copy and cite his meticulous unpublished doctoral dissertation, which rigorously reconstructs the process of expansion of the British army which took place during the Nine Years War and the War of the Spanish Succession.

[152] John Ehrman, *The Navy in the War of William III 1689–1697* (Cambridge: Cambridge University Press, 1953), pp. 201, 203–210, 243–244, 269–270, 278–279.

[153] Ibid., pp. 558–559, 644; Collinge, *Navy Board Officials*, pp. 21–23, 106, 140, 144; J. C. Sainty, *Admiralty Officials 1660–1870* (London: Athlone, 1975), pp. 2, 113.

[154] Ehrman, *The Navy*, p. xx.

of 1689 and 1690 were determined not to repeat the blunders of 1685, and so William was not voted a permanent revenue sufficient to live "of his own" even in peacetime.[155] The existing state of war meant that annual parliaments were a foregone conclusion, as every autumn new funds had to be voted for the coming year's campaign. Spokesmen for the military departments now had both to submit regular accounts detailing the previous year's expenditure to the House and to justify the estimates drawn up for the next fiscal year. Scrutiny of such estimates was accompanied by parliamentary inquiries into military setbacks like the naval defeat off Beachy Head in 1690 and the loss of the Straits Fleet in 1693.[156]

Though this level of parliamentary oversight was in keeping with the precedents of 1665–7 and 1672–4, it was supplemented by another measure which was qualitatively different. This was the creation of a Commission of Public Accounts (CPA) which was to operate *during* rather than simply after the war, and hence was designed to provide a running check on the central administration's activities.

The Commission turned out to be the instrument of the strong "country" sentiments, shared by both Whigs and Tories, present in the Parliaments of the 1690s. Country MPs were extremely concerned that the war might lead to an inordinate concentration of power in the hands of the executive, and at the same time provide an opening for corrupt interests waiting to appropriate for themselves a portion of the funds voted for national defense. The Commission was just one of a broad variety of measures (disqualification of placeholders from Parliament, frequent elections, property qualifications for MPs) proposed during the 1690s by country politicians like Robert Harley and Thomas Foley in an effort to prevent such an outcome.[157]

The CPA's regular and detailed examination of the accounts of the army and navy paymasters and other officials subjected the government departments to a degree of outside surveillance not hitherto experienced, and certainly made the Treasury's job easier. In 1695 the CPA's labors bore fruit when both the Secretary to the Treasury (Henry Guy) and the Speaker of the Commons himself (Sir John Trevor) were exposed for taking bribes. Meanwhile, inquiries carried out by the whole

---

[155] E. A. Reitan, "From Revenue to Civil List, 1689–1702: The Revolution Settlement and the 'Mixed and Balanced' Constitution," *Historical Journal*, vol. 13, no. 4 (December 1970), pp. 571–588.

[156] Henry Horwitz, *Parliament, Policy and Politics in the Reign of William III* (Manchester: Manchester University Press, 1977), pp. 87–88.

[157] Horwitz, *Parliament*, p. 88; J. A. Downie, "The Commission of Public Accounts and the Formation of the Country Party," *English Historical Review*, vol. 91, no. 358 (January 1976), pp. 33–51; Brewer, *Sinews*, pp. 151–152.

House resulted in the removal in 1694 of Viscount Falkland, the Treasurer of the Navy, for corrupt practices, and the uncovering of a scheme to endorse Exchequer Bills in a fraudulent manner devised by the past and present Cashiers of the Excise.[158]

The efforts of Parliament in general and the CPA in particular to search out corruption, mismanagement, and inefficiency received valuable support from another institution which gained even greater prominence after 1689 than it had enjoyed before: the press. While newssheets and pamplets had played a fundamental role in English life throughout the century, the freer political atmosphere following the Revolution, combined with the new permanency of Parliament and its refusal in 1695 to renew the old censorship law (the Licensing Act of 1685),[159] stimulated an explosion of political journalism. While constitutional and religious issues received due attention, the war also provoked an outpouring of literature on financial and administrative matters which was to last right up to 1714 and beyond.

Much attention was naturally directed at the management of the army and navy, and works with titles like *Naval Speculations and Maritime Politicks* (1691), *An Inquiry into the Causes of our Naval Miscarriages* (1707), and *An Essay on the Most Effectual Way to Recruit the Army...* (1707) appeared in great profusion.[160] While some of their authors were professional publicists (among whom Swift and Defoe were the most famous), many others were officers, merchants, and former officials with extensive technical knowledge.[161] Parliament paid serious attention to their ideas and allegations, and throughout both wars often called in such experts to testify before committees. Whereas during the 1660s, experts needed to gain access to the closed world of the Court in order to be heard, they now became public celebrities and, in the case of writers like the former Excise Commissioner Charles Davenant, a political force to be reckoned with. Thus from the 1690s onward, a standing Parliament, a freer press, and a more informed public opinion mutually reinforced one another in the role of watchdogs intent on preventing those within the charmed circles of central administration from profiteering from the war at the expense of the country as a whole.

The Financial Challenges of Large-Scale Warfare

There was one area where the government needed all the help it could get from experts or from any other quarter: finance. With the outbreak

---

[158] Horwitz, *Parliament*, pp. 128, 146–147, 229–231.   [159] Ibid., pp. 152–153.
[160] Ehrman, *The Navy*, provides a list nearly three pages long of pamphlets on naval matters from the 1690s (pp. 684–686).
[161] Ibid., pp. 595–598.

of the war, government expenditure quickly rose from just over 2 million pounds just prior to 1688 to over 4, then 6, and finally more than 8 million pounds per annum in 1696.[162] While the system of government finance constructed after 1667 was structurally sound, it was small-scale and unprepared for such demands. As a result, the 1690s were a period of often desperate improvisation.

The whole direction of Treasury development before 1688 and the open political atmosphere of the 1690s inclined the government to seek market-based solutions to the country's financial problems. William, however, seemed to care little about what financial methods were used as long as money was found to pay his troops. And there were many leading financiers in the City, like the goldsmith-banker Sir Charles Duncombe, who for personal reasons felt that private finance, like that of France, would provide a simpler solution to the state's problems.[163]

Initially, William placed the direction of the Treasury, as he had the Admiralty, in the hands of politicians with little knowledge of or experience in financial affairs. As the government's financial woes mounted, however, in 1690 he wisely gave command of the Treasury to Godolphin and Sir Stephen Fox, two mainstays of the 1679–85 Commission. Throughout most of the war these two, aided after 1692 by the brilliant young Whig politician Charles Montague, struggled to find the money to continue the conflict with France.[164]

Three interconnected problems faced the new Treasury team. First, they had to come up with enough revenue to fund a terribly costly war. Second, and more immediately, they had to find enough cash (i.e., coin) to meet the pressing demands for soldiers' and sailors' pay and for repayment of military contractors before that revenue could be collected. In the 17th and 18th centuries, this process could take a year or more to complete. Finally, they had to apportion the available resources among spending departments in such a way as to sustain the war effort and ensure that the departments were using those precious resources in an economical manner.

After 1689, the Treasury sought to solve the government's cash problem by extending and refining the Treasury Order system erected by Downing in 1665–8 and cautiously resurrected in the late 1670s following the Stop of the Exchequer. Orders carrying 6% interest and secured by act of Parliament on a specific revenue fund were in effect "sold" to the general public in return for cash loans brought to the Exchequer

---

[162] D. W. Jones, *War and Economy in the Age of William III and Marlborough* (Oxford: Basil Blackwell, 1988), p. 70.

[163] Hughes, *Studies*, pp. 164–166, 172–174; Brewer, *Sinews*, p. 94.

[164] Sainty, *Treasury Officials*, pp. 18–19; Clay, *Public Finance*, pp. 216–220, 228–231, 233.

and repaid "in course" as tax receipts from the fund flowed in. Other Orders were "imprested" (i.e., issued) to the army, navy, and Ordnance paymasters who could then offer them to suppliers as a form of payment or sell them on the open market to raise cash. Finally, the Treasury authorized the Navy, Victualling, and Transport Boards and the Ordnance Office to issue their own assignable, interest-bearing bills (the departmental equivalent of Treasury Orders) to their creditors. These bills would then be repaid "in course" as money arrived from the Treasury.[165] In effect, then, the existence of the Order system, even if underdeveloped, offered the Treasury the possibility, when large-scale war finally came, of raising the working funds needed to pay the armed forces from a multitude of small and medium-sized investors, rather than from the powerful goldsmith-bankers, tax farmers, or proprietary officials of old.

If this elaborate, interlocking system of short-term credit was to function properly, public confidence was essential. In order to engender such confidence, two things were necessary. First, the expanding credit system had to be backed by the full weight of parliamentary authority. As mentioned above, the Stop of the Exchequer and its aftermath had demonstrated quite clearly that only Orders and other forms of credit explicitly sanctioned and guaranteed by Parliament could be considered a safe investment.

Second, however, it became increasingly apparent after 1689 that general parliamentary guarantees alone were not sufficient to attract the huge amounts of money which the government now needed to carry on the fight against Louis XIV. Investors also needed to know that the tax funds upon which Treasury Orders were secured would actually produce enough revenue to pay back the principal and the interest due on them. For while it was almost certain that Parliament would honor its obligations to lenders if a particular loan fund ran dry, this process might prove to be long and drawn-out. As England's financial markets grew, the investing public wanted to be sure not only that they would eventually be repaid, but also that they would be repaid regularly and punctually. If this could not be convincingly demonstrated, investors would be loath to turn over their cash to the government or to buy Treasury Orders from departmental paymasters except at a discount.[166]

---

[165] John Sperling, "Godolphin and the Organization of Public Credit 1702 to 1710," unpublished Ph.D dissertation, Cambridge University, 1955, passim. I would like to thank Dr. Sperling for permission to consult and cite his brilliant dissertation. It has been of invaluable help in unraveling the complexities of English war finance under both William and Anne.

[166] That this was indeed a pressing concern of the Treasury is shown by the fact that Godolphin was moved to issue a personal guarantee that all investors who fell victim

Furthermore, departmental suppliers, fearful of the Exchequer's solvency, would demand ready money for their goods.[167] Thus as both Edward Hughes and John Brewer have forcefully argued, an efficient and reliable revenue collection system was as much a *sine qua non* for the expansion of public credit after 1688 as the establishment of parliamentary supremacy.[168]

Unfortunately, the government's revenue base, made up principally of excise, customs, and land tax receipts, was a source of continuous problems throughout the 1690s. The major funds consistently failed to produce the sums expected of them during the war.[169] In the case of the customs, this was due to the sharp decline in revenues brought about by the war-induced contraction in foreign trade and the initial difficulties in estimating the magnitude of that decline.[170]

The inability of either the excise or land tax to produce the amounts expected of them had deeper roots. While the government would have preferred the introduction of a general excise to generate more money, the Commons rejected this for political reasons (their fear that such a tax would be difficult to repeal in peacetime). Instead, they approved a piecemeal extension of the excise to several new products combined with a large increase in direct taxes on a number of forms of wealth, the collection of which lay in the hands of gentry committees in the counties. Such committees were in effect responsible for assessing the tax liabilities of its members and their neighbors, with the predictable result that tax receipts from this source fell consistently short of Treasury expectations.[171]

The difficulties at the Excise were of a different character. Because of the great technical difficulties involved in assessing and collecting

to insufficient tax revenues would be compensated. This illustrates how the expansion of the Order-based credit system created new and powerful incentives at the Treasury to ensure speedy and honest tax collection. See Sperling, "Godolphin," pp. 20–21.

[167] The situation of the investor in departmental debt, especially the all-important Navy Bills, was much more precarious than that of holders of Treasury Orders, for such bills possessed no direct parliamentary backing. Hence the value of Navy Bills, as well as of those issued by the Transport and Victualling Boards and the Ordnance, was dependent in part on public perception of how honestly and efficiently money was managed in those departments. Here again it was the credit system that created powerful incentives for rationalization. See ibid., pp. 78, 81, 85.

[168] Hughes, *Studies*, p. 167; Brewer, *Sinews*, p. 89.

[169] Sperling, "Godolphin," p. 8; Hughes, *Studies*, p. 180.

[170] Customs receipts dropped from an average annual level of about £1,000,000 just prior to the outbreak of the war to £657,000 p.a. between 1688 and 1691, and then fluctuated wildly between £689,000 and £1,028,000 over the course of the following six years. See Jones, *War and Economy*, p. 70.

[171] J. V. Beckett, "Land Tax or Excise: The Levying of Taxation in Seventeenth- and Eighteenth-Century England," *English Historical Review*, vol. 100, no. 395 (April 1985), pp. 285–308, here at pp. 292–293, 296–297, 298–300.

this tax, a highly professional and tightly supervised organization was essential.[172] Such an organization had been slowly built up after the Restoration, first under farmers and then, after 1683, under an Excise Commission controlled by the Treasury. Almost immediately upon his arrival in England, however, William was in need of ready cash, and so he fell back on Danby's old expedient of "inside" credit by introducing financiers directly into the Excise establishment in exchange for cash loans from them secured on the Excise receipts. Though William got his cash, the quality of Excise management suffered. In 1694, the Treasury tried to introduce several "reformers" into the Excise Commission, but their clashes with the "financiers" only made matters worse, as did politically motivated attempts, opposed by Godolphin, to remove Tories from the services.[173]

As if all of these difficulties were not enough, the Treasury itself worsened matters by failing to exercise strict enough control over the activities of departmental paymasters, especially those of the army and navy. These officials often released large numbers of Treasury Orders onto the market at inopportune times, thus driving up the discount on those Orders. In addition, the Earl of Ranelagh, Paymaster of the Forces (army), had, in pursuance of his own corrupt schemes, consistently failed to note down the interest accumulating on Orders as they lay in his hands. This led to unexpected charges at the Exchequer when these Orders were presented for payment.[174]

The interconnected problems of inadequate long-term revenue and public wariness about lending to the government short-term had put England in a parlous financial state by 1693–4. At the same time, there was no shortage of people with ideas about how to remedy this situation. Pamphlets on arcane financial matters poured from the presses and "projectors" tried to interest both Parliament and the Treasury in their schemes. One of the most common proposals was for a public bank, backed by parliamentary guarantees, which would be able to raise money on its own credit to aid the government.

In 1694, the Treasury decided, with the cooperation of Parliament, to act on the plans presented by William Paterson, a Scots promoter, and in April of that year a statute authorizing the establishment of the Bank of England was passed. The crucial point about this event for our purposes is that the Bank was created not to replace the Treasury-based system of public credit built up since 1665, but rather to buttress it.

---

[172] Brewer, *Sinews*, p. 101.

[173] Hughes, *Studies*, pp. 172–175, 185–189; Brewer, *Sinews*, p. 74.

[174] *The Manuscripts of the House of Lords* (London: HMSO, 1965), vol. V, pp. 58–64, 366–368; Sperling, "Godolphin," pp. 28–29.

The Bank's immediate purpose was to ease the government's revenue and short-term credit problems by advancing it £1.2 million, much of it in cash, raised through the sale of Bank stock to the general public. The dividends paid to Bank shareholders would derive mainly from the interest payments, guaranteed by Parliament, which the government was to make in perpetuity on this and any future loans. The Bank was also permitted to earn profits by dealing in securities, bullion, foreign exchange, and commercial loans.[175]

The enthusiasm of the investing public for Bank stock was immediate and overwhelming. The explanation for this lies in the fact that restrictions on trade imposed by the war had left large sums of capital idle in the City of London and elsewhere. Merchants and financiers who were wary of investing their cash directly in Treasury Orders or Navy Bills did not hesitate to place it with an institution provided by Parliament with a regular, guaranteed stream of income. These same investors agitated throughout the 1690s for the creation of a new, open East India Company, and the government acceded to these pressures in 1698 in return for a £2 million long-term loan from that organization.[176]

Chartered companies like the Bank of England and the New East India Company could help the state in a time of crisis by furnishing it with additional revenue and emergency injections of cash. But they could not, in and of themselves, correct the fundamental deficiencies which the Nine Years War revealed at the very heart of the system of government finance. Only after the war had ended could the Treasury set out to correct these deficiencies in preparation for the next conflict.

In 1698 the first steps in that direction were taken when, in conjunction with Parliament, it was decided to replace the old direct tax based on wealth with a new land tax raised by so-called assessment.[177] Under this method, first employed by Charles I to raise the Ship Money and revived numerous times during both the Interregnum and Restoration periods, the government required that each county raise and remit to the Exchequer a fixed sum in cash every month. Commissions in the county would then distribute the burden of this imposition among the local citizenry based on ability to pay.

While this inevitably led to inequities in the incidence of taxation both nationally and within counties, it at least guaranteed that the Exchequer would in the end receive a predictable amount of money,

[175] John Clapham, *The Bank of England: A History* (Cambridge: Cambridge University Press, 1945), vol. I, pp. 14–19; Jones, *War and Economy*, pp. 12–15.

[176] D. W. Jones, "London Merchants and the Crisis of the 1690s," in: Peter Clark and Paul Slack (eds.), *Crisis and Order in English Towns 1500–1700* (London: Routledge & Kegan Paul, 1972), pp. 311–355, here at pp. 334, 338–340, 342–345.

[177] Beckett, "Land Tax," pp. 294–296, 301–302, 308.

provided that the collection system was adequate. The Treasury attempted to ensure this outcome by placing all important members of the gentry, regardless of political persuasion, onto the county land tax commissions.[178] The results of this change were remarkable, as Land Tax receipts ran at 98.6% of their projected yield throughout most of the War of the Spanish Succession.[179] The land tax raised by assessment remained the primary form of direct taxation relied on by the British government throughout the 18th century.[180]

At the same time, the Treasury directed its attention towards the Excise in an effort to re-establish the professionalism which had characterized that organization before 1688. In several respects the strong "country" lobby present in the Commons aided the Treasury in this endeavor. First, in 1698, the Commission of Public Accounts forced the resignation of the Cashier of the Excise, a financier named Bartholomew Burton, after the CPA found him guilty of fraud and forgery. Next, a number of vocal Tory critics of Excise mismanagement, led by the former Commissioner, Charles Davenant, put together with the aid of City financiers a realistic proposal to return the Excise to farm.[181]

The Treasury responded to this direct threat to its authority with vigorous action to put the Excise's affairs in order. Its task was made easier by a place bill passed by Parliament in 1700 which barred excisemen from sitting in the House. This led to the resignation of the "politicians" on the Commission, leaving only the professional administrators. Taken together, these changes put the Excise back on track, allowing it quickly to regain its reputation as the most efficiently run department in the English government, a reputation it was to maintain throughout the 18th century.[182] Practically speaking, this also meant that the Excise could be counted on to produce regularly the receipts expected of it.

The revived Commission of Public Accounts of 1702–1704 provided a further service to the Treasury by revealing the irregularities and corrupt practices present in the navy and especially the army paymasters' offices during the last war. Ranelagh was forced to resign his position and was expelled from the House because of the cavalier way he had handled Treasury Orders.[183] This could not help but strengthen the Treasury's authority over paymasters in the new war that had just begun.

---

[178] Colin Brooks, "Public Finance and Political Stability: The Administration of the Land Tax, 1688–1720," *Historical Journal*, vol. 17, no. 2 (June 1974), pp. 281–300, here at pp. 289–291, 293–294, 296.
[179] Sperling, "Godolphin," p. 11.
[180] Beckett, "Land Tax," pp. 285, 301–303.
[181] Horwitz, *Parliament, Policy*, pp. 229–230; Hughes, *Studies*, pp. 190–195.
[182] Hughes, *Studies*, pp. 195–198; Brewer, *Sinews*, pp. 74, 102, 112.
[183] Geoffrey Holmes, *British Politics in the Age of Anne*, revised edition (London: Hambledon, 1987), pp. 138–139. Materials on the Commission's activities between 1702 and 1704

The New Administrative-Financial System Perfected

When Anne succeeded to the throne upon the death of William in March 1702, she immediately named Godolphin to head the Treasury. Over the next eight years he used the great powers now residing in that department to direct the British war effort, in conjunction with his close friend Marlborough. As John Sperling has pointed out, Godolphin was by this time one of the most experienced men ever to head the Treasury, having served there as a Commissioner for 17 of the previous 23 years. He was intimately acquainted with all the mistakes committed during the previous war, and was finally in a position to correct them. And with the aid of a now secure revenue base, he was to succeed in this to a remarkable degree.[184]

During the War of the Spanish Succession, the integrated administrative-financial system first conceived of by Downing was finally perfected. Every year Parliament voted supply of between 4 and 6 million pounds to prosecute the war, and every year the general public advanced to the government the full amount of supply voted *in cash* in exchange for Treasury Orders secured on the tax funds.[185] This, not the intermittent long-term loans floated by the Bank of England or the East India Company, was the essence of Britain's financial revolution.

The hidden foundation of the government's excellent credit was probity and efficiency in the key revenue and spending departments. The attractiveness of Treasury Orders ultimately depended on the ability of the Customs, Excise, and Land Tax establishments to send a steady stream of tax money to the Exchequer. Similarly, investors and suppliers were unlikely to place much confidence in Navy or Victualling Bills if those departments gained a reputation for mismanagement. After the difficulties of the 1690s, Godolphin understood this well and this time he tried to keep close watch over both the credit operations of particular paymasters and the contract and spending policies of the navy. If for any reason the price of Treasury Orders or departmental bills fell below par, the Bank of England stood ready to intervene at the Treasury's request to prop up the market.[186]

Over a period of 40 years, an interlocking system of bureaucratic administration and public finance was built up in England, held together by the triple pressures of parliamentary scrutiny, market forces, and informed public opinion. By 1710, the survival of this system no longer

can be found in: *Manuscripts of the House of Lords*, pp. 58–64, 128–133, 190, 209–217, 366–452, 560–561,
[184] Sperling, "Godolphin," pp. vii–viii and passim.
[185] Ibid., pp. 15, 21, 26.   [186] Ibid., pp. 33, 46–50, 70, 80, 83, 130.

depended on the skills or enlightened views of any one man. After Godolphin lost his post in 1710, a victim of court intrigue, his successor Harley followed the same policies against which he had railed while in opposition. By firmly resisting Tory calls for a political purge of the revenue departments and by establishing a new chartered company (the South Sea Company) to absorb outstanding departmental bills, Harley quickly re-established that public confidence in the Treasury lost through Godolphin's dismissal.[187] By 1714, it was clear that the innovative fiscal and administrative arrangements at the heart of the newly created British state had finally been institutionalized.

The existence of a quasi-one-party state from the 1720s through the 1750s certainly weakened the role of the Commons as a check on the executive. The era of Walpole and the Pelhams was of course the hey-day of patronage politics, the time when "influence" and "connection" came to dominate public life. Yet while there was certainly some decline in administrative standards during this period when compared to 1689–1713, the core institutions of the fiscal-military state continued to function at a high level, as the figures to be presented shortly will show. How was this possible, given the decline in parliamentary aggressiveness during stretches of the 18th century?

The answer to this question must lie in the fact that with the full development of the fiscal-military state between 1702 and 1710, other checks supplemented direct parliamentary oversight. With its position now more or less firmly established, the Treasury had both the power and the information to monitor standards in other departments. Even more important, however, public credit markets exerted considerable pressure on the central administration to maintain certain minimum standards of honesty and efficiency. The reasons for this were multiple. First, interest payments on government long-term debt were assigned on the income from various taxes, mainly the excise. Any investor skepticism over the ability of the revenue departments to collect those taxes in a predictable and honest manner would naturally send the government's credit rating plummeting.

Second, individual departments like the Ordnance and the Navy, Victualling, and Transport Boards derived their short-term credit from the circulation of bills, which were interest-bearing, assignable credit notes that, like Treasury Orders, were paid "in course." Rumors of corruption or mismanagement in one of these departments could also send the discount rate on their paper up, thereby imperiling government credit.

---

[187] Roseveare, *The Treasury 1660–1870*, p. 58; idem, *The Treasury*, pp. 76–77; Brian Hill, *Robert Harley: Speaker, Secretary of State and Premier Minister* (New Haven: Yale University Press, 1988), pp. 153–154; Brewer, *Sinews*, pp. 74, 160–161.

Table 4. *Government Spending as a Percentage of National Income,*
Britain and France, 1689–1783

| War | Annual spending as a % of national income | | Peak | |
	Britain	France	Britain	France
1689–1697	11	n.a.	15.7	n.a.
1702–1713	13	10	25	12.3
1741–1748	17	11/13	21	12/14
1756–1763	24	13/15	30.4	15/16
1778–1783	23.7	11/12	30	n.a.

Note: These figures were derived by adding together all government spending during the course of the war in question, then dividing this sum by the number of years during which the war lasted. This figure for average annual government spending was then divided by the estimated national income during the period of the war. "Peak" refers to the maximum level of annual spending reached during the war years, again expressed as a percentage of national income. These results can of course only be taken as orders of magnitude.

Sources:

British national income: Phyllis Deane and W. A. Cole, *British Economic Growth* (Cambridge: Cambridge University Press, 1967), p. 2; John Brewer, *The Sinews of Power* (London: Unwin Hyman, 1989), p. 41.

British government expenditure: B. R. Mitchell and Phyllis Deane, *Abstract of British Historical Statistics* (Cambridge: Cambridge University Press, 1962), pp. 389–391.

French national income: James C. Riley, "French Finances, 1727–1768," *Journal of Modern History*, vol. 59, no. 2 (June 1987), p. 228; idem, *The Seven Years War and the Old Regime in France* (Princeton: Princeton University Press, 1986), p. 21.

French government expenditure: Alain Guéry, "Les Finances de la Monarchie Française sous l'Ancien Régime," *Annales*, vol. 33, no. 2 (March–April 1978), p. 237; J.-J. Clamageran, *Histoire de l'Impôt en France* (Paris: Guillaumin, 1876), vol. III, pp. 117–119; Riley, "French Finances," pp. 224–225, 228; Michel Morineau, "Budgets de l'Etat et Gestion des Finances Royales en France au Dix-Huitième Siècle," *Revue Historique*, vol. 264, no. 536 (October–December 1980), pp. 312–313.

Because of the particular manner in which the British public credit system was constructed, then, the investing public had a direct interest in government standards and the ability to enforce that interest by withdrawing or transferring their funds.

The 18th-century British state thus possessed two features which lent it great strength in times of war. First, it enjoyed the benefits of a qualitatively new kind of administrative and financial system which was much more efficient than its predecessor of the early 1660s. Second, it contained the structural checks, in the form of a standing Parliament and credit markets, which ensured that this new system would not be undermined, even under the pressures of war.

To these two advantages must be added a third. While Parliament was crucial in both creating and maintaining the institutions which allowed Britain to wage war more effectively, it also contributed directly to the country's military prowess by serving as a center for consensus-building during international conflicts. The presence of Parliament forced the government to submit its foreign policy designs and military strategy to public scrutiny, which in turn made it much easier to generate broad public support for necessary wartime sacrifices such as tax increases.[188]

As the figures in Table 4 demonstrate, Britain's political system and its financial and administrative institutions endowed it with substantially greater military capacities than absolutist France. These rough figures indicate that the structural changes undergone by the British state in the late 1600s gave it a very substantial competitive advantage over the course of the next century. It was this advantage that provided the organizational and financial underpinnings for repeated victories over France of a magnitude not seen since the Hundred Years War, and which permitted the British to prevail in an arms race which drove the ancien régime to financial collapse and eventual extinction.

CONCLUSION

After 1660, the English government was confronted with a situation familiar to most European states of the period. It wished to increase its military capacity in the face of foreign threats. One way to do so was to make more intensive and systematic use of the established methods of governance already found among all of Europe's early statebuilders: proprietary officeholding, revenue farming, "inside" credit, military entrepreneurship. In countries like France, the members of powerful factions stood to gain politically, socially, and financially from a policy aimed at increasing the "irrationality" of many areas of the state in the interest of heightened royal control over the military. Such groups used their backstairs influence in the closed world of court politics to ensure that reformers wishing to follow a different path were defeated.

In England, such an outcome did not occur. Instead, a standing Parliament subjected the workings of key government departments to close scrutiny. Country MPs, who typically did not enjoy direct access to the Court and its bounty, branded age-old practices like the traffic

---

[188] Margaret Levi has presented a somewhat similar argument about the role played by Parliament in permitting England to mobilize resources more effectively than France in her important study *Of Rule and Revenue* (Berkeley: University of California Press, 1988), pp. 95–121.

in offices and tax farming "corrupt," and demanded their elimination. The attention generated by parliamentary inquiry and protest in turn strengthened the hand of those within the central administration who wished to found England's military might not upon an ever more vast series of "undertakings" on the model of Colbert, but upon a rationalized bureaucracy under Treasury supervision and a market-based system of public finance. In a word, the national representatives of England's self-governing local political communities, the lasting institutional legacy of a divergent pattern of state formation which set that country apart from its neighbors in Latin Europe, in the end triumphed over the centuries-old forces of appropriation and their usual ally, war.

After 1714, the long-term survival of these new patterns of administration and finance no longer depended on parliamentary oversight alone. The creation of a one-and-a-half-party state by Walpole in the wake of the Succession Crisis of 1714–5 resulted in a relative decline in the legislature's autonomy over the next half century, yet the gains of the previous 50 years were not reversed. While pockets of proprietary officeholding lingered on in some corners of the state, the core areas of the British administrative-financial system remained largely honest and efficient. The revenue departments continued to collect taxes in a very reliable way, and the navy was, by the organizational standards of the 18th century, in a class by itself.[189]

How can this resilience be explained, given the fact that powerful forces favoring "patrimonialism" were still present in Britain, as they were in all early modern societies? The answer seems to be that although the independence of Parliament had been weakened, financial markets continued to exercise strong pressures on government leaders not to sacrifice the good credit of the state, on which the defense of Britain ultimately rested, in the interests of personal or political gain. The savings of tens of thousands of individuals, not to mention the security of their property, depended on the probity and efficiency of Treasury, revenue, and military officials, and the investing public was now in a position to punish the government for reported cases of mismanagement by threatening to withdraw their funds, a threat that had to be taken seriously.

In a sense, then, the Parliaments of the 1690s had found a worthy structural equivalent in the flourishing coffeehouses of 'Change Alley. While not in themselves a force for positive change, the members of

---

[189] Brewer, *Sinews*, pp. 74–76, 79, 102, 112; Elizabeth Hoon, *The Organization of the English Customs System 1696–1786* (New York: Greenwood, 1968), p. 78; Daniel Baugh, *British Naval Administration in the Age of Walpole* (Princeton: Princeton University Press, 1965), pp. 2–3, 496–497.

the investing community, aided by a press already well trained to sniff out scandal, helped to preserve the modern core of the British state after 1714. In so doing, investors contributed more than just their money to Britain's military (and hence commercial) successes of the 18th century.

Chapter 5

⸺ ℭℑ ⸺

BUREAUCRATIC ABSOLUTISM IN GERMANY

In the decades prior to the French Revolution, principalities with absolutist political regimes dominated the complex world of states found within the borders of the confederal Holy Roman Empire of the German Nation. Germany's rulers had long since secured the unfettered powers of legislation – also enjoyed by monarchs in France, Iberia, and Italy – which were the *sine qua non* of absolutism. Unlike their counterparts in Latin Europe, however, German princes also had at their disposal administrative and financial infrastructures that were free of proprietary officeholding, tax farming, and "inside" finance. These infrastructures were instead built around proto-modern bureaucracies largely staffed by full-time, professional, university-trained officials, the so-called *Beamten*. As such, the states of Germany must be categorized as exemplars of *bureaucratic*, as opposed to patrimonial, absolutism.

In this chapter, I argue that two factors were responsible for this outcome: a pattern of administrative, top-down local government, itself the legacy of failed dark age statebuilding; and the late onset of sustained geopolitical competition. As in Latin Europe, the fact that the German principalities arose in an area previously occupied by large-scale – and ultimately unsuccessful – dark age polities predisposed them towards absolutism. This was so because the fragmented, decentralized political landscape which the collapse of these polities left in their wake led Germany's new generation of state-forming princes to adopt non-participatory, centralizing solutions to the problem of local integration. Nobles, churchmen, and burghers in turn responded to the threat posed by intrusive princely officials to their traditional rights by organizing themselves into corporate groups, thereby laying the groundwork for the later appearance of estate-based representative assemblies which were internally divided and defensive, and hence weak.

What ultimately sent the absolutist polities of central Europe down a path of development different from that of their counterparts to the west and south was the late arrival of interstate competition. Because the German principalities did not emerge as full-fledged states until the late 1400s, they also did not become subject to sustained geopolitical competition until that time, centuries later than the states of Latin Europe. This meant that when the German princes set out to expand and specialize their infrastructures in response to this late-arriving geopolitical pressure, they were in a position to borrow models from the statebuilding pioneers, learn from their mistakes, and benefit from the tremendous advances in finance, law, and education which had taken place since the early middle ages. More important still, they found themselves in a much stronger bargaining position vis-à-vis the skilled personnel they sought to employ than had the statebuilding rulers of Latin Europe and England during the 1100s, 1200s, and 1300s. This was so because the great shortages of administrative and financial skills characteristic of the central middle ages had now been overcome due to the proliferation of universities and the growth of financial and other markets. As a result, German rulers were in a position to construct nonproprietary bureaucracies which differed fundamentally from the patrimonial state apparatuses of France, Iberia, and Italy.

In building these bureaucracies, the rulers of central Europe encountered little resistance from the corporately organized estates of the nobility, clergy, and towns, which had emerged as early as the 13th century but institutionalized themselves as formal representative assemblies (*Landtage*) only in the 1400s and early 1500s. These often disunited bodies received confirmation of their group privileges and a say in the approval, collection, and even administration of new taxes. However, they were forced to concede considerable latitude in the areas of lawmaking, foreign policy, and military affairs to princes who laid claim to "imperial" powers of governance within their own lands in the interest of the common good and public order (*Polizei*).

In the aftermath of the Thirty Years War, many rulers sought to reduce still further or eliminate altogether the prerogatives of their Estates in the interests of national defense. Yet while it might at first glance seem that the combination of hard-line absolutism and nonproprietary bureaucracy would have been ideal from the point of view of maximizing military effectiveness, this was in fact not so, as the case of Brandenburg-Prussia illustrates. While this most absolutist and bureaucratic of German states was able to field armies that were out of all proportion to the size of its population, its capacity to wage war successfully was over the long term severely constrained by the inability of successive Prussian monarchs to construct an effective public credit system in the absence of those guarantees to investors that only a representative assembly could provide. In this respect as in others, bureaucratic absolutism proved itself inferior to the bureaucratic constitutionalism of Britain.

FAILED DARK AGE STATEBUILDING, EMPIRE, AND
THE EMERGENCE OF TERRITORIAL STATES IN GERMANY,
511–C. 1450

During the course of the 8th century, those portions of Germany
previously untouched by attempts at large-scale state formation were
Christianized, outfitted with a civil administration and ecclesiastical
infrastructure, and fully incorporated into the Frankish realm. As in the
west, the Carolingian system of rule was undermined in east Francia
during the 9th century by the widespread appropriation of public office. Following the advent of the Magyars in the 890s, large ethnically
based duchies appeared in the east that were comparable in some respects to the west Frankish territorial principalities. Under the rule of
the Ottonians (919–1024), however, it proved possible to overcome
these trends towards radical decentralization and even revive the empire of Charlemagne on a more limited scale by making use of royal
control of a Church that was all the more powerful due to the relative
backwardness of the eastern lands.

As the last of the great dark age states, the Ottonian-Salian Holy
Roman Empire was hit especially hard by the new forces unleashed by
the decline of its Carolingian predecessor, which included ecclesiastical
reform, the spread of markets, and the rise of bannal lordship (for an
extensive discussion of these developments, see Chapter 2). Whereas
the Salians (1024–1125) responded to their declining hold over the
Church by attempting to expand the royal domain and build up an
independent administrative network using a corps of royal knights (*ministeriales*), their Hohenstaufen successors (1137–1254) unsuccessfully
sought to buttress their position by deploying conceptions of feudal
hierarchy and imperial rulership derived from the recently revived Roman law, while at the same time seeking to subdue the wealthy cities of
northern Italy.

With the decline of authority at the center, the locus of power within
the Empire from the 13th century onward began to shift toward the
regional and local level. There, lay and ecclesiastical aristocrats used
rights and resources derived from allodial landownership, office, royal
grants of regalian rights and peacekeeping duties, and other sources to
build up territorial lordships from the rubble left by the near-collapse of
royal power. They were often assisted in this task by the nobles, prelates,
and towns of their lands, who organized themselves into corporate
estates in the same manner and at about the same time as their counterparts in Latin Europe, that other region of failed dark age state formation. By mid-1400s, these lordships had succeeded in transforming

themselves into the full-fledged states that would henceforth dominate the course of German political development.

Large-Scale, Post-Roman State Formation in Germany

Although they ultimately failed to conquer all Germany, the Romans did succeed from the 1st century B.C. onward in incorporating important parts of what would later be medieval and early modern central Europe – including Switzerland, Austria, and Germany west of the Rhine and south of the Danube – into their empire. Furthermore, the inhabitants of what was described as "free Germany" beyond the *limes* (imperial border) remained in close contact with the Romans not only as occasional enemies, but also as regular trading partners and military allies.[1] As mentioned in Chapter 2, many Germans came to occupy leading positions within the army and the state beginning in the 3rd century A.D., and whole tribal groups later crossed into the Empire and settled permanently within its borders.

The subjugation of much of Gaul by Clovis and the creation of a separate Frankish kingdom there during the last decades of the 5th century established a permanent institutional link between the Roman world and the lands to the east of the Rhine. During the course of the 6th century, the Franks defeated the three peoples then occupying most of central and southern Germany – the Alemannians (Swabians), Bavarians, and Thuringians – and reorganized them into tribal duchies owing tribute and military service. Missionaries were also sent into these territories, which won ever greater autonomy for themselves as Merovingian power declined, and by the early 700s all had become Christian.[2]

With the rise of the Carolingians, however, that autonomy was removed, for Charles Martel (714–741) campaigned vigorously to return Alemannia, Bavaria, and Thuringia to Frankish control. In addition, he was able to conquer and Christianize the heathen Frisians living in the northern Netherlands and begin the task of subduing and converting the Saxons of northern Germany, a process completed by Charlemagne in 803. Thus by the end of the latter's reign, direct Frankish rule, and

---

[1] Malcolm Todd, *The Northern Barbarians 100 B.C.–A.D. 300*, 2nd ed. (Oxford: Basil Blackwell, 1987), pp. 9–29.

[2] Eugen Ewig, "Das merowingische Frankenreich (561–687)," in: Theodor Schieder (ed.), *Handbuch der Europäischen Geschichte* (Stuttgart: Klett, 1975), vol. I, pp. 396–433, here at pp. 426–432; Friedrich Prinz, *Grundlagen und Anfänge: Deutschland bis 1056* (München: Beck, 1985), pp. 76–80; Heinz Löwe, *Deutschland im Fränkischen Reich* (= *Gebhardts Handbuch der Deutschen Geschichte*, 7th ed., vol. II) (Stuttgart: Deutscher Taschenbuchverlag, 1982), pp. 50–53, 95–101.

with it the institutions of the Carolingian church and state, had been successfully extended from Roman Gaul into the area (later to be called east Francia) now occupied by Switzerland, Austria, the northern Netherlands, and Germany up to the Elbe.[3]

In practice, this meant the eradication of paganism and the construction of an ecclesiastical hierarchy centering on the five archbishoprics of Cologne, Mainz, Trier, Bremen, and Salzburg, 17 bishoprics, and numerous richly endowed royal abbeys like Corvey and Fulda. Just as significantly, it also meant replacing the native governance structures of the subjugated Germanic groups with a single network of countries headed by Frankish counts and held together by the familiar institutions of vassalage, benefices and the *missi dominici*. As in the western portions of the empire, the Carolingians grouped those counties located in border regions into larger defensive units known as marches, and relied on bishops and abbots to monitor the activities of the local counts and margraves ("march counts").[4]

The Treaty of Verdun (843) which divided Charlemagne's empire among the three sons of Louis the Pious created a separate east Frankish kingdom, but the various Carolingian realms were reunited several times over the coming decades and east Francia did not establish a fully separate identity until Louis the Child became king there in 900. During this period, the east was subjected to the same general manifestations of declining central authority discussed in Chapter 2 in relation to west Francia. These included attempts to convert counties and marches into heritable property and the near disappearance of the use of *missi*. However, royal power actually remained stronger in the east, at least during the reigns of Louis the German (840–876) and Arnulf of Carinthia (887–899). This relatively primitive region was less affected than the more developed west by the 9th century decline of overseas commerce; furthermore, Louis' frequent campaigns against the Slavs and Arnulf's against the Vikings provided continuing opportunities for royal leadership and aristocratic profit lacking in west Francia since the early 800s.[5] It was only with the twin disasters of a royal minority (reign of Louis the Child 900–911) and intensified Magyar raiding after 899

[3]   Prinz, *Grundlagen*, pp. 78–82; Löwe, *Deutschland*, pp. 113–118, 130–133, 140–142; Timothy Reuter, *Germany in the Early Middle Ages 800–1056* (London: Longman, 1991), pp. 54–66.
[4]   Reuter, *Germany*, pp. 67, 92–93; Löwe, *Deutschland*, pp. 142–149; Hans Schulze, *Die Grafschaftsverfassung der Karolingerzeit in den Gebieten östlich des Rheins* (Berlin: Duncker & Humblot, 1973), pp. 301–309 and passim; Karl Bosl, *Franken um 800*, 2nd ed. (München: Beck, 1969), pp. 150–153.
[5]   Reuter, *Germany*, pp. 90–91, 94, 122–126; Löwe, *Deutschland*, pp. 181–182, 187–188; Prinz, *Grundlagen*, pp. 117, 120–121.

that central authority began to crumble in east Francia as well. The most immediate consequence of this was the rapid reemergence of ethnically based duchies (*Stammesherzogtümer*) – the eastern equivalent of the west's territorial principalities – in Bavaria, Saxony, Swabia, Lotharingia, and Franconia as waning Frankish power and the need for regional defense provided local aristocrats with the opportunity to establish themselves as the effective rulers of their peoples.[6]

Following the death of the last Carolingian, Louis the Child, in 911, the east Frankish aristocracy chose one of their number, Conrad of Franconia, as king and assigned to him the task of coordinating the defense of the realm. Over the next eight years, however, he had little success against either the Magyars or those dukes who refused to accept his rule. Not surprisingly, upon his death in 919, the aristocracy offered the throne to a member of another family, Henry of Saxony (919–936), who would establish the Ottonian dynasty that was to rule over east Francia until 1024. Henry's son, Otto the Great (936–973), rapidly transformed the kingdom into the West's most powerful polity by establishing hegemony over west Francia and Burgundy (940s), reimposing the tributary status of the Bohemians, conquering all of Italy as far south as Rome (951), destroying the military power of the Magyars at the Lechfeld (955), and, as his ultimate achievement, receiving the imperial crown and title from Pope John XII (962).[7]

It was during the reigns of Henry I and Otto the Great that the system of rule which the Saxon monarchs had inherited from the Carolingians was successfully modified so as to permit it to survive in east Francia until 1076, more than a century and a half after it had crumbled in its Gallic birthplace. In attempting to revitalize Carolingian institutions, the Ottonians benefited greatly from the fact that their realm was the most recently conquered, and hence least developed, region of the former Empire.[8] Unlike west Francia, much of the east was still a frontier zone, threatened by heathen peoples living to its east and north. This threat permitted the Ottonians from the 920s onward to continue the Carolingian tradition, already revived in more limited form by Louis the German and Arnulf, of regular military campaigns

[6] Herfried Stingl, *Die Entstehung der Deutschen Stammesherzogtümer am Anfang des 10. Jahrhunderts* (Aalen: Scientia Verlag, 1974), pp. 145–197, 217–218; Theodor Schieffer, "Die karolingischen Nachfolgerstaaten: Das Ostfränkische Reich (887–918)," in: Schieder, *Handbuch*, vol. I, pp. 633–642, here at pp. 637–639; Reuter, *Germany*, pp. 127–134.

[7] Reuter, *Germany*, pp. 135–137, 160–174.

[8] Karl Leyser, "Ottonian Government," in: idem, *Medieval Germany and Its Neighbours 900–1250* (London: Hambledon, 1982), pp. 69–101, here at p. 100.

against the pagan Slavs and Danes. Campaigns of this kind, which were no longer possible in the west, brought prestige to the monarchy and forged a sense of common purpose among the various Germanic tribes. This fact helped lay the groundwork for Otto's definitive defeat of the Magyars in 955 and the conquest of Italy in 961 that won him the imperial crown.[9]

Even with the advantages brought by regular military victories, however, the Ottonians still faced a formidable obstacle to effective rule in the entrenched power of dukes, margraves, and counts who, like their counterparts to the west, had taken advantage of Carolingian decline to render their offices largely hereditary.[10] Yet here again, relative backwardness worked to the advantage of the new dynasty. Because a comprehensive church organization had only been introduced relatively recently to the lands east of the Rhine, appointments to all its principal positions remained firmly in the hands of rulers whose caesaro-papist claims, inherited from the Carolingians, were only magnified by the acquisition of the imperial title. Yet the Ottonians were not content simply to employ their ecclesiastical clients to monitor the activities of counts and other officials, as their predecessors had done. Rather, they took the far more radical step of building up the Church as a direct, parallel instrument of rule by endowing it with extensive lands, jurisdictions, and regalian rights which, when combined with grants of immunity, removed whole areas of the country from the influence of the lay aristocracy.[11] This policy culminated in the practice of transferring entire counties to bishops, and at least 37 such secular jurisdictions were handed over to ecclesiastics in this way between 987 and 1056.[12] In return for the favors showered upon it, the Church was required to use its wealth to finance the bulk of the emperor's army.[13]

[9] Timothy Reuter, "Plunder and Tribute in the Carolingian Empire," *Transactions of the Royal Historical Society*, 5th series, vol. 35 (1985), pp. 75–94, here at pp. 92–94; idem, *Germany*, pp. 143–146, 160–166, 174; Josef Fleckenstein and Marie Luise Bulst, *Begründung und Aufstieg des Deutschen Reiches* (= *Gebhardts Handbuch der Deutschen Geschichte*, 7th ed., vol. III) (Stuttgart: Deutscher Taschenbuchverlag, 1983), pp. 33–36; Benjamin Arnold, *Princes and Territories in Medieval Germany* (Cambridge: Cambridge University Press, 1991), p. 119.

[10] Prinz, *Grundlagen*, pp. 252–254; Arnold, *Princes*, pp. 113–114; Reuter, *Germany*, pp. 193–195.

[11] Leo Santifaller, *Zur Geschichte des Ottonisch-Salischen Reichskirchensystems* (Wien: Böhlau, 1964), pp. 27–43 and passim; Josef Fleckenstein, *Grundlagen und Beginn der Deutschen Geschichte*, 2nd ed. (Göttingen: Vandenhoeck & Ruprecht, 1980), pp. 145–151; Prinz, *Grundlagen*, pp. 43, 228–230; Reuter, *Germany*, pp. 195–197, 218–219.

[12] Horst Fuhrmann, *Deutsche Geschichte in Hohen Mittelalter*, 2nd ed. (Göttingen: Vandenhoeck & Ruprecht, 1983), p. 52; Arnold, *Princes*, pp. 116–117.

[13] Heinrich Mitteis and Heinz Lieberich, *Deutsche Rechtsgeschichte*, 19th ed. (München: Beck, 1992), pp. 120–121.

The Salian-Hohenstaufen Empire and Its Failure

After Christian kingdoms were formed in Poland, Hungary, and Denmark around the year 1000, regular military campaigning could no longer play the integrative role it had in the 10th century. Thus, the Salian dynasty which succeeded the Ottonians in 1024 was left even more dependent than the latter had been on the so-called "imperial Church system" (*Reichskirchensystem*). After 1076, however, that system was irrevocably undermined by the Investiture Conflict between pope and emperor.[14] The roots of this conflict can be traced back to the decline of Carolingian power in west Francia and in Italy during the course of the 9th and early 10th centuries. As mentioned in Chapter 2, the most immediate impact of this decline was to open the Church, deprived of effective imperial protection, to the depredations of local aristocrats. These aristocrats engaged in the traffic in Church offices (simony) and filled the Church positions in their gift with relatives and retainers who more often than not ignored canonical prohibitions against clerical marriage.[15]

Yet the temporary disappearance of imperial tutelage also left the Church with a freedom of action which allowed reformers such as those at Cluny (see Chapter 2) to respond creatively to the problems they saw around them in both the secular and ecclesiastical spheres. The example of Cluny, with its call for spiritual renewal through the creation of a Church hierarchy independent of all secular powers, combined with the critical writing of clerics like Humbert of Silva Candida, soon won many ecclesiastics over to a program of radical Church reform built around demands for an end to simony, clerical marriage, and secular control of ecclesiastical appointments (lay investiture).[16]

Yet if advocates of radical reform were to have any hope of putting their ideas into practice, they would first have to secure positions of influence within the papacy itself. Ironically, it was the restoration of the Empire under the Ottonians and Salians, built upon the foundations of the imperial church system, that made this possible. Several emperors were in fact quite sympathetic to calls for moral renewal within the Church, and none more so than Henry III (1039–1056),

---

[14] Mitteis and Lieberich, *Deutsche Rechtsgeschichte*, p. 124.

[15] Colin Morris, *The Papal Monarchy: The Western Church from 1050 to 1250* (Oxford: Clarendon, 1989), pp. 20–28; Uta-Renate Blumenthal, *The Investiture Controversy* (Philadelphia: University of Pennsylvania Press, 1988), pp. 1–7; Malcolm Barber, *The Two Cities* (London: Routledge, 1992), pp. 85–86.

[16] Morris, *Papal Monarchy*, pp. 28–33, 80; Gerd Tellenbach, *Libertas: Kirche und Weltordnung im Zeitalter des Investiturstreites* (Stuttgart: Kohlhammer, 1936), pp. 91–104; Alfred Haverkamp, *Aufbruch und Gestaltung: Deutschland 1056–1273* (München: Beck, 1984), pp. 54–55, 58–60; Blumenthal, *Investiture Controversy*, pp. 64–70.

who in 1046 marched on Rome to free the papacy from the grip of the local aristocracy. He removed three pretenders who all claimed the title of pope, and two years later succeeded in placing a relative who was also a committed reformer, Leo IX (1048–1054), in the papal office. During his pontificate, Leo attracted a group of like-minded clerics to Rome and installed them in leading positions within the curia.[17]

In 1073, the most determined member of this reforming circle was swept into office by the Roman populace as Gregory VII (1073–1085). Almost immediately, he became embroiled in a dispute with Henry III's son Henry IV (1056–1106) over the latter's right to appoint the archbishop of Milan. This dispute soon escalated into a titanic struggle between pope and emperor over the whole issue of imperial control of the Church in Germany and northern Italy. Gregory excommunicated Henry twice, and Henry captured Rome and drove the pope from the city.[18] This struggle, commonly known as the Investiture Conflict, continued long after both Henry and Gregory were dead. It was only resolved in 1122 by the Concordat of Worms, which called for canonical elections to replace the imperial right to appoint higher Church officials. At the same time, the Empire's bishops and abbots were permitted to keep the lands, jurisdictions, and regalian rights previously granted to them, but henceforth would hold them as fiefs and thus would still be required to provide military service for them.[19]

In practical terms, this conflict dealt a fatal blow to the neo-Carolingian governance system of the Salians. For while many clerics remained loyal to the emperor, others did not, thereby creating a rift down the center of the imperial Church. More serious still, the conflict provided the perfect opportunity for Henry's aristocratic opponents to challenge his authority, cloaking their rebellion in the respectable mantle of ecclesiastical reform.[20] Soon all of Germany and Italy had formed itself into two armed camps and the cleavages which first arose during the 1070s were to reappear again and again in both countries over the coming two centuries, both up to and beyond the extinction of the Hohenstaufen in 1266.

The divisive impact of the Investiture Conflict was exacerbated by the fact that it occurred during a period of economic takeoff, which began in central Europe around the middle of the 1000s, about a century

---

[17] Tellenbach, *Libertas*, pp. 104–108, 118–128; Morris, *Papal Monarchy*, pp. 81–89; Barber, *Two Cities*, pp. 86–88; Blumenthal, *Investiture Controversy*, pp. 70–76.

[18] Morris, *Papal Monarchy*, pp. 109–121; Blumenthal, *Investiture Controversy*, pp. 113–127; Barber, *Two Cities*, pp. 90–94.

[19] Mitteis and Lieberich, *Deutsche Rechtsgeschichte*, pp. 123–124, 181, 201–202; Haverkamp, *Aufbruch*, pp. 139–140; Fuhrmann, *Deutsche Geschichte*, pp. 107–110.

[20] Fuhrmann, *Deutsche Geschichte*, pp. 76–83, 99–108; Haverkamp, *Aufbruch*, pp. 102–126.

later than in France. As in France, this takeoff provided local lords with the resources they needed to build expensive castles. With the weakening of imperial power after 1076 under near civil war conditions, the rate of castle-building accelerated across Germany.[21] In France, the decline of royal authority had led first to the appearance of regional principalities and only much later to the fracturing of local administrative districts with the rise of the castellans and (even later) of the cities. In Germany, by contrast, the survival of a neo-Carolingian state until the late 1000s meant that all of these processes occurred simultaneously, resulting in a fragmentation of the local political landscape far more severe than anything encountered by the Capetian kings. Thus, even after several centuries of concentration and consolidation, the German portion of the Empire would still contain some 2,400 separate political units in the early 1500s.[22]

The measures taken by the Salian and Hohenstaufen emperors to counteract these trends in the end proved ineffective, and may in fact have made the situation worse. The Salians sought to replace the administrative capacities they had lost due to Church reform by building a series of castles throughout their lands and manning them with a new class of dependent knights, the *ministeriales*.[23] But unlike the Capetians, whose own lands were heavily concentrated in the strategic Île-de-France, the estates of the emperors were scattered all across Germany and northern Italy, a consequence of the fact that three dynasties from entirely different areas of the country had occupied the east Frankish and imperial throne over the previous two centuries. Indeed, as under the Carolingians, the Empire did not even possess a fixed capital. Instead, its rulers were used to traveling regularly throughout their realm, staying in their widely scattered palaces or calling upon the hospitality of lay or ecclesiastical lords who owed them service.[24] As a result, neither

[21] Arnold, *Princes*, pp. 5, 140–146, 152–185; Prinz, *Grundlagen*, pp. 307–308; Haverkamp, *Aufbruch*, pp. 67–68; M. W. Thompson, *The Rise of the Castle* (Cambridge: Cambridge University Press, 1991), pp. 21–22.

[22] John Gagliardo, *Germany under the Old Regime 1600–1790* (London: Longman, 1991), p. 2. Gagliardo breaks this figure down into 136 ecclesiastical and 173 lay principalities, 85 free cities, and some 2,000 autonomous territories of imperial knights (*Reichsritter*). For lists of the Empire's constituent states in 1521, 1755, and 1792 see: Gerhard Oestreich, *Verfassungsgeschichte vom Ende des Mittelalters bis zum Ende des Alten Reiches* (= *Gebhardts Handbuch der Deutschen Geschichte*, 9th ed., vol. XI) (Stuttgart: Deutscher Taschenbuchverlag, 1974), pp. 137–155.

[23] Karl Bosl, *Die Reichsministerialität der Salier und Staufer*, 2 vols. (Stuttgart: Hiersemann, 1950), vol. I, pp. 74–112; Benjamin Arnold, *German Knighthood 1050–1300* (Oxford: Clarendon, 1985), pp. 209–212; Mitteis and Lieberich, *Deutsche Rechtsgeschichte*, pp. 201–202.

[24] Mitteis and Lieberich, *Deutsche Rechtsgeschichte*, pp. 151–153, 197–199; Haverkamp, *Aufbruch*, pp. 143–148; Carlrichard Brühl, *Fodrum, Gistum, Servitium Regis* (Köln: Böhlau, 1968), pp. 116–219.

the Salians nor the Hohenstaufen (whose private lands lay in yet another part of Germany) ever possessed a geographically compact base from which to reconquer their lost authority. They were forced instead to fight their enemies all across the length and breadth of Germany and Italy.

After securing the throne in 1137, the Hohenstaufen tried a new approach. Like the Capetians, they attempted to use feudalism to their advantage by bringing together those fiefs in the hands of lay aristocrats with those now held by churchmen following the Worms settlement and arranging the fiefs into a single hierarchy with a codified set of feudal rules and obligations (*Heerschildordnung*).[25] And, just as French rulers had sought to bolster further their new position as supreme feudal lord with a strategic redeployment of Carolingian conceptions of kingship, so too the Hohenstaufen seized upon a recently revived Roman law to lay claim to imperial prerogatives set down in the Justinian Code.[26]

While this approach in the end proved highly successful in Capetian France, this was not the case within the Empire. In response to geopolitical pressures, the Capetians had begun to construct, during the course of the 1100s, an independent administrative infrastructure which they then were able to use during subsequent centuries to enforce claims derived from feudal law. However, the devastating blow to central state power delivered by the Investiture Conflict and the subsequent 50-year civil war within Germany left the Salians and the Hohenstaufen too weak to do anything more than install a network of *ministeriales* in their scattered domain lands. Thus, they were left without a state apparatus capable of enforcing feudal obligations even on a regional basis, let alone across all of their vast realm. As a result, "feudalization" merely served to render irreversible the loss of central authority which began in 1076 by strengthening the rights of princely fief-holders vis-à-vis both their sovereign and their vassals.[27]

The most tangible consequence of Frederick I and Frederick II's

---

[25] Hans Schulze, *Grundstrukturen der Verfassung im Mittelalter*, 2nd ed., 2 vols. (Stuttgart: Kohlhammer, 1990), vol. I, pp. 63–67, 87–90; Karl Bosl, *Staat, Gesellschaft, Wirtschaft im Deutschen Mittelalter* (= *Gebhardts Handbuch der Deutschen Geschichte*, 9th ed., vol. VII) (Stuttgart: Deutscher Taschenbuchverlag, 1973), pp. 161–167; Mitteis and Lieberich, *Deutsche Rechtsgeschichte*, pp. 182–183.

[26] Hermann Krause, *Kaiserrecht und Rezeption* (Heidelberg: Carl Winter, 1952), pp. 26–49; J. P. Canning, "Introduction: Politics, Institutions, Ideas," in: J. H. Burns (ed.), *The Cambridge History of Medieval Political Thought c. 350–c. 1450* (Cambridge: Cambridge University Press, 1988), pp. 341–366, here at pp. 341–343; Mitteis and Lieberich, *Deutsche Rechtsgeschichte*, pp. 128–129, 328–329.

[27] Bosl, *Staat, Gesellschaft*, pp. 161–165; Mitteis and Lieberich, *Deutsche Rechtsgeschichte*, pp. 182–185.

new, more explicitly Roman conception of their imperial office was the ill-fated, century-long (1154–1254) attempt to reimpose direct control over northern Italy, Europe's wealthiest region at that time. The leading aristocrats of Germany in turn exploited every Hohenstaufen setback south of the Alps to obtain new privileges from the emperors, including most notably the *Statutum in Favorem Principum* (Statute in Favor of the Princes) of 1231. The statute confirmed the regalian rights already in aristocratic hands while permitting them to make new laws for their lands following consultations with the "good and great" (*meliores et maiores*) among their subjects.[28] Later, the princes and other territorial lords took up the strong, "imperial" conception of rulership revitalized by the Hohenstaufen and used it in support of their own state-forming activities.

Following the death of the last Hohenstaufen emperor, Conrad IV, in 1254, none of the families which, over the coming centuries, came to occupy the German and imperial thrones possessed private resources great enough to permit them to overcome the resistance of the other princes to any attempts at restoring effective central power. Using the freedom now afforded them by weakness at the center, lay and ecclesiastical lords great and small, as well as cities and even the strong peasant communities of the Alpine region, set about building up and consolidating their own local authority. The raw materials which they employed in this enterprise were of diverse origin: seigneurial jurisdiction over allodial lands, fiefs, and forests; titles to judicial offices such as those of count or advocate; peacekeeping authority over particular areas conferred by the emperor; grants of regalian rights over tolls, minting, mining, and safe passage; and powers to command vassals or retainers.[29]

Nascent territorial lordships thus first emerged as bundles of rights, often disputed by others and scattered over wide areas. A lingering consequence of the imperial Church system was the fact that, in contrast to the situation in other parts of Europe, churchmen within the

---

[28]   Herbert Grundmann, *Wahlkönigtum, Territorialpolitik und Ostbewegung im 13. und 14. Jahrhundert* (= *Gebhardts Handbuch der Deutschen Geschichte*, 9th ed., vol. V) (Stuttgart: Deutscher Taschenbuchverlag, 1973), pp. 50–52; Joachim Leuschner, *Deutschland im Späten Mittelalter*, 2nd ed. (Göttingen: Vandenhoeck & Ruprecht, 1983), pp. 82–88; Mitteis and Lieberich, *Deutsche Rechtsgeschichte*, pp. 133–136; Barber, *Two Cities*, pp. 207–221.

[29]   Benjamin Arnold, *Count and Bishop in Medieval Germany: A Study of Regional Power 1100–1350* (Philadelphia: University of Pennsylvania Press, 1991), passim; idem, *Princes*, pp. 72, 88–132, 282–283 and passim; Götz Landwehr, "Mobilisierung und Konsolidierung der Herrschaftsordnung im 14. Jahrhundert. Zusammenfassung," in: Hans Patze (ed.), *Der Deutsche Territorialstaat im 14. Jahrhundert*, 2 vols. (Sigmaringen: Jan Thorbecke, 1971), vol. II, pp. 484–505; Mitteis and Lieberich, *Deutsche Rechtsgeschichte*, pp. 264–270.

Empire often held considerable bundles of such "secular" rights. The micro-history of central Europe between the mid-1200s and the close of the middle ages thus consisted of attempts to solidify and concentrate these rights through marriage, exchange, purchase, litigation, or conquest. The administrative means which lords possessed to do this were everywhere the same and quite rudimentary: they consisted of networks of castles manned by knights and a few subordinate officials which served as multipurpose administrative, judicial, and military centers for the seigneurial lands located in the surrounding area. Meanwhile, the lord in question traveled ceaselessly from castle to castle, accompanied by a small court, dispensing justice and overseeing his possessions. A small writing office headed by a chancellor was usually sufficient to accomplish all necessary clerical tasks.[30]

The privileged subjects of the territorial lords played an important role in the emergence of durable states from the debris of the Salian-Hohenstaufen Empire. Beginning as early as the late 1200s, the nobility, clergy, and towns of the Empire's highly fragmented territories began to organize themselves into status-based groups, just as their counterparts in Latin Europe had done, in order to protect their interests in the face of the increasingly intense efforts of their lords to consolidate and extend their own authority. Though these estates were usually *not* brought together into a single representative assembly until the late 1400s or after, they nonetheless were able to influence the process of state formation by winning the right to be consulted before taxes were imposed and, most important of all, by opposing the common lordly practice of dividing their lands among surviving male heirs.[31] Under pressure from the privileged orders, Germany's state-forming princes abandoned this practice beginning in the late 1400s, a clear indication that the Empire's territories were now more than just overblown private domains. They had become states in their own right and as such

[30] Hans Patze, "Die Herrschaftspraxis der deutschen Landesherren während des späten Mittelalters," in: Werner Paravicini and Karl Ferdinand Werner (eds.), *Histoire Comparée de l'Administration (IVe–XVIIIe Siècles)* (München: Artemis, 1980), pp. 363–391; Gerd Theuerkauf, "Zur Typologie spätmittelalterlicher Territorialverwaltung in Deutschland," *Annali dell Fondazione Italiana per la Storia Amministrativa*, vol. 2 (1965), pp. 37–76, here at pp. 50–66; Arnold, *German Knighthood*, pp. 184–208; Mitteis and Lieberich, *Deutsche Rechtsgeschichte*, pp. 270–271.

[31] Hans Spangenberg, *Vom Lehnstaat zum Ständestaat* (Aalen: Scientia, 1964), passim; Robert Folz, "Les Assemblées d'États dans les Principautés Allemandes (Fin XIIIe–Début XVIe Siècle)," *Gouvernés et Gouvernants*, vol. 25 (1965), pp. 163–191, here at pp. 176–183, 186–187; F. L. Carsten, *Princes and Parliaments in Germany from the Fifteenth to the Eighteenth Century* (Oxford: Clarendon, 1959), pp. 425–428; Leuschner, *Deutschland*, pp. 163–164; Bosl, *Staat, Gesellschaft*, pp. 222–228; Theuerkauf, "Typologie," pp. 71; Mitteis and Lieberich, *Deutsche Rechtsgeschichte*, pp. 273–277.

possessed an identity which transcended the person of individual rulers, an identity which the interaction between those rulers and their estates had helped bring about.[32]

By the close of the middle ages, the centuries-long process of state formation involving hundreds of lay and ecclesiastical lordships of widely varying sizes and configurations was finally drawing to a conclusion. Over the course of half a millennium, Germany had been transformed, under the lasting impact of the Investiture Conflict, economic expansion, and private castle-building, from a single, vast dark age polity organized along neo-Carolingian lines into a confederation dominated by approximately two dozen increasingly sovereign territorial states. During the coming centuries, those states would remain the undisputed focus of political development in central Europe.

REPRESENTATIVE INSTITUTIONS, GEOPOLITICAL
COMPETITION, AND THE CONSOLIDATION OF BUREAUCRATIC
ABSOLUTISM IN THE GERMAN TERRITORIAL STATES,
C. 1450–1789

The new generation of states that solidified across central Europe after the mid-1400s were embroiled almost immediately in sustained geopolitical competition. Initially this took the form of local tensions and conflicts as lay and ecclesiastical princes moved to consolidate and extend their territories at the expense of their neighbors. Beginning in the mid-1500s, however, the rise of Habsburg power and the forces unleashed by the Reformation soon rendered the Empire the principal arena for larger, continent-wide rivalries which eventually culminated in the devastating Thirty Years War of 1618–1648. It was in response to these new pressures that Germany's territorial rulers first sought to expand and improve their administrative and financial infrastructures beyond the rudimentary institutional arrangements which had sufficed to complete the process of state formation.

Whereas in England and Latin Europe representative assemblies did not arise until a century or more after the onset of sustained geopolitical competition, in Germany they were present right from the start, formed from the corporately organized estates which had long negotiated individually with their lords. While this was also true, as will be

---

[32] Leuschner, *Deutschland*, pp. 165–166; Oestreich, *Verfassungsgeschichte*, p. 67; Folz, "Assemblées d'Etats," p. 178; Theuerkauf, "Typologie," pp. 70–71; Ernst Klein, *Geschichte der Oeffentlichen Finanzen in Deutschland (1500–1870)* (Wiesbaden: Franz Steiner, 1974), p. 3; Winfried Schulze, *Deutsche Geschichte im 16. Jahrhundert* (Frankfurt am Main: Suhrkamp, 1987), pp. 205, 211.

seen in Chapter 6, of Poland and Hungary, rulers in Germany found themselves in a much more favorable position vis-à-vis their assemblies than did the kings of those countries. This was due to the fact that the German princes had inherited a strong, imperial conception of rulership present in central Europe since the 8th century and earlier, and because the German assemblies did not represent autonomous local political communities, as did the British Parliament and the Polish and Hungarian Diets. Rather, representative assemblies in Germany were joint gatherings of separate, legally defined orders interested above all in protecting their rights and privileges.

The result of this balance of forces was, at least initially, a division of labor within the new territorial states. The Estates retained significant influence in the area of greatest common concern to them – extraordinary taxation – while the rulers kept wide powers over lawmaking, internal order, defense, and foreign affairs. The latter then used their freedom of maneuver to construct large new state apparatuses which, thanks to the educational and legal advances of the later middle ages, were nonproprietary and hence susceptible to bureaucratic organization. The further increase in princely power which these bureaucracies brought with them in turn led many princes to reduce or eliminate altogether the remaining prerogatives of their Estates during the period between the end of the Thirty Years War and the French Revolution.

Representative Assemblies in the New German Territorial States

The manner in which the German states had come into being made future conflicts almost inevitable, for there was hardly a prince within all of the Empire who did not harbor a claim against lands or rights in the possession of one of his colleagues, and very few whose territories were not intermingled with those of other rulers. The result was a pattern of frequent though limited wars between neighbors throughout the late 15th and early 16th centuries, such as those, for example, between Württemberg and the Palatinate, the Palatinate and Bavaria, Hessen and Mainz, Cologne and Cleves and Mark, and the Rhine duchies among themselves.[33] While these wars may have been small by international standards, they frequently had a devastating impact on the finances of the combatants, for the accumulated costs of the process of

---

[33] Carsten, *Princes and Parliaments*, pp. 6, 263–265, 343; Herbert Helbig, "Fürsten und Landstände im Westen des Reiches im Uebergang vom Mittelalter zur Neuzeit," *Rheinische Vierteljahrsblätter*, vol. 29, no. 1 (1964), pp. 32–72, here at p. 41; Georg Droege, "Die finanziellen Grundlagen des Territorialstaates in West- und Ostdeutschland an der Wende vom Mittelalter zur Neuzeit," *Vierteljahrschrift für Sozial- und Wirtschaftsgeschichte*, vol. 53, no. 2 (Juli 1964), pp. 145–161, here at p. 153.

state formation had already left most German principalities with massive debts and depleted domain revenues as a result of the widespread practice of pawning assets to raise cash. Furthermore, the advent of paid professional armies had rendered even local feuds extremely costly.[34] In response to their conflict-induced financial difficulties, rulers all over the Empire moved during this period to gather their estates into formal representative assemblies in order to facilitate negotiations with them about the levying of new taxes. Thus, institutionalized assemblies (*Landtage*) first appeared in the electoral archbishopric of Trier in 1456, in that of Cologne in 1463, in Württemberg in 1457, Alsace in 1463/ 1472, Brandenburg in 1472, Mecklenburg in 1489, and Bavaria in 1505.[35] The dominant form which these *Landtage* took was the curially organized, three-order model already familiar from Latin Europe, though in some states in the eastern areas of the Empire (the Habsburg lands and Bohemia) and in Prussia, which technically lay beyond its borders, the nobility was divided into a lordly (*Herrenkurie*) and knightly (*Ritterkurie*) estate. Two kinds of subsequent changes also sometimes modified the original tricurial composition of a given assembly. In a minority of Protestant territories (e.g., Mecklenburg), the clerical order disappeared altogether after the Reformation. Also, in a number of states located in the southwest of Germany (Trier, Württemberg), the nobility succeeded in freeing itself from the authority of the local ruler by gaining the status of *Reichsritter* (imperial knights), and as a result dropped out of the *Landtag*. None of these developments, however, altered the fundamentally curial, corporate structure common to all of the German Estates, regardless of how many chambers they in the end retained.[36]

---

[34] Droege, "Die finanziellen Grundlagen," pp. 148–153; E. B. Fryde and M. M. Fryde, "Public Credit, with Special Reference to North-Western Europe," in: M. M. Postan, E. E. Rich, and Edward Miller (eds.), *The Cambridge Economic History of Europe. Volume III: Economic Organization and Policies in the Middle Ages* (Cambridge: Cambridge University Press, 1963), pp. 430–553, here at pp. 518–526; Klein, *Geschichte*, pp. 5–6.

[35] Folz, "Assemblées d'Etats," pp. 186–190; Helbig, "Fürsten und Landstände," pp. 42, 48; Oestreich, *Verfassungsgeschichte*, pp. 77–79; Ulrich Lange, "Der ständische Dualismus – Bemerkungen zu einem Problem der deutschen Verfassungsgeschichte," *Blätter für Deutsche Landesgeschichte*, vol. 117 (1981), pp. 311–334, here at pp. 312, 315, 323; Volker Press, "Vom 'Ständestaat' zum Absolutismus: 50 Thesen zur Entwicklung des Ständewesens in Deutschland," in: Peter Baumgart (ed.), *Ständetum und Staatsbildung in Brandenburg-Preussen* (Berlin: Walter de Gruyter, 1983), pp. 319–326, here at p. 319.

[36] Gerhard Buchda, "Reichsstände und Landstände in Deutschland im 16. und 17. Jahrhundert," *Gouvernés et Gouvernants*, vol. 25 (1965), pp. 193–226, here at pp. 208– 209, 221; Volker Press, "Formen des Ständewesens in den deutschen Territorialstaaten des 16. und 17. Jahrhunderts," in: Baumgart, *Ständetum*, pp. 280–318, here at pp. 284–288; Georg von Below, "System und Bedeutung der landständischen Verfassung," in: idem, *Territorium und Staat*, 2nd ed. (München: R. Oldenbourg, 1923), pp. 53– 160, here at pp. 69–100; Helbig, "Fürsten und Landstände," pp. 34–40.

Over the next century and a half, the representative assemblies within the Empire devoted the bulk of their attention to financial matters ("Landtag ist Geldtag"). During this period their rulers' need for funds grew steadily as a result not only of continuing local wars but also of a series of much larger conflicts, many of them linked to the Reformation and looming Habsburg hegemony in western Europe (Knights' War 1522–1523, Peasants' War 1525–1526, Schmalkaldic War 1546–1547, Princes' War 1552–1555, Thirty Years War 1618–1648). The territorial states were also forced to contribute sizable sums to the imperial effort against the Turks, and, if all these burdens were not enough, the inflationary trend of the 16th century played its part in eroding the real value of princely incomes.[37]

Against this background, the Estates were called upon again and again to approve new taxes during the 1500s and early 1600s. Indeed, it was at this time that the revenue base of the Empire's principalities shifted decisively from domain and regalian income to regular taxation. Furthermore, at the start of this period the rudimentary infrastructures of the recently crystallized German states did not possess the means either to gather or to administer such tax flows. The Estates in most territories were therefore able to step in and take over these functions themselves, employing their own collection agents and setting up separate treasuries under their direct control from which the revenues were then to be disbursed.[38]

The German rulers were hardly in a position to block this development, since in many cases, such as those of Württemberg (1514, 1525, 1554), Brandenburg (1549), Mecklenburg (1555), Bavaria (1557, 1563), Saxony (1570), and Baden-Durlach (1588), a considerable portion of the income from new extraordinary taxes was earmarked for princely debts which the Estates had agreed to repay. Turning over financial and debt management to the Estates was also a way to restore the creditworthiness of the nascent territorial states, for while bankers and private citizens were reluctant to lend funds directly to rulers who had acquired a reputation for profligacy and irresponsibility during the later middle ages, they were often willing to entrust their funds to Estates who could provide them with legally binding guarantees of

---

[37] Klein, *Geschichte*, pp. 5–6, 15; Schulze, *Deutsche Geschichte*, pp. 205–207; Kersten Krüger, "Public Finance and Modernisation: The Change from Domain State to Tax State in Hesse in the Sixteenth and Seventeenth Centuries – A Case Study," in: Peter-Christian Witt, *Wealth and Taxation in Central Europe* (Leamington Spa, UK: Berg, 1987), pp. 49–62, here at p. 50.

[38] Klein, *Geschichte*, pp. 12–16; Krüger, "Public Finance," pp. 50–60; Carsten, *Princes and Parliaments*, pp. 35, 358, 368; Oestreich, *Verfassungsgeschichte*, p. 79; von Below, "System und Bedeuting," pp. 134–135.

repayment.[39] In order to oversee on a day-to-day basis their growing responsibilities and provide quick responses to emergency requests for funds, most Estates created permanent standing committees (*Ausschüsse*) to represent them between plenary meetings, thereby further institutionalizing their position within the new German polities.[40]

While the Estates did take advantage of meetings – called primarily to approve taxes – to present grievances (*gravamina*) and offer advice on matters of policy, and while rulers often voluntarily presented major pieces of legislation such as new law codes to their assemblies for discussion and approval, it is a striking fact that the *Landtage* never succeeded in translating their considerable financial leverage into effective participation in areas of government other than direct taxation. In effect, they never attained the status of "co-rulers" achieved by their English, Polish, Hungarian, and Swedish counterparts. The reasons for this were twofold. First, while the different orders which comprised the German assemblies may have been bound together by the defensive desire to protect their group privileges and limit their masters' ability to tax them or their tenants, their interests were opposed to one another in most other areas. Furthermore, the status-group-based organization of the German assemblies served to heighten and perpetuate those differences rather than moderate them, thereby rendering positive cooperation across the different *curiae* very difficult to achieve.[41]

Second, the claims of the Empire's territorial rulers to exclusive prerogatives in the area of legislation, defense, and foreign policy were bolstered by a tradition of the proper rights and duties of rulers – also present in Latin Europe – which had its roots in the Roman Empire and was very different from the one found in England, Poland, or Hungary. As discussed in Chapter 2, that conception, which was passed on (with some modifications) directly from the late Romans through the Merovingians to the Carolingians, charged the prince with the preservation of peace and order and the promotion of the public good (*salus, utilitas publica*) and endowed him with absolute legislative powers in order that he might accomplish those tasks. In Germany, this tradition

---

[39] Volker Press, "Steuern, Kredit und Repräsentation: Zum Problem der Ständebildung ohne Adel," *Zeitschrift für Historische Forschung*, vol. 2, no. 1 (1975), pp. 59–93, here at pp. 65–72; idem, "Formen des Ständewesens," pp. 291–292; Klein, *Geschichte*, pp. 18–19; Lange, "Ständestaatlicher Dualismus," pp. 329–330, 333; Droege, "Finanzielle Grundlagen," pp. 158–159; Carsten, *Princes and Parliaments*, pp. 17, 34, 379.

[40] Lange, "Ständestaatlicher Dualismus," pp. 319–334; von Below, "System und Bedeutung," pp. 103–106; Oestreich, *Verfassungsgeschichte*, p. 78; Press, "Formen des Ständewesens," p. 293.

[41] Helbig, "Fürsten und Landstände," pp. 41–45, 52, 59–67, 71–72; von Below, "System und Bedeutung," pp. 69, 114–116, 153–154; Press, "Formen des Ständewesens," pp. 290–291; Carsten, *Princes and Parliaments*, pp. 430, 441.

was reinvigorated by the revival of the Empire in 962 under the Ottonians, by the imperialist propaganda directed against the pope during the Investiture Conflict, and by the Hohenstaufen mobilization – in support of their own political aims – of arguments concerning the absolute and sovereign powers of the emperor derived directly from the rediscovered *Corpus Iuris*.[42]

When imperial authority declined after 1254, the territorial princes appropriated these arguments (e.g., the tag *princeps imperator in territorio suo*, "every prince an emperor in his own territory") and employed them against both their own subjects and the emperor himself, much as the king of France did at about the same time.[43] Beginning in the later middle ages, the princes of the Empire reinforced their claims to be Roman-style *principes* by replacing the customary law of their lands directly with Roman law, a process known as the *Rezeption* that accelerated after 1495 when a new Imperial Chamber Court (*Reichskammergericht*) was created which directly applied the *Corpus Iuris*. When combined with the structural weaknesses of the Estates mentioned above, this long tradition of "imperial" rulership permitted German rulers to assert successfully, during the course of the late 1400s and 1500s, their right to make new laws and exercise wide-ranging executive powers without first seeking the approval of the *Landtage*. At approximately the same time, one of the most characteristic features of German absolutism, the *Landes-* and *Polizeiordnungen*, began to appear. These government ordinances, which were issued by the ruler for the most part without consultation and set down rules and guidelines for every sphere of life from private dress to the operation of the economy, made up the largest single body of legislation promulgated in early modern Germany.[44]

Infrastructural Expansion and Mature Bureaucratic Absolutism

While the ideological position of the Empire's territorial rulers may have been a strong one, their ability to convert prerogatives into actual

---

[42] Percy Ernst Schramm, *Kaiser, Rom und Renovatio*, 4th ed. (Darmstadt: Wissenschaftliche Buchgesellschaft, 1984), passim; Canning, "Introduction," pp. 341–343; Hermann Krause, *Kaiserrecht und Rezeption*, pp. 26–147; Mitteis and Lieberich, *Deutsche Rechtsgeschichte*, pp. 328–329.

[43] Kurt Jeserich, Hans Pohl, Georg-Christoph von Unruh (eds.), *Deutsche Verwaltungsgeschichte*, 6 vols. (Stuttgart: Deutsche Verlags-Anstalt, 1983), vol. I, p. 288.

[44] Wilhelm Ebel, *Geschichte der Gesetzgebung in Deutschland* (Göttingen: Otto Schwarz, 1988), pp. 58–65, 68–75; Michael Stolleis, "Condere leges et interpretari. Gesetzgebungsmacht und Staatsbildung in der frühen Neuzeit," in: idem, *Staat und Staatsräson in der Frühen Neuzeit* (Frankfurt: Suhrkamp, 1990), pp. 167–196; here at pp. 188–196; Mitteis and Lieberich, *Deutsche Rechtsgeschichte*, pp. 327–331, 379–380, 389; Schulze, *Deutsche Geschichte*, pp. 224–226; Oestreich, *Verfassungsgeschichte*, pp. 72–74; Marc Raeff, *The Well-Ordered Police State* (New Haven: Yale University Press, 1983), pp. 43–56 and passim.

governing capacities depended on the possession of effective, independent state infrastructures. During the late 1400s and 1500s, Germany's princes set out to construct such infrastructures in response to geopolitical pressures. It was Emperor Maximilian I (1493–1519) who, in financial difficulties as a result of large-scale conflicts with France over the Burgundian inheritance and control of northern Italy, first set out during the 1490s to increase the efficiency with which his Austrian lands were managed. In carrying out comprehensive administrative reform, Maximilian drew on models familiar to him from the more advanced southern Netherlands. No sooner had these reforms been completed (1497), than they were promptly imitated by two geopolitical competitors of the Austrians – Saxony (1499) and Bavaria (1501) – and thereafter by nearly every principality in the Empire.[45]

As a result of this great wave of infrastructural expansion, the states of central Europe came to possess, by the early part of the 17th century, administrative, fiscal, and judicial apparatuses which, despite some differences in nomenclature, were remarkable in their uniformity. At the center of these new apparatuses stood the *Hofrat* (court or privy council), composed largely of trained jurists, which served both as the chief organ of administrative coordination and oversight and as a high court of appeal. During the course of the late 1500s and early 1600s, a smaller *Geheimer Rat* (secret council) in which the ruler held confidential discussions with a few close advisers separated itself off from the *Hofrat*. Ordinary finances (as opposed to the extraordinary finances most often in the hands of the Estates), defense, and ecclesiastical affairs were all administered by separate boards – respectively the *Hofkammer* (court chamber), *Kriegsrat* (war council), and *Konsisterei* (consistory) – and a *Kanzlei* or chancellory carried out the clerical work of the central government. Finally, a new network of courts was put in place at the local and/or regional level, and specialized fiscal and military field staffs were created or expanded.[46]

What permitted these new infrastructures to function in a relatively

---

[45] Oestreich, *Deutsche Verfassungsgeschichte*, pp. 83–85; Fritz Hartung, "Der französisch-burgundische Einfluss auf die Entwicklung der deutschen Behördenorganisation," in: idem, *Staatsbildende Kräfte der Neuzeit* (Berlin: Duncker & Humblot, 1961), pp. 78–92, here at pp. 79–81 and passim; Jeserich et al., *Deutsche Verwaltungsgeschichte*, vol. I, pp. 307–309.

[46] Jeserich et al., *Deutsche Verwaltungsgeschichte*, vol. I, pp. 300–346; Oestreich, *Verfassungsgeschichte*, pp. 84–87; Georg von Below, "Die Neuorganisation der Verwaltung in den deutschen Territorien des 16. Jahrhunderts," in: idem, *Territorium und Staat*, pp. 194–208; Gustav Schmoller, "Der deutsche Beamtenstaat vom 16. bis 18. Jahrhundert," in: idem, *Umrisse und Untersuchungen zur Verfassungs-, Verwaltungs- und Wirtschaftsgeschichte besonders des Preussischen Staates im 17. und 18. Jahrhundert* (Hildesheim: Georg Olms, 1974), pp. 289–313; Schulze, *Deutsche Geschichte*, pp. 211–214; Stolleis, "Condere leges," pp. 179–180.

bureaucratic manner was the fact that the officials employed within them, in contrast to their counterparts in Latin Europe and pre-Civil War England, possessed no proprietary rights over their offices.[47] Not only were the German princes fully aware of the French system of *vénalité des offices* and determined to avoid it,[48] but over the past several centuries a concept of office and officeholding had developed that was free of the influence of the ecclesiastical benefice.[49] Finally, and most importantly, the administrative and legal skills which government officials possessed were no longer the rare commodities they had been in the 13th and 14th centuries, and hence could not be used to extort concessions from their rulers. Between 1348 and 1498, 16 universities had been founded within central Europe, and between 1502 and 1648 another 18 would open, thus producing a steady stream of graduates trained in Roman and canon law suitable for positions in government service. Furthermore, the cultural and legal unity of this region made it possible for officials to move from country to country with relative ease.

Armed with their new, bureaucratically organized apparatuses, the German princes moved, in the period following the Thirty Years War, to eliminate the remaining constraints on their behavior. Thus, they reduced the remaining influence of the Estates and in some cases eliminated those bodies altogether. This was made all the easier by the fact that the *Landtage* in most parts of the Empire had ruined themselves financially over the previous half-century by providing credit guarantees and debt-servicing facilities to their sovereigns without securing for themselves any meaningful checks over these rulers' foreign and domestic policy decisions. Having exhausted the credit of their Estates and with the capacity to collect taxes directly themselves, the princes could afford to neutralize the assemblies by taking over the separate, Estate-controlled tax administrations and/or by replacing plenary sessions with meetings of the small, easily corruptible standing committees. Where no committee system had developed, as in the Kurmark (Brandenburg), Prussia, Schleswig, and Holstein, rulers ceased to convoke the Estates altogether after securing long-term grants of taxation.[50]

---

[47] Klaus Malettke (ed.), *Aemterkäuflichkeit: Aspekte Sozialer Mobilität im Europäischen Vergleich (17. und 18. Jahrhundert)* (Berlin: Colloquium, 1980), pp. 179–180; K. W. Swart, *The Sale of Offices in the 17th Century* (Utrecht: HES, 1980), pp. 94–96.

[48] Michael Stolleis, "Grundzüge der Beamtenethik (1550–1650)," in: idem, *Staat und Staatsräson*, pp. 197–231, here at pp. 217–218.

[49] Jeserich et al., *Deutsche Verwaltungsgeschichte*, vol. I, pp. 81–92, 347–359; Oestreich, *Verfassungsgeschichte*, p. 160.

[50] Lange, "Der ständestaatliche Dualismus," passim; Press, "Formen des Ständewesens," pp. 299–302; Carsten, *Princes and Parliaments*, pp. 439–444; idem, "The Causes of the Decline of the German Estates," in: *Album Helen Maud Cam* (Louvain: Publications Universitaires de Louvain, 1961), pp. 287–296; Ronald Asch, "Estates and Princes after 1648: The Consequences of the Thirty Years War," *German History*, vol. 6, no. 2 (August 1988), pp. 113–132.

The bureaucratic absolutist polities which came to maturity within the Empire during the late 17th and 18th centuries were the logical outcome of a specific statebuilding process. Like their Latin European counterparts several centuries earlier, German rulers increasingly confronted intense geopolitical competition. In order to give themselves more flexibility to respond to such pressures, Germany's princes endeavored to consolidate coercive and financial resources under their direct control. In this process, they benefited greatly from the advantages of the latecomer. Not only were they able to borrow statebuilding models from other regions, but they also successfully avoided the burden of proprietary officeholding which had doomed the rationalizing efforts of reformers in Latin Europe. Although the bureaucratic absolutist system was initially able to amass resources at the center, it eventually withered under the strain of sustained warfare. This was so because the absolutist nature of the regime could not ensure the continual, yet consensual, flow of resources during wartime that Britain's bureaucratic constitutionalism was capable of delivering. In the next section, I illustrate this point by briefly examining the case of Brandenburg-Prussia, the most bureaucratic and absolutist – and also most militarily threatened – of all the states within the 18th-century Empire.

THE LIMITS AND CONTRADICTIONS OF BUREAUCRATIC ABSOLUTISM: THE CASE OF BRANDENBURG-PRUSSIA

It was during the reign of the Great Elector Frederick William (1640–1688) that the modern state of Brandenburg-Prussia actually came into being. Over the course of many decades, 11 disparate territories, acquired by marriage and diplomacy, were welded together through the establishment of a standing army and a national administrative and financial system designed to support it. In realizing this centralizing project, Frederick William felt it necessary to undermine those representative bodies within his realm which were hostile to it. While the new political entity which he created proved to be militarily competitive during his own lifetime – and was to become even more so during the reigns of his grandson and great-grandson Frederick William I and Frederick the Great – its absolutist character burdened the famed Prussian war machine with internal contradictions which eventually led to its collapse after the crushing defeat at Jena in 1806.

The Great Elector and the Foundations of the Prussian State

The roots of the dramatic expansion in Prussian power which occurred during the course of the 17th century lay in dynastic claims made by the Hohenzollern rulers of the medium-sized German electorate of

Brandenburg upon the Rhine territories of Kleve, Mark, Jülich, and Ravensberg in 1609, upon the Polish-held duchy of Prussia in 1618, and upon Pomerania in 1637. In 1648, Frederick William was granted half of Pomerania in the Treaty of Westphalia, as well as the former ecclesiastical states of Halberstadt and Magdeburg, but control of the other territories remained in dispute.[51] It was clear that if he wished to secure them, the elector would have to increase his military power sufficiently to hold his own against the Baltic's two regional powers, Sweden and Poland, as well as against his neighbor Saxony. The Estates of the Kurmark (i.e., Brandenburg) were generally hostile to this design, both because they feared that it would in the end limit the autonomy of their own land and, perhaps more importantly, because they sensed that it would involve the country in costly and bloody warfare.[52]

Over the next two decades, Frederick William set out to win long-term or permanent grants of taxation from the representative assemblies found in each of his many territories. These grants would support a standing army and obviate the need for frequent future meetings of such bodies, thereby reducing the potential influence of the various Estates over foreign affairs. The grants would have critical implications in the case of the Kurmark Estates, which were the most consistent opponents of the elector's expansionist policies. Frederick William's eventual 1653 agreement with the Kurmark Estates (the so-called *Recess*) served as the basis for similar accords negotiated with the Estates of Prussia in 1663 and those of Kleve-Mark in 1660–1.

The Brandenburg *Recess* of 1653 called for new direct taxes of 530,000 Thaler, to be levied over a period of six years by the government rather than the Estates. In return for this concession, Frederick William confirmed the nobility's tax-exempt status. He also promised to support landowners in efforts to force their peasants to meet feudal obligations. It was this last concession which probably led the Estates in the end to grant Frederick William's demand for new taxes sufficient to support a modest standing army. The Thirty Years War had left Brandenburg severely depopulated, and in its aftermath the nobility was attempting to use every legal means at their disposal to coerce peasants into taking up abandoned farms, a campaign that proved none too successful. While the *Recess* may not, as is often alleged, have encouraged the spread of serfdom in the Mark Brandenburg, it did help to shore up the manorial

---

[51] A concise overview of Brandenburg's acquisitions and its claims to each is provided by Gustav Schmoller in his *Preussische Verfassungs-, Verwaltungs- und Finanzgeschichte* (Berlin: Verlag der Täglichen Rundschau, 1921), pp. 45–53.

[52] F. L. Carsten, *The Origins of Prussia* (Oxford: Clarendon, 1954), p. 184; Christoph Fürbringer, *Necessitas und Libertas. Staatsbildung und Landstände im 17. Jahrhundert in Brandenburg* (Frankfurt am Main: Peter Lang, 1985), p. 59.

system at a time when it was under severe economic and demographic strain.[53]

Despite the time limits and other safeguards built into this agreement and those made with the other Estates, Frederick William soon began to levy direct taxes without prior consent, first in Brandenburg after 1659 and then in Prussia in the 1670s. These taxes were supplemented after 1667 with an excise levy, the *Akzise*, first introduced voluntarily into a number of towns in the Mark and then extended by the government without consultation to all of Brandenburg, Magdeburg, and Pomerania in 1681–6. This indirect tax on various food items and on commercial activity had been brought to Germany from Holland in the early 17th century, and the Brandenburg ordinance of 1684 was copied almost word for word from a Dutch law of 1683.[54]

By 1688, the three largest Hohenzollern provinces of Brandenburg, Prussia, and Kleve-Mark were paying about 1 million Thaler per year in total taxes, with smaller territories contributing another 600,000.[55] Practically all of the circa 1.6 million Thaler that the government now received annually through direct and indirect taxation was new income, since prior to 1640 nearly all tax revenues were controlled by the Kurmark Estates and employed by them to pay off royal debts. Frederick William continued to allow the older taxes to flow into the Estates treasury for this purpose, but now brought that treasury under direct electoral control. With the disappearance of the Kurmark Estates after 1659, their role as guarantor of future credits also vanished, and the activities of the former *Ständisches Kreditwerk* (Estates' Credit Agency) slowly wound down as old debts were reimbursed.[56]

This treatment of the *Kreditwerk* was only one aspect of a much broader drive by the Great Elector to create a new, government-controlled administrative apparatus encompassing all of his territories. At the top of the state, the character of the royal (inner) council or *Geheimer Rat* was

---

[53] William Hagen has recently thrown new light on the economic and social backround to the *Recess* in his article "Seventeenth-Century Crisis in Brandenburg: The Thirty Years War, the Destabilization of Serfdom, and the Rise of Absolutism," *American Historical Review*, vol. 94, no. 2 (April 1989), pp. 302–335.

[54] Willi Boelcke, "'Die Sanftmütige Accise': Zur Bedeutung und Problematik der 'indirekten Verbrauchsbesteuerung' in der Finanzwirtschaft der deutschen Territorialstaaten während der frühen Neuzeit," *Jahrbuch für die Geschichte Mittel- und Ostdeutschlands*, vol. 21 (1972), pp. 93–139, here at p. 112; Schmoller, *Preussische Verfassungs-....*, pp. 94–97.

[55] Kurt Breysig, "Der brandenburgische Staatshaushalt in der zweiten Hälfte des siebzehnten Jahrhunderts," *Jahrbuch für Gesetzgebung, Verwaltung und Volkswirtschaft im Deutschen Reich* (*"Schmollers Jahrbuch"*), vol. 16, no. 1 (1892), pp. 1–42; no. 2, pp. 449–545, here at p. 458.

[56] Conrad Bornhak, *Geschichte des Preussischen Verwaltungsrechts* (Berlin: Julius Springer, 1884), vol. I, pp. 404–405.

transformed from a coterie of powerful Brandenburg nobles into an
administrative body staffed by professional officials and career statesmen – many of them aristocrats and academics from other German
states – that was now responsible for all aspects of policy throughout
the Hohenzollern lands. At the same time, governors (*Statthalter*) responsible directly to the *Geheime Rat* were sent to the territories outside
the Mark, most of which had previously been ruled by councils or high
officials like chancellors who were beholden to the local Estates.[57]

Similar changes were introduced into the new composite state's
financial institutions as well. In the Kurmark, overall administration of
both the royal domain and regalian income like customs and tolls lay
in the hands of the domain chamber or *Amtskammer*, formally established in 1615. Beginning in 1651, this body was reorganized and staffed
with a number of leading officials who also sat on the *Geheime Rat*. Over
the next three decades, similar *Amtskammer* were set up in Pomerania,
Magdeburg, and Prussia, and the one already present in Kleve-Mark
since 1612 was reformed. Each of these bodies was directed to send its
surplus income directly to Berlin. Finally, shortly after the death of the
Great Elector, a collegial board, the *Hofkammer*, was created to direct
the activities of the provincial *Amtskammer* under the reforming minister Dodo von Knypenhausen.[58]

Knypenhausen also succeeded after 1684 in removing the administration of the Elector's landed estates (or at least those that had not
been pawned) from the hands of the bailiffs, leasing them instead to
private farmers in return for fixed money rents.[59] These changes
allowed total revenues from electoral estates (including *regalia*) to be
raised from under 600,000 Thaler in 1640 to over 1.6 million Thaler
at the end of the reign.[60] In addition, money rents finally permitted
Brandenburg-Prussia to free itself from the bane of in-kind payments
which had remained at the center of state finances long after they had
been abandoned in much of the West.

The most famous reform introduced under the Great Elector, however, and the one that would exercise the greatest influence on the character of the Prussian state for centuries to come, was the creation of a
new national bureaucracy that combined the tasks of revenue collection

[57] Ibid., pp. 316–320; Schmoller, *Preussische Verfassungs-*..., pp. 68–72; Peter-Michael
Hahn, "Landesstaat und Ständetum im Kurfürstentum Brandenburg während des 16.
und 17. Jahrhunderts," in: Peter Baumgart (ed.), *Ständetum und Staatsbildung in
Brandenburg-Preussen* (Berlin: Walter de Gruyter, 1983), pp. 41–79, here at pp. 65–66.
[58] This whole process is documented with Prussian thoroughness in: Kurt Breysig,
*Geschichte der Brandenburgischen Finanzen in der Zeit von 1640 bis 1697. Band I: Die
Centralstellen der Kammerverwaltung. Die Amtskammer, das Kassenwesen und die Domänen
der Kurmark* (Leipzig: Duncker & Humblot, 1895), pp. 5–190.
[59] Ibid., pp. 352ff.   [60] Breysig, "Der brandenburgische Staatshaushalt," p. 35.

and military administration. It was called the *Kriegskommissariat* or war commissary. Although centralized war councils with broad powers had existed in 16th-century Austria and other German states, it was the Swedish military administration during the Thirty Years War that seems to have provided the direct inspiration for the *Kommissariat.*

Whenever the Swedish army took over a new area, a commissary would be responsible for organizing the orderly collection of war taxes or "contributions" from the occupied population. While all late medieval and early modern armies were accompanied by similar civilian officials responsible for mustering the troops, distributing their pay, and organizing their marches, the widespread use of the contribution system to support armies during the Thirty Years War gave the commissaries vast new financial powers as well. Not only did the long Swedish occupation of Brandenburg provide both that country's ruler and his officials with first-hand knowledge of Swedish methods, but in 1631 Gustavus Adolphus himself seems to have presented Frederick William's father with a concrete plan for introducing a commissary system into the Hohenzollern territories.[61]

The opportunity to do so was provided by the First Northern War of 1655–1660, during which the Great Elector was finally able to wrest Prussia from Polish overlordship. Because of this conflict, sizable numbers of troops were stationed in Brandenburg, Pomerania, and Prussia, and provincial commissaries were named to ensure that they were paid and accommodated. After the war, the contingents of the expanded standing army remained scattered throughout the realm, and commissaries were gradually introduced into all provinces. Their principal task soon became to organize the transfer of tax revenues from the local receivers to the regiments in their respective areas according to orders sent from the commissary-general (*Generalkommissar*) in Berlin.

Over the next several decades, both the provincial and the central commissariats were transformed, in typical Prussian fashion, into collegial boards. These boards came to acquire responsibility for tax collection and all aspects of military administration. Soon after, they also gained wide regulatory authority not only over the local economy but also over law and order, all in the name of greater military effectiveness.[62] It was at the provincial and new, supra-territorial levels, where existing

---

[61] Friedrich Wolters, *Geschichte der Brandenburgischen Finanzen in der Zeit von 1640–1697. Band II: Die Zentralverwaltung des Heeres und der Steuern* (Munich and Leipzig: Duncker & Humblot, 1915), pp. 2–9.

[62] The standard works on the development and functioning of the commissariat system are: Wolters, *Geshichte,* passim; and Kurt Breysig, "Die Organisation der brandenburgischen Kommissariate in der Zeit von 1660 bis 1697," *Forschungen zur Brandenburgischen und Preussischen Geschichte,* vol. 5, no. 1 (1892), pp. 135–156.

administrative bodies were weak or nonexistent, that the Great Elector
had been most successful in his efforts at infrastructural expansion.
At the local level of the district or *Kreis*, he had left tax collection and
general administration in the hands of local nobles.

Yet despite these achievements in the area of central administration,
the absence of permanent representative institutions within the new
Prussian state had important structural ramifications. The most significant of these were the financial difficulties that were already visible
under the Great Elector. Throughout his reign, the amount of money
Frederick William received in the form of direct or indirect taxes proved
insufficient to support the 30,000-man standing army he sought to
maintain, as well as the costs of two major wars, thus forcing him to
employ a range of questionable measures in order to fill the gap.

A persistent mismatch between ordinary revenues and expenses is a
common feature of fully absolutist regimes. In the absence of an institutional counterweight to their powers such as a permanent representative assembly, rulers will commonly be driven by the external forces of
geopolitical or artistic-cultural competition to undertake policies without regard to their subjects' ability to pay for them through ordinary
taxes. Furthermore, political necessity almost always prevents an absolutist regime from attacking the fiscal privileges of various powerful
groups, hence limiting the available tax base. Thus absolutist prerogatives leave rulers unconstrained in their spending, but the need to
maintain élite support constrains government revenue sources.

In the absence of present or future tax flows sufficient to meet all of
their needs, absolutist regimes must resort to a variety of expedients to
raise additional funds. Such expedients inevitably have structural consequences, however, which make it ever more difficult for absolutist
governments to construct an orderly tax system based on regular revenue flows capable of sustaining military power *over the long term*. The
revenue problems are particularly acute during periods of war because
large amounts of cash are necessary in order to pay troops in the field.
In Britain, Parliament was able legally to guarantee short- and long-
term loans made to the Crown from domestic public credit markets. As
a result, the British armed forces could be paid without weakening state
capacities. In absolutist France, where no representative bodies existed
capable of guaranteeing loans in a convincing way, rulers resorted to
"inside credit." As argued in Chapter 3, this move had devastating
consequences for state authority. Thus whereas Britain's political system
provided a secure and reliable means of financing expensive military
campaigns over the long term, those of France and Prussia did not.

Prussia's financial predicament was already visible during the reign
of the Great Elector, and became more pronounced as the military

ambitions of Prussia's leaders grew. Frederick William chose to maintain an army of 30,000 men in a poor country of less than 1.5 million people who were largely hostile to this design. As a result, he was consistently forced to resort to four expedients to solve his interlocking revenue and cash problems: military entrepreneurship, borrowing from royal officials, subsidy payments from foreign powers, and the levying of contributions in money and kind from his own subjects.

The army of the Elector, the instrument with which he was able eventually to secure possession of Prussia and Kleve-Mark, was a wholly contract force of the kind which dominated the Thirty Years War.[63] Colonels ran their units as profit-making ventures, always seeking to widen the margin between the lump-sum payments provided by their employers and the actual cost of raising and equipping a regiment. The government had little or no influence over a colonel's choice of his subordinate officers, and captains also attempted to earn a profit from their companies. This kind of military organization was preferred by hard-pressed rulers because if a cash shortage ensued, the enterpriser-officers could be expected to continue to pay their men out of their own pockets, at least for a time, since they possessed a proprietary interest in their units.

In addition to exploiting the credit potential found within his army, Frederick William was not averse to borrowing sums directly from both wealthy officers and officials. Thus Breysig has uncovered a series of cash loans of between 10,000 and 31,000 Thaler provided to the government by two royal councillors, a commissary-general, a tax receiver, a general, and a captain for the express purpose of meeting military costs.[64] In the case of both military organization and internal borrowing, there was an obvious conflict between the Great Elector's long-term desire to build a strong, independent state apparatus based on a high degree of central control, and the short-term pressures of financial need. Similar tensions are also evident in Frederick William's willingness, beginning in 1666, to compromise his newly won foreign-policy freedom by agreeing to provide troops to Holland, Spain, and Austria in return for military subsidies amounting to many millions of Thaler.[65]

None of these methods were sufficient, however, fully to support the Great Elector's oversized army, especially during the wars of 1655–1660 and 1672–1679. One response to this problem would have been to rely heavily on contributions from conquered territories, as had been the common practice during the Thirty Years War. As the military situation

---

[63] Gustav Schmoller, "Die Enstehung des preussischen Heeres von 1640 bis 1740," in: idem, *Umrisse und Untersuchungen*, pp. 247–313, here at pp. 261–267.
[64] Breysig, "Der brandenburgische Staatshaushalt," pp. 166–168.
[65] Ibid., pp. 173–176.

did not allow this, Frederick William instead turned his developing commissary network on his own people. Between 1655–1660, the recalcitrant provinces of Prussia and Kleve-Mark as well as Brandenburg were subject to heavy exactions above and beyond ordinary taxes in order to support the troops stationed in their midst. The same fate befell Prussia once again between 1676 and 1679.[66] During peacetime as well, it became standard practice to force the population to contribute free food and other necessities to the soldiers garrisoned in their town or village.[67]

The financial tensions present at the core of the Prussian state were sharpened in some respects under Frederick III/I,[68] because unlike his father this monarch wished to maintain both a strong army and a lavish court. Funds that would in the past have been spent exclusively on the military were now diverted to the royal household.[69] Frederick, whose foreign policy aspirations were few, thought that he could square this circle by in effect leasing his army to the Allies in their struggle against Louis XIV. Thus during the Nine Years War and the War of the Spanish Succession, it is estimated that he received over 14 million Thaler in subsidies from Holland, Britain, and Austria.[70] Yet these funds proved insufficient to prevent the government's financial near-collapse in 1710.[71]

Prussia's Military Absolutism at Its Height

The contradictions inherent in the Prussian form of bureaucratic absolutism were pushed to new heights during the reigns of that country's two great 18th-century monarchs. On the one hand, both King Frederick William I and his son Frederick the Great wanted to expand dramatically the size of their army, an army which had consistently strained the resources of the realm to the breaking point in the past. At the same time, they wished to avoid at all costs many of the methods used by

---

[66] Gustav Schmoller, "Die Epochen der preussischen Finanzgeschichte bis zur Gründung des deutschen Reiches," in: idem, *Umrisse und Untersuchungen*, pp. 104–246, here at p. 141; Carsten, *The Rise*, pp. 206–207, 221, 245.

[67] Otto Hintze, "Staat und Gesellschaft unter dem ersten König," in: idem, *Regierung und Verwaltung*, pp. 313–418, here at p. 384; Schmoller, *Preussische Verfassungs-* . . . , pp. 117–119.

[68] This somewhat cumbersome title is traditionally employed because in 1701, elector Frederick III raised his province of Prussia, which stood outside the Holy Roman Empire, to the status of a kingdom. He then became Frederick I, king *in Prussia* (i.e., but not in Brandenburg or the other territories).

[69] Hintze, "Staat und Gesellschaft," pp. 367–368.   [70] Klein, *Geschichte*, p. 48.

[71] Walther Koch, *Hof und Regierungsverfassung: König Friedrich I. von Preussen (1697–1710)* (Breslau: Verlag von M. & H. Marcus, 1926), pp. 104ff.

their predecessors (and by their counterparts in Latin Europe) to raise additional revenues and much-needed cash, so as not to compromise in any way either their domestic or international freedom of action. The organizational and financial solutions they employed to realize these goals brought Prussia great military success in the short term, but fatally undermined its ability to defend itself against other major powers over the long term.

In 1710, 1.6 million Prussians had proved incapable of supporting an army of 40,000 men despite substantial foreign aid. Yet in 1740, the country, whose population had expanded in the interim to 2.2 million, was able to field without subsidies a first-class army of over 83,000 that would soon win great victories over a power many times its size.[72] How had Frederick William I been able to achieve this? He had done so by employing methods that for the next century at least, set Prussia decisively apart from all other states in western Europe.

There were three principal components to the new fiscal-military system created by Frederick William. First, patrimonialist tendencies were rooted out of the core areas of the state through a thoroughgoing militarization of all levels of administration. Second, a new method of recruiting and maintaining the army was introduced: the *Kantonsystem*, which allowed the number of men under arms to be increased at a faster rate than state spending. Finally, all court expenditures were reduced to the absolute minimum and the budget surplus thus achieved used to purchase new domain lands. The profits from these capital acquisitions were then saved to create a "state treasure" (*Staatsschatz*) that, it was hoped, would obviate the need for short-term borrowing during wartime.

The principal structural change which Frederick William I brought to the administrative apparatus built up by the Great Elector was the amalgamation, in 1723, of the entire domains board system with the commissarial bureaucracy to form the so-called General Directory (*Generaldirektorium*). In effect, this meant that all areas of civil administration outside the sphere of justice had been formally subordinated to the interests and needs of the army. This step pushed Prussia in a direction opposite to that being taken in the rest of Europe, where separate, specialized ministerial bureaucracies were emerging as the dominant organizational feature of most central governments.[73]

This formal militarization of the Prussian administration was accompanied by an informal one as well. On the one hand, the king treated his officials as if they were soldiers, demanding absolute loyalty and

---

[72] Schmoller, "Die Epochen," p. 180; Klein, *Geschichte*, p. 49.
[73] Hans Haussherr, *Verwaltungseinheit und Ressorttrennung* (Berlin: Akademie-Verlag, 1953), pp. 1–30 and passim.

strict obedience from them. He paid no attention to claims of either rank or privilege in his personnel decisions, and felt free to hire and dismiss his officials as he chose.[74] On the other hand, large numbers of real soldiers, from retired officers and noncommissioned officers to war invalids, were appointed to positions at all levels of the bureaucracy, from simple doormen to members of the General Directory itself. This trend accelerated under Frederick II, when the number of invalid soldiers within the kingdom increased dramatically. Finally, special commissions composed of military men were employed to investigate alleged wrongdoing among civilian administrators.[75]

This militarization of the Prussian bureaucracy was accompanied by a militarization of much of society itself as a consequence of the new system of military recruitment, the *Kantonsystem*, introduced in 1732–3. When Frederick William, a firm opponent of the old regimental economy, began to curb the powers of colonels, the captain and his company became the new cornerstone of the Prussian army. In the 1720s, Junker-captains had taken to recruiting their own peasants into their units, and then releasing them for farm work for most of the year. Rather than punish this practice, the king used it as a means greatly to increase army size. From 1733, each company was assigned a fixed recruiting district, the canton. All peasant men in the area of military age would then be entered on a muster roll and would be successively called up for military service whenever openings in the company arose. After an initial period of military training, they would be "vacationed" (*beurlaubt*) for nine months, only to return to the colors once a year for the army's annual maneuvers.

The great advantage of this system, aside from the fact that it forced a higher percentage of the native population into the army, was that it permitted captains to fill their companies with large numbers of foreign recruits as well. During the nine months during which the native soldiers were not on duty, their captains kept their pay and used it to recruit new men abroad. This was a very expensive operation, but one that was necessary to circumvent the natural limits on army size imposed by Prussia's small population. Most of the foreign recruits, who

---

[74] Otto Hintze, "Einleitende Darstellung der Behördenorganisation und allgemeinen Verwaltung in Preussen beim Regierungsantritt Friedrichs II.," in: *Acta Borussica*, vol. VI, pt. 1 (Berlin: Paul Parey, 1901), pp. 277–279; Gustav Schmoller, "Einleitung: Ueber Behördenorganisation, Amtswesen und Beamtenthum im Allgemeinen und speciell in Deutschland und Preussen bis zum Jahre 1713," in: *Acta Borussica*, vol. I (Berlin: Paul Parey, 1894), pp. 13–143, here at pp. 132–138.

[75] Otto Büsch, *Militärsystem und Sozialleben im Alten Preussen* (Berlin: Walter de Gruyter, 1962), pp. 138–139, 170; Wilhelm Naudé, "Zur Geschichte des preussischen Sub-alternbeamtentums," *Forschungen zur Brandenburgischen und Preussischen Geschichte*, vol. 18, no. 2 (1905), pp. 1–22, here at p. 3.

were garrisoned in towns, were also released during the year to work as craftsmen, thus freeing up yet more money for recruiting. By 1740, there were about 26,000 foreigners serving the Prussian crown, thereby accounting for one-third of Frederick the Great's army. At times, this figure could rise to as high as two-thirds.[76]

In the area of finance as well, Frederick William I was capable of unusual innovations. By the beginning of his reign, the amount of direct taxes that could be imposed on the population without their consent seemed to have reached its limit, for neither the king nor his son attempted to raise the level of the *Kontribution* throughout either of their reigns.[77] While some increased revenue could be expected from indirect taxes, which automatically expanded with the growth in trade and population, the monarchy's financial prospects appeared dim, especially since Frederick William refused to consider accepting foreign subsidies.

In order to get around this problem, the king reduced all civilian expenditures from a level of 1.5 million Thaler under his father to an annual average of only 1 million. Nine million Thaler derived from these savings were then used to purchase new landed estates, which were in turn leased to improving farmers. In this manner, Frederick William I increased the revenue derived from his domains from 1.8 million to 3.3 million Thaler per year, which permitted him to accumulate a hoard of 8.7 million Thaler in coin which he could bequeath to his son.[78]

The combination of the king's military and financial innovations produced almost incredible results over the course of Frederick William's reign. Although total revenues grew by only 44% between 1713 and 1740, from 4.8 to 6.9 million Thaler, the size of the army was increased to 83,000 (+107.5%), thanks to the *Kantonsystem*, and a sizable war chest created.[79]

Yet the price paid for these successes was in the long run quite high. Frederick William's policies linked Prussia's military might more than ever to the continued existence of a backward manorial economy and a rigid, stereotyped social system where all social groups, including the nobility, were assigned preordained roles. Most importantly, the local landowner/captain and his estate became the cornerstone of the *Kantonverfassung* and hence of the entire Prussian army. The coercive

---

[76] Schmoller, "Die Entstehung," pp. 276–278; Curt Jany, "Die Kantonverfassung des altpreussischen Heeres," in: Otto Büsch and Wolfgang Neugebauer (eds.), *Moderne Preussische Geschichte 1648–1947* (Berlin: Walter de Gruyter, 1981), pp. 767–809, here at p. 802 and passim.

[77] Hahn, "Landesstaat und Ständetum," p. 70.

[78] Klein, *Geschichte*, pp. 47, 51–52.   [79] Ibid., pp. 49, 51.

power of manorial courts helped enforce peasant deference. Without these mutually reinforcing institutions of coercion, it would have proved impossible, within the context of an absolutist society of orders, to drive a considerable proportion of the population into an army legendary for its brutality. The limits on economic growth and social development which this social system imposed curtailed Prussia's capacity, even after it had achieved substantial gains, to generate the kind of resources that would allow the country to hold its own against other powers in a series of protracted conflicts.

The achievements of Frederick William I were fraught with other contradictions as well. The proper functioning of both the war chest and *Kanton* system were predicated on conditions of peace. Indeed, except for a brief participation in the Great Northern War, the king never actually risked his overblown army in battle. While he was able, thanks to his closely supervised bureaucracy, to mobilize all available domestic resources to maintain a huge standing army (much of which was of course no longer really standing), even his budget surpluses were unable to provide a realistic solution to the problem of war finance and credit, given the huge cost of any great-power conflict.

Frederick the Great well understood the limitations inherent in the state his father had bequeathed to him. He realized that in its present condition, Prussia was simply incapable of generating the revenue necessary to fight a major war, and that if this situation was ever to be remedied, the country would have to acquire new territory. The Great Elector had seen this as early as 1672, and had in fact drawn up a plan for the conquest of the wealthy and populous Austrian province of Silesia.[80] In 1740, Frederick moved decisively to put this plan into action, invading the province without warning and immediately installing an occupation bureaucracy designed to extract every possible Groschen for his own war effort. It was the 3.2 million Thaler levied each year in Silesia, together with about 4 million Thaler in contributions demanded from occupied Bohemia and Saxony, that, when added to the 8.7 million Thaler left by Frederick William to his son, permitted Frederick to carry his first war against Austria (1740–1745) to a successful conclusion.[81] After the Peace of Dresden in 1745, the permanent incorporation of Silesia's 1.3 million inhabitants increased Prussia's population by almost 60%, from 2.2 to about 3.5 million, and lifted total state

[80] Otto Hintze, *Die Hohenzollern und ihr Werk 1415–1915* (Berlin: Paul Parey, 1915), p. 324.
[81] Reinhold Koser, "Der preussische Staatsschatz von 1740–1756," *Forschungen zur Brandenburgischen und Preussischen Geschichte*, vol. 4, no. 1 (1891), pp. 207–229, here at pp. 208, 211, 222. On the Silesian bureaucracy, see: Hubert Johnson, *Frederick the Great and His Officials* (New Haven: Yale University Press, 1975), pp. 134–155.

revenues by 42%, to over 11 million Thaler in 1756.[82] This higher income level in turn allowed Frederick to expand his army still further, to 137,000 men at the start of the Seven Years War.[83]

Frederick was well aware that the Austrians would soon attempt to win back Silesia. To meet the costs of the next conflict, he planned quickly to occupy wealthy Saxony, which would then be annexed after the war, and to conquer the kingdom of Bohemia, from which sizable contributions could be extracted. To Saxony the king also hoped some-day to add the Polish province of West Prussia (the "Polish Corridor" of the interwar period), which lay between the Prussian provinces of Brandenburg and Pomerania and East Prussia.[84] In August 1756, Saxony was duly invaded and the Seven Years War set in motion.

Although the Saxons were forced to pay between 48 and 70 million Thaler over the course of the conflict, and the occupied Mecklenburg and Swedish Pomerania a further 5 to 12 million Thaler,[85] Frederick's mixed military fortunes during this war did not permit him to extract the funds he had hoped for from rich Bohemia. As early as 1757, when the war chest accumulated since the last war had been spent, the coun-try found itself in dire financial straits. From 1758, the king was forced to violate one of his father's sternest strictures and accept £2.7 million in subsidies from Britain. In 1762, however, Frederick decided to re-nounce these subsidies when the British attempted to pressure him into returning Silesia.

Even this foreign aid was not sufficient, however, to fill the gap be-tween Prussia's resources and the total costs of the war. Thus, from 1757 onward Frederick decided to engage in a large-scale debasement of first the Saxon, then his own, currency. This operation produced an estimated profit of 40 million Thaler, thereby accounting for nearly one-third of the 125 million Thaler which the Seven Years War is believed to have cost Prussia.[86] This massive debasement, the actual

---

[82] Population: Schmoller, "Die Epochen," p. 180; Walther Hubatsch, "Verwaltungsent-wicklungen von 1713–1803," in: Jeserich et al., *Deutsche Verwaltungsgeschichte*, pp. 892–941, here at p. 921. Hubatsch, op. cit., claims that total Prussian population was only 1.6 million in 1739, a figure which seems unreasonably low, given future population developments, compared to Schmoller's 2.2 million. Revenue: Klein, *Geschichte*, p. 54.

[83] Curt Jany, *Geschichte der Preussischen Armee vom 15. Jahrhundert bis 1914* (Osnabrück: Biblio Verlag, 1967), vol. II, p. 195.

[84] Hintze, *Die Hohenzollern*, pp. 361–362.

[85] The lower estimates are from: Reinhold Koser, "Die preussischen Finanzen im siebenjährigen Krieg," *Forschungen zur Brandenburgischen und Preussischen Geschichte*, vol. 13 (1900), pp. 153–217 (no. 1), 329–375 (no. 2), here at pp. 217, 370; the higher are found in: Schmoller, "Die Epochen," p. 182.

[86] Koser, "Die preussischen Finanzen," p. 371; A. O. von Loehr, "Die Finanzierung des siebenjährigen Kriegs: Ein Versuch vergleichender Geldgeschichte," *Numismatische Zeitschrift*, Neue Folge, vol. 18 (1925), pp. 95–110, here at pp. 98–99 and passim.

implementation of which had been farmed out to a group of Jewish factors,[87] was a novelty in the 18th century. Most princes had by that time come to understand the damaging effects of such an expedient not only on the country's economy, but also on the government's creditworthiness.

If the pressures of war had produced a very negative effect on Prussian finances, they had also served to complicate the unitary fiscal-military administrative apparatus perfected by Frederick William I. As mentioned above, Frederick installed a special Silesian administration shortly after invading the province, and he specifically commanded its directors to report directly to him, thus creating a new bureaucracy independent of the General Directory which persisted after 1745. This approach was repeated in 1756 with the occupation of Saxony, and though the Saxon administration disappeared with the loss of that territory in 1763, a separate board was set up for East and West Prussia following the acquisition of the latter from Poland in 1772.[88]

These moves were prompted by Frederick's disillusionment with the capacities and personnel of the General Directory, a sentiment that was increased by the performance of that organization during the two wars against Austria. Many officials had succumbed to the temptations present during wartime both to enrich themselves and to establish greater freedom of action from their superiors.[89] In 1748, the king attempted to counter this tendency by issuing new guidelines for the General Directory which chastised its "laziness . . . , partisan spirit, and insufficient reliability" and ordered that all matters that could not be resolved within six minutes [!] be referred directly to him for a decision.[90] Finally, in a last attempt to improve the quality of the department's personnel, Frederick took the momentous step in 1770 of establishing an examination commission (*Oberexaminationskommission*) charged with testing aspirants for higher administrative positions to determine their fitness for office. This commission was the first of its kind in Europe, and its creation brought a fully modern bureaucracy one step closer in Prussia.

Yet at the same time the proliferation of independent and parallel administrative organizations (General Directory, Silesian, Saxon, Prussian administrations), which growing fiscal-military pressures had promoted,

---

[87] On these Jewish financiers at the court of Frederick the Great, see: Heinrich Schnee, *Die Hoffinanz und der Moderne Staat* (Berlin: Duncker & Humblot, 1953), vol. I, pp. 117ff.

[88] Johnson, *Frederick the Great*, pp. 136ff., 169–173, 203.

[89] Hans Rosenberg, *Bureaucracy, Aristocracy, and Autocracy* (Cambridge: Harvard University Press, 1958), p. 179.

[90] Fritz Hartung, "Studien zur Geschichte der preussischen Verwaltung," in: idem, *Staatsbildende Kräfte der Neuzeit* (Berlin: Duncker & Humblot, 1961), pp. 178–344, here at pp. 198, 202.

inevitably led to strife and discord at the heart of Prussian government as the various bureaucracies competed for jurisdiction, resources, and the attention of the monarch.[91] In fact, this growing administrative confusion rendered the personal intervention of the monarch ever more crucial if the government was to continue to function at a minimum level of effectiveness. Under Frederick William I, responsibility for overall coordination of state activities had passed from the royal council (*Geheimer Rat*) to the General Directory. With the decline of this body, however, the government lacked an institutional center. Rather than return to a council system, Frederick chose instead to make himself the indispensable unifying force within the Prussian state. He foreswore personal contacts with his leading official altogether and made all important policy decisions alone, based only on written reports submitted by individual department heads.[92] This insistence on personal control was apparently motivated by the king's desire to avoid at all costs the kind of "ministerial absolutism" which he believed had weakened the France of Louis XV.[93] While such a personalist system of rule may have been capable of functioning under an exceptional monarch like Frederick, it was very ill-suited to the lesser talents of his two successors.

It was in the area of finance that the institutional developments sketched out above had their most notable effect. The proliferation of bureaucracies also meant the proliferation of new treasuries, and Prussia possessed no body equivalent to the British Treasury capable of overall financial planning and coordination. Thus only Frederick himself was in a position to know the true condition of his state's finances. Yet here the king's mania for secrecy in all matters related to money and his habit of appropriating cash surpluses from various departments and depositing them in his private treasure (the *Dispositionskasse*) acted as a source of confusion rather than order.[94]

Despite this mounting administrative dissonance, Frederick was able to achieve a marked increase in total revenues following the period of the Seven Years War, from 13.8 million Thaler in 1768 to 21.7 million in 1784, just prior to his death.[95] This was due in part to the acquisition

[91] Johnson, *Frederick the Great*, pp. 267–274, especially p. 274, and passim.
[92] Haussherr, *Verwaltungseinheit*, pp. 142–143.
[93] Otto Hintze, "Das preussische Staatsministerium im 19. Jahrhundert," in: idem, *Regierung und Verwaltung*, pp. 530–619, here at pp. 533–534.
[94] Schmoller, "Die Epochen," p. 185; Haussherr, *Verwaltungseinheit*, pp. 141–142; Reinhold Koser, "Die preussischen Finanzen von 1763 bis 1786," in: *Forschungen zur Brandenburgischen und Preussischen Geschichte*, vol. 16 (1903), pp. 101–132, here at pp. 112ff., 119.
[95] Koser, "Die preussichen Finanzen von 1763 bis 1786," pp. 119–121. Here Koser presents a critique of the oft-used figures found in: Adolph Friedrich Riedel, *Der Brandenburg-Preussische Staatshaushalt in den beiden letzten Jahrhunderten* (Berlin: Ernst & Korn, 1866), pp. 132–133 and Beilage XIV.

in 1772, following the first partition of Poland, of the new province of West Prussia. The latter, with its 520,000 inhabitants, helped boost the total Prussian population to 4.76 million in 1776; by 1786, it had reached 5.4 million.[96] In accordance with long-standing Prussian practice, the king took advantage of these increases to expand the size of his standing army from 137,000 men in 1756 to 200,000 in 1786.[97]

What Frederick did not do, however, was attempt to alter in any way the basic character of the financial system upon which Prussia's military power rested. He continued after 1763 to direct the budget surpluses achieved each year into a special war chest, which contained 51 million Thaler by 1786. Yet even Frederick did not believe that this treasure would be sufficient to pay for a large-scale war. In two sets of comments on a future war written in 1768 and in 1777, Frederick stated clearly that the invasion and exploitation of Saxony would have to feature once again in any future military plans.[98] Nor was this key structural flaw ignored by contemporary observers. In his detailed analysis of the Prussian army written in about 1790 for Mirabeau's *De la Monarchie Prussienne sous Frédéric le Grand*, the professional officer and social theorist Johann von Mauvillon asserted that, despite its large army, Prussia was incapable of fighting a defensive war, and could only find military security in an offensive strategy.[99]

During the decades following the Seven Years War, Frederick the Great made clever use of diplomacy in order to keep his fragile state out of large-scale conflicts. This was made easier by the rough balance of power which existed on the continent during the 1770s and 1780s. The emergence, in the early 1790s, of a thoroughly modernized French state armed with a revolutionary ideology quickly upset this delicate balance. After 1792, the Prussian state, despite its standing army of over 200,000 men, proved itself utterly incapable of meeting this French threat. As early as 1795, it was already clear to the rest of Europe that the Prussia which Frederick the Great had bequeathed to his successor possessed feet of clay.

The revolution in France had driven Prussia into an alliance with its traditional enemy Austria, and in April 1792, the French government declared war on these powers. The Prussians responded in their traditional

---

[96] Walther Hubatsch, *Friedrich der Grosse und die Preussische Verwaltung* (Cologne: Grote, 1982), p. 180; idem, "Preussen von 1713–1803," p. 921; Schmoller, "Die Epochen," p. 180.

[97] Schmoller, *Preussische Verfassungs-* . . . , p. 112.

[98] Koser, "Die preussischen Finanzen von 1763 bis 1786," pp. 181–182.

[99] Dietmar Stutzer, "Das preussische Heer und seine Finanzierung in zeitgenössischer Darstellung 1740–1790," *Militärgeschichtliche Mitteilungen*, vol. 24, no. 2 (1978), pp. 23–47, here at pp. 25, 43.

fashion by invading French territory, but after their defeat at Valmy in September they were driven back into Germany. Throughout the rest of the war Prussia was on the defensive, attempting to defend the Rhineland from the French armies. For the first time since the 17th century, Prussia was unable to rely on contributions extracted from the enemy or from innocent neutrals to help support its armed forces. The country was thrown back entirely upon its own means.

Yet how was Prussia, its resources already stretched tight to pay for a huge standing army, to meet the expenses of a major war, most of which would have to be paid in cash? In Frederick William I's scheme, the war chest was supposed to fulfill this function. During over 20 years of peace, Frederick the Great had succeeded in filling this chest up once again with over 50 million Thaler.[100] In 1787, Frederick's successor had spent 6 million of this on an expedition to put down the recent revolution in the Netherlands, and several million more were spent on mobilizations in 1790 and 1791 against Russia and Austria. The country was left in 1792 with perhaps 40 million Thaler in cash with which to meet the French threat. By 1794, this money was gone.[101]

In response, Frederick William II resorted to a number of financial expedients, just as Frederick the Great had done during the latter half of the Seven Years War. First, large quantities of debased coins (*Scheidemünzen*) were minted, and a desperate search for loans was begun. While the government was able to borrow 8 million Gulden in Holland, another 5 million in Frankfurt, and smaller amounts in other parts of Germany and within the country itself, these proved insufficient. By early 1795, Prussia had run out of cash, and could find few people willing to lend more. In April, Frederick William had little choice but to agree to a separate armistice, the Peace of Basel, which ceded to the French all Prussian territory on the west bank of the Rhine.[102] In many respects this defeat was more telling than the purely military ones suffered at Jena and Auerstedt 11 years later, for on this occasion it was not the tactical genius of Napoleon which forced the country to sue for peace, but the internal failure of the Prussian fiscal-military state itself.

The foregoing analysis of Brandenburg-Prussia's bureaucratic absolutism has stressed that while the Great Elector and his successors may have succeeded, thanks to the advantages of the latecomer, in constructing a durable, nonproprietary bureaucracy to administer their

---

[100] Koser, "Die preussischen Finanzen von 1763 bis 1786," p. 130.
[101] Riedel, *Der Brandenburg-preussische Staatshaushalt*, p. 191.
[102] Riedel, *Der Brandenburg-preussische Staatshaushalt*, pp. 192–195; Krug, *Geschichte der Preussischen Staatsschulden*, pp. 32–45, contains a description of all loans contracted during the war and its immediate aftermath and their exact terms.

oversized army, these rulers proved unable to build the stable tax and credit system which was just as essential to the country's defense. None of the Prussian monarchs were willing to tolerate representative assemblies, even if only to provide independent loan guarantees to potential lenders, yet without such guarantees the creation of a public credit market, a *sine qua non* of military effectiveness over the long term, was beyond reach. The belief that this contradiction – which lay at the heart of all fully absolutist regimes – could be overcome by building up cash hoards or invading neighboring territories proved to be an illusion. In addition, the society of orders and manorial economy upon which the Prussian military system rested ultimately acted as a constraint on their state's military capacity by limiting the prospects for long-term economic development. It was in the period after 1789, when Prussia suddenly faced the challenge of a radically reformed France, that these weaknesses were to be starkly revealed, leading to the bankruptcy of 1795 and the crushing military defeat of 1806.

CONCLUSION

East Francia was the latecomer among the large-scale states of the dark ages. As the last area incorporated into the Romano-Frankish world, it enjoyed certain advantages of relative backwardness which allowed it to survive and, as the Ottonian-Salian Empire, even flourish long after other great dark age polities like those of Charlemagne and the Umayyads had passed into history. But the longevity of the new Holy Roman Empire was its undoing. Whereas in Latin Europe the postmillennial forces of Church reform, market expansion, and castle-building came to the assistance of those rulers like the Capetians or the Sicilian Normans who were attempting to rebuild on a grand scale following the failure of large-scale dark age statebuilding, in central Europe they served to strengthen centrifugal tendencies, thereby ensuring that the Empire would never regain its former authority.

From the perspective of the nascent territorial states, this late demise of the Empire brought distinct advantages, for it led to a new round of state formation at the regional and local level. This in turn meant that by the time the newly consolidated German principalities were ready to embark on a course of infrastructural expansion in response to geopolitical competition among themselves, they were in a position to benefit fully from those medieval advances in the law, education, and finance which permitted them to construct nonproprietary, bureaucratic apparatuses but which had come too late to save their counterparts in Latin Europe from the clutches of patrimonial officialdom.

The result of this sequence of developments in central Europe was the predominance there of a state form – bureaucratic absolutism – which would seem to have been ideally suited to the warlike, fiercely competitive world of early modern power politics. Yet this was not true, as the case of Brandenburg-Prussia shows. For while preparations for war may have been the driving force behind the emergence of polities of this kind, the realities of war confronted it over the long term with insurmountable problems. Although absolutist rulers were able, under the right circumstances, to build nonproprietary bureaucracies, the very nature of absolutism prevented them from complementing those bureaucracies with the kind of credit systems necessary to survive drawn-out conflicts. Ironically, then, avoiding war was the key to survival not only for the patrimonial form of absolutism, but for its more "modern," bureaucratic variant as well.

Chapter 6

———— ⟨⟩ ————

THE TRIUMPH OF PATRIMONIAL CONSTITUTIONALISM IN HUNGARY AND POLAND AND ITS PREMATURE DEMISE IN SCANDINAVIA

It is one of the most remarkable features of European political development that the two states within western Christendom whose political regimes most resembled that of 18th-century Britain – the kingdoms of Poland and Hungary – were among the farthest removed from it not only geographically, but also culturally, socially, and economically.[1] Like Britain, Poland and Hungary possessed bicameral representative assemblies which enjoyed substantial rights of co-determination in matters of taxation, foreign affairs, and legislation, and the statutes which these bodies drafted and approved served to expand a corpus of national customary law which, as in England, successfully resisted the reception of Roman law. Like the British Parliament, the Polish and Hungarian Diets consisted of an upper chamber comprising ecclesiastical and lay worthies and a lower chamber composed of the elected representatives of royal towns and of territorially integrated rural districts. Finally, the assemblies of these districts (*ziemie* or provinces[2] in Poland, counties in Hungary) and the nonprofessional officials chosen from among their members exercised extensive powers in the spheres of justice, finance, and military affairs, as they did in Britain.

---

[1] Otto Hintze, "Typologie der ständischen Verfassungen des Abendlandes," in: idem, *Staat und Verfassung*, 3rd ed. (Göttingen: Vandenhoeck & Ruprecht, 1970), pp. 120–139, here at pp. 128, 139; Heinrich Marczali, *Ungarische Verfassungsgeschichte* (Tübingen: J. C. B. Mohr, 1910), p. 82; Hans Roos, "Ständewesen und parlamentarische Verfassung in Polen (1505–1772)," in: Dietrich Gerhard (ed.), *Ständische Vertretungen in Europa im 17. und 18. Jahrhundert*, 2nd ed. (Göttingen: Vandenhoeck & Ruprecht, 1974), pp. 310–367, here at pp. 311, 313.

[2] There is no perfect English equivalent for *ziemia*, which in Polish documents written in Latin is normally translated as *terra* ("land") or *provincia* ("province"). "Land" is awkward in English, and "province" can be misleading, since it is sometimes used in the historical literature to refer to large historical regions containing many *ziemie* like Greater Poland (Wielkopolska) and Lesser Poland (Malopolska). Nevertheless, following the lead of Adam Zamoyski (*The Polish Way* [London: John Murray, 1987]), I have chosen the latter translation.

Yet despite these similarities, the Hungarian and Polish polities of the 18th century were in other respects quite different from their British counterpart. Whereas in Britain the organs of local self-government merely served to complement a large, bureaucratically organized administrative infrastructure, in Poland and Hungary such a bureaucracy was entirely lacking. Instead, the nobility of these countries, in their capacity both as private landowners and as the sole participants in county and *ziemia* political life, had succeeded – with the assistance of their respective Diets – in appropriating nearly all state functions, leaving their central governments with only meager capacities for direct rule. Hence these two polities conform to an early modern state type I call *patrimonial* constitutionalism, in contrast to the bureaucratic constitutionalism of Britain.

How can we account for the striking similarities as well as the sharp differences between 18th-century Britain on the one hand and Poland and Hungary on the other? The answer lies in a common experience of unencumbered state formation, which resulted in both strong, participatory organs of local government, territorially based parliaments, and ultimately constitutionalism in all three countries; and in the early onset of sustained geopolitical competition in England as opposed to Poland and Hungary, which led to the construction of a centralized, bureaucratic state apparatus in the English case and a successful defense against this step by an entrenched nobility in the two east-central European monarchies.

Like England, Poland and Hungary were founded – in 1076 and 1000, respectively – upon territory that had not known large-scale, dark age state formation. All three kingdoms were constructed around organizational forms, such as the county, borrowed from the more advanced polities of Latin Europe and Germany. New instruments of rule, such as the castle, helped geographically unified units of local government to survive and even flourish among the unencumbered state formers. The emergence of elite, rural, political communities within these units of local government in turn meant that when national representative assemblies arose in England, Poland, and Hungary during the 1200s, 1300s, and 1400s, they would be structured along territorial lines rather than by estate, as was the case in Latin Europe and Germany.

Yet whereas from the 12th century onward the English kings were in possession, thanks to the early onset of sustained geopolitical pressure, of an increasingly large and powerful central administrative apparatus capable of holding the power of the counties – and of the leading nobles within those counties – in check, the Polish and Hungarian monarchs enjoyed no such advantage. Once the nobility of both countries had gained full control of local government, these rulers proved incapable – due to their lack of adequate, independent coercive capacities – of preventing that nobility from first expanding the powers of the Diets which it dominated, and then using those powers to render the monarchy fully elective and the peasant population entirely subservient.

Hence by the time Hungary and Poland finally came under sustained geopolitical pressure in the period after 1450, many centuries later than England, their nobilities and the parliaments that represented them had already gained the upper hand vis-à-vis rulers who had always lacked the instruments of rule possessed by their English counterparts. The mighty Hungarian and Polish parliaments ensured that the new challenges of large-scale warfare would be met through the expansion of existing, noble-controlled organs of local government rather than through the construction of centralized administrative and financial systems – whether proprietary or nonproprietary – as was the norm across the rest of western Christendom.

The most direct consequence of this failure to build a more extensive, centralized administrative and financial infrastructure in either Poland or Hungary was a weakened capacity for self-defense which first became evident in the 1520s, when the latter was almost completely overrun by the armies of the Ottoman Empire. The country was in the end only saved by the ascension to the Hungarian throne of the Habsburgs, who were able to draw on resources from their other possessions and from the Holy Roman Empire in order to reconquer, in a process lasting several centuries, the lands lost to the Turks. Help from the Habsburgs proved to be a mixed blessing, for rulers from this family repeatedly attempted to alter Hungary's constitution in an absolutist direction. However, the institutions of noble self-government proved sufficiently strong and cohesive to surmount this challenge and to permit the Hungarian ancien régime to continue until 1848.

For Poland, the almost total appropriation of public authority by the nobility and the resulting failure to build an effective state apparatus had far more tragic consequences. After 1648, a Polish government increasingly paralyzed by the frequent use of the notorious *liberum veto* proved unable to respond with effective reforms to the rising military power of Russia, Sweden, and Brandenburg-Prussia. As a result, by 1717 the country was no longer capable of defending itself and was forced to turn to Russia for protection. Yet even this desperate move could not prevent the three partitions of 1772, 1793, and 1795 which would temporarily eliminate from the map of Europe a Polish state long since privatized by a narrow and self-serving elite.

The cases of Denmark and Sweden pose a problem for the argument developed above, for both exhibited the same combination of factors –

participatory forms of local government during the early period of statebuilding and the late onset of sustained geopolitical competition – as did Hungary and Poland, and yet neither can be classified as examples of patrimonial constitutionalism at the end of the early modern period. Denmark was at that time one of the continent's most absolutist and bureaucratic states, while Sweden oscillated between a bureaucratic constitutionalism close to that of Britain and a bureaucratic absolutism similar to that of its southern neighbor.

How can these unexpected outcomes be explained? I will argue below that while both polities initially started down the same path as that trodden by Hungary and Poland, the unexpected intervention of contingent historical factors – the political and cultural impact of the nearby German nobility in Denmark, the after-effects of the national liberation struggle in Sweden – later propelled the two Scandinavian kingdoms off in rather different directions. However, it will also be shown that despite the distorting effects of contingency, the causal relationships posited throughout this study between local government organization and political regime on the one hand and between the timing of infrastructural expansion and the character of the resulting state apparatus on the other hold true for these "aberrant" cases as well.

UNENCUMBERED STATE FORMATION AND THE
CONSOLIDATION OF LOCAL ELITE SELF-GOVERNMENT IN
HUNGARY AND POLAND, C. 1000–1387

The acceptance of Christianity by Mieszko of Poland in 966 and Stephen of Hungary in 997 marked the beginning of a process of unencumbered state formation that would transform both countries into western-style polities over the course of the next century. Heavy institutional borrowing, both direct and indirect, from more advanced polities like the Carolingian realm enabled this process to reach its speedy, and successful, conclusion. Although Stephen converted 31 years later than did Mieszko, Hungary's path to full internal consolidation and stability proved to be far smoother than neighboring Poland's. Hungary was acknowledged as a kingdom by pope and emperor in the year 1000 and was freed from all ties of vassalage vis-à-vis the latter in 1053. Furthermore, the new state was troubled by few external threats until the 13th century, when it suffered episodic attacks fom the nomadic Mongols and Kumans. In spite of these favorable conditions, however, the power of the initially quite strong Hungarian crown declined substantially during the early 1200s in the wake of repeated succession conflicts. The principal beneficiary of this decline was the emerging aristocracy. In order to check the growing influence of this group, successive Hungarian monarchs chose to bolster the position of the lesser fighters within the counties. Yet this action merely furthered the creation of a single noble class which, by the late 1300s, was already well on its way to collectively appropriating the instruments of royal authority.

Whereas Hungary had achieved a high degree of cohesion by the early 1100s, the task of domestic consolidation in Poland was fraught with difficulties, due above all to repeated interference from an imperial Germany reluctant to see a strong new neighbor on its eastern border. Although the ruling Piast family had become Christians considerably earlier than their counterparts in Hungary, they were not definitively elevated to regal status until 1076, nearly three-quarters of a century after the Árpáds. Furthermore, in 1138 the recently formed kingdom was divided among the sons of Boleslaw III, and not reunited again until 1320.

Poland's disintegration into a series of petty duchies controlled by rival Piast princes only served to strengthen the hand of the most influential aristocratic families within the new, small-scale polities. The same had occurred under similar circumstances in Merovingian Gaul over 600 years earlier. Władysław the Short was only able to overcome resistance to reunification from regional aristocrats and restore the unity of the kingdom in 1320 due to support from the Church and the knightly class. Over the next half-century, this latter group came to play an ever greater role in the life of the *ziemie*, the former duchies which now became the provinces of the new kingdom. By the late 1300s, these bodies were well on their way to becoming powerful noble political communities like the Hungarian counties, and would soon be in a position to undermine the recently restored public character of the Polish state.

Hungary

As with so much else in the political history of the West, the origins of the Catholic kingdom of Hungary can be traced back to developments within the Carolingian Empire. During the late 700s, Charlemagne destroyed the power of the Avars, a people which at that time ruled over the Carpathian basin on the eastern border of his own domain. The decline of east Carolingian authority over this border region in the late 800s was exploited by newcomers from the East, the Hungarians, who occupied this area during the 890s and quickly subjugated the resident Slavic population. The Hungarians were a confederation of seven tribes of mixed ethnic origin, one of which – the Megyeri – had established its political and linguistic hegemony over the others and led them westward under the command of their prince, Árpád.[3]

From new bases in what had, in part, been the former Roman provinces of Pannonia and Dacia, Hungarian horsemen launched repeated raids into both halves of a now-divided Carolingia until the rulers of Germany defeated them first at Merseburg in 933 and then at Lechfeld near Augsburg in 955. A further defeat in 970 at the hands of the Byzantines, which put an end to Hungarian attempts at expansion towards the southeast, seems to have convinced prince Géza, the grandson of Árpád, to abandon his people's tradition of raiding and instead seek an accommodation with his increasingly powerful Ottonian neighbors to the west. In 973, Géza made peace with Otto I and opened his territories to Christian missionaries, a process which culminated in the baptism in 997 of his son and successor under the name Stephen, and the latter's marriage to an Ottonian princess. Three years later, on Christmas day 1000, Stephen was crowned king of Hungary by the authority of both pope and emperor.[4]

During the 38 years of his reign, Stephen used tools provided by his more advanced neighbors to lay the groundwork for a state of the Western type. The most powerful of these tools was the aggressive and self-confident Christianity of the post-Carolingian period. The new religion was instrumental in helping him destroy the tribal and clan basis of Hungarian society, which was inextricably linked to pagan religious cults and rituals. Ruthless repression of pagan practices further strengthened the position as hereditary princes which the Árpáds had built up over the previous century, a position bolstered still further after 1106 when primogeniture was introduced to govern the royal succession.[5] Stephen was also permitted to construct his own independent church administration of eight (later ten) bishoprics subject to the two archbishoprics of Kalocsa and Esztergom (Primate). The task was completed by 1030 with the help of churchmen imported from Germany, Italy, and Lorraine who brought Latin with them.[6] As in Poland, Latin remained the language of government until the end of the ancien régime.

Complementing this ecclesiastical infrastructure was a secular one

3   Hence the Hungarians' name for themselves and their language, *Magyar*. See: Manfred Hellmann, "Die politisch-kirchliche Grundlegung der Osthälfte Europas," in: Theodor Schieder (ed.), *Handbuch der Europäischen Geschichte* (Stuttgart: Ernst Klett Verlag, 1976), vol. I, pp. 857–938, here at p. 899; Ervin Pamlényi (ed.), *A History of Hungary* (London: Collet's, 1975), pp. 15–27.

4   Hellmann, "Die politisch-kirchliche Grundlegung," pp. 899–900; Pamlényi, *History*, pp. 31–34; Malcolm Barber, *The Two Cities* (London: Routledge, 1992), pp. 373–374.

5   Colin Morris, *The Papal Monarchy: The Western Church from 1050 to 1250* (Oxford: Clarendon, 1989), pp. 264–265.

6   Hellmann, "Die politisch-kirchliche Grundlegung," p. 900.

indirectly based, it appears, on Carolingian models.[7] Stephen divided the country into 45 (later 72) counties (originally called *civitates*, later *comitatus*), each centered on a royal castle commanded by a count. Following the Frankish paradigm, each count served as chief judge and financial administrator of his district, aided in these tasks by members of the local free population which, under his command, also constituted the armed forces of the county. However, in an innovation typical of all states formed around the turn of the millennium or thereafter, the count was neither granted a benefice nor was he bound to his ruler by ties of vassalage. Instead, he was permitted to retain one-third of the income from local royal estates and the royal court for his own use before turning over the remaining two-thirds to the king. Since the county network was built up in parallel to that of the Church hierarchy, these two forms of territorial organization could be harmonized to a degree almost unique in the West. Each diocese was coterminous with a certain number of counties, the ecclesiastical affairs of which were overseen by an archdeacon responsible to the local bishop.[8]

Government at the center was organized along familiar Carolingian lines, with the high officials of the king's household doubling as the state's principal administrators. Chief among them was the count of the palace (*comes palatinus*), who headed the household; the junior court count (*comes curialis minor*) who later became the royal judge; the chamberlain, later the royal treasurer; the notary, later the royal chancellor; and a range of other Frankish household officers like the butler, cupbearer, and marshall. Important decisions were made by the king in consultation with these officials and the other lay and ecclesiastical worthies who made up the royal council (*consilium regale*).[9]

The establishment of the Christian kingdom also brought with it significant social and economic changes. Following the dissolution of the tribes and clans their extensive common property came into the

[7] Charles d'Eszlary, *Histoire des Institutions Publiques Hongroises*, 3 vols. (Paris: Marcel Rivière, 1959–1965), vol. I, p. 94; Marczali, *Ungarische Verfassungsgeschichte*, p. 3. It is interesting to note that both the Hungarian and Slavic words for king, *karolyi* and *kral*, are derived from Karl, the German name for Charlemagne, who was obviously believed to embody the very essence of kingship. See: Louis Leger, "Hungary, 1000–1301," in: J. R. Tanner, C. W. Previté-Orton, and Z. N. Brooke (eds.), *The Cambridge Medieval History, Volume VI: Victory of the Papacy*, pp. 463–472, here at p. 463.

[8] Erik Fügedi, *Castle and Society in Medieval Hungary (1000–1437)* (Budapest: Akadémiai Kiadó, 1986), pp. 18–20, 37–39; Bálint Hóman, *Geschichte des Ungarischen Mittelalters* (Berlin: De Gruyter, 1940), vol. II, pp. 208–211; Akos von Timon, *Ungarische Verfassungs- und Rechtsgeschichte mit Bezug auf die Rechtsentwicklung der Westlichen Staaten* (Berlin: Puttkammer und Mühlbrecht, 1904), pp. 202–212; Marczali, *Ungarische Verfassungsgeschichte*, pp. 3–4.

[9] Eszlary, *Histoire*, vol. I, pp. 109–117; Timon, *Ungarische Verfassungs- und Rechtsgeschichte*, pp. 171–178; Marczali, *Ungarische Verfassungsgeschichte*, p. 3.

possession of the monarch. Indeed, it has been estimated that the royal domain under Stephen covered about three-quarters of the entire country.[10] The first king and his successors made substantial grants from this patrimony to the Church and to their intimates and officials, who henceforth came to form a class of landowning aristocrats. Unlike their counterparts in many other areas of the West, however, the members of this new elite did not hold their lands as fiefs, but rather as allodial (i.e., fully private) property; nor were they bound to the king by ties of vassalage which implied specific legal obligations. As a result, this group – the later higher nobility or magnates – proved extremely difficult to control after the power of the monarchy had declined.[11] Such a decline was nowhere in evidence in the late 1100s, however. At that time, despite two centuries of land grants made from the domain, the profits of justice, customs, and tolls, the rich royal mines, and other sources remained immense. Indeed, the income of Béla III (1173–1196) was larger than that of the king of France and only slightly smaller than that of the English and German monarchs. In addition, the Árpáds could draw on an authority built up after nearly two centuries of unbroken rule over a realm which they themselves had founded.[12]

In the 25 years following the death of Béla III, however, all this changed. A bitter struggle between his two sons over the succession degenerated into a civil war as both sides competed with one another to gain supporters for their respective claims to the throne. The conflict resulted in the massive alienation of royal property, particularly when the eventual winner of the civil war, Andrew II (1205–1235), bestowed lavish gifts on the aristocrats who had championed his cause. Thus, events of the early 1200s markedly strengthened the landowning and officeholding elite.[13]

In the manner of their contemporaries in Latin Europe and Germany, some well-connected counts then attempted to convert their offices, and the income attached to them, into heritable private property. This move would have placed the free royal knights (*servientes*

[10] Eszlary, *Histoire*, vol. I, p. 150.
[11] Timon, *Ungarische Verfassungs- und Rechtsgeschichte*, pp. 109, 120–122; Eszlary, *Histoire*, vol. I, p. 188.
[12] János Bak, "Das Königreich Ungarn im Hochmittelalter 1060–1444," in: Schieder, *Handbuch*, vol. II, pp. 1103–1124, here at pp. 1107–1108; Eszlary, *Histoire*, vol. I, pp. 129–131; Marczali, *Ungarische Verfassungsgeschichte*, pp. 17–18; Claude Michaud, "L'Europe Centrale et le Cas Hongrois," in: Noël Coulet and Jean-Philippe Genet (eds.), *L'État Moderne: Le Droit, L'Espace et les Formes de L'État* (Paris: Éditions du C.N. R.S., 1990), pp. 189–207, here at p. 197.
[13] Eszlary, *Histoire*, vol. I, pp. 187–188; Pamlényi, *History*, pp. 54–56; Marczali, *Ungarische Verfassungsgeschichte*, pp. 19–20; Michaud, "L'Europe Centrale," pp. 197–198; Barber, *Two Cities*, p. 377.

regales) and the dependent castle soldiers (*iobagiones castri* – equivalent to the German *ministeriales*), the lesser landowners of the country, at the mercy of the aristocratic families. In response to such a threat, these two groups revolted against their royal master with the support of dissident aristocrats. In the aftermath of his disastrous participation in the Fifth Crusade of 1217–18, Andrew was forced in 1222 to concede the Golden Bull, Hungary's Magna Carta.[14]

While the Golden Bull is sometimes characterized as the bill of rights of the Hungarian nobility, this description is misleading.[15] It was above all the rights of the *servientes* and *iobagiones castri* that were confirmed and strengthened in this document, while those of the officeholding aristocracy were in fact curtailed. Thus the Golden Bull forbade hereditary grants of the office of count, reaffirmed the royal claim to two-thirds of the county's income, insisted on the king's right to remove incompetent or exploitative officials at will, and banned the cumulation of offices. At the same time, it protected the property of *servientes* and *iobagiones* from the depredations of both rulers and aristocrats and shielded their persons from arrest without due process of law, while also exempting them from extraordinary taxes and releasing them from the obligation to serve in military campaigns abroad unless paid. Finally, the Golden Bull obliged the king to hold a national assembly once a year on St. Stephen's Day at which *servientes* had the right to appear with their grievances.[16]

While this document does indeed exhibit many parallels with the nearly contemporaneous Magna Carta, the differences between the two are more telling. In England, the barons appeared at Runnymede as spokesmen for the entire "community of the realm," concerned to constrain the actions of a monarch whose greatest source of strength lay in the fact that he had at his disposal a powerful, independent administrative and financial apparatus built up over the previous century. In Hungary, by contrast, the king lacked such an apparatus. He thus came to rely ever more heavily on the aristocratic officeholders who occupied key positions in a minimal state infrastructure which had hardly expanded, due to the lack of a sustained geopolitical stimulus,

---

[14] Herbert Helbig, "Ungarns Goldene Bulle von 1222 und die Adelsrechte in Siebenbürgen 1291," in: *Album Elemér Malyusz* (Bruxelles: Éditions de la Librairie Encyclopédique, 1976), pp. 109–121, here at p. 111; Pamlényi, *History*, pp. 56–57; Bak, "Königreich Ungarn," pp. 1107–1108; Hóman, *Geschichte*, vol. II, pp. 46–79; Marczali, *Ungarische Verfassungsgeschichte*, pp. 20–21; Fügedi, *Castle and Society*, p. 43; Barber, *Two Cities*, p. 377.

[15] József Gerics, "Von den Universi Servientes Regis bis zu der Universitas Nobilium Regni Hungariae," in: *Album Elemér Malyusz*, pp. 97–108, here at p. 101.

[16] Marczali, *Ungarische Verfassungsgeschichte*, pp. 21–23; Hóman, *Geschichte*, vol. II, pp. 79–85; Helbig, "Ungarns Goldene Bulle," pp. 111–112.

since its creation by St. Stephen 200 years earlier. This alliance between ruler and aristocracy provoked a counterreaction from the knightly classes of the kingdom, whose aspiration was above all to secure the same rights as their aristocratic superiors. In England, Magna Carta set in motion a dynamic in which the power of the Crown was counterbalanced by a "community of the realm" which became progressively more inclusive – first encompassing all barons, then all free men, and finally all royal subjects. In Hungary, on the other hand, the Golden Bull paved the way for a unification of the aristocracy and lesser fighting men into a single, equally privileged noble class against which a weak Hungarian monarch – and an even weaker peasantry – proved incapable of defending themselves. When a sustained geopolitical stimulus finally did come to affect Hungary in the late 1400s, it was too late for this stimulus to benefit the Crown, as had been the case in England during the 1100s. Rather, as will be seen below, the continuous threat posed by the Turks served only to strengthen the nobility still further.

That process of unification between the aristocracy and the lesser fighting men was furthered by the after-effects of a devastating Mongol attack on the country in 1241. Though the Mongols withdrew in 1242 as suddenly as they had come, their victories highlighted the deficiencies of Hungary's traditional defenses built around primitive castles and light cavalry. One way in which the new king, Béla IV (1235–1270), sought to overcome these deficiencies was by amalgamating the *servientes* and *iobagiones castri* into a new class of heavily armored, well-trained knights of the western type.[17] This transformation not only brought a new unity and heightened coercive power to the ranks of the lesser fighting men, but also improved their material condition, for the king helped defray the cost of new equipment with generous grants of land.

The other step taken by Béla was to initiate a massive building program in order to outfit the realm as quickly as possible with a network of stone castles better capable of withstanding prolonged sieges than the older wood, earthen, and shard variety. Given the weakened state in which the Hungarian Crown already found itself vis-à-vis a wealthy and powerful aristocracy, it could not possibly hope to construct dozens of massively expensive castles within a reasonable amount of time by drawing solely on its own resources. Knowing this, the king reluctantly licensed private groups and individuals to build fortifications, a step all previous monarchs had sought to avoid. As Eric Fügedi's research has shown, Béla's initiative was a great success, with 55 new castles erected

---

[17] Elemér Malyusz, "Die Entstehung der Stände im mittelalterlichen Ungarn," in: *L'Organisation Corporative du Moyen Âge à la Fin de l'Ancien Régime* (Louvain: Bibliothèque de l'Université, 1939), pp. 13–30, here at pp. 25–26.

and 13 more reconstructed in stone between 1242 and the end of his reign in 1270. However, of the 63 castles whose ownership is known, 30 or nearly half were in private hands, built and garrisoned for the most part by leading aristocrats and churchmen. This trend, once begun, only accelerated after the death of Béla, as at least 88 of the 110 new castles constructed between 1270 and 1300 were private.[18]

The rapid spread of mainly aristocratic fortifications brought profound social and economic changes to Hungary. Above all, it provided castle owners with both the incentive and the means to extend their control over the peasants of the surrounding countryside, for maintaining these potent centers of coercive power was very costly. It was this period which saw the beginnings of a new class of hereditary dependent peasants, the *jobbágyok*, formed from men who had previously been free, semi-free, or slaves, and who now labored on the latifundia grouped around the castles of the great lords. The lords also quickly succeeded in extending their seigneurial jurisdiction over these dependents for all but the most serious crimes – just as the bannal lords of France had done three centuries earlier – thereby removing much of the county population from the direct judicial authority of the count and, indirectly, of the king.[19] At the same time, many of the new western-style knights who were emerging to replace the old *servientes regales* and *iobagiones castri* were drawn into the orbit of the castle-centered estates as castellans, armed retainers, or simply clients of the dominant local family.[20]

Béla IV actively sought to bolster the social and political standing of these knights in order to counterbalance the renewed expansion of aristocratic power provoked by the Mongol invasion. Thus in a royal decree of 1267, Béla conferred upon the former *servientes* and *iobagiones castri* the status of *nobiles* or nobles, previously reserved only for aristocrats. He thereby created a single noble class encompassing all free fighting men. Members of the aristocracy, the new "higher nobility," immediately sought to set themselves apart from their humbler cousins by referring to themselves as *barones* in imitation of the French and Sicilian usage.[21] The same decree also granted to the lesser nobility of every county the right to elect judges (*iudices nobilium* or *szolgabiró*)

---

[18] Fügedi, *Castle and Society*, pp. 50–62.
[19] Fügedi, *Castle and Society*, pp. 61–62, 73–76; Eszlary, *Histoire*, vol. I, pp. 281–284, 373–381; Malyusz, "Entstehung der Stände," p. 24; Pamlényi, *History*, pp. 70–71.
[20] Fügedi, *Castle and Society*, pp. 76–80; Barber, *Two Cities*, p. 379.
[21] Joseph Holub, "La Formation des Deux Chambres de l'Assemblée Nationale Hongroise," in: *Album Helen Maud Cam* (Louvain: Publications Universitaires de Louvain, 1961), pp. 347–358, here at pp. 349–350; Gerics, "Von den Universi Servientes Regis," pp. 101–104; Malyusz, "Entstehung der Stände," pp. 25–26, 28–29; Pamlényi, *History*, pp. 65–66.

from among their number to assist the count (usually an aristocrat) in his court, and to select two or three representatives to carry their grievances to the national judicial assembly traditionally held once a year at Székesfehérvar.[22]

This line of policy was taken up again in the 1290s by Andrew III after the weak and divisive rule of Ladislas the Kuman (1272–1290) had contributed to another surge in aristocratic power marked by a wave of unchecked private castle-building.[23] In 1290, Andrew began his reign by taking up a practice used twice before (1277, 1279) by his hapless predecessor in order to counterbalance baronial influence:[24] he called members of the clergy and lower nobility from the whole country to Buda in order to discuss the state of the kingdom and deliberate over new legislation alongside the royal council made up entirely of *barones*. In a decree submitted to and approved by this assembly, called a *parlamentum publicum* or *congregatio generalis* in the documents of the time, he weakened the position of the count by providing him with a deputy, the viscount (*vicecomes*), chosen from among the local nobility and empowered to carry out the count's duties whenever the latter was absent. At the same time, Andrew made provisions for the royal palatine to visit the counties and call together assemblies (*congregationes*) of all free and semi-free men, both nobles and non-nobles, to judge important cases and present local grievances.[25]

At the next meeting of the nascent Hungarian parliament in 1298, the lesser nobility and clergy themselves drew up a law which established the right of free assembly in the counties. This permitted meetings of the *congregatio* to be held to discuss matters of pressing importance, without the presence of the palatine. Even more significantly, it also decreed that in the future the royal council should be composed of two bishops, two members of the lesser nobility chosen by parliament, and only two barons. Furthermore, the king was required to gain the approval of this reformed council before making any important decisions or issuing any new decrees or edicts, which effectively limited the royal right of legislation. This draft law was subsequently passed by both the king and the barons, who had been excluded from the initial meetings

[22] Marczali, *Ungarische Verfassungsgeschichte*, p. 30; Timon, *Ungarische Verfassungs- und Rechtsgeschichte*, pp. 214–217, 318; Eszlary, *Histoire*, vol. I, pp. 268–269, 367; Barber, *Two Cities*, p. 379.

[23] Thus of the 74 castles constructed between 1271 and 1290, only 9 were royal and at least 58 were in private hands. See: Fügedi, *Castle and Society*, p. 54.

[24] Ferenc Eckhart, "La Diète Corporative Hongroise," in: *L'Organisation Corporative*, pp. 211–224, here at pp. 215–216.

[25] Timon, *Ungarische Verfassungs- und Rechtsgeschichte*, pp. 199–200, 214–218, 318–319; Eszlary, *Histoire*, vol. I, pp. 227–231; 267–271; Helbig, "Ungarns Goldene Bulle," p. 118.

of the lesser nobility and clergy, in what amounts to the first instance in Hungarian history of the joint exercise of legislative powers by the king and the national assembly.[26] It is no coincidence that it was precisely during this period of increased political involvement that the nobility – excepting a small number of overweening barons – came to see itself, whether in the counties or in parliament, as a single group with common interests and began to refer to itself (and be referred to by clerical commentators) as the *universitas nobilium*, the community of nobles.[27]

The parliamentary dominance of the 1290s proved to be short-lived, however, for the death in 1301 of Andrew III, the last Árpád in the direct male line of descent, ushered in a period of de facto civil war in which competing baronial leagues supported rival claimants to the throne. In the end, it was Charles of Anjou (1308–1342), grandson of the king of Naples but born of an Árpád mother and raised in Hungary, who finally succeeded in securing the throne in 1308, though he did not overcome all of his baronial opposition until 1321.[28] As a military victor at the head of his own forces, Charles was able to reestablish royal authority in Hungary by seizing the castles of his defeated opponents and placing them under the control of castellans who were his faithful followers. Whereas in 1310 fewer than one-fourth of the country's castles (43 of 185 with known owners) were in royal hands and the greatest magnate possessed as many castles as the king, by 1321 Charles had 100 castles at his disposal while no single aristocrat maintained more than 10. Charles's son and heir Louis (1342–1382) was able to consolidate his father's gains by retaining ownership over more than half of all the realm's castles throughout his long reign.[29]

Under the Angevins, castles once again became centers of royal power in the counties, with castellans often simultaneously granted the office of count and placed in charge of all royal estates and revenues in the area. This new generation of castellans, whether counts or not, was also given the powers of higher jurisdiction over the population of the royal

---

[26] Timon, *Ungarische Verfassungs- und Rechtsgeschichte*, pp. 200–201, 218, 319; Eszlary, *Histoire*, vol. I, pp. 193–194, 231, 270; Marczali, *Ungarische Verfassungsgeschichte*, p. 31; Barber, *Two Cities*, p. 380; Ekhart, "Diète Corporative," pp. 215–216; Holub, "Formation des Deux Chambres," p. 351; Helbig, "Ungarns Goldene Bulle," p. 119.

[27] Joseph Holub, "La Représentation Politique en Hongrie au Moyen Âge," in: *Xe Congrès International des Sciences Historiques, Rome, 1955: Etudes Présentées à la Commission Internationale pour l'Histoire des Assemblées d'États* (Louvain: Publications Universitaires de Louvain, 1958), pp. 77–121, here at p. 89, Gerics, "Von den Universi Servientes Regis," pp. 104–106.

[28] On Charles's long struggle to gain the throne and consolidate his position upon it, see: Bálint Hóman, *Gli Angioini di Napoli in Ungheria 1290–1403* (Roma: Reale Accademia d'Italia, 1938), pp. 80–148.

[29] Fügedi, *Castle and Society*, pp. 54, 82, 113–114, 123.

estates. Such powers were to be retained by noble landowners following their appropriation of much of the royal domain after 1387.[30]

Having restored royal authority in Hungary by repossessing the castes of hostile aristocrats, the Angevins were little disposed to share this authority with a national parliament. Indeed, while great judicial assemblies continued to be held every year at Székesfehérvar, no more parliaments like those of 1290 and 1298 were convened by the Angevins after 1323, despite repeated demands from the clergy that the king do so. Without sustained foreign military pressure and enjoying a substantial regalian income thanks to an upsurge in gold and silver mining after 1327, the Angevins saw no reason to comply with such demands.[31] Yet that same financial security and absence of military pressure also meant that neither Charles nor Louis possessed the incentive to solidify their power base by attempting to build up an extensive, independent administrative infrastructure. In the absence of such a structural foundation, royal power in Hungary was predestined to decline again as soon as it was necessary to alienate royal properties and castles in order to shore up aristocratic support, as would be the case after 1387.

While the nascent Hungarian Diet may have vanished temporarily from the political stage between 1323 and 1387, the privileges of the nobility continued to grow. Like all of their predecessors since Béla IV, the Angevins sought to bolster the position of the (lesser) nobles as a counterweight to the influence of an aristocracy consisting of some 30 families who still controlled over 100 castles and 3,000 villages at the time of Louis's death (1382).[32] The monarchs therefore made no effort to reverse the transformation of the counties into local, largely self-governing branches of one nationwide "community of nobles."[33] And Louis's decree of 1351, which finally granted full legal equality to all members of the nobility, from lowliest knight to mightiest aristocrat while at the same time confirming all privileges found in the Golden Bull, only served to entrench noble strength. In the same decree, Louis also played the traditional royal role of protector of the weak by reaffirming the right of dependent peasants to leave their masters whenever they chose as long as they had paid all of their seigneurial dues.[34]

Although royal power in Hungary appeared to reach its height under the Angevin kings, the groundwork was being laid for the appropriation

[30] Ibid., pp. 103–115; Timon, *Ungarische Verfassungs- und Rechtsgeschichte*, pp. 694–695.
[31] Eszlary, *Histoire*, vol. II, pp. 76–78, 140; Homan, *Angioini di Napoli*, pp. 194–195.
[32] Homan, *Angioini di Napoli*, p. 248.
[33] Holub, "Représentation Politique," pp. 88–89.
[34] Hóman, *Angioini di Napoli*, pp. 353–358; Timon, *Ungarische Verfassungs- und Rechtsgeschichte*, pp. 557, 597; Marczali, *Ungarische Verfassungsgeschichte*, pp. 36–38; Pamlényi, *History*, pp. 82–83; Eszlary, *Histoire*, vol. II, pp. 77–78, 311.

of much of the Crown's authority and practical capacities for rule after 1387. Lacking sufficient external stimulus, neither the Angevins nor their predecessors had succeeded in equipping themselves with the kind of independent state apparatus which their western cousins had long possessed, and which could have provided a firm structural basis for their continued strength. At the same time, while the national parliaments which had first appeared during the 13th century may have momentarily faded, the efforts of successive monarchs to check the power of an immensely wealthy and influential aristocracy had led to the creation of a large, privileged, and increasingly assertive noble class which had already converted what had been royal administrative districts into units of local elite self-government. From this base of operation, the noble class stood poised to appropriate further state power when the opportunity next presented itself.

Poland

Despite the lack of any strong cultural similarities, other than a shared Catholicism, between the Polish and Magyar peoples, the history of Poland down to the late 14th century exhibits many parallels to that of Hungary because of their common experience of late state formation. Considering that the Slavic tribes who would later become the Poles had established themselves between the Odra and Vistula rivers by the 8th century, well before the Hungarians arrived in Europe, it is surprising that the two states were established at approximately the same time. The vast areas of thick forest and marshland in this region, as well as its relative isolation from the Carolingian Empire and other more advanced western polities, prevented the construction of large-scale forms of social and political organization until well into the 10th century.[35]

The revival of Carolingian power in Germany under the Ottonians – the same revival that spelled defeat for the Magyars – combined with European-wide forces of ecclesiastical and economic renewal, eventually led to the rapid emergence of a Western-style state in Poland during the second half of the 900s. During this period, the Piast family, tribal leaders of the Polonians, sought to weld together surrounding tribes into a viable political unit in the face of threatened Ottonian

---

[35] Norman Davies, *God's Playground: A History of Poland* (New York: Columbia University Press, 1982), vol. I, pp. 37–48; Juliusz Bardach, "L'État Polonais aux Xe et XIe Siècles," in: Institut d'Histoire de l'Académie Polonaise des Sciences, *L'Europe aux IXe–XIe Siècles: Aux Origines des États Nationaux* (Varsovie: Pánstwowe Wydawnictwo Naukowe, 1968), pp. 279–319, here at pp. 281, 283; Jörg Hoensch, *Geschichte Polens*, 2nd ed. (Stuttgart: Verlag Eugen Ulmer, 1990), pp. 13–16; Oskar Kossmann, *Polen im Mittelalter*, 2 vols. (Marburg: J. G. Herder-Institut, 1971–1984), vol. II, pp. 5–16.

expansion towards the east.[36] The crucial step in realizing this project came in 965, when the Piast duke Mieszko decided to draw on the superior expertise of the neighboring Bohemian state – itself built around Carolingian borrowings – by marrying the daughter of the Bohemian ruler and simultaneously converting himself and his people to Christianity. As in Hungary, both the anti-clan character of Christian doctrine and the sophisticated nature of Church organization played a crucial role in Polish state formation.[37] At about the same time, Mieszko established a friendly, albeit tribute-paying, relationship with the Ottonian emperors of Germany, a relationship later solidified by Mieszko's second marriage to the daughter of a Saxon aristocrat, the margrave of the Nordmark. And in the year 1000 Otto III personally initiated the creation of an independent Polish archbishopric in Gniezno like the one which Hungary had received three years earlier, and implied that the elevation of the Piasts into the family of kings – shortly to be achieved by the Árpáds – might soon follow.[38]

Otto's death in 1002 put an end to such hopes, however, for his imperial successors were opposed to the emergence of a powerful, independent new polity on Germany's eastern borders. Although Mieszko's son Bohuslaw Chroby was able to exploit the interregnum within the Empire in 1025 to have himself crowned king with the approval of Pope John XIX, his successor Mieszko II was forced to relinquish this honor in 1033 following military defeat at the hands of the emperor Conrad II. It was only in 1076, during the height of the Investiture Controversy and just days before Henry IV's humiliating trip to Canossa, that Pope Gregory VII rewarded Duke Boleslaw II for his support against the emperor by raising him to the rank of king. This time, the Piasts were able to keep their new title thanks to the permanent weakening of the Empire resulting from protracted conflict with the Church.[39]

The internal organization of the nascent Polish kingdom strongly

---

[36] Bardach, "L'État Polonais," pp. 283–284; Davies, *God's Playground*, pp. 62–63; Aleksander Gieysztor, "En Pologne Médiévale: Problèmes du Régime Politique et de l'Organisation Administrative du Xe au XIIIe Siècle," *Annali della Fondazione Italiana per la Storia Amministrativa*, vol. 1 (1964), pp. 135–156, here at pp. 146–147; idem, "Aspects Territoriaux du Premier État Polonais," *Revue Historique*, vol. 226, no. 2 (Octobre–Décembre 1961), pp. 357–381, here at pp. 366–367.

[37] Morris, *Papal Monarchy*, pp. 264–265, 271–273.

[38] Herbert Ludat, "Piasten und Ottonen," in: Institut d'Histoire, *L'Europe aux IXe-XIe Siècles*, pp. 321–359, here at pp. 326–342; Kossmann, *Polen im Mittelalter*, vol. II, pp. 86–96; Hellmann, "Die politisch-kirchliche Grundlegung," pp. 906–908; Hoensch, *Geschichte*, pp. 17–21.

[39] Hoensch, *Geschichte*, pp. 21–27; Kossmann, *Polen im Mittelalter*, vol. II, pp. 97–101; Hellmann, "Die politisch-kirchliche Grundlegeung," pp. 908–911; Ferdinand Seibt, "Polen von der Jahrtausendwende bis 1444," in: Schieder, *Handbuch*, vol. II, pp. 1042–1070, here at pp. 1051–1052.

resembled its Hungarian counterpart. This was especially true in the area of central administration since both the Piasts and the Árpáds made use of the same Carolingian models – in the case of the Piasts most likely passed along by the Bohemians and Bavarians. As in Hungary, the king was advised by a royal council made up of lay and ecclesiastical worthies, and his household was headed by a count of the palace or palatine under whose authority stood the usual range of officials: chancellor, chamberlain, treasurer, judge, steward, cup-bearer, marshall.[40] Local administration was likewise constructed around a network of royal castles which functioned as judicial, military, and fiscal centers and as headquarters from which royal estates located in the surrounding area could be overseen. Yet unlike in Hungary, these castles where not the seats of counties, but rather of somewhat smaller castellanies, each headed by a multipurpose official, the castellan. There were approximately 120 castellanies in 12th-century Poland, compared to 72 Hungarian counties spread over a somewhat larger area.[41] The castellanies were grouped into eight large *ziemie* or provinces, each headed by a "provincial count" (*comes provinciae*). This two-tiered pattern of local administration in Poland seems to have been modeled on the eastern German pattern, not on the organization of the Carolingian heartland as was the case in Hungary. The eastern regions of the Empire, the area closest to the Piast realm, were divided into larger "marches" (e.g., the Nordmark or "north march" of which Mieszko I's father-in-law was margrave or "march count") which in turn comprised numerous smaller castellanies.[42]

Unlike its Árpád counterpart, the early Piast kingdom proved unable to maintain its initial unity. Throughout the 1000s and early 1100s, Poland was troubled by a series of protracted succession struggles which were often instigated and encouraged by the neighboring German emperors. As was typical in medieval Europe, such conflicts served to strengthen the hand of a nascent aristocracy whose support was crucial to anyone hoping to secure and then hold onto the throne. The more rapid development of a powerful aristocracy in Poland, as compared to

---

[40] Gieysztor, "En Pologne Médiévale," pp. 146–147, 149–152; Stanislaus Kutrzeba, *Grundriss der Polnishen Verfassungsgeschichte* (Berlin: Puttkammer & Mühlbrecht, 1912), pp. 19–21; Seibt, "Polen," p. 1054.

[41] Pre-1920 Hungary, which was roughly the same size as the kingdom had been during the later middle ages, was 325,411 square kilometers in size, whereas early Piast Poland covered (very roughly) 250,000 square kilometers. See: Davies, *God's Playground*, p. 51; Joseph Rothschild, *East Central Europe between the Two World Wars* (Seattle: University of Washington Press, 1974), p. 155.

[42] Kossmann, *Polen im Mittelalter*, vol. II, pp. 243–256, 282–283, 310–311; Gieysztor, "En Pologne Médiévale," pp. 153–155; Kutrzeba, *Grundriss*, pp. 21–25; Hellmann, "Die politisch-kirchlichen Grundlegung," pp. 911–912.

Hungary, at a critical historical juncture helps explain Poland's centuries-long partition. The aristocracy lent crucial support to Boleslaw III's decision in 1138 to divide his kingdom among his sons and to the continued existence of the separate Piast duchies once they had been created.[43]

Boleslaw's original intention seems to have been to introduce a Merovingian-style "collective rulership" wherein the Polish provinces would be regularly redistributed among the male members of the family, with the senior member always assigned the capital Kraków, the title of "grand duke," and general authority over all of his younger relatives. This would have provided some hope that a single "Crown of Poland" might continue to be a reality, much as a "kingdom of the Franks" had survived Clovis's division of 511. Yet without the Merovingians' strong collective charisma, this schema could not work. Instead, the individual *ziemie* soon became – with the blessing of Emperor and Pope in 1181–1184 – autonomous, hereditary duchies that were later subdivided into even smaller duchies comprising only a few castellanies each.[44]

As in the Merovingian and Carolingian realms, the existence of a series of neighboring political units all controlled by members of the same extended family was a sure recipe for interminable conflict and competition as individual Piast princes – as well as the offspring and husbands of Piast princesses – sought to enlarge their patrimony through alliance, marriage, or conquest. Aside from the Empire, two groups gained from this perpetual discord among the Piasts: the still united Church, which was able to extract important privileges and land grants from the weak territorial princes; and the aristocracy, which came to dominate the political life of the duchies.[45]

The new polities offered attractive prospects for influential local families, for each duke insisted on setting up his own court with a full range of lucrative household offices (palatine, chancellor, treasurer, chamberlain, judge, steward). Furthermore, since support from one's own powerful subjects was a prerequisite for external expansion, the dukes actively courted such support by calling together all of the leading men of their realms (court officials, castellans, bishops) for consultations (*colloquia*) and made liberal grants to them from the ducal domains. The elites of each duchy also established the principle that if, as frequently happened,

[43] Aleksander Gieysztor, Stefan Kieniewicz, Emanuel Rostworowski, Janusz Tazbir, and Henryk Wereszycki, *History of Poland* (Warszawa: PWN, 1968), pp. 79–81; Zamoyski, *Polish Way*, pp. 18–19.

[44] Zamoyski, *Polish Way*, p. 24; Seibt, "Polen von der Jahrtausendwende," p. 1052; Hoensch, *Geschichte*, pp. 30–31; Gieysztor, "En Pologne Médiévale," p. 148.

[45] Davies, *God's Playground*, vol. I, p. 70; Hoensch, *Geschichte*, p. 32; Kossmann, *Polen im Mittelalter*, vol. II, p. 412.

their own territory was united with that of another prince, all of their duchy's court offices would be preserved and meetings of the local *colloquia* would continue to take place. This was a sure sign that the duchies were on their way to becoming territorially integrated, self-governing elite communities comparable to the contemporaneous Hungarian counties. And as in Hungary, aristocratic officeholders as well as the lesser fighters or knights (Latin *milites*, Polish *rycerz*, derived from German *Ritter*) aspired to play an active role in local government.[46]

Like the case of the Merovingians, sustained intra-family competition inevitably led to a general depletion of resources, and by the late 1200s the ducal domains of the Piast duchies lay exhausted, most of their lands having been alienated either to the Church or to the leading local families.[47] Yet, as in late 7th- and 8th-century Gaul, the weakening of the regional princes created favorable conditions for the reunification of the kingdom. Between 1305 and 1320, the Piast prince Władysław the Short was able, thanks to support from the Church and the knightly class, to unite all of the central Polish lands under his control. Though the Church had initially benefited from the kingdom's disunity, it later came to see that disunity as a threat to its own future independent existence due to the rise of the new German territorial states to the west, the state of the Teutonic Order to the north, and an aggressive Bohemia to the south. As in Hungary, the lesser nobility looked to a strong central authority to prevent it from falling into total subservience to an overmighty aristocracy. Thus the same constellation of forces that in 13th-century Hungary had sought to curb aristocratic power coalesced somewhat later in Poland around the goal of restoring the country's unity under a revitalized Piast monarchy.[48]

Władysław realized this goal in 1320, when he was crowned king of a much reduced Poland (minus Pomerania, Silesia, and Masovia) with papal approval. Yet the task of reforging the lands he had brought together into an effective, unified state fell to his son Casimir (1333–1370). The building blocks for the restored kingdom were of necessity provided by all of the territories, about 18 in number by the end of the reign, that at one time or another had been independent duchies. As mentioned above, these territories, now called *ziemie*, had retained their court officials[49] and *colloquia* and attained a high degree of participatory

---

[46] Kutrzeba, *Grundriss*, pp. 30–33, 49–51, 54–56; Juliusz Bardach, "Gouvernants et Gouvernés en Pologne au Moyen Âge et aux Temps Modernes," *Gouvernés et Gouvernants*, vol. 25 (1965), pp. 255–285, here at pp. 259–260.

[47] Kossmann, *Polen im Mittelalter*, vol. II, pp. 409–412.

[48] Gieysztor et al., *History*, pp. 114–118; Zamoyski, *Polish Way*, pp. 34–36; Kossmann, *Polen im Mittelalter*, vol. II, p. 348.

[49] While all of the former duchies had retained a complement of former court officials, not all had retained a palatine. After reunification, those territories that still possessed

self-government by local elites prior to reunification. While Casimir could not hope to reverse this development, he did have at his disposal a new official, the *starosta*, borrowed from neighboring Bohemia and introduced by his father Władisław into the *ziemie*. The *starosta* was to be a kind of count of the new provinces, acting as a multipurpose judicial and administrative officer answerable directly to the king.[50] Casimir also reformed the Polish monetary system, commissioned the first codifications of Polish "common law," founded the University of Kraków, and gave refuge to many Jews fleeing persecution in Germany, all of which helped earn him the predicate "the Great."[51] Yet what he did not attempt to do, for want of a sufficient external stimulus, was to construct the kind of central administrative apparatus that would have provided a permanent structural foundation for royal power.

Although Casimir's father had relied on the knightly class (*milites*) during his campaigns to reunite the country, Casimir derived the bulk of his support from the provincial aristocracy, especially that of Lesser Poland (*Małopolska*) around Kraków. The knightly class made only one substantial advance during Casimir's reign: they gained the right to participate in local judicial administration as lay assessors, deciding cases together with the *ziemia* judge, usually a local aristocrat. It was only under Casimir's successor that the *milites* would begin to make the legal gains that would eventually bring them social and political equality with their wealthier brethren. That successor was none other than Louis of Anjou, king of Hungary and a nephew of Casimir. Lacking a son, Casimir chose Louis as his heir despite the better claims of several Piast princes. Louis knew that in order to rule effectively, he would have to win widespread domestic support in his realm, and he chose to do this using the same method he had already employed in Hungary. He thus granted broad-based charters of privilege to an inclusively defined nobility – something that had not previously been done in Poland – with the aim of extending to the knightly class rights already enjoyed by their aristocratic cousins.[52]

a palatine were referred to as "palatinates," while those that had lost this official were called simply *ziemie*, the term that was also used collectively for all of the former duchies that had now become the "provinces" or *pays* of the restored kingdom. On this knotty problem of nomenclature, see: Kutrzeba, *Grundriss*, pp. 49–50, 124–127.

50 In Latin documents, the *starosta* was sometimes referred to as *bracchium regale*, or "royal arm." See: Kutrzeba, *Grundriss*, pp. 50–52, 114–116; Paul Knoll, *The Rise of the Polish Monarchy: Piast Poland in East Central Europe, 1320–1370* (Chicago: University of Chicago Press, 1972), pp. 26–27.

51 Hoensch, *Geschichte*, pp. 49–53; Zamoyski, *Polish Way*, pp. 37–40.

52 Davies, *God's Playground*, p. 111; Hoensch, *Geschichte*, p. 52; Zamoyski, *Polish Way*, pp. 41–43; Karol Górski, "Les Chartes de la Noblesse en Pologne aux XIVᵉ et XVᵉ Siècle," in: *Album Elemér Malyusz*, pp. 247–271, here at pp. 251–252.

Louis issued the first of these charters at Buda in 1355, to come into effect after he gained the throne, and the second at Košice in 1374. In the Statute of Buda, he promised not to impose himself on noble families while traveling throughout the country, not to name foreigners to Polish offices, and to provide compensation for any costs incurred in foreign military expeditions. The Statute of Košice was much more substantial, granted in order to gain approval for the succession of one of his daughters to the Polish Crown. It was this charter which extended to all aristocrats and knights privileges – including seigneurial jurisdiction and freedom from various fiscal exactions – previously enjoyed by only some of their number. In return, these groups were required to provide unpaid military service in defense of the country and to pay a small regular land tax of 2 *grossi* a year per mansum. Furthermore, the king stated that he would impose no taxes beyond this sum without their explicit approval.[53]

The charters of 1355 and 1374 mark the formal birth of the Polish nobility or *szlachta*[54] as a legally defined class. While the way for this amalgamation had been paved beginning in the late 13th century by the formation of patron/client-based noble "clans" employing common coats of arms and encompassing unrelated members of both aristocratic and knightly families, its consummation at law was undoubtedly aided by the arrival of a foreign ruler whose own nobility had received de jure recognition three-quarters of a century earlier.[55] In a clear example of transnational learning, it was in 1382 – during Louis of Anjou's reign – that the term *communitas nobilium* made its first appearance in Poland, and that the first meetings of a Polish Diet (*Sejm*) – also inspired by Hungarian precedents – took place during 1384–1386, just after his death. Yet the makeup of that Diet, composed almost entirely of the aristocratic officials of the royal court and the *ziemie*, shows that the lesser nobility did not yet possess the political influence of its counterpart in Hungary.[56]

At the end of this first period of their development, Hungary and

---

[53] Górski, "Chartes de la Noblesse," pp. 252–254; Kutrzeba, *Grundriss*, pp. 30–31, 70–71; Davies, *God's Playground*, p. 111; Kossmann, *Polen im Mittelalter*, vol. II, pp. 341–343; Hóman, *Angioini di Napoli*, pp. 397–398; Hoensch, *Geschichte*, p. 56.

[54] The term *szlachta* is sometimes erroneously translated as "gentry" when in fact it was a collective term for all nobles, from the greatest magnate to the landless *Lumpenadel*. It is derived from the Czech *slehta*, etymologically related to the modern German *Geschlecht* (family, lineage). See the discussion in Davies, *God's Playground*, pp. 206–207.

[55] Bak, "Königreich Ungarn," p. 1117.

[56] Juliusz Bardach, "La Formation des Assemblées Polonaises au XVᵉ Siècle et la Taxation," *Anciens Pays et Assemblées d'Etats*, vol. 70 (1977), pp. 249–296, here at pp. 260–262; Kutrzeba, *Grundriss*, pp. 30–33.

Poland had achieved a kind of convergence aptly symbolized by their brief period of joint rulership between 1370 and 1382. Both countries had experienced a period of unencumbered state formation which had permitted the emergence of participatory, though markedly elitist, forms of local government built around territorially integrated administrative units (the county and the *ziemia*/castellany). On the other hand, neither polity had experienced early, sustained geopolitical pressure, which in England and Latin Europe had provoked the construction of large-scale central state infrastructures by the end of the 13th century. As a result, both Hungary and Poland were kingdoms ruled by monarchs who – whatever their personal qualities – were in structurally weak positions because they lacked substantial, independent apparatuses of coercion. To make up for this deficiency, they had tried to build up the position of their lesser fighters as counterweights to a powerful, allodial aristocracy over which they had no feudal hold. In so doing, however, successive Hungarian and Polish rulers only succeeded in creating large, unified noble classes that, by the late 1300s, already dominated local government and now stood poised to extend their influence still further.

THE ADVENT OF SUSTAINED GEOPOLITICAL COMPETITION
AND THE TRIUMPH OF PATRIMONIAL CONSTITUTIONALISM
IN HUNGARY AND POLAND, 1387–1648

Although Hungary and Poland had remained relatively free of sustained geopolitical pressure during the first four centuries of their existence, such pressure finally manifested itself after 1450. At this time, the northerly advance of the Ottomans through the Balkans came to pose a direct and persistent threat to the Magyars. Meanwhile, the appearance of an increasingly potent Muscovy to the east, when combined with a still persistent rivalry with the Teutonic Knights, and – somewhat later – the rise of Vasa Sweden to the north, forced a kind of geopolitical competition upon Poland which the country had not hitherto experienced. Yet the resulting wars and preparations for war did not lead in either case, as they had in the rest of Europe, to the construction of large, centrally controlled administrative, fiscal, and military infrastructures manned by either patrimonial or bureaucratic officials. Rather, they simply accelerated the flow of state functions and state authority away from structurally weak monarchs and towards self-governing local political communities and their national representatives, the Diets. Both were made up exclusively of members of one privileged social group, the nobility.

This period witnessed the full maturation of a pattern of governance I call patrimonial constitutionalism. In such a system, nominally public institutions and tasks are appropriated by narrow groups of local elites pursuing their own private interests and operating through representative bodies. In the case of Hungary, the immediate effect of this appropriation was a decline in military capacity which contributed to a decisive defeat at the hand of the Turks in 1526. This defeat brought the Habsburgs to the Hungarian throne and marked the beginning of a long, and largely successful, struggle by the Hungarian nobility to maintain their power and privileges in the face of repeated Habsburg attempts at modernizing, bureaucratic reform. Poland, faced with a somewhat less acute military threat in the northeastern Europe of the 16th and early 17th centuries, was able for the moment to avoid such a dramatic fate, but would eventually pay for its patrimonial constitutionalism a price even greater than that extracted from its neighbor.

Hungary

The Turkish victory over the Serbs in 1389 laid the groundwork for the expansion of the Ottoman Empire into central Europe. Regular armed conflict between Hungary and the Turks did not, however, result until the middle of the 15th century, when the Hunyadis organized a number of successful military expeditions (1442–1443, 1456, 1463–1464, and 1504) against their new Islamic foes. Yet none of these victories came even close to relieving Ottoman pressure on Hungary, for the vast Turkish military machine remained largely intact.[57]

At the moment when the Ottoman Empire was enjoying its first triumphs further to the south, Hungary was ruled by Sigismund of Luxemburg (1387–1437), husband of Louis the Great's daughter Mary. He had only been able to secure the throne for himself and his wife because of support provided by 15 baronial families and their retainers against an Angevin claimant. After their common victory, these families had to be rewarded. Thus, in the period up to 1408 Sigismund granted away 80 of the 130 castles he controlled to his aristocratic allies, thereby reversing in a decade the century-long work of the Angevins to rebuild monarchial power through a network of royal strongholds. What is more, the new private owners of these castles often acquired not only the dues previously owed to the castellan, but also the capital jurisdiction over the entire surrounding area.[58]

Given the recent successes of the Turks, Sigismund was careful not to alienate castles in the crucial southern border region.[59] Yet the approach he took to national defense betrayed his weakness vis-à-vis the

[57] Bak, "Königreich Ungarn," p. 1118; Pamlényi, *History*, pp. 97–99, 113.
[58] Fügedi, *Castle and Society*, pp. 107, 112, 123–130.   [59] Ibid., pp. 132–133.

aristocratic forces to which he owed his crown. The king did little to alter the nature of the army inherited from the Angevins. This army was built around units called *banderia* recruited and commanded by lay and ecclesiastical barons at the county level, but paid for from the public purse. To these Sigismund added new *banderia* raised by officials such as the *voivode* of Transylvania and the *bán* of Croatia. To pay for these troops, the king levied extraordinary taxes nine times, but only once (1423) did he seek approval for this action from a full Diet which included deputies chosen by the counties. Like the Angevins, he preferred to consult with a grand council of all the principal barons and bishops rather than with a larger assembly in which the lesser nobility carried much more weight.[60]

Only after the death of Sigismund did the Diet regain the place it had briefly won for itself in the 1290s. When Sigismund's successor Albrecht of Habsburg died suddenly without an heir in 1439, the national assembly asserted its right to choose a new king. They proceeded to select a prince (Władysław III of Poland) unrelated to his predecessors, and thereby strengthened the elective character of the office. At the same time, the concept of the "Holy Crown of Hungary" (*sacra corona regni*) was developed to embody a conception of state sovereignty independent of any particular monarch. Sovereignty rested with a "community of the realm" which possessed the right to select its own ruler. This "community" was increasingly seen as synonymous not with all free men, as in England, but exclusively with the *communitas nobilium*.[61]

In contrast to Sigismund, the new king sought to build a broader basis of support for his rule by calling annual meetings of the Diet. In 1443, he found the perfect ally for his policies in János Hunyadi (also know as Jan Corvinus, 1407/9–1456). During Sigismund's reign, Hunyadi received vast royal donations, which ever since has led many to believe that he was in fact an illegitimate son of the king. By the 1440s, he was the country's wealthiest magnate – in possession of 28 castles, 57 towns, and over 1,000 villages – and its greatest soldier. Although Hunyadi was despised as a parvenu by many of the older aristocratic families, his military exploits had made him the hero of the lesser nobility.[62]

---

[60] Elemér Malyusz, "Les Débuts du Vote de la Taxe par les Ordres dans la Hongrie Féodale," in: *Nouvelles Etudes Historiques* (Budapest: Maison d'Edition de l'Académie des Sciences de Hongrie, 1965), pp. 55–82, here at pp. 55–61; Eszlary, *Histoire*, vol. II, pp. 100–104, 154–166; Holub, "Représentation Politique," pp. 82–83; Michaud, "L'Europe Centrale," p. 198.

[61] Marczali, *Ungarische Verfassungsgeschichte*, pp. 46–48; Eszlary, *Histoire*, vol. II, pp. 7–15, 32–33.

[62] Eszlary, *Histoire*, vol. II, pp. 302–303; Pamlényi, *History*, pp. 96–97.

In 1443, Hunyadi was placed in command of the kingdom's defenses. Following the death of Wladyslaw at the battle of Varna in 1444, Hunyadi became regent for the infant Ladislas of Habsburg, Albrecht's posthumous son who now succeeded to the throne. As regent and later captain-general, he enjoyed near-regal powers, and employed a mercenary army financed entirely from his own resources to inflict a number of significant defeats on the Turks, most notably the successful defense of Belgrade in 1456 against overwhelming odds. The prestige gained by the Hunyadi name from this triumph was so great that, following the death of Ladislas Habsburg in 1457, János's 18-year-old son Mátyás (Matthias Corvinus) was elected king with the support of the lesser nobility. While the leading baronial families had acquiesced in this choice because they believed Mátyás too young to rule effectively, he in fact became one of Hungary's greatest leaders. He ruled for 32 years and continued his father's successes on the battlefield with victories over the Ottomans, the Bohemians, and the Austrians.[63]

It was Mátyás Hunyadi (reigned 1458–1490) who finally responded to the external threats facing the country by attempting to increase the military capacities directly controlled by the central government. Building on the forces assembled by his father, he replaced the quasi-private *banderia* troops of the barons with the largest, most effective professional fighting force in east-central Europe, the Black Army of some 28,000 men. To pay his men, Mátyás introduced national customs duties in 1467, and levied a series of heavy new direct taxes, which were collected in the counties under the supervision of royal officials. As a result, his Hungarian revenues increased fivefold compared to those enjoyed by Ladislas of Habsburg. At the center, royal secretaries and chancery and treasury personnel – generally university-educated humanists of humble background – came to play a greater role in administration at the expense of the magnate-dominated royal council.[64]

In introducing these reforms, Mátyás chose to work closely with the full Diet, in which the lesser nobility was represented by county deputies, rather than with the aristocratic Grand Council preferred by Sigismund. In the years up to 1471, assemblies were called together almost annually, and Mátyás respected the principle, first stated explicitly in 1453, that all new taxation required the assent of that body. In

---

[63] Gotthold Rhode, "Ungarn vom Ende der Verbindung mit Polen bis zum Ende der Türkenherrschaft (1444–1699)," in: Schieder, *Handbuch*, vol. III, pp. 1061–1117, here at pp. 1069–1074; Pamlényi, *History*, pp. 96–100; Michaud, "L'Europe Centrale," p. 198.

[64] Pamlényi, *History*, pp. 101–102, 107–109; Eszlary, *Histoire*, vol. II, pp. 145–147, 183–185, 238–239; Rhode, "Ungarn," p. 1077.

addition, his practice of submitting new laws to the Diet for approval firmly established its position as the king's legislative partner. Yet as the burden of taxation became heavier and more permanent, and the independent coercive capacity of the king grew stronger, many of the middling and lesser nobility began to accept the baronial view that Mátyás's innovations represented a threat to noble interests. As resistance to each new imposition waxed, the king called fewer and fewer meetings of the assembly, extracting revenues instead from territories conquered in Silesia and Moravia. His humanist advisers even began to argue that their master possessed a just claim to *absoluta potestas*.[65]

Yet these efforts at reform, which bear a close resemblance to those that were introduced with such success into the German principalities after the 1490s, would fail both in Hungary and, later, in Poland. The power of the barons and the institutional position and prerogatives of the nobility, rooted as they were in powerful organs of local government and a strong, cohesive, territorially based national assembly, were already too great for any Hungarian ruler to overcome, even one with the will, prestige, and resources of a Mátyás Hunyadi. Thus Hunyadi had thought it necessary to introduce tax exemptions for the privileged orders, and did not even attempt to replace a system of tax collection built largely around county-appointed amateurs with one staffed entirely with royal officials. What is more, near the end of his reign he was forced to dilute his own prerogatives by increasing the powers of the palatine and allowing him to be elected by the Diet. Hunyadi also eliminated royal judicial inquisitions and assizes in the counties, thereby converting the latter into almost entirely self-regulating bodies in the legal sphere.[66]

Upon Mátyás's death in 1490, his baronial opponents, supported by many other nobles, moved quickly to reverse what remained of his reforms. His illegitimate son János Corvinus was rejected as successor and a pliant foreign prince, Władysław Jagiełło of Bohemia, was elected in his place after promising to cancel Mátyás's innovations and never to levy extraordinary taxes. For good measure, responsibility for tax assessment, collection, and disbursement was turned over entirely to the counties. The absence of new taxes, combined with the change in administrative methods, quickly led to a precipitous fall in central government

---

[65] Holub, "Représentation Politique," p. 83; György Bónis, "The Hungarian Feudal Diet (13th–18th Centuries)," *Gouvernés et Gouvernants*, vol. 25 (1965), pp. 287–307, here at pp. 294, 298; Malyusz, "Débuts du Vote," p. 67; Pamlényi, *History*, pp. 107–108; Rhode, "Ungarn," p. 1077.

[66] Pamlényi, *History*, pp. 109–110; Michaud, "L'Europe Centrale," p. 199; Rhode, "Ungarn," pp. 1076, 1079; Eszlary, *Histoire*, vol. II, pp. 118, 202–203.

revenue from a level of 800,000–1,000,000 florins per annum achieved under Mátyás to less than 200,000 florins.[67] This fall in income in turn set the stage for the destruction of the feared Black Army. In 1493, the latter was sent into battle against the Turks and then starved of funds, at which point baronial forces fell upon and destroyed the mutinous troops. With their 'rival eliminated, these privately controlled, publicly subsidized baronial armies (*banderia*) once again became the country's sole source of defense.[68]

With their political power no longer held in check by a strong ruler, the nobility were now free to use this power to their economic advantage. Thus, the period after 1490 saw a notable increase in the exploitation of the dependent rural population in the form of rising unpaid labor dues. In 1514, this poor treatment provoked a bloody peasant revolt (Dózsa's Rebellion). The nobility responded by tying the peasantry to the soil and by cataloging and reaffirming all of their own privileges in a document known as the *Tripartitum* (1514), a kind of constitution of the Hungarian ancien régime which exercised a profound influence until 1848 and beyond. The *Tripartitum* set out in its most elaborate form the theory of the Sacred Crown which designated the *communitas nobilium* as the collective sovereign of Hungary. In consequence, the *communitas* possessed the right – acting through its organ, the Diet – to elect the country's ruler, make new laws and raise taxes together with him, and oppose him with force if he failed to live up to his obligations. Over the difficult centuries to come, the *Tripartitum* proved to be a powerful source of noble unity and a ready-made program of resistance to the Habsburgs.[69]

The destruction of Mátyás's army and his proto-bureaucratic administrative and financial system together with the election of two weak Jagiellonian monarchs may have brought the Hungarian nobility to the height of its political power, but it also left the country's defenses in ruins. In 1526, at the battle of Mohács, the Turks finally took advantage of this situation. The 70,000-strong army of Suleiman the Magnificent utterly destroyed a Hungarian force of 26,000, killing King Louis II in the process. The latter's death without issue meant that the terms of an agreement approved by the Diet in 1491 – whereby the Habsburgs

[67] Marczali, *Ungarische Verfassungsgeschichte*, pp. 56–57; Rhode, "Ungarn," pp. 1080–1081; Pamlényi, *History*, p. 114; Eszlary, *Histoire*, vol. II, pp. 148–149; György Bónis, "Ständisches Finanzwesen in Ungarn im frühen 16. Jahrhundert," in: *Nouvelles Etudes Historiques* (Budapest: Maison d'Édition de l'Académie des Sciences de Hongrie, 1965), pp. 83–103.

[68] Pamlényi, *History*, pp. 113–114; Michaud, "L'Europe Centrale," pp. 200–201; Rhode, "Ungarn," p. 1083.

[69] Marczali, *Ungarische Verfassungsgeschichte*, pp. 60–66; Eszlary, *Histoire*, vol. II, pp. 348–351; Pamlényi, *History*, pp. 116–118.

would assume the Hungarian throne if and when the Bohemian line of the Jagiellonians died out – came into force. Following another crushing defeat at Buda in 1541, the country was divided into three parts: Transylvania, a Turkish vassal state ruled by a Hungarian prince; central Hungary, under direct Ottoman control; and the west and north of the country, which remained free under a Habsburg monarch. This tripartite division would only be overcome in 1699 with the final defeat of the Turks.[70]

The arrival of the Habsburgs to the Hungarian throne brought notable benefits. With their substantial family lands and position as Holy Roman emperors, the Habsburgs were able to provide the military might necessary to protect the country in the future and, eventually, to drive out the Ottomans. Initially, they seemed content, as absentee rulers, to leave the domestic order laid down in the *Tripartitum* largely untouched. In fact, the degree of local elite control was increased substantially in 1548 when it was decreed that the viscount, leader of the county during the frequent absences of the count, would henceforth be elected by all of the local nobility rather than appointed by his superior. Yet with the growing fervor of the Counter-Reformation during the late 16th century, the Habsburgs became ever more determined to stamp out religious pluralism and impose absolutism upon Hungary, if necessary with the help of the foreign troops garrisoned there to protect the country against the Turks.[71]

While the ideology of noble liberty and equality may have masked the reality of baronial dominance in the past, it now served to unite the nobility around a defense of their common privileges, which they of course linked to the defense of the nation as a whole against domination by a foreign dynasty. Moreover, the institutions of local noble self-government, when combined with the still-substantial resources of the great families, proved ideally suited to organizing armed resistance to central authority. In 1606, encouraged by the Diet and led by the aristocrat Stefan Bocskay, the country revolted against the persecution of the Protestants by a high-handed government, and succeeded in forcing the removal of King Rudolf and his replacement in 1608 by his brother Matthias. Matthias reconfirmed – as did his elected successor Ferdinand in 1618 – all of the traditional Hungarian privileges, including the Diet's powers in the areas of taxation and legislation and its right to choose the palatine who acted as the country's chief executive during the almost constant absences of the Habsburgs. The Diet exploited its

---

[70] Rhode, "Ungarn," pp. 1081–1089.
[71] Marczali, *Ungarische Verfassungsgeschichte*, pp. 77–79; Pamlényi, *History*, pp. 144–146; Eszlary, *Histoire*, vol. II, p. 226.

strong position after the Bocskay Rebellion by passing new laws which
increased the role of the rank-and-file nobleman in the county courts,
and extended the judicial powers of the nobility over both their peasants and the economic life of the county towns, many of which had
previously enjoyed a degree of autonomy in that area.[72]

It was also at this time that the internal composition of Hungary's
national representative assembly was permanently fixed. Henceforth
(until 1848), the Diet consisted of two chambers or "tables." The first
or upper table was made up of the bishops, chief officers of state, and
the titled nobility (the former barons); the second consisted of two representatives from each county elected by its nobility, two representatives
from each of the 14 (later 39) royal towns, one from each cathedral
chapter, the abbots appearing personally, and – most curiously – the
proxies for titled nobles not able to appear in person at the upper
table. In 1721, the upper table numbered 156 members and the lower
table 242.[73] It was now up to the Hungarian nobility to ensure that the
powers of their parliament remained undiminished in the future, for
Rudolf of Habsburg's attempt to impose absolutism would not be the
last.

Poland

Unlike its Hungarian counterpart, the Polish kingdom did not face a
sustained geopolitical threat of a magnitude capable of inducing attempted changes to the state apparatus until the 1500s. However,
throughout the 1300s and 1400s, Poland engaged in intermittent clashes
with its neighbors the Teutonic Knights, clashes which played a significant role in the country's constitutional development. The Knights were
a German military order founded in the Holy Land but forced to return to Europe following the fall of Jerusalem in 1187. In 1226, they
accepted, with papal and imperial approval, an invitation by the Piast
duke Conrad of Mazovia to establish themselves in the frontier regions
to the northeast of Poland to act as the vanguard of Christendom
against the pagan Slavic tribes (Prussians, Lithuanians, Latvians) found
there. Relations between the Piast duchies and the Order were initially
quite good but soured in 1308 when the Knights conquered the previously Polish area of Eastern Pomerania and briefly spilled over into
active warfare between 1327 and 1333. However, upon his ascension to

[72] Marczali, *Ungarische Verfassungsgeschichte*, pp. 79–80; Pamlényi, *History*, pp. 147–150; Rhode, "Ungarn," pp. 1103–1105.
[73] Marczali, *Ungarische Verfassungsgeschichte*, pp. 81–82; György Bónis, "Die ungarischen Stände in der ersten Hälfte des 18. Jahrhunderts," in: Gerhard, *Ständische Vertretungen*, pp. 286–309, here at pp. 295–299.

the throne, Casimir the Great arranged a truce with the Order and signed a treaty in 1343 which secured peace between the two states throughout his long reign and that of his successor.[74]

The 1386 marriage of Louis of Anjou's daughter and successor Jadwiga with the Lithuanian grand duke Władysław Jagiełło altered the relationship between Poland and the Teutonic Knights. Under the terms of this marriage, which linked Lithuania in personal union with the Polish kingdom, Jagiełło and his subjects agreed to be baptized. A large new Christian polity was thereby created which virtually surrounded the Knights and eliminated their justification for further expansion. The result was a series of low-intensity conflicts (1389–1404, 1409–1422, 1454–1466, 1519–1525) which continued until the Order's secularization in 1525 in the wake of the Reformation, when Poland was finally able to regain Eastern Pomerania and convert Prussia into a Polish fief.[75]

The most tangible result of these conflicts was, as in Hungary, an increase in the hold of the nobility over the state, but the manner in which this occurred was more complicated than in the Hungarian case. As mentioned earlier, a national representative assembly (Sejm) first appeared in Poland between 1384 and 1386, during the confused period following the death of Louis of Anjou. At its birth, the assembly was already powerful enough to force upon Queen Jadwiga its own choice of a husband, the heathen Władysław Jagiełło. During his long reign (1386–1434) that foreign prince found it wise, given his own weak political standing and the pressures of war with the Order, to consult annually with the Sejm on matters of legislation, taxation, and general government policy. In 1425, and again in 1430 and 1433, he was even required to submit his choice of a successor to this body for approval, even though he had produced male heirs. At approximately the same time, the idea of the "Crown of Poland" (*corona regni Poloniae*) came to be used as an impersonal symbol of state sovereignty. As in Hungary, sovereignty was vested in the community of nobles as represented in the Sejm.[76]

Like the royal council of which they were a kind of expanded version, the early Polish parliaments were in fact heavily aristocratic in

---

[74] Hans Patze, "Der Deutschordenstaat Preussen 1226–1466," in: Schieder, *Handbuch*, vol. II, pp. 468–489, here at pp. 469–476; Davies, *God's Playground*, pp. 87–91, 95; Zamoyski, *Polish Way*, pp. 28–34, 36; Hoensch, *Geschichte*, pp. 40–41, 47–49, 54.

[75] Hoensch, *Geschichte*, pp. 75–78, 85–86, 101–103; Zamoyski, *Poland's Way*, pp. 46–47; Davies, *God's Playground*, pp. 116–117, 120–124, 143.

[76] Bardach, "Formation des Assemblées," pp. 262, 264–265; idem, "Gouvernants et Gouvernés," pp. 263, 266–268; Kutrzeba, *Grundriss*, pp. 109–110, 122; Gieysztor, *History*, 133, 145; Davies, *God's Playground*, pp. 117–118.

character, composed mainly of the officeholders of the *ziemie* supplemented by a small number of lesser nobles and, occasionally, by representatives of the cities and lesser clergy. As such, these assemblies were an accurate reflection of the weak position of the lesser nobility, despite the charters of 1355 and 1374, vis-à-vis their wealthier brothers. It was above all the conflict with the Teutonic Knights which, over the course of the 15th century, helped to alter this balance of forces. Already in 1404, when Władysław sought to levy a tax in order to buy back the district of Dobrzyn from the Knights, he thought it necessary to seek approval beyond the Sejm. To this end, he called meetings of the local *colloquia* which, against the older practice, were made up not just of local aristocratic officeholders, but rather of all members of the *ziemia* nobility, just like the county assemblies of Hungary. Once called into being, these new bodies – later called *sejmiki* or "little Sejms" – soon supplanted the traditional *colloquia* as the basic forum for local administrative, judicial, financial, and military business.[77]

Yet the lesser nobility was not satisfied with this increased influence in local affairs, and soon learned to exploit its position as the backbone of the Polish military to extract further concessions from the king and the aristocracy. In 1422, while on a campaign against the Order, the assembled army suddenly converted itself into a massive, armed Sejm dominated by the former knightly class. This impromptu Sejm forced Władysław to grant a charter protecting all noble property from occupation or confiscation without due process of law, a measure directed against aristocratic expropriation of their weaker neighbors' land. In the aftermath of this show of strength, the king sought the explicit approval of the *sejmiki* for his son's succession, and in 1430 conceded to the whole nobility the right of *neminem captivabimus*, the equivalent of habeas corpus. Finally, in 1454, another army revolt forced the king to grant the Privilege of Nieszawa, which stated that no new taxes could be levied or troops mobilized without the consent of the *sejmiki*, thereby elevating the latter to the status of "co-rulers" (Bardach) with the aristocratic Diet.[78]

In consequence, after 1454 Władysław's son Casimir IV (1446–1492) was required to consult both the Diet and the *sejmiki* on all important matters of state and to gain their approval for any new impositions. In 1493, this cumbersome arrangement was superceded when the *sejmiki*

[77] Bardach, "Formation des Assemblées," pp. 262–264, 269–272; idem, "Gouvernants et Gouvernés," pp. 264–266; Górski, "Chartes de la Noblesse," p. 258; Kutrzeba, *Grundriss*, pp. 123, 125.
[78] Górski, "Chartes de la Noblesse," pp. 258–266; Bardach, "Formation des Assemblées," pp. 265–266, 272–275; idem, "Gouvernants et Gouvernés," pp. 267, 269; Hoensch, *Geschichte*, pp. 81, 85–86.

agreed to send representatives to form a separate Chamber of Deputies in the Diet. The old Diet, its membership reduced to the bishops and officers of state comprising the royal council and the palatines and castellans of the *ziemie*, then chose to call itself the Senate. In 1505, the Chamber, stronghold of the lower nobility, ensured its future equality with the aristocratic Senate by engineering passage of the statute known as *Nihil Novi*, which declared that no new legislation could be passed nor taxes imposed without the consent of both houses of the new, expanded Sejm.[79] At that time, the assembly numbered 123 members (87 senators and 36 deputies, two from each of the 18 *ziemie*). After the extension of *ziemie* to Lithuania and its representation in the Sejm following the full union of the two countries in 1569, this figure rose to 283 (140 senators, 143 deputies). In the 18th century, when there were 64 *ziemie* (30 Polish, 34 Lithuanian), the number of deputies increased yet again to 236.[80]

Throughout the remainder of the 16th century, the nobility continued to expand its political power at the expense of the king. In 1518, it deprived the royal courts of any appellate jurisdiction over peasants on noble lands – which covered 60% of the country – thereby leaving those peasants entirely at the mercy of their lords, even in cases of crimes carrying the death penalty. Since Church property (15%) had also long since acquired full legal immunity, this effectively meant that royal judicial authority of any kind now applied only to the 25% of Polish territory (18th century: 19%) that remained part of the ruler's domain, and much of that was leased out to noble tenants.[81]

While the conflict with the Teutonic Knights exercised a profound influence on the future shape of Poland's political regime, it was the intensification of geopolitical competition associated with the rise of Muscovy/Russia and Sweden to the east and north and the growth of Habsburg and Ottoman power to the south which led to repeated royal attempts to build up the power of the central government in order to defend the country more effectively. Following the victory of Muscovy over its Russian rivals during the last decades of the 15th century, the Grand Duchy turned its ambitions to the west, towards Lithuania, now united in personal union with the Polish Crown. The result was a series of wars between Poland and Muscovy which began in 1486 and

[79] Bardach, "Formation des Assemblées," pp. 275–280, 285–287, 290–295; idem, "Gouvernants et Gouvernés," pp. 270–271; Kutrzeba, *Grundriss*, pp. 111–112, 121–126; Hoensch, *Geschichte*, pp. 97–98.

[80] Kutrzeba, *Grundriss*, pp. 121, 124, 127; Davies, *God's Playground*, p. 330; Roos, "Ständewesen," p. 361; Zamoyski, *Polish Way*, pp. 97, 100.

[81] Hoensch, *Geschichte*, p. 95; Kutrzeba, *Grundriss*, p. 83; Davies, *God's Playground*, p. 218; Roos, "Ständewesen," pp. 343–344.

continued on and off throughout the 1500s. While the long conflict with the Order was finally laid to rest in 1525, the Ottoman victory at Mohács the following year not only extended the Turkish threat to the border of Poland, it also brought the ambitious and wealthy Habsburgs to the thrones of neighboring Bohemia and unoccupied Hungary.

In order to meet these new geopolitical challenges, both Kings Sigismund the Old (reigned 1506–1548) and his son Sigismund Augustus sought the approval of the Sejm, most notably between 1510 and 1515 and again in the early 1560s, for the permanent taxes needed to finance a professional army to supplement the noble forces raised in the *ziemie*. In spite of the number and strength of the country's foreign rivals, these efforts yielded little. The legislature, fearful of placing a powerful military instrument in the hands of the king, grudgingly agreed in 1563 to introduce a single modest tax (the *kwarta*) capable of supporting a token force of 4,000 men. The size of the army was only permitted to rise to 12,000 by the mid-1600s, despite the pleas for action of successive monarchs and the appearance in the interim of new threats from Sweden, Denmark, and the Brandenburg-Prussia of the Great Elector.[82]

The death of Sigismund Augustus, last of the Jagiellonians, in 1572 presented another opportunity to weaken royal power, for the Sejm decided that henceforth the monarch should be elected by all nobles appearing in person (*viritim*). This move underlined the fact that the nobility saw itself as the collective owners of the state and the king merely as their chosen manager. In keeping with this view, the successful candidate would also be presented with a set of conditions to which he would have to agree before assuming the throne. These conditions, called the Henrician Articles after the first king (Henry de Valois 1573–1574) to whom they were put, henceforth functioned as a kind of constitution for a polity now popularly referred to as the "republic of nobles" (*respublica nobilium*).[83] The Articles declared that the ruler could neither raise taxes, call out the army, nor make new laws touching on the privileges of the nobility without the consent of the Sejm, which he was obliged to convoke at least once every two years. The Articles also

---

[82]   Gotthold Rhode, "Polen-Litauen vom Ende der Verbindung mit Ungarn bis zum Ende der Vasas (1444–1669)," in: Schieder, *Handbuch*, vol. III, pp. 1003–1060, here at pp. 1021, 1027; Kutrzeba, *Grundriss*, pp. 144–145; Hoensch, *Geschichte*, p. 142; Gieysztor et al., *History*, p. 224; Davies, *God's Playground*, vol. I, p. 445.

[83]   Bardach, "Gouvernants et Gouvernés," p. 275. The new polity formed in 1569 through the full unification of Poland and Lithuania was officially termed a *Rzeczpospolita*, a direct translation of the Latin *res publica*, though many commentators prefer to translate this as "commonwealth" rather than "republic." As Norman Davies has pointed out, "monarchical republic" is probably the most accurate way to describe the Polish form of government. See his *God's Playground*, pp. 369–370.

assigned a group of 16 senators to advise the king between meetings of the assembly. Most significant of all, the Articles permitted nobles to refuse to obey the monarch if he failed to respect any of the terms of his electoral agreement, thereby legalizing the formation of armed confederations (*confederationes, rokoszy*) as a means of bringing errant rulers to heel.[84]

During the last decades of the 16th century, already meager royal powers were reduced still further. In legislation of 1578 and 1601, the Sejm claimed the exclusive right to admit new members to the nobility, and shortly thereafter the king lost the last vestiges of his judicial authority over that group. As far back as the reign of Casimir the Great, the powers of *ziemie* judges had been circumscribed by the presence on the bench of lay assessors chosen from among the local elite, and by the early 1400s the king was forced to choose the *ziemie* judges from among four candidates proposed by the *sejmik*. In 1501, the last significant local official answerable directly to the monarch, the *starosta*, had won life tenure, thereby freeing himself from royal influence. After that date, Poland's kings still retained the right to hear appeals from the nobility and try them for high crimes and misdemeanors in his court, but in 1579 the Sejm transferred these prerogatives to a Crown Tribunal made up of judges elected by the *ziemie*. Finally, in 1590, the assembly took full control of the state's finances, setting aside a number of income sources for the king's personal use and assigning all other revenues to a new parliamentary treasury (the Rawa Chamber).[85] It is hardly surprising in this context that the Sejm repeatedly rejected demands by the Vasa kings Sigismund III (1587–1632) and Władysław IV (1632–1648) for reforms aimed at strengthening the executive in the interest of national defense, despite the fact that these rulers had involved their country in a series of murderous wars with their Swedish cousins which would last until 1660 and which were pursued in parallel to the endemic conflict with Muscovy/Russia.[86]

Throughout these centuries, the nobility sought to exploit its growing control of political institutions to strengthen its position vis-à-vis other social groups. Thus in 1459, the Diet declared its right to pass legislation affecting the royal cities without their explicit consent, and in 1496 and again in 1538 burghers were forbidden to buy landed estates. Throughout this period, the nobility used legal restrictions to favor its own

---

[84] Gieysztor et al., *History*, pp. 190–192; Kutrzeba, *Grundriss*, pp. 165–169; Davies, *God's Playground*, pp. 334–335, 339–340.

[85] Kutrzeba, *Grundriss*, pp. 60, 113, 121, 131, 134–136, 139–140, 147, 174, 183–185, 189–190, 237; Davies, *God's Playground*, pp. 335, 349; Górski, "Chartes de la Noblesse," pp. 258, 266, 268.

[86] Gieysztor et al., *History*, p. 209.

commercial interests at the expense of those of the (free) towns. Such efforts culminated in the full noble exemptions from the import tariffs introduced in 1507 and 1509 and the 1565 attempt (largely unsuccessful) to ban Polish merchants from both the grain export and foreign import trades. More effective were a series of laws which by 1563 had left the local (aristocratic) palatine with the power to set prices in all of the *ziemia*'s towns, and in 1565 made the smaller free cities answerable to the *starosta*.[87]

As one would expect, a similar torrent of self-serving legislation fell upon the defenseless heads of Poland's peasantry. In 1421, the first statute was passed introducing mandatory unpaid labor service, in this case in Mazovia, and in 1520 the Sejm generalized this requirement to one day of labor service per week applicable throughout the country. In 1423, the nobility granted itself permission to remove without replacement an unruly *soltys*, a kind of village mayor, and during the next century and a half this office was progressively eliminated. Beginning in 1496, peasant mobility was also restricted by law, the first step in a process of tying peasants to the soil that would be completed in 1543. Finally, as mentioned above, in 1518 the Sejm eliminated all rights to appeal against the judgments issued by one's lord in his seigneurial court. Taken together, these exploitive measures left the country's rural population entirely at the mercy, both economic and political, of the landowning nobility by the end of the 16th century.[88] They also illustrate quite clearly the fact that, as in Hungary, the extraordinary socioeconomic power which the Polish nobility enjoyed over peasants and towns in the 18th century was a *consequence* of its earlier conquest of political power, rather than the other way around, as traditional Marxist historiography has often asserted.

Although the Sejm's exploitation of its political supremacy to weaken the position of the king, the burghers, and the peasantry brought short-term gains to the nobility as a whole, in the longer term it only served to enhance the position of the higher nobility, and especially its wealthiest members, the magnates. This occurred for two reasons. On the one hand, the higher nobility possessed the resources to derive the greatest economic advantage from restrictions placed on city dwellers and the rural population. On the other hand, the decline of the king and the towns deprived the lesser nobility of potential allies with whom they could have made common cause against the magnates. Thrown back

---

[87] Kutrzeba, *Grundriss*, pp. 87–94, 152–154; Gieysztor, *History*, pp. 177–178; Hoensch, *Geschichte*, pp. 95–96.
[88] Kutrzeba, *Grundriss*, pp. 82–87, 157–161; Gieysztor, *History*, p. 177; Hoensch, *Geschichte*, pp. 95–96; Davies, *God's Playground*, pp. 211–212.

entirely on their own resources, the lesser nobles proved unable to defend themselves either politically or materially against the great families of the realm. By 1648, nearly 60% of all nobles owned little or no land, and many were forced to place themselves in the hands of their wealthier brothers in order to survive. Even those lesser nobles who still possessed property often found it advantageous to become the clients of one of the aristocratic families of their *ziemie*, just like their counterparts in Hungary.[89]

In fact, the first signs of rising magnate power in the political sphere date to the decision in 1573 to permit all nobles to participate in person (*viritim*) in the selection of a new king. It was the great families who stood behind this constitutional change, for they correctly surmised that they would be able to exercise greater control over thousands of poor, landless electors than over an independent-minded Sejm. It was this same period that also saw increasingly successful attempts by the *sejmiki*, themselves ever more under the sway of local aristocrats, to tie the hands of their representatives by depriving them of the full powers of decision (*plena potestas*) they had acquired in the early 1500s and instead imposing imperative mandates upon them. Most ominously of all, the magnates also began during the latter part of the century to insist that all decisions taken by the Sejm required unanimity, a principle which after 1648 would lead to the infamous *liberum veto*.[90]

This strategy of undermining a Sejm which had itself just finished undermining the king was an attractive one to the magnates. It permitted nearly all of what remained of state authority to be concentrated in the *ziemie*, from whence it could be more readily swallowed up by the vast private power of the magnates. As mentioned earlier, by the late 1500s *ziemia* officials and local nobles had assumed from the ruler all judicial functions not already taken over by the landowners themselves, and in the period up to 1648 the locus of financial administration also shifted to the provinces, with tax assessment, collection, and administration in the hands of local notables or officials responsible to the *sejmiki*.[91]

Increasingly, however, control over these organs of local government fell entirely into the hands of the magnates, and those organs came to look like nothing more than "public" adjuncts of their great private empires. This development is hardly surprising given the fact that the

[89] Roos, "Ständewesen," pp. 329, 340; Gieysztor, *History*, pp. 223–224; Bardach, "Gouvernants et Gouvernés," p. 278; Davies, *God's Playground*, pp. 226–227, 229.

[90] Gieysztor, *History*, pp. 188–190, 192, 225; Bardach, "Formation des Assemblées," pp. 288–289; idem, "Gouvernants et Gouvernés," p. 272; Kutrzeba, *Grundriss*, pp. 171–173.

[91] Kutrzeba, *Grundriss*, pp. 176, 187–188; Gieysztor, *History*, p. 225.

leading magnate families all owned properties of between 5,000 and
25,000 square kilometers, each of which contained dozens of towns,
hundreds of villages, and, on average, about 50,000 "subjects." Indeed,
by the early 1600s the holdings of the greatest aristocrats had come to
resemble small states, complete with capital cities, court systems, hundreds of officials and retainers, and private armies numbering several
thousand men.[92] In order to guarantee the smooth functioning of their
own "states," the magnates wished the institutions of the Polish Commonwealth to remain as weak as possible, and in the *liberum veto* they
were soon to discover the weapon that would ensure just that.

Thus in both the Hungarian and Polish cases, the primary effect of late-
arriving geopolitical pressure on states with structurally weak central
authorities but strong, independent organs of local government was to
permit the numerically large (5–10% of population) nobilities who had
rendered those organs their exclusive domain to gain complete control
of their respective political systems. By the end of the 1500s, the Hungarian and Polish nobilities exercised power at the national level through
bicameral, territorially based parliaments. In Hungary, this outcome
quickly led to military defeat and a loss of external sovereignty which,
paradoxically, helped preserve total noble domination of domestic
political and economic life. In Poland, noble domination soon gave way
to magnate domination, a dynamic of development that would ultimately lead to a disaster far greater than that of Mohács.

INTERNAL AND EXTERNAL THREATS TO PATRIMONIAL
CONSTITUTIONALISM IN HUNGARY AND POLAND,
1648–1795

After 1648 the well-entrenched Hungarian and Polish variants of
patrimonial constitutionalism faced very different kinds of challenges.
In Hungary, the main threat to the nobility's continuing hold over the
state came from the country's Habsburg rulers, who attempted repeatedly to introduce absolutism from above by force. However, numerous
noble-led rebellions, combined with the emergence of a class of Catholic magnates acceptable to the Austrians as domestic political leaders,
succeeded in safeguarding the Hungarian elite's internal control at the
cost of relinquishing most influence over foreign and military affairs.
    In Poland, by contrast, the threat to the established order came not

---

[92] Roos, "Ständewesen," pp. 330–331, 340–341; Davies, *God's Playground*, pp. 219–228;
Gieysztor, *History*, p. 224; Hoensch, *Geschichte*, pp. 126–127, 142.

from authoritarian monarchs but from foreign enemies. The Commonwealth found itself surrounded by four major powers: Sweden, Brandenburg-Prussia, Austria, and Russia. While other polities across the continent were busy reacting to similar pressures by concentrating resources in the hands of central governments in order to increase their military capacities, the private interests of Poland's overweening magnates dictated the opposite course of action. Instead of centralizing power, they devolved it more and more to noble-controlled organs of local government. As a result, the country soon proved incapable of defending itself and, between 1773 and 1795, was partitioned out of existence by its ambitious neighbors.

Hungary

After the end of the Thirty Years War and the victory of the Counter-Reformation throughout most of the Habsburg lands, the Austrians turned their attentions once again to the eyesore of Hungary's patrimonial constitutionalism. It was during the reign of Leopold I (1655–1690 in Hungary, 1657–1705 in the Empire) that a pattern of political development first appeared that would last until 1711. In that pattern, Habsburg military successes against the Turks encouraged heightened political and religious coercion in Hungary, which in turn provoked noble-led rebellions in defense of local "liberties."

Thus, the victories of 1663 and 1664 led to an increased persecution of Protestants, a neglect of the Diet and a record of violence by foreign troops which in turn spawned the Wesselényi Revolt of 1670 that attracted both Protestant and Catholic aristocrats. Once this poorly organized challenge to his authority was put down, Leopold did away with the Hungarian constitution altogether (1673), but this step was soon met by a much more powerful rebellion – under the leadership of the Lutheran magnate Pál Thököly – which lasted for eight years (1674–1682) and forced the king to restore the old order intact in 1681. Renewed military successes in 1685–1687, combined with constitutional guarantees and promises to restore religious tolerance, finally allowed Leopold to achieve one lasting alteration to Hungary's informal constitution. In 1687, he persuaded the Diet to make the throne hereditary in the male line for the first time since the Árpáds and to strike the right of resistance (article 31) from the still valid Golden Bull.[93]

[93] Marczali, *Ungarische Verfassungsgeschichte*, pp. 86–89; Rhode, "Ungarn," pp. 1112–1115; R. J. W. Evans, *The Making of the Habsburg Monarchy 1550–1700: An Interpretation* (Oxford: Clarendon, 1979), pp. 237–238, 261–264; Jean Bérenger, *Finances et Absolutisme Autrichien dans la Seconde Moitié du XVIIe Siècle* (Paris: Publications de la Sorbonne, 1975), pp. 222–228.

Over the next 12 years, the reconquest of of Turkish-occupied Hungary (with the exception of the Banat) was completed, and the country finally reunited after more than 150 years of division through the Peace of Karlowitz (January 26, 1699). Yet as usual with the Habsburgs, success led to excess, and during the 1690s troops were used to round up recruits and to collect taxes without the approval of the Diet. Meanwhile, a plan was drawn up to eliminate Hungarian particularism, by force if necessary, following the final victory over the Turks. This last attempt to impose Counter-Reformation absolutism on the country was met by the greatest rebellion of all, that of Ferenc Rákóczi (1703–1711). In what amounted to a national uprising, Rákóczi was able to fight the Austrian forces to a standstill. The Peace of Szatmár (1711) provided the basis for a permanent settlement between ruler and local elites, worked out over the next 12 years, that would remain undisturbed until Joseph II's reform attempts in the 1780s.[94]

According to the terms of this settlement, the Habsburgs were permitted to raise permanent, professional regiments in Hungary that were, however, integrated into a single imperial army administered from Vienna. In order to finance these troops, the Diet granted in 1715, and regularly renewed thereafter, a direct tax (the contribution) from which the nobility was exempted. Foreign policy, of course, remained in royal hands. In all other respects, however, the old order was fully restored and guaranteed. The day-to-day direction of the country lay with a regency council headed by a palatine elected for life by the Diet, and the consent of that body was still required for any new taxes or legislation. More important still, tax collection, military recruitment, and local justice remained entirely in the hands of the self-governing county communities and of private noble landlords: no bureaucratic infrastructure was ever permanently introduced into Hungary until the 19th century.[95]

The dominant role in 18th-century Hungarian government at both the national and county levels was played by a group of 30 to 40 magnate families whose wealth and standing were comparable to their Polish counterparts. Unlike the latter, however, aristocrats like the Esterházy and Károlyi had a strong interest in ensuring that the key institutions

---

[94] Pamlényi, *History*, pp. 171–178; Marczali, *Ungarische Verfassungsgeschichte*, pp. 89–91; Rhode, "Ungarn," p. 1116.

[95] Marczali, *Ungarische Verfassungsgeschichte*, pp. 93–103, 112–113; Michaud, "L'Europe Centrale," pp. 190, 201–204; Jean Bérenger and Daniel Tollet, "La Genèse de l'État Moderne en Europe Orientale: Synthèse et Bilan," in: Jean-Philippe Genet (ed.), *L'État Moderne: Genèse* (Paris: Editions du CNRS, 1990), pp. 43–63, here at pp. 55–56, 62; P. G. M. Dickson, *Finance and Government under Maria Theresia 1740–1780*, 2 vols. (Oxford: Clarendon, 1987), vol. II, pp. 255–258.

of patrimonial constitutionalism – the Diet and the county assembly – functioned well, for the alternative was direct rule from Vienna through an alien (or native) professional bureaucracy. Following the return of nearly all the great noble families to Catholicism by the late 1600s, their forging of cultural and personal links with the aristocracies of other Habsburg dominions, and their support of Maria Theresia's ascension to the throne in 1740, Habsburg rulers became reconciled to leaving a substantial measure of local power in magnate hands.[96]

It was Maria Theresia's son, Joseph II, who presented the final challenge to the Hungarian ancien régime under the banner of enlightened absolutism. Between 1785 and 1787, he launched a direct assault on the county, converting it into a simple administrative district overseen by royal officials alone. At the same time, he put an end to justice by amateurs, creating instead a professional judiciary manned by trained jurists. In 1787, however, a war broke out with Turkey, and the new government machinery proved incapable of accomplishing the tasks thrust upon it, due above all to the noncooperation of the county nobility. In 1790, Joseph was forced to withdraw all of his reforms and return the country to the status quo ante of 1780. The old order, well entrenched after seven centuries, had once again demonstrated its capacity for resistance. In 1791, in the midst of a revolutionary age, the Hungarian Diet solemnly reaffirmed the rights and privileges of the native nobility.[97]

Poland

While the protection from external threats provided by the Habsburg military umbrella permitted the Hungarian nobility to devote all its energies to defending patrimonial constitutionalism at home, their Polish counterparts enjoyed no such luxury. It was precisely during the period from 1648 to 1721, when the Austrians finally succeeded in removing the Turkish presence from Hungary, that the Polish Commonwealth suffered a series of reverses on the battlefield – reverses attributable largely to the country's sociopolitical system – from which it was never really to recover.

In 1648, the Cossacks of the Ukraine revolted against the local Polish aristocracy, and in 1654 Russia invaded the Commonwealth in support of the Cossacks. Seeking to take advantage of this situation, Poland's other neighbors – Sweden, Brandenburg-Prussia, and Transylvania – all

[96]   Evans, *Habsburg Monarchy*, p. 240; Dickson, *Finance and Government*, vol. I, pp. 104–114.
[97]   Marczali, *Ungarische Verfassungsgeschichte*, pp. 114–122; Pamlényi, *History*, pp. 201–204.

launched attacks on the country. This unleashed a period of unparalleled suffering known as "the Deluge" which was comparable to German experiences during the Thirty Years War. However, when King Jan Casimir attempted to take advantage of this terrible experience to introduce changes aimed at restoring some power to the central government, he was opposed by the aristocratic confederation led by the Marshall of the Crown Jerzy Lubomirski, which successfully fought its own government for two years (1665–1667) to prevent reform.[98]

Miraculously, the Commonwealth was able to survive, albeit with substantial territorial losses, and peace was concluded with Sweden in 1660 and Russia in 1667. However, these horrific conflicts served only to increase the power of the magnates. The defense of the country lay on the one hand with their private armies, which as mentioned earlier could often number several thousand men; and on the other with the *sejmiki*, largely under aristocratic control. These bodies not only levied and retained their own taxes, but also hired their own troops, a practice that would continue until 1717.[99] The true locus of power in the country during this time was revealed by the election of two successive magnates to the Polish throne, Michal Wiśniowiecki (1669–1673) and Jan Sobieski (1674–1696).

Sobieski, himself a great general and the victor over the Turks at Vienna in 1683, attempted to make a virtue of necessity by incorporating magnate forces into the Commonwealth's standing army, thereby raising its size from 18,000 to as many as 54,000 soldiers.[100] Yet with Poland now surrounded by three hostile powers, each possessing an army of over 100,000 men, this was too little, too late. In 1699, Sobieski's successor, the Saxon August the Strong, decided to seek out Russia as an ally against Sweden and Brandenburg-Prussia. Even with Russian assistance, however, the country proved unable to defend itself during the Great Northern War of 1700 to 1721. In 1717, August was forced to place the future of his subjects in the hands of the Russians, who henceforth became the "protectors" of Poland and guarantors of her constitution.[101]

In practice, this meant that the Russians would tolerate no attempts to reverse the developments of the past two centuries and introduce the reforms necessary to build up central state power. Thus, while the occupiers did permit the transfer of some measure of financial control

---

[98] Davies, *God's Playground*, pp. 463–469; Hoensch, *Geschichte*, pp. 143–152; Gieysztor et al., *History*, pp. 242–253; Roos, "Ständewesen," pp. 347–348.
[99] Kutzeba, *Grundriss*, pp. 186–187, 194–195.
[100] Davies, *God's Playground*, p. 478.
[101] Davies, *God's Playground*, pp. 495–504; Hoensch, *Geschichte*, pp. 155–160; Gieysztor et al., *History*, pp. 272–283.

from the *sejmiki* back to the Rawa Chamber, they reduced the size of the Polish army to 24,000 and did nothing to prevent the ever more frequent use of the *liberum veto* (the right of any single Sejm member to block legislation), employed at the behest of the magnates to ensure that the central authorities remained almost entirely powerless. First invoked in 1652 and then again in 15 of 44 Sejm sessions through the end of the century, the *veto* disrupted more than half of all parliaments under August the Strong and all but one under his successor August III (1733–1763), thereby completely paralyzing government activity.[102]

With the advent of the native-born Stanisław August Poniatowski (1764–1795) to the throne in 1764, the final drama of the Commonwealth commenced as desperate attempts were made to head off the complete disintegration of the Polish state by introducing long-overdue reforms. While these attempts were repeatedly sabotaged by the actions of Russia and Prussia and their agents within Poland, in both the 1760s and again in the early 1790s outside intervention provoked the formation of pro-reform confederations which could only be put down by the combined forces of anti-reform magnates and/or the Russian army.

Once the reformers had been defeated, the price imposed on a defenseless nation was repeated annexations by Russia, Prussia, and Austria.[103] Yet the Polish Commonwealth which finally disappeared from the map of Europe in 1795 had long since died, its governing capacities and authority drained away over many centuries by a narrow and self-serving elite. In a competitive geopolitical environment, the inevitable fate of this particularly pure form of patrimonial constitutionalism was extinction.

ABORTIVE PATRIMONIAL CONSTITUTIONALISM IN SCANDINAVIA

In light of the preceding analysis of Hungary and Poland, the cases of Denmark and Sweden must appear problematic. Both of these kingdoms were, like Hungary and Poland, "new foundations"; that is, they arose upon territories not previously encumbered by failed large-scale, post-Roman state formation. As a result, just like their counterparts in east-central Europe and the British Isles, they were built around territorially integrated, increasingly participatory forms of local government. Furthermore, just like Hungary and Poland, Denmark and Sweden only became subject to persistent geopolitical pressures of a magnitude

---

[102] Davies, *God's Playground*, pp. 346–347, 502; Gieysztor, *History*, p. 259; Kutrzeba, *Grundriss*, pp. 172–173, 177, 187–188.
[103] Davies, *God's Playground*, pp. 517–542; Hoensch, *Geschichte*, pp. 162–168.

great enough to induce changes in their administrative and financial infrastructures relatively late, during the 1500s and 1600s.

Given these facts, one would expect the Scandinavian kingdoms of the 18th century very much to resemble their Polish and Hungarian counterparts to the southeast. Yet by and large they did not. While, as will be shown below, the trajectory followed by Denmark and Sweden during the middle ages did indeed parallel closely that of Hungary and Poland, both began to follow different paths during the early modern period. After a kind of coup d'état in 1660, Denmark was transformed from a noble-dominated polity with a minimal state apparatus into an absolutist monarchy equipped with a proto-modern bureaucracy constructed largely along German lines. While Sweden also introduced a similarly structured bureaucracy at about this time, a relatively strong national representative body (the Riksdag) ensured that the country moved increasingly in the direction of the bureaucratic constitutionalism pioneered in England rather than the bureaucratic absolutism of Germany and Denmark. However, Sweden's constitutionalism was twice interrupted (1681–1718, 1772–1809) by royal initiatives, ultimately unsuccesssful, aimed at introducing absolutism there as well. In the remainder of this section, a brief attempt will be made to account for these unexpected Scandinavian outcomes.

Denmark

The early histories of the Danish and Polish kingdoms exhibit striking parallels to one another. It was in the same year, 966, that their respective founding figures, Harold Bluetooth and Mieszko, converted to Christianity, in both cases to forestall the threat of invasion from an Ottonian Germany then at the height of its powers. Extensive ecclesiastical infrastructures, constructed with the help of foreign churchmen, then permitted these state-forming rulers and their successors to consolidate their control over far-flung territories which had long been divided among rival tribal groupings. In Denmark, as in Poland, and nearly all other western polities of the period, a central administration soon emerged which was built around a number of court officials (indirectly) modeled on those of the Carolingians: a chancellor, chamberlain, marshall, and justiciar.[104]

---

[104] Malcolm Barber, *The Two Cities* (London: Routledge, 1992), pp. 380–382; Lucien Musset, *Les Peuples Scandinaves au Moyen Âge* (Paris: Presses Universitaires de France, 1951), pp. 126–127; Aksel Christensen, H. P. Clausen, Svend Ellehøj, and Søren Mørch (eds.), *Danmarks Histoire*, 5 vols. (Copenhagen: Gyldendal, 1977), vol. I, pp. 274–275.

More importantly still, the new Danish kingdom rested, just as did its Polish, Hungarian, and English counterparts, upon the foundations of territorially integrated, participatory organs of local government. These were the *landskaber* or provinces, corresponding roughly to Poland's *ziemie*; and the *herreder*, similar to the "hundreds" which made up the English counties. Within both circumscriptions, the entire free male population played a role in the business of governance by serving on juries, heeding the call to the general levy (the *leding*), acting as revenue collectors, and taking part in regular general assemblies (the *landthing* and *herredthing*). Of these, the *landthing* were especially significant because they both elected the king and approved changes to the distinctive body of traditional law associated with each province. Links between the localities and the center were provided by the *ombudsmaend*, royal officials responsible for administering the royal domain.[105]

What soon seems to have sent Denmark off down a path of development different from that of other states also characterized by participatory forms of local government during the early period of statebuilding was the strong influence – cultural, political, and economic – exercised upon the country by the territories of northern Germany. During the first half of the 12th century, the first German cavalrymen appeared in Denmark, thereby introducing into the country the fighting techniques and lifestyle associated with European knighthood. Later in the century, both the king and members of the nobility began to construct castles in imitation of their southern neighbors. Perhaps most important of all, in 1241 the office of the *ombudsmand* was reinterpreted as a fief or *len* (from German *Lehen*) and his position upgraded, inspired by German models, to that of an all-purpose local administrator responsible for revenue collection, public order, and the supervision of the royal domain within his area. Complementary to this development was the large-scale immigration of German nobles which began in the late 1200s and continued into the 1300s. Many of these newcomers were granted lands at feudal tenure, sometimes with rights of jurisdiction over their peasants. The ascension of a German prince, the count of Oldenburg, to the Danish throne in 1448, followed by the permanent attachment to the crown in 1460 of the German county (later duchy) of Holstein ensured a steady influx of German elites into the kingdom for the next three centuries.[106]

---

[105] Musset, *Peuples Scandinaves*, pp. 100–107, 114; Barber, *Two Cities*, pp. 383–385.

[106] Aksel Christensen, *Korngemagt og Aristokrati* (Copenhagen: Ejnar Munksgaards Forlag, 1945), pp. 157–178; Johan Hvidtfeldt, Ib Koch-Olsen, and Axel Steensberg, *Danmarks Historie*, 2 vols. (Copenhagen: Det Danske Forlag, 1950), vol. I, pp. 163–166, 174–181; Carl-Ferdinand Allen, *Histoire de Danemark*, 2 vols. (Copenhagen: Host, 1878), vol. I, pp. 138–140, 238; Musset, *Peuples Scandinaves*, pp. 106, 114–115, 118, 265–267.

The cumulative effect of these foreign-induced changes in administration and in noble prerogatives was progressively to undermine the autonomous political communities of the *landskab* and the *herred*, as more and more of the business of local governance was now carried out by the *lensmand* and his assistants and an increasing number of formerly free peasants came under the tutelage of noble landlords. As one would expect from the cases examined earlier, this basic change from a participatory to a top-down, administrative pattern of local government in turn had profound implications for the development of a national representative assembly and, ultimately, for the political fate of early modern Denmark.

During the early 1200s, the Danish kings, like their English, Hungarian, and Polish counterparts, began to call together much enlarged royal councils (*magna consilia*) which included all of the country's leading nobles and churchmen to provide advice on important matters. In 1282 this body, commonly known as the *parlamentum danorum* or *danehof*, extracted the so-called "Magna Carta of Denmark" from Eric V, in which the latter promised to rule the country in collaboration with its leading men, call together annual parliaments, and respect the rights of his subjects. By the early 1300s, the *danehof* had already acquired certain powers of co-legislation for itself.[107]

In England, Hungary, and Poland, similar elite representative bodies were soon expanded to include deputies from the basic units of local self-government, whether shire, *sejmniki*, county, or borough. But in Denmark this never happened because the noncongruent and nonparticipatory *len* had already succeeded in eclipsing the participatory *landskaber* and *herreder*. Instead, the *danehof* was supplanted by a *smaller* body, a council of the realm (*rigsråd*) of some 20 to 30 members which was dominated by the great noble families. Since in the absence of early, sustained geopolitical pressure the Danish state apparatus, and with it the independent capacities of the king, had remained rudimentary, the *riksråd* soon became the most powerful institution in the land, winning for itself most of the prerogatives later enjoyed by the Hungarian Diet and the Polish Sejm. Thus in 1376 the *riksråd* successfully asserted its sole right to elect the Danish sovereign and to bind him or her through a coronation oath to seek the *råd*'s approval before declaring war, raising taxes, or admitting new members to the nobility. During the 1400s, the council established de facto powers of co-legislation, and

---

[107] Thomas Riis, *Les Institutions Politiques Centrales du Danemark 1100–1332* (Odense: Odense University Press, 1977), pp. 237–239, 252, 256–260; Ludvig Krabbe, *Historie de Danemark* (Copenhagen: Ejnar Munksgaard, 1950), pp. 77–78.

was able to ensure that all court offices and *lensmand* positions were filled from the ranks of its members or their relatives and clients.[108]

As in Hungary and Poland, the Danish nobility also successfully sought to convert political dominance into even greater economic power. Thus it was during the course of the 15th century, as the *rigsråd* was institutionalizing its superiority vis-à-vis the Crown, that noble landowners began to bind their peasants to the soil and subject them to labor dues or *hoveri* (from German *Hofdienst*, which betrays their origin) just as their Hungarian and Polish counterparts were to do over the coming century.[109] In addition, the nobility of course jealously protected its freedom from all taxation, and even sought to gain advantages for itself in its competition with non-noble traders in livestock.[110]

Most significant of all for the future development of the Danish state, the *rigsråd* consistently resisted, just like the Hungarian Diet and the Polish Sejm, all royal attempts to expand and bureaucratize the country's administrative, financial, and military infrastructure in response to massive increases in geopolitical pressure beginning in the 1500s.[111] When taken together, the emergence of an independent and increasingly powerful Sweden after 1523, the mounting Habsburg threat to all central European states which (like Denmark in 1536) had adopted Lutheranism, and the growing influence of Poland in the Baltic following the demise of the Teutonic Order – all posed a qualitatively new kind of threat to long-standing Danish interests. Yet despite repeated royal entreaties, the nobility refused either to lighten its self-serving and inefficient grip on the country's undersized infrastructure or consider giving up its tax exemptions despite a mounting crisis of royal finances. Just as in Hungary and Poland, the inevitable result of such obstructionism was, over the long run, military disaster.

Thus during the two wars which they fought with Denmark between 1657 and 1660, the Swedes succeeded in conquering nearly all of the country, and in the peace settlement of 1658 and 1660 the Danes were

---

[108] Jens Olesen, *Rigsråd, Kongemagt, Union* (Aarhus: Universitetsforlaget, 1980), pp. 1, 318–322, 432–433; John Evjen, *Die Staatsumwälzung in Dänemark im Jahre 1660* (Leipzig: Emil Glausch, 1903), pp. 31–34; Dietrich Gerhard, "Probleme des dänischen Frühabsolutismus," in: idem, *Gesammelte Aufsätze* (Göttingen: Vandenhoeck & Ruprecht, 1977), pp. 89–111, here at pp. 95–96, 102–103.

[109] Anders Bogh, "Feudalisering og Bondekommunalisme," in: Per Ingesman and Jens Villiam Jansen (eds.), *Danmark i Senmiddelalderen* (Aarhus: Universitetesforlag, 1994), pp. 88–105; Allen, *Histoire*, pp. 234–239; Musset, *Peuples Scandinaves*, p. 279.

[110] Gerhard, "Probleme," p. 96.

[111] Ibid., pp. 96, 102; E. Ladewig Petersen, "War, Finance and the Growth of Absolutism: Some Aspects of the European Integration of Seventeenth Century Denmark," in: Göran Rystad (ed.), *Europe and Scandinavia: Aspects of the Process of Integration in the 17th Century* (Lund: Esselte Studium, 1983), pp. 33–49, here at pp. 39–40.

forced to turn over their valuble northern provinces to the victor. To add
insult to injury, the lost conflict had left Denmark practically bankrupt.
In this desperate situation, King Frederick III sought to outflank the
råd by calling together a meeting of a national representative assembly.
This tactic had been employed on several occasions during the course
of the 1500s and early 1600s, but the council had always been able to
prevent such a body from gaining a permanent foothold within the
government. Mirroring the alteration in Danish local government –
under German influence – from a territorially based, participatory
pattern of organization to a nonparticipatory, administrative one, this
assembly was not built around territorial representation but rather
assumed the tricurial, estate-based form dominant among the polities
of Germany and Latin Europe.[112]

When the Danish Estates came together under conditions of extreme
crisis in 1660, the inherent structural weaknesses of curially based assemblies played into the hands of King Frederick. By this time burghers
and clergy had become so disgusted with the unwillingness of the nobility
to sacrifice any of its privileges in the interest of national defense that
they were willing to support the creation of an absolute monarchy in
order to break the *riksråd*'s hold on power. Taking advantage of their
noble opponents' weakness in the wake of two defeats at the hands of
the Swedes, the two lower estates approached Frederick with their plan
and, not surprisingly, gained his ready support. With the backing of
burghers and clergy assured, the king forced the nobility to agree to
the transformation of the country into a hereditary monarchy in which
the ruler would possess full and undivided powers to make new laws,
raise and lower taxes, control all administrative appointments, and
conduct foreign and military policy without consulting with or obtaining the approval of either the Estates or the *råd*.[113] Having failed to
build their hegemony upon the surer foundation of a territorially based
assembly with roots in (elite-dominated) units of local self-government,
as had their counterparts in Hungary and Poland, the Danish nobles
were routed in the closest thing to a coup d'état found in early modern
Europe. Within the space of a few months, Denmark was transformed
from a western variant of patrimonial constitutionalism into a paradig-
matic case of absolutism.

A thoroughgoing reconstruction and expansion of the Danish state

---

[112] Kersten Krüger, "Absolutismus in Dänemark – ein Modell für Begriffsbildung und
Typologie," in: Ernst Hinrichs (ed.), *Absolutismus* (Frankfurt am Main: Suhrkamp,
1986), pp. 65–94, here at p. 74; Evjen, *Staatsumwälzung*, pp. 34–35, 39–45; Gerhard,
"Probleme," pp. 90–92.

[113] Evjen, *Staatsumwälzung*, pp. 11, 90–106 and passim; Krüger, "Absolutismus," pp. 74–78;
Gerhard, "Probleme," pp. 92–93.

apparatus soon followed this dramatic change in the political sphere. Fully exploiting the advantages of the latecomer, Frederick III and his successors reorganized central administration along German and Swedish lines, introducing a privy council, a new high court and exchequer, and army, navy, and commerce boards. These bodies were all staffed by nonproprietary officials of mainly non-noble origin with university-based legal training who could be hired, fired, promoted, and demoted at will.[114]

This new, nonproprietary bureaucracy at the center was complemented by a suitable field service as well. The former system of local administration built around the noble-dominated *len* was abolished and replaced by one based upon the *Amt* – once again borrowed from Germany – staffed by an all-purpose official, the *amtmand*, and his full-time, professional assistants. However, in a concession to the nobility already encountered in Prussia, the noble estate or *god* (from German *Gut*) was retained as the lowest unit of local government. In practical terms this meant that the local landlord was granted the right to judge, collect taxes from, and recruit for military service not only his own peasants, who remained bound to the soil, but also anyone else living in the area of his estate.[115] Despite this typical compromise with the old order at the local level, the Danish absolutist state has been judged by knowledgeable observers to be among the most thoroughly bureaucratic (and in that sense modern) in 18th-century Europe.[116]

Sweden

Despite some differences in detail, the path of development which the Swedish kingdom followed during the early and central middle ages was broadly similar to that of its southern neighbor. The first Christian king of what would become Sweden is traditionally considered to be Olaf Skötkonung, who was baptized in 1006, but the task of converting and of unifying the rest of the country proved to be much more difficult than in Denmark, requiring more than a century to accomplish.[117]

---

[114] Hvidtfeldt et al., *Danmarks Historie*, vol. I, pp. 346–348; Birgit Bjerre Jensen, *Udnaevnelsesretten i Enevaeldens Magtpolitiske System 1660–1730* (Copenhagen: Riksarkivet/G. E. C. Gads Forlag, 1987), pp. 296–307 and passim; Tim Knudsen, *Dansk Statsbygning* (Copenhagen: Jurist- og Okonomforbundets Forlag, 1995), pp. 117–123.

[115] Birgit Løgstrup, *Jorddrot og Offentlig Administrator* (Copenhagen: G. E. C. Gads Forlag, 1983), pp. 373–379 and passim; Knudsen, *Dansk Statsbygning*, pp. 112–113; Gerhard, "Probleme," pp. 102–105.

[116] Bjerre Jensen, *Udnaevnelsesretten*, pp. 305–307; Knudsen, *Dansk Statsbygning*, pp. 121, 123.

[117] Franklin Scott, *Sweden: The Nation's History* (Carbondale: Southern Illinois University Press, 1988), pp. 39–44; T. K. Derry, *A History of Scandinavia* (Minneapolis: University of Minnesota Press, 1979), pp. 35, 40.

Once a durable polity of the western type had emerged by the mid-1100s, thanks in no small measure to the efforts of the Church, it contained all of the institutions familiar from the Danish case. Thus central administration was in the hands of the great court officials, the chancellor (*kansler*), justiciar (*drot*), and marshall (*marskalk*). At the local level the country was divided into largely self-governing provinces (*landskap*), which in assemblies of all free men (the *ting*) chose their own leaders (the *lagmän*) and were also responsible for electing the king; and the *häreder* or hundreds, also built around their own assemblies. Royal estates were administered by local officials, here called bailiffs (*bryte*).[118]

As in Denmark, Swedish rulers began calling together large meetings (*parlamenta*) of the kingdom's bishops and leading aristocrats to provide advice and counsel on matters of policy and law as early as the mid-1200s if not before, and a smaller council of the realm (*riksråd*) emerged shortly thereafter. It is at this point, however, that Danish and Swedish paths of development begin to diverge. For given the continued vigor in Sweden of the participatory *landskap* and *häreder*, undisturbed by imported feudal influences, it soon became necessary for the king to invite local government representatives to the *parlamenta* in order to gain the widest possible support for the measures decided upon there. Thus, whereas by the 1400s in Denmark the *danehof* had been eclipsed by the more aristocratic *rigsråd* at the center of political life, in Sweden a single-chamber national representative assembly was beginning to emerge. While clearly dominated by members of the nobility and higher clergy, it also contained within it burgher delegates from the towns and peasant representatives chosen by the various *landskap*.[119]

Whether, as in Hungary and Poland, the nobility would ultimately have succeeded in forcing all other social groups out of the organs of local government and of this nascent national assembly is impossible to say, for at this point a sharp break occurred in Swedish development comparable to the events of 1660 in Denmark. Since 1397 the Norwegian and Swedish kingdoms had been linked to Denmark through the Union of Kalmar, and in 1521, following a complex series of events that

---

[118] Sten Carlsson and Jerker Rosén, *Svensk Historia*, 2 volumes (Stockholm: Svensk Bokförlaget, 1962), vol. I, pp. 130, 134–137, 170–171; Erik Lönnroth, "Government in Medieval Scandinavia," *Gouvernés et Gouvernants*, vol. 24 (1966), pp. 453–460, here at pp. 453–456.

[119] Erik Lönnroth, "Representative Assemblies in Medieval Sweden," *Xe Congrès International des Sciences Historiques, Rome, 1955* (Louvain: Publications Universitaires de Louvain, 1958), pp. 123–131; Herman Schück, "Sweden's Early Parliamentary Institutions from the Thirteenth Century to 1611," in: Michael Metcalf (ed.), *The Riksdag: A History of the Swedish Parliament* (New York: St. Martin's Press, 1987), pp. 5–60, here at pp. 5–6, 11–37.

need not be recounted here, a kind of national revolution broke out in Sweden directed against Danish rule. This uprising was led by the noble Gustav Vasa, but was strongly supported by local peasant communities and the country's miners.[120]

Having driven out the Danes and been elected king, Vasa was in a position to introduce major changes to Swedish government. Interestingly, the one institution he chose to alter in a fundamental way, in addition to the newly reformed Church, was the country's nascent national representative body. In 1527 and again in 1544, 1547, and 1560 he called together an assembly, the Riksdag, which differed substantially in form from the assemblies of the 1400s. Unlike the former, in which all participants met in a single group, the Riksdag was divided into separate status-based curia along German lines. Indeed, it is now believed that the Estates of Prussia provided the model for this reform of Sweden's national assembly. Given the nature of Swedish local government, which remained unaltered, it was not possible even for a ruler as powerful as Gustav Vasa simply to transform the Swedish assembly from a territorially based to an estate-based body at the stroke of a pen. Hence in addition to the separate chambers for the nobility (meeting in person), the clergy (higher clergy and representatives of the lower clergy), and the towns (delegates from the town councils), the new Riksdag also included a fourth chamber of peasant proprietors chosen by the *häred* assemblies.[121]

The Riksdag was thus a hybrid institution, a curial body with an important territorial element rooted in participatory units of local government. It was the assembly's hybrid character which rendered it stronger than the Estates of Germany or Latin Europe but weaker than the parliaments of England, Hungary, and Poland. This combination of strengths and weaknesses helps explain, I would argue, the subsequent Swedish vacillations during the late 17th and 18th centuries between constitutionalism (the dominant political regime) and absolutism.

While it is not known whether Gustav consciously intended to weaken Sweden's national assembly by dividing it into separate status-based chambers, this seems to have been the practical effect of his actions. Thus, unlike in Hungary and Poland, there was little resistance from that body to the fundamental transformation and expansion of the Swedish state apparatus undertaken first after 1538 and then again after 1611 to meet the threats first from a hostile Denmark and then

---

[120] Michael Roberts, *The Early Vasas* (Cambridge: Cambridge University Press, 1968), pp. 1–24.

[121] Schück, "Sweden's Early Parliamentary Institutions," pp. 39–52, 58–60; Roberts, *Early Vasas*, pp. 191–193, 433–434.

from Poland and the Habsburgs of Germany. The first wave of reforms was carried out by Gustav's German minister Conrad von Pyhy, who reorganized the central administration around the usual set of institutions found in the states of the Empire: a government council, chancery, chamber, high court, and consistory.[122]

These changes were partially reversed after 1560, but with the ascension of Gustavus Adolphus to the throne in 1611, a major period of state expansion began which saw government at the center, restructured around a series of collegial boards according to more recent German and Dutch models. In addition, a bureaucratic element was introduced into local governments when royal officials were placed at the heads of the *landskap* and the *härad*, but the essentially participatory character of these bodies was preserved. Most important, all these new positions at the center and in the localities were manned by professional, often university-trained, officials who possessed no proprietary claims to their offices.[123]

It was above all this new proto-modern bureaucracy, the felicitous product of the late onset of sustained geopolitical competition in the Swedish case, which provided the structural underpinnings to that country's rise to the rank of a great power during the reign of Gustavus Adolphus. But it was also this instrument of rule which permitted successive kings, most notably Charles XI (1672–1697) and Charles XII (1697–1718), to rule largely without consulting the Riksdag, though not to abolish that body altogether. The death in battle of Charles XII in 1718, however, opened the door to a restoration of the assembly's power and the inauguration of a period ("the age of liberty," 1719–1772) when the Swedish state, with its mix of parliamentary co-rule, a nonproprietary infrastructure, and a currency-issuing national bank directly answerable to the Riksdag, was the closest equivalent in Europe to the bureaucratic constitutionalism of Britain.[124]

CONCLUSION

Despite similarities in parliamentary institutions and patterns of local government stretching back into the middle ages, Poland and Hungary

---

[122] Carlsson and Rosén, *Svensk Historia*, vol. I, pp. 400–401; Roberts, *Early Vasas*, pp. 122–124.

[123] Carlsson and Rosén, *Svensk Historia*, vol. I, pp. 490–494; David Gaunt, *Utbildning till Statens Tjänst* (Uppsala: Almquist & Wiksell, 1975), pp. 43–47, 50–56, 67–69, 83–91 and passim; Michael Roberts, *The Swedish Imperial Experience 1560–1718* (Cambridge: Cambridge University Press, 1979), pp. 56–62.

[124] On this period, see: Michael Roberts, *The Age of Liberty* (Cambridge: Cambridge University Press, 1986); Michael Metcalf, "Parliamentary Sovereignty and Royal Reaction, 1719–1809," in: idem (ed.), *The Riksdag*, pp. 109–164; Claude Nordmann, *Grandeur et Liberté de la Suède* (Paris: Béatrice-Nauwelaerts, 1971).

in the end followed a path of political development radically different from that of England. As we have seen, the roots of this divergence can be traced to the 12th and 13th centuries, when all three polities already possessed comparable organs of territorially integrated local government thanks to their common experience as unencumbered state formers. It was at this time that, unlike their Polish and Hungarian counterparts, successive English monarchs began to construct a large, specialized, and professionally staffed state apparatus in response to sustained geopolitical competition.

The consequences of this step were far-reaching, for it left the kings of England with an instrument of rule – independent of the elite-dominated bodies of the county – which would allow them in future to defend their own institutional position in an effective way and to extend royal protection to weaker social groups such as peasants and townsmen. By contrast, Polish and Hungarian rulers remained structurally weak, thanks to a lack of geopolitical incentives for infrastructural expansion, and were forced to compensate for this weakness by furthering the drive of nascent lesser nobilities for equality with their aristocratic brothers. Yet once a large and privileged noble class had come into being, the kings of Poland and Hungary did not possess the independent administrative, fiscal, or military resources necessary to prevent this group both from taking full control of local government and from imposing their will at the center as well through strong, territorially based parliaments.

Ironically, this noble conquest of political power by means of national and local organs of self-government was aided by the delayed arrival during the late 14th and 15th centuries of sustained geopolitical competition. Once the nobility had established its supremacy within the state, there was nothing to stop it from using that supremacy to weaken still further its political and economic rivals – townsmen, peasants, and the king himself – through the introduction from above of discriminatory economic policies, serfdom, and an elective monarchy. Hence the existence of these last two phenomena in Poland and Hungary, often cited as the *cause* of their unique pattern of political development, was in fact one of its consequences.

The logical endpoint of this pattern of development is best exemplified by the case of Poland, where the dictatorship of a single (socially and legally defined) class, trumpeted as a form of democracy, did indeed lead to the overcoming of the state, though not in the way Marx would have expected. In England, by contrast, it was the parallel growth of both participatory local government *and* a strong and bureaucratic center – a product of the confluence of late state formation and early geopolitical pressure – that made possible the coexistence of constitutionalism and a strong state in a polity where "liberty" meant more than just a license to dominate.

Yet as the Scandinavian cases underline, these outcomes were less inevitable than they might at first glance seem. In both Sweden and Denmark, the two factors highlighted throughout this book also operated, broadly speaking, in the manner expected. In Sweden, unencumbered state formation produced participatory local government which in turn brought forth a territorially based national representative assembly during the course of the 1400s, while there were signs during the 1200s and early 1300s at least that Denmark was moving in the same direction. Once in place, the roots of the Swedish Riksdag in a still-vibrant, participatory local government *did* prevent the definitive triumph of monarchical absolutism, though the rivalries and animosities among the verious estates furthered by that assembly's curial form also opened the door to two extended quasi-absolutist interludes over the course of the 17th and 18th centuries. Finally, the late onset of sustained geopolitical and hence state expansion did indeed permit rulers to introduce modernizing reforms where assemblies were curially organized (Sweden) or non-existent (Denmark).

Yet in both cases contingent historical circumstances intervened to shunt these states off the path leading to noble dominance and patrimonial constitutionalism and onto rather different roads. In Sweden, it was the alteration in the form of the assembly which weakened that body sufficiently to allow bureaucratization and, with it, a substantial increase in monarchical power – an increase which nonetheless still fell short of what would have been needed for true absolutism. As the Danish case emphasizes, the complete victory of absolutism in Sweden would have required a disabling of the participatory organs of local government of the kind which, under German influence, was to occur in Denmark over the course of the late middle ages.

Chapter 7

CONCLUSION

What lessons does the long and complex process of European state-building hold for the study of political development more generally? Before addressing this question, it may be useful to summarize this book's principal findings once again. From the 11th century onward, Europe was divided into a multiplicity of political units which remained locked in conflict with one another throughout the medieval and early modern period. In response to war and preparation for war, rulers sought to monopolize political power in order to gain exclusive control over foreign, military, and financial policy. At the same time, they attempted to construct ever larger and more specialized state apparatuses so as to guarantee order at home and battlefield success abroad. A dynamic, autonomous market economy furnished the resources necessary for such an expansion of military, administrative, and financial infrastructures.

Yet precisely because geomilitary competition and the resulting tendencies towards absolutism and the growth of the state were so ubiquitous, they cannot in themselves explain *differences* in the paths of development followed by the various European polities. Attempts to do so either through variations in the intensity of geomilitary competition and/or variations in socioeconomic structure have not proven successful. In this book, I have argued that a combination of three factors can account for such differences in a more convincing way.

First, the kind of *political regime* which a given state came to possess by the 18th century was determined by the ability of national representative assemblies to resist royal pressures for absolutism, which was in turn a function of the nature of local government. Where local government was organized during the early period of a state's development in a participatory manner – as was the case in England, Scotland, Hungary, Poland, and Scandinavia – the result was cooperative interaction across status groups at both the local and national level. This interaction generated reserves of social capital[1] as well as financial and

---

[1] On the nature and origins of social capital in general and its role in the development of the Italian city-states in particular, see: Robert Putnam, *Making Democracy Work* (Princeton: Princeton University Press, 1993), pp. 163–185.

317

military resources which could then be mobilized to combat absolutism and force royal acceptance of constitutionalist power sharing. Where, on the other hand, local government was structured in a top-down, nonparticipatory way – as was true in Latin Europe and Germany – status-based representative assemblies remained internally divided and hence weak, and rulers were always able over the long run to push them aside and realize their absolutist designs.

These all-important variations in the initial character of local government in turn resulted from differences in the pattern of state formation found across the European continent. Where, as in Latin Europe and Germany, new polities were created after about the year 1000 upon the ruins of collapsed dark age kingdoms, the hostility of already entrenched local elites to the centralizing goals of a new generation of rulers rendered participatory local government impossible. In those areas of the continent such as the British Isles, Scandinavia, and east-central Europe where no such large-scale, dark age kingdoms had existed, new states were formed as a cooperative enterprise among political leaders, the Church, the aristocracy, and the entire free male population. The participatory nature of government at the local level was a direct consequence of these cooperative beginnings.

Second, the kind of *state apparatus* which emerged in a given European polity in response to geomilitary competition was determined in the first instance by the conditions under which such apparatuses were first constructed, and these conditions changed substantially between the 1100s and the 1700s. During the middle ages (prior to about 1450), resources like administrative and financial know-how and ready cash were in short supply. Rulers who, under military pressure, first expanded their infrastructures during this period were in a weak position vis-à-vis those groups which possessed such resources and hence were forced, all other things being equal, to concede to them substantial direct control over the emerging state apparatus.[2]

On the other hand, rulers who were not forced to enlarge their infrastructures until after about 1450 found themselves in a much stronger position vis-à-vis their future staffs. This was so because the supply of trained personnel and short-term funds increased substantially after 1450, thanks to the growth of universities and financial markets. At the same time, the experience of those states which had built apparatuses earlier provided the latecomers with valuable lessons – both positive

---

[2]   Douglass North has recently stressed the crucial impact of initial bargaining strength in the creation of long-lasting institutional frameworks in his book *Institutions, Institutional Change and Economic Performance* (Cambridge: Cambridge University Press, 1990), pp. 16, 47–48.

and negative – and new administrative and financial models not available to the pioneers. Rulers who built up their apparatuses later were therefore better able to resist pressures for staff-dominated (patrimonial) administrative and financial arrangements and instead construct proto-modern bureaucracies over which they themselves retained substantial control.

Finally, another factor also helped determine the ultimate character of a given state's apparatus: the independent influence of representative assemblies on administrative and financial infrastructures. Where such assemblies were weak or non-existent, as in absolutist Latin Europe and Germany, this influence was insufficient to alter apparatuses the character of which had already been dictated by the timing of their construction. Thus in Latin Europe, state infrastructures were built early, in the unfavorable circumstances of the 13th and 14th centuries, and in consequence quickly acquired a patrimonial taint. They retained that taint – thanks to determined resistance to reform on the part of their staffs – until after the French Revolution despite periodic protests from the Estates General, the Castilian Cortes, and other representative bodies. France, Spain, and the other territorial states of Latin Europe must thus be classified as examples of *patrimonial absolutism*. In Germany and Denmark, infrastructural expansion occurred during the early modern period, under conditions more favorable to rulers, and hence the latter successfully introduced proto-modern bureaucracies, often over the objections of their Estates. This region was hence the homeland of *bureaucratic absolutism*.

In polities with stronger national assemblies, however, the interests and goals of those assemblies carried much more weight. Thus the English Parliament, largely representing as it did taxpayers with little sympathy for full-time officeholders, opposed right from the start the patrimonial infrastructure which it already found in place at the moment of its creation during the late 1200s. During the late 1600s, Parliament provided the crucial measure of support which allowed reformers within the central government to overcome the resistance of entrenched patrimonial officials and construct the new, proto-modern administrative and financial system which permitted Britain – the prime example along with Sweden of *bureaucratic constitutionalism* – to become a world power during the 18th century.

In Hungary and Poland, by contrast, sustained geomilitary pressures came later than in England, and hence those countries' assemblies found no substantial state infrastructures in place when they first established themselves permanently on the national political stage during the 1300s. Both assemblies later mobilized all of the substantial resources which participatory local governments placed at their disposal in order to block rulers' attempts to build proto-modern bureaucracies, because the latter would have substantially increased royal power. The assemblies of Hungary and Poland were equally successful in this enterprise, and both polities must hence be classified as cases of *patrimonial constitutionalism*. In both countries noble-controlled organs of local government took over most administrative, financial, and military functions, with tragic consequences for the ability of Hungary and Poland to defend themselves.

How can the pattern of statebuilding found in medieval and early modern Europe, when taken as a whole, be characterized? Over the past decade, a number of scholars working in international relations and in Latin American studies have challenged pluralist and functionalist theories of long-term political development. Drawing on the earlier thinking of Sidney Verba, Stein Rokkan, and Seymour Martin Lipset as well as on ideas from fields as diverse as economic history and evolutionary biology, they have proposed a branching tree, path-dependent model of long-term political change which stresses the way in which institutional choices made at "critical junctures" lay down a given state's course of development for decades and even centuries to come by limiting the range of viable policy options open to future leaders.[3] In effect, states are often unable, due to the burdens of the past, to respond quickly and efficiently to changes in their environment, and are forced instead to operate within the constraints imposed by sometimes dysfunctional institutional frameworks.[4]

---

[3] Stephen Krasner, "Approaches to the State: Alternative Conceptions and Historical Dynamics," *Comparative Politics*, vol. 16, no. 2 (January 1984), pp. 223–246; idem, "Sovereignty: An Institutional Perspective," *Comparative Political Studies*, vol. 21, no. 1 (April 1988), pp. 66–94; Ruth Berins Collier and David Collier, *Shaping the Political Arena* (Princeton: Princeton University Press, 1991), pp. 27–39; also Terry Lynn Karl, "Dilemmas of Democratization in Latin America," *Comparative Politics*, vol. 23, no. 1 (October 1990), pp. 1–21, here at pp. 5–8. The term "branching tree model" stems from Sidney Verba, "Sequence and Development," in: Leonard Binder et al. (eds.), *Crises and Sequences in Political Development* (Princeton: Princeton University Press, 1971), pp. 283–316, here at p. 308. Lipset and Rokkan's analysis of the development of European party systems is often cited as a classic example of a branching tree or branching path model. See: Seymour Martin Lipset and Stein Rokkan, "Cleavage Structures, Party Systems, and Voter Alignments: An Introduction," in: idem (eds.), *Party System and Voter Alignments: Cross National Perspectives* (New York: Free Press, 1968), pp. 1–64, esp. pp. 37–41.
    Two articles from economic history which have inspired this new political science literature are: Paul David, "Clio and the Economics of QWERTY," *American Economic Review*, vol. 75, no. 2 (May 1985), pp. 332–337; W. Brian Arthur, "Competing Technologies, Increasing Returns, and Lock-in by Historical Event," *The Economic Journal*, vol. 99 (March 1989), pp. 116–131.

[4] The reasons behind the persistence of dysfunctional institutional arrangements have also been explored by Douglass North in *Institutions, Institutional Change*, pp. 51–53, 92–104 and passim.

European statebuilding can be understood as a form of path-dependent change analogous to the continent's later process of industrialization. In that process, the experience of the first cohort of industrializers (the pioneers) not only influenced their own future path of development; it also generated the practices and institutions which allowed other countries, thanks to "transnational learning"[5] driven by economic competition, to industrialize as well. These latecomers, however, were forced to make their way in a world already transformed and structured by the achievements of the pioneers; the path which they followed thus necessarily diverged from that of the early industrializers. In a similar way, the pressures of geomilitary competition brought forth new organizational forms (the representative assembly, the nonproprietary conception of office, the Treasury Order) and resources (trained personnel, ready cash) as well as creating incentives for imitation, borrowing, and the retrospective analysis of the successes and failures of earlier statebuilders. As a result, the world of the early modern period was already very different from that of the middle ages, and hence confronted a later generation of leaders attempting to expand and refine their infrastructures with a new set of constraints and challenges when compared to those faced by rulers who had built up their apparatuses centuries earlier.

What more general conclusions can be drawn from the European statebuilding experience? Above all, the pervasiveness across much of the continent until the 19th century and beyond of patrimonial practices like proprietary officeholding, tax farming, and "inside" finance, with their accompanying inefficiency, arbitrariness, and diversion of substantial public revenues into private hands, underlines just how difficult it is to construct effective and honest administrative and financial infrastructures as part of the process of political development. The ubiquity of parasitical or rent-seeking behavior on the part of those connected with the state in medieval and early modern Europe and in many parts of Africa, Asia, and Latin America today is best understood by viewing statebuilding from the perspective of the government official rather than from that of the ruler.

Considered in this way, the creation and expansion of administrative and financial institutions represents a unique opportunity for personal and familiar enrichment and social aggrandizement because it inevitably involves the extraction of wealth from the population at large and its concentration – ostensibly for the public good – in the coffers of state organizations. Once amassed, such wealth presents an inviting target to rent-seeking groups, be they government officials, financiers, the military,

---

[5]   Krasner, "Approaches to the State," p. 241, citing Hugh Heclo.

local political bosses, or the employees of subsidized state enterprises. Indeed, it was with good reason that contemporary observers considered the emerging administrative and financial institutions of early modern Europe to be "new Perus," overflowing with riches greater than those of the Indies. As the European case illustrates all too well, rent-seeking groups will, unless checked, structure the state apparatus in the way that best suits their own interests, with little concern for the long-term consequences for their country's defense capabilities, domestic services, or international economic competitiveness. Furthermore, once entrenched, they will fiercely resist all attempts aimed at reform and instead seek to reorganize patrimonial infrastructures in such a way as to increase their effectiveness without altering their fundamental nature, a procedure I characterized in Chapter 3 as the "rationalization of irrationalization."[6]

Patrimonial infrastructures can prove to be extremely durable. Just because the military, administrative, and financial arrangements associated with various forms of patrimonialism are suboptimal from the point of view of more modern, bureaucratic institutions does not mean that they are doomed to immediate collapse, even under conditions of sustained geomilitary pressure. This is especially true if one's principal rivals are also constrained by a rent-seeking state apparatus. Thus the French monarchy operated for over 300 years as one of Europe's greatest powers – despite massive levels of inefficiency and the vast diversion of public revenues into private pockets – thanks to the great reserves of men, money, and matériel found within the country and the similarly patrimonial infrastructure possessed by its main competitor, Spain. When a new enemy, namely Britain, did appear equipped with a proto-modern bureaucracy and a market-based financial system, ancien régime France was finally driven into bankruptcy, but only after a century of intense conflict.

Patrimonial institutions can also have nagging long-term consequences. Despite the reforms of the 19th century, patron-client relations, lack of clear boundaries between politics and administration, and redistribution of public funds towards political insiders remain a serious problem in Spain, Portugal, France, and Italy – not to mention the former Spanish and Portuguese colonies of Latin America and Asia – down to the present day. Indeed, while the practices involved may be

---

[6] Douglass North has similarly written of "organizations that . . . will become more efficient – but more efficient at making the society ever more unproductive and the basic institutional structure ever less conducive to productive activity." See his *Institutions, Institutional Change*, p. 9.

different, the extent and complexity of rent-seeking behavior in some parts of Italy seems to have changed little since the early modern period.

How then might it be possible to resist the rent-seeking deformation of state institutions during and after the completion of the statebuilding process? The European experience points to two possibilities. The first of these is an "authoritarian" solution of the kind found in the absolutist states of Germany – Brandenburg-Prussia above all – and in Denmark after 1660, where a monocratic executive maintains a close watch over the activities of government employees and dismisses those who fail to meet certain standards of honesty and efficiency. In addition to the objections that one might have to monocratic systems of rule on philosophical grounds, they also exhibit a number of shortcomings as far as the construction of durable modern bureaucracies is concerned. First, as the cases of France, Spain, and the other absolutist polities of Latin Europe illustrate, the mere existence of a monocratic political regime is not a sufficient condition for successful bureaucratization. Favorable circumstances regarding the supply of trained personnel and of available financial resources are also necessary. Second, under monocratic rule a lasting defense against patrimonialist tendencies depends almost entirely on the degree of vigilance and the quality of supervision exercised by the executive, a condition subject to a high degree of contingency in such a system. Thus following the death of Frederick the Great, his successors were far less interested in the day-to-day business of administration, and as a result the quality of the Prussian bureaucracy suffered noticeably. Third, in order to sustain themselves, monocratic regimes often must enter into compromises with powerful socioeconomic groups, compromises which – as in both the French and Prussian cases – serve to hinder economic development and to reinforce status hierarchies, thereby preventing the status-leveling which, as Max Weber observed, is a key prerequisite for bureaucratization.

In all these respects, constitutionalist (power-sharing) regimes like those found in Britain and Sweden would seem to have an advantage over their monocratic counterparts with regard to the construction of modern bureaucracies. As these two European cases suggest, such regimes are capable not only of building nonproprietary administrations under favorable circumstances (Sweden), but are also able to eliminate patrimonial practices already in place (England). Furthermore, constitutionalist polities offer a variety of checks to appropriationist tendencies: scrutiny by representative assemblies themselves under pressure from a taxpaying electorate suspicious of government officials and their designs; investigations by a public sphere more developed and open than that found under monocratic rule; and pressure for efficiency from domestic financial markets of a kind that cannot really emerge in monocratic systems. Finally, such regimes usually contain within them a strong, politically driven tendency toward status-leveling of the kind favorable for bureaucratization.

Yet this insight merely begs the larger question of what conditions give rise to the bureaucratic constitutionalism characteristic of 18th-century Britain (and, with some reservations, Sweden). This book points to the key role played by the organization of local government during the early period following state formation in bringing about such an outcome. The involvement of a broad segment of the population in the management of its own affairs at the local level, I have argued, creates bonds of solidarity and commonalities of interest which, when combined with the material resources at the disposal of participatory local bodies, allow effective resistance to be mobilized against the monocratic designs of statebuilding political leaders.

As the patrimonialist fate of Hungary and Poland illustrate, however, the mere presence of participatory local government is in itself not enough to ensure the triumph of bureaucratic constitutionalism. It is only the combination of participatory local government with a strong center equipped with independent capacities of rule that, the British case implies, can assure such an outcome. This is so because only a strong center is capable of intervening to prevent the oligarchization of local government by the community's most powerful elements, as happened in the Hungarian and Polish kingdoms. In England, it was the consistent support provided by the Crown to non-elite groups which permitted the continued participation of free-born commoners in county institutions and in the life of Parliament itself long after the representative assemblies of Hungary and Poland had become nothing more than organs for the protection and extension of noble privileges. Thus if the European past holds one overriding lesson for today's statebuilders, it would be this: it is the combination right from the start of a strong center and strong, participatory localities which, over the long run, will best permit states to balance the demands of infrastructural expansion, political participation, economic growth, and geopolitical competition. Perhaps this was the message that Tocqueville was attempting to communicate to the old continent itself over a century and a half ago.

BIBLIOGRAPHY

Adams, Simon. "Faction, Clientage and Party: English Politics, 1550–1603." *History Today,* vol. 32, no. 12 (December 1982), pp. 33–39.

Allen, Carl-Ferdinand. *Histoire de Danemark.* 2 vols. Copenhagen: Host, 1878.

Alsop, J D. "Government, Finance and the Community of the Exchequer." In: *The Reign of Elizabeth I.* Ed. Christopher Haigh. London. Macmillan, 1984, pp. 101–123.

"The Revenue Commission of 1552." *Historical Journal,* vol. 22, no. 3 (1979), pp. 511–533.

Arnold, Benjamin. *Count and Bishop in Medieval Germany: A Study of Regional Power 1100–1350.* Philadelphia: University of Pennsylvania Press, 1991.

German Knighthood 1050–1300. Oxford: Clarendon, 1985.

Princes and Territories in Medieval Germany. Cambridge: Cambridge University Press, 1991.

Anderson, Perry. *Lineages of the Absolutist State.* London: New Left Books, 1974.

Passages from Antiquity to Feudalism. London: New Left Books, 1974.

Ardascheff, Paul. *Les Intendants de Province sous Louis XVI.* Paris: Félix Alcan, 1909.

Arthur, W. Brian. "Competing Technologies, Increasing Returns, and Lock-in by Historical Event." *The Economic Journal,* vol. 99 (March 1989), pp. 116–131.

Artola, Miguel. *La Hacienda del Antiguo Régimen.* Madrid: Alianza, 1982.

Historia de España Alfaguara V: La Burguesía Revolucionaria (1808–1874). Madrid: Alianza Universidad, 1973.

Asch, Ronald. "Estates and Princes after 1648: The Consequences of the Thirty Years War." *German History,* vol. 6, no. 2 (August 1988), pp. 113–132.

Ashley, Maurice. *Financial and Commercial Policy under the Cromwellian Protectorate.* 2nd ed. Oxford: Oxford University Press, 1962.

Ashton, Robert. *The Crown and the Money Market 1603–1640.* Oxford: Clarendon, 1960.

"Deficit Finance in the Reign of James I." *Economic History Review.* 2nd ser. Vol. 10, no. 1 (August 1957), pp. 15–29.

"The Disbursing Official under the Early Stuarts: The Cases of Sir William Russell and Philip Burlamachi." *Bulletin of the Institute of Historical Research,* vol. 30, no. 82 (November 1957), pp. 162–174.

"Revenue Farming under the Early Stuarts." *Economic History Review.* 2nd ser. Vol. 8, no. 3 (April 1956), pp. 310–322.

Autrand, Françoise. "Office et Officiers Royaux en France sous Charles VI." *Revue Historique,* vol. 93, no. 242 (October–December 1969), pp. 285–338.

Aylmer, G. E. "Attempts at Administrative Reform, 1625–1640." *English Historical Review,* vol. 72, no. 283 (April 1957), pp. 229–259.

"Charles I's Commission on Fees, 1627–1640." *Bulletin of the Institute for Historical Research,* vol. 31, no. 83 (May 1958), pp. 58–67.

The King's Servants. London: Routledge & Kegan Paul, 1974.

The State's Servants: The Civil Service of the English Republic 1649–1660. London: Routledge & Kegan Paul, 1973.

Bak, János. "Das Königreich Ungarn im Hochmittelalter 1060–1444." In: *Handbuch der Europäischen Geschichte.* Ed. Theodor Schieder. Vol. II. Stuttgart: Ernst Klett Verlag, 1976, pp. 1103–1124.

Baker, Robert. "The English Customs Service 1307–1343: A Study of Medieval Administration." *Transactions of the American Philosophical Society*. New Series. Vol. 51, part 6 (October 1961), pp. 3–76.

Baldwin, John W. *The Government of Philip Augustus*. Berkeley: University of California Press, 1986.

Barber, Malcolm. *The Two Cities: Medieval Europe 1050–1320*. London: Routledge, 1992.

Bardach, Juliusz. "L'État Polonais aux Xe et XIe Siècles." In: *L'Europe aux IXe–XIe Siècles: Aux Origines des États Nationaux*. Ed. Institut d'Histoire de l'Académie Polonaise des Sciences. Varsovie: Państwowe Wydawnictwo Naukowe, 1968, pp. 279–319.

"La Formation des Assemblées Polonaises au XVe Siècle et la Taxation." *Anciens Pays et Assemblées d'États*, vol. 70 (1977), pp. 249–296.

"Gouvernants et Gouvernés en Pologne au Moyen-Âge et aux Temps Modernes." *Gouvernés et Gouvernants*, vol. 25 (1965), pp. 255–285.

Barnes, Frederic Richard. "The Taxation of Wool, 1327–1348." In *Finance and Trade Under Edward III*. Ed. George Unwin. Manchester: Manchester University Press, 1918, pp. 137–177.

Barnwell, P. S. *Emperors, Prefects and Kings*. London: Duckworth, 1992.

Batchfelder, Ronald and Herman Freudenberger. "On the Rational Origins of the Modern Centralized State." *Explorations in Economic History*, vol. 20 (1983), pp. 1–13.

Baugh, Daniel. *British Naval Administration in the Age of Walpole*. Princeton: Princeton University Press, 1965.

Baumgart, Peter, ed. *Ständetum und Staatsbildung in Brandenburg-Preussen*. Berlin: Walter de Gruyter, 1983.

Baumgartner, Frederic. *Henry II*. Durham, N.C.: Duke University Press, 1988.

Baxter, Douglas. *Servants of the Sword: The French Intendants of the Army 1630–1670*. Urbana: University of Illinois Press, 1976.

Baxter, Stephen, ed. *England's Rise to Greatness 1660–1763*. Berkeley: University of California Press, 1983.

Bayard, Françoise. *Le Monde des Financiers au XVIIe Siècle*. Paris: Flammarion, 1988.

Bean, Richard. "War and the Birth of the Nation State." *Journal of Economic History*, vol. 23, no. 1 (March 1973), pp. 202–221.

Beckett, J. V. "Land Tax or Excise: The Levying of Taxation in Seventeenth- and Eighteenth-Century England." *English Historical Review*, vol. 100, no. 395 (April 1985), pp. 285–308.

Beeler, John. *Warfare in Feudal Europe 730–1200*. Ithaca: Cornell University Press, 1971.

Beik, William. *Absolutism and Society in Seventeenth Century France: State Power and Provincial Aristocracy in Languedoc*. Cambridge: Cambridge University Press, 1985.

von Below, Georg. "Die Neuorganisation der Verwaltung in den deutschen Territorien des 16. Jahrhunderts." In *Territorium und Staat*. 2nd ed. München: R. Oldenbourg, 1923, pp. 194–208.

"System und Bedeutung der landständischen Verfassung." In: *Territorium und Staat*. 2nd ed. München: R. Oldenbourg, 1923, pp. 53–160.

Bendix, Reinhard. *Max Weber: An Intellectual Portrait*. Berkeley: University of California Press, 1977.

Beneyto, Juan. "Les Cortes d'Espagne du XVIe au XIXe Siècle." In: *Receuils de la Société Jean Bodin, XXIV: Gouvernés et Gouvernants, Troisième Partie: Bas Moyen Âge et Temps Modernes (I)*. Bruxelles: Éditions de la Librairie Encyclopédique, 1966, pp. 461–481.

Bennett, Martyn. "Contribution and Assessment: Financial Exactions in the English Civil War, 1642–1646." *War and Society*, vol. 4, no. 1 (May 1986), pp. 1–9.

Bérenger, Jean. "Charles Colbert, Marquis de Croissy." In: *Le Conseil du Roi de Louis XII à la Révolution*. Ed. Roland Mousnier. Paris: Presses Universitaires de France, 1970, pp. 153–174.

Finances et Absolutisme Autrichien dans la Seconde Moitié du XVIIe Siècle. Paris: Publications de la Sorbonne, 1975.

Bérenger, Jean and Daniel Tollet, "La Genèse de l'État Moderne en Europe Orientale: Synthèse et Bilan." In: *L'État Moderne: Genèse*. Ed. Jean-Philippe Genet. Paris: Editions du CNRS, 1990, pp. 43–63.

Beresford, John. *The Godfather of Downing Street.* London: Richard Cobden-Sanderson, 1925.
Beumann, Helmut, ed. *Karl der Grosse: Lebenwerk und Nachleben. Band I: Persönlichkeit und Geschichte.* Düsseldorf: Verlag L. Schwann, 1965.
Bluche, François. *Les Magistrats du Parlement du Paris au XVIIIᵉ Siècle.* Paris: Economica, 1986.
Blumenthal, Uta-Renate. *The Investiture Controversy.* Philadelphia: University of Pennsylvania Press, 1988.
Binder, Leonard, et al. *Crises and Sequences in Political Development.* Princeton: Princeton University Press, 1971.
Bindoff, S. T., J. Hurstfield, and C. H. Williams, eds. *Elizabethan Government and Society: Essays Presented to Sir John Neale.* London: Athlone, 1961.
Bisson, Thomas. *The Medieval Crown of Aragon.* Oxford: Clarendon, 1986.
Bodin, Jean. *Les Six Livres de la République.* Aalen: Scientia Verlag, 1977.
Boelcke, Willi. "'Die Sanftmütige Accise': Zur Bedeutung und Problematik der 'indirekten Verbrauchsbesteuerung' in der Finanzwirtschaft der deutschen Territorialstaaten während der frühen Neuzeit." *Jahrbuch für die Geschichte Mittel- und Ostdeutschlands,* vol. 21 (1972), pp. 93–139.
Böer, Joachim. "Aspekte der Aemterkäuflichkeit in Valladolid (Altkastilien) im 18. Jahrhundert: Das Beispiel der *Regidores.*" In: *Aemterkäuflichkeit: Aspekte Sozialer Mobilität im Europäischen Vergleich (17. und 18. Jahrhundert).* Ed. Klaus Malettke. Berlin: Colloquium Verlag, 1980, pp. 122–124.
Bogh, Anders. "Feudalisering og Bondekommunalisme." In: *Danmark i Senmiddelalderen.* Ed. Per Ingesman and Jens Villiam Jensen. Aarhus: Universitetsforlag, 1994, pp. 88–105.
Bois, Guy. *La Mutation de l'An Mil.* Paris: Fayard, 1989.
Bónis, György. "Ständisches Finanzwesen in Ungarn im frühen 16. Jahrhundert." In: *Nouvelles Études Historiques.* Budapest: Maison d'Édition de l'Académie des Sciences de Hongrie, 1965, pp. 83–103.
"Die ungarischen Stände in der ersten Hälfte des 18. Jahrhunderts." In: *Ständische Vertretungen in Europa im 17. und 18. Jahrhundert.* Ed. Dietrich Gerhard. 2nd ed. Göttingen: Vandenhoeck & Ruprecht, 1974, pp. 286–309.
Bonney, Richard. *The King's Debts.* Oxford: Clarendon, 1981.
Political Change in France under Richelieu and Mazarin. Oxford: Oxford University Press, 1978.
Bornhak, Conrad. *Geschichte des Preussischen Verwaltungsrechts.* Berlin: Julius Springer, 1884.
Böse, Kuno. "Die Aemterkäuflichkeit in Frankreich vom 14. bis 16. Jahrhundert." In *Aemterhandel im Spätmittelalter und im 16. Jahrhundert.* Ed. Ilja Mieck. Berlin: Colloquium Verlag, 1984, pp. 83–111.
Bosher, John. *French Finances 1770–1795.* Cambridge: Cambridge University Press, 1970.
The French Revolution. New York: Norton, 1988.
"Jacques Necker et L'État Moderne." *Report of the Canadian Historical Association.* 1963, pp. 162–175.
Boshof, Egon. "Einheitsidee und Teilungsprinzip in der Regierungszeit Ludwigs des Frommen." In: *Charlemagne's Heir.* Ed. Peter Goodman and Roger Collins. Oxford: Clarendon, 1990, pp. 161–189.
Bosl, Karl. *Franken um 800.* 2nd ed. München: Beck, 1969.
Die Reichsministerialität der Salier und Staufer. 2 vols. Stuttgart: Hiersemann, 1950.
Staat, Gesellschaft, Wirtschaft im Deutschen Mittelalter. Gehardts Handbuch der Deutschen Geschichte. 9th ed. Vol. VII. Stuttgart: Deutscher Taschenbuchverlag, 1973.
Bosl, Karl, ed. *Der Moderne Parlamentarismus und seine Grundlage in der Ständischen Repräsentation.* Berlin: Duncker & Humblot, 1977.
Brewer, John. *The Sinews of Power.* London: Hutchinson, 1989.
Brewer, John and Eckhart Hellmuth, eds. *Rethinking Leviathan: The British German States of the Eighteenth Century.* Oxford: Oxford University Press, forthcoming.
Breysig, Kurt. "Der brandenburgische Staatshaushalt in der zweiten Hälfte des siebzehnten Jahrhunderts." *Jahrbuch für Gesetzgebung, Verwaltung und Volkswirtschaft im Deutschen Reich [Schmollers Jahrbuch],* vol. 16, no. 1 (1892), pp. 1–42; no. 2, pp. 449–545.

Geschichte der Brandenburgischen Finanzen in der Zeit von 1640 bis 1697. Band I: Die Centralstellen der Kammerverwaltung. Die Amtskammer, das Kassenwesen und die Domänen der Kurmark. Leipzig: Duncker & Humblot, 1895.
"Die Organisation der brandenburgischen Kommissariate in der Zeit von 1660 bis 1697." *Forschungen zur Brandenburgischen und Preussischen Geschichte,* vol. 5, no. 1 (1892), pp. 135–156.
Brooks, Colin. "Public Finance and Political Stability: The Administration of the Land Tax, 1688–1720." *Historical Journal,* vol. 17, no. 2 (June 1974), pp. 281–300.
Brown, A. L. *The Governance of Late Medieval England 1272–1461.* London: Edward Arnold, 1989.
"Parliament, c. 1377–1422." In: *The English Parliament in the Middle Ages.* Eds. R. G. Davies and J. H. Denton. Manchester: Manchester University Press, 1981, pp. 109–140.
Brown, Peter. *The World of Late Antiquity.* London: Thames and Hudson, 1971.
Browning, Andrew. "The Stop of the Exchequer." *History,* vol. 14, no. 56 (January 1930), pp. 333–337.
Thomas Osborne Earl of Danby and Duke of Leeds 1632–1712. Glasgow: Jackson, Son & Co., 1944–1951.
Bruguière, Michel. *Gestionnaires et Profiteurs de la Révolution.* Paris: Olivier Orban, 1986.
Brühl, Carlrichard. *Deutschland-Frankreich: Die Geburt zweier Völker.* Wien: Böhlau, 1990.
Fodrum, Gistum, Servitium Regis. Köln: Böhlau, 1968.
"Zentral- und Finanzverwaltung im Franken- und Langobardenreich." In: *I Problemi dell'Occidente nel Secolo VIII – Settimane di Studio del Centro Italiano di Studi sull'Alto Medioevo.* No. XX. Spoleto: Presso la Sede del Centro, 1973, vol. I, pp. 61–94, 169–185.
Bryant, Arthur. *Samuel Pepys: The Man in the Making.* Cambridge: Cambridge University Press, 1933.
Samuel Pepys: The Saviour of the Navy. Cambridge: Cambridge University Press, 1938.
Samuel Pepys: The Years of Peril. Cambridge: Cambridge University Press, 1935.
Buchda, Gerhard. "Reichstände und Landstände in Deutschland im 16. und 17. Jahrhundert." *Gouvernés et Gouvernants,* vol. 25 (1965), pp. 193–226.
Burnet, Gilbert. *History of My Own Time.* Ed. Osmund Airy. Oxford: Clarendon, 1897–1900.
Burns, J. H., ed. *The Cambridge History of Medieval Political Thought c. 350–c. 1450.* Cambridge: Cambridge University Press, 1988.
Burton, Ivor. "The Secretary at War and the Administration of the Army during the War of the Spanish Succession." Diss. University of London, 1960.
Büsch, Otto. *Militärsystem und Sozialleben im Alten Preussen.* Berlin: Walter de Gruyter, 1962.
and Wolfgang Neugebauer, eds. *Moderne Preussische Geschichte 1648–1947.* Berlin: Walter de Gruyter, 1981.
Calabria, Antonio. *The Cost of Empire.* Cambridge: Cambridge University Press, 1991.
Cam, Helen Maud. "The Theory and Practice of Representation in Medieval England." In: *Historical Studies of the English Parliament. Volume I: Origins to 1399.* Eds. E. B. Fryde and Edward Miller. Cambridge: Cambridge University Press, 1970, pp. 262–278.
Campbell, James. "Observations on English Government from the Tenth to the Twelfth Centuries." In: *Essays in Anglo-Saxon History.* London: Hambledon Press, 1986, pp. 155–170.
"The Significance of the Anglo-Norman State in the Administrative History of Western Europe." In: *Essays in Anglo-Saxon History.* London: Hambledon Press, 1986, pp. 171–189.
Canning, J. P. "Introduction: Politics, Institutions, Ideas." In: *The Cambridge History of Medieval Political Thought c. 350–c. 1450.* Ed. J. H. Burns. Cambridge: Cambridge University Press, 1988, pp. 341–366.
Carande, Ramón. *Carlos V y sus Banqueros.* Madrid: Sociedad de Estudios y Publicaciones, 1949.
Carlsson, Sten and Jerker Rosén. *Svensk Historia.* 2 vols. Stockholm: Svenska Bokförlaget, 1962.

Carrere, Claude. "Aux Origines des Grandes Compagnies: La Compagnie Catalane de 1302." In: *Recrutement, Mentalités, Sociétés*. Ed. Centre d'Histoire Militaire et d'Études de Défense Nationale de Montpellier. Montpellier: Université Paul Valéry, n.d., pp. 1–7.

Carsten, F. L. "The Causes of the Decline of the German Estates." In: *Album Helen Maud Cam*. Louvain: Publications Universitaires de Louvain, 1961, pp. 287–296.

The Origins of Prussia. Oxford: Clarendon, 1954.

Princes and Parliaments in Germany from the Fifteenth to the Eighteenth Century. Oxford: Clarendon, 1959.

Casey, James. *The Kingdom of Valencia in the Seventeenth Century*. Cambridge: Cambridge University Press, 1979.

Castillo, Álvaro. "Dette Flottante et Dette Consolidée en Espagne de 1557 à 1600." *Annales*, vol. 18, no. 4 (July–August 1963), pp. 745–759.

"Los Juros de Castilla: Apogeo y Fin de un Instrumento de Crédito." *Hispania*, vol. 23, no. 89 (1963), pp. 43–70.

Cauwès, Paul. "Les Commencements du Crédit Public en France: Les Rentes sur l'Hôtel de Ville au XVIᵉ Siècle." *Revue d'Économie Politique*, vol. 9, no. 10–11 (October–November 1895), pp. 825–865; vol. 10, no. 5 (May 1896), pp. 407–479.

Cazelles, Raymond. *Société Politique, Noblesse et Couronne sous Jean le Bon et Charles V*. Geneva: Droz, 1982.

Chabod, Federico. *Carlo V e il suo Impero*. Torino: Einaudi, 1983.

"Stipendi Nominali e Busta Paga Effettiva dei Funzionari dell'Amministrazione Milanese alla Fine del Cinquecento." In: *Carlo V e il suo Impero*. Torino: Einaudi, 1983, pp. 281–450.

"Usi e Abusi nell'Amministrazione dello Stato di Milano a mezzo il Cinquecento." In: *Carlo V e il suo Impero*. Torino: Einaudi, 1983, pp. 451–521.

Chamberlayne, John. *Magnae Britanniae Notitia: Or, the Present State of Great Britain*. 27th ed. London: D. Midwinter et al., 1726.

Chandaman, C. D. *The English Public Revenue 1660–1688*. Oxford: Clarendon, 1975.

Charmeil, Jean-Paul. *Les Trésoriers de France à l'Époque de la Fronde*. Paris: Picard, 1964.

Chaussinand-Nogaret, Guy. *Les Financiers de Languedoc au XVIIIᵉ Siècle*. Paris: S.E.V.P.E.N., 1970.

Childs, John. *The Army, James II and the Glorious Revolution*. Manchester: Manchester University Press, 1980.

The Army of Charles II. London: Routledge & Kegan Paul, 1976.

Christensen, Aksel. *Kongemagt og Aristokrati*. Copenhagen: Ejnar Munksgaards Forlag, 1945.

and H. P. Clausen, Svend Ellehøj, and Søren Mørch, eds. *Danmarks Historie*. 5 vols. Copenhagen: Gyldendal, 1977.

Church, Clive. *Revolution and Red Tape: The French Ministerial Bureaucracy 1770–1850*. Oxford: Clarendon, 1981.

Cipolla, Carlo. *Before the Industrial Revolution*. 2nd ed. New York: Norton, 1980.

Clamageran, J.-J. *Histoire de L'Impôt en France*. Paris: Guillaumin, 1867–1876.

Clapham, John. *The Bank of England: A History*. Cambridge: Cambridge University Press, 1945.

Clark, Peter and Paul Slack, eds. *Crisis and Order in English Towns 1500–1700*. London: Routledge Kegan and Paul, 1972.

Clay, Christopher. *Public Finance and Private Wealth: The Career of Sir Stephen Fox 1627–1716*. Oxford: Clarendon, 1978.

Colby, Andrew. *Central Government and the Localities: Hampshire 1649–1689*. Cambridge: Cambridge University Press, 1987.

Coleman, Christopher. "Artifice or Accident? The Reorganization of the Exchequer of Receipt c. 1554–1572." In: *Revolution Reassessed: Revisions in the History of Tudor Government and Administration*. Oxford: Clarendon, 1986, pp. 163–198.

and David Starkey, eds. *Revolution Reassessed: Revisions in the History of Tudor Government and Administration*. Oxford: Clarendon, 1986.

Coleman, D. C. and Peter Mathias, eds. *Enterprise and History: Essays in Honour of Charles Wilson*. Cambridge: Cambridge University Press, 1984.

Collier, David. "The Comparative Method." In: *Political Science: The State of the Discipline II.* Ed. Ada Finifter. Washington: American Political Science Association, 1993, pp. 105–119.

Collier, Ruth Berins and David Collier. *Shaping the Political Arena.* Princeton: Princeton University Press, 1991.

Collinge, J. M. *Navy Board Officials 1660–1870.* London: Institute of Historical Research, 1978.

Collins, James. *The Fiscal Limits of Absolutism.* Berkeley: University of California Press, 1988.

Collins, Roger. *The Arab Conquest of Spain 710–797.* Oxford: Basil Blackwell, 1989.

Early Medieval Europe 300–1000. New York: St. Martin's Press, 1991.

Early Medieval Spain. London: Macmillan, 1983.

"Literacy and Laity in Early Medieval Spain." In: *The Uses of Literacy in Early Medieval Europe.* Ed. Rosamond McKitterick. Cambridge: Cambridge University Press, 1990, pp. 109–133.

Comparato, Vittor Ivo. *Uffici e Società a Nâpoli (1600–1647).* Firenze: Leo Olschki, 1974.

Contamine, Philippe. *La Guerre au Moyen Âge.* Paris: Presses Universitaires de France, 1980.

Contamine, Philippe, ed. *Guerre, État, et Société à la Fin du Moyen Âge: Études sur les Armées des Rois de France 1337–1494.* Paris: Mouton, 1972.

Histoire Militaire de la France I: Des Origines à 1715. Paris: Presses Universitaires de France, 1992.

Corvisier, André. *Louvois.* Paris: Fayard, 1983.

Coulet, Noël and Jean-Philippe Genet, eds. *L'État Moderne: Le Droit, L'Espace et les Formes de L'État.* Paris: Éditions du C.N.R.S., 1990.

Crone, Patricia. *Pre-Industrial Societies.* Oxford: Basil Blackwell, 1989.

D'Arms, John. *Commerce and Social Standing in Ancient Rome.* Cambridge: Harvard University Press, 1981.

David, Paul. "Clio and the Economics of QWERTY." *American Economic Review,* vol. 75, no. 2 (May 1985), pp. 332–337.

Davies, Norman. *God's Playground: A History of Poland.* New York: Columbia University Press, 1982.

Davies, R. G. and J. H. Denton, eds. *The English Parliament in the Middle Ages.* Manchester: Manchester University Press, 1981.

Deane, Phyllis and W. A. Cole. *British Economic Growth 1688–1959.* Cambridge: Cambridge University Press, 1967.

Dering, Sir Edward. *The Papers and Diaries of Sir Edward Dering Second Baronet 1664 to 1684.* Ed. Maurice Bond. London: Her Majesty's Stationery Office, 1976.

Derry, T. K. *A History of Scandinavia.* Minneapolis: University of Minnesota Press, 1979.

Dessert, Daniel. *Argent, Pouvoir et Société au Grand Siècle.* Paris: Fayard, 1984.

"Colbert Contre Colbert." In: *Un Nouveau Colbert.* Ed. Roland Mousnier. Paris: C.D.U. et SEDES réunis, 1985, pp. 111–118.

Fouquet. Paris: Fayard, 1987.

and Jean-Louis Journet. "Le Lobby Colbert: Un Royaume ou une Affaire de Famille?" *Annales,* vol. 30, no. 6 (November–December 1975), pp. 1303–1336.

D'Eszlary, Charles. *Histoire des Institutions Publiques Hongroises.* 3 vols. Paris: Marcel Rivière, 1959–1965.

Dhondt, J. *Études sur la Naissance des Principautés Territoriales en France.* Bruges: De Tempel, 1948.

Dickson, P. G. M. *Finance and Government under Maria Theresia 1740–1780.* 2 vols. Oxford: Clarendon, 1987.

Dietz, Frederick C. *English Government Finance 1485–1558.* New York: Barnes and Noble, 1964.

Domínguez Ortíz, Antonio. *Instituciones y Sociedad en la España de los Austrias.* Barcelona: Ariel, 1985.

Politica y Hacienda de Felipe IV. Madrid: Pegaso, 1983.

Doucet, Roger. "Le Grand Parti de Lyons au XVIᵉ Siècle." *Revue Historique,* vol. 171, no. 3 (May–June 1933), pp. 473–513; vol. 172, no. 1 (July–August 1933), pp. 1–41.

Les Institutions de la France au XVIᵉ Siècle. Paris: Picard, 1948.

Downie, J. A. "The Commission of Public Accounts and the Formation of the Country Party." *English Historical Review*, vol. 91, no. 358 (January 1976), pp. 33–51.

Downing, Brian. "Constitutionalism, Warfare, and Political Change in Early Modern Europe." *Theory and Society*, vol. 17, no. 1 (January 1988), pp. 7–56.

The Military Revolution and Political Change: Origins of Democracy and Autocracy in Early Modern Europe. Princeton: Princeton University Press, 1992.

[Downing, Sir George]. *A State of the Case between furnishing His Majesty with Money by way of Loan, or by way of Advance of the Tax of any particular Place, upon the Act for the £1,250,000 passed at Oxford, October 9, 1665*. London, 1666.

Doyle, William. *Origins of the French Revolution*. 2nd ed. Oxford: Oxford University Press, 1988.

The Parlement of Bordeaux and the End of the Old Regime 1771–1790. London: Ernest Benn, 1974.

Droege, Georg. "Die finanziellen Grundlagen des Territorialstaates in West- und Ostdeutschland an der Wende vom Mittelalter zur Neuzeit." *Vierteljahrschrift für Sozial- und Wirtschaftsgeschichte*, vol. 53, no. 2 (July 1966), pp. 145–161.

Duby, Georges. *L'Économie Rurale et la Vie des Campagnes dans L'Occident Médiéval*. 2 vols. Paris: Flammarion, 1977.

Guerriers et Paysans. Paris: Gallimard, 1973.

Le Moyen Âge 987–1460. Paris: Hachette, 1987.

Les Trois Ordres ou L'Imaginaire du Féodalisme. Paris: Gallimard, 1978.

La Société aux XIᵉ et XIIᵉ Siècles dans la Région Mâconnaise. Paris: S.E.V.P.E.N., 1971.

Dunbabin, Jean. *France in the Making 843–1180*. Oxford: Oxford University Press, 1985.

Dupont-Ferrier, Gustave. *Les Officiers Royaux des Baillages et Sénéchaussées et les Institutions Monarchiques Locales en France à la Fin du Moyen Age*. Paris: Bouillon, 1902.

Durand, Yves. *Les Fermiers Généraux au XVIIIᵉ Siècle*. Paris: Presses Universitaires de France, 1971.

Dyson, Stephen. *Community and Society in Roman Italy*. Baltimore: Johns Hopkins University Press, 1992.

Ebel, Wilhelm. *Geschichte der Gesetzgebung in Deutschland*. Göttingen: Otto Schwarz, 1988.

Echeverria, Durand. *The Maupeou Revolution*. Baton Rouge: Louisiana State University Press, 1985.

Eckhart, Ferenc. "La Diète Corporative Hongroise." In: *L'Organisation Corporative du Moyen Âge à la Fin de l'Ancien Régime*. Louvain: Bibliothèque de l'Université, 1939, pp. 211–224.

Edwards J. G. et al. *Historical Essays in Honour of James Tait*. Manchester: n.p., 1933.

Égret, Jean. *Louis XV et l'Opposition Parlementaire*. Paris: Armand Colin, 1970.

Ehrenberg, Richard. *Das Zeitalter der Fugger*. Hildesheim: Georg Olms, 1963.

Ehrman, John. *The Navy and the War of William III 1689–1697*. Cambridge: Cambridge University Press, 1953.

Eisenstadt, S. N. and Stein Rokkan, eds. *Building States and Nations*, 2 vols. Beverly Hills: Sage, 1973.

Elias, Norbert. *Ueber den Prozess der Zivilisation*. 2 vols. Frankfurt am Main: Suhrkamp, 1976.

Elliott, J. H. *Imperial Spain 1469–1716*. New York: St. Martin's Press, 1964.

Elton, G. R. *The Parliament of England 1559–1581*. Cambridge: Cambridge University Press, 1986.

Studies in Tudor and Stuart Politics and Government. Cambridge: Cambridge University Press, 1974.

The Tudor Revolution in Government. Cambridge: Cambridge University Press, 1953.

Engrand, Charles. "Clients du Roi. Les Colberts et L'État 1661–1715." In: *Un Nouveau Colbert*. Ed. Roland Mousnier. Paris: C.D.U. et SEDES réunis, 1985, pp. 85–97.

Ennen, Edith. *Die Europäische Stadt des Mittelalters*. 3rd ed. Göttingen: Vandenhoeck & Ruprecht, 1979.

Ensslin, Wilhelm. "The End of the Principate." In: *The Cambridge Ancient History. Volume XI: The Imperial Crisis and Recovery A.D. 193–324*. Ed. S. A. Cook, F. E. Adcock, M. P. Charlesworth, and N. H. Baynes. Cambridge: Cambridge University Press, 1939, pp. 352–382.

Bibliography

Erbe, Michael. "Aspekte des Aemterhandels in den Niederlanden im späten Mittelalter und in der Frühen Neuzeit." In: *Aemterhandel im Spätmittelalter und im 16. Jahrhundert.* Ed. Ilja Mieck. Berlin: Colloquium Verlag, 1984, pp. 112–131.

Ertman, Thomas. "Explaining Variation in Early Modern State Structure: The Cases of England and the German Territorial States." In: *Rethinking Leviathan: The British and German States of the Eighteenth Century.* Ed. John Brewer and Eckhart Hellmuth. Oxford: Oxford University Press, forthcoming.

"*The Sinews of Power* and European State-building Theory." In: *An Imperial State at War.* Ed. Lawrence Stone. London: Routledge, 1993, pp. 33–51.

"War and Statebuilding in Early Modern Europe." Diss. Department of Sociology, Harvard University, 1990.

Evans, Peter, Dietrich Rueschemeyer, and Theda Skocpol, eds. *Bringing the State Back In.* Cambridge: Cambridge University Press, 1985.

Evans, R. J. W. *The Making of the Habsburg Monarchy 1550–1700: An Interpretation.* Oxford: Clarendon, 1979.

Evjen, John. *Die Staatsumwälzung in Dänemark im Jahr 1660.* Leipzig: Emil Glausch, 1903.

Ewig, Eugen. "Das merowingische Frankenreich (561–687)." In: *Handbuch der Europäischen Geschichte.* Ed. Theodor Schieder. Vol. I. Stuttgart: Ernst Klett Verlag, 1976, pp. 396–433.

Feenstra, Robert. "Law." In: *The Legacy of Rome: A New Appraisal.* Ed. Richard Jenkyns. Oxford: Oxford University Press, 1992, pp. 399–420.

Feiling, Keith. *A History of the Tory Party 1640–1714.* Oxford: Clarendon, 1924.

Finifter, Ada, ed. *Political Science: The State of the Discipline II.* Washington: American Political Science Association, 1993.

Finley, M. I. "The Ancient City: From Fustel de Coulanges to Max Weber and Beyond." In: *Economy and Society in Ancient Greece.* London: Chatto & Windus, 1981, pp. 3–23.

The Ancient Economy. 2nd ed. Berkeley: University of California Press, 1985.

Firth, C. H. *Cromwell's Army.* 4th ed. London: Methuen, 1962.

Fisher, D. J. V. *The Anglo-Saxon Age c. 400–1042.* London: Longman, 1973.

FitzNigel, Richard. *Dialogus de Scaccario.* Ed. Charles Johnson. Oxford: Oxford University Press, 1983.

Fleckenstein, Josef and Marie Luise Bulst. *Begründung und Aufstieg des Deutschen Reiches. Gebhardts Handbuch der Deutschen Geschichte.* 7th ed. Vol. III. Stuttgart: Deutscher Taschenbuchverlag, 1983.

Folz, Robert. "Les Assemblées d'États dans les Principautés Allemandes (Fin XIIIᵉ–Début XVIᵉ Siècle). *Gouvernés et Gouvernants,* vol. 25 (1965), pp. 163–191.

Fortescue, Sir John. *The Governance of England: Otherwise Called the Difference between an Absolute and Limited Monarchy.* Ed. Charles Plummer. Oxford: Oxford University Press, 1885.

Fossier, Robert. *Enfance de l'Europe.* 2 vols. 2nd ed. Paris: P.U.F., 1989.

Fouracre, Paul. "'Placita' and the Settlement of Disputes in Later Merovingian Gaul." In: *The Settlement of Disputes in Early Modern Europe.* Ed. Wendy Davies and Paul Fouracre. Cambridge: Cambridge University Press, 1986, pp. 23–43.

Franklin, Julian. "Sovereignty and the Mixed Constitution: Bodin and His Critics." In: *The Cambridge History of Political Thought 1450–1700.* Ed. J. H. Burns. Cambridge: Cambridge University Press, 1991, pp. 298–328.

Fryde, E. B. "The English Farmers of the Customs, 1343–1351." *Transactions of the Royal Historical Society.* 5th ser. Vol. 9 (1959), pp. 1–17.

"Parliament and the French War, 1336–40." In: *Historical Studies of the English Parliament.* Eds. E. B. Fryde and Edward Miller. Vol. I. Cambridge: Cambridge University Press, 1970, pp. 242–261.

Fryde, E. B. and M. M. Fryde. "Public Credit, with Special Reference to North-Western Europe." In: *The Cambridge Economic History of Europe. Volume III: Economic Organization and Policies in the Middle Ages.* Ed. M. M. Postan, E. E. Rich, and Edward Miller. Cambridge: Cambridge University Press, 1963, pp. 430–553.

Fryde, E. B. and Edward Miller, eds. *Historical Studies of the English Parliament.* 2 vols. Cambridge: Cambridge University Press, 1970.

Fügedi, Erik. *Castle and Society in Medieval Hungary (1000–1437)*. Budapest: Akadémiai Kiadó, 1986.

Fuhrmann, Horst. *Deutsche Geschichte in Hohen Mittelalter*. 2nd ed. Göttingen: Vandenhoeck & Ruprecht, 1983.

Fürbringer, Christoph. *Necessitas und Libertas. Staatsbildung und Landstände im 17. Jahrhundert in Brandenburg*. Frankfurt am Main. Peter Lang, 1985.

Gagliardo, John. *Germany under the Old Regime 1600–1790*. London: Longman, 1991.

Ganshof, François Louis. "Charlemagne et l'Administration de la Justice dans la Monarchie Franque." In: *Karl der Grosse: Lebenswerk und Nachleben. Band I: Persölichkeit und Geschichte*. Ed. Helmut Beumann. Düsseldorf: Verlag L. Schwann, 1965, pp. 394–419.

"Charlemagne et les Institutions de la Monarchie Franque." In: *Karl der Grosse: Lebenswerk und Nachleben. Band I: Persönlichkeit und Geschichte*. Ed. Helmut Beumann. Düsseldorf: Verlag L. Schwann, 1965, pp. 349–393.

"L'Immunité dans la Monarchie Franque." In: *Recueils de la Société Jean Bodin, I: Les Liens de Vassalité et les Immunités*. 2nd ed. Brussels: Éditions de la Librairie Encyclopédique, 1958.

Qu'est-ce que la Féodalité?. 5th ed. Paris: Tallandier, 1982.

García de Cortázar, José Ángel. *Historia de España Alfaguara II: La Época Medieval*. 9th ed. Madrid: Alianza, 1983.

García Marín, José María. *El Oficio Público en Castilla durante la Baja Edad Media*. Seville: University of Seville, 1974.

Garnsey, Peter, Keith Hopkins, and C. R. Whittaker, eds. *Trade in the Ancient Economy*. Berkeley: University of California Press, 1983.

Garnsey, Peter and Richard Saller. *The Roman Empire*. Berkeley: University of California Press, 1987.

Gaunt, David. *Utbildning till Statens Tjänst*. Uppsala: Almquist & Wiksell, 1975.

Gaussin, Pierre-Roger. *Louis XI: Roi Méconnu*. Paris: Librairie Nizel, 1976.

Geary, Patrick. *Before France and Germany*. Oxford: Oxford University Press, 1988.

Genet, Jean-Philippe, ed. *L'État Moderne: Genèse*. Paris: Éditions du C.N.R.S., 1990.

and Michel Le Mené, eds. *Genèse de l'État Moderne: Prélèvement et Redistribution*. Paris: Éditions du C.N.R.S., 1987.

Gerhard, Dietrich. "Assemblies of Estates and the Corporate Order." In: *Gesammelte Aufsätze*. Göttingen: Vandenhoeck & Ruprecht, 1977, pp. 38–54.

"Probleme des dänischen Frühabsolutismus." In: *Gesammelte Aufsätze*. Göttingen: Vandenhoeck & Ruprecht, 1977, pp. 89–111.

ed. *Ständische Vertretungen in Europa im 17. und 18. Jahrhundert*. 2nd ed. Gottingen: Vandenhoeck & Ruprecht, 1974.

Gerics, József. "Von den Universi Servientes Regis bis zu der Universitas Nobilium Regni Hungariae." In: *Album Elemér Malyusz*. Bruxelles: Éditions de la Librairie Encyclopédique, 1974, pp. 97–108.

Gerschenkron, Alexander. "Economic Backwardness in Historical Perspective." In: *Economic Backwardness in Historical Perspective*. Cambridge, Mass.: Harvard University Press, 1962, pp. 5–30.

Gerth, H. H. and C. Wright Mills, eds. *From Max Weber*. New York: Oxford University Press, 1946.

Giddens, Anthony. *The Nation-State and Violence*. Berkeley: University of California Press, 1985.

Gieysztor, Alexander. "Aspects Territoriaux du Premier État Polonais." *Revue Historique*, vol. 226, no. 2 (October–Décember 1961), pp. 357–381.

"En Pologne Médiévale: Problèmes du Régime Politique et de l'Organisation Administrative du Xe au XIIIe Siècle." *Annali della Fondazione Italiana per la Storia Amministrativa*, vol. 1 (1964), pp. 135–156.

Gieysztor, Aleksander, Stefan Kieniewicz, Emanuel Rostworowski, Janusz Tazbir, and Henryk Wereszycki. *History of Poland*. Warszawa: PWN, 1968.

Gillmann, Franz. *Die Resignation der Benefizien*. Mainz: Verlag von Franz Kirchheim, 1901.

Given-Wilson, Chris. *The Royal Household and the King's Affinity*. New Haven: Yale University Press, 1986.

Goffart, Walter. *Barbarians and Romans* A.D. *418–584: The Techniques of Accommodation.* Princeton: Princeton University Press, 1980.

Göhring, Martin. *Die Aemterkäuflichkeit im Ancien Régime.* Berlin: Verlag Dr. Emil Ebering, 1938.

Goldscheid, Rudolf and Joseph Schumpeter. *Die Finanzkrise des Steuerstaats.* Ed. Rudolf Hickel. Frankfurt: Suhrkamp, 1976.

Goodman, Anthony. "The Military Subcontracts of Sir Hugh Hastings, 1380." *English Historical Review,* vol. 95, no. 374 (January 1980), pp. 114–120.

Goodman, Peter and Roger Collins, eds. *Charlemagne's Heir.* Oxford: Clarendon, 1990.

Górski, Karol. "Les Chartes de la Noblesse en Pologne aux XIVᵉ et XVᵉ Siècle." In: *Album Elemér Malyusz.* Bruxelles: Éditions de la Librairie Encyclopédique, 1976, pp. 247–271.

Gras, Norman S. B. *The Early English Customs System.* Cambridge: Harvard University Press, 1918.

Grimm, Dieter. *Deutsche Verfassungsgeschichte 1776–1866.* Frankfurt: Suhrkamp, 1988.

Gruder, Vivian. *The Royal Provincial Intendants.* Ithaca: Cornell University Press, 1968.

Grundmann, Herbert. "Rotten und Brabanzonen: Söldnerheere im 12. Jahrhundert." *Deutsches Archiv für die Geschichte des Mittelalters,* vol. 5 (1941–1942), pp. 418–492.

Wahlkönigtum, Territorialpolitik und Ostbewegung im 13. und 14. Jahrhundert. Gebhardts *Handbuch der Deutschen Geschichte.* 9th ed., vol. V. Stuttgart: Deutscher Taschenbuchverlag, 1973.

Guenée, Bernard. *Tribunaux et Gens de Justice dans le Baillage de Senlis à la Fin du Moyen Âge.* (Strasbourg: University of Strasbourg, 1963.

Guéry, Alain, "Les Finances de la Monarchie Française sous l'Ancien Régime." *Annales,* vol. 33, no. 2 (March–April 1978), pp. 216–239.

Guy, Alan. *Oeconomy and Discipline: Ownership and Administration in the British Army 1714–1763.* Manchester: Manchester University Press, 1985.

Haigh, Christopher, ed. *The Reign of Elizabeth I.* London: Macmillan, 1984.

Hagen, William. "Seventeenth-Century Crisis in Brandenburg: The Thirty Years War, the Destabilization of Serfdom, and the Rise of Absolutism." *American Historical Review,* vol. 94, no. 2 (April 1989), pp. 302–335.

Hahn, Peter-Michael. "Landesstaat und Ständetum im Kurfürstentum Brandenburg während des 16. und 17. Jahrhunderts." In: *Ständetum und Staatsbildung in Brandenburg-Preussen.* Ed. Peter Baumgart. Berlin: Walter de Gruyter, 1983, pp. 41–79.

Struktur und Funktion des Brandenburgischen Adels im 16. Jahrhundert. Berlin: Colloquium Verlag, 1979.

Haliczer, Stephen. *The Comuneros of Castile.* Madison: University of Wisconsin Press, 1981.

Hall, John. *Powers and Liberties: The Causes and Consequences of the Rise of the West.* Harmondsworth: Penguin, 1986.

Hallam, Elizabeth. *Capetian France 987–1328.* London: Longmans, 1980.

Hamscher, Albert. "The Conseil Privé and the Parlements in the Age of Louis XIV: A Study in French Absolutism." *Transactions of the American Philosophical Society,* vol. 77, part 2 (1987), pp. 1–162.

The Parlement of Paris After the Fronde 1653–1673. Pittsburgh: University of Pittsburgh Press, 1976.

Harding, Robert. *Anatomy of a Power Elite: The Provincial Governors of Early Modern France.* New Haven: Yale University Press, 1978.

Harouel, Jean-Louis, Jean Barbey, Eric Bournzel, and Jacqueline Thibaut-Payen. *Histoire des Institutions de l'Époque Franque à la Révolution.* 3rd ed. Paris: Presses Universitaires de France, 1990.

Harris, Robert D. "French Finances and the American War, 1777–1783." *Journal of Modern History,* vol. 48, no. 2 (June 1976), pp. 233–258.

Necker: Reform Statesman of the Ancien Regime. Berkeley: University of California Press, 1979.

"Necker's *Compte Rendu* of 1781: A Reconsideration." *Journal of Modern History,* vol, 42, no. 2 (June 1970), pp. 161–183.

Harriss, G. L. "The Formation of Parliament 1272–1377." In: *The English Parliament in the Middle Ages*. Ed. R. G. Davies and J. H. Denton. Manchester: Manchester University Press, 1981, pp. 29–60.

Henry V: The Practice of Kingship. Oxford: Oxford University Press, 1985.

King, Parliament and Public Finance in Medieval England to 1369. Oxford: Clarendon Press, 1975.

"War and the Emergence of the English Parliament 1297–1360." *Journal of Medieval History*, vol. 2, no. 1 (March 1976), pp. 35–56.

Hart, Marjolein 't. *The Making of a Bourgeois State: War, Politics and Finance during the Dutch Revolt*. Manchester: Manchester University Press, 1993.

Hartung, Fritz. "Der französisch-burgundische Einfluss auf die Entwicklung der deutschen Behördenorganisation." In: *Staatsbildende Kräfte der Neuzeit*. Berlin: Duncker & Humblot, 1961, pp. 78–92.

Staatsbildende Kräfte der Neuzeit. Berlin: Duncker & Humblot, 1961.

Haussherr, Hans. *Verwaltungseinheit und Ressorttrennung*. Berlin: Akademie-Verlag, 1953.

Haverkamp, Alfred. *Aufbruch und Gestaltung: Deutschland 1056–1273*. München: Beck, 1984.

Heather, Peter. *Goths and Romans 332–489*. Oxford: Clarendon, 1991.

Heidenheimer, Arnold J., Michael Johnston, and Victor T. LeVine, eds. *Political Corruption: A Handbook*. New Brunswick, N.J.: Transaction, 1989.

Heinzelmann, Martin. "Bischof und Herrschaft vom spätantiken Gallien bis zu den karolingischen Hausmeiern. Die institutionellen Grundlagen." In: *Kirche und Herrschaft*. Ed. Friedrich Prinz. Stuttgart: Anton Hiersemann, 1988, pp. 24–82.

Helbig, Herbert. "Fürsten und Landstände im Westen des Reiches im Uebergang vom Mittelalter zur Neuzeit." *Rheinische Vierteljahrsblätter*, vol. 29, no. 1 (1964), pp. 32–72.

"Ungarns Goldene Bulle von 1222 und die Adelsrechte in Siebenbürgen 1291." In: *Album Elemér Malyusz*. Bruxelles: Éditions de la Librairie Encyclopédique, 1976, pp. 109–121.

Hellmann, Manfred. "Die politisch-kirchliche Grundlage der Osthälfte Europas." In: *Handbuch der Europäischen Geschichte*. Ed. Theodor Schieder. Vol. I. Stuttgart: Ernst Klett Verlag, 1976, pp. 857–938.

Henneman, John Bell. *Royal Taxation in Fourteenth Century France: The Captivity and Ransom of John II 1356–1370*. Philadelphia: American Philosophical Society, 1976.

Royal Taxation in Fourteenth Century France: The Development of War Financing 1322–1356. Princeton: Princeton University Press, 1971.

Herrin, Judith. *The Formation of Christendom*. Oxford: Basil Blackwell, 1987.

Hespanha, António Manuel. *História das Instituções. Épocas Medieval e Moderna*. Coimbra: Livraria Almedina, 1982.

Vísperas del Leviatán: Institutiones y Poder Político (Portugal, Siglo XVII). Madrid: Taurus, 1989.

Hill, Brian. *Robert Harley. Speaker, Secretary of State and Premier Minister*. New Haven: Yale University Press, 1988.

Hillgarth, J. N. *The Spanish Kingdoms 1250–1516*. 2 vols. Oxford: Clarendon, 1976.

Hinrichs, Ernst, ed. *Absolutismus*. Frankfurt: Suhrkamp, 1986.

Hintze, Otto. *The Historical Essays of Otto Hintze*. Ed. Felix Gilbert. New York: Oxford University Press, 1975.

Die Hohenzollern und ihr Werk 1415–1915. Berlin: Paul Parey, 1915.

"Einleitende Darstellung der Behördenorganisation und allgemeinen Verwaltung in Preussen beim Regierungsantritt Friedrichs II." In: *Acta Borussica*. Vol. VI, pt. 1. Berlin: Paul Parey, 1901.

"Machtpolitik und Regierungsverfassung." In: *Staat und Verfassung: Gesamelte Abhandlungen zur Allgemeinen Verfassungsgeschichte*. 3rd. ed. Gottingen: Vandenhoeck & Ruprecht, 1970, pp. 424–456.

"Military Organization and the Organization of the State." *The Historical Essays of Otto Hintze*. Ed. Felix Gilbert. New York: Oxford University Press, 1975, pp. 178–215.

Regierung und Verwaltung: Gesammelte Abhandlungen zur Staats-, Rechts-, und Sozialgeschichte Preussens. Göttingen: Vandenhoeck & Ruprecht, 1967.

Staat und Verfassung: Gesammelte Abhandlungen zur Allgemeinen Verfassungsgeschichte. 3rd ed. Göttingen: Vandenhoeck & Ruprecht, 1970.

"Staatenbildung und Kommunalverwaltung." In: *Staat und Verfassung: Gesammelte Abhandlungen zur Allgemeinen Verfassungsgeschichte.* 3rd ed. Göttingen: Vandenhoeck & Ruprecht, 1970, pp. 216–241.

"Typologie der Standischen Verfassungen des Abendlandes." In: *Staat und Verfassung: Gesammelte Abhandlungen zur Allgemeinen Verfassungsgeschichte.* 3rd ed. Göttingen: Vandenhoeck & Ruprecht, 1970, pp. 120–139.

"Verfassungsgeschichte Polens vom 16. bis 18. Jahrhundert." In: *Staat und Verfassung: Gesammelte Abhandlungen zur Allgemeinen Verfassungsgeschichte.* 3rd ed. Göttingen: Vandenhoeck & Ruprecht, 1970, pp. 511–562.

"Weltgeschichtliche Bedingungen der Repräsentativverfassung." In: *Staat und Verfassung: Gesammelte Abhandlungen zur Allgemeinen Verfassungsgeschichte.* 3rd ed. Göttingen: Vandenhoeck & Ruprecht, 1970, pp. 140–185.

"Die Wurzeln der Kreisverfassung in den Ländern des nordöstlichen Deutschland." In: *Staat und Verfassung: Gesammelte Abhandlungen zur Allgemeinen Verfassungsgeschichte.* 3rd ed. Göttingen: Vandenhoeck & Ruprecht, 1970, pp. 186–215.

Hodges, Richard. *The Anglo-Saxon Achievement.* London: Duckworth, 1989.

Dark Age Economics. London: Duckworh, 1982.

Hodges, Richard and Davis Whitehouse. *Mohammed, Charlemagne and the Birth of Europe.* Ithaca: Cornell University Press, 1983.

Hoensch, Jörg. *Geschichte Polens.* 2nd ed. Stuttgart: Verlag Eugen Ulmer, 1990.

Hofmann, Hans, ed. *Die Entstehung des Modernen Staates.* Koln: Kiepenheuer & Witsch, 1967.

Holdsworth, W. S. *A History of English Law.* 7th ed. London: Methuen, 1956.

Hollister, C. Warren and John Baldwin. "The Rise of Administrative Kingship: Henry I and Philip Augustus." *American Historical Review,* vol. 83, no. 4 (October 1978), pp. 867–905.

Holmes, Geoffrey. *Augustan England.* London: George Allen & Unwin, 1982.

British Politics in the Age of Anne. Rev. ed. London: Hambledon, 1987.

Holmes, George, ed. *The Oxford Illustrated History of Medieval Europe.* Oxford: Oxford University Press, 1988.

Holt, J. C. *Magna Carta.* 2nd ed. Cambridge: Cambridge University Press, 1992.

Holub, Joseph. "La Formation des Deux Chambres de l'Assemblée Nationale Hongroise." In: *Album Helen Maud Cam.* Louvain: Publications Universitaires de Louvain, 1961, pp. 347–358.

"La Représentation Politique en Hongrie au Moyen Age." In: *Xe Congrès International des Sciences Historiques, Rome, 1955: Études Présentées à la Commission Internationale pour l'Histoire des Assemblées d'Etats.* Louvain: Publications Universitaires de Louvain, 1958, pp. 77–121.

Hóman, Bálint. *Geschichte des Ungarischen Mittelalters.* 2 vols. Berlin: De Gruyter, 1940–1943.

Gli Angioini di Napoli in Ungheria 1290–1403. Roma: Reale Accademia d'Italia, 1938.

Hoon, Elizabeth. *The Organization of the English Customs System 1696–1786.* New York: Greenwood, 1968.

Horwitz, Henry. *Parliament, Policy and Politics in the Reign of William III.* Manchester: Manchester University Press, 1977.

Hubatsch, Walther. *Friedrich der Grosse und die Preussische Verwaltung.* Cologne: Grote, 1982.

"Verwaltungsentwicklungen von 1713–1803." In: *Deutsche Verwaltungsgeschichte.* Eds. Kurt Jeserich, Hans Pohl, and Georg-Christoph von Unruh. Stuttgart: Deutsche Verlags-Anstalt, 1983, pp. 892–941.

Hughes, Edward. *Studies in Administration and Finance 1558–1825.* Manchester: Manchester University Press, 1934.

Hurstfield, Joel. *Freedom, Corruption and Government in Elizabethan England.* Cambridge: Harvard University Press, 1973.

Hutton, Ronald. *The Restoration.* Oxford: Oxford University Press, 1985.

The Royalist War Effort 1642–1646. London: Longman, 1982.

Hvidtfeldt, Johan, Ib Koch-Olsen, and Axel Steensberg. *Danmarks Historie.* 2 vols. Copenhagen: Det Danske Forlag, 1950.

Hyde, Edward, Earl of Clarendon. *The Life of Edward, Earl of Clarendon.* Oxford: Clarendon, 1827.

Institut d'Histoire de l'Académie Polonaise des Sciences. *L'Europe aux IXe–XIe Siècles: Aux Origines des Etats Nationaux.* Varsovie: Państwowe Wydawnictwo Naukowe, 1968.

Isaacsohn, Siegfried. "Die Finanzen Joachim II. und das Ständische Kreditwerk." *Zeitschrift für Preussische Geschichte und Landeskunde,* vol. 16, no. 4 (July–August 1879), pp. 455–479.

Geschichte des Preussischen Beamtentums vom Anfang des 15. Jahrhunderts bis auf die Gegenwart. 3 vols. Berlin: Puttkammer & Muhlbrecht, 1874–1884.

Israel, Jonathan. *The Dutch Republic: Its Rise, Greatness, and Fall 1477–1806.* Oxford: Oxford University Press, 1995.

Jacobsen, Gertrude. *William Blathwayt: A Late Seventeenth Century English Administrator.* New Haven: Yale University Press, 1932.

Jago, Charles. "Habsburg Absolutism and the Cortes of Castile." *American Historical Review,* vol. 86, no. 2 (April 1981), pp. 307–326.

James, Edward. *The Franks.* Oxford: Basil Blackwell, 1988.

The Origins of France. London: Macmillan, 1982.

Jany, Curt. *Geschichte der Preussischen Armee vom 15. Jahrhundert bis 1914.* Osnabruck: Biblio Verlag, 1967.

"Die Kantonverfassung des altpreussischen Heeres." In: *Moderne Preussische Geschichte 1648–1947.* Ed. Otto Büsch and Wolfgang Neugebauer. Berlin: Walter de Gruyter, 1981, pp. 767–809.

Jenkyns, Richard, ed. *The Legacy of Rome: A New Appraisal.* Oxford: Oxford University Press, 1992.

Jensen, Birgit Bjerre. *Udnaevnelsesretten i Enevaeldens Magtpolitiske System 1660–1730.* Copenhagen: Riksarkivet/G. E. C. Gads Forlag, 1987.

Jeserich, Kurt, Hans Pohl, and Georg-Christoph von Unruh, eds. *Deutsche Verwaltungsgeschichte.* 6 vols. Stuttgart: Deutsche Verlags-Anstalt, 1983.

Johnson, Hubert. *Frederick the Great and His Officials.* New Haven: Yale University Press, 1975.

Jones, A. H. M. *The Late Roman Empire 284–602.* Balitimore: Johns Hopkins University Press, 1986.

Jones, D. W. "London Merchants and the Crisis of the 1690s." In: *Crisis and Order in English Towns 1500–1700.* Ed. Peter Clark and Paul Slack. London: Routledge & Kegan Paul, 1972, pp. 311–355.

War and Economy in the Age of William III and Marlborough. Oxford: Basil Blackwell, 1988.

Jones, E. L. *The European Miracle.* 2nd ed. Cambridge: Cambridge University Press, 1987.

Jones, J. R. *Charles II: Royal Politician.* London: Allen & Unwin, 1987.

Court and Country: England 1658–1714. Cambridge: Harvard University Press, 1978.

ed. *The Restored Monarchy 1660–1688.* London: Macmillan, 1979.

Kaeuper, Richard, *Bankers to the Crown: The Riccardi of Lucca and Edward I.* Princeton: Princeton University Press, 1973.

War, Justice and Public Order: England and France in the Later Middle Ages. Oxford: Clarendon, 1988.

Kagan, Richard. *Students and Society in Early Modern Spain.* Baltimore: Johns Hopkins University Press, 1974.

Kaiser, Reinhold. "Königtum und Bischofsherrschaft im frühneuzeitlichen Neustrien." In: *Kirche und Herrschaft.* Ed. Friedrich Prinz. Stuttgart: Anton Hiersemann, 1988, pp. 83–108.

Kamen, Henry. *Spain 1469–1714: A Society of Conflict.* London: Longmans, 1983.

Karl, Terry Lynn. "Dilemmas of Democratization in Latin America." *Comparative Politics,* vol. 23, no. 1 (October 1990), pp. 1–21.

King, Gary, Robert Keohane, and Sidney Verba. *Designing Social Inquiry.* Princeton: Princeton University Press, 1994.

Klein, Ernst. *Geschichte der Oeffentlichen Finanzen in Deutschland (1500–1870)*. Wiesbaden: Franz Steiner Verlag, 1974.

Von der Reform zur Restauration. Berlin: Walter de Gruyter, 1965.

Klüpfel, Ludwig. *Verwaltungsgeschichte des Königreichs Aragon zu Ende des 13. Jahrhunderts*. Stuttgart: Kohlhammer, 1915.

Knecht, R. J. *Francis I*. Cambridge: Cambridge University Press, 1982.

Knoll, Paul. *The Rise of the Polish Monarchy: Piast Poland in East Central Europe, 1320–1370*. Chicago: University of Chicago Press, 1972.

Knudsen, Tim. *Dansk Statsbygning*. Copenhagen: Juristog Okonomforbundets Forlag, 1995.

Koch, Walther. *Hof und Regierungsverfassung: König Friedrich I. von Preussen (1697–1710)*. Breslau: Verlag von M. & H. Marcus, 1926.

Koenigsberger, H. G. "Dominium regale or dominium politicum et regale? Monarchies and Parliaments in Early Modern Europe." In: *Der moderne Parlamentarismus und seine Grundlagen in der Ständischen Repräsentatation*. Ed. Karl Bosl. Berlin: Dunker & Humbolt, 1977, pp. 43–68.

Estates and Revolutions. Ithaca: Cornell University Press, 1971.

"The Parliament of Piedmont during the Renaissance, 1460–1560." In: *Estates and Revolutions*. Ithaca: Cornell University Press, 1971, pp. 19–79.

"The Parliament of Sicily and the Spanish Empire." In: *Estates and Revolutions*. Ithaca: Cornell University Press, 1971, pp. 80–93.

The Practice of Empire. Ithaca: Cornell University Press, 1969.

Konetzke, Richard. "Territoriale Grundherrschaft und Landesherrschaft im spanischen Spätmittelalter. Ein Forschungsproblem zur Geschichte des spanischen Partikularismus." In: *Histoire Économique du Monde Méditerranéan 1450–1650. Mélanges en L'Honneur de Fernand Braudel*. Toulouse: Privat, 1973, pp. 299–310.

Koser, Reinhold. "Der preussische Staatschatz von 1740–1756." *Forschungen zur Brandenburgischen und Preussischen Geschichte*, vol. 4, no. 1 (1891), pp. 207–229.

"Die preussischen Finanzen im siebenjährigen Krieg." *Forschungen zur Brandenburgischen und Preussischen Geschichte*, vol. 13, no. 1 (1900), pp. 153–217; no. 2, pp. 329–375.

"Die preussischen Finanzen von 1763 bis 1786." In: *Forschungen zur Brandenburgischen und Preussischen Geschichte*, vol. 16 (1903), pp. 101–132.

Kosselleck, Reinhart. *Preussen zwischen Reform und Revolution*. 3rd. ed. München: Deutscher Taschenbuch Verlag, 1989.

Kossmann, Oskar. *Polen im Mittelalter*. 2 vols. Marburg: J. G. Herder-Institut, 1971–1984.

Krabbe, Ludvig. *Histoire de Danemark*. Copenhagen: Ejnar Munksgaard, 1950.

Krasner, Stephen. "Approaches to the State: Alternative Conceptions and Historical Dynamics." *Comparative Politics*, vol. 16, no. 2 (January 1984), pp. 223–246.

"Sovereignty: An Institutional Perspective." *Comparative Political Studies*, vol. 21, no. 1 (April 1988), pp. 66–94.

Krause, Hermann. *Kaiserrecht und Rezeption*. Heidelberg: Carl Winter, 1952.

Kriedte, Peter. *Spätfeudalismus und Handelskapital*. Göttingen: Vandenhoeck & Ruprecht, 1980.

Kroener, Bernhard. *Les Routes et les Etapes*. Münster: Aschendorff, 1980.

Krug, Leopold. *Geschichte der Preussischen Staatsschulden*. Breslau: Verlag von Eduard Trewendt, 1861.

Krüger, Kersten. "Absolutismus in Danemark – ein Model fur Begriffsbildung und Typologie." In: *Absolutismus*. Ed. Ernst Hinrichs. Frankfurt: Suhrkamp, 1986, pp. 65–94.

"Public Finance and Modernisation: The Change from Domain State to Tax State in Hesse in the Sixteenth and Seventeenth Centuries – A Case Study." In: *Wealth and Taxation in Central Europe*. Ed. Peter-Christian Witt. Leamington Spa, UK: Berg, 1987, pp. 49–62.

Kubler, Jean. *L'Origine de la Perpétuité des Offices Royaux*. Nancy: Université de Nancy, 1958.

Küchler, Winfried. "Aemterkäuflichkeit in den Ländern der Krone Aragons." In: *Gesammelte Aufsätze zur Kulturgeschichte Spaniens*. Ed. Johannes Vincke. Münster: Aschendorffsche Verlagsbuchhandlung, 1973, pp. 1–26.

Die Finanzen der Krone Aragon während des 15. Jahrhunderts (Alfons V. und Johann II.). Münster: Aschendorffsche Verlagsbuchhandlung, 1983.

Kutrzeba, Stanislaus. *Grundriss der Polnischen Verfassungsgeschichte.* Berlin: Puttkammer & Mühlbrecht, 1912.
Labande-Mailfert, Yvonne. *Charles VIII et son Milieu.* Paris: Klincksieck, 1975.
Ladero Quesada, Miguel Ángel. *Castilla y la Conquista del Reino de Granada.* Valladolid: Universidad de Valladolid, 1967.
España en 1492. Madrid: Hernando, 1978.
La Hacienda Real de Castilla en el Siglo XV. Tenerife: Universidad de La Laguna, 1973.
El Siglo XV en Castilla. Barcelona: Editorial Ariel, 1982.
Landwehr, Götz. "Mobilisierung und Konsolidierung der Herrschaftsordnung im 14. Jahrhundert. Zusammenfassung." In: *Der Deutsche Territorialstaat im 14. Jahrhundert.* Ed. Hans Patze. 2 vols. Sigmaringen: Jan Thorbecke, 1971, vol. II, pp. 484–505.
Lange, Ulrich. "Der ständische Dualismus – Bemerkungen zu einem Problem der deutschen Verfassungsgeschichte." *Blätter für Deutsche Landesgeschichte,* vol. 117 (1981), pp. 311–334.
LaPalombara, Joseph, ed. *Bureaucracy and Political Development.* Princeton: Princeton University Press, 1963.
Lavisse, Ernest. *Histoire de la France depuis les Origines jusqu'à la Révolution.* Paris: Hachette, 1911.
Lebigre, Arlette. "Colbert et les Commissaires du Roi." In: *Un Nouveau Colbert.* Ed. Roland Mousnier. Paris: C.D.U. et SEDES réunis, 1985, pp. 133–144.
Leger, Louis. "Hungary, 1000–1301." In: *The Cambridge Medieval History, Volume VI: Victory of the Papacy.* Ed. J. R. Tanner, C. W. Previté-Orton, and Z. N. Brooke. Cambridge: Cambridge University Press, 1968, pp. 463–472.
Legohérel, Henri. *Les Trésoriers de la Marine (1517–1788).* Paris: Editions Cujas, 1965.
Lemarignier, Jean-François. *La France Médiévale: Institutions et Société.* Paris: Armand Colin, 1970.
"Structures Monastiques et Structures Politiques dans la France de la Fin du Xe Siècle et des Débuts du XIe Siècle." In: *Il Monachesimo nell'Alto Medioevo e la Formazione della Civiltà Occidentale* (= Settimane di Studio del Centro Italiano di Studi sull'Alto Medioevo IV). Spoleto: Presso la Sede del Centro, 1957, pp. 357–400.
Léonard, Émile. *Les Angevins de Naples.* Paris: Presses Universitaires de France, 1954.
Leuschner, Joachim. *Deutschland im Späten Mittelalter.* 2nd ed. Göttingen: Vandenhoeck & Ruprecht, 1983.
Levi, Margaret. *Of Rule and Revenue.* Berkeley: University of California Press, 1988.
Lewis, N. B. "An Early Indenture of Military Service, 27 July 1287." *Bulletin of the Institute of Historical Research,* vol. 13, no. 38 (November 1935), pp. 85–89.
Lewis, P. S. *Essays in Late Medieval French History.* London: Hambledon, 1985.
Late Medieval France. London: Macmillan, 1968.
Leyser, Karl. "Ottonian Government." In: *Medieval Germany and Its Neighbours 900–1250.* London: Hambledon, 1982, pp. 69–101.
Liehr, Reinhard. "Aemterkäuflichkeit und Aemterhandel im kolonialen Hispanoamerika." In: *Aemterhandel im Spätmittelalter und im 16. Jahrhundert.* Ed. Ilja Mieck. Berlin: Colloquium Verlag, 1984, pp. 159–180.
Lipset, Seymour Martin, and Stein Rokkan. "Cleavage Structures, Party Systems, and Voter Alignments: An Introduction." In: *Party System and Voter Alignments: Cross National Perspectives.* Ed. Seymour Martin Lipset and Stein Rokkan. New York: Free Press, 1968, pp. 1–64.
Litchfield, R. Burr. *The Emergence of a Bureaucracy: Florentine Patricians 1530–1790.* Princeton: Princeton University Press, 1986.
Livermore, H. V. *A History of Portugal.* Cambridge: Cambridge University Press, 1947.
von Loehr, A. O. "Die Finanzierung des siebenjährigen Kriegs: Ein Versuch vergleichender Geldgeschichte." *Numismatische Zeitschrift.* Neue Folge, vol. 18 (1925), pp. 95–110.
Lönnroth, Erik. "Representative Assemblies of Medieval Sweden." In: *Xe Congrès International des Sciences Historiques. Rome, 1955.* Louvain: Publications Universitaires de Louvain, 1958, pp. 123–131.
"Government in Medieval Scandinavia." *Gouvernés et Gouvernants,* vol. 24 (1966), pp. 453–460.

Løgstrup, Birgit. *Jorddrot og Offentlig Administrator.* Copenhagen: G. E. C. Gads Forlag, 1983.
Lopez, Robert. *The Commercial Revolution of the Middle Ages, 950–1350.* Cambridge: Cambridge University Press, 1976.
"The Trade of Medieval Europe: The South." In: *The Cambridge Economic History of Europe. Volume II: Trade and Industry in the Middle Ages.* Ed. M. M. Postan and Edward Miller. Cambridge: Cambridge University Press, 1987, pp. 306–401.
Lot, Ferdinand. *L'Art Militaire et les Armées au Moyen Âge.* Paris: Payot, 1946.
Recherches sur les Effectifs des Armées Françaises des Guerres d'Italie aux Guerres de Réligion 1494–1562. Paris: S.E.V.P.E.N., 1962.
and Robert Fawtier, *Histoire des Institutions de la France au Moyen Âge.* Paris: Presses Universitaires de France, 1958.
Löwe, Heinz. *Deutschland im Fränkischen Reich. Gebhardts Handbuch der Deutschen Geschichte.* 7th ed. Vol. II. Stuttgart: Deutscher Taschenbuchverlag, 1982.
Loyn, H. R. *The Governance of Anglo-Saxon England 500–1087.* London: Edward Arnold, 1984.
Ludat, Herbert. "Piasten und Ottonen." In: *L'Europe aux IXe–XIe Siècles: Aux Origines des Etats Nationaux.* Ed. Institut d'Histoire de l'Académie Polonaise des Sciences. Varsovie: Państwowe Wydawnictwo Naukowe, 1968, pp. 321–359.
Luethy, Herbert. *La Banque Protestante en France.* Paris: S.E.V.P.E.N., 1959.
Lynch, John. *Bourbon Spain 1700–1808.* Oxford: Basil Blackwell, 1989.
Spain under the Habsburgs. 2nd ed. 2 vols. New York: New York University Press, 1981.
Lyon, Bryce and A. E. Verhulst. *Medieval Finance: A Comparison of Financial Institutions in Northwestern Europe.* Providence: Brown University Press, 1967.
MacCaffrey, Wallace. "Place and Patronage in Elizabethan Politics." In: *Elizabethan Government and Society: Essays Presented to Sir John Neale.* Eds. S. T. Bindoff, J. Hurstfield, and C. H. Williams. London: Athlone, 1961, pp. 95–126.
Mack Smith, Denis. *A History of Sicily.* New York: Dorset, 1988.
MacKay, Angus. *Spain in the Middle Ages.* London: Macmillan, 1977.
MacMullen, Ramsay. *Corruption and the Decline of Rome.* New Haven: Yale University Press, 1988.
Maitland, F. W. *The Constitutional History of England.* Cambridge: Cambridge University Press, 1908.
Major, J. Russell. *Representative Institutions in Renaissance France 1421–1559.* Madison: University of Wisconsin Press, 1960.
Malement, Barbara C., ed. *After the Reformation: Essays in Honor of J. H. Hexter.* Philadelphia: University of Pennsylvania Press, 1980.
Malettke, Klaus, ed. *Aemterkäuflichkeit: Aspekte Sozialer Mobilität im Europäischen Vergleich (17. und 18. Jahrhundert).* Berlin: Colloquium Verlag, 1980.
Mallett, Michael. *Mercenaries and their Masters.* London: The Bodley Head, 1974.
Malyusz, Elemér. "Les Débuts du Vote de la Taxe par les Ordres dans la Hongrie Féodale." In: *Nouvelles Études Historiques.* Budapest: Maison d'Édition de l'Académie des Sciences de Hongrie, 1965, pp. 55–82.
"Die Entstehung der Stände im mittelalterlichen Ungarn." In: *L'Organisation Corporative du Moyen Âge à la Fin de l'Ancien Régime.* Louvain: Bibliothèque de l'Université, 1939, pp. 13–30.
Mann, Michael. *The Sources of Social Power.* Vol. I. *A History of Power from the Beginning to A.D. 1760.* Cambridge: Cambridge University Press, 1986.
"State and Society, 1130–1815: An Analysis of English State Finances." *Political Power and Social Theory,* vol. 1 (1980), pp. 165–208.
Mantelli, Roberto. *Burocrazia e Finanze Pubbliche nel Regno di Napoli a Metà del Cinquecento.* Napoli: Lucio Pironti, 1981.
The Manuscripts of the House of Lords. London: H.M.S.O., 1965.
Marczali, Heinrich. *Ungarische Verfassungsgeschichte.* Tübingen: J. C. B. Mohr, 1910.
Marion, Marcel. *Dictionnaire des Institutions de la France aux XVIIe et XVIIIe Siècles.* 1923, rpt. Paris: Picard, 1984.
Histoire Financière de la France depuis 1715. Paris: Arthur Rousseau, 1914.
Machault d'Arnouville. Paris: Hachette, 1891.

Marongiu, Antonio. *Medieval Parliaments: A Comparative Study.* London: Eyre and Spottiswoode, 1968.

Il Parlamento in Italia nel Medio Evo e nell'Età Moderna. Milano: Guiffrè, 1962.

Martin, Olivier. "La Nomination aux Offices Royaux au XIVe Siècle et d'après les Pratiques de la Chancellerie." *Mélanges Paul Fournier.* Paris. Recueil Sirey, 1929, pp. 487–501.

Matthew, Donald. *The Norman Kingdom of Sicily.* Cambridge: Cambridge University Press, 1992.

Matthews, George. *The Royal General Farms in Eighteenth Century France.* New York: Columbia University Press, 1958.

McIlwain, C. H. "Medieval Estates." In: *The Cambridge Medieval History. Volume VII: Decline of Empire and Papacy.* Ed. J. R. Tanner, C. W. Previté-Orton, and Z. N. Brooke. Cambridge: Cambridge University Press, 1968, pp. 664–715.

McKisack, May. *The Fourteenth Century 1307–1399.* Oxford: Clarendon, 1959.

McKitterick, Rosamond. *The Frankish Kingdoms under the Carolingians, 751–987.* London: Longman, 1983.

Meisner, Heinrich Otto. "Die monarchische Regierungsform in Brandenburg-Preussen." In: *Forschungen zu Staat und Verfassung: Festgabe für Fritz Hartung.* Ed. Richard Dietrich and Gerhard Oestreich. Berlin: Duncker & Humblot, 1958, pp. 219–245.

Merritt, Richard and Bruce Russett, eds. *From National Development to Global Community.* London: George Allen & Unwin, 1981.

Metcalf, Michael. "Parliamentary Sovereignty and Royal Reaction, 1719–1806." In: *The Riksdag: A History of the Swedish Parliament.* Ed. Michael Metcalf. New York: St. Martin's, 1987, pp. 109–164.

ed. *The Riksdag: A History of the Swedish Parliament.* New York: St. Martin's, 1987.

Mettam, Roger. *Power and Faction in Louis XIV's France.* Oxford: Basil Blackwell, 1988.

Michaud, Claude. "L'Europe Centrale et le Cas Hongrois." In: *L'État Moderne: Le Droit, L'Espace et les Formes de l'État.* Ed. Noël Coulet and Jean-Philippe Genet. Paris: Éditions du C.N.R.S., 1990, pp. 189–207.

Mieck, Ilja, ed. *Aemterhandel im Spätmittelalter und im 16. Jahrhundert.* Berlin: Colloquium Verlag, 1984.

Millar, Fergus. *The Emperor in the Roman World.* London: Duckworth, 1977.

Mitchell, B. R. and Phyllis Deane. *Abstract of British Historical Statistics.* Cambridge: Cambridge University Press, 1962.

Mitterauer, Michael. "Grundlagen politischer Berechtigung im mittelalterlichen Ständewesen." In: *Der Moderne Parlamentarismus und seine Grundlage in der Ständischen Repräsentation.* Ed. Karl Bosl. Berlin: Duncker & Humblot, 1977, pp. 11–41.

Mitteis, Heinrich and Heinz Lieberich. *Deutsche Rechtsgeschichte.* 19th ed. Munich: Beck, 1992.

Morineau, Michel. "Budgets de l'État et gestion des finances royales en France au dix-huitième siècle." *Revue Historique,* vol. 264, no. 546 (October–December 1980), pp. 289–336.

Morris, Colin. *The Papal Monarchy: The Western Church from 1050 to 1250.* Oxford: Clarendon, 1989.

Morris, Rosemary. "Northern Europe Invades the Mediterranean, 900–1200." In: *The Oxford Illustrated History of Medieval Europe.* Ed. George Holmes. Oxford: Oxford University Press, 1988, pp. 175–234.

Mousnier, Roland. *L'Assassinat d'Henri IV.* Paris: Gallimard, 1964.

ed. *Le Conseil du Roi de Louis XII à la Révolution.* Paris: Presses Universitaires de France, 1970.

ed. *Un Nouveau Colbert.* Paris: C.D.U. et SEDES reunis, 1985.

"Le Trafic des Offices à Venise." *Revue Historique du Droit Français et Étranger,* vol. 30, no. 4 (1952), pp. 552–565.

La Vénalité des Offices sous Henri IV et Louis XIII. 2nd ed. Paris: Presses Universitaires de France, 1971.

de Moxó, Salvador. *La Alcabala.* Madrid: Consejo Superior de Investigaciones Cientificas, 1963.

Musset, Lucien. *Les Peuples Scandinaves au Moyen Âge.* Paris: Presses Universitaires de France, 1951.

Myers, A. R. *Parliaments and Estates in Europe to 1789.* London: Thames & Hudson, 1975.
"The Parliaments of Europe in the Age of the Estates." *History,* vol. 60, no. 198 (February 1975), pp. 11–27.
Myres, J. N. L. *The English Settlements.* Oxford: Clarendon, 1986.
Näf, Werner, "Frühformen des 'modernen Staates' im Spätmittelalter." In: *Die Entstehung des Modernen Staates.* Ed. Hans Hofmann. Köln: Kiepenheurer & Witsch, 1967.
Naudé, Wilhelm. "Zur Geschichte des preussischen Subalternbeamtentums." *Forschungen zur Brandenburgischen und Preussischen Geschichte,* vol. 18, no. 2 (1905), pp. 1–22.
Neale, J. E. *Elizabeth and Her Parliaments 1584–1601.* London: Jonathan Cape, 1957.
Essays in Elizabethan History. London: Macmillan, 1958.
Nelson, Janet. "Kingship and Empire." In: *The Cambridge History of Medieval Political Thought c. 350–c. 1450.* Ed. J. H. Burns. Cambridge: Cambridge University Press, 1988, pp. 211–251.
Newhall, Richard. *Muster and Review.* Cambridge: Harvard University Press, 1940.
North, Douglass. *Structure and Change in Economic History.* New York: W. W. Norton, 1981.
Nordmann, Claude. *Grandeur et Liberté de la Suède (1660–1792).* Paris: Béatrice-Nauwelaerts, 1971.
North, Douglass and Robert Paul Thomas. *The Rise of the Western World.* Cambridge: Cambridge University Press, 1973.
Obenaus, Herbert. *Die Anfänge des Parlamentarismus in Preussen bis 1848.* Düsseldorf: Droste, 1984.
"Finanzkrise und Verfassungsgebung: Zu den sozialen Bedingungen des frühen deutschen Konstitutionalismus." In: *Preussische Reformen 1807–1820.* Ed. Barbara Vogel, N.p.: Verlagsgruppe Athenäum-Hain-Scriptor-Hanstein, 1980, pp. 244–265.
O'Callaghan, Joseph. *The Cortes of Castile-Leon 1188–1350.* Philadelphia: University of Pennsylvania Press, 1989.
A History of Medieval Spain. Ithaca: Cornell University Press, 1975.
Oestreich, Gerhard. "Ständestaat und Ständewesen im Werk Otto Hintzes." In: *Ständische Vertretungen in Europa im 17. und 18. Jahrhundert.* Ed. Dietrich Gerhard. Göttingen: Vandenhoeck & Ruprecht, 1974, pp. 56–71.
Verfassungsgeschichte vom Ende des Mittelalters bis zum Ende des Alten Reiches. Gebhardts Handbuch der Deutschen Geschichte. 9th ed. Vol. XI. Stuttgart: Deutscher Taschenbuchverlag, 1974.
Ohnishi, Takeo. "Die preussische Steuerreform nach dem Wiener Kongress." In: *Preussische Reformen 1807–1820.* Ed. Barbara Vogel. N.p.: Verlagsgruppe Athenaum-Hain-Scriptor-Hanstein, 1980, pp. 266–284.
Olesen, Jens. *Rigsrad, Kongemagt, Union 1434–1449.* Aarhus: Universitetsforlaget, 1980.
Olivier-Martin, François. "La Nomination aux Offices Royaux au XIVᵉ Siècle et d'après les Pratiques de la Chancellerie." In: *Mélanges Paul Fournier.* Paris: Recueil Sirey, 1929, pp. 487–501.
Oppenheim, M. *A History of the Royal Navy and of Merchant Shipping in Relation to the Navy from 1509 to 1660 with an Introduction Treating of the Preceding Period.* London: The Bodley Head, 1896.
Ormrod, W. M. *The Reign of Edward III.* New Haven: Yale University Press, 1990.
Pacaut, Marcel. "Structures Monastiques, Société, et Église en Occident aux XIᵉ et XIIᵉ Siècles." *Cahiers d'Histoire,* vol. 20, no. 2 (1975), pp. 119–136.
Pamlényi, Ervin. ed. *A History of Hungary.* London: Collet's, 1975.
Paravicini, Werner and Karl Ferdinand Werner, eds. *Histoire Comparée de l'Administration (IVᵉ–XVIIIᵉ Siècles).* München: Artemis, 1980.
Parker, Geoffrey. *The Army of Flanders and the Spanish Road 1567–1659.* Cambridge: Cambridge University Press, 1972.
The Military Revolution. Cambridge: Cambridge University Press, 1988.
Parrott, D. A. "The Administration of the French Army During the Ministry of Cardinal Richelieu." D.Phil. thesis. Oxford, 1985.
Partner, Peter. *The Pope's Men.* Oxford: Clarendon, 1990.
Patze, Hans. "Der Deutschordenstaat Preussen 1226–1466." In: *Handbuch der Europäischen Geschichte.* Ed. Theodor Schieder. Vol. II. Stuttgart: Ernst Klett Verlag, 1976, pp. 468–489.

ed. *Der Deutsche Territorialstaat im 14. Jahrhundert.* 2 vols. Sigmaringen: Jan Thorbeck, 1971.

"Die Herrschaftspraxis der deutschen Landesherren während des späten Mittelalters." In *Histoire Comparée de l'Administration (IVᵉ–XVIIIᵉ Siècles).* Ed. Werner Paravicini and Karl Ferdinand Werner. München; Artemis, 1980, pp. 363–391.

Peck, Linda Levy. "Corruption at the Court of James I: The Undermining of Legitimacy." In: *After the Reformation: Essays in Honor of J. H. Hexter.* Philadelphia: University of Pennsylvania Press, 1980, pp. 75–90.

Pelorson, Jean-Marc. *Les Letrados: Juristes Castillans sous Philippe III.* Poitiers: Université de Poitiers, 1980.

Pepys, Samuel. *The Diary of Samuel Pepys.* Ed. Robert Latham and William Matthews. 11 vols. London: Bell and Hyman, 1970–1983.

Petersen, E. Ladewig. "War, Finance and the Growth of Absolutism: Some Aspects of the European Integration of Seventeenth Century Denmark." In: *Europe and Scandinavia: Aspects of the Process of Integration in the 17th Century.* Ed. Göran Rystad. Lund: Esselte Studium, 1983, pp. 33–49.

Picot, Georges. *Histoire des États Généraux.* 2nd ed. Paris: Hachette, 1888.

Pieri, Piero. "Consalvo de Cordova e le Origini del Moderno Esercito Spagnolo." In: *Fernando el Católico e Italia.* Zaragoza: Institución "Fernando el Católico," 1954, pp. 209–225.

Pillorget, René. "Henri Pussort, Oncle de Colbert (1615–1697)." In: *Le Conseil du Roi de Louis XII à la Révolution.* Ed. Roland Mousnier. Paris: Presses Universitaires de France, 1970, pp. 255–274.

di Pinto, Mario, ed. *I Borbone di Napoli e i Borbone di Spagna.* 2 vols. Napoli: Guida Editori, 1985.

Piskorski, Wladimiro. *Las Cortes de Castilla en el Período de Tránsito de la Edad Media a la Moderna 1188–1520.* Barcelona: El Albir, 1977.

Poggi, Gianfranco. *The Development of the Modern State.* Stanford: Stanford University Press, 1978.

The State: Its Nature, Development and Prospects. Stanford: Stanford University Press, 1990.

Pollock, Sir Frederick and Frederick William Maitland. *The History of English Law before the Time of Edward I.* 2nd ed. Cambridge: Cambridge University Press, 1968.

Poly, Jean-Pierre and Eric Bournazel. *La Mutation Féodale: Xᵉ–XIIᵉ Siècles.* Paris: Presses Universitaires de France, 1980.

Porter, Stephen. "The Fire-raid in the English Civil War." *War and Society,* vol 2, no. 2 (September 1984), pp. 27–40.

Post, Gaines. "*Plena Potestas* and Consent in Medieval Assemblies." In: *Studies in Medieval Legal Thought.* Princeton: Princeton University Press, 1964, pp. 91–162.

"Roman Law and Early Representation in Spain and Italy, 1150–1250." In: *Studies in Medieval Legal Thought.* Princeton: Princeton University Press, 1964, pp. 61–90.

Postan, M. M. "The Trade of Medieval Europe: The North." In: *The Cambridge Economic History of Europe. Volume II: Trade and Industry in the Middle Ages.* Ed. M. M. Postan and Edward Miller. Cambridge: Cambridge University Press, 1987, pp. 168–305.

Postan, M. M. and Edward Miller, eds. *The Cambridge Economic History of Europe. Volume II: Trade and Industry in the Middle Ages.* 2nd ed. Cambridge: Cambridge University Press, 1987.

Postan, M. M., E. E. Rich, and Edward Miller, eds. *The Cambridge Economic History of Europe. Volume III: Economic Organization and Policies in the Middle Ages.* Cambridge: Cambridge University Press, 1963.

Pounds, N. J. G. *An Historical Geography of Europe 450 B.C.–A.D. 1330.* Cambridge: Cambridge University Press, 1973.

The Medieval Castle in England and Wales. Cambridge: Cambridge University Press, 1990.

Powicke, M. R. "Lancastrian Captains." In: *Essays in Medieval History Presented to Bertie Wilkinson.* Ed. T. A. Sandquist and M. R. Powicke. Toronto: University of Toronto Press, 1969, pp. 371–382.

Press, Volker. "Formen des Ständewesens in den deutschen Territorialstaaten des 16. und 17. Jahrhunderts." In: *Ständetum und Staatsbildung in Brandenburg-Preussen.* Ed. Peter Baumgart. Berlin: Walter de Gruyter, 1983, pp. 280–318.

"Steuern, Kredit und Repräsentation: Zum Problem der Ständebildung ohne Adel." *Zeitschrift für Historische Forschung.* vol. 2, no. 1 (1975), pp. 59–93.

"Vom 'Ständestaat' zum Absolutismus: 50 Thesen zur Entwicklung des Ständewesens in Deutschland." In: *Ständetum und Staatsbildung in Brandenburg-Preussen.* Ed. Peter Baumgart. Berlin: Walter de Gruyter, 1983, pp. 319–326.

Prestwich, J. O. *Edward I.* Berkeley: University of California Press, 1988.

The Three Edwards. London: Methuen, 1980.

"War and Finance in the Anglo-Norman State." *Transactions of the Royal Historical Society.* 5th ser. Vol. 4 (1954), pp. 19–54.

Prince, A. E. "The Indenture System under Edward III." In: *Historical Essays in Honour of James Tait.* Ed. J. G. Edwards et al. Manchester: n.p., 1933, pp. 283–297.

Prinz, Friedrich. *Grundlagen und Anfänge: Deutschland bis 1056.* München: Beck, 1985. ed. *Kirche und Herrschaft.* Stuttgart: Anton Hiersemann, 1988.

Procter, Evelyn. *Curia and Cortes in Leon and Castile 1072–1295.* Cambridge: Cambridge University Press, 1980.

Quatrefages, René. *Los Tercios Españoles (1567–77).* Madrid: Fondación Universitaria Española, 1979.

Quesada, Miguel Ángel Ladero. *Castilla y la Conquesta del Reino de Granada.* Valladolid: Universidad de Valadolid, 1967.

El Siglo XV en Castilla. Barcelona: Editorial Ariel, 1982.

"Ingreso, Gasto y Politica Fiscal de la Corona de Castilla. Desde Alfonso X a Enrique III (1252–1406)." In: *El Siglo XV en Castilla.* Barcelona: Editorial Ariel, 1982, pp. 13–57.

"Instituciones Fiscales y Realidad Social en el Siglo XV Castellano." In *El Siglo XV en Castilla.* Barcelona: Editorial Ariel, 1982, pp. 58–87.

La Hacienda Real de Castilla en el Siglo XV. Tenerife: Universidad de La Laguna, 1973.

"Los Judíos Castellanos del Siglo XV en el Arrendamiento de Impuestos Reales." In *El Siglo XV en Castilla.* Barcelona: Editorial Ariel, 1982, pp. 143–167.

Raeff, Marc. *The Well-Ordered Police State.* New Haven: Yale University Press, 1983.

Randsborg, Klavs. *The First Millennium A.D. in Europe and the Mediterranean.* Cambridge: Cambridge University Press, 1991.

Redlich, Fritz. *The German Military Enterpriser and His Workforce.* Wiesbaden: Franz Steiner Verlag, 1964.

Reilly, Bernard. *The Kingdom of Leon-Castilla under Queen Urraca 1109–1126.* Princeton: Princeton University Press, 1982.

Reinhard, Wolfgang. "Aemterhandel in Rom zwischen 1534 und 1621." In: *Aemterhandel im Spätmittelalter und im 16. Jahrhundert.* Ed. Ilja Mieck. Berlin: Colloquium Verlag, 1984, pp. 42–60.

"Staatsmacht als Kreditproblem. Zur Struktur und Funktion des frühneuzeitlichen Aemterhandels." In: *Absolutismus.* Ed. Ernst Hinrichs. Frankfurt: Suhrkamp, 1986, pp. 214–248.

Reitan, E. A. "From Revenue to Civil List, 1689–1702: The Revolution Settlement and the 'Mixed and Balanced' Constitution." *Historical Journal,* vol. 13, no. 4 (December 1970), pp. 571–588.

Renouard, Yves. "1212–1216: comment les traits durables de l'Europe occidentale moderne se sont définis au début du XIIIᵉ siècle." *Annales de l'Université de Paris,* vol. 28, no. 2 (January–March 1952), pp. 21.

Reuter, Timothy. "The End of Carolingian Military Expansion." In: *Charlemagne's Heir.* Ed. Peter Goodman and Roger Collins. Oxford: Clarendon, 1990, pp. 391–405.

Germany in the Early Middle Ages 800–1056. London: Longman, 1991.

"Plunder and Tribute in the Carolingian Empire." *Transactions of the Royal Historical Society.* 5th ser. Vol. 35 (1985), pp. 75–94.

Rhode, Gotthold. "Ungarn vom Ende der Verbindung mit Polen bis zum Ende der Türkenherrschaft (1444–1699)." In: *Handbuch der Europäischen Geschichte.* Ed. Theodor Schieder. Vol. III. Stuttgart: Ernst Klett Verlag, 1976, pp. 1061–1117.

Ribbe, Wolfgang. "Burg und Amtsverpfändungen in der Mark Brandenburg." In: *Aemterhandel im Spätmittelalter und im 16 Jahrhundert.* Ed. Ilja Mieck. Berlin: Colloquium Verlag, 1984, pp. 211–230.

Riedel, Adolph Friedrich. *Der Brandenburg-Preussische Staatshaushalt in den Beiden Letzten Jahrhunderten.* Berlin: Ernst & Korn, 1866.
Riis, Thomas. *Les Institutions Politiques Centrales du Danemark 1100–1332.* Odense: Odense University Press, 1977.
Riley, James C. *International Government Finance and the Amsterdam Capital Market.* Cambridge: Cambridge University Press, 1980.
"French Finances, 1727–1768." *Journal of Modern History,* vol. 59, no. 2 (June 1987), pp. 209–243.
The Seven Years War and the Old Regime in France. Princeton: Princeton University Press, 1986.
Roberts, Clayton. "Party and Patronage in Late Stuart England." In: *England's Rise to Greatness 1660–1763.* Ed. Stephen Baxter. Berkeley: University of California Press, 1983, pp. 185–212.
Roberts, Michael. *The Age of Liberty: Sweden 1719–1772.* Cambridge: Cambridge University Press, 1986.
The Early Vasas: A History of Sweden 1523–1611. Cambridge: Cambridge University Press, 1968.
The Swedish Imperial Experience 1560–1718. Cambridge: Cambridge University Press, 1979.
Robinson, I. S. "Church and Papacy." In: *The Cambridge History of Medieval Political Thought c. 350–c. 1450.* Ed. J. H. Burns. Cambridge: Cambridge University Press, 1988.
Rokkan, Stein. "Cities, States and Nations: A Dimensional Model for the Study of Contrasts in Development." In: *Building States and Nations.* Ed. S. N. Eisenstadt and Stein Rokkan. 2 vols. Beverly Hills: Sage, 1973, vol. I, pp. 73–97.
"Dimensions of State Formation and Nation-Building: A Possible Paradigm for Research on Variations in Europe." In: *The Formation of National States in Western Europe.* Ed. Charles Tilly. Princeton: Princeton University Press, 1975, pp. 562–600.
"Territories, Nations, Parties: Toward a Geoeconomic-Geopolitical Model for the Explanation of Variations within Western Europe." In: *From National Development to Global Community.* Ed. Richard Merritt and Bruce Russett. London: George Allen & Unwin, 1981, pp. 70–95.
Roos, Hans. "Ständewesen und parlamentarische Verfassung in Polen (1505–1772)." In: *Ständische Vertretungen in Europa im 17. und 18. Jahrhundert.* Ed. Dietrich Gerhard. 2nd ed. Göttingen: Vandenhoeck & Ruprecht, 1974, pp. 310–367.
Rosenberg, Hans. *Bureaucracy, Aristocracy and Autocracy: The Prussian Experience 1660–1815.* Cambridge: Harvard University Press, 1958.
Roseveare, Henry. "Prejudice and Policy: Sir George Downing as Parliamentary Entrepreneur." In: *Enterprise and History: Essays in Honour of Charles Wilson.* Ed. D. C. Coleman and Peter Mathias. Cambridge: Cambridge University Press, 1984.
The Treasury: The Evolution of a British Institution. New York: Columbia University Press, 1969.
The Treasury 1660–1870: The Foundations of Control. London: George Allen & Unwin, 1973.
Rothschild, Joseph. *East Central Europe between the Two World Wars.* Seattle: University of Washington Press, 1974.
Roy, Ian. "England Turned Germany? The Aftermath of the Civil War in Its European Context." *Transactions of the Royal Historical Society,* vol. 28 (1978), pp. 127–144.
Ruíz Martín, Felipe. "Los Hombres de Negocios Genoveses de España durante el Siglo XVI." In: *Fremde Kaufleute auf der Iberischen Halbinsel.* Ed. Hermann Kellenbenz. Cologne: Böhlau, 1970, pp. 84–99.
Rubinstein, Nicolai, ed. *Florentine Studies.* London: Faber and Faber, 1968.
Ryder, Alan. *The Kingdom of Naples under Alfonso the Magnanimous.* Oxford: Clarendon, 1976.
Sagnac, Philippe, "Le Crédit d'État et les Banquiers à la Fin du XVIIᵉ et au Commencement du XVIIIᵉ Siècle." *Revue d'histoire moderne et contemporaine,* vol. 10, no. 4–5 (June–July 1908), pp. 257–272.
Sainty, J. C. "A Reform of the Tenure of Office during the Reign of Charles II." *Bulletin of the Institute of Historical Research,* vol. 41, no. 104 (November 1968), pp. 150–171.

"The Tenure of Office in the Exchequer." *English Historical Review*, vol. 80, no. 316 (July 1965), pp. 449–475.

Treasury Officials 1660–1870. London: Athlone, 1972.

Salmon, J. H. M. *Society in Crisis: France in the Sixteenth Century.* London: Methuen, 1979.

Sandquist, T. A. and M. R. Powicke, eds. *Essays in Medieval History Presented to Bertie Wilkinson.* Toronto: Toronto University Press, 1969.

Santifaller, Leo. *Zur Geschichte der Ottonisch-Salischen Reichskirchensystems.* Wien: Hermann Böhlaus Nachfolger, 1964.

Schieder, Theodor. "Die karolingischen Nachfolgerstaaten: Das Ostfränkische Reich (887–918)." In: *Handbuch der Europäischen Geschichte.* Ed. Theodor Schieder. Vol. I. Stuttgart: Ernst Klett Verlag, 1976, pp. 633–642.

—— ed. *Handbuch der Europaischen Geschichte.* 7 vols. Stuttgart: Ernst Klett Verlag, 1976.

Schissler, Hanna. "Preussische Finanzpolitik nach 1807." *Geschichte und Gesellschaft*, vol. 8, no. 3 (1982), pp. 367–385.

Schmidt, Steffen W., James C. Scott, Carl Landé, and Laura Guasti, eds. *Friends, Followers, and Factions: A Reader in Political Clientelism.* Berkeley: University of California Press, 1977.

Schmoller, Gustav. "Der deutsche Beamtenstaat vom 16. bis 18. Jahrhundert." In: *Umrisse und Untersuchungen zur Verfassungs-, Verwaltungs- und Wirtschaftsgeschichte besonders des Preussischen Staates im 17. und 18. Jahrhundert.* Hildesheim: Georg Olms, 1974, pp. 289–313.

—— "Die epochen der preussischen Finanzgeschichte bis zur Gründung des deutschen Reiches." In: *Umrisse und Untersuchungen zur Verfassungs-, Verwaltungs- und Wirtschaftsgeschichte besonders des Preuisschen Staates im 17. und 18. Jahrhundert.* Hildesheim: Georg Olms, 1974, pp. 104–246.

—— "Die Enstehung des preussischen Heeres von 1640 bis 1740." In *Umrisse un Untersuchungen zur Verfassungs-, Verwaltungs- und Wirtschaftsgeschichte besonders des Preuisschen Staates im 17. und 18. Jahrhundert.* Hildesheim: Georg Olms, 1974, pp. 247–313.

—— "Einleitung: Ueber Behördenorganisation, Amtswesen und Beamtenthum im Allgemeinen und speciell in Deutschland und Preussen bis zum Jahre 1713." In *Acta Borussica.* Vol. I. Berlin: Paul Parey, 1894, pp. 13–143.

—— "Historische Betrachtungen über Staatenbildung und Finanzentwicklung." *Jahrbuch für Gesetzgebung, Verwaltung und Volkswirtschaft im Deutschen Reich [Schmollers Jahrbuch],* vol. 33, no. 1 (1909), pp. 1–64.

—— *Preussische Verfassungs-, Verwaltungs- und Finanzgeschichte.* Berlin: Verlag der Täglichen Rundschau, 1921.

—— *Umrisse und Untersuchungen zur Vergassungs, Verwalttungs- und Wirtschaftsgeschichte besonders des Preussischen Staates im 17. und 18. Jahrhundert.* Leipzig: Duncker & Humblot, 1898, pp. 247–313.

Schnapper, Bernard. *Les Rentes au XVIe Siècle: Histoire d'un Instrument de Crédit.* Paris: S.E.V.P.E.N., 1957.

Schnee, Heinrich. *Die Hoffinanz und der Moderne Staat.* Berlin: Duncker & Humblot, 1953.

Schramm, Percy Ernst. *Kaiser, Rom und Renovatio.* 4th ed. Darmstadt: Wissenschaftliche Buchgesellschaft, 1984.

Schück, Herman. "Sweden's Early Parliamentary Institutions from the Thirteenth Century to 1611." In: *The Riksdag: A History of the Swedish Parliament.* Ed. Michael Metcalf. New York: St. Martin's Press, 1987, pp. 5–60.

Schulze, Hans. *Die Grafschaftsverfassung der Karolingerzeit in den Gebieten östlich des Rheins.* Berlin: Duncker & Humblot, 1973.

—— *Grundstrukturen der Verfassung im Mittelalter.* 2nd ed. 2 vols. Stuttgart: Kohlhammer, 1990.

Schulze, Winfried. *Deutsche Geschichte im 16. Jahrhundert.* Frankfurt am Main: Suhrkamp, 1987.

Schumpeter, Joseph. *Aufsätze zur Soziologie.* Tübingen: J. C. B. Mohr, 1953.

—— "Die Krise des Steuerstaates." In: *Aufsätze zur Soziologie.* Tübingen: J. C. B. Mohr, 1953, pp. 1–71.

Schwarz, Brigide. "Aemterkäuflichkeit, eine Institution des Absolutismus und ihre mittelalterlichen Wurzeln." *Staat und Gesellschaft in Mittelalter und früher Neuzeit: Gedankschrift für Joachim Leuschner.* Göttingen: Vandenhoeck & Ruprecht, 1983, pp. 176–196.

"Die Entstehung der Aemterkäuflichkeit an der Römischen Kurie." In: *Aemterhandel im Spätmittelalter und im 16. Jahrhundert.* Ed. Ilja Mieck. Berlin: Colloquium Verlag, 1984, pp. 61–65.

Die Organisation kurialer Schreiberkollegien von ihrer Entstehung bis zur Mitte des 15 Jahrhunderts. Tübingen: Max Niemeyer, 1972.

Scott, Franklin. *Sweden: The Nation's History.* Carbondale: Southern Illinois University Press, 1988.

Scott, James. *Comparative Political Corruption.* Englewood Cliffs, N.J.: Prentice Hall, 1972.

Scott, W. R. *The Constitution and Finance of English, Scottish and Irish Joint-Stock Companies to 1720.* Cambridge: Cambridge University Press, 1912.

Seibt, Ferdinand. "Polen von der Jahrtausendwende bis 1444." In: *Handbuch der Europäischen Geschichte.* Ed. Theodor Schieder. Vol. II. Stuttgart: Ernst Klett Verlag, 1976, pp. 1042–1079.

Shefter, Martin. "Party and Patronage: Germany, England and Italy." *Politics and Society,* vol. 7, no. 4 (1977), pp. 403–451.

Skalweit, Stephan. "Der preussische Staat im politischen Denken des ausgehenden 'Ancien régime' in Frankreich." In: *Moderne Preussische Geschichte.* Ed. Otto Büsch and Wolfgang Neugebauer. Berlin: Walter de Gruyter, 1981, pp. 197–242.

Skocpol, Theda. "Bringing the State Back In: Strategies of Analysis in Current Research." In *Bringing the State Back In.* Ed. Peter Evans, Dietrich Rueschemeyer, and Theda Skocpol. Cambridge: Cambridge University Press, 1985, pp. 3–37.

Social Revolutions in the Modern World. Cambridge: Cambridge University Press, 1994.

States and Social Revolutions. Cambridge: Cambridge University Press, 1979.

Skocpol, Theda and Margaret Somers. "The Uses of Comparative History in Macrosocial Inquiry." In: *Social Revolutions in the Modern World.* Cambridge: Cambridge University Press, 1994, pp. 72–95.

Sonnino, Paul. *Louis XIV and the Origins of the Dutch War.* Cambridge: Cambridge University Press, 1988.

Sorge, Amedeo. "La Venalità degli Uffici nel Regno di Napoli: Un Tentativo di Reforma nel Primo Decennio Borbonico." In: *I Borbone di Napoli e i Borbone di Spagna.* 2 vols. Vol. I. Ed. Mario Di Pinto. Napoli: Guida Editori, 1985, pp. 291–304.

Spangenberg, Hans. *Vom Lehnstaat zum Ständestaat.* Aalen: Scientia, 1964.

Sperling, John. "Godolphin and the Organization of Public Credit 1702 to 1710." Diss. Cambridge University, 1955.

Spruyt, Hendrik. *The Sovereign State and Its Competitors.* Princeton: Princeton University Press, 1994.

Stacey, Robert. *Politics, Policy and Finance under Henry III 1216–1245.* New Haven: Yale University Press, 1987.

Starkey, David. "From Feud to Faction." *History Today,* vol. 32, no. 11 (November 1982), pp. 16–22.

Stenton, F. M. *Anglo-Saxon England.* 3rd ed. Oxford: Clarendon, 1971.

Stone, Lawrence, ed. *An Imperial State at War.* London: Routledge, 1993.

Steward, Paul. "The Soldier, the Bureaucrat, and Fiscal Records in the Army of Ferdinand and Isabella." *Hispanic American History Review,* vol. 49, no. 2 (May 1969), pp. 281–292.

Stingl, Herfried. *Die Entstehung der Deutschen Stammesherzogtümer am Anfang des 10. Jahrhunderts.* Aalen: Scientia Verlag, 1974.

Stocker, Christopher. "Public and Private Enterprise in the Administration of a Renaissance Monarchy: The First Sales of Offices in the Parlement of Paris (1512–1524)." *Sixteenth Century Journal,* vol. 9, no. 2 (July 1978), pp. 4–29.

"Office as Maintenance in Renaissance France." *Canadian Journal of History,* vol. 6, no. 1 (March 1971), pp. 21–43.

Stolleis, Michael. "Condere leges et interpretari. Gesetzgebungsmacht und Staatsbildung in der frühen Neuzeit." In: *Staat und Staatsräson in der Frühen Neuzeit.* Frankfurt: Suhrkamp, 1990, pp. 167–196.

"Grundzüge der Beamtenethik (1550–1650)." In: *Staat und Staatsräson in der Frühen Neuzeit.* Frankfurt: Suhrkamp, 1990, pp. 197–231.

Storey, Robin. "England: Aemterhandel im 15. und 16. Jahrhundert." In: *Aemterhandel im Spätmittelalter und im 16 Jahrhundert.* Ed. Ilja Mieck. Berlin: Colloquium Verlag, 1984, pp. 186–207.

Strayer, Joseph. *The Reign of Philip the Fair.* Princeton: Princeton University Press, 1980.

and Charles Taylor. *Studies in Early French Taxation.* Cambridge: Harvard University Press, 1939.

Stumpo, Enrico. *Finanza e Stato Moderno nel Piemonte del Seicento.* Roma: Istituto Storico Italiano, 1979.

Stutzer, Dietmar. "Das preussische Heer und seine Finanzierung in zeitgenössischer Darstellung 1740–1790." *Militärgeschichtliche Mitteilungen,* vol. 24, no. 2 (1978), pp. 23–47.

Swart, K. W. *Sale of Offices in the 17th Century.* Utrecht: HES Publishers, 1980.

Symcox, Geoffrey. *The Crisis of French Sea Power 1688–1697.* The Hague: Martinus Nijhoff, 1974.

Victor Amadeus II: Absolutism in the Savoyard State 1675–1730. Berkeley: University of California Press, 1983.

Tanner, J. R. *A Descriptive Catalogue of the Naval Manuscripts in the Pepysian Library at Magdalene College, Cambridge.* London: Naval Records Society, 1903.

Tanner, J. R., C. W. Previté-Orton, and Z. N. Brooke, eds. *The Cambridge Medieval History. Volume VII: Decline of the Empire and Papacy.* Cambridge: Cambridge University Press, 1986.

eds. *The Cambridge Medieval History. Volume VI: Victory of the Papacy.* Cambridge: Cambridge University Press, 1986.

Tellenbach, Gerd. *Libertas: Kirche und Weltordnung im Zeitalter des Investiturstreites.* Stuttgart: Kohlhammer, 1936.

Theuerkauf, Gerd. "Zur Typologie spätmittelalterlicher Territorialverwaltung in Deutschland." *Annali dell Fondazione Italiana per la Storia Amministrativa,* vol. 2 (1965), pp. 37–76.

Thompson, E. A. *The Goths in Spain.* Oxford: Clarendon, 1969.

Thompson, I. A. A. "Crown and Cortes in Castile, 1590–1665." *Parliaments, Estates and Representation,* vol. 2, no. 1 (June 1982), pp. 29–45.

War and Government in Habsburg Spain, 1560–1620. London: Athlone, 1976.

Thompson, M. W. *The Rise of the Castle.* Cambridge: Cambridge University Press, 1991.

Tilly, Charles. *Big Structures, Large Processes, Huge Comparisons.* New York: Russell Sage Foundation, 1984.

Coercion, Capital and European States A.D. 990–1990. Oxford: Basil Blackwell, 1990.

ed. *The Formation of National States in Western Europe.* Princeton: Princeton University Press, 1975.

"War Making and State Making as Organized Crime." In: *Bringing the State Back In.* Ed. Peter Evans, Dietrich Rueschemeyer, and Theda Skocpol. Cambridge: Cambridge University Press, 1985, pp. 169–191.

Tilly, Charles and Wim Blockmans, eds. *Cities and the Rise of States in Europe, A.D. 1000 to 1800.* Boulder: Westview, 1994.

von Timon, Akos. *Ungarische Verfassungs- und Rechtsgeschichte mit Bezug auf die Rechtsentwicklung der Westlichen Staaten.* Berlin: Puttkammer und Mühlbrecht, 1904.

Todd, Malcolm. *The Northern Barbarians 100 B.C. – A.D. 300.* 2nd ed. Oxford: Basil Blackwell, 1987.

Tomás y Valiente, Francisco. *Gobierno e Instituciones en la España del Antiguo Régimen.* Madrid: Alianza, 1982.

"Origen Bajomedieval de la Patrimonialización y la Enajenación de Oficios Públicos en Castilla." *Actas del I Symposium de Historia de la Administración.* Madrid: Instituto de Estudios Administrativos, 1970, pp. 125–159.

"Les Ventes des Offices Publics en Castile aux XVIIe et VIIIe Siècles." In: *Aemterkäuflichkeit: Aspekte Sozialer Mobilität im Europäischen Vergleich (17. und 18. Jahrhundert).* Ed. Klaus Malettke. Berlin: Colloquium Verlag, 1980, pp. 89–121.

Tomlinson, Howard. "Financial and Administrative Developments in England, 1660–88." In: *The Restored Monarchy.* Ed. J. R. Jones. London: Macmillan, 1979.

Guns and Government: The Ordnance Office under the Later Stuarts. London: Royal Historical Society, 1979.

"Place and Profit: An Examination of the Ordnance Office, 1660–1714." *Transactions of the Royal Historical Society.* 5th ser. Vol. 25 (1975), pp. 55–75.

Tout, T. F. "The English Civil Service in the Fourteenth Century." In: *The Collected Papers of Thomas Frederick Tout.* Manchester: Manchester University Press, 1934, pp. 191–221.

Trebilcock, Clive. *The Industrialization of the Continental Powers 1780–1914.* London: Longman, 1981.

Ullmann, Hans-Peter. *Staatsschulden und Reformpolitik.* Göttingen: Vandenhoeck & Ruprecht, 1986.

Ulloa, Modesto. *La Hacienda Real de Castilla en el Reinado de Felipe II.* 3rd. ed. Madrid: Fundación Universitaria Española, 1986.

Unwin, George, ed. *Finance and Trade under Edward III.* Manchester: Manchester University Press, 1918.

Valdeavellano, Luis García de. *Curso de Historia de las Instituciones Españolas. De los Orígines al Final de la Edad Media.* Madrid: Alianza Editorial, 1986.

van Caenegem. *The Birth of the English Common Law.* 2nd ed. Cambridge: Cambridge University Press, 1988.

Van Doren, Llewain Scott. "War Taxation, Institutional Change and Social Conflict in Provincial France – The Royal *Taille* in Dauphiné, 1494–1559." *Proceedings of the American Philosophical Society,* vol. 121, no. 1 (February 1977), pp. 70–96.

Verba, Sidney. "Sequence and Development." In: *Crises and Sequences in Political Development.* Ed. Leonard Binder et al. Princeton: Princeton University Press, 1971, pp. 283–316.

Veríssimo Serrão, Joaquim. *História de Portugal. Volume I: Estado, Patria e Nação (1080–1415).* 3rd ed. Lisbon: Editorial Verbo, 1979.

Villiers, Robert. "Colbert et les Finances Publiques." In: *Un Nouveau Colbert.* Ed. Roland Mousnier. Paris: C. D. U. et SEDES reunis, 1985, pp. 177–187.

Vincke, Johannes, ed. *Gesammelte Aufsätze zur Kulturgeschichte Spaniens.* Münster: Aschendorffsche Verlagsbuchhandlung, 1973.

Visconti, Alessandro. *La Pubblica Amministrazione nello Stato Milanese durante il Predominio Straniero (1541–1796).* Roma: Athenaeum, 1913.

Vittinghoff, Friedrich, ed. *Stadt und Herrschaft: Römische Kaiserzeit und Hohes Mittlealter.* München: R. Oldenbourg Verlag, 1982.

Vogel, Barbara, ed. *Preussische Reformen 1807–1820.* N.P.: Verlagsgruppe Athenäum-Hain-Scriptor-Hanstein, 1980.

Vührer, A. *Histoire de la Dette Publique en France.* Paris: Berger-Levrault, 1886.

Vuitry, Adolphe. *Le Désordre des Finances et les Excès de la Spéculation à la Fin du Règne de Louis XIV et au Commencement du Règne de Louis XV.* Paris: Calman Levy, 1885.

Wacquet, Jean-Claude. *De la Corruption: Morale et Pouvoir à Florence aux XVIIe et XVIIe Siècle.* Paris: Fayard, 1984.

"Note sur les Caractères Originaux du Système Financier Toscan sous les Médicis." In: *Genèse de l'État Moderne: Prélèvement et Redistribution.* Ed. Jean-Philippe Genet and Michel Le Mené. Paris: Éditions du C.N.R.S., 1987, pp. 111–114.

Waley, Daniel. "The Army of the Florentine Republic from the Twelfth to the Fourteenth Century." In: *Florentine Studies.* Ed. Nicolai Rubinstein. London: Faber and Faber, 1968, pp. 70–108.

"Le Origini della Condotta nel Duecento e le Compagnie di Ventura." *Rivista Storica Italiana,* vol. 88, no. 3 (1976), pp. 531–538.

Wallace-Hadrill, J. M. *Early Germanic Kingship in England and on the Continent.* Oxford: Clarendon, 1971.

The Long-Haired Kings. Toronto: University of Toronto Press, 1982.

Ward, W. R. "The Office for Taxes, 1665–1798." *Bulletin of the Institute of Historical Research,* vol. 25, no. 72 (November 1952), pp. 204–212.

Warren, W. L. *The Governance of Norman and Angevin England 1086–1272.* London: Edward Arnold, 1987.
Weber, Max. "Agrarverhältnisse im Altertum." In: *Gesammelte Aufsätze zur Sozial- und Wirtschaftsgeschichte.* Tübingen: J. C. B. Mohr, 1924.
The City. Glencoe: Free Press, 1958.
Economy and Society. Berkeley: University of California Press, 1978.
Gesammelte Politische Schriften. 4th ed. Tübingen: J. C. B. Mohr, 1980.
"Politics as a Vocation." In: *From Max Weber.* Eds. H. H. Gerth and C. Wright Mills. New York: Oxford University Press, 1946, pp. 77–128.
Wirtschaft und Gesellschaft. 5th ed. Tübingen: J. C. B. Mohr, 1976.
Wehler, Hans-Ulrich. *Deutsche Gesellschaftsgeschichte 1700 bis 1815.* Munich: Beck, 1987.
Werner, Karl Ferdinand. *Histoire de France, Tome I: Les Origines.* Paris: Fayard, 1984.
"Missus-Marchio-Comes." In: *Vom Frankenreich zur Entfaltung Deutschlands und Frankreichs.* Sigmaringen: Jan Thorbecke, 1984, pp. 109–156.
White, Eugene. "Was There a Solution to the Ancien Regime's Financial Dilemma?" *Journal of Economic History,* vol. 49, no. 3 (September 1989), pp. 545–568.
White, Lynn. *Medieval Technology and Social Change.* Oxford: Clarendon, 1962.
Wickham, Chris. *Early Medieval Italy.* London: Macmillan, 1981.
"Land Disputes and Their Social Framework in Lombard-Carolingian Italy, 700–900." In: *The Settlement of Disputes in Early Medieval Europe.* Ed. Wendy Davies and Paul Fouracre. Cambridge: Cambridge University Press, 1986, pp. 105–124.
Willard, James Field. *Parliamentary Taxes on Personal Property 1290 to 1334.* Cambridge: Medieval Academy of America, 1934.
Williams, Penry. *The Tudor Polity.* Oxford: Clarendon, 1978.
Willms, Johannes. *Die Politik der Officiers Royaux auf den États Généraux 1576–1614.* Heidelberg: n.p., 1975.
Witcombe, D. T. *Charles II and the Cavalier House of Commons 1663–1674.* Manchester: Manchester University Press, 1966.
Witt, Christian. *Wealth and Taxation in Central Europe.* Leamington Spa: Berg, 1987.
Wolfe, Martin. *The Fiscal System of Renaissance France.* New Haven: Yale University Press, 1972.
Wood, Ian. "Administration, Law and Culture in Merovingian Gaul." In: *The Uses of Literacy in Early Medieval Europe.* Ed. Rosamond McKitterick. Cambridge: Cambridge University Press, 1990, pp. 63–81.
"Disputes in Late Fifth- and Sixth-Century Gaul: Some Problems." In: *The Settlement of Disputes in Early Modern Europe.* Ed. Wendy Davies and Paul Fouracre. Cambridge: Cambridge University Press, 1986, pp. 7–22.
"Kings, Kingdoms and Consent." In: *Early Medieval Kingship.* Ed. P. H. Sawyer and I. N. Wood. Leeds: School of History, University of Leeds, 1977, pp. 6–29.
Woolf, Stuart. *A History of Italy 1700–1860.* London: Methuen, 1979.
Wolters, Friedrich. *Geschichte der Brandenburgischen Finanzen in der Zeit von 1640–1697. Band II: Die Zentralverwaltung des Heeres und der Steuern.* München and Leipzig: Duncker & Humblot, 1915.
Wrigley, E. A. and R. S. Schofield. *The Population History of England, 1541–1871.* Cambridge: Harvard University Press, 1981.
Wyduckel, Dieter. *Princeps Legibus Solutus.* Berlin: Duncker & Humblot, 1979.
Wyluda, Erich. *Lehnrecht und Beamtentum.* Berlin: Duncker & Humblot, 1969.
Zamoyski, Adam. *The Polish Way.* London: John Murray, 1987.
Zeller, Gaston. *Les Institutions de la France du XVIe Siècle.* Paris: Presses Universitaires de France, 1948.
Zolberg, Aristide. "Strategic Interaction and the Formation of Modern States: France and England." In: *The State in Global Perspective.* Ed. Ali Kazancigil. London: Gower, 1986, pp. 72–106.

INDEX

Note: The order of subheadings follows the structure of the argument.